RGVEDIC CULTURE

ABINAS CHANDRA DAS

GYAN

Published by

Gyan Publishing House
5, Ansari Road
Daryaganj, New Delhi-110002
Phone: 011-47034999, 9811692060
E-mail: books@gyanbooks.com

Distribution Network
gyanbooks.com
India, USA, Canada, UK, Australia

ISBN: 978-93-7316-659-9 (PB)

First Published, 1925

2nd Impression 2025

Printed at: Gyan Press, Delhi.

RGVEDIC CULTURE
Author: ABINAS CHANDRA DAS

RGVEDIC CULTURE

BY

ABINAS CHANDRA DAS, M.A., PH.D.,

Author of "Rgvedic India," and Lecturer in Ancient Indian History and Culture, Calcutta University.

CALCUTTA AND MADRAS.

R. CAMBRAY & Co.,

PUBLISHERS & BOOKSELLERS.

1925.

TO

THE SACRED MEMORY

OF MY FATHER WHO INSPIRED IN ME

A LOVE OF ANCIENT INDIA.

PREFACE.

THIS book was to have formed the second volume of *Ṛgvedic India*, but as the subject-matter dealt in it is mainly cultural, I have designated it as *Ṛgvedic Culture*, forming as it does a complete volume by itself.

I have attempted in the First Chapter, with what success I do not know, to meet the objections raised against the acceptance of my theory regarding the original cradle of the Aryans in ancient Sapta-Sindhu (or the Punjab) by such distinguished European savants as Dr. Sten Konow of Christiana University and Prof. M. Winternitz of Prague University.

In the light of the opinions of some modern Geologists, I have consistently brought down the age of a different distribution of land and water (evidences of which are revealed in the Ṛgveda) and hence of the real beginnings of Ṛgvedic culture itself, to about 20,000 or 25,000 B. C., a date which, following the method adopted by Prof. Flinders Petrie in calculating the earliest age of ancient Egyptian culture, can be reached back approximately by assigning 1500 years to the duration of each of the *ten* different periods of Vedic culture, that I have pointed out in this book.

From astronomical calculations, based on the position of certain stars mentioned in some of the Ṛgvedic *mantras*, the vast antiquity of the Ṛgveda and Ṛgvedic culture can also be inferred. Profs. Pischel and Geldner in their *Vedische Studien* (Vol. VII, Part I) recognised the value and importance of such calculations. In India, the late Mr. B. G. Tilak attempted to prove in his *Orion* the antiquity of some hymns of the Ṛgveda by a similar process. In his opinion, the Vṛṣākapi hymn (Rv. x. 68) "gives us not only a description of the constellations of Orion and Canis (verses 4 and

5), but clearly and expressly defines the position of the Sun when he passed to the north of the Equator in old times (verse 22)." Mr. V. B. Ketkar of Poona, another Vedic scholar, has proved from a statement in the *Taittirīya Brāhmaṇa* (iii., 4, 1, 5) that Bṛhaspati, or the planet Jupiter, was first discovered when confronting or nearly occulting the star Tiṣya about 4650 B. C. This veteran scholar also read a paper before the First Oriental Conference held at Poona in 1917, "wherein (he states) I have proved on Astronomical evidence and Paurāṇic account that the Rajputana and Gangetic Seas nearly separating the Jambu-dvīpa from the Punjab and the Himalayas disappeared after 7500 B.C. by the upheaval, partly volcanic and partly seismic, of their beds." The above extracts from his letter, addressed to the author soon after the publication of his book *Ṛgvedic India*, go to prove and confirm the internal evidences in the Ṛgveda of a different distribution of land and water in the Punjab in Ṛgvedic times, which have been pointed out in that book. Mr. D. Mukhopādhyāya, in an article on "Hindu Nakṣatras" published in the *Journal of the Department of Science* (Calcutta University, Vol. vi, pp. 19-20), holds the opinion that "the Vṛṣākapi hymn takes us back to the period even beyond 16000 B.C." Prof. Bloomfield pointed out, while reviewing Mr. Tilak's *Orion*, that "the language and literature of the Vedas is by no means so primitive as to place with it the real beginnings of Aryan life... These in all probability and in all due moderation *reach back several thousands of years more*" than 4500 B.C. which was assigned by Mr. Tilak to the composition of some of the Ṛgvedic *mantras*.

From a cultural point of view also, it will be seen from a perusal of this book that Ṛgvedic culture passed through all the different stages of its evolution in Sapta-Sindhu from the early Neolithic to the recent, and that there was a continuity in this culture, without break, for over 20,000 years. Considered from all these different stand-points, the date assigned by me to the beginnings of this culture will, I trust, not be found by scholars to be either improbable, or too early.

If the proofs, adduced by me, be found convincing, or even probable, I think it will not be unreasonable for me to hope that they will sufficiently justify the necessity for starting a fresh enquiry with regard to the original cradle of the Aryans on their basis, or on the basis of such other fresh proofs as may be forthcoming or available. During the last one hundred years, the cradle has been shifted by generations of Oriental Scholars from one country to another, from Kashmir and Bactria to Central Asia, from Central Asia to Mesopotamia, from Mesopotamia to the Arctic regions, from the Arctic regions to Northern and Central Europe, and from there to a region, said to have been lost in the Mediterranean Sea. I have tried to shift it back again to ancient Sapta-Sindhu or the Punjab, which included Kashmir, Gandhāra and Bactria in Ṛgvedic times. It is for Oriental Scholars to judge whether I have made out a case for the revision of the current theory.

This highly controversial matter apart, the book, it is hoped, will be found interesting by Vedic students and scholars in so far as it seeks to reconstruct the life of the ancient Aryans, as it was actually lived by them in the Punjab in Ṛgvedic times, and also gives glimpses of the different phases of their all-round wonderful culture. I have depended on the results of my own researches, supplemented by those of renowned Vedic scholars, Indian, European and American, to all of whom I acknowledge my indebtedness. I have availed myself of the valuable materials embodied in Profs. Macdonell and Keith's *Vedic Index*, and Prof. Macdonell's *Vedic Mythology*, and adopted their views where I have agreed, and criticized them where I have differed. All authorities quoted or referred to have been mentioned in the foot-notes and Bibliography.

I cannot conclude without expresssing my thanks to Mr. H. G. Wells who has kindly permitted me to reproduce two maps from his excellent work, *The Outline of History*, and to make some excerpts from it in support of some of my points. His two maps of India will be found wonderfully to tally in their broad outlines with the map I drew up for *Ṛgvedic India*, consistently with the geographical evidences found in the Ṛgveda, and the results of investigations made by Geologists. I have also reproduced from his work three sketches, viz., those of *Pithecanthropus erectus*, the Neanderthal man and the Cro-Magnon man, for which I beg to acknowledge to him my indebtedness.

Lastly, I would humbly bespeak the patience, indulgence and tolerance of such Vedic students and scholars as may not agree with me in the views propounded in this book and in *Ṛgvedic India*. There is nothing like finality in views that are mainly based on mere intelligent guesses, surmises and probabilities rather than on positive and incontestable historical proofs, and there should be room enough for a fresh view, based on fresh materials, in an arena where so many have struggled and are still struggling for existence and recognition. Truth can only be arrived at, not certainly by stifling any independent opinion, boldly expressed and formulated, but by encouraging it and giving it a patient hearing. Time alone can show whether any view has its justification or not, and to the verdict of this great Tribunal, I humbly submit myself.

CALCUTTA UNIVERSITY.
October, 1925.

A. C. DAS.

CONTENTS.

PREFACE ... ... P. v—viii

CHAPTER I.

INTRODUCTION : The Antiquity of Ṛgvedic Culture P. 1—44

CHAPTER II.

Glimpses of some of the early stages of Aryan culture in the Ṛgveda ... ... P. 45—118

CHAPTER III.

A brief account of the Aryan people in the ancient Punjab; the different clans and classes; primitive pastoral existence; village life and village industries; gradual evolution of castes according to different occupations; social intercourse; trades and industries; the Paṇis, Dāsas, Dasyus and numerous Aryan tribes, both Vedic and non-Vedic ... ... P. 119—172

CHAPTER IV.

Further accounts of the Vedic people in Ṛgvedic times: some aspects of material art and culture P. 173—199

CHAPTER V.

Food, drink, dress, sports and amusements of the Vedic Aryans ... ... P. 200—236

CHAPTER VI.

Domestic and social life, marriage and morals during Ṛgvedic times ... ... P. 237—259

CHAPTER VII.

Agriculture and the value of cattle in Ṛgvedic times P. 260—293

CHAPTER VIII.

The King and the State, the Sage-priests, and Wars and mode of Warfare ... ... P. 294—351

CHAPTER IX.

Warring Aryan tribes and the War of Ten Kings with Sudās, King of the Tṛtsus ... ... P. 352—367

CHAPTER X.

Manners, customs, rites and beliefs; family-life; wedding rites; child-life; hospitality and liberality; student-life and learning; origin of the idea of religion; the region of Yama, or Heaven; Nirṛti or Hell; burial-rites; demons and goblins; cremation-rites; transmigration, *Karma* and re-birth ... ... P. 368—428

CHAPTER XI.

A further account of some manners, customs and beliefs of the Ṛgvedic Aryans ... ... P. 429—449

CHAPTER XII.

The Vedas and Vedic Gods; philosophical speculations regarding the origin of the Universe and realisation of the unity of the Godhead ... ... P. 450—484

CHAPTER XIII.

Yajña or Vedic Sacrifice ... ... P. 485—512

CHAPTER XIV.

Ṛgvedic Poetry ... ... P. 513—538

CHAPTER XV

Concluding remarks ... ... P. 539—540
Bibliography ... ... P. 541—545
INDEX ... ... P. 546—561

ṚGVEDIC CULTURE.

CHAPTER I.

INTRODUCTION : THE ANTIQUITY OF ṚGVEDIC CULTURE.

THREE objections seem, at present, to stand out against the acceptance of the theory propounded by me in my book *Ṛgvedic India*[1] about the original cradle of the Aryan race in ancient Sapta-Sindhavah or the Punjab. The *first* objection is with regard to the geological evidence of a different distribution of land and water in Northern India, which coincides, in my opinion, with the internal evidence of the Ṛgveda about the *actual* existence of such a distribution in Ṛgvedic times, and the consequent inference of the vast antiquity of Ṛgvedic culture and civilisation. The *second* objection is the difficulty felt by modern scholars in believing (admitting that the geological evidence was correct) that the Aryans, who were a highly intellectual race, were so slow in developing their culture through several millenniums. And the *third* objection is that advanced by Professor M. Winternitz of Prague University in his Readership Lecture delivered at the University of Calcutta in August 1923, to the effect "that it is absolutely impossible that the language of the Ṛgveda should be so little different as it is from the Old Persian in the 6th Century B. C, and from the Sanskrit of Pāṇini and Patañjali, if it had been the language of a people that lived even only in the Quaternary, to say nothing of the Miocene or Pliocene epochs" (*vide* also *Calcutta Review*, November 1923, P. 137). I admit the

[1] *Ṛgvedic India*, Calcutta University, 1921.

apparent force of these objections, and take this opportunity for making a few observations on the points.

I.

First, as to the geological evidence. Having found the clearest mention in the Ṛgveda (vii. 95, 2) that the Sarasvatī flowed from the Himālaya right *into the sea*, I naturally inferred that in Ṛgvedic times there must have been a sea, occupying that part of the desert tract of Rajputana where the Sarasvatī now loses herself in its sands. Then, there is also the clearest mention of the existence of an *Eastern Sea* (*Pūrva Samudra*) in the Ṛgveda (x. 136, 5); but as this sea could not have been the Bay of Bengal, because a knowledge of this sea presupposed a knowledge of the alluvial provinces lying between the Punjab and the Bay, of which, however, there is no mention at all in the Ṛgveda, and as its contiguity to the Punjab in Ṛgvedic times is clearly indicated by a number of verses,[1] I naturally inferred its existence to the immediate east of the Punjab. There is also mention in the *Ṛgveda* of the prevalence of a cold climate in this ancient province to such an extent as to have necessitated the year to have been named *Hima* or Winter,[2] and of the existence of *Four Seas*[3] round about the country, inhabited by the Ṛgvedic Aryans. With all these data and a few others before me, I investigated such Geological records of India as I could lay my hands on for any proofs as to the existence of a sea or seas to the south and the east of the Punjab, and in other directions. The existence of a Miocene Sea, cutting off the Punjab from Southern India, was asserted by some old Geologists,[4]

---

[1] Rv. i. 46, 2. 8; iii. 55, 1; iv. 43. 5; v 80, 5; vii. 55 7; x. 72, 7; 136, 5; 155, 3; Das, *Ṛgvedic India*, Chaps. i, ii, iii.

[2] Rv. i. 64, 14; ii. 1, 11; 33, 2; v. 54, 15; vi. 10, 7; 48, 8, &c.

[3] Rv. ix. 33, 6; x. 47, 2.

[4] Wallace, *The Geographical Distribution of Animals*, &c., i. 76-77 (1870). H. F. Blanford, *Quarterly Journal of the Geological Society*, xxxi 534-540 (1875). *Ency. Brit.* xii, 736 (9th Edn.)

but this period seemed to me too early and remote for the development of a civilisation like that depicted in the Ṛgveda; and I surmised that this sea must have existed down to later Geological periods, probably the Pleistocene, and even the Post-Pleistocene, when the ancestors of modern man undoubtedly flourished in many parts of the world, especially in India and Europe, with a civilisation not unlike the *early beginnings* of Ṛgvedic civilisation. After the publication of *Ṛgvedic India* early in January 1921, I accidently came across Mr. Wadia's *Geology of India*[1] which mentions the existence of a *Pleistocene Sea* covering the Gangetic trough at the foot of the Himalayan Range,—a sea that undoubtedly lasted for several thousand years till it was gradually filled up by "the waste of the high lands" and the alluvium brought down by the Himalayan rivers,[2] and the two large rivers of Central India, *viz.*, the Sone and the Chambal. This unexpectedly confirmed the surmise I had made in *Ṛgvedic India* about the existence of this sea down to a very late Geological period.[3] As regards the existence of a sea in Rajputana in the Pleistocene period, the evidence is still very meagre; but Mr. Wadia speaks of "marine transgressions" which caused portions of Rajputana to be invaded occasionally by the encroachments of the Arabian Sea, such encroachments lasting probably for thousands of years at a time.[4] My surmise is that in Ṛgvedic times when the Sarasvatī flowed right into the sea, there was probably one such "marine transgression" or encroachment made by the sea. As deserts

---

1 Wadia, *Geology of India*. London: Macmillan & Co. (1919).

2 *Op. cit.* 248.

3 *Ṛgvedic India*, pp. 114 & 567 (1st Edn).

4 *Geology of India*, P. 108, where Mr. Wadia says: "Such invasions of the sea on land known as 'marine transgressions' are of comparatively short duration and invade only low level areas converting them for the time being into epi-continental seas." The duration of these encroachments was "short," only geologically speaking. It must be computed by at least thousands of years.

are also mentioned in the Ṛgveda, the physical features of Rajputana must have consisted of patches of sandy deserts, a sea or the arm of a sea projecting inland, salt lakes and low swampy levels, occasionally inundated by the sea, all of which combined to cut off the Punjab from Southern India. In fact, very few relics of the Stone Age of civilisation have been discovered in Rajputana, which goes to show that it was not inhabited, but completely shunned by the Palæolithic and Neolithic savages of Southern India, the more so, because the deserts did not supply them with any food, nor afford them enough game upon which they could subsist.[1] Lastly, the ancient tradition which ascribes to Agastya the extraordinary feat of sipping up the ocean dry, and depressing the top of the Vindhya Hills in order to be able to go to the south unmistakably pointed to the existence of a sea in Rajputana in Ṛgvedic times and even later.

On the top of all these evidences unexpectedly come independent proofs, or, at least, very intelligent guesses about the existence of a sea about 50,000 years ago extending from the Arabian Sea right through Rajputana and Northern India to the Bay of Bengal, cutting off the Punjab, such as it then was, from Southern India, in an interesting and fascinating volume entitled the *Outline of History* written by Mr. H. G. Wells,[2] and published in 1920. I have not seen any previous editions of this book, but the present edition must have been in the press about the same time as *Ṛgvedic India*, and it is remarkable that both of us agree in several important matters, looked at from different stand-points, though, of course, our conclusions are different. Mr. Wells gives two maps in his book, one at page 39, showing a "possible outline of Europe and Western Asia at the maximum of the

[1] Memoirs of the Geological Survey of India xlv. Part I, P. 103.

[2] H. G. Wells' *Outline of History*, Cassel and Co., Ltd., 1920.

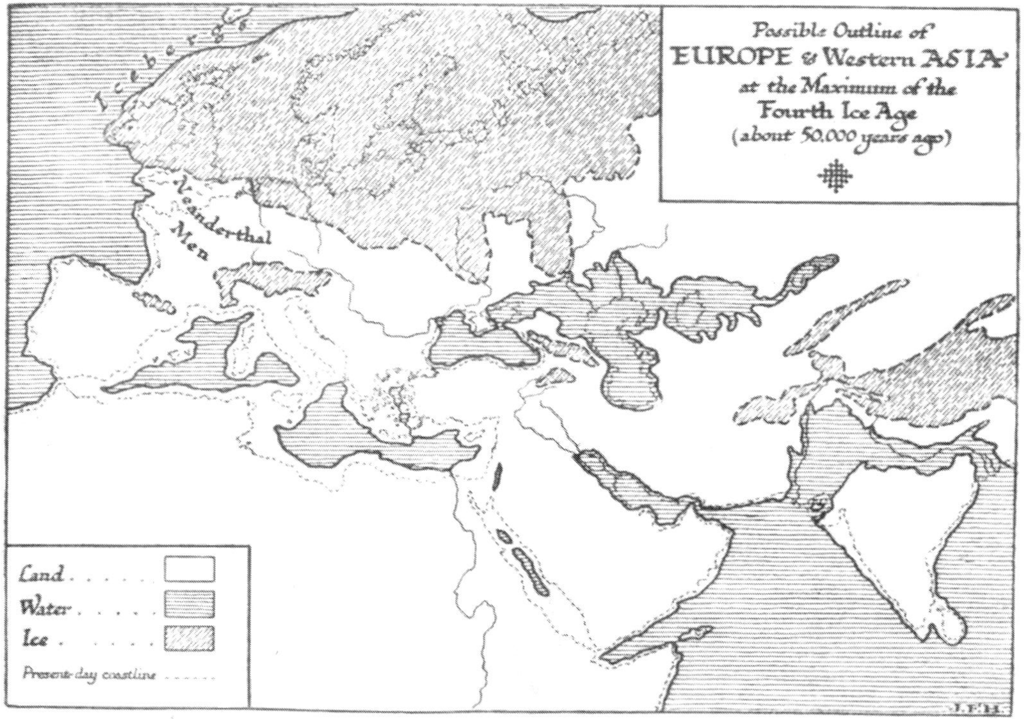
Possible Outline of
EUROPE & Western ASIA
at the Maximum of the
Fourth Ice Age
(about 50,000 years ago)
Icebergs
Neanderthal
Men
Land
Water
Ice
Present-day coastline
J.F.H.

P. 4.

Fourth Ice Age (about 50,000 years ago)." and another at page 45, which shows their possible outline "in the later palæolithic age (35,000 to 25,000 years ago)." The first map shows Southern India entirely cut off from the Punjab, Kāshmir and Gandhāra by a sea connecting the Arabian Sea with the Bay of Bengal, which closely resembles the two maps I have sketched and printed in my book *Ṛgvedic India*. The high lands of Bactria and Turkestan and parts of Central Asia and the whole of the Tibetan plateau are shown in Mr. Wells' map as covered by deep ice, and hence uninhabitable. The Asiatic Mediterranean Sea occupies an immense area from the western confines of Mongolia to South-Eastern Russia. Asia Minor is broadly connected with Turkey and the Balkan Peninsula including Greece. The European Mediterranean Sea is divided into two inland lakes or seas, and Northern Africa is connected with Southern Europe through Italy and Spain. The Alpine region and the Pyrenees and the whole of Northern Europe, including North-Western Russia, Germany, Scandinavia, Great Britain and Ireland and parts of Central Europe are all covered by a vast sheet of ice. Great Britain and Ireland form parts of the Continent, and Neanderthal men only live in and roam over Central and Northern Gaul. Mr. Wells observes that the map "represents the present state of our knowledge of the geography of Europe and Western Asia at a period which we guess to be 50,000 years ago" and which according to him corresponds to "the Neanderthaler Age."

The second map at page 45 of Mr. Wells' book, which represents a possible outline of Europe and Western Asia about 35,000 to 25,000 years ago, "when the true men were replacing the Neanderthalers in Western Europe," shows the physical features of the two continents to be nearly the same as 50,000 years ago, excepting for a few alterations here and there. For example, the sea that separated the Punjab and the Himalayas from Southern India, and was stretched from end to end, has had its uninterrupted continuity broken, and a sea to the immediate east of the Punjab (which is undoubtedly the "Eastern Sea" of the Ṛgveda) covers a large portion of the Gangetic plains, and a broad gulf covers a part of Rajputana and the whole of the province of Lower Sindh. There is thus some land connection between the Punjab and parts of Rajputana that must have emerged from the sea. The Asiatic Mediterranean remains much the same as before. The two inland seas or lakes in the region now covered by the European Mediterranean have had only slight alterations, and Asia Minor and South-Eastern Europe remain as much connected with each other as 50,000 years ago. Great Britain and Ireland still remain annexed to the continent, and the present North Sea and the British Channel are being slowly and gradually outlined. Glacial conditions are receding to the north of Great Britain and Ireland, Germany, and Central and Northern Russia, most of which is frozen land. A wide belt of steppes runs from the confines of Mongolia along the southern coasts of the Asiatic Mediterranean, right through Asia Minor and Southern and Central Europe, to Gaul, occupying the grounds uncovered by ice, and forests are advancing immediately to the south of this belt. These were approximately the physical features of the two continents about 35,000 to 25,000 years ago, according to Mr. Wells, when "the true men were replacing the Neanderthalers in Western Europe."

But who were these Neanderthalers and their successors, "the true men"? As Northern or Central Europe is regarded by European and American scholars as the original cradle of the Aryan race, it will not be uninteresting to give here a brief account of the Neanderthalers and their predecessors in Europe, as well as their successors "the true men". For this purpose I will have recourse again to the pages of Mr. Wells' book, the *Outline of History*: "Among the earliest evidences of some creature, either human or at

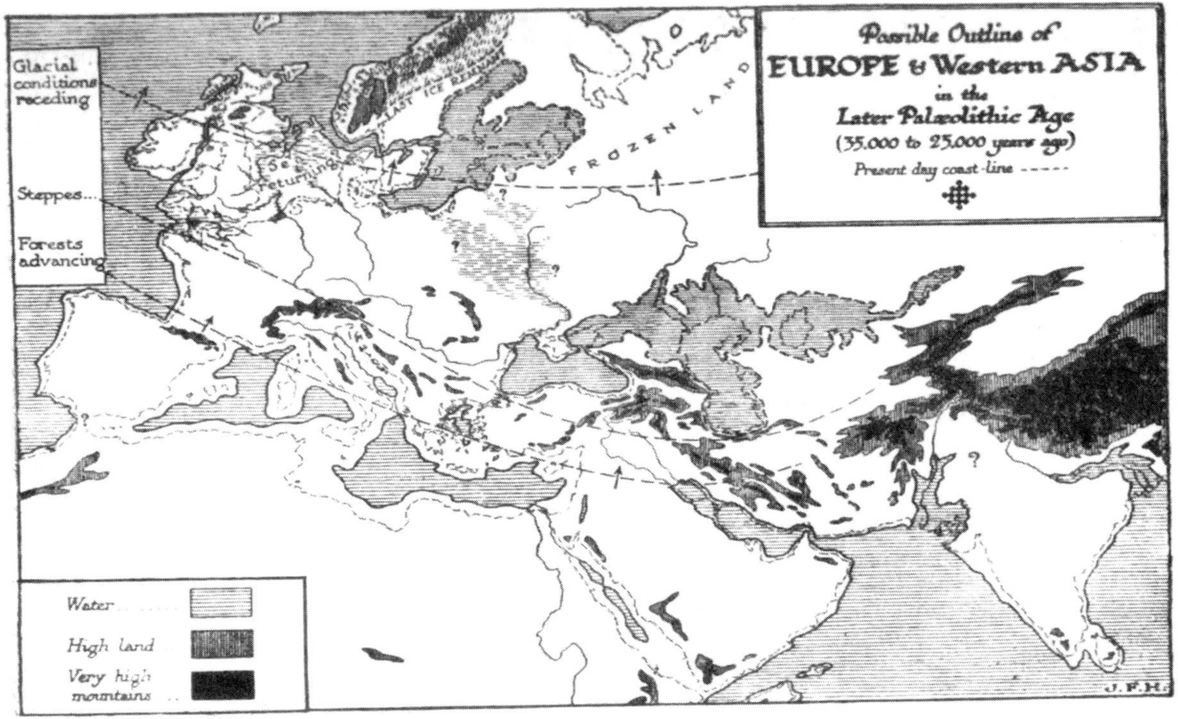
Possible Outline of
EUROPE & Western ASIA
in the
Later Palæolithic Age
(35,000 to 25,000 years ago)
Present day coast-line
Glacial conditions receding
Steppes
Forests advancing
FROZEN LAND
Water
High land
Very high mountains
J. F. H.

P. 6.

least more man-like than any living ape upon earth, are a number of flints and stones very roughly chipped and shaped so as to be held in the hand. These were probably used as hand-axes. These early implements ('eoliths') are often so crude and simple that there was for a long time a controversy whether they were to be regarded as natural or artificial productions. The date of the earliest of them is put by geologists as Pliocene, that is to say, before the First Glacial Age. They occur also throughout the First Interglacial Period." (p. 35).

"At Trinil in Java, in strata which are said to correspond either to the later Pliocene, or to the American and European First Ice Age, there have been found some scattered bones of a creature, such as the makers of these early implements may have been........The creature was not a man, nor was it an arboreal ape like the chimpanzee. It has been named by naturalists *Pithecanthropus erectus* (the walking ape-man). We cannot say that it is a direct human ancestor, but we may guess that the creatures who scattered these first stone tools over the world must have been closely similar and kindred, and that our ancestor was a beast of like kind.......While these early men or 'submen' were running about Europe four or five hundred thousand years ago, there were mammoths, rhinoceroses, a huge hippopotamus, a giant beaver, and a bison and wild cattle in their world. There were also wild horses, and the sabre-toothed tiger still abounded. There are no traces of lions or true tigers at that time in Europe, but there were bears, otters, wolves and a wild boar"......(p. 35-36).

Next, we come across a human jaw-bone, found in a sand-pit at Heidelberg at a depth of 80 feet from the surface in deposits which are said to belong to the Second Interglacial Period, 200,000 years later, or about 200,000 to 250,000 years ago. The owner of this jaw-bone has been named *Homo Heidelbergensis*. "He lived in a world not remotely unlike the world of the still earlier sub-man of the first implements; the deposits in which it is found show that there were elephants, horses, rhino ceroses, bison, a moose, and so forth with it in the world, but the sabre-toothed tiger was declining and the lion was spreading over Europe. The implements of this period (known as the Chellian period) are a very considerable advance upon those of the Pliocene Age. They are well-made but *very much bigger* than any truly human implements. The Heidelberg man may have had a very big body and large forelimbs"......(p. 36).

Next, "in a deposit ascribed to the Third Interglacial Period, which may have begun 100,000 years ago, and lasted 50,000 years, the smashed pieces of a whole skull turn up" at Piltdown in Sussex. According to Dr. Keith, there was "a fairly large brain in the Piltdown man with an arrangement and development of convolutions, not very unlike those of modern man," and "we shall be justified in drawing the conclusion that, so far as potential mental ability is concerned, he had reached the modern standard."[1] This creature has been named *Eoanthropus* or the Dawn man. Then in the Fourth Glacial Age, about 50,000 years ago, flourished a type of man who is called *Homo Neanderthalensis* or Neanderthal man (so called on account of the human remains having been found among other places at Neanderthal near Düsseldorf) "He was certainly not descended from *Eoanthropus*, but his jaw-bone is so like the Heidelberg jaw-bone, as to make it possible that the clumsier and heavier *Homo Heidelbergensis*, a thousand centuries before him, was of his blood and race."[2]

Mr. Wells says that "if the Heidelberg jaw was that of a Neanderthaler, and if there is no error in the estimate of the age of that jaw, then the Neanderthal Race lasted out for more than 200,000 years." (*Op. cit.* p. 43).

[1] Keith, *The Antiquity of Man.*, p. 401.

[2] Wells, *The Outline of History*, p. 39.

P, 8.

The Neanderthal men were acquainted with the use of fire, and sought shelter under rock-ledges and in caves. They hunted and killed such giant creatures as the mammoth or the cave bear, or even the rein-deer, with "spears of wood, wooden clubs, and those big pieces of flint they left behind them, the 'Chellian' and 'Moustierian' implements" (p. 40). They partly ate their kill where it fell; "but they brought back the big marrow bones to the cave to crack and eat at leisure." They did not speak at all or very sparingly, and had nothing that we should call a language. They used skins to wrap about them, and the women probably dressed the skins.

The type of the "first true men" (*Homo Sapiens*) who supplanted or exterminated the Neanderthalers was, according to Mr. Wells, "probably developed in *South Asia* or *North Africa*, or in lands now submerged in the Mediterranean basin.........For hundreds of centuries they were acquiring skill of hand and limb, and power and bulk of brain in that *still unknown environment*. They were already far above the Neanderthal level of achievement and intelligence, when first they come into our ken, and they are already split into two or more very distinctive races. These new-comers did not migrate into Europe in the strict sense of the word, but rather, as century by century the climate ameliorated, they followed the food and plants to which they were accustomed, as those spread into the new realms that opened to them. The ice was receding, vegetation was increasing, big game of all sorts was becoming more abundant. Steppe-like conditions, conditions of pasture and shrub, were bringing with them vast herds of wild horse. Ethnologists (students of race) class these new human races in one same species as ourselves, and with all human races subsequent to them, under one common specific name of *Homo Sapiens*. They had quite human brain-cases and hands. Their teeth and their necks were anatomically as ours are" (pp. 43 and 44). It is supposed that they entered into Europe from their original home or environments between 40,000 and 25,000 years ago.

As in the grotto of Cro-Magnon were first discovered the complete skeletons of one main type of these Later Palæolithic men,—these true men,—they are spoken of as Cro-Magnards. They were "a tall people with very broad faces, prominent noses, and all things considered, astonishingly big brains. The brain capacity of the woman in the Cro-Magnon cave exceeded that of the average male to-day." (p. 44).

This was one type of the Later Palæolithic True Men in Europe. But there was also another type of them, and their skeletons have been discovered in the Grimaldi cave near Mentone. Hence they are spoken of as the Grimaldi Race. These skeletons are "of a widely contrasted type, with Negroid characteristics that point rather to the Negroid type. There can be no doubt that we have to deal in this period with at least two, and probably more, highly divergent races of true men" (p. 44). The Cro-Magnards had probably been an Asiatic race, and the Grimaldis an African. "Both of these main races had a human fore-brain, a human hand, an intelligence very like our own. They dispossessed *Homo Neanderthalensis* from his caverns and his stone quarries. And they agreed with modern Ethnologists, it would seem, in regarding him as a different species. Unlike most savage conquerors, who take the women of the defeated side for their own and interbreed with them, it would seem that the true men would have nothing to do with the Neanderthal race, women or men. There is no trace of any intermixture between the races" (p. 46).

These Later Palæolithic men of Europe hunted and killed wild horses, as they were very fond of horse-flesh, and they probably also tamed some of them. They could make nice drawings and carvings. They carved on bones and horns, and they drew and painted on the cliffs and cave-walls.

P 10.

Probably they also painted their bodies. "They had no properly domesticated animals at all. They watched and drew and killed and ate. They do not seem to have cooked their food. Perhaps they scorched and grilled it, but they could not have done more, because they had no cooking implements. Although they had clay available, and although there are several Palæolithic clay figures on record, they had no pottery.... They had no cultivation of grain or vegetables of any sort.... These hunters lived on open steppes for two hundred centuries or so, ten times the length of the Christian era. They were, perhaps, overtaken by the growth of the European forests, as the climate became milder and damper. When the wild horse and the rein-deer diminished in Europe, and a newer type of human culture, with a greater power over food-supply, a greater tenacity of settlement, and probably a larger social organization arose, the Rein-deer men had to learn fresh ways of living or disappear . . . Apparently the Grimaldi type of men has disappeared altogether from Europe" (pp. 50-51). As regards the Cro-Magnon race, it is surmised that they may have mingled with their successors, the Neolithic men, or moved away with the rein-deer to Siberia and North America which was connected with Asia in those days. "There is a streak of their blood in most European peoples to-day, and there is a much stronger streak, if not a predominant strain in the Mongolian and American races" (p. 15).

Mr. Wells is of opinion that "the Neolithic phase of human affairs began in Europe about 10,000 or 12,000 years ago. But probably men had *reached the Neolithic stage elsewhere some thousands of years earlier.* Neolithic men came slowly into Europe *from the south or south-east* as the rein-deer and the open steppes gave way to forest and modern European conditions" (p. 52). These Neolithic people possessed polished stone implements, knew the rudimentary arts of agriculture, though they mainly lived by the chase, made pottery and cooked their food, domesticated cattle, sheep, goats and pigs and tamed the dog. "There is no great break," says Mr. Wells, "no further sweeping away of one kind of man and replacement by another kind between the appearance of the Neolithic way of living and our own time. There are invasions, conquests, extensive emigrations and intermixtures, but the races as a whole carry on and continue to adapt themselves to the areas into which they began to settle in the opening of the Neolithic Age. The Neolithic men of Europe were white men ancestral to the modern Europeans. They may have been of a darker complexion than many of their descendants; of that we cannot speak with certainty. But there is no real break in culture from their time onward until we reach the age of coal, steam, and power-driven machinery that began in the eighteenth century" (p. 53).

Further on Mr. Wells writes: "We do not know yet the region in which the ancestors of the white and whitish Neolithic peoples worked their way up from the Palæolithic stage of human development. Probably it was somewhere about *South-Western Asia*, or in some region now submerged beneath the Mediterranean Sea or the Indian Ocean; that while the Neanderthal men still lived their hard lives in the bleak climate of a glaciated Europe, the ancestors of the white men developed the rude arts of *their* Later Palæolithic period. But they do not seem to have developed the artistic skill of their more northerly kindred, the European Later Palæolithic races. And through the hundred centuries or so, while Rein-deer men were living under comparatively unprogressive conditions upon the steppes of France, Germany and Spain, these more favoured and progressive people to the south were mastering agriculture, learning to develop their appliances, taming the dog, domesticating cattle, and, as the climate to the North mitigated, and the equatorial climate grew more tropical, spreading northward. All these early chapters of our story have yet to be disinterred. They will probably be found in Asia Minor, *Persia*, Arabia, *India* or

North Africa, or they lie beneath the Mediterranean waters. Twelve thousand years ago, or thereabouts—we are still too early for anything but the roughest chronology—Neolithic peoples were scattered all over Europe, North Africa and Asia. They were peoples at about the level of many of the Polynesian islanders of the last century, and they were the most advanced peoples in the world." (p. 54).

Mr. Wells is quite definite in his statement that the white Neolithic people of Europe who were the direct ancestors of the modern European races had not their original cradle in Europe, but in *South-Western Asia* or some submerged region in the Mediterranean Sea or the Indian Ocean. Most of the modern European races speak different forms of the Aryan tongue, and claim to have descended from the original stock of the Aryan race. The white Neolithic peoples of Europe were, therefore, undoubtedly Aryans and had their original cradle, *not certainly in Europe*, but either in some submerged regions or in South-Western Asia including Persia and India. The mention of the submerged regions becomes necessary for the sake of argument, and a fair presentation of the case; but it has absolutely no practical value. For nobody would ever be able to ascertain whether any region, long ago submerged, had ever been the original cradle of a race; and hence all speculations on the subject would be extremely idle and futile. We have, therefore, to search *South-Western Asia* for the original cradle of the Aryan race. Mr. Wells suggests the names of Asia Minor, *Persia*, Arabia, *India* or North Africa as the probable places of this cradle. But North Africa may be left out of the reckoning, as it was probably peopled by the Negroid race, the same to which the Grimaldi men had belonged. For similar reasons Asia Minor, Mesopotamia and Arabia also should be eliminated, as it is admitted on all hands that these countries were the cradles of the Semitic people. If there are traces of Aryan culture and civilisation still to be found here and there in Asia Minor and

Mesopotamia, they must be due to other causes than the probability of their having been the original cradles of the Aryans, viz. emigration, colonization, and conquests etc. The only other two regions of *South-Western Asia* which may claim to be the original cradle of the Aryans are, therefore, India and Persia. Both Northern India and Persia were inhabited in ancient times by a people who called themselves *Aryans*, and claimed to have lived in these regions, and therein developed their civilisation from time immemorial. The Iranians of Persia and the Aryans of Sapta-Sindhavah (the ancient Punjab) were ethnologically one people, speaking nearly one and the same language or different *dialects* of it, having nearly the same myths, and worshipping nearly the same Gods. The descendants of the people still inhabit these regions with a literature and civilisation which are regarded as the earliest of the Aryan race. It seems, therefore, extremely strange that Mr. Wells, while diligently searching the Aryan cradle in South-Western Asia, and *naming India and Persia as two of the probable cradles*, did not take the ancient history, literature and culture of the Aryans of India and the Iranians of Persia into his consideration to come to a definite conclusion on the subject, and declare with unfaltering voice that the original cradle of the Aryan race was either the two contiguous regions of Persia and the Punjab, or some other region close to them. But probably the verdict of modern Oriental Scholarship in Europe and America, which has fixed the original cradle of the Aryans either in Northern or Central Europe without much show of reason, deterred him from making such a bold and consistent declaration, and compelled him to seek refuge under a vague and general statement that the original cradle of the Aryans must remain "unknown." Yes, "unknown" it will remain for ever, or, at any rate, for so long as the present angle of vision of the prominent Oriental scholars of Europe and America remains unchanged. They have turned their research-telescopes to all possible directions from Central Asia to the Arctic regions, and from the Arctic regions to Northern and Central Europe, and even to Asia Minor and Mesopotamia, *excepting India and Persia*, and are content to believe that Central Europe was the original cradle of the race, in spite of unmistakable and even positive geological and ethnological proofs and evidences to the contrary! They could not but declare the Ṛgveda to be the earliest work extant of the Aryan race; but probably not studying it with that spirit of detachment absolutely necessary for the discovery of historical truths, and having their vision limited, circumscribed or turned away by their telescope being focussed to a wrong point, they have failed to be struck and impressed by the many startling and wonderful proofs, found interspersed in the pages of the above-named ancient Scripture, about the hoary antiquity of Ṛgvedic culture and civilisation, and about their origin and development in the Land of the Seven Rivers or the Punjab from Later Palæolithic and Neolithic times. If they had done this, and allowed their vision a broad sweep in all directions, they would undoubtedly have come to the conclusion that the original cradle of the white Neolithic peoples of Europe, the ancestors of the present European races, was in the Punjab and Iran, situated *in South-Western Asia*, whence they entered into Europe with Aryan speech and Neolithic culture about 15,000 or 20,000 years ago, when the ice had permanently receded to the North from Southern and Central Europe.

It has been pointed above that the map of India of 50,000 years ago, as sketched by Mr. Wells, agrees in its salient features with the geographical description of the Punjab or Sapta-Sindhavah, as can be gathered from the Ṛgveda. These salient features must have continued to exist down to 35,000 or 25,000 years ago, and even later, and it is quite natural and reasonable to infer that the composition of some of the ancient hymns or verses of the Ṛgveda must be as old as that period. Of course, the language in which the present hymns of the Ṛgveda have been clothed was not exactly the language of those ancient times, and there is evidence in the Ṛgveda itself of the old archaic language having been transformed, recast and polished into the language of later times, so as to make it intelligible to all. The great sage Viśvāmitra declares: "Born from the heaven e'en in the days aforetime, wakening, sung aloud in holy synod, auspicious, *clad in white and shining raiment*, this is the ancient hymn of our forefathers." (Rv. iii. 39, 2). Nothing can be more explicit than this about the recasting of the old archaic language. There is also distinct mention of Three Ages in the Ṛgveda viz., the Ancient, the Mediæval, and the Later, during which the Ṛgvedic hymns were composed. One verse says: "The worshipper, by his conservatory sacrifice, has made Indra present. May I bring him to my presence to obtain new wealth, him who has been exalted by praises, whether *ancient, mediæval or recent*." (Rv. iii. 32, 13). Yet another verse points to the same three Ages: "Yea, here were they who, born of old, have served thee, thy friends of ancient time, thou active Worker. Bethink thee now of these, Invoked of many, the midmost and the recent, and the youngest." (Rv. vi. 21, 5). The present hymns of the Ṛgveda were, therefore, not the oldest literature of the Aryans, but there were older and still older hymns which came down to the Ṛgvedic Aryans from generations to generations "clad in white and shining raiment," and the period when the hymns first began to be composed is now lost in the impenetrable darkness of the past. As Professor Bloomfield once observed: "The language and literature of the Vedas is, by no means, so primitive as to place with it the real beginnings of Aryan life.........These in all probability and in all due moderation, *reach back several thousands of years more*" and "this curtain, which seems to shut off our vision at 4,500 B. C., may prove in the end a veil of thin gauze."[1] We can, therefore, safely take it for granted that the mention of the Eastern Sea

[1] Quoted in Tilak's *Arctic Home in the Vedas* Preface ii.

to the immediate east of the Punjab, and of a sea in Rajputana carries us back to a period about 35,000 or 25,000 years ago, when these seas may have actually existed.

"Between 40,000 and 25,000 years ago" says Mr. Wells "as the Fourth Glacial Age softened towards more temperate conditions, a different human type came upon the scene (of Europe), and, it would seem, exterminated *Homo Neanderthalensis*. This new type was probably developed in *South Asia or North Africa*, or in lands now submerged in the Mediterranean basin" (p. 43). These men, as already pointed out, were divided into two distinct types, one of which was Negroid to which the Grimaldi men belonged, and the other Asiatic to which belonged the men called Cro-Magnards, who had come from South Asia. It is very difficult to say from which part of South Asia these people had emigrated to Europe. Arabia was the early cradle of the Semites who only came into prominence after the Sumerians had established a kingdom in Chaldea in comparatively recent times. Mesopotamia had been peopled by primitive savages before the Sumerians came there by sea, and founded a colony. The only other country in South Asia must, therefore, be India, or to speak more correctly, the ancient Punjab including Gandhāra, which was the cradle of the Aryans, and where a higher type of civilisation was being evolved by them. Of the numerous Aryan tribes that inhabited that land, only five were developing a homogeneous civilisation, while the other tribes lagged behind in the race and remained in the various stages of their evolution, Palæolithic and Neolithic. These tribes proved a clog in the wheel of Aryan progress, and the advanced or advancing tribes thought it necessary to purge and remove them altogether from the country, and a war of extermination or expulsion went on vigorously for a considerable length of time. Tribes after tribes of savage Aryan nomads and hunters were expelled from the country, who passed through the Western mountain passes out into Western

Asia and the wide world beyond. Probably they commingled their blood with that of the Mongolian nomadic savages in a similar state of evolution in Western Asia, and the amalgamated type became Mongolian on account of the pre-potence of the latter race, though the language of this mixed humanity became Aryan in its crudest form. These men must have poured into Europe, as the ice gradually receded towards the north, laying bare the vast plains which were gradually converted into grassy steppes, attracting thereto vast herds of wild horses, deer and other herbivorous animals which supplied the new-comers with plenty of game. These men gradually dispossessed the Neanderthalers from their caves and haunts, and drove them away. No intermixture appears to have taken place between these "True Men" and the Neanderthalers. The Cro-Magnards then became the masters of the situation, and held Europe for thousands of years with the men of the Grimaldi race who had emigrated to the north from Africa and were probably the ancestors of the Iberians. The reason why there is a Mongolian streak in the blood of the modern European races is best explained by the theory of Aryo-Mongolian emigration from India and Western Asia into Europe between 40,000 and 30,000 years ago. This race of the First True Men in Europe lived undisturbed for about 20,000 years until they were ousted from possession in their turn, and amalgamated by batches of Neolithic Aryan savages who kept pouring into the continent, with a higher type of civilisation, "from the South or South-East as the rein-deer and the open steppes gave way to forest and modern European conditions." These Neolithic Aryans also undoubtedly emigrated from their original cradle in the Punjab and Gandhāra, and took with them such Aryan culture and language as they possessed. They could not help mixing their blood with that of the Aryo-Mongolian Cro-Magnards and the Iberians or the Grimaldi people, and became the ancestors of the modern civilised races of Europe. The advanced settled Aryans of the Punjab were a white race, but the nomadic Aryan savages were of a dark complexion in consequence of their wandering habits and exposure to the inclemencies and various vicissitudes of climate. Hence they were called "blacks," and "black-skinned" *Dāsas* and *Dasyus* by the Ṛgvedic Aryans. They changed the colour of their skin, however, by long residence in the northern latitudes of Europe, which were colder than the comparatively hot plains of the Punjab and the temperate wilds of Gandhāra and Iran.

We thus find that the geological evidences that I have cited in my book, *Ṛgvedic India*, in support of the physical description of the ancient *Sapta Sindhavah* as found in the Ṛgveda, are perfectly applicable to the history of the ancient Aryans inhabiting that country from time immemorial, and there is nothing absurd about them. If I was mistaken anywhere, it was in the fixing of the age when there was actually a different distribution of land and water in Northern India, for which geologists (more than the present humble writer) were responsible. The reference in the Ṛgveda to the existence of seas to the immediate east, west and south of the Punjab, and the prevalence of a cold climate in Ṛgvedic times, is undoubted. Whatever doubts may have existed in the minds of scholars on these points have now been dispelled by our present geological knowledge which has brought the proofs well within the range of historical speculation, if not actual historical record; and there is no reason why European and American Oriental scholars should not view the question of the original cradle of the Aryans from this altogether new stand-point. I have no doubt that they would arrive at the same conclusion as I have done, especially when it is admitted that the Neolithic Aryan-speaking peoples, the ancestors of the modern European races, came to Europe from the *south or south-west of Asia* about 10,000 or 12,000 years ago. If Mr. Wells' account of the peopling of Europe by the Neolithic races be found and admitted to be correct, the theory of a European cradle of the Aryan race must be given up for good as untenable, absurd, and unhistorical.

II.

I will now deal with the second objection, viz. if the Aryans in India had begun to develop a comparatively decent civilisation some 25,000 or 30,000 years ago, how is it that they have not been able to advance more than they have actually done during this long period? Dr. Sten Konow of Christiana University, while reviewing my book, *Ṛgvedic India*, in the pages of a Calcutta periodical,[1] made the following observations: "I have always admired the Indian mind for its high intellectual faculties. During the periods which I am able to control, I see how it has always been capable of producing new and fresh fruits. Now, however, we are asked to believe that the same Aryan mind had, to all effects, reached the higest development hundreds of millenniums ago. The only possible inference would be that it has remained practically stationary during untold millenniums, that it has, during the greater part of its existence, been unproductive and barren, and that its growth and development, which we were wont to admire, has extended over such a vast period that it becomes insignificant in comparision with such nations, as for instance, the Germanic ones. For they were certainly still barbarians less than two thousand years ago, and in spite of that they may now compare, and in some respects even favourably, with the Indo-Aryans who had developed, we are told, a marvellous civilisation hundreds of thousand years ago."

I gave a reply to the point raised by the learned reviewer, in the August number of the same periodical, which I cannot do better than partly reproduce here. But before doing so, I must frankly state here that I was consistently led to speak of "hundreds of millenniums" by the wrong geological

---

[1] *Modern Review*, Calcutta, July 1921, (Vol. xxx, No. 1, p. 69).

proofs at my disposal about the existence of a sea over the Gangetic trough in a remote geological period. But subsequent geological proofs have considerably modified my estimate, and the beginnings of Ṛgvedic civilisation may now be put down at a period, some 25,000 or 30,000 years ago, as already discussed in the previous pages. But even this period would probably appear too early and too long to Dr. Sten Konow not to apply to it his observations quoted above. Hence the reply I gave him, which is partly reproduced below, may still be found apposite :

"I have nowhere said in my book (*Ṛgvedic India*) that the Aryan mind 'had reached the *highest* development' in Ṛgvedic times. All that I have said is that the Aryans, during this period, after emerging from the state of a nomadic existence 'attained a comparatively high state of culture' (p. 557). Further, 'the Ṛgvedic hymns were composed during a long period, as there is distinct reference in the sacred Scripture to hymns that had been composed in the early and the middle ages and to hymns that were composed in the later age of Ṛgvedic times (Rv. iii. 32, 13). The language of the ancient hymns also underwent a thorough change, and had to be recast in the more refined dialect of the later age. In fact, the old hymns came down to the Aryans of the later age *in new graceful robes*, as a Ṛṣi has felicitously expressed the idea. All the hymns that we find in the Ṛgveda were collected and redacted in comparatively recent times, not certainly according to their sequence and dates of composition, but according to their happening to fall in with certain groups, and we need not, therefore, be surprised if we occasionally come across certain hymns that bear in them the stamp of modernity along with hymns that are admittedly more ancient' (p. 557). The above extracts from *Ṛgvedic India* would go to show that the development of Ṛgvedic civilisation extended over a long period of time, consisting of three ages. Of course, we do not know anything about the extent of each age; but we may safely surmise, considering how slowly did early civilisation move, that each age must have extended over some thousands of years. We should always bear in mind that progress was necessarily extremely slow in early human, or for the matter of that, early Aryan society on account of its complete isolation from, and the absence of communication with the outer world which also, by the way, had not made much advance towards civilisation. And this brings us to the question raised by Dr. Sten Konow about the improbability of the extremely slow development of the Aryan mind during an enormously long period of time. Certain modern nations, it is true, have advanced by leaps and bounds on the path of progress and attained a high degree of culture in the course of a few centuries by coming into contact with the original high culture of peoples who, in their isolation, had developed it by their own independent exertions slowly and laboriously through long untold centuries, nay millenniums. The history of modern Japan may be cited here as an instance. She has taken less than three-quarters of a century to come to the front-rank of the civilised nations of the world. If left to herself and her own resources in her island home, she would probably have taken millenniums to reach the present stage of her development. The Germanic nations also owed their present culture and civilisation to a successful assimilation of the high Roman, Celtic and Slavonic cultures with which they had come into contact; but, if left to themselves in their splendid isolation, they would probably not have advanced, during the last two thousand years, much beyond the stage of civilisation, as revealed in their ancient kitchen-middens. The aboriginal tribes like the Juangs of Orissa and the Puliyers and Mundavers of Southern India are still in the stone age of civilisation in consequence of their isolation, though some Dravidian peoples like the Cholas and the Pandyas attained a high culture thousands of years ago through their having come into contact with higher Aryan culture and civilisation. It is, therefore, extremely misleading to compare the rate of progress made by some modern nations with that made by an ancient people like the Indo-Aryans who, having been completely cut off from the outer world and surrounded by savage neighbours, had, through their unaided exertions, to develop a civilisation of their own, consistently with their peculiar genius. One need not, therefore, be surprised to find the slow growth of civilisation and the slow rate of progress of the Indo-Aryans during a long period of time. Before the last three thousand years, they had not come into contact with any peoples who might be regarded as their superiors or even equals. They moved in the same old groove, cut out by their fore-fathers thousands and thousands of years ago, carefully and religiously preserving the treasures bequeathed to them by countless generations of their ancestors, and developing a unique civilisation with unique religious rites and social customs which have no counterparts in any human society on the face of the globe. Only those Indo-Aryan tribes who emigrated to foreign countries from time to time took with them a portion of their culture which, having been transplanted in foreign soils, either did not flourish amidst uncongenial environments, or was transformed into some thing else beyond recognition. But this process also helped to uplift the then ancient world, and to spread civilisation over Western Asia, Egypt and Europe.

"It is against the Law of Nature to produce continually, or in quick succession, without sufficient rest and recuperation. And this law also holds good in the case of human communities. It is wrong to suppose that the Aryan mind 'has always been capable of producing new and fresh fruits.' This is reading history on a wrong line. The Indo-Aryan mind has undoubtedly produced new and fresh fruits, but only after sufficiently long intervals, as is evidenced by the production of the different Vedas which bear unmistakable internal evidence, both geographical and historical, of having been composed in different periods separated from one another by long stretches of time. The *Brāhmaṇas* were composed when the Vedic rituals became too complicated to be easily understood from a perusal of the *Mantras*, and they were followed by the *Āraṇyakas*, the *Upaniṣads* and the *Sūtras*, not surely in quick succession, but after long intervals, covered by thousands of years. This shows the gradual and natural growth of the Aryan mind. Nothing can be more misleading from an historical point of view than to apply the measure of progress made in modern times within a limited period to the circumstances of ancient times, which were so different from those of our own.

"The putting forth of a stupendous amount of energy is invariably succeeded by a period of inactivity, languor and depression both in the life of nations as of individuals. 'Professor Flinders Petrie' says the *Times* of January 8, 1921 'has insisted that culture is intermittent. He estimates the average duration of any period of culture at about 1500 years. He has traced eight such periods in ancient Egypt.' This may be true of ancient Egypt. But as regards India, the periods of production and non-production must have been far larger in number, during which the Aryan mind oscillated and progressed slowly but surely towards a higher culture, both material and spiritual, but more spiritual than material, which it was destined to achieve. Dr. Sten Konow's objection, therefore, against accepting my view about the long period of the slow development of the Aryan mind, stage by stage, does not seem to stand on firm ground.

"There is historical evidence of periods of national activity and inactivity extending over centuries. Has Rome achieved anything very great after the downfall of the Empire? Does Greece still lead the van of civilisation in

Europe? Where is the greatness of the ancient Persians now? And where is the greatness of ancient Egypt, Babylonia and Assyria? What has become again of the ancient civilisations of Peru and Mexico? The last sparks of their lives have probably been extinguished for ever, to revive no more. But there was and has been an uninterrupted continuity in the life of the ancient civilisation of the Indo-Aryans, showing that it possesses a strong vitality, acquired in the course of ages, through strenuous self-exertion and hard self-culture."[1]

If we apply Professor Flinders Petrie's estimate of the average duration of any period of culture (which, by the way, is a very modest estimate) to the growth and development of Vedic culture, we shall find that there were at least *ten* periods of this culture from the time of the composition of the earliest Ṛgvedic hymns down to the period of the *Sūtras*, which European scholars have put down at 500 B. C., with which, of course, I do not agree. Admitting for the sake of argument that this estimate is correct, we find that the period of the composition of the earliest hymns of the Ṛgveda goes back to 15,000 years before 500 B. C., or to about 17,500 years ago from our present time. The ten periods of Vedic culture roughly consisted of the three ages, mentioned in the Ṛgveda itself, during which the hymns were composed, and culture gradually advanced from the nomadic and pastoral to the agricultural stage of its evolution, and the different periods of the *Sāma-veda*, the *Yajur-veda*, the *Atharva-veda*, the *Brāhmaṇas*, the *Āraṇyakas*, the *Upaniṣads* and the *Sūtras*. No further comments are necessary on the hymns of the Ṛgveda. The *Sāma-veda* which derives its contents chiefly from the Eighth and especially the Ninth Book which is the Soma-book of the Ṛgveda "resembles the *Yajur-veda* in having been compiled exclusively for ritual applications; for the verses, of which its consists, are all meant to be chanted at the ceremonies of the Soma sacrifice. Removed from their

[1] *Modern Review* (Calcutta), Vol. XXX, No. 2, pp. 213-214.

context in the Ṛgveda, they are strung together without internal connection, their significance depending solely on their relation to particular rites. In form these stanzas appear in the text of the Sāma-veda, as if they were to be spoken or recited, differing from those of the Ṛgveda only in the way of marking the accent. The *Sāma-veda* is, therefore, only the book of words employed by the class of Udgātṛ priests at the Soma sacrifice. Its stanzas assume their proper character of musical *Sāmans* or chants only in the various song-books called *gānas*, which indicate the prolongation, the repetition, and the interpolation of syllables necessary in singing, just as is often done in European publications when the words are given below the musical notation."[1] While in the Ṛgveda we find mention of various sacrifices, viz. the horse-sacrifice, the bull-sacrifice, as well as the Soma-sacrifice, the last only was selected for elaboration in a later age with probably a change of culture, which resulted in the compilation of the *Sāma-veda*. "The hymns of the Ṛgveda being mainly invocations of the Gods, their contents are largely mythological. Special interest attaches to this mythology, because it represents an earlier stage of thought than is to be found in any other literature. . . . Though the mythological phase presented by the Ṛgveda is comparatively primitive, it yet contains many conceptions *inherited from previous ages*."[2] There is no indication in the *Ṛgveda* of the existence of the caste-system in the sense in which we now understand it, and the life led by the people was partly pastoral and partly agricultural, with the patriarchal stamp impressed on their domestic, social and political institutions.

While the *Ṛgveda* does not mention any of the provinces to the east of the Punjab, except casually mentioning the name of the Gangā and the Yamunā, or any river, mountain or province of Southern India, "the *Yajur-veda* introduces us not

---

[1] Macdonell's *Hist. of Sansk. Lit.*, Ch. vii, 171.

[2] *Op. Cit.*, Ch. iv, p. 67.

only to a geographical area different from that of the *Ṛgveda*, but also to a new epoch of religious and social life in India. The centre of Vedic civilisation is now found to lie farther to the east. We hear no more of the Indus and its tributaries, for the geographical data of all the recensions of the *Yajurveda* point to the territory in the middle of Northern India occupied by the neighbouring peoples of the Kurus and Pañchālas."[1] We find in it the existence of the Hindu caste-system, and " not only do we find the four castes firmly established as the main divisions of Indian society in the *Yajurveda*, but, as one of the later books of the Vājasaneyī Samhitā shows, most of the mixed castes known in later times are already found to exist. The social as well as the religious condition of the Indian people, therefore, now bear an aspect essentially different from those revealed to us in the *Ṛgveda*[2] . . . . . . Snake-worship which is unknown in the *Ṛgveda* now appears as an element in Indian religion. That, however, which impresses on the *Yajurveda* the stamp of a new epoch is the character of the worship which it represents. The relative importance of the Gods and of the sacrifice in the older religion has now become inverted. In the *Ṛgveda* the object of devotion was the Gods, for the power of bestowing benefits on mankind was believed to lie in their hands alone, while the sacrifice was only a means of influencing their will in favour of the offerer. In the *Yajurveda*, the sacrifice itself has become the centre of thought and desire, its correct performance in every detail being all important. Its power is now so great that it not merely influences but compels the Gods to do the will of the officiating priest. By means of it the Brahmans may, in fact, be said to hold the Gods in their hands."[3] There are also introduced altogether new ceremonies " such as the human sacrifice, the universal sacrifice, and the sacrifice to the Manes." The God Rudra is called by the names of Īśāna and Mahādeva. " The language of the Mantra portion of the

[1] *Op. Cit.*, Chap. vii, p. 174.

[2] *Ibid.*, pp. 184-185.

[3] *Ibid.*, p. 182-183.

Yajurveda, though distinctly representing a later stage, yet on the whole agrees with that of the *Ṛgveda*, while separated from that of classical Sanskrit by a considerable interval."[1]

The *Atharva-veda* was composed in a still much later period when the Aryans knew the whole country from Gandhāra, the Mujavat and Balhika in the north and west down to Magadha and Anga in the east. (Av. v. 22). It was possible for the Aryans to advance as far as Magadha and Anga in this period, as the lands began to be gradually reformed from the sea covering the Gangetic trough. The language of this Veda is "from a grammatical point of view decidedly later than that of the Ṛgveda, but earlier than that of the Brāhmaṇas. In vocabulary it is chiefly remarkable for the large number of popular words which it contains, and which from lack of opportunity do not appear elsewhere. . . . . .[2] It does not represent the most advanced religious beliefs of the priestly class, but is a collection of the most popular spells current among the masses, who always preserve more primitive notions with regard to demoniac powers. The spirit which breathes in it is that of a prehistoric age."[3] Besides containing many spells "directed against hostile agencies, such as diseases, noxious animals, demons, wizards, foes, oppressors of Brahmans, it also contains many spells of an auspicious character, such as charms to secure harmony in family and village life, reconciliation of enemies, long life, health and prosperity" and "prayers for protection on journeys and for luck in gambling. Thus it has a double aspect, being meant to appease and bless as well as to curse."[4]

As regards the different periods in which the *Brāhmaṇas*, the *Āraṇyakas*, the *Upaniṣads* and the various *Sūtras* were composed, I refer the reader for an elaborate account of them to Macdonell's *History of Sanskrit Literature* Chapters VIII

---

[1] *Ibid.*, p. 181.
[2] *Ibid.*, p. 185.
[3] *Ibid.*, p. 196.
[4] *Ibid.*, p. 185.

and IX. These periods unmistakably point to different stages of culture and were separated from one another by centuries, if not millenniums. It will not be out of place to refer here to an account of the eastward migration of the Aryans from the Punjab, as related in the *Śatapatha Brāhmaṇa*. The geographical data of this Brahmaṇa "point to the land of the Kuru-Pañchālas being still the centre of Brahmanical culture. Janmejaya is here celebrated as a king of the Kurus, and the most renowned Brahmanical teacher of the age, Āruṇi, is expressly stated to be a Pañchāla. Nevertheless, it is clear that the Brahmanical system had by this time spread to the countries to the east of Madhyadeśa, to Kosala, with its capital Ayodhyā (Oudh), and Videha (Tirhut or Northern Behar), with its capital, Mithilā...... The *Śatapatha Brāhmaṇa* contains reminiscences of the days when the country of Videha was not yet Brahmanised. Thus Book I. relates a legend in which three stages in the eastward migration of the Aryans can be clearly distinguished. Māṭhava, the King of Videgha (the older from of Videha), whose family priest was Gotama Rāhūgaṇa, was at one time on the Sarasvatī. Agni Vaiśvānara (here typical of Brahmanical culture) thence went burning along this earth towards the east, followed by Māṭhava and his priest, till he came to the river Sadānīrā (probably the modern Gandak, a tributary running into the Ganges near Patna), which flows from the northern mountain, and which he did not burn over. This river Brahmans did not cross in former times, thinking 'it has not been burnt over by Agni Vaiśvānara.' At that time the land to the eastward was very uncultivated and marshy, but now many Brahmans are there, and it is highly cultivated, for the Brahmans have caused Agni to taste it through sacrifices. Māṭhava, the Videgha, then said to Agni, 'Where am I to abide?' 'To the east of this river be thy abode' he replied. Even now, the writer adds, this river forms the boundary between the Kosalas (Oudh) and the Videhas (Tirhut)." [1]

[1] Macdonell, *Hist. of Sansk. Lit.*, pp. 213-215

It would thus appear that the Vedic Aryans gradually advanced towards the east, as the Gangetic plains began to be reformed from the sea. At the time to which the *Śatapatha Brāhmaṇa* refers (more than 3,000 B.C.), the sea must have been in the vicinity of Tirhut, as the latter was marshy land, unfit for cultivation and human habitation.[1] This time must have been anterior to the period when the Atharva-veda which mentions Magadha and Anga was composed.

If the Vedic civilisation had grown and flourished in one and the same territory like the ancient Egyptian, the estimate of the average duration of any period of culture which Professor Flinders Petrie has applied to the latter could also be applied with equal force to the Vedic. But we have to take into our consideration the fact of the gradual expansion and advance of the Vedic Aryans to the east simultaneously with the formation of new land in the Gangetic Sea. The age of the later Vedas, viz. the *Yajurveda* and the *Atharva-veda* must, therefore, be computed according to the actual time taken by the plains to form and emerge from the depth of the sea. If the Gangetic Sea existed, as it undoubtedly did, to the immediate east of the Punjab in Ṛgvedic times, the formation of the alluvial plains and their emergence from the sea down to Magadha and Anga, mentioned in the *Atharva-veda*, must have taken from 15,000 to 20,000 years, which places the beginning of Ṛgvedic civilisation in a period which is removed from our times by 30,000 to 35,000 years, and this nearly agrees with the period fixed by Mr. Wells, "when the true men were replacing the Neanderthalers." These "true men" were in the later Palæolithic stage of civilisation, and if they drifted to Europe from the outlying regions of ancient Sapta-Sindhu, which is extremely probable, we may take it that the early Ṛgvedic Aryans were about this time

[1] The date of the composition of the *Śatapatha Brāhmaṇa* was fixed at 2,500 B.C. by Mr. Tilak from the fact that it assigns to the Kṛttikās or Pleiades a position in the due east, but Mr. Dixit pointed out that this calculation was wrong and the date should be 3,000 B.C. Videgha Māṭhava's emigration to Tirhut must have taken place long long before 3,000 B.C., probably in the fourth millennium B.C. or even earlier.

in the Neolithic stage of culture, their God, Indra, having been represented as armed at first with a *stone* and then with a *bone* weapon for his *vajra*.[1] These Neolithic Aryans were then changing a pastoral and nomadic state of existence for a settled agricultural state. Though Neolithic culture with Aryan language may have been taken to Europe about 10,000 or 12,000 years ago, that period does not necessarily synchronize with the beginning of Neolithic culture in the Punjab or elsewhere, which is stated by Mr. Wells to be "some thousands of years earlier." According to Montelier "the deposits at Susa show Neolithic remains perhaps more than 20,000 years old."[2] Sir Arthur Evans also says that the Neolithic age began in Crete more than 14,000 years ago.[3] It is therefore just possible that Neolithic culture began in Ṛgvedic India some 30,000 years ago, or even earlier. Though Mr. Wells' map, as sketched for this period, does not show the existence of a continuous sea from the Arabian Sea to the Bay of Bengal over the regions now occupied by Rajputana and the Gangetic plains, yet the Rajputana Sea and the Gangetic Sea have been shown to be large enough to answer to the general conditions of Ṛgvedic times, and had probably mutual communication through a narrow channel, as I have pointed out in my maps in *Ṛgvedic India*. It is also extremely doubtful whether the Bay of Bengal in its present shape existed in Ṛgvedic times, and the Gangetic Sea was connected with it. Very probably it was an inland sea at the foot of the Himalayan Range. However this may have been, we can safely infer from the internal evidences of the Ṛgveda and subsequent Vedic literature that Ṛgvedic culture had begun in Sapta-Sindhu some 30,000 years ago, and the first "true men" of the later Palæolithic age had gone to Europe from India at about this period, and were subsequently followed by tribes of Neolithic Aryans at a much later period. These Palæolithic

---

[1] See *Infra*, Chap. II.

[2] *Congrès Internat. d' Anthrop. Prehist*, 1906, p. 22, quoted by Mr. Wells in his *Outline of History* in a Foot-note, p. 52.

[3] Wells, *Outline of History*, Foot-note, p. 52.

and Neolithic Aryan tribes were compelled to leave, or were driven out from the land of their birth by the advanced Aryans who had constituted themselves into "Five Tribes" or the Pañcajanāḥ or *Pañcakṛṣṭayaḥ* of the Ṛgveda, and had been determined to rid the country of all discordant elements. Almost the whole of the *Ṛgveda* is a record of this struggle which must have lasted for several thousand years.

As the ancient Aryans were autochthonous to the Punjab, they must have passed there through all the different stages of human culture viz. Eolithic, Palæolithic, later Palæolithic and Neolithic. We find the early Aryans in the Neolithic stage of culture, as will appear from a perusal of the next Chapter; but this subsequently gave place to the next stage, when metals and their different uses were discovered. The savage Aryan tribes whom the Five Tribes did their best to expel from the country were probably in the later Palæolithic stage, as they have been frequently described as *anāyudhāḥ* weaponless, *anāsāḥ*, mouthless, or speechless (showing that they had not as yet developed a tolerable language to express their ideas), *Kākṣasāḥ* or monsters subsisting on raw meat, *avratāḥ*, riteless, and living in the deep recesses of mountains and forests, because they were a hunting people, and game was plentiful in those regions. As in the Post-Glacial age there grew up an extensive belt of steppes extending in an uninterrupted line from the confines of Mongolia, along the southern coasts of the Asiatic Mediterranean, right into the heart of Europe, we can easily guess that it attracted vast herds of horses and deer from Central Asia, which the later Palæolithic Aryans followed in their onward march to Europe, along with the Mongolian savages with whom they mixed their blood, which developed the "type Mongoloid" of the early European populations. The Neolithic Aryans, with their rude wagons drawn by oxen, and their cattle, dogs and skin-tents followed them several thousand years later, and settling down in the various localities of Europe, and probably mingling their blood with the Aryo-Mongolian tribes and the Iberians, became the ancestors of most of the modern European races who speak different forms of the Aryan language. The theory of the original Aryan cradle in Sapta-Sindhu, therefore, fully explains the geological and ethnological facts discovered in Europe.

III.

Lastly, I will deal with Professor Winternitz's objections against the acceptance of my theory about the hoary antiquity of Ṛgvedic Culture. He says: "It is absolutely impossible to use geological evidence as Abinas Chandra Das does in his book 'Ṛgvedic India' (published by the University of Calcutta, 1921), in order to prove an age of the Ṛgveda which is not to be measured by thousands but by ten thousands, nay hundred thousands or even millions of years. He would have us believe that the Ṛgveda is 'as old as the Miocene or the Pliocene epoch whose age is to be computed by some hundreds of thousands, if not, millions of years.' Now why is this impossible? First of all, it is extremely doubtful whether man existed at all in the Miocene or Pliocene epoch. Most anthropologists and archæologists agree that the earliest existence of man on earth cannot be traced further than to the Quaternary or Glacial epoch. But apart from this, it is absolutely impossible that the language of the Ṛgveda should be so little different as it is from the Old Persian in the 6th Century B. C., and from the Sanskrit of Pāṇini and Patañjali, if it had been the language of a people that lived even in the Quaternary, to say nothing of the Miocene or Pliocene epochs. For languages, as a rule, change very rapidly; there are languages (and these are exceptions) that have changed comparatively little in the course of a thousand years, but never have languages been known to have remained almost unchanged for thousands or ten thousands of years. Merely from a linguistic point of view the theory of Abinas Chandra Das must be rejected. It must also be rejected from a historical point of view." [1]

---

[1] Readership Lecture delivered by Prof. Winternitz at the Calcutta University in August 1923. Published in the *Calcutta Review*, Nov. 1923.

It is said that errors, like prejudices, die very hard, and the truth of this remark has been best illustrated in my case. I have already explained elsewhere how I was naturally led by the wrong estimate of old Geologists as to the age of a different distribution of land and water in the Punjab and Northern India, of which unmistakable evidence is found in the Ṛgveda, to infer a vast antiquity of some of the Ṛgvedic hymns which, however, I candidly doubted, and attempted to bring down to the Pleistocene and even the Post-Pleistocene or Quaternary epoch in my book *Ṛgvedic India.*[1] But the error seems to have got a firm hold on the mind of my critics, and in spite of my clearly expressing my own modified opinion, they persist in mentioning the Miocene and Pliocene epochs as the probable age ascribed by me to some of the early Ṛgvedic hymns, evidently with the object of holding up my theory to ridicule. I do not know whether this could be called fair criticism, compatible with a genuine spirit of research for truth. I firmly relied, as I still do, upon the geographical data as revealed in the Ṛgveda, which I challenge any Vedic scholar to disprove; and if there was any error at all, it lay in my mis-reading the ancient geological epochs in the absence of more trustworthy evidence which, however, has since been available, to a certain extent. The geographical data, as brought forward by me, should have arrested the attention of my critics sufficiently strongly to induce them to examine them in the light of fresh geological evidence, if available, before passing them by with an indifference which is really amazing. It is, therefore, a matter for deep regret to me, and to a large number of students of Ancient Indian History and Culture in the University of Calcutta, that Professor Winternitz should have remained profoundly silent on the value of the several geographical data advanced by me, and content himself only by expressing what seems to be a mere dogmatic

[1] *Ṛgvedic India*, P. 567. Read also my article on "The Antiquity of the Ṛgvedic Age" published in the *Journal of the Department of Letters*, Vol. VIII, pp. 277-295 (Calcutta University).

assertion that "it is absolutely impossible to use geological evidence" (as I have done), in order to prove the ancient age of the Ṛgveda. The reason he adduces is that the Miocene or the Pliocene age was too early for the evolution of civilised man or of a culture as described in the Ṛgveda. I admit (as I have admitted in *Ṛgvedic India*) the force of this objection. But the geographical evidence of a different distribution of land and water in the Punjab in Ṛgvedic times is still there, which cannot be ignored, and must be explained correctly, if recourse cannot be had to geological evidence. Either the geographical evidence must be satisfactorily explained, or you must have recourse to geological evidence. There is no third alternative. The geological age may not have been (as it is certainly not, in the light of recent proofs) the Miocene or the Pliocene; but it must have been an age, subsequent to them and more recent. Mr. Wadia in his *Geology of India* (P. 248) says that there was a Pleistocene sea over the Gangetic trough which lasted for thousands of years, and Mr. Wells also is of opinion that such a sea existed so long as 50,000 to 25,000 years ago.[1] Taking the lower estimate as correct, it would not be unreasonable to guess that some of the Ṛgvedic hymns were as old as 25,000 years. Let us hope, Professor Winternitz will not now consider it to be "absolutely impossible to use geological evidence" with a view to explain the geographical data revealed in the *Ṛgveda*, and prove its hoary antiquity.

Next, with regard to the language of the Ṛgveda, Professor Winternitz holds that it is so little different from the Old Persian in the 6th Century B. C., and from the Sanskrit of Patañjali that it could not have been the language of a people that lived in the Quaternary epoch. For, according to him, "languages, as a rule, change very rapidly; there are languages (and these are exceptions) that have changed comparatively little in the course of a thousand years;

---

[1] Mr. H. G. Wells' *Outline of History*, pp. 39 & 45.

but never have languages been known to have remained almost unchanged for thousands or ten thousands of years."

Let us examine the above dictum of the Professor a little closely. He evidently proceeds on the assumption that the Ṛgvedic hymns were composed about 2,000 B.C., or 2,500 B. C., at most. If his surmise be correct, then his statement that it is very little different from the Old Persian in the 6th Century B. C., and from the Sanskrit of Pāṇini and Patañjali militates against his theory that "languages as a rule change very rapidly." For we find on his own admission that the Ṛgvedic language remained unchanged for about 2,000 years. And if it remained practically unchanged for 2,000 years, what is there to disprove that it had remained unchanged for 5,000, 10,000 or even 15,000 years? And the same query may be put with regard to Old Persian, and the language of the Avesta. As to the language of the latter, the Professor remarks: "The date of the Avesta is itself not quite certain." Further on, he remarks: "Languages differ very much as to how long old forms of speech may be kept up, and there is a great difference between the languages of one family as to the time they want for differentiation. Lithuanian is one of those Indo-European languages which are nearest related to the ancient Indo-Iranian. But yet it is not an old language, and its literature is of quite recent growth." If Lithuanian is very closely related to the ancient Indo-Iranian, it is extremely difficult to understand why it is "not an old language," though its literature may be of recent growth. The very fact that Lithuanian still retains its old forms, being "nearest related to the ancient Indo-Iranian" goes clearly to show that language can remain unchanged for thousands of years.

It is a pity that, for reasons best known to them, Western Vedic scholars seem generally unwilling to attach much importance to clear astronomical evidence, found in the Vedic Literature, which would have helped them in fixing the date of some of the old compositions. For example, in his *Orion* Mr. B. G.

Tilak has proved from astronomical statements found in the Vedic Scriptures that " the Vernal Equinox was in the constellation of Mṛga or Orion about 4,500 B. C." when, he believes some of the hymns of the Ṛgveda were composed. And in this opinion he has been indirectly supported by another Vedic scholar, Mr. V. B. Ketkar, who has proved from a statement in the *Taittiriya Brāhmaṇa* (III. 4, 1, 5) that Bṛhaspati, or the planet Jupiter, was first discovered when confronting, or nearly occulting the star Tiṣya " about 4650 B. C.[1] Mr Dhirendranath Mukhopādhyāya also proves from the Vṛṣakapi hymn (Rv. x. 68) that " when the vernal equinoctial colure passed through the group Orion (this was an extremely ancient date B. C. 30,000), sacrifices were offered to Vṛṣākapi (this was allowed by Indra because of the vernal equinoctial colure passing through it). But later on the vernal equinox having retreated a long way, Vṛṣākapi rose on the Equator (about B. C. 23,000), and people were still sacrificing to Vṛṣākapi . . . . Later on Vṛṣākapi was again going slowly to the south, as if by the orders of Indra, and was almost invisible with the exception of the head about B. C. 10,000. Later on still, it was slowly rising (at present it has coincided again with the Equator), and at this time the hymns to Vṛṣakapi were sung. Here the description of the penomenon is exquisite :

'O Vṛṣākapi, go to the house, the celestial sphere which is cut off and which contains some (unknown) *yojanas* or stages. From your nether house come to our house. Indra is in the upper (portion) of the Universe. O Vṛṣākapi, you, the destroyer of sleep, who are going to the house, come back again, again by your way. We would perform the sacrifices. (Indra is, &c). O Mighty Vṛṣakapi, when you rising upwards (or rather northwards) would come to (our) house, where would that great sinner Mṛga be ? Where he, who misleads people, would go ? (Indra is, &c.).' The explanation of the phenomenon—when Vṛṣākapi returns in his upward march

[1] Tilak's *Arctic Home in the Vedas*. Preface, ii.

to the house of Indra, the impertiment (sinner) Mṛga is not to be seen—is that the vernal equinox passing through the group at the time, Mṛga (Orion) is not to be seen at night being in company of the Sun. This Vṛṣākapi hymn takes us back to the period even beyond 16,000 B. C."[1] Mr. Tilak says that "the latest attempt of the kind is that of Pischel and Geldner in their Vedic Studies, Vol. VII, Part I. These scholars hold that the hymn narrated a legend current in old times. In other words, they take it, and I think rightly, to be a historic hymn....Pischel and Geldner understand the hymn to mean that Vṛṣākapi went down to the south and again returned to the house of Indra."[2]

Mr. D. Mukhopādhyāya further refers to another astronomical evidence in a verse of the Ṛgveda (x. 85, 13) which indicates a period about 15,000 B. C. The verse is as follows :

Sūryáyá vahatuḥ prágát Savita yam avásṛjat Agháṣu hanyante gávah Arjunyoḥ paryuhyate.

" Here, ' Aghā ' means the group ' Maghā ' and ' Arjunī ' the two Phalgunīs as interpreted by Sāyaṇa. Astronomically it means, when the Sun enters Maghā, the rays (*gávah*) of the Sun are almost powerless, indicating Winter Solstice (B. C. 15,000), and on his entrance into Phalgunī they are again revived, symbolically representing Sūryā being carried to her husband's house as if in a Palanquin formed of the Phalgunī *nakṣatras*. The seventh case-ending here is in place of the instrumental."[3]

---

[1] *The Hindu Nakṣatras*, in the "Journal of the Department of Science" (Calcutta University), Vol. vi, pp. 19-20.

[2] Tilka's *Orion*, P. 176. Vṛṣākapi, according to Mr. Tilak is "the Sun as represented by the constellation of Orion." (P. 178).

"The (Vṛṣākapi) hymn gives us not only a description of the constellation of Orion and Canis (verses 4 & 5), but clearly and expressly defines the position of the Sun when he passed to the north of the Equator in old times. (verse 22)."

[3] *The Hindu Nakṣatras* in the "Journal of the Department of Science" (Calcutta University), Vol. vi, P. 22.

I need not multiply more instances to prove that there are allusions in the Ṛgveda to such ancient times as would stagger those European and American scholars who are unwilling to take back Ṛgvedic culture and civilisation to more than 2,000 B. C. or 2,500 B. C. On the mere fact that there are some real vestiges of Aryan language and culture in many parts of Europe, they have built a theory of the original Aryan cradle in Europe, consistently with the state of culture of the Neolithic people in that continent and have made the Indo-Aryans and the Iranians mere immigrants to the Punjab and Iran respectively from that country in comparatively very recent times, resolutely shutting their eyes against the many geographical, astronomical and cultural evidences in the Ṛgveda, that directly militate against their theory. It may be a convenient theory for explaining the existence of the Aryan language and culture in some forms in Europe, but it is certainly *not ancient history*, and no structure based on it can stand for any length of time. It is bound to topple over sooner or later, and the original cradle of the Aryans will have ultimately to be sought, not certainly in any parts of Europe, but elsewhere—very probably in the sacred Land of the Seven Rivers, as revealed by various evidences in the Ṛgveda itself. The antiquity of Ṛgvedic culture must also be taken back to about 25,000 B. C., or more, in spite of hazy and not very convincing arguments regarding the rapid changeability of language.

Turning again to Professor Winternitz's objections against the acceptance of my theory regarding the vast antiquity of Ṛgvedic culture, on the ground of the rapid changeability of language, I must point out to my readers that though spoken dialects may be liable to frequent changes, the language of any literary composition, whether recorded or not, especially if it relates to religious matters and holy sacrificial formulas, is seldom or only very slowly changed. In fact, such language is regarded as too sacred to be frequently handled, changed, polished or modernized, and the very quaintness of its wording and structure seems to add a peculiar sanctity, force and mystic fascination to it. There were three distinct ages,—the Ancient, the Mediæval and the Later,—during which the Ṛgvedic *mantras* were composed (Rv. iii, 32, 13; vi. 21, 5) and these three ages covered so vast a period of time that in spite of the extreme reluctance on the part of Ṛṣis to make any change in the wording of the sacred texts and formulas, there is clear evidence in the Ṛgveda itself of some such change having been *actually* effected in the Later age, with a view to make the *mantras* more intelligible to the learned of that period. This is clearly indicated in a verse (Rv. iii. 39. 2) which says that the *mantra* came down to the Ṛṣi from his ancient ancestors, clothed in white and graceful robes. This means, if it means anything, that the language had to be polished in order to make it intelligible to the holy men of that later period. The very necessity for doing this implied the vast antiquity of the *mantra* itself. It has been held by Dr. Martin Haug and others that the present Ṛgvedic hymns are not the oldest, but there were *mantras* that were older still. I will let Dr. Haug speak on the subject:

"Now the question arises, are the finished and polished hymns of the Ṛgveda with their artificial metres the most ancient relics of the whole religious literature of the Brahmans, or are still more ancient pieces in the other Vedic writings to be found? It is hardly credible that the Brahmanical priests employed at their sacrifices in the earliest times hymns similar to those which were used when the ritual became settled. . . . . .

"Now if we compare the sacrificial formulas as contained in the Yajurveda, and principally the so-called *Nigadas* and *Nivids*, preserved in the Brāhmaṇas and Sūtras with the bulk of the Ṛgveda hymns, we come to the conclusion that the *former are more ancient*, and served the Ṛsis as a kind of sacred text, just as passages of the Bible suggest ideas to religious poets among Christians. That Vedic poets were perfectly acquainted with several of such formulas and addresses which are still extant, can be proved beyond any doubt.

"I must lay particular stress on the *Nivids* which I believe *to be more ancient than almost all the hymns contained in the Ṛgveda*.

"The word *Nivid* frequently occurs in the hymns, and even with the epithet *pūrva* or *pūrvya*, old. (Rv. i. 89, 3; 96, 2; ii. 36, 6). The *Marutvatīya Nivid* is, as it appears, even referred to by Vāmadeva (Rv. vi. 18, 7); the repetition of the *Nivids* is juxtaposed with the performance of the chanters, and the recital of the Śastras (Rv. vi. 67, 10). The (Aitareya) Brahmaṇam regards the Nivids, particularly that one addressed to Agni, as those words of Prajāpati, by means of which he created all beings (*Ait. Brāh.* 2, 33-34). The old Ṛṣi, Kutsa, who is already in many Vedic songs looked upon as a sage of the remote past, says (Rv. i. 96, 2) that Agni created by means of the 'first *Nivid*' the creatures of the Manus. In i. 89, 3-4, an old *Nivid* appears to be quoted.

"Many *Nivids*, even the majority of them, are certainly lost. But the few pieces of the kind of religious literature which are still extant, are sufficient to show that they must be very ancient, and are not to be regarded as fabrications of the sacrificial priests at the times when the Brāhmaṇas were composed. Their style is, in the main, just the same in which the hymns are composed, and far more ancient than that of the Brāhmaṇas. They contain in short sentences the principal names, epithets and feats of the deity invoked. They have no regular metre but a kind of rhythmus, or even a *parallelismus membrorum* as the ancient Hebrew poetry.

"The *Nivids* along with many so-called *Yajus* formulas which are preserved in the Yajurveda, the *Nigadas*, such as as the Subrahmaṇya and the so-called Japa formulas (*Aitareya Brāhmaṇa* 2, 38) which are muttered with a low voice only, are doubtless the most ancient pieces of Vedic poetry

The Ṛṣis tried their poetical talent first in the composition of the *Yājyās*, or verses recited at the occasion of an offering being thrown into the fire. Thence we meet so many verses requesting the deity to accept the offering, and taste it. These *Yājyās* were extended into little songs, which on account of their finished forms, were called *Sūktam*, *i.e.*, well, beautifully spoken. The principal ideas for the *Yājyās* were furnished by the sacrificial formulas in which the Yajurveda abounds, and those of the hymns suggested by the *Nigadas* and *Nivids*. There can be hardly any doubt that the oldest hymns which we possess are purely sacrificial, and made only for sacrificial purposes. Those which express more general ideas, or philosophical thoughts, or confessions of sins, such as many of those addressed to Varuṇa, are comparatively late."[1]

From the above discussion it would appear that the Ṛgvedic hymns are not the oldest, but there were still older verses called Nivids and Nigadas, the proto-types of the Ṛgvedic hymns, whose language was more archaic than that of the hymns themselves. Though most of the Nivids are now lost, having been either amplified or absorbed in the Ṛgvedic hymns, even those that remain and are found in the Brāhmaṇas and Sūtras bear in them the unmistakable impress of vast antiquity. There may have been still older verses than the *Nivids* themselves, but no relics of them have so far been discovered. Though the changeability of language is thus proved, the changes in the language of religious and sacrificial verses were certainly not so rapid as Professor Winternitz would make them out to be. The changes were necessarily extremely slow, partially suited to the needs of changing time, so as to make the language intelligible, at any

---

[1] *Aitareya Brāhmaṇam* ; *Introduction*, by Dr Martin Haug, Vol. I, pp. 30-39 (Bombay 1863) I am indebted for the above extracts to my esteemed friend and colleague Mr. Narayanchandra Bannerjea M.A., Lecturer, Calcutta University.

rate, to the hereditary custodians of the ancient sacred verses in later times. The majority of the common people or the lay folk, who spoke a different dialect, did not understand the language of the *mantras* any better than an illiterate Hindu would understand Sanskrit, or an ordinary Englishman would understand old Anglo-Saxon at the present day. In fact the language, with its complicated rules for recitation and accentuation, was regarded by the lay folk as too sacred and mysterious to be uttered, especially when the efficacy of the *mantras* was believed to depend upon how, when and by whom they were pronounced. This ultimately must have led to the formation of a distinct class, that of the priests, who were the custodians of the *mantras* and were carefully versed in the art of correctly pronouncing them and applying them to the various rites and sacrifices. And no one was entitled to be called a Ṛṣi or Seer, who could not clothe his thoughts, or the truths discovered by him, in the conventional antique language of the ancient *mantras*, and in the recognised style and metres of old. It is extremely probable that the art of writing existed in some form or other in Ṛgvedic times, as there is reference in the Ṛgveda to Speech *(Vāc)* having been *seen*, yet not understood, and heard yet not comprehended by the uninitiated (Rv. x. 71, 4), thereby showing that the spoken dialect of Ṛgvedic times was different from the old literary language of the *mantras*.[1] And this old literary language was imitated not only by the Ṛṣis, but even by some of the commentators and expositors in later ages, with a view to give their compositions a sacred character. This will explain why the literary language of the Ṛgvedic hymns and the Nivids was adopted with more or less variations in the later Vedic Saṃhitās, the Brāhmaṇas, the Upaniṣads and the Sūtras, and why even Pāṇini, who wrote his Vedic grammar, adopted a style that closely resembled that of the *mantras*. But it is a mistake to suppose, as Professor Winternitz has

[1] *Vide* my article on the "Art of Writing in Ancient India" (Jour. of the Department of Letters, Calcutta University, Vol. X).

done, that the language of the later Vedic literature was exactly the same as that of the Ṛgvedic hymns. There is noticed a general family likeness between them, no doubt; but there is also a marked difference in style, diction, metre, and even vocabulary among the various sections of what is ordinarily known as Vedic Literature, thus showing that they were composed in different periods of time, removed from one another by several centuries, and hence they could not help bearing in them the impress of the particular periods. Pāṇini and Lord Buddha were born with comparatively a small interval between them, but the language in which the Buddha preached his doctrines to the people was not the language in which Pāṇini wrote his Grammar. The latter was the sacred old literary language of the Vedas which had become unintelligible even to the learned who had, therefore, begun to reform and polish it into what is known as Sanskrit (Lit. Polished). This afterwards became the literary language of the Epics and the Purāṇas, though the dialects spoken by the people were different. It is, therefore, quite clear that the use of an ancient literary language and style in a later age does not necessarily prove that it was a spoken living language in that age, and it is not at all safe to base any chronology or history on such loose and slender ground.

It is useless further to deal with the objections raised by Professor Winternitz against the vast antiquity of Ṛgvedic culture, which on close examination do not appear to be either strong or sound. As regards the history of this vast period, the materials are necessarily too meagre to construct it. But, nevertheless, the Ṛgveda contains sufficient internal evidence to prove the various early stages through which ancient Aryan culture had passed, reference to which will be made in the next and subsequent Chapters. Whatever may be the date of this culture, it is absolutely certain that it is older than that of any other culture that the world has ever known or possessed any records about.

CHAPTER II.

GLIMPSES OF SOME OF THE EARLY STAGES OF ARYAN CULTURE IN THE ṚGVEDA.

The Pañcajanāḥ or Five Clans.—In the Ṛgveda we find evidences of a comparatively high state of culture of the Aryans who appear to have been divided into five principal clans or tribes *(Pañcajanāḥ or Pañcakṛṣṭayaḥ)*[1] possessing a homogeneous civilisation, worshipping common gods, performing common religious rites, observing common social customs, subsisting on the products of agriculture, and living in well-organized village communities (*grāmas*)[2] under the guidance of *Grāmaṇīs*[3] (lit. leaders of *grāmas* or multitudes), and in fortified cities *(purs)*[4] under the protection of kings or rulers. Sāyaṇa, the great commentator of the Ṛgveda, has interpreted the word *Pañcajanāḥ* to mean the four principal castes, and the *Niṣ ādas* as the fifth caste; but this interpretation does not seem to be tenable in the face of the fact that the caste-system, as we know it now, did not exist in early Ṛgvedic socie ty. The four castes have certainly been mentioned, though clearly only once, in the Tenth Maṇḍala of the Ṛgveda (x. 90, 12); but Western Vedic scholars are of opinion that the verse in question is of later origin, the language not being as archaic as that of most other Ṛgvedic verses. It must, therefore, have been composed at a period of Ṛgvedic times when the caste-system had become somewhat developed and well-marked in ancient Aryan society.

---

[1] Rv. iii, 37, 9; 59, 8; viii, 32, 22; ix, 65, 23; x, 45. 6; *Pañca-carṣaṇyaḥ*—Rv. v. 86, 2; vii. 15, 2; ix. 101, 9, *Pañca-kṛṣṭayaḥ*—Rv. ii. 2, 10; iii, 53, 16; iv. 38, 10; x. 60, 4; 119, 6. *Pañca-kṣitayaḥ* Rv. i, 7, 9; 176, 3; v. 35, 2; vi. 46, 7; vii. 75, 4; 79, 1.

[2] Rv. i. 44, 10; 114, 1; ii. 12, 7; x. 146, 1; 149, 4; etc.

[3] Rv. x. 62, 11; 107, 5.

[4] Rv. i. 53, 7; 58, 8; 131, 4; 166, 8; iii. 15, 4; iv. 27, 1.

The system, however, had existed in embryo from the very beginning, as it still exists in some form or other in all human societies, either savage or civilised, being based on certain in-born tendencies of the human mind and temperament *(guṇas)*, that make some men choose a certain profession or career in preference to another and stick fast to it. The verse in question did not certainly create or sanction the four castes, but only indicated their existence in a somewhat developed form in the *Later period* of the Ṛgvedic age. The system was the product of economical causes rather than of social or religious movements, and was highly elastic, not standing in the way of inter-dining or inter-marriage. It should be remembered in this connection that the Ṛgvedic age was divided into three periods, *viz.*, (1) the Early, (2) the Mediæval and (3) the Later, during which the Ṛgvedic verses were composed.[1] The verse regarding the four castes must have been composed in the Later period, when they were emerging into and assuming distinctive forms.

This having been the case, the *Pañcajanāh* and *Pañcakṛṣṭayah*, frequently mentioned in the Ṛgveda, did not refer to the five castes of later Aryan society, but to the five clans or tribes whose frequent mention is met with in the sacred Scripture. These five tribes or clans were most likely the Bharatas and Tṛtsyus, the Purus, the Anus, the Druhyus and the Turbaśes. There were also other Aryan tribes like the Cedis and the Yadus, etc., but they were probably comprised in one or another of the five principal clans. For instance, the Yadus are frequently mentioned and coupled with the Turbaśes, and they were probably regarded as one clan. The very fact that the hymns were composed by Ṛṣis who belonged to one or another of the clans, and that their compositions were collected together into the Ṛgveda Saṃhitā, goes to show that the *Pañcajanāh* referred to the five principal clans only, and not to the five castes, as remarked by Sāyaṇa.

---

[1] Rv. iii. 32, 13; vi. 21, 5.

Other Aryan clans.—As already stated, these five tribes developed a comparatively high state of culture in Ṛgvedic times; but there were other Aryan clans, some of whom were not as advanced as they. We find mention, however, of certain Aryan tribes in the Ṛgveda, some of whom, though not subscribing to the orthodox Vedic faith, were nevertheless as advanced as the Ṛgvedic Aryans. But they were hated by the latter, and called by the hateful names of *Asuras Dāsas* and *Dasyus*, terms which seemed to have been applied to all persons, savage or civilised, who were not one with the Vedic Aryans in religious sentiments, or who performed different religious rites, and observed different social customs, just as the Greeks called all people "barbarians," who were not Greeks, or as the early and mediæval Christians designated all persons as "heathens", who did not profess the Christian faith.[1]

Savage Aryan tribes.—The savage Aryan tribes who were also, for similar reasons, called *Dāsas* and *Dasyus* by the Vedic Aryans, were mostly hunters and nomads who either roamed about, or lived in mountain-caves and in the deep recesses of forests, from which they occasionally came out, and descended upon the peaceful agricultural population who lived in the plains below, and carried off their cattle and goods.[2] The very fact that these savage Aryan tribes existed in Sapta-Sindhu, side by side with the more advanced Aryan tribes, goes to show that the Aryans were autochthonous to the Punjab, and that the savage tribes were only the remnants—the dross as it were—cast out by the Aryan race in the course of its long evolution and advancement towards a higher civilisation. As inhabitants of Sapta-Sindhu, the savage Aryan tribes were probably acquainted with the use of the same weapons as the advanced Aryans used, and hence they proved formidable enemies of the settled tribes who found it very difficult at first to drive

---

[1] *Ṛgvedic India*, Chap. vii; also Chap. iii of this book.

[2] *Ṛgvedic India*, Ch. vii.

them out of the country, but succeeded in the long run in getting rid of them.

Dispersion of the savage Aryan tribes.—After their expulsion from Sapta-Sindhu, the savage Aryan tribes, called "black" or "black-skinned" on account of their dark complexion which was the result of their constant exposure to the sun and all the inclemencies of the different seasons, inevitable in a nomadic existence, took refuge in the mountainous regions and wilds of Afghanistan, Baluchistan, Persia and Asia Minor where they found abundant scope for hunting, on which they mainly lived; but they followed other savage Aryan tribes in a still more primitive stage of civilisation, who had left Sapta-Sindhu in a far earlier age. These, having already commingled their blood with Turanian and Mongolian savages to whom, however, they gave their Aryan speech and such little Aryan culture as they possessed, had moved into Europe through Asia Minor which was broadly connected with it in those days, and dispersed over the various regions of the continent, carrying with them an Aryan speech, but distinctly Turanian or Mongolian type.[1]

The Aryans autochthonous to Sapta-Sindhu.—From the above brief summary, it would appear that the Aryans were autochthonous to Sapta-Sindhu which comprised Gandhāra in the west, and Kashmir and Bactria in the north, and their evolution as a race began in that region from very primitive times when man had been scarcely much removed from the condition of anthropoid apes. The Aryan man, therefore, had passed through all the stages of development, *viz.*, eolithic, palæolithic, and neolithic, before he knew the uses of metals and emerged into the earliest stage of culture and civilisation. The Ṛgveda no doubt represents a high state of culture; but if it be a fact that the Aryans were autochthonous to the Punjab, and passed through all

[1] *Ibid.*, Ch. viii.

the different stages of civilisation, it is probable that there would be at least some fossils in the different strata of the Ṛgveda and in the Vedic myths and stories, unmistakably pointing to the existence of those stages. It will be our endeavour in this Chapter to find out a few of these fossils, if possible, and read their meanings.

Sticks, stones and bones used as weapons by early man.—First of all, let us speak of weapons by which primitive man set great store, not only for the purposes of offence but also of defence. Primitive man was not a carnivorous animal by nature. He primarily subsisted on fruits, edible herbs and nutritious roots of plants, which he dug up with the help of a pointed stick, or a pointed flint flake which he picked up for the purpose. As the latter was more durable than the former, he would naturally prefer to use the pointed stone and keep it for future operations. He was also fond of honey which he procured by plucking down the bee-hives hanging down from the branches of trees with the help of a long stick. The honey as well as the hive with the larvæ or young bees in the cells formed his favourite meal, as they do with monkeys. It was only when fruits became rare that he had recourse to flesh for food,—flesh of small birds and animals that he could easily kill. Those that lived on the sea-coasts or near lakes and rivers ate snails, oysters, shells, tortoises and fish. Rev. Mr. E. O. James says: "*Homo primigenius* was probably at first mainly a vegetarian, till through the deficiency of the food-supply caused by the advancing glacial period (in Europe), he was obliged to acquire flesh-eating propensities, and thus added animal food to his original diet......It can be pretty safely assumed, judging from the teeth of the earliest skulls, and from the lack of implements that prior to the Chellean Age primeval man was chiefly a vegetarian, except for such flesh as was furnished by small animals." [1]

[1] E. O. James' *Intro. to Anthropology* (1919), pp. 65-65.

So it was from a lack of suitable implements that primeval man was chiefly a vegetarian. But necessity being the mother of inventions, he invented weapons and methods for killing animals whose flesh he required for his consumption, when roots and fruits were no longer available, or became scanty. For purposes of offence and defence, a small broken branch of a tree would naturally be got hold of, or a stone picked up and thrown against the object to be hit; and thus sticks and stones would be the first natural weapons of primitive man. Says Professor Henry Drummond: "When threatened by a comrade or pressed by an alien species, he (primitive man) called in a simple foreign aid to help him in the struggle—the branch of a tree. Whether the discovery was an accident, whether the idea was caught from the falling of a bough or a blow from a branch waving in the wind, is of no consequence. The broken branch became the first *weapon*. It was the father of all *clubs*. The day this discovery was made, the struggle for life took a new departure. Hitherto animals fought with some specialized parts of their own bodies—tooth, limb, claw. Now they took possession of the armoury of material nature."[1]

The stick being easily perishable, primitive man would pick up, when available, and prefer to have either a stone-flake, found in its natural state, or the bone of an animal for his weapons. The ribs, and the femur and the tibia would naturally be preferred to other bones for this purpose. The pointed horns of animals like cattle and the stag would also be picked up and used as weapons. But as primitive man had not as yet domesticated animals, their bones could only be casually and accidentally procured from the carcasses of animals that had died natural deaths, or been killed in the chase for food. As human bodies were either interred or thrown away on account of the repugnance and sorrow felt at the sight of a dead relative or comrade, and were sometimes eaten up, when

---

[1] Henry Drummond's *The Ascent of Man*, Chap. vi.

they happened to belong to enemies, human bones were at first not much used as weapons. It was the handy rough stone-weapons found in their natural state that were commonly used by primitive man for offence or defence. Bone-weapons came to be extensively used later on, when cattle and horses were domesticated, and their bones were more easily available. The polish of these bones probably suggested to primitive man the idea of chipping natural stone-weapons into polished shapes. This undoubtedly marked the dawn of the neolithic stage, but primitive man probably took thousands of years to arrive at this stage of development from the palæolithic, when stones in their natural shapes only were used as weapons.

Hence, I think that I shall not be far wrong if I say that the neolithic stage implied the domestication of wild animals like cattle and horses, and also the development of the rudimentary art of agriculture. The digging for roots with a pointed stick or stone suggested agriculture, as Prof. Henry Drummond says. Agriculture necessarily implies the exchange of a nomadic life for a settled existence in homesteads near corn-fields. But neolithic man was not necessarily an agriculturist. He was generally a nomad, wandering about with his domesticated cattle and dogs and skin-tents, and living mainly by the chase, in which the hunting dog and the hawk played most prominent parts.

Indra's "vajra" originally a stone-made and then a bone-made weapon.—Applying these conditions to the state of early Aryan civilisation, we find it mentioned in the Ṛgveda that the *vajra*, the formidable weapon of Indra, which was employed to kill Vṛtra, the Demon of Drought, was originally made of stone, and then of bone. It was quite natural for primitive men to arm their gods with the weapons that they themselves used and knew and believed to be most formidable and effective. The stone-made and bone-made *vajras* which are mentioned in the Ṛgveda as the original weapons of Indra must, therefore, necessarily reveal the stage of civilisation in which the early Aryans were placed, when the first conception of Indra was formed. This stage was neolithic, when weapons of stones and bones were commonly used by the early Aryans.

There is a word, *parśu*, in the Ṛgveda (vii. 83, 1) which, according to Sāyaṇa, means "the rib-bone of the horse, the edge of which is as sharp as a sword and fit for cutting." *(tacca khaḍgavat tīkṣṇadhāratvāt lavane samartham).* Wilson says: "The *aśva-parśu* is an implement for cutting the *kuśa* grass, either the rib of a horse, or an instrument like it; it is frequently alluded to in the *Brāhmaṇas* and the *Sūtras*" The *mantra*, *ghoṣad asi*, occurring in the the *Taittirīya Saṃhitā* (i. 1, 2) is said by Baudhāyana to be addressed to the *aśva-parśu*, and means, "thou art the implement," the priest having taken it in hand.[1] In neolithic times the rib-bone of the horse must have been used as a sickle not only to cut *kuśa* grass, but also as a war-implement. Probably when the use of iron became known, an implement was made from it after the shape of a horse-rib, which also came to be known as *parśu*. The word, *pṛthu-parśavaḥ*, occurring in Rv. vii. 83, 1, very likely means a broad and heavy iron sickle with which men armed themselves in war.

I have already said that the naturally polished bones suggested the idea of chipping rude stone weapons into polished shapes. The use of bone-weapons, therefore, marked the transitional period from the palæolithic to the neolithic stage. It is said in the Ṛgveda that Indra's *vajra* or bolt was fashioned from the bones of Dadhīci, a great sage, or whoever he might have been. Nay, his very bones were used as *vajra* by Indra with which he killed Vṛtra nine-and-ninety times. A Ṛgvedic verse (i. 84, 13) says:

"With *bones* of Dadhyac for his arms, Indra, resistless in attack, struck nine-and-ninety Vṛtras dead." (Griffith).

---

[1] *Vide* Foot-note, Wilson's *Rigveda* (vii. 83, 1).

It was Tvaṣṭṛ, the Indian Hephaistos, the artificer of the gods, who fashioned the dreaded thunderbolt for Indra from Dadhīci's bones. But the *vajra* is sometimes described as "golden" (Rv. i. 57, 2; 85, 9; viii. 57, 3; x. 23, 3), probably on account of the golden flashes that emanate from it, when struck or hurled; sometimes as ruddy (*harita* Rv. x. 96, 3) for the very same reason; and sometimes as made of iron (*āyasa* Rv. i, 52, 8; 80, 12; 81, 4; 121, 9; viii. 85, 3; x. 48, 3; 96, 3; 113, 5) "Sometimes" says Dr. Muir "it is represented as four-angled (*caturaśrī* iv. 22, 2), sometimes as hundred-angled (*śataśrī* vi. 17, 10), sometimes as hundred-jointed (*śataparvan* i. 80, 6; viii. 6, 6; 65, 2; 78, 3) and sometimes as having a thousand points (*sahasrabhṛṣṭi*, i. 80, 12; 85, 9; v. 34, 2; vi. 17, 10)." [1] But nowhere else, except in the above verse (Rv. i. 84, 13) has it been described as fashioned from the bones of Dadhīci. Though the use of metals was well-known in Ṛgvedic times, the verse in question contains fossil-history of a bye-gone age when bone and stone weapons had been in common use in early Aryan society. This legend of Dadhīci formed the basis of later Paurāṇic tales about the great renunciation and sacrifice made by the sage for the benefit of the gods and mankind, in as much as he immolated himself to enable Tvaṣṭṛ to fashion a thunderbolt for Indra out of his bones, so that the God might successfully wage war with Vṛtra and kill him. Now, there is a curious myth about this Dadhīci in the Ṛgveda. It is said that he was made by the Aśvins to assume the head of a horse in order to save himself from Indra's wrath, because he had taught the twin Gods *pravargya-vidyā* and *madhu-vidyā*, contrary to the distinct injunction of Indra, from whom he had learnt them himself. (Rv. i. 116, 12 and Sāyaṇa's commentary thereon.) Indra, however, cut off the horse-head near Śaryaṇāvat Lake situated in Kurukṣetra (Rv. i. 84, 14). Whatever

---

[1] Muir's O. S. T., v. 86.

may be the import of this myth, one thing stands out clear and certain, viz., that Indra's *vajra* was made from the bones of Dadhīci, and the latter, though apparently a sage, had for sometime fixed on to his neck the head of a horse. The inference that can be drawn from the myth is that Dadhīci was the name of the horse, and that the bones of the horse having been in early Aryan society used as weapon, they are described as having furnished the materials for fashioning Indra's thunderbolt.[1] The myth, therefore, contains a reference to the neolithic stage of Aryan civilisation in Sapta-Sindhu, when the use of metals was unknown, and bones and stones only were used as weapons. The word *vajra* is sometimes also used to mean a hard unbreakable stone like diamond; and there is evidence that Indra's *vajra* had at first been made of hard stone like flint which afterwards gave place to bone—the bone of a horse which was probably the largest animal known to the Aryans of this period.

With regard to the fact of Indra's *vajra* having also been made of stone, the attention of the reader is drawn to the following descriptions of his bolt:—

"O Indra and Soma, hurl about your weapons from the sky. Pierce the sides of the demons with your *stone-made weapons*, undecaying, firey and scorching and let them (the demons) depart without a sound."[2]

---

[1] "Dadhyac, or in later form Dadhīca, was a Ṛṣi, son of Atharvan, he and his father being regarded as the first founders of sacrifice. He is described as having the head of a horse given to him by the Aśvins which was afterwards cut off by Indra. With his bones, or as the legend says, the bones of this horse's head, converted into a thunderbolt, Indra slew the Vṛtras or demons who withheld the rain. The Vedic legend, which was modified and amplified in later times, appears to have been connected in its origin with that of Dadhikrās, often mentioned in the Veda and described as a kind of divine horse, probably a personification of the morning Sun in his rapid course." (Griffith).

[2] Rv. vii. 104, 5.

The word used here for weapon is *aśma*, which literally means a stone.

In verse 22 of the same hymn, the *vajra* has been compared with stone (dṛṣad). In another verse again, the *vajra* has been identified with *aśma* or stone. [1]

Writing about weapons made of stones and bones, I am reminded of another verse of the Ṛgveda (vi. 75, 11) which speaks of the horn-tipped arrow-head. This was undoubtedly also a relic of the stone and bone age of Aryan civilisation. All these evidences point to an age when iron or steel was unknown and flint and bone weapons were in common use.

The chipped flint weapons, as I have already said, must have followed the bone-weapons which furnished models to primitive men for fashioning flints into shapes. The bones were naturally more brittle than hard flints which gradually replaced the former after they had been polished and shaped.

We find certain hymns in the Ṛgveda (Rv. iv. 38; 40; vii. 44) describing the divine war-horse under the name of *Dadhikrās*, which word bears a close resemblance to the word *Dadhīci*. Hence I am disposed to think that *Dadhīci* was the name of the horse, and this surmise is supported by the myth which says that the Aśvins caused a horse's head to be fixed on to the neck of Dadhīci. But even if Dadhīci was a man and sage, the fact that his bones were used to fashion Indra's thunderbolt goes to prove unmistakably the neolithic stage of Aryan civilisation in Sapta-Sindhu when human bones were probably used as weapons for offence and defence. The mention of the Śaryaṇāvat Lake, situated in Kurukṣetra, in connection with Dadhīci's story clearly points to the locality of this neolithic civilisation as Sapta-Sindhu or the ancient Punjab.

In this connection another curious verse may be cited here from the Ṛgveda (x. 73, 10) which says that Indra

---

[1] Rv. ii. 14, 6.

himself had his origin from the horse. The word *aśva* (horse) in the verse may mean the sun who is emblematical of power or vigour. But from the fact that Indra's bolt was made from the bones of Dadhīci who had a horse's head fixed on to his neck, and that the bolt represented the power of Indra, it can be surmised that the horse was regarded as the source of Indra's power.

The "vajra" afterwards made of metals.—The Ṛgveda says that Indra's thunderbolt was made of gold (*hiraṇmaya*), was of ruddy colour (*harit*) and was also made of iron (*āyasa*). These descriptions, besides indicating in the first two cases the red flashes of lightning, very probably refer to the different stages of civilisation when metals like gold, copper or bronze and iron successively came to be known and used by the Aryans, and they, therefore, also fully represent fossil-history. From a careful study of Indra's weapons, we thus find the clear outline of the different stages of Aryan civilisation from the neolithic to the most recent.

The origin of the Indra-cult.—The supreme position assigned to Indra in the Ṛgveda points to another phase of the neolithic stage of Aryan civilisation. Indra certainly does not belong to the pantheon of the oldest Aryan gods, in which Dyus or Dyāvā and Pṛthivī, Mitra and Varuṇa, Aṃsa, Bhaga, Aryaman and Dakṣa are included and figure greatly. Mitra and Varuṇa have been described in the Ṛgveda as the earliest or oldest (*jyeṣthatamāh*) of the Aryan gods (Rv. vi. 67, 1). But Indra is far younger, and is spoken of as having been born of a father and mother, like ordinary mortals. A Ṛgvedic verse (vii. 20, 5) says: "A vigorous (god) begot him a vigorous (son) for the battle; a heroic female (*nārī*) brought him forth, a heroic (son)." As *Dyāvā* and *Pṛthivī* have frequently been described as the divine parents of some of the gods, probably these two deities respectively represented "the vigorous father" and "the heroic female," referred to in the above verse. There is an account of the origin of the Gods in Rv. x. 72, in which it is said that Aditi gave birth to eight sons, of whom seven became divine and immortal, and the eighth was cast out for repeated births and deaths. Of the seven "divine and immortal" sons, Indra was one and regarded as a *Deva Āditya*. It is curious, however, that in the earlier portion of the Ṛgveda (ii. 27, 1), only six Ādityas have been mentioned, and Indra is not one of them. There can be no doubt, therefore, that Indra was discovered and included among the Ādityas, later on. Aditi was his mother who probably took the place of the old *Pṛthivī*; and *Brahmaṇaspati* who probably replaced the old *Dyus* or *Dyāvā* has been described in a Ṛgvedic verse (x. 72, 2) as the deity who created the Gods, including Indra. It is said that as soon as Indra was born, he drank the Soma juice before even sucking his mother's breasts. (Rv. iii. 48, 2; vii. 98, 3). It would thus appear that the Soma cult had existed in early Aryan society even before Indra was ushered into existence, and his worship promulgated.

Now, what was it that led to the birth and discovery of Indra? The principal feat attributed to Indra, that made him famous in the ancient Vedic world, was the killing of Vṛtra, the Demon of Drought, who in his black cloud-body, pent up the rains, and thereby caused very great distress. Vṛtra is said to have been a Brāhmaṇa, being the son of Tvaṣṭṛ, the Fire-god, who forged the thunderbolt for Indra with which, however, he subsequently killed Tvaṣṭṛ's son who was also known by the name of *Viśvarūpa* or the Omniform. Now this killing of Vṛtra made Indra incur the odium and displeasure of Tvaṣṭṛ and his votaries who ceased worshipping him or offering him the Soma juice of which the god was very fond. But it is said that Indra afterwards forcibly partook of the Soma juice (Rv. iii. 48, 4; *Ait. Brāh.* vii. 35, 2). It would be very interesting to unravel the meaning of this strange myth. It appears that the followers of Tvaṣṭṛ did not want Vṛtra to be killed, while the followers of Indra strengthened him by the offer of the Soma juice to successfully wage a war with the demon and kill him. This was no doubt the result of a schism among two important sects or clans of the ancient Aryans. But what really led to it? My surmise is that the cleavage was due to a difference in the culture of the two clans. Vṛtra represented clouds which overspread the sky in the rainy season after the hot days of summer, and was thus known as *Viśvarūpa* or the Omniform. Cloudy days were highly welcome to a pastoral people like the ancient Aryan nomads after the burning summer months, during which it was not at all possible or convenient for them to take out the herds of cattle and flocks of sheep and goats for grazing on the parched-up plains and hill-sides. Clouds, covering up the blazing sun and occasionally drizzling rains, sufficient to make the grass grow and the herbs sprout, present ideal weather conditions for pasturing cattle and flocks on the plains and hill-sides. A name for cloud in the Ṛgveda is *gotra* (i. 62, 13) which literally means that which protects cows or cattle. When the Aryans were a pastoral people, without any fixed habitations, and kept wandering about in the country with their herds and flocks, the advent of clouds after the hot and burning summer months was hailed with delight and many mysterious rites and religious ceremonies were probably performed in honour of the season with offerings of the Soma juice, honey, wine and victuals, which went to establish the character of Vṛtra as a priest of the Devas and the Asuras (both words originally possessing nearly identical meanings), having three mouths representing probably the three months of the rainy season, with the help of which he consumed respectively the Soma juice, the wine and the victuals offered to him. *Ekata*, *Dvita* and *Trita* were the three gods probably connected with the three months of rain, the last month having been assigned to *Āptya Trita* or *Traitana* who poured down copious rain during that month. So far, no hostile feeling was entertained against Vṛtra by the nomadic and pastoral Aryans.

But the angle of vision gradually changed, when a few Aryan tribes, the Pañcajanaḥ of the Ṛgveda, took to agriculture, and settled down in rude homesteads near their corn-fields, depending more upon the products of agriculture for their living than upon precarious means of livelihood like the collection of roots and fruits, the flesh of animals killed in the chase, or of their domesticated herds and flocks, and the milk of cows, buffaloes and goats. Timely rains were needed for carrying on successful agricultural operations, but the rains were never regular in coming and were sometimes too scanty for cultivating the fields. The agricultural population thus came to look upon the rain-withholding clouds with anything but favour, and in fact, regarded them as the root of all mischief, and the main cause of their sufferings and distress. Vṛtra thus assumed a malevolent form in the eyes of these people who thought that it was he who was withholding the rains with the deliberate object of tormenting them. It was, therefore, essentially necessary to invoke the aid of a powerful God who could not only counteract the evil influences exercised by the magical powers of the dark-complexioned and evil-minded Vṛtra, but also vanquish him, releasing the captive waters and the Sun and the Dawn, all enveloped in his cloud-body. Such a powerful God was not long in being discovered: He was the great Wielder of the Thunderbolt who was seen to rend open the clouds with his deadly weapon, and pour down rains for the benefit of beasts and men.[1] But Vṛtra was

[1] Says Muir: "At the close of the long hot weather, when every one is longing for rain to moisten the earth and cool the atmosphere, it is often extremely tantalising to see the clouds collecting and floating across the sky day after day without discharging their contents. And in the early ages when the Vedic hymns were composed, it was an idea quite in consonance with the other general conception which their authors entertained, to imagine that some malignant influence was at work in the atmosphere to prevent the fall of the showers, of which their parched fields stood so much in need. It was but a step further to personify both this hostile power and beneficent agency by which it was at last overcome. Indra is thus at once a terrible warrior and

too powerful and wily an enemy to be easily vanquished, as he carried on the struggle with *Vajrī* (or the Wielder of the Thunderbolt) with great tact and vigour, often eluding his aim, and thus prolonging the conflict. The agricultural people who watched this great struggle with the keenest interest thought that *Vajrī* who had been disinterestedly carrying on this struggle, almost single-handed, required to be strengthened by earnest and grateful prayers, and the performance of sacrifices with the Soma juice, the exhilerating drink that made them strong and hilarious. And so the Soma sacrifice was inaugurated and performed in honour of Indra not only during the three months of the rainy season, but also subsequently, throughout the whole year, in order that he might be able and ready to put up a tough fight with Vṛtra from the very commencement of the struggle. The annual and the periodical *Sattras*, as these Soma sacrifices were called, had thus a very utilitarian origin in ancient Vedic society, their object being the pouring of timely rain for the benefit of the agricultural population. It has been distinctly stated in a verse of the Ṛgveda (v. 45, 11): "I offer to you (Gods), *for the sake of water*, an all-bestowing sacrifice whereby the Navagvas (the nine months' ministrants) have completed the ten months' rite."[1] The Gods in the verse included, besides Indra, all those who assisted him in his fight with Vṛtra, viz. the Maruts, Parjanya, Sarasvatī, Bṛhaspati, Viṣṇu, Āptya Trita and others.

Trita and Parjanya earlier than Indra.—By the way, it may be stated here that Trita or Āptya Trita was an early God of rain—the God who poured down copious rain in the

---

a gracious friend, a god whose shafts deal destruction to his enemies, while they bring deliverance and prosperity to his worshippers. The phenomena of thunder and lightning almost inevitably suggest the idea of a conflict between opposing forces; even we ourselves, in our more prosaic age, often speak of the war or strife of the elements." (O. S. T, Vol. v, p. 98).

[1] M. N. Dutt's Translation of the *Ṛgveda*.

"third" (Gk. *trito-s*) month of the rainy season. Trita is also called Traitana, but the latter name occurs only once in the Ṛgveda (i. 158, 5). The equivalent of Vedic Traitana is Thraetaona in the Zend-avesta wherein he is described as *Ajihantā*, like Indra who is called Ahi-hantā (the killer of Ahi or the serpent, Vṛtra) in the Ṛgveda. We can also trace his shadow in the Greek and Roman *Triton* who was a Sea-deity, so powerful as to be able to calm the ocean and abate storms at pleasure. But Trita or Traitana, the god of rain, holds a subordinate position to Indra in the Ṛgveda, for in a verse (x. 8, 8), the latter commissions the former, the son of Āpta (or Water), to take up his father's weapons and kill the three-headed monster whose name is Viśvarūpa or Vṛtra. Parjanya seems to me to be another early God of rain, belonging very probably to the pre-Vedic period, for we find the name of Perkunas, the God of thunder, in Lithuanian. The name also occurs in Gothic as *Fairguni*, and in Norse as *Fiörgyn*, which means thunder. In the Ṛgveda the word *Parjanya* at first meant simply a rain-cloud (Rv. i. 38. 9), but later on the word came to mean the God of both thunder and rain, as the following translation of a Ṛgvedic hymn (v. 83) will go to show :—

"1. Address the powerful (god) with these words; laud Parjanya; worship him with reverence; the procreative and stimulating fructifier, resounding, sheds his seed and impregnates the plants. 2. He splits the trees, he destroys the Rākṣasas; the whole creation is afraid of the mighty stroke; even the innocent man flees before the vigorous god, when Parjanya thundering smites the evil-doers. 3. Like a charioteer urging forward his horses with a whip, the god brings into view his showery scouts. From afar the lion's roarings arise, when Parjanya charges the clouds with rain. 4. The winds blow, the lightnings fall, the plants shoot up; the heaven fructifies; food is produced for all created things, when Parjanya, thundering, replenishes the earth with moisture. 5. Parjanya, before whose agency the earth bows down, at whose operation all hoofed cattle quiver, by whose action plants (spring up) of every form, do thou grant us thy mighty protection. 6. Grant to us, Maruts, the rain of the sky; replenish the streams of the procreative horse; come hither with this thy thunder, our divine father, shedding waters. 7. Resound, thunder, impregnate, rush hither and thither with thy watery chariot. Draw on forward with thee thy opened and inverted water-skin; let the hills and dales be levelled. 8. Raise aloft thy vast water-vessel, and pour down showers; let the discharged rivulets roll on forward; moisten the heaven and earth with fatness; let there be well-filled drinking places for the cows. 9. When thou, Parjanya, resounding and thundering, dost slay the evil-doers, the whole universe rejoices, whatever lives upon the earth. 10. Thou hast shed down rain; now desist; thou hast made the waterless wastes fit to be traversed; thou hast generated plants for food, and thou hast fulfilled the desires of living creatures."[1]

Here we see that from the original significance of rain-cloud, the word *Parjanya* came to mean the deity that presided over rain-clouds, and poured down rains with the help of thunder, lightning and storm. Indra in later Vedic mythology was the only wielder of the thunder. Hence it is not unreasonable to suppose that Parjanya was older than Indra himself by whom he was superseded in later times. The existence of the word Perkunas in Lithuanian meaning the god of thunder, and of Fairguni in Gothic and Fiörgyn in Norse lends a strong support to this supposition. "Dr. Bühler holds Parjanya to have been decidedly distinct from Indra (Transact. Phil. Soc., P. 167 and Or. and Occ. 299)."[2] My opinion is that Parjanya was the god of rain, thunder and lightning of the early Aryans at a time when they had been in a nomadic and pastoral stage, and did not settle down as agriculturists.

---

[1] Muir's translation (O. S. T., Vol. v, pp. 140-141).

[2] Muir's O. S. T., Vol. v, p. 142.

He is praised for filling well the drinking places for the cows, and for making "the waterless wastes fit to be traversed." He is, of course, also praised for "impregnating the plants" and producing "food for all created things." But this description does not necessarily imply the existence of agriculture; it simply means that rain-water caused plants, herbs and grass to grow, furnishing food for cattle and also for men by making the plants bear fruits. On the other hand, Indra was essentially the god of the Aryans when they settled down as agriculturists, when timely rain was required for agricultural operations, when *Sattras* were performed with the main object of obtaining an adequate supply of rain, and when Vṛtra assumed a malevolent character by withholding timely rain. Indra thus became not only the god of thunder, lightning, storm and rain like Parjanya, but also the God in whose honour sacrifices were performed, who released the Sun and the Dawn from the clutches of Vṛtra every morning and at the end of every rainy season, who gave fertile lands to the agriculturists for cultivation and settlement (Rv. iv. 26, 2), who drove away or killed the nomadic Dāsas and Dasyus that had been inimical to the settled Aryans, and who gave them wealth and plenty in times of peace and victory in battle. This was how Indra came to be distinguished not only from Parjanya, but also from Trita or Traitana. As I have already said, the worship of Indra was firmly established in Sapta-Sindu in the Neolithic age when stone-made and bone-made weapons were freely used. Hence there can be no doubt that Ṛgvedic civilisation began from this very age in Sapta-Sindhu.

Trita and Parjanya superseded by Indra.—We have now been able to understand how Indra came to occupy a supreme position in the Vedic Pantheon, ousting Trita or Traitana and Parjanya from the high positions that they had respectively once occupied. Indra's power and usefulness were thus far above those of the early gods of rain, and it is to beneficent power and capacity for doing good that men always bend their knees, and offer their homage. We are also able to understand how and why Vṛtra was metamorphosed from a benevolent into a malevolent power by a certain section of the ancient Aryans, and why the killing of Vṛtra by Indra was extremely resented by another section, and why Indra was not at all acknowledged as a god, but rather regarded as a devil-incarnate by them.

Vṛtra as Deva.—It would thus appear that those Aryan tribes who led a nomadic existence, and roamed about in the country with their cattle and flocks which they took out for pasturing on the advent of the rainy season, came to look upon Vṛtra as a *Deva* in as much as he caused the sky to be covered up with clouds, and the plains and hill-sides to be decorated with green grass and shooting herbs, and made the days cool and pleasant. They were however in need of only moderate rain that would cause the grass to grow and the plants to bear fruits, and not of heavy rain that would flood the rivers and make them and the adjoining country impassable, causing great distress to them and their cattle and flocks. A long drought, with scanty rain and barren clouds, often presented an ideal weather to the pastoral Aryans for pasturing their cattle and roaming about from place to place. The agricultural population, on the other hand, were in need of copious rain, and cursed Vṛtra when there was a long drought. This difference of culture gave rise to a conflict of religious sentiments, which afterwards was turned into implacable hatred for one another, even though the conditions that had produced it no longer existed.

A word of explanation with regard to the epithet *Deva* applied to Vṛtra (Rv. i. 32, 12) is necessary here. The verse in which the epithet *Deva* occurs, has been translated by Wilson as follows: "When the single resplendent Vṛtra (*Deva ekah*) returned the blow (which had been inflicted), Indra, by thy thunderbolt, thou becamest (furious) like a horse's tail." The word *Deva* naturally connotes the idea of brightness, as it is derived from the root *div*, to shine. As Vṛtra is usually identified with clouds and darkness, his complexion is dark, and he has been rightly described as "black-skinned." His epithet *Deva*, therefore, would seem at first sight to be incongruous. But we should remember that clouds and darkness only represented his external body, and the real Vṛtra lay concealed behind them, occasionally revealing himself in zigzag lightning that flashed through the clouds in the shape of a hydra-headed angry serpent (*Ahi*), and in the different phases of the moon from its crescent serpent-like form to the gradually growing and full moon and *vice versa*. The lightning and the moon are bright in appearance. Hence Vṛtra was called a *Deva*. "Professor Hillebrandt has recently advanced a new theory of Indra, Vṛtra and the waters, which he expounds with great ingenuity and learning. (*Vedische Mythologie*, vol. iii. P. 157 ff). He argues that the streams of India and the neighbouring Iranian countries are at their lowest level in the winter; that the confiner of their waters is the frozen winter, conceived as a winter monster by the name of Vṛtra, 'confiner'; that Vṛtra holds captive the rivers on the heights of the glacier mountains; and that, consequently Indra can be no other than the spring or summer sun who frees them from the clutches of the winter dragon."[1] This theory no doubt looks very plausible and ingenious at first sight, for it explains the dragon (*Ahi*) in the form of a glacier or frozen river with the bright and white colour of ice to justify his epithet *Deva*, and Indra as the spring or summer sun who melts the ice and thus kills the dragon, Vṛtra. But this theory does not explain all the feats of Vṛtra, consisting as they did in imprisoning not only the waters, but also the Sun and the Dawn (Rv. i. 32, 4; vi. 30, 2; 17, 5). It also does not explain how, why and when

---

[1] Bloomfield's *The Religion of the Vedas*, P. 179.

Indra had to wield his thunderbolt in killing the dragon, when the hot solar rays were themselves sufficient to cause the ice to thaw, and how the battle was waged in *antarikṣa* (sky) where the dreaded dragon usually resided. (Rv. i. 52, 6) The epithets, "black-skinned" and "black," applied to Vṛtra in the Ṛgveda cannot also be explained by identifying him with mountain-glaciers, frozen rivers or frozen winter. Hillebrandt's theory, therefore, though plausible, cannot be accepted as correct.

It is, however, possible that from the original significance of the word Vṛtra, encompasser or obstructor, anything that caused obstruction to the free flow of water, either in rivers by their getting frozen up in winter, or from fountains by their getting dried up, or from clouds on account of drought, was ascribed to the action of Vṛtra, and sometimes also identified with him. Hillebrandt's hypothesis, therefore, may only partially be true; but it is not wholly true, as it does not explain the imprisonment of the Sun and the Dawn by Vṛtra, the deities whom Indra had to release from his clutches. (Rv. i. 32, 4; vi. 17, 5).

Indra looked upon as a demon by the Parsis.—We find that the ancient Parsis looked upon Indra (or Āndra) as a demon, and did not acknowledge his supremacy as a god. This was probably originally due to the fact that they were still nomadic cattle-keepers, with crude ideas of agriculture, while the Vedic Aryans had settled down as advanced agriculturists. They did not feel called upon to invoke the aid of a God like Indra to break up the spell of a long drought. They also came to detest the Soma juice for sometime, because it was offered by the Vedic Aryans to Indra to strengthen him in his fight with Vṛtra with the object of dispelling the drought. This abhorrence against Indra continued even when the Parsis in a later age advanced a step forward in their culture, and became agriculturists themselves like the Vedic Aryans. As agriculturists, they could not of course help feeling a repugnance for Vṛtra, the Demon of Drought, whom they caused to be vanquished by Tishtrya, the god of rain. The vanquisher of Vṛtra was called *Veretraghna* (the killer of Vṛtra), like the Vedic Indra, but their early prejudice against the latter having persisted, they continued to look upon him as a demon, and never acknowledged him as a god. This, however, made a world of difference, and separated the two tribes for ever.

Culture among the Neolithic Aryan nomads.—I have already said that the neolithic Aryan nomads and cattle-keepers, not having been able to keep pace with the advanced Aryan tribes (*Pañcajanāḥ* or *Pañcakṛṣṭayaḥ*), and having found the environments in their original home highly uncongenial, wandered out and away from Sapta-Sindhu with their cattle and dogs, and passed into Western Asia at a period when probably with the receding ice in Europe and the northern regions of Asia in the Post-Glacial epoch, a wide and long belt of grassy steppes extended from Central Asia along the Southern coasts of the Asiatic Mediterranean Sea right into the heart of Southern and Central Europe which was broadly connected in those days with Asia Minor. This broad and extensive grassy belt naturally provided them with plentiful game of various sorts, viz. the wild horse, hog, deer and antelope, and their cattle with abundant pasture. They took with them such culture as they possessed, and the names of the Gods that they worshipped, viz., Sūryas, Agni, Dyāvā, Pṛthivī, Dyus, Mitra, Varuṇa, Vala, Atri, Maruts, Day and Night, Dawn and Parjanya, etc., and the religious myths connected with them. Along with their Aryan speech they also carried with them the names of the different family relationships like father, mother, son, brother, wife, sister, daughter, father-in-law, widow and so on, showing that, though not settled as agriculturists, they were well advanced in their domestic life and institutions even as nomads. The names of animals like the ox, cow, dog, horse, etc., were also carried by them, showing that in the neolithic stage these animals had already been domesticated by them. They also knew the names of birds like the owl, and of rodents like the mouse. The use of metals was not as yet known either to the nomads or the agriculturists (the *Pañcakṛṣṭayaḥ*), and hence this knowledge did not go with them. The names of trees like the birch etc. were familiar to them. They could also count up to hundred (*śatam*). They used skins or barks for clothing, knew the use of fire, and either buried or cremated their dead. With these social, domestic and religious customs and mental, moral and linguistic equipments, the Neolithic Aryan nomads started in their wanderings towards the west, driving before them still ruder Aryan tribes who had preceded them from time to time, and had commingled their blood with the Turanian or Mongolian savages in a similar state of culture. There were, however, still left in the mother country many savage nomadic Aryan tribes who either hung about in the outskirts of the villages and towns, or lived in the deep recesses of the forests or the inaccessible portions of the mountainous regions, from which they occasionally swooped down upon the peaceful inhabitants, carrying off their cattle, or stealing their goods and chattels. These gave a lot of trouble to the Vedic Aryans who made a determined effort to drive them out of the country.

Horses and Cattle.—The horse appears to have played a great part in the Neolithic civilisation of the ancient Aryans. This animal was probably the last to have been domesticated, the first having been the goat, the second the ram or sheep, the third the cow, and last, though not least, the horse. There is an anecdote in the *Taittirīya Saṃhitā* (vii. 1, 1, 4-6) which says that Prajāpati first created Brahmans among men, and goats among beasts; then he created Kṣatriyas and sheep; next he created Vaiśyas and cows, and last of all were created Śūdras and horses. The order in which the animals have been mentioned as having been created by Prajāpati probably shows the order in which they were really domesticated from their wild state by the Neolithic Aryans. Of all animals, the goat is the most harmless, and as it lived both on the mountains and in the plains, it was easily caught and domesticated by the nomadic Aryans. The next animal caught and domesticated was the sheep which, though equally harmless with the goat, was difficult to catch, as its natural habitat was the inaccessible heights of the mountains. Then came the cow, a fierce animal in its wild state, and lastly the horse which, on account of its swiftness and vicious nature, was difficult to catch and bring under control. The domestication of the cow and the horse did not necessarily imply the inauguration of agriculture. Nomads would possess large herds and flocks, without knowing anything of agriculture for several generations. They would subsist on roots and fruits of trees, the milk of goats, cows and buffaloes, and the flesh of animals, either killed in the chase, or slaughtered from their live stock. Of all domestic animals, the horse struck their imagination the most. It is a noble and splendid animal, possessing great speed, indomitable energy and dashing vigour, unsurpassed by any other animal. The horse, therefore, formed a basis of comparison to denote power, vigour, brightness, or speed. The Sun, the Fire, the Aśvins and the Maruts were each and all compared to the horse. The very name of the Aśvins (the precursors of Dawn) was derived from a word, meaning the horse. The Sun was the aërial steed; Fire was like a red horse advancing with thundering speed; the Maruts in their mad career came riding on fleet and dashing horses; Indra had a pair of horses on which he rode. The horse, therefore, figured much in ancient Aryan society, and was highly prized as a useful animal. It was sometimes used to draw the plough; but it was mostly employed for riding and drawing the chariot and also as a beast of burden. In the nomadic state of society, the horse was invaluable, in as much as it helped the wanderers to move from one place to another with great ease and swiftness. We can imagine a whole cavalcade of Aryan nomads moving on horseback with their families and goods, driving their herds and flocks before them, and halting at sun-down on an open heath under their rude skin-tents. They would tarry at a place for a long period, if it afforded ample pasturage and water to their cattle and flocks, and provided facilities to the men for hunting. Otherwise they would keep on moving from place to place on horseback, never stopping anywhere longer than was necessary. Thus we find that the horse had been known to the Aryans from Neolithic times, before they settled down as agriculturists, or before even Indra was discovered and worshipped. As we have already seen, Indra was pre-eminently the God of the agricultural section of the ancient Aryans, and the horse had been known to them long before they knew Indra, as Dadhici had a horse's head fixed on to his neck, and it was from the bones of Dadhici that Indra's thunder was made.

The Dog and the Hawk.—The dog was probably the earliest beast, as the hawk was the earliest bird, to have been tamed by the Palæolithic savage nomad. There is evidence of the dog having been a constant companion of the Palæolithic savages in Europe. The wild dogs lived and hunted in packs, as they do even to this day in places where they are found in large numbers; and no animal was safe from their combined, ferocious and determined attack. The nomadic savage, in the course of his wanderings in quest of animal food, must have observed how the wild dogs hunted down an animal in packs, and he must have eagerly wished to possess some young puppies which could be tamed and trained to assist him in the hunt. And so some would be procured and brought up with the children who were naturally very fond of them. When they grew up into adult animals, they would be taken out by the savage hunter and let loose upon a quarry which would be pursued by the pack with the speed of lightning and run down. The hunter would follow them as fast as his legs could carry him, and would probably be just in time to see the young dogs tear up and begin to devour the prey. He would wrest the mangled carcass from them, and give them a portion of it to eat, carrying the remainder home, followed by the pack which were eager to have some more share of the meat. In this way were dogs domesticated, and trained to assist in the hunt. Having been cared for by their masters, they developed a wonderful instinct of attachment for him and obeyed his becks and calls like a domestic. In Neolithic times, they were also trained to guard the herds and flocks and prevent them from straying. The large-sized dogs were also employed in Sapta-Sindhu for carrying heavy burdens on their back (Rv. viii. 46, 8). Yama, the God of Death, had a pair of dogs which guarded the regions of death, each having four eyes, which probably meant that it was extremely vigilant, and nothing could escape its watchful eyes. (Rv. x. 14, 10. 11).

The conception of Yama is certainly very old; but the domestication of the wild dog and its use as a guard for keeping watch, and as a hunter for tracking and running down a victim, must be older still.

The hawk was tamed and employed to catch or knock down small flying birds. The employment of the dog and the hawk in the hunt goes to show that the primitive Aryans, like other primitive savages, had no effective weapons to kill animals and birds with, and had recourse to the device of taming the dog and the hawk for killing animals and birds for them. Bird-catching, of which frequent mention is made in the Ṛgveda, was an art that was subsequently developed. The hawk is frequently mentioned in the Ṛgveda.

Skin cloths and utensils.—Nomads who possessed herds of cattle and flocks of goats and sheep were never in want of food or clothing. The flesh of animals killed would supply them with meat, and their skins would serve as wraps for protection from the inclemencies of winter, or as tents to protect them from rain or the burning rays of the sun.

Vastra or cloth probably originally meant the skin only, as one of its etymological significance seems to be the natural covering that protects the *vasā* or fat of the body. The skin used as a wrap probably thus came to be known as *vastra*. Besides skin-clothing, skin utensils were in great use in ancient Aryan society. There were leather-bags (*krivi* Rv. v. 44, 4), and domestic utensils, such as curd-skins (*dṛti* Rv. i. 191, 10; vi. 48, 18), vessels for storing water (*bhastrā*, occurring in *Śat. Bṛhā.* i, 1, 2, 7), wine, honey, and even the Soma-juice (Rv. i. 28, 9; ix. 66. 29; 79, 4). Thus there was absolutely no prejudice against the use of skin-vessels for domestic purposes, showing that the Aryans were in close proximity to the Neolithic age when such vessels were in common use as a matter of necessity. There is also mention of skin-gloves (*hastaghna*, Rv. vi. 75, 5), and the cow-gut or cow-hide was used for manufacturing a string to the bow. (Rv. vi. 75, 11). Probably bone-needles were used for stitching skins. Cloths were woven from the fibres of barks, or from woollen threads made from sheep-wool. (Rv. x. 26. 6). "It may be reasonably supposed" says Rev. Mr. E. O. James "that clothing like cave-dwelling was one of the arts of life learnt by men in the Pleistocene, probably early in the Mousterian phase."[1]

It must have cost the Neolithic Aryans a stupendous effort to invent a rude contrivance for weaving cloths. The idea of weaving was very likely suggested by the weaving of baskets and mats in which savage man was proficient and the rude contrivance for weaving came into being in course of time. At first fibres of barks would be used as threads for weaving what was known as bark-cloths (*valkala*). The word *valka* in the sense of bark occurs in the Taittirīya Saṃhitā (ii. 5, 3, 5) and the Taittirīya Brāhmaṇa (i. 4, 7, 6). These bark-cloths were largely used, as the materials for weaving them were more easily available than woollen threads.

---

[1] James, *Intro. to Anthropology*, p. 98.

Cotton-cloth was a later production when people became acquainted with tree-cotton and learnt to produce yarn from the woolly stuff found in the pods.

Origin of Fire.—"Fire" says Rev. Mr. E. O. James, "though familiar to man from the beginning was not used by him till he had learnt the secret of its property and devised some means of obtaining it. How and when this was accomplished is not known. In the early Pleistocene there is evidence of its existence, as for example, in the hearths discovered in Mousterian sites. There are two obvious sources of natural fire, lightning and volcanic lava. The latter is limited to certain areas, and the former would be but sporadic. Moreover, at such conflagrations he would be so terrified that he would not be in a position to appreciate the result. Another way in which forest-fires are accidentally kindled is by friction of boughs in a stormy wind creating a dust that in due course would ignite. In the sort of climate in which earliest man apparently lived, bamboo and the sort of wood that most readily ignites by attrition would be plentiful, and, therefore, it is possible that the observant mind experimented in the generation of heat, and the consequent manufacture of fire by rubbing together two pieces of wood. The suggestion is supported by the widely distributed custom of frictional fire-making among primitive people to-day, and, all things considered, appears to be the most probable explanation of the origin of fire." [1]

In the Ṛgveda, Fire has been described to be the youngest of the Gods. (Rv. x. 20, 2). This means, if it means anything, that the God was raised to, and included in the Vedic Pantheon last of all, though the element had been discovered and brought to human use long long ago. It is said that the sage Atharvan was the first to produce fire. (Rv. x. 21, 5). How did he produce it is not known, though it may be surmised that he produced it either by

[1] James, *Intro. to Anthropology*, pp. 98-99.

striking two flint stones together, or by the friction of two pieces of dry stick, which was and still is the orthodox method for producing sacrificial fire. A Ṛgvedic verse (vi. 16, 13) says that "Atharvan drew thee (Agni) forth, from the lotus flower by rubbing," and the next verse says: "Thee (Fire) Dadhyañc, the son of Atharvan, kindled." How did Atharvan draw Agni forth from the lotus flower passes our comprehension, unless we suppose that the sparks emitted by striking two flint-stones together were caught by the dry lotus-petals which were thus ignited. Griffith says that the *lotus flower* is "probably a figurative expression for heaven." If the interpretation be correct, how could Atharvan bring forth Agni from heaven by *rubbing*? The Aṅgirases are also said to be the originators of Fire-worship (Rv. i. 31, 1. 2; 71,3). The same feat is also ascribed to the Bhṛgus and to Manu. A Ṛgvedic verse (i. 58,6) says: "The Bhṛgus have placed thee among men." Another verse (Rv. i. 36,19) says: "Manu has placed thee (here) a light to all (generations of) men." And yet a third verse (Rv. vii. 2,3) says: "Let us, like Manu, ever attract to the sacrifice Agni who was kindled by him" Fire is identified with lightning in the sky, and the sun in heaven (Rv. i. 79, 1-3; x. 45,3). It is further said that fire was first born in the sky in the shape of lightning (Rv. x. 45, 1). This tallies with the story of the first discovery of fire by savages in lightning when it struck a tree and set it a-blazing.

In another verse (Rv. x. 20,7) Fire has been described as "the son of stone" (*adreḥ sūnuḥ*). A similar idea occurs in another verse, Rv. ii. 12,3, which means that Indra produced fire between two stones,[1] though the word *aśmanaḥ* may also mean "clouds," in which case the sentence would mean that "Indra produced fire between two clouds," which can only be identified with lightning. However this may be,

[1] Griffith translates the passage thus: "(who) begat the fire between two stones."

there can be no doubt that the ancient Aryans knew the method of producing fire by striking two flint-stones against each other. There was also the other method of producing fire by the friction of two dry sticks against each other, which earned for Fire the epithet of *Dvimātrika* (Rv. i. 34, 2. 4) which means "the son of two mothers," and this method was always adopted for producing Fire for sacrifice. In a hymn (Rv. iii. 29) we come across the following verses:—

"1. This process of friction, of generation has begun; bring this mistress of the people (the lower *araṇi*, or wood for friction); let us rub out Agni as heretofore. 2. This God is deposited in the two pieces of wood, as the embryo in pregnant woman. Agni is daily to be lauded by men bringing oblations and awaking (early). 3. Skilled (in the process), bring (the upper piece of wood) into contact with the lower, lying recumbent; being impregnated, she speedily brings forth the vigorous (Agni)." In a verse (Rv. i. 68, 2), it is noticed as remarkable that a living being should spring out of dry wood, and in another verse (Rv. v. 9, 3) it is related that Agni is produced from the two sticks as a new-born infant. [1]

It would not be uninteresting to recall here a similar method of producing fire, current among the savage Tasmanians. Says Rev. Mr. E. O. James: "They (the Tasmanians) were certainly acquainted with fire, which they made by rubbing the pointed end of a stick to and fro in a groove cut out in another piece of wood; by rotating one stick on another in a hole." [2] Captain Cook also mentions a similar method existing among the savage inhabitants of New South Wales in Australia. The Esquimaux of Pondi Bay also produce fire by rubbing two dry sticks together, and their implements, obtained by Sir Edward Belcher C. B., may be seen in the "Arctic collection" presented by Mr. Barrow

---

1 *Uta sma yam śiśum yathā navam janiṣṭāraṇi* (Rev. v. 9,3).

2 James, *Intro. to Anthropology*, pp. 102-103.

to the British Museum, and deposited in the Ethnographical Room. It would thus appear that human mind always worked on similar lines, whether in Tasmania, the Polar regions, or Sapta-Sindhu.

There was another source or dwelling place of Fire, known to the ancient Aryans, which is worth mentioning here, and this was water i.e. the water of the ocean where Varuṇa lived. A verse (Rv. x. 45,3) says: "Varuṇa, the benefactor of mankind has kept thee (Fire) burning in the waters of the ocean." The ancient Aryans probably observed some phosphorescent light burning in the sea-water,[1] or must have noticed huge tongues of fire belching out from some sunken volcano, which afterwards gave rise to many Pauraṇic myths. The other two dwelling places of Fire have been described in the above verse to be the sun, and the clouds where he is said to live and flourish in rain-water.

These references to the dwelling place and origin of Fire in the Ṛgveda point to the early stage of Aryan civilisation, which was probably synchronous with the Pleistocene or Post-Pleistocene epoch when the human savages in other parts of the world became acquainted with the use of Fire.

---

[1] The *Scientific American* writes: "In the animal kingdom, in groups ranging from the protozoa to the vertibrates, there are more than three hundred genera which contain one or more species that are known to be phosphorescent By far the great majority are those forms which live in the sea. Of these perhaps the best known are Noctiluca, a microscopic animal which causes the phosphorescent light in the wake of a vessel; jelly-fishes which produce flashes of light when colliding with a boat or struck with an oar; marine worms and small crustaceans." Captain Cook in his first voyage in 1768 discovered a similar phenomenon in the Atlantic near the equator: "On the 25th of October, they crossed the line with the usual forms. On the 29th in the evening the luminous appearance of the sea, mentioned by navigators, was observed by them: it emitted rays of light resembling those of lightning. Mr. Banks and Dr. Solander threw out a casting-net, when a species of the Medusa was caught, resembling a metallic substance greatly heated, emitting a whitish light. Some crabs were also caught at the same time, which were exceedingly small, yet gave a glittering appearance." Captain Cook's *Voyages of Discovery*. P. 11 (J. M. Dent & Sons, London).

They also go to show that the Vedic Aryans were fully acquainted with the ocean from very early times.

Some Early Aryan Gods—Dyāvā-Pṛthivī.—If the ancestors of the Greeks, Romans, Celts, Slavs, Lithuanians and Teutons migrated from a central home to Europe in the Neolithic Age, the Gods that they worshipped with the Indo-Aryans would be amongst the earliest of the Pantheon known to them. The budding Aryan mind was doubtless greatly impressed by the vastness of the bright Sky above, and of the Earth below, which seemed to be joined with each other in the distant horizon, and to have produced by their union not only the animals and plants of the earth, but also the bright sun, moon, planets and stars, representing the shining ones or *Devas*, that moved between them. The Sky was known as Dyuś, Dyaus and Dyava; and the Earth was called *Pṛthivī* on account of her vast extent. *Dyāvā-Pṛthivī* are thus very ancient Aryan divinities, and in many passages of the Ṛgveda described as the parents of all the Gods. The translation of the first and second verses of Rv. i. 159 is as follows:—

"1. At the festivals (I worship) with offerings, and celebrate the praise of Heaven and Earth, the promoters of righteousness,—the great, and wise, energetic, who, having Gods for their offspring, thus lavish with the Gods the choicest blessings in consequence of our hymn. 2. With my invocations I adore the thought of the beneficent Father, and the mighty inherent power of the Mother. The prolific parents have made all creatures, and through their favours (have coferred) wide immortality on their offspring." The two (Heaven and Earth) together are styled parents *pitarā* (Rv. i. 159, 2; iii. 3, 11; vii. 53, 2 and x. 65, 8), or *mātarā* (Rv. i. 155, 3; ix. 85, 12; x. 1. 7) or *Janitrī* (Rv. x. 110, 9). In other passages the Heaven is separately styled father, and the Earth, mother. (Rv. i. 89, 4; 90, 7; 159, 2, &c.)[1] *Dyus* or *Dyaus* is equivalent to the Greek Zeus, and *Dyaus Pitar*

[1] Muir's O. S. T., Vol. V, pp. 21-23.

to the Latin Jupiter, showing that the ancestors of the Greeks, Romans and Indo-Aryans (Hindus) drew the names of their Gods from a common source, and worshipped the same Gods before their separation. They had also a common mythology. In the *Aitareya Brāhmaṇa* (iv. 27) the marriage of Heaven and Earth is thus referred to: "These two worlds (Heaven and Earth) were once joined. (Subsequently) they separated. (After their separation) there fell neither rain, nor was there sunshine. The five classes of beings (Gods, men, etc.), then did not keep peace with one another. (Thereupon) the Gods brought about a reconciliation of both these worlds. Both contracted with one another a marriage according to the rites observed by the Gods."[1]

A doctrine partly similar to that of the Aitareya Brāhmaṇa, adduced above, regarding Heaven and Earth, is ascribed to the philosopher Anaxagoras, and was thus expressed by his disciple, the poet Euripedes:

"Euripedes frequented the lectures of Anaxagoras. Now it was the theory of that philosopher that all things were confounded (lit. all things were in all things), but afterwards became separated. Euripedes afterwards associated with Socrates, and became doubtful regarding the theory. He accordingly admits the ancient doctrine by the mouth of Melanippe: 'The saying is not mine but came from my mother, that formerly the Heaven and Earth formed one substance, but when they were separated from each other, they gave birth to all things, and brought them forth into the light,—trees, birds, beasts, fishes and the race of mortals.'"

According to the Theogony of Hesiod (116 ff) the first thing that arose out of Chaos was "the board-bosomed Earth, the firm abode of all things." She, in her turn, "produced the starry Heaven, co-extensive with herself, to envelop her on every part." From the union of these two powers sprang Oceanos, Kronos, the Cyclopes, Rheia etc., and from Kronos

---

[1] Dr. Haug's "Translation of the Aitareya Brāhmaṇa," Vol. II. p. 308.

and Rheia again were produced Zeus, Here and other deities. In his "Works and Days" (561) Hesiod speaks of the Earth as the mother of all things. Among the Homeric hymns there is one of 19 lines addressed to "the mother of all things" which begins thus: "I will sing of the Earth, the Universal Mother, the firmly based, the most venerable, who feeds all creatures that are on the ground," etc. In verse 16 she is addressed as a venerable goddess and in verse 17 as "the mother of the Gods and the spouse of the starry Ouranos."

In the 41st fragment of Æschylus (from the Danaides) Aphrodite is introduced as saying: "The pure Heaven loves to inflict on the Earth an amorous blow; and desire seizes the Earth to obtain the nuptial union. Rain falling from the moist Heaven impregnates the Earth who brings forth for mortals the food of sheep and the sustenance of Demeter. The verdure of the woods also is perfected by the showers proceeding from this marriage. Of all these things I (Aphrodite) am in part the cause."[1]

In the *Atharva-veda* Parjanya takes the place of Dyaus as the husband of Pṛthivī. Parjanya is here equivalent to what Æschylus describes as "the moist Heaven," that pours down rain. In a verse of the Atharva-veda (xii. 1, 12) the poet says: "The Earth is the mother, and I am the son of the Earth: Parjanya is the father. May he nourish us." In verse 42 of the same hymn he says: "Reverence be paid to the Earth, the wife of Parjanya, to her who draws her richness from showers." It would thus appear that the idea of the union of Heaven and Earth as father and mother from whom everything was produced was common among the ancestors of the Hindus, the Greeks and the Romans. It may, therefore, be conjectured that Dyāvā-Pṛthivī were undoubtedly very ancient Aryan deities.

---

[1] Muir's O. S. T., Vol. v, pp. 23-26. I am indebted to Dr. Muir for these classical references.

Varuṇa.—Another ancient Aryan divinity is Varuṇa. But he is very often associated with Mitra, and only occasionally with Indra. The frequent association of Mitra and Varuṇa will be easily explained when we remember that Mitra represented the Day, and Varuṇa the Night. Mitra and Varuṇa are both Ādityas, *i.e.*, the sons of Aditi. Sāyaṇa comments on Rv. i. 89, 3 as follows :—"Mitra is the God who presides over the day, according to the Vedic text 'the day is Mitra's,'" and again "Varuṇa is derived from the root *vri*, to cover; he envelops the wicked in his snares, and is the God who rules over the night, according to the text 'the night is Varuṇa's.'" The commentator on the *Taittirīya Saṃhitā* (i. 8, 16, 1) also says that "the word Mitra denotes the Sun," and that "the word Varuṇa signifies one who envelopes like darkness." Mitra is therefore the day, and Varuṇa the night. Varuṇa also signifies the sky which covers the Earth, darkness which envelops both the Earth and the Sky, clouds which cover the sky, and waters which cover the ocean. Varuṇa's sway is, therefore, extensive like that of a *Samrāt* or Universal Monarch. (Rv. i. 25, 10; ii. 28, 6; v. 85, 1; vi. 68, 9 and viii. 42 1). He is described as King of all, both gods and men (Rv. ii. 27, 10), and as King of the Universe (Rv. v. 85, 3). His house has a thousand doors (Rv. vii. 88, 5), and he is described as occupying with Mitra a stable palace supported by a thousand columns. Mounted in their car, he and Mitra behold all things in heaven and earth (Rv. v. 62, 4. 8.; 63, 1); but Varuṇa is said to be far-sighted (Rv. i. 25, 5. 16; viii. 90, 2) and thousand-eyed (Rv. vii. 34, 10), which epithet probably refers to the thousand stars that glitter in the sky at night. Elsewhere, the Sun is called "the eye of Mitra and Varuṇa" (Rv. vii. 61, 1; 63, 1; x. 37, 1). So nothing can escape the penetrating vision of these two gods.

Varuṇa's power and omniscience are thus discribed in the Atharva-veda (iv. 16).—"1. The great one who rules over these worlds beholds as if he were close at hand. When any man thinks he is doing aught by stealth, the gods know it all; 2. (and they perceive) everyone who stands or walks, or glides along secretly, or withdraws into his house, or into any lurking place. Whatever two persons, sitting together, devise, Varuṇa, the king, knows it, (being present there as) a third. 3. This earth, too, belongs to the king Varuṇa, and that vast sky whose ends are so remote. The two oceans (the aerial and terrestrial) are Varuṇa's stomachs; he resides in this small pool of water. 4. He who should flee far beyond the sky would not there escape from Varuṇa, the king. His messengers, descending from heaven traverse this world; thousand-eyed, they look across the whole earth. 5. King Varuṇa perceives all that exists within heaven and earth, and all that is beyond. The winkings of men's eyes are all numbered by him," etc. [1]

Varuṇa is thus the Moral Governor of the Universe, who upholds everything on the path of *ṛta* (right), and punish those who transgress the moral laws, and from whose far-seeing gaze nothing can escape. This conception of Varuṇa is indeed grand. But he is also gracious to those who have committed sins and supplicate him in a penitent spirit (Rv. vii. 87, 7). Vasiṣṭha's prayer to Varuṇa, imploring his forgiveness for the sins committed by him, are indeed highly touching. (Rv. vii, 86, 88 & 89).

The following are the functions and attributes of Varuṇa:—He upholds heaven and earth and dwells in all worlds as sovereign ruler (Rv. viii. 42, 1). He made the golden and revolving sun to shine in the firmament (Rv. vi. 70, 1; vii. 86, 1; 87, 6. &c.). The wind which resounds through the atmosphere is his breath (Rv. vii. 87, 2). He has opened boundless paths for the sun, and has hollowed out channels for the rivers which flow by his command. (Rv. i. 24, 8; ii. 28, 4; vii. 87, 1). By his wonderful contrivance the rivers pour their waters into one ocean, but

[1] Muir's translation, (O. S. T., Vol. v, pp. 63-64).

never fill it (Rv. v. 85, 6). His ordinances are fixed and unassailable (Rv. iii. 54, 18). Through their operation, the moon walks in brightness, and the stars which appear in the nightly sky mysteriously vanish in day-light. (Rv. i. 24, 10). He knows the flight of birds in the sky, the path of ships on the ocean, the course of the far-travelling wind, and beholds all the secret things that have been or shall be done. (Rv. i. 25, 7). No creature can even wink without him (Rv. ii. 28, 6) and he witnesses men's truth and falsehood (Rv. vii. 49, 3).[1]

It has already been said that in the Ṛgveda Varuṇa has also been identified among other things with the Ocean. He is described with Mitra as "Lords of the Seas" (*Sindhupati* vii. 64, 2). These seas probably refer to both the aerial and terrestrial seas, as indicated in Rv. vii. 64, 1, where it is said that Mitra and Varuṇa are the lords of waters both in heaven and earth. But Mitra has never been known to be the lord of the terrestrial sea, though he may fitly be described as the lord of the aerial ocean through which he moves. Varuṇa is said to reside and move in the midst of waters which are celestial, as well as waters which are terrestrial, *viz.*, those which flow, those for which channels are dug, those which are self-produced, and those which are proceeding to the ocean and are bright and purifying (Rv. vii. 49, 2 and 3). In a Ṛgvedic verse (viii, 41, 8) Varuṇa is identified with a hidden ocean *(Samudro apīcyaḥ)*.

It would thus appear that Varuṇa was the Supreme Lord of the Universe, *i.e.*, of land, water and the sky, and was omnipresent and omniscient, regulating and controlling all the natural phenomena by his immutable laws. I have already said that he and Mitra have been described as the oldest of the Gods (Rv. v. 65, 3; vi. 67, 1) though Dyāvā-Pṛthivī appear to be older still.

---

[1] Muir's O. S. T., Vol. v, pp. 61-63.

From some of the hymns addressed to Varuṇa, it does not appear that the ancient Aryans were agriculturists when they worshipped Varuṇa as their Supreme Diety. Though a prayer in Rv. vii. 64, 2 addressed to Mitra and Varuṇa says, "Send us food and rain from the sky," it has probably no reference to the requirements of agriculture, but is a simple prayer for food and water. In a Ṛgvedic verse (v. 63, 3) Varuṇa and Mitra have been described as "Ṣhowerers" (*Vṛṣava)* and as coming to the place of sacrifice, accompanied by multi-coloured clouds and pouring down rain from heaven with the help of the Asura's magic power (*asurasya māyayā*), whatever this may mean. Sāyaṇa interprets the last passage to mean "with the help of Parjanya 's power." This interpretation is plausible, as in the next verse there is a reference to Parjanya (the god of rain) from whom it is said, rain comes down according to the desire of Mitra and Varuṇa. The latter are also said to conceal the Sun "the wondrous weapon" behind clouds: "Ye hide him in the sky with cloud and flood of rain, and water-drops, Parjanya! full of sweetness, flow." (Rv. v. 63, 4).[1] The absence of any ill-feeling against Mitra and Varuṇa for covering up the Sun with clouds, such as is noticed against Vṛtra later on, is significant and remarkable. There is present the same grateful feeling towards the Gods as is entertained by a nomadic pastoral people for the days being made cool by clouds shutting out the burning rays of the Sun, and by occasional showers of rain. There is a prayer in Rv. vii. 62, 5 and 6, addressed to Mitra and Varuṇa, which invokes them to moisten the *grazing grounds for cattle* with rain, and to make the paths of the worshippers easy and safe. (*Sugā no viśvā supathāni santu*). The same sentiments are also expressed in Rv. vii. 64, 3 and 65, 4. It should also be noted that there is no mention of Vṛtra in connection with Varuṇa, and the latter performs no valorous deeds like Indra by killing him and releasing the pent-up waters. Varuṇa also

---

[1] Griffith 's "Translation of the Ṛgveda."

does not take any active part in killing or defeating the Dāsas and Dasyus who proved such intolerable pests to the settled agriculturists in a later age, though in a general way he, with Mitra and Aryaman, is said to destroy the forts of inimical persons and remove the troubles of the worshippers. (Rv. i. 41, 3).[1]

Varuṇa's authority gradually usurped by Indra.—These, then, are some of the relics of the ancient functions of Mitra and Varuṇa, mixed up with much that appertained to a later age when the present hymns were composed. Varuṇa became exclusively the Lord of the Ocean in a much later age after civilisation had far advanced, and the conditions of Aryan life also had considerably changed. His seat was probably transferred from the sky and the aerial ocean to the terrestrial ocean below at the time when Indra first appeared on the scene and usurped a great many of Varuṇa's functions. But the transition was extremely slow and gradual. Indra's name at first came to be coupled with that of Varuṇa as in hymns, i. 17 and iii. 38 of the Ṛgveda, which goes to show that though people acknowledged Indra to be the greatest God of the time, conformably to the change of their outlook on life and the comparatively advanced stage of their civilisation, they could not as yet altogether discard the name of Varuṇa who had hitherto occupied the supreme position in the pantheon of the early gods, and was still looked upon by ancient Ṛṣis like Vasiṣṭha as the Supreme Moral Governor of the Universe. When Indra's supreme position was firmly established, he became *Samrāt*, the Universal Monarch, and Varuṇa only *Svarāt* or a self-dependent ruler, possessing only limited powers and jurisdiction, (Rv. ii. 28, 1 and 82, 2). It was then that Varuṇa's name was dropped out altogether from the couple "Indra-Varuṇa," and Indra alone reigned supreme.

---

[1] Rv. i. 41, 3:- *vi durgā vi dviṣah puro ghnanti rājāna eṣām nayanti duritā tirah.*

It may be stated here in this connection that before Indra's supremacy was finally established, a struggle had been going on between the two Gods, or more correctly speaking, among their worshippers as to who should occupy the supreme position. There is a colloquy between Indra and Varuṇa, found in Rv. iv. 42, "in which each of these leading Gods puts forward his claim to pre-eminence." Says Varuṇa: "I am the Royal Ruler, mine is empire, as mine who sway all life, are all Immortals. Varuṇa's will the Gods obey and follow. I am the King of men's most lofty cover, (*i.e.*, the highest heaven). I am King Varuṇa. To me were given these first existing high celestial powers . . . . I, Varuṇa, am Indra: in their greatness, these the two wide deep fairly fashioned regions, these the two world-halves have I, even as Tvastṛ knowing all beings, joined and held together. I made to flow the moisture-shedding waters, and set the heaven firm in the seat of Order, (*i.e.*, in the place appointed by Law or the general Order of the Universe). By Law, the son of Aditi, (*i.e.*, I, Varuṇa) Law-Observer, hath spread abroad the world in three-fold measure." To this Indra replies: "Heroes with noble horses, fain for battle, selected warriors, call on me in combat. I, Indra Maghavan, excite the conflict; I stir the dust, Lord of surpassing vigour. All this I did. The Gods' own conquering power never impedeth me whom none opposeth. When lauds and Soma juice have made me joyful, both the unbounded regions are affrighted." (Griffith's translation). While Varuṇa bases his claim to supremacy on his power to uphold the Eternal Laws and Order of the Universe, compelling physical Nature to perform her functions properly, Indra vaunts on his ability to lead men to war and victory, and to command the allegiance of all the Gods who never oppose him. He also refers to the performance of the Soma sacrifice by men who offer him copious libations of the Soma juice in order to make him strong and hilarious. The poet finding Indra's reply not very satisfactory and comprehensive, goes to the very root of the question, and says in the next verse: "All beings know these deeds of thine: thou tellest this unto Varuṇa, thou Great Disposer! *Thou art renowned as having slain the Vṛtras. Thou madest flow the floods that were obstructed.*" In other words, Indra's real greatness lay in causing timely rains to fall for agricultural operations by killing Vṛtra who had obstructed them. He not only carried on a deadly conflict with Vṛtra in mid-heaven, but also helped his votaries on the earth below to kill the nomadic Dasas and Dasyus who caused them great trouble and mischief by pillaging their agricultural products and stealing their cattle, and opposed them in the performance of their sacrifice. The above verses undoubtedly refer to a changed order of things, which indicated and was the result of a marked change in the culture of the people.

Causes of the decline of Varuṇa's power.—It would not be uninteresting to speculate here on the causes that led to Varuṇa's dethronement from his supreme position in the hierarchy of the Vedic Gods. As I have already pointed out, the word "Varuṇa" etymologically means *that which covers.* The god Varuṇa was, therefore, (1) darkness which *covers* the earth at night; (2) clouds or waters of the aerial ocean, which *cover* the sky; (3) the sky with millions of glittering stars, which *covers* the earth at night, and (4) waters which *cover* the sea. But darkness afterwards came to be regarded as a malevolent deity, in as much as it not only extinguished the light of the Sun, but brought many attendant horrors in its train, viz., wolves, wild animals and robbers. Professor Oldenberg has advanced the theory that as Mitra was the Sun, the lord of day, so Varuṇa was the Moon, the lord of night. There may be some truth in this speculation, indicating as it does separate worships of the Sun (Mitra) and of the Moon (Varuṇa), which afterwards probably gave rise to two schools of worshippers, viz., the Sun-worshippers and the Moon-worshippers, or to state it more clearly in Paurāṇic parlance, the worshippers of Viṣṇu and of Śiva ("the Sun of the night," probably identified with the Moon). But Vṛtra came in Ṛgvedic times to be identified with darkness which shut up the Sun and the Dawn in its bosom, and the Moon as the presiding deity over darkness came to be identified with Vṛtra, being in eternal enmity with the Sun, as the *Śatapatha Brāhmaṇa* says (i. 5, 3, 18). There was consequently a nightly struggle between Indra and Vṛtra, as the former wanted to release the Sun and the Dawn from the clutches of the latter, and invariably succeeded in doing so, having been strengthened by the libations of Soma juice offered to him by his worshippers. In the next place, Vṛtra came to be identified with clouds, as they covered up the Sun and the Dawn, and also confined the rains in their bosom, which were required for agricultural purposes. Indra, with his thunderbolt, rent open the black skin of the demon and released the waters, as well as the Sun and the Dawn. But this struggle was carried on for months together during the rainy season before the final victory was achieved by Indra. Varuṇa thus gradually came to be ousted from his functions as enveloper in the shapes of darkness and clouds. We have already said that Vṛtra was at first regarded as a *Deva* and Brāhmaṇa, but his functions having proved detrimental to the performance of sacrifice and to the successful carrying on of agricultural operations, he was regarded as a malevolent power, inimical to the interests of both Gods and men. Varuṇa, having been stripped of some of his functions by Vṛtra, came as a matter of course to be identified with the broad Ocean below, and the expanded Sky above, with his eye as Mitra (Rv. i. 53, 6) in the day-time, and his thousand eyes glittering in the darkness at night as stars. Thus was Varuṇa's power crippled, and he came to occupy a secondary position in the hierarchy of the Vedic gods, when the Aryans had changed their mode of life and passed on from a pastoral to an agricultural, and from a non-sacrificial to a sacrificial stage, and Indra had been discovered and his divine services requisitioned to suit the changing needs of the time.

Varuṇa still remained supreme with certain Aryan clans.—Though shorn of some of his functions and attributes by the agricultural and sacrifice-performing sections of the Aryans, Varuṇa still remained the Supreme God with those who did not take to agriculture, and were fond of roving about either from habit or necessity. The *Paṇis* were the Aryan merchants in Ṛgvedic times, trading in their own country and in foreign lands across the seas which they negotiated in their own vessels. Some of them were also cattle-keepers, moving from place to place with their herds, and occasionally augmenting their stock by stealing cattle belonging to the tribes through whose territories they passed. As they were not agriculturists by occupation, they did not feel the necessity of worshipping Indra or performing any sacrifice in his honour. In fact, they did not recognize even the existence of Indra. "Who is he?" the Paṇis asked Saramā who had gone to them as Indra's messenger, "what looks he like, this Indra, whose herald you have hastened from afar? Let him come here," said they probably jestingly, "we will make friends with him; then he may be the herdsman of our cows." (Rv. x. 108,3.) This shows the spirit in which Indra was regarded by certain sections of the Aryans, even in Ṛgvedic times. The Paṇis went on worshipping the ancient Varuṇa as their Supreme God, firstly because Varuṇa was the Lord of the Ocean which the sea-going merchants had to cross under his protection and guidance, as he knew the path of the ships on the ocean and "the course of the far-reaching winds" (Rv. i. 25, 7. 9); and secondly because he guided their ships in the watery waste at night by means of the stars which he revealed in the sky. Hence the Phœnicians who were the descendants of the Paṇis, and the product of an amalgamation of the Aryan and Semitic races, [1] continued to worship Varuṇa or

[1] *Ṛgvedic India*, Ch. xi.

Ouranus as their Supreme God. There were others, even Ṛṣis in Sapta-Sindhu, who did not believe in the existence of Indra. For instance, the Ṛṣi, known as Nema, used to say: "There is no such god as Indra. Who has seen him? Why should we laud him?" (Rv. viii. 100, 3). This unbelief in Indra was also shared by another powerful branch of the Aryans, the worshippers of Ahura Mazda, who not only not regarded him as a god, but positively put him down as the devil-incarnate. This was one of the causes that led to the great schism, separating the two branches for ever. The Ormuzdians believed in the supremacy of only one God, named Ahura Mazda. By the way, the words *Ahura Mazda* are believed by some to be a corruption of the words *Asura Mahā*, used as epithets of Agni, Rudra or Fire (Rv. ii. 1, 6), or of the words *Asura Maghavā* (the Asura, fit to be worshipped). But the word *Asura*, though applied to other Gods also in the early portions of the Ṛgveda, was mainly used as an epithet of Varuṇa to denote his all-pervading power. Hence some European savants are disposed to identify *Ahura Mazda* with Varuṇa. Says Dr. Muir: "Varuṇa also, in the opinion of certain writers, is connected, at least indirectly, with the Ahura Mazda of the old Persian mythology; and in support of this it may alleged,—(1) that the name of Asura, the divine being, is frequently applied to Varuṇa, as an epithet; (2) that the class of Indian gods called Ādityas, of whom Varuṇa is the most distinguished, bears a certain analogy to the Amshaspands of the Zend mythology, of whom Ahura Mazda is the highest; and (3) that a close connection exists between Varuṇa and Mitra, just as, according to Professor Roth, Ahura and Mithra are frequently associated in the Zend Avesta, though the position of the two has otherwise become altered, and Mithra is not even reckoned among the Amshaspands.[1]

Says Professor Roth in his paper on "The Highest Gods of the Arian Races" (Journal of the German Oriental

[1] Muir's, O. S. T., Vol. v, Sec. 8, p. 72.

Society, vi, p. 70 f): "Within the circle of the Ādityas there subsists the closest connection between Mitra and Varuṇa who are invoked more frequently together than Varuṇa is invoked singly. We find only one hymn in which Mitra is invoked by himself (Rv. iii. 59). The fact that this dual invocation is preserved in the Zend Avesta, in regard to Ahura and Mitra, though the position of both has become entirely altered, and Mithra is not even reckoned among the Amshaspands,—this fact proves how close the ancient connection of the two was, when it has been maintained even after the reason for it had ceased."[1]

On the Zend word Varena, Professor Westergaard thus remarks: "The Zend word *Varena* corresponds also etymologically, on the one hand, to the Greek *Ouranos* and, on the other, to the Indian Varuṇa, a name which in the Vedas is assigned to the god who reigns in the farthest regions of the heaven, where air and sea are, as it were, blended; on which account he has, in the later Indian Mythology, become god of the sea, whilst in the Vedas he appears first as the mystic lord of the evening and the night." And he adds: "Possibly the Iranian Varena, in opposition to Yima's home on the remotest mountains of the east, denotes originally the distant western region of the heaven and the air, where every evening, the Sun and light conceal themselves, and so much the rather as the epithet Varenya, derived from Varena, is in the Zend Avesta applied only to the evil spirits of darkness."[2]

Professor Bloomfield says on this subject: "Greek *Ouranos* is Indo-European Uoru-nnos or Uoruenos; Sanskrit Varuṇas is Indo-European Uoru-nos . . . . . It shows that Varuṇa belongs not only to the Indo-Iranian (Aryan) time,

---

[1] Muir's, O. S. T., Vol. v, Sec. 6, p. 70.

[2] Paper originally published in 1852, and translated by Prof. Spiegel from the Danish, and published in Weber's *Indische Studien*, Vol. iii, (Quoted in Muir's, O. S. T., Vol. v, pp. 75-76).

but reaches back to the Indo-European time, and that he represents, on the impeccable testimony of *Ouranos*, some aspect of the heavens, probably the encompassing sky, in accordance with the stem *Uoru*, which is its essential element."[1]

"Uranos" says Professor, Max Müller "in the language of Hesiod, is used as a name for the sky. He is made or born that he should 'be a firm place for the blessed gods.' It is said twice that Uranos covers everything (v. 127), and that when he brings the night, he is stretched out everywhere, embracing the earth. This sounds almost as if the Greek myth had still preserved a recollection of the etymological power of Uranos. For Uranos is in the Sanskrit Varuṇa, and is derived from a root, *var*, to cover, Varuṇa being in the Veda also a name of the firmament, but especially connected with the night, and opposed to Mitra, the day."[2] We have, however, seen that Varuṇa has always been associated with Mitra, and never acted in opposition to him, as wrongly described by Professor Max Müller.

We thus find the existence of the name of Varuṇa, (Varena, Ouranos or Uranos) not only among the Vedic Aryans but also among the Iranians, the Phœnicians, the Greeks and other races, which goes to show that this name was taken by the various peoples at the time of their dispersion from their central home which was in Sapta-Sindhu, and that this God was worshipped according to the conception that each tribe had formed of him.

Agni, Parjanya, Bhaga, Mitra, Vala, Sūrya, Atri etc. There were other Vedic Gods whom we find dispersed over ancient Europe and Western Asia under the same or similar names among various tribes who were either Aryans, or who imbibed Aryan culture. Some of these gods are named as follow: Agni, Parjanya, Bhaga, Mitra, Vala, Sūrya, Atri etc.

---

[1] Bloomfield's *The Religion of the Vedas* (1908), pp. 136-137.

[2] Max Müller's *Chips from a German Workshop*, ii, 65.

Agni, the god of Fire, is the same as the *Ignus* of the Latins, and the *Ogni* of the Slavonians. Parjanya, the god of rain and storm in the Ṛgveda (v. 83; vii. 101 and 102) is, as we have already pointed out, the same as the Lithuanian god, *Perkunas*, the god of thunder. Dr. G. Bühler wrote a paper in English on the subject, which was published in the "Transactions of the London Philological Society" for 1859 (pp. 154 ff) and another paper in German which was published in Benfy's "Orient and Occident" (vol. i, pp. 214 ff). According to him, Parjanya was decidedly distinct from Indra (Trans. Phil. Society p. 167 and Or. and Occ. p. 229), and I perfectly agree with him in this view, in as much as Parjanya was undoubtedly far more ancient than Indra, and the latter had wider and more complex functions to perform than the former. Indra killed Vṛtra with his thunderbolt and released the waters pent up by the demon in his bosom, as well as the Sun and the Dawn and the solar rays encompassed by him. He also helped his worshippers to defeat and kill the Dasas and the Dasyus who proved intolerable pests to them in ancient Aryan society. Further, he gave lands to the Aryans, probably for cultivation, and helped them to perform their sacrifice. But Parjanya's functions were limited. "Taking a review of the whole" says Dr. Bühler in the English paper, "we find that Parjanya is a god who presides over the lightning, the thunder, the rain, and the procreation of plants and living creatures." (P. 161) Dr. Bühler, however, was not at first quite certain whether the god was originally a god of rain or god of thunder, and inclined to think from the etymology of his name and the analogy between him and Perkunas that he was originally the thunder-god; but he subsequently concluded in his German essay that Parjanya was "the god of thunderstorm and rain, the generator and nourisher of plants and living creatures." (P. 226).[1]

[1] *Vide* Muir's, O. S. T., Vol. v, p. 142.

If Parjanya is the God of rain and thunderstorm, the question still remains to be answered, why was the God Indra conceived to perform the very same functions? The answer to this question is that Parjanya was an ancient conception of the God of rain and thunder, when the Aryans were probably nomads, and noticed the clouds to be rent by the God with his thunderbolt, which caused rains to fall for the growth of grass and plants on which their flocks and cattle grazed. Indra's conception was more complex, due to the later culture and advancement of the Aryans as a sacrifice-loving and agricultural people who wanted the Dawn and the Sun to rise regularly to enable them to perform their sacrifices in time, and were in need of timely rains for cultivating the lands. Moreover, the settled Aryans were in need of the assistance of a powerful God of war who would defeat the Dāsas and the Dasyus, and lead them to victory so that they might peacefully live and prosper. Hence Indra became the greatest God of the time, and usurped Parjanya's functions to a great extent, or rather made him a helping hand in carrying on his work, just as he was assisted by the Maruts, Viṣṇu and Brahmaṇaspati in defeating Vṛtra. Parjanya thus remained the old God of rain, with limited functions, while Indra was his later development, with wider powers, and more extensive jurisdiction. The very fact that Perkunas, and not Indra, was the God of rain among the Lithuanians, and Fairguni in Gothic and Fiörgyn in Norse mean thunder, lends support to this view. There can be no doubt that the Lithuanians and the Indo-Aryans derived the names Parjanya and Perkunas from the same common stock.

The name of the god *Bhaga* seems also to have been derived from the same common stock, the Vedic Aryans and the Iranians calling him *Bhaga*, the Kossæans *Bugash*, the Phrygians *Bagaios*, and the Slavs *Bogu*. This goes to prove that they were all one people in some remote age, or derived their culture from a common source.

The God *Mitra* of the Vedic Aryans was the same as *Mithra* of the Iranians and *Medeus* of the Lydians. The worship of Mitra prevailed down to the 4th century in the Roman Empire. Prof. A. A. Macdonell says that from Zoroastrianism was developed the worship of the Sun-god Mithras in Western Europe. "This, introduced to Rome in the first century B. C., began to be spread very widely throughout the Roman Empire, before the end of the first Christian century, by the army, slave population, and traders as the worship of the 'Sun-god, the unconquered Mithra.' Thus by the end of the third century A. D., it bade fair to become a world religion. At the beginning of the 4th century several Roman Emperors were votaries of Mithraism, but after the adoption of Christianity by Constantine, who became Emperor in 326, and made Christianity the official religion of the State, Mithraism declined and disappeared from Rome by the end of the 4th century." [1]

Atri is a solar deity in the Ṛgveda, being a friend of the Sun whom he released from the clutches of *Svarbhânu* or eclipse (Rv. v. 40. 7). There is also a myth connected with Atri in the Ṛgveda (i. 100. 8), which goes to show that he was the summer Sun whom the Asuras tortured by confining him in a torture-house, and whom the Aśvins subsequently released by causing rains to fall, which extinguished the fire that tortured him. This *Atri* is found as *Attys* among the Phrygians and Lydians. The god Sûryas is the same as the Kossæan *Suryash*, the Greek *Helius*, the Latin *Sol*, and Egyptian *Horus*.

Vala was another ancient Vedic god who is identified with the Sun. The *Ṛbhus*, whom Sâyaṇa has identified with the solar rays, were the sons of Vala. (Rv. iv. 33, 34, 35, 36, and 37). Fire was also called a son of Vala. (Rv. iv. 18). The Paṇis were the worshippers of *Vala* and the *Ṛbhus*.

---

[1] ***Brahmanism and Buddhism***, an address delivered at Lahore and published in the *Hindustan Review*, xlvii July 1923.

This God Vala or Baal was also the God of the Phœnicians who identified him with *Ouranus* or Varuṇa. He was also worshipped under the same name or under the name of *Bel* by the ancient Chaldeans and later Babylonians. The earlier walls for the Temple of Bel (Baal) at Nippur are said to date from 6000 or 7000 years B. C.[1]. Professor Nilsson finds traces of Baal worship in Scandinavia. "Indeed, the festival of Baal or Balder was, he tells us, celebrated on Midsummer's night in Scania, and far up into Norway, almost to the Loffoden Islands, until within the last fifty years. A wood fire was made upon a hill or mountain, and the people of the neighbourhood gathered together in order, like Baal's prophets of old, to dance round it, shouting and singing. The Midsummer's-night fire has even retained in some parts the ancient name cf 'Balders-baal' or Balders-fire....A similar custom also prevailed until lately in some parts of our islands. Baal has given his name to many Scandinavian localities, as, for instance, the Baltic, the Great and Little Belt, Belteberga, Baleshaugen, Balestranden, &c."[2]

All these coincidences in the names of the gods as well as of domestic relations and domesticated animals go to show that the different races derived them from a common source, and as *all* these names are to be found in that language only, in which the Vedic hymns were composed, the natural inference would be that these different races, among whom the words are found, must have borrowed them from this common language, before dispersing to the different parts of Western Asia and Europe in different times and different stages of Aryan civilisation. That this dispersion had taken place long before the Vedic hymns were composed goes without saying. Of course most of these races afterwards commingled their blood with races

---

[1] *Hist. Hist. of the World*, vol. I, p. 329.

[2] Lord Avebury's *Prehistoric Times*, pp. 67-71 (Ed., 1912).

other than Aryan ; but the culture that they carried remained essentially Aryan.

Domestic life, Marriage and the Origin of the Home.—In the account of the domestic life of the Ṛgvedic Aryans, we also come across a few relics of an earlier stage of civilisation. In the Ṛgvedic period, we find the home well-established, with the father as patriarch, possessing supreme control of the household, and marriage-laws fully observed and recognised. In fact, it was on the custom of marriage that the foundations of the home were laid. A merely passing or temporary union of the sexes like that of the lower animals would not have necessitated the creation of the home. It was the natural instinct or desire of woman to have adequate protection for herself in her critical delicate condition, and for the child in its helpless state of infancy, that undoubtedly guided her in the selection of her partner, and led to mutual understanding before she could think of giving herself away. She was, therefore, naturally cautious, undemonstrative, shy and retiring, and would take a long time to make a choice from among her suitors. She would naturally select one who was not only young, but physically strong, and endowed with sufficient mental vigour and resource to face an emergency. When once assured of his fitness, the woman would feel a strong attachment for him, and her heart would flow out in love, and she would attract her man towards her in her thousand and one fascinating ways. Her sentiments would, of course, be duly reciprocated, resulting in a union both of the heart and body. This union of man and woman, based as it is on mutual understanding and love, is the real germ of the home, be it a natural cave, a leafy shade, a rude hut, or an open heath under the wide sky. The pair would support each other by collecting roots or fruits, or killing small animals in the course of their wanderings, which they would share between them, and would nurse each other in times of sickness. This constant companionship and association of each other in all matters would strengthen the bond of their love and union, and make their hearts beat in unison, teaching them self-sacrifice and self-denial, without which no home would ever exist or grow. When the interesting event of the advent of a little new-comer was expected, they would seek out a natural cave or other place of protection, where mother and child could find shelter from heat, cold or rain, and the attacks of wild animals, and the child could be safely nursed and reared up till such time as it could trot along with its parents, or take care of itself. This natural cave or shelter was the origin of the home, and the home afterwards became the unit of society. The home, therefore, primarily owed its origin to woman who was like the very embodiment of that great moral and spiritual force that ultimately worked itself out in the creation and development of modern civilised society.

It was the renowned sage Viśvāmitra who realised this moral and spiritual force of woman thousands of years ago, and ecstatically declared *Jāyetastam*, *i.e.* "The wife is the home" (Rv. iii 53, 4), and nobody has spoken a greater truth since those remarkable and memorable words were uttered. The wife is verily the home, and woman is the mainspring of those human activities that have uplifted the race from its savage condition. The ancient Aryans never looked upon woman as the cause of human downfall. On the other hand, the important part that she played in advancing human civilisation and converting the earth into a paradise was fully appreciated and recognised. The very creation of the Universe was ascribed by the Aryans to the union of *Prakṛti* and *Puruṣa* "Nature beneath, and Will or Power above" (Rv. x. 129, 5). Woman is Prakṛti, and man is Puruṣa, and the union of these two has created the home and made the world what it is to-day.

Promiscuous Intercourse.—It does not appear that intercourse between man and woman in primitive society was originally promiscuous. Says Westermarck: "It is not of course impossible that among some peoples, intercourse between the sexes may have been almost promiscuous. But there is not a shred of genuine evidence for the notion that promiscuity even formed a general stage in the history of mankind. ....Although polygamy occurs among most existing peoples, and polyandry among some, monogamy is by far the most common form of human marriage. It was so among the ancient peoples of whom we have any direct knowledge. Monogamy is the form which is generally recognised and permitted. The great majority of peoples are, as a rule, monogamous, and other forms of marriage are usually modified in a monogamous direction." [1]

Howard also makes the following observations on the subject.—"The researches of several recent writers, notably those of Starcke and Westermarck, confirming in part and further developing the earlier conclusions of Darwin and Spencer, have established a probability that marriage, or pairing between one man and one woman, though the union be only transitory, and the rule frequently violated, is the typical form of sexual union from the infancy of the human race."[2]

Rev. Mr. E. O. James says: "Man is, in the words of Aristotle, 'naturally a civic animal.' Some kind of community is necessary for him to live the fulness of his life, and therefore marriage is not an artificial regulation of civilised society, but a natural necessity in all ages of man's terrestrial history. Were the human species constituted as the lower animals, a merely passing union of the sexes would suffice, but more than this is required. The offspring needs long continued care after birth. A parallel is, of course, to be found in some of the lower animals, but in a less degree. Child-bearing in the human organism continues for sometime,

---

[1] Westermarck's *History of Human Marriage*, pp. 133, 459.

[2] Howard's *History of Matrimonial Institutions*, pp. 90, 91.

while the elder children are growing to maturity, whereas in the other animals the young are usually independent of the mother before other offspring are born. The connexion of human parents is, therefore, indefinitely prolonged, extending beyond the age of child-bearing. As a consequence of this prolonged intimacy, there appears the phenomenon of human love apart from sexual desire. In the same way the parental and filial affections of the human species pass the bounds of mere devoted care, as seen in the case of the lower animals, which terminates with the period of protection."[1]

Monogamy, therefore, is natural and the rule, while the other forms of marriage, *viz.*, polygamy, polyandry or only temporary connexions are unnatural and regarded as exceptions. They represent an extremely low, almost bestial stage of human evolution, or mark a degradation or retrogression to the primitive condition of brutes. Promiscuity never creates the home, nor evokes those noble sentiments of self-sacrifice and self-denial that have helped to uplift the human race. If such tribes exist as indulge in promiscuous connexions, they must have been like the dross cast out by the human race in its evolution towards progress, and left as relics of the primitive brutish stage through which it had to pass. Such tribes are destined to remain for ever in their primitive condition or to perish, unless they are uplifted by being brought into contact with a higher form of civilisation, and assimilating it.

Promiscuity condemned by the Aryans.—In the Mahābharata which is a veritable store-house of ancient legends, we come across an account of sexual intercourse which savours of promiscuity.[2] It is therein stated that the women were in early primitive times free and not bound to be faithful to their husbands. They could have intercourse with any man they chose, even though they were bound by ties of marriage. This revolting custom, however, was abolished

---

[1] James' *Introduction to Anthropology*, pp. 128-129.

[2] *The Mahābhārata*, Bk. I, Chap. 122.

by Śvetaketu, son of Uddālaka, who clearly saw the colossal immorality of the whole thing, and probably voiced public opinion that had been formed on the subject but had remained inarticulate. This story goes to show that primitive Aryan society also probably passed through a stage in which promiscuity was tolerated as a necessary evil, if not approved. But we do not find any evidence in the Ṛgveda, showing that promiscuity was in vogue in early Aryan society. The Mahābhārata story must, therefore, have reference to pre-Ṛgvedic times. In the Ṛgveda, however, we find in the story of Yama and Yamī (x. 10) an echo of primitive times when promiscuous and what we now call incestuous connexions were probably tolerated. Yama and Yamī were brother and sister, born as twins. The latter was strongly enamoured of the former, and wanted him to co-habit with her. But Yama strongly set his face against her importunate, unholy and immoral proposal, saying that sexual connexion between brother and sister was sinful and condemned by men. Mr. R. C. Dutt says that this myth of Yama and Yamī probably refers to the twins, Day and Night, the latter always following the former, but never coming in contact with it. This fact may have suggested to the poet the revolting and uncanny picture of a sister sinfully craving the company of her brother. An interpretation like this is possible, especially when we find some of the Vedic bards indulge in revolting metaphors of a father having sexual connexion with his daughter (Rv. x. 61, 7) in order to explain certain natural phenomenon in a very odd and ugly fashion. But the myth of Yama and Yamī itself may also be interpreted to refer to a primitive state of society in by-gone times, when such a connexion was probably not condemned; for Yamī distinctly says in verse 3 that though the custom is prohibited among men, there is no such prohibition against it among the Devas or Gods! Of course this refers, as I have already said, to the odd and fanciful way in which the Vedic bards loved to indulge in revolting descriptions of the relations between a God and a

Goddess who could be explained, like the Sun and the Dawn, as performing the parts of both husband and wife, father and daughter, and son and mother. Uṣas or the Dawn first appears on the horizon like a lovely maiden, followed by the Sun, who is looked upon as her lover eager to possess her. (Rv. i. 71, 5; 91, 1). Again Uṣas is looked upon as the Primordial Force that produced everything. She is called the "first" (Rv. i. 123, 5), "the mother of the Gods" (Rv. i. 113, 19) "the ancient damsel" (Rv. iii. 61, 1; iv. 51. 6) "the mother of Sūrya" (Rv. i. 113, 2) and "the producer of the Sun, Fire and Sacrifice" (Rv. vii. 78, 3). Here, then, we come across two conflicting descriptions of the Dawn, according to two different view-points of the Vedic bards. Yamī's words, therefore, do not mean much. Whatever may have been the custom in early human society, it is certain that marriage or sexual connexion between brother and sister was condemned in Ṛgvedic times as highly immoral and sinful. It may be stated here in passing that even in such a primitive co mmunity as that of the Australian savages, ths custom does not exist, and even marriage between a man and woman belonging to the same tribe is strictly prohibited. Incestuous connexions must, therefore, have been in vogue among tribes who were little removed from anthropoid apes and were only just emerging into the human state. The instance of an Egyptian or a Persian king marrying his own sister is only an exception to the general rule, and shows a retrogression to the brute-like savage state beyond any hope of redemption. Such connexions were, nevertheless, strongly condemned by public opinion.

Marriage by contract.—We find, however, in the Ṛgveda an instance of marriage by contract, which goes to show that such marriage was of a temporary nature, terminable only on the violation of the term of the contract on which it was based. The story of Urvaśī and Purūravā in the Ṛgveda (x. 95) shows that their marriage was based on contract, and that Urvaśī left her husband because he had failed to perform his part of the contract and keep his promise. This form of marriage which was not current in Ṛgvedic times must have been a relic of ancient times when temporary marriages were probably in vogue.

Exogamy.—A word on exogamy will not be quite out of place here. We find that from very ancient time the custom of marrying outside one's own clan or *gotra* was in vogue in Aryan society. How did the custom come into being it is very difficult to ascertain ; but we find it existing in such a primitive community as that of the Australian aborigines. One clan is distinguished from another by the sign of a certain *totem* or animal, from which the clan is supposed to have derived its origin. These clans were often at war with one another, during which it was usual with the victorious men to carry off the young damsels of the defeated tribe. Association with women, won as spoils of war, probably gave a greater zest to the indulgence of sexual propensities than association with women of one's own clan, whom it was very difficult to secure owing to their having been strongly protected by their parents, brothers or near relations. Hence probably arose the custom of marrying outside one's own clan, which is observed in primitive communities as well as in such a highly developed community as that of the Vedic Aryans. The *Pirrauru* relationship to be found among Australian aborigines "is one in which a group of men and women have the right of sexual intercourse with one another. But a *Pirrauru* is always a wife's sister, or a brother's wife, or in some such definite relationship to her partner."[1] In developed Aryan society a wife's sister or a brother's widow could occupy the position of a wife, probably because they originally belonged to different clans, and were eligible for marriage.

It has been suggested that in the primitive stages of Aryan society the different clans were known by different

[1] E. O. James' *Intro. to Anthropology*, p. 120.

totem names; but there is no reliable evidence in the Ṛgveda to prove their existence. The later Aryans called certain tribes *Garudas* and *Sarpas*, probably on account of their migratory habits, and also because they were constantly at war with one another like the king of birds and the serpents. It is not probable that they had also these different *totem* names. Dr. R. Shama Śāstrī traces the existence of *totem* names in the species that go to form the *yoni-kūta* or species harmony of Hindu astrologers.[1] But it is extremely doubtful whether the names of the animals represent the names of the different Aryan clans, for they really represent the characteristics of *individuals* only rather than of clans.

In this connexion, the following remarks of Professor Bloomfield in the *Religion of the Veda* (p. 138) will be found interesting: "Totemism is founded on the belief that the human race, or, more frequently, that given clans or families derive their descent from animals: totemic names like 'Bear' and 'Wolf' carry traces of this sort of belief into our time. This particular question is a splendid theme of universal ethnology, but I have never been able to discover that it has any considerable bearing upon the ancient religion of India. The many hints at its possible importance should be substantiated by a larger and clearer body of facts than seems at present available."

Polyandry.—It is possible, as I have said, that at a certain stage in early Aryan society promiscuity may have been in vogue and society in that stage was, according to Dr. Śāstrī, "maternal or matriarchal rather than paternal or patriarchal. Words such as Daityas, son of Diti, Vainateyas, sons of Vinatā, Kādraveyas, sons of Kadru, Ānjaneya, son of Anjanā, Jabāla, son of Jabālā, and Jaratkāra, son of Jaratkāru are

[1] Dr. Shama Śastri's *Evolution of Indian Polity*, p. 6. Prof. Macdonell sees traces of totemism in the Vedic names Kaśyapa (tortoise), the Matsyas (fishes), the Ajas (goats), the Śigrus (Horse-radish), the Śunakas (dogs), the Kauśikas (owls), etc. (V. M. 65); but Hopkins and Bloomfield express doubts.

taken as indicative of the uncertainty of the real begetter and of the unsettled condition of the society which rendered promiscuity among women a necessary evil."[1] But some of the names selected in the above extract by Dr. Śāstrī belong to non-Aryan tribes, e.g. Vinatā, Kadru, Anjanā etc., and cannot be cited to prove that the matriarchal form of family existed in Aryan society. The story of Jabālā is too well known to need an explanation why her son Jābala was named after her.

It must be frankly stated, however, that there are indications in the Ṛgveda of polyandry, though the custom was extremely rare in Ṛgvedic times. There is a verse (Rv. viii. 29, 8.) which says that two men lived with one woman. It is probable that the woman was a harlot, and the two men were her paramours who alternately visited her. There are three other verses (Rv. i. 167, 4. 5. 6) which say that the Maruts had one common wife named Rodasī who was devotedly attached to her husbands, and probably lived with them by turns. Rodasī stands for lightning, and the description may be a mere metaphor; but it may have been suggested to the poet by some concrete examples before him. Though instances of ployandry may have existed here and there in Ṛgvedic times, the custom was certainly very rare, and, we may take it, the matriarchal form of family did not at all exist in Ṛgvedic times. Nevertheless, it must be admitted that sexual morality was somewhat low and lax even in Ṛgvedic times. There are many references in the Ṛgveda to women having paramours, and unmarried girls casting away their fœtus or infants delivered in secret,[2] revealing a state of society that shocked the better mind of the cultured Aryans, and roused lady-Ṛṣis like Lopamudrā to place nuptial relations on a firmer and sounder basis. (Rv. v. 28, 3).

---

[1] Dr. R. Śāstrī, *Evolution of Indian Polity*, p. 2.

[2] Rv. ii. 29, 1; v. 5, 5; ix. 32, 5; 38, 4; 96, 22; 101, 12; &c.

Women as chattels.—Women captured in war from rival clans, or otherwise forced to matrimonial connexion, were necessarily kept in subjection and treated more like chattels than human beings. They were virtually treated as slaves, over whose life and liberty their husbands had complete control. This was the lowest form of marriage, if it could be called by that name at all. Even in such later times as the age of the Epics, we find Draupadī, the royal consort of the five Pāṇḍavas, pawned by Yudhiṣṭhira in a game of dice which he played with Śakuni, and lost. The Kurus for whom the game was won forcibly brought out the queen from her royal apartments, and subjected her to a series of inhuman insults and indignities that made the blood of her royal husbands boil. But they were utterly demoralized and could not raise their voice, nor even their little finger in protest, because, forsooth, they had lost her in the game! Even Rāma, the ideal hero, has been made by Vālmīki to say that he would fain give away his wife Sītā, his royal inheritance, and even his life and all that he valued to Bharata, of his own free accord, without being requested by anybody; how much more ready and willing would he therefore be to do the same things, if commanded by his father, the king himself.[1] How could Rāma give away his own wife to another man, be he a brother or a stranger, unless he was perfectly conscious of the fact that he had complete control over her life and liberty? These incidents and sentiments were undoubtedly the relics of a by-gone barbarous age when a wife was regarded no better than a chattel. Whether wives used to be pawned in the games of dice of which the Ṛgvedic Aryans were exceedingly fond is not quite clear from a perusal of the Ṛgveda; but certain verses (Rv. x. 34, 2 and 4) may be made to bear an interpretation like that. In one verse the gambler laments that he had to abandon a wife who was not only beautiful and loving but highly

[1] The Rāmāyaṇa, ii. 19, 7-8.

serviceable to him and his friends. In another verse he says that when love of gambling gets the better of his reason, other persons lay their hands on his wife. Whatever may be the real import of these passages, there can be no doubt that in the very early stages of civilisation, the position of the wife as a rule was scarcely better than that of a slave. No wonder, therefore, that she entertained scarcely any love or good feeling towards her husband, and often went astray and proved faithless, giving occasion for the expression of such uncomplimentary sentiments as the following: "woman's mind is uncontrollable" (Rv. viii. 33, 17); and "woman's love is never stable; and her heart is like that of a hyena." (Rv. x. 95, 15). It was only when woman came to be treated with respect, and was allowed freedom in making her choice of a husband that society made real progress towards civilisation. The Ṛgveda reveals a stage showing that Aryan women, at any rate of the higher and better classes, enjoyed equal freedom with the men in all matters, social and religious. It was this feeling of equality and freedom that evoked the highest virtues of Aryan womanhood, and lifted society to a high state of culture.

Patria Potestas and Human-sacrifice.—The father was the supreme ruler of the household, and, as I have already said, possessed complete power over the life and liberty of his wife and also of his children, in the early stages of Ṛgvedic civilisation. There is a story of Śunaḥśepa in the Ṛgveda (i 24) which bears reference to his having been bound to the *yūpa* or sacrificial post, preparatory to being sacrificed. But there is no clear reference to the performance of human sacrifice in the verses, though the story was subsequently expanded in the *Aitareya Brāhmaṇa*, giving full details which go to show that human sacrifice, if it was not a common practice, was occasionally resorted to in ancient Aryan society. In the early stages, probably those who had been captured in war were sacrificed to propitiate the God of victory. That the flesh of these victims was not partaken of by the victors after the manner of the Australian aborigines who resort to this revolting practice "in order to acquire the strength of a dead man, or to establish a vital union with the dead"[1] may be taken as certain. But with a view to make human sacrifice more efficacious, meritorious, and acceptable to the Gods, the victim probably came gradually to be selected from among the nearest and dearest relations of the sacrificer, especially his sons over whose life he had complete power. Thus the story in the *Aitareya Brāhmaṇa* says that a certain king named Hariścandra vowed to Varuṇa to sacrifice his first-born son; but when that son was born and Varuṇa demanded the sacrifice, the king put off the ceremony on one excuse or another till the boy grew sufficiently old to think for himself and understand his own interests. When the father, unable to put off the demand of Varuṇa any further, asked his son Rohita to be the victim of the sacrifice, the latter took fright and fled into the woods where he remained in hiding for full six years. Meanwhile, the king, not having been able to fulfil his vow, incurred the displeasure and wrath of Varuṇa who afflicted him with an incurable disease. Rohita, hearing of his father's affliction, hurried to the town probably with the object of enabling his father to redeem his vow, and accidentally met on the way a poor Brahman family, famished with hunger. Rohita asked the father, whose name was Ajīgarta, to part with one of his sons for one hundred cows, so that he may be his substitute at the sacrifice. The offer was too tempting to be rejected. But the father was unwilling to part with the eldest son whom he claimed as his own as a matter of right, and the mother was unwilling to part with the youngest, as she was very fond of him. So the second son was sold to Rohita for one hundred cows, and taken to the king as his vicarious offer to Varuṇa. The offer was accepted by Varuṇa, and

[1] E. O. James' *Intro. to Anthropology*, p. 107.

arrangements for the sacrifice were accordingly made. But as no one came forward to bind the victim to the sacrificial post, Ajīgarta, the inhuman father, offered to do so, if he were given another hundred cows for the act. His demand having been complied with, he securely bound his own son to the post. But no one was found willing to decapitate the poor victim at the sacrifice. So, the inhuman father, Ajīgarta, offered to perform the decapitation with his own hands, if he were given another one hundred cows! His offer having been accepted, he sharpened the sacrificial knife, and was ready to strike the fatal blow. Śunaḥśepa who saw all these ghastly preparations for his sacrifice, invoked, in his despair, divine help and prayed to Prajāpati for his release. Prajāpati directed him to pray to Agni (Fire), and he invoked his help with *mantras*; Agni directed him to pray to Savitṛ, and he invoked Savitṛ's help with *mantras*; Savitṛ told him to pray to Varuṇa for his release, and he invoked Varuṇa's help accordingly. Varuṇa advised him to pray to Agni again, and Śunaḥśepa invoked his help. Agni directed him to pray to the *Viśvadeváḥ*. And the latter directed him to pray to Indra, and Indra directed him to pray to the Aśvins, and the Aśvins directed him to pray to Uṣas for his release. Śunaḥśepa offered his prayers to all these deities, and lo, the straps with which he was bound fell off, one by one, from his body, and he was released from the sacrificial post. The king's incurable disease also was cured at the same time.

From the above story it is clear (1) that human sacrifice was occasionally resorted to in ancient Aryan society; and (2) that the father had complete power over the life and liberty of his sons. This type of the primeval paternal authority resembled the *Patria Potestas* of the Romans. The father had the *jus vitæ necésque*, the power of life and death, over his children in the early stages of Aryan civilisation. He could sell them or give them away for adoption by another family, or even as victims of sacrifice.

Animal sacrifice.—Writing on human sacrifice, we are led to refer to animal sacrifice which was extensively in vogue in Ṛgvedic times, and had come down as a relic of ancient pastoral times when animal flesh formed the staple food of the people. It is stated in the Ṛgveda that on certain occasions Indra consumed as many as twenty bulls (Rv. x. 86, 14), or three hundred roasted buffaloes (Rv. v. 29, 7). This means that twenty bulls and three hundred buffaloes were sacrificed in honour of Indra, and their flesh consumed by his votaries. Horses also were sacrificed and their flesh partaken of with great relish (Rv. i. 162, 12). In course of time, however, this slaughter of animals created in the mind of a certain section of the Aryans a strong repugnance for and abhorrence against the custom, which led to a religious and social schism, ultimately separating the two sections for ever.

Gotra and Goṣṭhī.—The early Aryans were divided into numerous clans and tribes. The early name of a clan is *gotra* which etymologically means "a place for the protection of cows." My conjecture is that those families that possessed a common place for the protection of cows, i.e. a common cow-stall, belonged to the same *gotra*.[1] We must remember that in the nomadic and even a later stage of Aryan civilisation, cattle formed the principal property of the people. A man was considered rich or poor according to the number of cattle he possessed. It was not possible for every family to erect a strong barricade or enclosure for the protection of cows at night from the attacks of wild beasts like wolves, hyenas, &c., or from robbers (Rv. vi. 28, 3. 7), and make adequate arrangements for guarding it. So a group of families entered into an agreement or mutual understanding

[1] "Roth interprets the word by 'cowstall,' while Geldner thinks 'herd' is meant. The latter sense seems to explain best the employment which the term shows in the later literature as denoting the 'family' or 'clan,' and which is found in the *Chāndogya Upaniṣad*" Macdonell & Keith's *Vedic Index*, i, pp. 235-236.

with one another to erect a common enclosure or stall for their cattle and guard it against wolves and robbers at night. There was a leader among them, who took the initiative in the matter, and issued necessary directions to all. This man was called the *gotra-pati* or lord of the *gotra* or cattle-enclosure, and all the families that shared the same enclosure and acted under the direction of their common leader belonged to the same *gotra*. It was essential and a matter of necessity for each family to belong to either one *gotra* or another. This was how clans were evolved in ancient Aryan society from a sense of common interest, common necessity, and mutual protection. In the day time, the cattle were released from the *gotras* or enclosures, and taken out to the grazing grounds for pasture. Certain grazing grounds were used for pasturing the cattle of a number of *gotras*, which were common to them all. They were thus the ancient commons known by the name of *goṣtha*, *i.e.* the place where the cattle used to graze or *stand* or *lie down* for rest.[1] The *goṣtha* was also known by the name of *vraja* *i.e.* the place where cattle were taken out for grazing. Those clans or *gotras* that used the same common for pasturing their cattle were known as *belonging to the same goṣtha*, which is the meaning of the word *goṣthī*. The clan or *gotra* was thus an aggregate of a number of families (*kulas*) and the *goṣthī* was an aggregate of a number of *gotras*. These social institutions were in the nature of guilds, but their evolution was quite natural, and there was no artificiality about them. The families included in a *gotra* were regarded as one large family (*mahákula*) under the guidance of one leader, and the daughters and sons belonging to the same *gotra* stood in the

---

1 "Go-ṣṭha—'standing place for cows' denotes not so much a 'cowstall,' as the 'grazing ground for cows,' as Geldner shows from a passage of the *Aitareya Brâhmaṇa* (iii. 18, 4) and from a note of Mahidhara on the *Vâjsaneyî Samhitā* The sense suits adequately all the passages of the Ṛgveda where it occurs. (i. 191, 4; vi. 28, 1; viii. 43, 17), and it greatly improves the interpretation of a hymn of the Atharvaveda, besides being accepted elsewhere." Macdonell & Keith's *Vedic Index* i, p. 240.

relation of cousins, and hence marriage in the same *gotra* came to be prohibited in later times. There was no room here for totems, and no *gotra* was ever named after an animal as in the case of the aborigines of Australia and America. Each *gotra* was named after a Ṛṣi or seer who was originally the leader or head of the institution.

The conglomeration of a number of *goṣṭhīs* formed a *grāma* which etymologically means "a collection" or "aggregate"[1]. In the nomadic stage of Aryan civilisation, the whole *grāma* or collection of *goṣṭhīs* moved from one place to another under the guidance of a leader who was styled Grāmaṇī (Rv. x. 62, 11; 107, 5), or leader of the *grāma* or collection of *goṣṭhīs*. When the Aryans settled down in particular areas as agriculturists, the villages in which the various *goṣṭhīs* settled down under a common leader came to be known as *grāmas*.

The inhabitants of the various villages were commonly known as *viśah*, translated by Weber as "settlers," or simply *janāḥ*, and the territory in which was situated a group of villages possessing a homogeneity of culture and civilisation came to be known as a *janapada*. These inhabitants formed a tribe. The Ṛgveda frequently mentions Five Tribes, or *Pañcajanāh*, who were also known by the names of *Pañca-kṣitayah* (Five Territories), and *Pañca-kṛṣṭayah*, or Five *Agricultural* Tribes, implying thereby that there were other

---

[1] "Zimmer tends to regard the *Grāma* as a clan, and as standing midway between the family and the tribe (*viś*). The *Grāma* may, however, perhaps be regarded more correctly as an aggregate of several families, not necessarily forming a clan, but only part of a clan (*viś*), as is often the case at the present day." (Macdonell & Keith's *Vedic Index*, i, p 245). My idea is that the family or *kula* was the unit of a tribe. A collection of families having a common object and acting in concert formed a *gotra*. An aggregate of *gotras* having a common object and acting in concert formed a *Goṣṭhī* and an aggregate of *goṣṭhīs* formed a *grāma*. An aggregate of *grāmas* formed a *viś* or district, and an aggregate of the latter formed a *jana*, *i.e.*, tribe. The *Yadus* were a tribe and have been called *Yādva-jana* in the Ṛgveda (viii. 6, 46. 48); so the *Bharatas* were another tribe, and have been called *Bharata-jana* (Rv. iii. 53. 12).

Aryan tribes who possessed no territories and were not agriculturists. These Five Tribes had a homogeneous civilisation and culture, speaking the same language, believing in the same Gods, and performing the same religious rites. They occupied different parts of Sapta-Sindhu or the ancient Punjab, watered and fertilized probably by the five large rivers, under the protection and guidance of rulers called *Viśpatis* or *Rājans*, who belonged to certain well-known ancient families, after which the tribes were named, as the Anus, the Druhyus, the Bharatas, the Tṛtsyus, the Yadus, &c. These tribes were independent of one another. But they sometimes quarrelled among themselves through simple vanity or greed of territory, or on occasions formed a strong combination or coalition against a common enemy. How did these Five Tribes develop a homogeneous civilisation is a question which does not admit of an easy answer, as the circumstances that favoured and the causes that led to the slow and gradual growth of this civilisation are shrouded in the darkness of the past. We may however guess that it was the keen struggle for existence, and the necessity for mutual protection that brought these Five Tribes into close contact with one another, and made them hold together in times of common danger. There were numerous Aryan tribes who were in extremely low stages of civilisation, leading nomadic lives of savage hunters or cattle-keepers and indulging in loot and pillage. These proved veritable pests to the Five Tribes who made a common cause against them with a view to extirpate them from the country. The aid of their Gods was invoked with many incantations, rites and ceremonies for this purpose. When they succeeded in the long run in getting rid of these discordant elements, they settled down as agriculturists in the various fertile regions of the country. It was then that they discovered the powers of a new mighty God, named Indra, whom they worshipped not only to help them in their struggle with such inimical Aryan tribes as remained in the country, but also to pour down timely rains to enable them to carry on their agricultural operations with success. This gave rise to a series of sacrifices called *Sattras*, mainly performed for strengthening Indra in his fight with the malevolent power, named Vṛtra, who withheld the rains. A peaceful atmosphere having been created in the country, the thoughtful among the Aryans began to indulge in speculations about the cosmic forces by which they were surrounded, and to discover the intimate relations that they had with them. This ushered in the period of the *mantras* or hymns which we find collected in the Ṛgveda Saṃhitā. The old beliefs and superstitions that still had their firm hold on the mind of the common people were afterwards collected in the *Atharva-veda Saṃhitā*, though some could not help finding their way into the Ṛgvedic collection also. The period of the Ṛgvedic *mantras* extended over a vast expanse of time, divided as it was into three ages, the Early, the Mediæval and Later.[1] This was how the Ṛgvedic Aryans developed a civilisation and culture of their own, which is unique in the world, and has no counterpart anywhere among the various Aryan peoples that were scattered over Western Asia and Europe.

Summary.—Let us now sum up some of the early stages of Aryan culture, of which we find glimpses in the Ṛgveda. There is reference in it to the early period when fire was first artificially produced, and Fire-worship first started. Reference is also found to stone and bone weapons, to skin gloves and skin utensils, to the hunting, nomadic, and pastoral stages of civilisation, through which the ancient Aryans had passed, to a loose form of marriage, to the worship of primitive Gods common to most of the neolithic Aryan tribes scattered over Europe and Western Asia, to the eating of beef and horse-flesh, indispensable to a people who were not acquainted with the art of agriculture, to the custom of human sacrifice, which must have been at one

---

[1] Rv. iii. 32, 13; vi. 21, 5.

time in vogue, and to many crude manners and rude customs associated with the low culture of savages. It was only when the ancient Aryans settled down as agriculturists in primitive homesteads, with common cattle-enclosures (*gotras*), and common pasture-lands (*goṣṭhas*) that they were able to form themselves into organized communities and make some real advancement as a semi-civilised people. The necessity of regular rain-fall for the cultivation of crops led to the discovery and worship of Indra by the advanced Aryan tribes living in Sapta-Sindhu, in as much as this deity was found able to defeat Vṛtra who withheld the rains in his cloud-body. The worship of Indra which was peculiar to the Ṛgvedic Aryans marked a definite step in their progress towards civilisation, and inaugurated a new epoch in the life of the people. But this worship was begun in neolithic times when stone and bone weapons had been in common use, and the Aryans did not know the use of metals like bronze or iron. Indra's *vajra* was at first made of stone or hard flint *(aśma)*, and afterwards of bone,—the bone of Dadhyañc or Dadhīci who had a horse's head fixed on to his neck. As I have already said, Dadhīci was probably the name of the horse, and as the horse's head or bones were found near the Śaryaṇāvat Lake situated in *Kurukṣetra*, there can be no doubt that the neolithic stage of Ṛgvedic civilisation commenced in Sapta-Sindhu or the ancient Punjab. It was during this stage that the ancient Aryans learnt the art of agriculture, for Indra was pre-eminently the God of an agricultural people. It was during this stage also that Varuṇa was ousted from his supreme position in the hierarchy of the ancient gods, and Vṛtra who had at first been regarded as a *Deva* and priest of the gods came to be regarded as a malevolent power who withheld the rains. Thus the outlook on life was completely changed with the adoption of agriculture by the ancient Aryans who settled down in organized communities in the different parts of the country, and took to the regular performance of sacrifice. The discovery made by Hugh Winckler at Boghaz Keui in 1909 of a clay-tablet containing the terms of a treaty made in the Fifteenth century B. C. by a Mitannian king, in which the Vedic gods Mitra-Varuṇa, Indra and the Nāsatyas (the twin Aśvins) were invoked, unmistakably points to the emigration of a Vedic Aryan tribe from Sapta-Sindhu, and cannot be interpreted to indicate the immigration of an Aryan tribe with Vedic culture into India from abroad. A supposition like this, in the face of the evidences discussed above, is absurd to a degree, and must be put down to the eagerness of some scholars to prove their pet theory that the original cradle of the Aryans was situated somewhere in Northern or Central Europe whence the Vedic Aryans and Iranians emigrated to Sapta-Sindhu and Persia respectively. The discovery of Indra by the Ṛgvedic Aryans in Sapta Sindhu was certainly far earlier than 1500 B. C., as they had been in the early neolithic stage of civilisation which commenced in Europe, according to some anthropologists, about 12000 or 15000 B. C. and, as Mr. H. G. Wells has shown, was taken to that continent by an Aryan-speaking people from *South Asia*, probably *India* or *Persia* at about that period. As these migrating neolithic Aryans were savage nomads, and knew very little of agriculture, they did not feel the necessity for worshiping a God like Indra who alone could force out timely rains from the reluctant clouds (Vṛtra). Hence we do not find any trace of the names of either Indra or Vṛtra in any of the Aryan languages of Europe. As I have already pointed out, Indra was evidently an Indo-Aryan God, and was discovered nowhere else excepting India. The name of Indra, as found in a clay-tablet at Boghaz-Keui, must therefore have been taken to that place by a migrating Aryan tribe from India, or more correctly speaking, Sapta-Sindhu.

The beginnings of Neolithic culture in India must have been far earlier than 15000 B. C. Considering the fact that there was a different distribution of land and water in the Punjab when some of the ancient hymns of the Ṛgveda were composed, and that an extremely cold climate prevailed there at that time, we are disposed to take them back to several thousand years earlier than this period. This surmise is strengthened by reference in the Ṛgveda itself to such primitive times when fire was first artificially produced and brought to human use, and when some of the manners and customs of the people did not remove them very far from the state of nomadic savages.

That the Vedic civilisation was evolved in Sapta Sindhu does not admit of any doubt. The frequent mention of some of the well-known Punjab rivers in the hymns of the Ṛgveda and of the Himālaya mountain and of the Mujavat peak on which Indra is said to have been born, and of Gandhāra, and some of the rivers of Bactria goes firmly to establish the original cradle of the Aryans in Sapta-Sindhu which included the beautiful valley of Kashmir and parts of Bactria on the north, and Gandhāra on the west. In a recent lecture delivered by Professor Sir Arthur Keith at the Royal Institution, he has expressed his opinion, shared by many modern anthropologists, that the cradle-land of humanity was situated near or within the Northern Frontiers of India, where the finds of fossil-remains of extinct kinds of anthropoid apes have been numerous, though, so far, no trace of fossil-man has been discovered.[1] Whether the Northern Frontiers of India were the original cradle of humanity or not, we can safely surmise that they were the original cradle-land of the Aryan race. The absence of any traces of fossil-man in these

---

[1] "There may be, there probably are thousands of deposits still untouched containing countless fragments and vestiges of man and his progenitors. In Asia particularly, in India or the East Indies there may be hidden the most illuminating clues. What are known to-day of early man is the merest scrap of what will presently be known." H. G. Wells' *Outline of History*, p. 34, (1920).

"In the Siwalik Hills in Northern India remains of some very interesting apes have been found, of which Sivapithecus and Palæopithecus were possibly related closely to the human ancestors. Possibly these animals already used implements." *Ibid.*, p. 35.

regions can probably be explained by the fact that the Aryans were from the earliest times in the habit of cremating their dead, and thus left no traces of fossil-man. If these regions were the cradle-land of the human race, and especially of the Negro race, as is supposed by the learned Professor, there would certainly have been found traces of fossil-man to the same extent as they are found in other parts of the world.

In this connection it would not be uninteresting to refer to the recent discovery made in the Gobi desert of China by an American Museum of Natural History expedition, led by Dr. Roy Chapman Andrews, the American explorer, of the prehistoric homeland of the animals that lived millions of years before the advent of man on earth. In this desert have been found the remains of giant reptiles and the first mammals. So valuable is the achievement to science that Professor Henry Fairfield Osborn calls it "of epoch-making importance" and "a kind of realisation of the discovery of the palæontological Garden of Eden, the birth-place or Asiatic homeland from which many kinds of mammals and reptiles spread westward and eastward." In this animal Garden of Eden, says an American paper, Nature tried a new experiment. She "scrapped" the monstrous reptilian dinosaurs—the most destructive creatures ever known—and in their places started to re-people the earth with the first warm-blooded mammals, including the pen-tailed tree-shrew, a strange little animal from which, by long processes of evolution during untold ages, was to come the human race. The discovery in the Gobi desert of a stratum of the closing age of reptiles, overlaid by two fossil-bearing strata of the early age of mammals has led scientists to conjecture that "on that very spot in Asia succeeding generations of life existed over a period of many millions of years," and that "the last of the old order and first of the new dwelt once together there." The causes that converted this animal Garden of Eden into a desert must have brought about the dispersion of the surviving mammals all over the earth, and the mammals of the Simian tribe must have migrated in large numbers to the south of the Asiatic continent, and swarmed, among other places, over the North-Western frontiers of India, where the finds of fossil-remains of extinct kinds of anthropoid apes have been numerous. If man was evolved in this region, he must have belonged to a particular family. It is probably incorrect to suppose that the entire human race was evolved from one and the same stock. There must have been not one but several cradles of the human race, each producing a different family with different characteristics physical, mental and moral, consistently with those of the original simian stock [1] from which the particular human family was evolved. The North-Western frontiers of India was most probably the original cradle of the Aryan race, as the ancient Aryans of India had no traditions among themselves of any foreign cradle.

---

[1] Mr. H. G. Wells thus writes in his *Outline of History*, p. 33: "Some anthropologists have even indulged in a speculation whether mankind may not have a double or treble origin; the Negro being descended from a Gorilla-like ancestor, the Chinese from a Chimpanzee-like ancestor and so on These are very fanciful ideas, to be mentioned only to be dismissed.' I do not know why it should be so summarily dismissed. If human ancestry is to be traced back to anthropoid apes, a theory like this only can satisfactorily explain the different features and characteristics of the different races of mankind, all of which may not be due to mere climatic influence and environments.

CHAPTER III.

A BRIEF ACCOUNT OF THE ARYAN PEOPLE IN THE ANCIENT PUNJAB; THE DIFFERENT CLANS AND CLASSES; PRIMITIVE PASTORAL EXISTENCE; VILLAGE LIFE AND VILLAGE INDUSTRIES; GRADUAL EVOLUTION OF CASTES ACCORDING TO DIFFERENT OCCUPATIONS; SOCIAL INTERCOURSE; TRADES AND INDUSTRIES; THE PAṆIS, DĀSAS, DASYUS AND NUMEROUS ARYAN TRIBES, BOTH VEDIC AND NON-VEDIC.

Division of the Vedic People.—We have seen in the preceding Chapter that the Aryans were divided in Ṛgvedic times into *Janāḥ* or tribes, and the *Janāḥ* into *Viśaḥ i.e.* cantons or districts, the *Viśaḥ* into *Grāmas*, the *Grāmas* into *Goṣṭhīs* (or *Vrājas*), the *Goṣṭhīs* into *Gotras* and the *Gotras* into *Kulas* or families. Professor Macdonell and Keith say that the word *Kula*, as an uncompounded word, does not occur before the period of the Brāhmaṇas.[1] But the word "Kula-pā (lit. 'house-protector') or chief of the family is mentioned in the Ṛgveda (x. 179, 2) as inferior to and attendant on the Vrājapati in war, the latter being perhaps the leader of the village contingent of the clan."[2] When the compound word Kula-pā occurs in the Ṛgveda, we can safely conjecture that the word *Kula* also was in use in Ṛgvedic times to denote the 'home' or 'house' of the family, and even the family itself. There is no distinct mention of *Goṣṭhī* in the sense of an aggregation of Kulas or Gotras in the Ṛgveda, though the word Goṣṭha in the sense of 'standing place for cows' occurs in several verses (Rv. i. 191, 4; vi. 28, 1; viii. 43, 17). The word *Vraja* in the sense of 'a place where cows go for pasture' is equivalent to *Goṣṭha*, and the *Vrājapati* occupied the same position as the *Goṣṭhīpati* of later times, the Kulapā having been

---

[1] *Vedic Index*, i, p 171.

[2] *Ibid.* Rv. x. 179, 2; (*kulapā na vrājapati carantam*)

inferior to and attendant on him. (Rv. x. 179, 2). The Kula, or family, was therefore the unit of the Tribe or *Jana*.

The Roman Gens and Vedic Jana.—The Roman *Gens* bears some resemblance to the Vedic *Jana*. Writing about the constitution of the ancient Roman Commonwealth, Sir Henry Sumner Maine observes: "The elementary group is the family, connected by common subjection to the highest male ascendant. The aggregation of families forms the *Gens* or House. The aggregation of Houses makes the Tribe. The aggregation of Tribes constitutes the Commonwealth."[1] The division of the Vedic Aryan Tribe into its different constituents was, however, more elaborate and natural. The Vedic *Jana* was a term of wider significance than the Roman *Gens*, in as much as it meant the Tribe itself and not a mere aggregation of families as signified by the word *Gens*. An aggregation of Vedic families formed a *Gotra*, and an aggregation of *Gotras* formed a *Goṣṭhī* or *Vrāja*. An aggregation of *Goṣṭhīs* or *Vrājas* formed a *Grāma*, and a number of *Grāmas* formed a *Viś*. Lastly, an aggregation of *Viśah* formed a *Jana* or Tribe.

Primitive Vedic communities mainly pastoral.—We have already stated in the preceding Chapter that the combination of families into a *Gotra* and of *Gotras* into a Goṣṭhī (or *Vrāja*) dated back from pastoral times when the early Aryans were unacquainted with the art of agriculture, and set great store by the possession of a large number of cattle which provided them with not only food and drink, but also wraps and clothing. The early Aryans, therefore, formed themselves into primitive pastoral communities, actuated by common interest which was centred in their cattle; and their Families and Clans were respectively named Gotras and Goṣṭhīs or Vrājas, simply because they used common enclosures and common grazing grounds for their cattle. The possession of cattle, therefore, furnished the bond by which

[1] Maine's *Ancient Law*, Ch. V.

families were grouped into clans (*Gotras*) and clans into *Goṣṭhīs* or larger clans.

The Grāma.—An aggregate of Goṣṭhīs or Vrājas formed a *Grāma* which literally means 'a collection' or 'body of men.' A *Grāma* ordinarily connotes a settled and not a nomadic state of existence, and the word in the sense of a village has been used in several verses of the Ṛgveda.[1] A Ṛgvedic *Grāma* or village, therefore, consisted of a number *gṛhas* or houses, tenanted by several families or *Kulas*, under the leadership of Kulapās, and all living under the leadership of the *Grāmaṇī*, or the leader or head of the village. Each *Kula* was subdivided into a number of householders or Gṛhapatis (Rv. vi. 53, 2) who were probably independent of one another, holding separate property and having independent means of livelihood. The mistress of the household was called Gṛhapatnī (Rv. x. 85, 26). As already stated, in the early stages of civilisation, a number of families had a common *gotra*, where their cows were kept during the night for protection from the attacks of wild beasts or robbers. But sometimes cows were also kept within the compound of the house, as there is distinct mention of playful calves and children in the house. (Rv. vii. 56, 16), There is also mention in the Ṛgveda of cows passing the night in Goṣṭhas which were generally situated at a distance from the village. The following verse (Rv. i. 191, 4) will corroborate our view: "The cows had settled in their stalls (goṣṭha); the beasts of prey had sought their lairs. Extinguished were the lights of men, when things unseen infected me." (Griffith). The Goṣṭhas must have been well guarded to enable cows to pass the nights without molestation. The villages were surrounded in olden times, as now, by corn-fields (*kṣetras*) which were owned by the families in separate and well-marked holdings (Rv. iii. 31, 15; x. 33, 6). The fields also were carefully measured off (Ṛv. i. 110, 5), and the deity, *Kṣetrasya Pati*,

[1] Rv. i. 44, 10; i. 141, 1; i. 149, 4; x. 146, 1, etc.

(Rv. iv. 37, 1. 2; vii. 35, 10, etc.) or Lord of the Field, presided over each field. "It is a fair conclusion" say Professors Macdonell and Keith "from the evidence that the system of separate holdings already existed in early Vedic times."[1]

The villages were "scattered over the country, some close together, some far apart, and were connected by roads."[2] The roads were not mere foot-paths, but cart-roads, as carts were constantly used as conveyance by the Vedic Aryans. The headman of the village and the nobles and rich merchants also possessed chariots, drawn by horses. So it may be safely conjectured that the villages were connected by roads (*rathyās*), all leading to the *Pur* or fortified town where the king ordinarily resided.

The villages were full of cows, buffaloes, horses, flocks of sheep and goats as well as watch-dogs which guarded the houses, the *gotras* and the *goṣthas* at night. The cows were taken out from the *gotras*, and the sheep and goats from their folds for pasture in the morning (Rv. i. 25, 16; x. 97, 8) by *Go-pās*, or protectors of cows (Rv. i. 164, 21; ii. 23, 6; iii. 10, 2; v. 12, 4, etc.) after the milch-cows had been milked. The cows ordinarily returned to the *gotras* in the evening, (Rv. x. 149, 4) and were milked again. But some of them were also milked in the forenoon, as milk was required thrice daily for pouring libations into the sacred Household Fire. Milking in the morning was called *Prātardoha*, in the forenoon *Saṃgava*, and in the evening *Sāyam-doha* (*Taitt. Saṃ.* vii. 5, 3, 1). "Thrice a day they (the cows) were driven out to graze, according to the *Taittirīya Brāhmaṇa*[3] (*pratah, saṃgave, sāyam*). The first milking was productive, the last two scanty. According to the *Aitareya Brāhmaṇa* (iii. 18, 14), among the Bharatas the herds in the evening are in the

---

[1] *Vedic Index*, i. p. 211.

[2] *Ibid*, p. 24.

[3] i. 4, 9, 2.

goṣṭha, at mid-day in the *saṃgavinī*. This passage Sāyaṇa expands by saying that the herds go to the *śāla*, or house for animals at night so far as they consist of animals giving milk, while the others stayed out in the Goṣṭha, or open pasturage; but both were together in the cattle-shed during the heat of the day. The time before the Saṃgava, when the cows were grazing freely on the pasture-lands, was called *svasara*.[1] When the cows were out feeding, they were separated from the calves which were, however, allowed to join them at the Saṃgava,[2] and sometimes in the evening."[3] The ears of the cattle were marked to indicate ownership. (Rv. vi. 28, 3).

As I have already said, there was in the early stages of society only one *gotra* or cow-shed for a certain number of families, where the milking was usually done both in the morning and evening. It was usually the duty of the grown-up daughters (Duhitṛ) to milk the cows, as *Duhitṛ* literally means "the milker." (Rv. ix. 97, 47). Macdonell and Keith are of opinion that the word has "the sense of one who nourishes a child," but its etymology does not support this view. We can picture the daughters of the several families wending their way to the *gotra* with their milk-pails, and letting loose the claves from their tethers, and drawing down the milk from the udders of the cows into the pails. They were probably assisted in the task by their big brothers who accompanied them to the *gotra*. The scene that was presented there must have been very picturesque and animating. What with the lowing of the cows, and response of the calves eager to be let loose from the cords that tied them (Rv. vii. 86, 5), what with the sonorous gurgling sound of milking and what with the mutual greetings and merry laughter of the boys and girls as they met one another or left for their respective homes with pailfuls of milk, the

---

[1] Rv. ii. 2, 2; 34, 8. v. 62, 2, vii, 88, 1; ix. 14, 2.

[2] Rv. ii. 2, 2; viii, 81, 1.

[3] *Vedic Index*, i, p 232.

picture was that of a happy pastoral life, unique in the history of the Aryans. The use of a common *gotra* by a number of families drew the men and women, and the boys and girls together, all of whom came to regard themselves as the members of one large family, standing in the relation of cousins, and living under the guidance of the *Gotrapati*. It was thus how Sa-gotra marriage, or marriage within the same clan came to be prohibited in later times, though probably it was not put under a strict ban in the early days. Milking time brought the young folk of both sexes together in the *gotra*, and it would be strange if it were not availed of by some for romantic love-making or mutual attraction.

Moving villages.—During the nomadic stage of Aryan civilisation, the Grāma which, as we have said, literally meant "a body of men" or "a collection" i. e. a collection of families or clans, kept on moving from place to place with their cattle, goods and skin-tents under the leadership of the *Grāmaṇī*. The main object of this movement was the search for "fresh fields and pastures new" for their cattle. Pūṣan, one of the Ādityas, or Sūrya, was the guide of these pastoral people. He has been called *Pathaspati* or 'Lord of the path.' (Rv. vi. 53. i). The following verses will more clearly explain his functions: "1. Shorten our ways, O Pūṣan, move aside obstruction in the path; go close before us, cloud-born God. 2. Drive, Pūṣan, from our road the wolf, the wicked inauspicious wolf, who lies in wait to injure us. 3. Who lurks about the path we take, the robber with a guileful heart; far from the road chase him away. 4. Past all pursuers lead us, make pleasant our path and fair to tread: O Pūṣan, find thou power for this. 8. Lead us to meadows rich in grass: send on our way no early heat; O Pūṣan, find thou power for this. 9. Be gracious to us, fill us full, give, feed us, and invigorate; O Pūṣan, find thou power for this."[1] Forays were sometimes made by the

[1] Rv. i. 42 (Griffith's translation). The other translations also are Griffith's.

nomads for cattle and wealth, and Pūṣan was invoked to aid them in their enterprise: "Clear paths that we may win the prize: scatter our enemies afar. Strong God, be all our thoughts fulfilled" (Rv. vi. 53, 4). Again, "Lead on this company of ours that longs for kine, to win the spoil: thou, Pūṣan, art renowned afar." (Rv. vi. 56, 5). But their main concern was the protection of their own cattle: "May Pūṣan follow near our kine, may Pūṣan keep our horses safe; may Pūṣan gather gear for us. Follow the kine of him who pours libations out and worships thee; and ours who sing thee songs of praise. Let none be lost, none injured, none sink in a pit and break a limb. Return with these all safe and sound." (Rv. vi. 54, 5. 6. 7). Pūṣan must have been an early God of the nomadic Aryans, as his car was drawn by goats, and not horses or oxen. (Rv. vi. 55, 3. 4; 57, 3; 58, 2). The goat, as we have already pointed out, was the first animal to have been tamed; and it was quite natural for early nomads to make goats the drawers of their God's car. Pūṣan was also conceived to pour down rain, not certainly to help agricultural operation, as the art of agriculture was then unknown, but for the growth of grass in the pasture-lands (*vraja*, Rv. x. 26, 2. 3,). It is also significant that Mitra and Varuṇa, two of the most ancient Gods, were invoked simply to wet the *grazing grounds* with rain-water. (Rv. vii. 62, 5). When, at last, the nomadic Aryans became settled agriculturists, and Indra came to be worshipped as the giver of timely rains, they could not all at once discard the worship of Pūṣan, but coupled his name with that of Indra, and invoked them jointly. (Rv. vi. 57). In this connection, the following verses will be found significant: 1. "Indra and Pūṣan will we call for friendship and prosperity, and for winning of the spoil. ...3. Goats are the team that draws the one: the other hath bay steeds at hand....4. When Indra, wondrous strong, brought down the streams, the mighty water-floods, Pūṣan was standing by his side. To this, to Pūṣan's favouring love, and Indra's, may we closely cling, as to a tree's extended bough. As one who drives a car draws in his reins, may we draw Pūṣan near, and Indra for our great success." (Rv. vi. 57). The joint-worship of Pūṣan and Indra undoubtedly indicated a marked change in the life of the people. Cattle and the products of agriculture constituted the wealth of the early Vedic Aryans, when they settled down in the villages, and changed a nomadic for a settled existence; and the protection of Pūṣan and Indra was rightly invoked by them in the joint-hymn mentioned above.

The Grāma self-contained.—A Vedic *grāma* or village was self-contained. The wants of the people, which were few, were supplied by the people themselves. They cultivated corns like barley (*yava* Rv. v. 85, 3; x. 69, 3; 131, 2), rice (*dhāna* or *dhānya*, (Rv. v. 53, 13; vi. 13, 4; x. 94, 13), beans (*mudga*, *māsa*, etc.), sesamum (*tila*), etc. The grains were stored in granaries (*sthivi*) from which quantities were extracted as necessity arose (Rv. x. 68, 3). From the possession of large herds of cows by each family, we can easily infer that it had an abundant supply of milk from which curds, *ghee*, etc., were prepared. Meat also was supplied from the live-stock. Sheep's wool was spun into yarns, and woolen cloths were woven with them (Rv. x. 26, 6). There were men who learnt the art of weaving, took it up as a profession, and were called weavers (*vāya* Rv. x. 26, 6; 106, 1). The loom was called *tantra* (Rv. x. 71, 9) or *vimāna* (*Vāj. Sam.* xix. 83). But each family also wove the cloths required for its ordinary use, and the weaving was usually entrusted to and done by the women (Rv. ii. 3, 6; 38, 4; v. 47, 6; cf. Av. x. 7, 42; xiv. 25, 1). It is distinctly said in one verse that the mother wove cloths for her sons (Rv. v. 47. 6). There were carpenters (*tvaṣṭṛ* Rv. x. 119, 5; *takṣa* Rv. ix. 112, 1) who made chariots, wheels, boats and wooden vessels (*druṇa* Rv. ix. 65, 6), and smiths (*karmāra*, Rv. ix. 112, 2; x. 72, 2) who made agricultural implements and weapons for war. There were also potters who made pots and vessels of clay, which were easily broken (Rv. x. 89, 7). There is frequent mention of *kalaśa* or pots, either made of clay or wood (Rv. i. 117, 12; iii. 32, 15), of *kumbha* or earthen jar or vessel (Rv. i. 116, 7; 117, 6; vii. 33, 13), as well as of *ukhā* or cooking pot (Rv. i. 162, 13. 15; iii. 53, 22) which was also "made of clay" (*mṛnmaya*, *Vāj. Sam.* xi. 59; *Taitt. Sam.* iv. 1, 5, 4). There were also goldsmiths who made gold ornaments like *niṣka*, ear-rings, etc. (Rv. viii. 47, 15; 78, 3). There were also men whose profession it was to make flower-garlands or wreaths (Rv. viii. 47, 15) which must have been in great requisition among fashionable and luxurious men and women. We find numerous mention of skin-vessels (Rv. vi. 48, 17; viii. 5, 19; ix. 66, 29) which were manufactured by men who knew the art of tanning leathers (*mlā* Rv. viii. 55, 3) and sewing them into shapes. The tanner was known by the name of *carmamna* (Rv. viii. 5, 38). Barbers (*vaptā*) are also mentioned in the Ṛgveda (x. 142, 4). There were also physicians (*bhiṣak* Rv. ix. 112, 1. 3) who, it is jestingly said, were eager to see the outbreak of diseases. But their services were in great requisition and valued, as one Ṛṣi most earnestly says that he would readily give a physician cows, horses, clothes, nay, his very person (Rv. x. 95, 4). The physicians claimed a scientific knowledge, so far as it went in those days, of the properties of the various herbs and drugs, from which they prepared their nostrums and medicines. (Rv. x. 95).

In the absence of flowing rivers in the vicinity of a village, water was supplied from wells (Rv. i. 105, 17) which were dug deep into the earth, and from which water was raised by means of a stone-wheel to which pots were attached, (*aśmacakram* Rv. x. 101, 5, 7; cf. x. 93, 13). There is also mention of people digging lakes for the purpose of supplying pure drinking water (Rv. ix. 110, 5), as well as of natural lakes having full-blown white lotuses on their bosom. (*Puṣkariṇī*, Rv. x. 142, 8). The washing of the clothes was probably done by the householders themselves, though the work has been strangely ascribed to the God Pūṣan (Rv. x. 26, 6).

There were also drummers and musicians in the village, as there is mention of drums (*dundubhi*, Rv. i 28, 5; vi. 47, 29. 31), fifes and other instruments of music, from which it can be inferred that the musicians were professional men who played on their instruments both in wars, and on festive occasions in the piping times of peace.

From the above account it would appear that a Ṛgvedic Grāma or village was completely self-contained and supplied all the ordinary wants of its inhabitants.

Classes and not Castes.—The people were divided into classes, and not castes, and each class was named after the work it had to perform. "The word *Brāhmaṇa*, the regular name for a 'man of the first caste'" says Prof. Macdonell "is still rare in the Ṛgveda, occurring only eight times, while *Brahman*, which simply means sage or officiating priest, is found forty-six times."[1] *Rājanya* or *Kṣatra* meant the class which was concerned with the government of the country in all its various departments. *Viś* was the general name of the people. All these classes performed the Vedic sacrifices, and subscribed to the orthodox Vedic faith. Those who did not perform any sacrifice, or believe in the Vedic Gods were put down as *Dāsas*, and latterly *Śūdras*, although they belonged to the Aryan stock. The *Yadus* and the *Turbaśes* were designated as Dāsas, because they had seceded from the Vedic faith for a time (Rv. x. 62, 10). Every Vedic householder was a priest unto himself so far at least as the performance of daily ordinary religious duties was concerned, viz., the lighting up of the sacred Household Fire, and the pouring of libations of *habis* into it thrice during the day,—one in the morning, one in the

[1] Macdonell's *Hist of Sansk. Lit*, pp 161-162.

mid-day, and another in the evening,—along with his wife who was called the *Gṛha-patnī* or the mistress of the house. It was only on special occasions when any *Sattra* or big religious sacrifice had to be performed that the vicarious services of experts (*Brahmans* or priests), well versed in the *mantras*, and well acquainted with the detailed process of performing it, were requisitioned and paid for in kine, grains or food cooked over *dakṣiṇāgni* (the fire lighted on the south of the altar), and hence called *dakṣiṇā*, as well as in gold and silver.[1] These experts formed a class by themselves, who spent their time in learning and properly reciting the *mantras*, aud mastering the intricate processes of performing the various *yajnas* strictly in accordance with long-standing practice. There was no caste-system in the sense in which we now understand it, with its exclusiveness and strict elaborate rules as regards eating, drinking, association by marriage, and touchability. The four castes have certainly been mentioned in a verse of the Tenth Maṇḍala of the Ṛgveda (x. 90. 12). But these came to be regarded as distinct social institutions towards the close of the Ṛgvedic period, when civilisation had become far more complex, and society was looked upon as a living organism, whose various limbs could be distinctly differentiated as the head, body, arms, thighs and legs, all possessing separate functions, but forming essential parts of and necessary adjuncts to the organism. The verse need not at all be taken as an interpolation, for it merely marked the stage at which social progress had arrived. The castes, though emerging into shapes, were still in a fluid condition, and grouping themselves round the principal occupations of the people. There were still simple divisions of labour and the pursuit of a particular occupation according to individual bent of mind and aptitude, and no odium was ever attached to the fact of a Ṛṣi's father having been a physician or his mother a grinder

[1] *Dakṣiṇā* was afterwards equivalent to a milch-cow, which was the fee of the priest. The price of cow in gold or silver ultimately took the place of the cow.

of corn. (Rv. ix. 112, 3). A verse (Rv. i. 113, 6) clearly says that Uṣas (the Dawn) has awakened one person to apply himself to the attainment of high sway, one to perform sacrifices, one to pursue his gain and one his labour, in a word, all to pursue their respective vocations. Viśvāmitra who belonged to the ruling class (*rājanya*) acted as a priest (Rv. iii. 53, 9). So also did Devāpi (Rv. x. 98). The descendants of the great Ṛṣi Bhṛgu were master-carpenters, having been experts in making chariots. (Rv. x. 39, 14). A sage advised gamblers to take to agriculture for want of any better occupation rather than ruin themselves by gambling (Rv. x. 34, 13). Even a Ṛṣi like Mudgala did not hesitate to take up his arms in pursuit of robbers who had stolen his cows, and his valiant wife drove the car for him, and came to his rescue when the situation had become somewhat embarrassing for him (Rv. x. 102). Ṛṣis prayed to the Gods for the birth of brave and heroic sons who would be able to defeat their enemies in battle, and rout whole aggressive armies (Rv. v. 23, 1. 2; vi. 31, 1). The great sage Viśvāmitra himself led the vast combined army of the confederacy of Ten Kings against Sudās, the King of the Tṛtsyus (Rv. vii. 18 & 33), and Vasiṣṭha also was present at the battlefield, offering prayers to Indra for victory. (Rv. vii. 83). As Tvastṛ was the God who forged the thunderbolt for Indra, no odium was attached to the work of the *karmāra* or smith who manufactured weapons for men.[1] Every art was noble, because it was useful. The

[1] From the Dravidian name for a smith, *Karuma*, it is inferred by some scholars that the Ṛgvedic word *Karmāra* was derived from it. But why not draw just the opposite inference and say that the Dravidian name *Karuma* is only a corruption of the Vedic word *Karmāra*? The word can be perfectly derived from Sanskrit roots. Unfortunately the tendency of most scholars, either Indian or foreign, has been to ascribe the origin of the Vedic civilisation to a comparatively recent age, which is far beside the truth. The Vedic smith or *Karmāra* "smelted (dhmá) the ore in the fire; hence he is called *dhmātṛ*, the smelter. Mention is also made of his bellows of birds' feathers (Rv. ix. 112, 2). He made metal vessels *gharma ayasmaya*, (Rv. v. 30, 15) to be put on the fire; even the Soma cup could occasionally be made of hammered metal (*ayohata* Rv. ix. 1, 2)." *Vedic Index*, i, pp. 140-141.

dignity of labour was well understood, and every one was free to pursue any calling, for which he had a natural inclination and aptitude. It is true that a certain degree of squeamishness and fastidiousness with regard to certain occupations, *e.g.*, agriculture and weaving, is noticeable in the later portions of the Ṛgveda, which probably marked the close of the Ṛgvedic period (Rv. x. 71, 9), when the learned began to indulge in higher philosophical speculations and obtain bright glimpses of higher spiritual truths, which made them look askance and cavil at materialistic culture to some extent; but these outbursts should be regarded in the light of strong protests against the development of an exclusively materialistic tendency at the sacrifice of higher spiritual yearnings which alone can lead to the full realisation and attainment of the ideal of true manhood. Otherwise, no odium was attached in Ṛgvedic times to any calling, however low, if it was useful, and conducive to communal welfare.

It must, however, be conceded that even in early Ṛgvedic times, the Brahmans commanded the respect of all classes, including the kings, for their high spiritual attainments and culture, and their supposed ability to propitaiate the Gods by *mantras*. "In his own house he dwells in peace and comfort, to him for ever holy food flows richly, to him the people with free will pay homage,—the king, with whom the *Brahman* hath precedence. He, unopposed, is master of the riches of his own subjects and of hostile people. The Gods uphold that king with their protection, who helps the *Brahman* when he seeks his favour." (Rv. iv, 50, 8. 9). The original word in the text is *Brahman* and not *Brāhmaṇa*. In another verse (Rv. x. 85, 29) there is injunction to distribute treasure to the *Brahmans* (*brahmabhyah*). But the word *Brāhmaṇa* occurs in the following verses of the Ṛgveda (x. 71, 8. 9): "When friendly Brāhmaṇas sacrifice together with mental impulse which the heart hath fashioned, they leave one far behind through their attainments, and some who count as Brāhmaṇas wander elsewhere. Those men who step not back and move not forward, nor Brāhmaṇas nor preparers of libations, having attained to *vāc* in sinful fashion, spin out their thread in ignorance like spinsters." The supremacy of the Brāhmaṇas over the other classes or castes was gradually acquired by mental, moral and spiritual culture, and the homage they commanded was willingly paid. For it is the spirit that always dominates the body and the mind. Whoever attained to a high degree of spiritual culture could become a Ṛṣi or Brāhmaṇa in ancient times. Echoes of this process of recruitment to the rank of the Brahmaṇas are to be found even in the later Purāṇas. The *Bhāgavata Purāṇa* says that the Kṣatriya clan known as Dhāṣtra became Brāhmaṇas. (ix. *Story of Ilā*). Gargya, Taryāruṇi, Kavi and Puṣkarāruṇi, though originally Kṣatriyas, became Brāhmaṇas (*Ibid*, ix. *Story of the Purus*). Bharadvāja, though a Brāhmaṇa, was adopted by the Kṣatriya king Bharata as his son. (*Ibid*) Nābhāga, though originally a Kṣatriya, became a Vaiśya. (ix. *Story of Ilā*). In the *Aitareya Brāhmaṇa* (ii. 8. 1) and the *Kauṣītakī Brāhmaṇa* (xii. 3) it has been mentioned that Kavaṣa, the son of a slave girl (*dāsyāh putrah*), was acknowledged as a Ṛṣi by such renowned sages as Gṛtsamada, Viśvāmitra, Vāmadeva, Atri, Bharadvāja, and Vasiṣṭha, all of whom saluted him (*namaste astu*), and admitted his superiority in spiritual knowledge and culture (*tvam vai nah śresthosi*, thou art superior to us all). We thus find that in the early Vedic times recruitments to the rank of the Brāhmaṇas and Ṛṣis were made from all classes on the basis of superior spiritual culture and acquirements, and there were no hard and fast rules about castes.

The early use of the word Kṣatriya in the Ṛgveda (iv. 12 3; 42, 1; v. 69. 1; vii. 64. 2; viii. 25, 8, &c.), is exclusively connected with royal authority or divine authority. According to Macdonell and Keith, it included the royal house and the various branches of the royal family. It also included the nobles and their families. Rājanya and Kṣatriya are identical. In the Ṛgveda there are instances of others than

Kṣatriyas fighting. The people (*viś*) also fought. (Rv. i. 69, 3; 126, 5; iv. 24, 4; vi. 26, 1, &c.). The Grāmaṇī was usually a Vaiśya. "In the early stages of development of the nobility, it was probably not unusual or impossible for a Vaiśya to become a Kṣatriya; at least this assumption best explains the phrase 'claiming falsely a Kṣatriya rank'." (Rv. vii. 109, 13). The word *Śūdra* occurs only once in the Ṛgveda (x. 90, 12). The Dāsas and the Dasyus were either savage or non-Vedic Aryan tribes. (see *infra*). Those of them that were captured in war were probably made slaves and formed the *Śūdra* caste. In later times, other tribes, not necessarily Aryan, who adopted the Vedic religion and Aryan mode of life, were recruited into the caste and probably formed its rank and file, with this distinction that the Aryan *Śūdras* enjoyed special privileges which the non-Aryan did not.

Inter-marriage.—From the above accounts it follows that intermarriage among the different classes was common and to a certain extent unrestricted, and this could not but have been the case in a society which did not tolerate infant marriage, and in which girls were not married before they reached puberty, or were developed into full-grown young women (Rv. x 85, 21. 22), and were allowed to make a free choice of their husbands from among a number of suitors (Rv. x. 27, 12). Young ladies attracted young men to themselves by their coquetry and personal charms, (Rv. viii. 3?, 5; 62, 9), and there was a good deal of love-making among young folks (Rv. viii. 62, 9; ix. 56, 3; x. 30, 6) and sometimes jilting also, which probably led to the expression of such sentiments as "woman's love is never stable and her heart is like that of a hyæna" (Rv x 95, 15). Even the disciplined hearts of Ṛṣis also were not impervious to penetrating feminine charms, and in three successive verses of a hymn prayers were repeated for winning beautiful damsels. (Rv. ix. 67, 10. 11. 12). In a community in which such social conditions prevailed, intermarriage among the different classes could never be restricted.

The story of Śyāvāśva.—With reference to hymn 61 of the Fifth Maṇḍala Sāyaṇa relates a beautiful story of love, which would bear reproduction here. Śyāvāśva, the Ṛṣi of the above hymn, had once attended a sacrifice performed by King Rathavīti, son of Darbha, in which his father Arcanānā of the Atri clan had been employed by the King to perform the functions of Hotṛ. Arcanānā noticed the beautiful daughter of the King seated by her father's side, and, probably finding his son Śyāvāśva love-sick at the sight of the young Princess, requested her father to give her away to his son in marriage. The King, probably finding the Princess equally attracted to the young man, was agreeable to the proposal, but he thought it proper and prudent to refer the matter to his Queen first of all. The latter, however, sternly set her face against the proposal, probably on account of the poverty of the young suitor, and this so much grieved the unfortunate love-sick youth that he left the place at once, and roamed about the country with an eager and earnest craving for wealth. In the course of his wanderings, he reached the kingdom of King Taranta, whose Queen was named Śaśīyasī. The Queen noticed the helpless youth wandering evidently in great distress of mind, but withal bearing the stamp of greatness on his forehead, and of sparkling genius in his countenance. She was struck by the remarkable appearance of this young stranger, and summoning him to her side asked his name and the object of his visit. Encouraged by her kindness and sympathy, the simple-minded young man straightway narrated to her the woful tale of his love, mentioning how and why his suit, presented to the King on his behalf by his father, the great sage Arcanānā, was rejected by the Queen, the mother of the Princess. Queen Śaśīyasī could not help feeling very deep sympathy with the distress of the love-sick youth, and introduced him to her royal husband, King Taranta, after making a gift to him of horses, kine and a flock of one hundred sheep. (Rv. v. 61, 5). Śyāvāśva lauded the kind-hearted Queen above those men who did not worship the Gods, or make valuable gifts to the poor and needy, or syampathise with their distress in consequence of the very hardness of their hearts. (Rv. v. 61, 6. 7). The King also, duly apprised of the cause of the youth's distress, made him suitable gifts in gold and silver. Strengthened and encouraged by the enthusiastic support of the Queen who wished him good luck and full success in his mission, Śyāvāśva alternately mounted the two bay horses presented to him by the Queen, and, as directed by her, proceeded to the kingdom of the wise King Purumintha, son of Vidadaśva. Purumintha also made him rich and valuable gifts in gold and silver, like King Taranta, besides giving him one hundred cows. Elated with unexpected success in his mission, Śyāvāśva was proceeding home with his rich gifts, cattle, horses and flock of sheep, when the Maruts, the powerful Gods of wind, suddenly appeared before him. Śyāvāśva, in the ecstacy of his joy, offered them a beautiful prayer which is embodied in hymn 61 of the Fifth Maṇḍala of the Ṛgveda (verses 1-4 and 11-16). The Maruts were immensely pleased with his prayer, and declared him fit to be called a *Ṛṣi* or sage-seer. He then offered a prayer to the Goddess Night, commissioning her to convey his hymn, addressed to the Maruts, to King Rathavīti, son of Darbha, who lived on the bank of the river Gomatī (or Gomal) flowing through Gandhāra, in a palace built by the side of the mountain, and to inform him, on his behalf, at the end of the Soma sacrifice he had been performing, that he (Śyāvāśva) was still steadfast and loyal in his love for his beautiful daughter, the Princess. (Rv. v. 61, 17-19). Needless to say that Rathavīti and his Queen, being deeply touched by his single-minded devotion to, and warm love for their daughter, and hearing that he had been declared fit to be styled a Ṛṣi by the Maruts, invited him to their palace with great honour, and joined the Princess in holy wedlock with him. It was thus how love became triumphant in the long run.

The stories of Vimada and Ghoṣā.—This is not the only solitary instance of intermarriage in the Ṛgveda. Śundhyu or Kamadyu, the daughter of King Purumitra, was married to the sage Vimada, and it is said that the Aśvins conveyed her in their chariot to her husband. (Rv. x. 39, 7). The story has thus been narrated by Sāyaṇa (Rv. i. 116, 1): Kamadyu chose the sage Vimada for her husband in a *Svayamvara Sabhā* held for the purpose. As Vimada was returning with his bride, he was attacked on the way by the disappointed Kings and Princes who had been suitors for the hand of the Princess. The Aśvins helped Vimada in the skirmish, and taking up the bride in their own chariot, conveyed her to her husband's home. Ghoṣā, the celebrated lady Ṛṣi, also was a Princess; but as she was afflicted by an incurable disease, she did not find a husband willing to marry her until she reached the middle age, when through the grace of the Aśvins, she became thoroughly cured and was restored to youth. Her fame as a Ṛṣi was soon established, and a Ṛṣi married her (Rv. x. 39 & 40). Her sons, Suhasta and Bhṛgu, also became Ṛṣis. (Rv. i. 120, 5). It is further useless to multiply instances, and it will suffice only to say here that this custom of inter-marriage lasted till after Ṛgvedic times. The story of King Yayāti (Rv. x. 63, 1) marrying Devayānī, the daughter of Śukrācarya, is well known, though it is not mentioned in the Ṛgveda. Śaśvatī, the daughter of the Ṛṣi Angiras, became the queen of King Asanga. (Rv. viii. 1, 34). Kakṣīvant was a Ṛṣi, frequently mentioned in the Ṛgveda (i. 18, 1; 51, 13; 112, 11; iv. 26, 1; viii. 9, 10; ix. 74, 8; x. 25, 10; 61, 16). He appears to have been a descendant of a female slave, named Uśij, and was called Auśija. The King Śvanaya Bhāvya who dwelt in the land of Sindhu[1] bestowed

[1] *Sindhāvadhikṣiyataḥ* in the text has been explained by Sāyaṇa thus: *Sindhudeśe yadvā lakṣaṇayā Sindhutīre Samudratīre adhikṣiyataḥ adhinivasataḥ, &c.*, which "means living either in the country, known as Sindhu or on the sea-coast." Dr. S. K. Chatterji of Calcutta University has wrongly

magnificent gifts on him. (Rv. i. 126, 1-4.) In his old age he obtained as a wife the maiden Vṛcayā (Rv. i. 51, 13), and lived to be a hundred. (Rv. ix. 74. 8). We may, therefore, take it for granted that inter-marriage among the higher respectable classes was common in Ṛgvedic times. There was no bar against the marriage of a high-born youth with a low-born damsel, though such unions were usually discouraged. There seemed to exist in Ṛgvedic times an aristocracy of wealth as well as of intellect, and inter-marriage among these classes was common. The union of a high-born girl with a low-born youth was discountenanced, and in a later age strongly condemned.

Principal occupations, professions and trade.—The principal occupations of the people in Ṛgvedic times were cattle-rearing and agriculture. Every respectable householder was eager to possess a number of cattle and plots of fertile land (*urvarā*, Rv. i. 127, 6; iv. 41, 6, etc.,) for cultivating corn. But there were also professions like those of the carpenter, blacksmith, physician, priest, poet, female grinder of corn, goldsmith, potter, tanner, weaver, &c., which the people pursued according to the individual bent of their mind. "We different men have all our various imaginations and designs" declares a Ṛgvedic bard. "The carpenter seeks

---

explained the phrase as 'living on the bank of the Sindhu or the Indus,' holding that the Vedic Aryans did not advance as far south as the province of Sindh in Ṛgvedic times. (*Mod. Rev.* Dec 1924 and March 1925) His object is to prove that the recent finds at Mahenjo-Daro in Sindh, which are said to be more than 3000 B C. old, could not have any connexion with the Aryans, but that they were the relics of Sumerian civilisation in Sindh. Whether the particular finds appertained to Aryan or Sumerian culture, I am not competent to say. But it is entirely wrong to affirm that the Ṛgvedic Aryans were not acquainted with the province of Sindh or the sea-coast in their own times. The province is still famous for fine breed of horses, some of which were presented to Kakṣivan by King Svanaya of Sindh (Rv. i. 126, 2.) The banks of the Sindhu are thousands of miles long, and it cannot be said that King Svanaya lived in and ruled over this vast and indefinite region.

something that is broken, the doctor a patient, the priest some one who will offer libations ...With dried-up sticks, with birds' feathers, with metals and fire, the artisan (smith) continually seeks after a man with plenty of gold...I am a poet, my father is a doctor, and my mother is a grinder of corn. ...With our different views, seeking to get gain, we run after (our respective objects) as after cattle. The draught-horse desires an easy-going carriage; merry companions a laugh; the female sex the male [1], and frogs a pond" (Rv. ix 112, 1-4).

The following free metrical rendering of these verses by Dr. Muir will probably be found interesting :—

"Men's tastes and trades are multifarious,
And so their ends and aims are various.
The smith seeks something cracked to mend,
The leech would fain have sick to tend.
The priest desires a devotee,
From whom he may extract his fee.
Each craftsman makes and vends his ware,
And hopes the rich man's gold to share.
My sire's a leech; and I a bard;
Corn grinds my mother, toiling hard.
All craving wealth, we each pursue,
By different means the end in view,
Like people running after their cows,
Which too far off have strayed to browse.
The draught-horse seeks an easy yoke,
The merry dearly like a joke.
Of lovers youthful belles are fond,
And thirsty frogs desire a pond."

Every work of art was appreciated, if it was useful, and the original designer and artisan applauded. The Ṛbhus were celebrated as skilful workmen, and in consequence of

[1] Dr. Muir has incorrectly translated this passage. The correct rendering, divested of all indecency, would be: "The male sex desires the female." Muir's, O. S. T. v, pp. 424-425

a promise made by the Gods, were rewarded "by their exaltation to divine honours" (Rv. i, 161, 1-5) for accomplishing a most difficult feat in art, viz, making into four a single new sacrificial cup which Tvaṣṭṛ had formed (Rv. i. 20, 6). It has been mentioned above that the Bhṛgus were the celebrated chariot-makers, and the art of chariot-making was so much appreciated that the skill in the composition of hymns was compared to it. (Rv. i. 61, 4; 62, 13; 130, 6; 171, 2; ii. 19, 8; iv. 16, 20; v. 29, 15; vi. 32, 1, &c.). Reference has already been made to weaving. Boat-making or ship-building also was well-known, as there is frequent mention of boats and sea-going ships. Agriculture was also reduced to an art.

The Paṇis and trade by barter.—Trade was carried on by barter, and a cow was originally the unit of exchange. The Paṇis formed the great trading class among the Ṛgvedic Aryans, and traded both on land, and by sea. But they were not popular, as they were "greedy like the wolf" (Rv. vi. 51, 14), "extremely selfish and niggardly" (Rv. vi. 61, 1), and "non-sacrificing, voluble, of cruel and unkind speech, devoid of reverential sentiments, and not multiplying" (Rv. vii. 6, 3). Sometimes when they roamed about in the country with their merchandise, exchanging their articles for cattle, they used to steal other people's cows and mixing them with their own herd, swiftly moved away from the locality. This frequently led to conflicts, and in one such conflict they were completely defeated and punished by Indra (Rv. vi. 39, 2). The Paṇis were probably also ship-builders, and constructed boats and sea-going vessels. Bṛbu was their leader who lived on the high banks of the Gangā, probably on the coast of the Eastern Sea covering the entire Gangetic trough, and subscribed to the othodox Vedic faith. Sāyaṇa describes him as the master-carpenter, rich and liberal. (*Vide* also *Manu* x. 107). His liberality has been highly praised in three verses of the Ṛgveda (vi. 45, 31-33).

Coins: the Niṣka and Manā.—The cow did not form the only unit of exchange. Gold and silver coins were also in use. The *Niṣka* was originally a gold neck-ornament. A number of square or round gold pieces were strung together into a necklet which was worn both by men and women. The isolated pieces, of fixed weight and standard, were afterwards used as coin. According to Professors Macdonell and Keith,[1] *Niṣka* originally denoted "a gold ornament worn on the neck." (Rv. ii. 33, 10; viii. 47, 15), as is shown by the epithet *Niṣka-grīva* (Rv. v. 19, 3) 'having a gold ornament on the neck.' "As early as the Ṛgveda (i. 126, 2) traces are seen of the use of Niṣkas as a sort of currency, for a singer celebrates the receipt of a hundred Niṣkas and a hundred steeds: he could hardly require the Niṣkas merely for purposes of personal adornment. Later the use of Niṣkas as currency is quite clear."[2] A Ṛṣi praises King Bibhindu for giving him forty thousand coins on one occasion, and eight thousand on another (Rv. viii. 2, 41). *Manā* was the name of another gold coin. This was probably taken by the Paṇis to Babylonia and Assyria, where it was known as *Minā*. Afterwards it passed into the Greek monetary system under the name of *manā*. The word Manā occurs in the following verse of the Ṛgveda (viii. 78, 2): "O Indra, bring us jewels, cattle, horses and *manās* of gold." (*Saca manā hiranyayā*). This word is derivable from the Sanskrit root *man*, to measure, or *man* to prize or value, and the coin must have been of a fixed and recognized weight or standard. There must also have been some sort of impression on it, authorized and approved by the king, to make it pass as genuine current coin. Very probably the impression was that of a cow or bull, the original unit of exchange or barter, and the coin itself represented, as it still does, the price of a cow or bull (*kāncana mūlyam*), when a live one

---

[1] *Vedic Index* i. pp. 454-55.

[2] A. V. xx. 127. 3 Lāt. Śra Sūt ix. 9. 20. Śat Brā. xi. 4, 1, 1, 8. Gop. Brā. i. 3. 6, &c. *Vedic Index* i. pp. 454-55.

could not be given or presented to a Brahman or priest. It is a mistake to suppose that the gold coin *Manā* was brought by Dravidian merchants from Babylonia, and passed on to the Ṛgvedic Aryans in Sapta-Sindhu.[1] Macdonell and Keith observe: "Manā may very well be identical with the word *Manā* which occurs several times in the Ṛgveda (i. 173, 2; iv. 33, 2; x. 6, 3) in the sense of 'desire' (from the root *man*, to think), and which may have in this one passage (Rv. viii. 78, 2) the concrete sense of 'desirable object'." (*Vedic Index* ii. 129). There were also silver coins, and a *niṣka* of silver is mentioned in the Pañcaviṃśa Brāhmaṇa. (xvii. 1, 14). Probably silver coins called *rayis* were also in vogue in Ṛgvedic times. (Rv. v. 33, 6).

Agricultural and Industrial products.—The following description of the Sindhu river is typical of the prosperity that the ancient Aryans enjoyed in Ṛgvedic times: "The Sindhu is rich in horses, rich in chariots, rich in clothes, rich in gold ornaments, well-made, rich in food, rich in wool, ever fresh, abounding in Silama plants, and the auspicious river wears honey-growing flowers" (Wilson, Rv. x. 75, 8). From this it appears that there were excellent horses and cattle and chariots in the land. The rich soil of the Punjab produced bumper crops which amply fed the people. Wool was produced in vast quantities, from which excellent cloths, blankets, shawls and garments were manufactured. The description presents a beautiful picture of busy industrial life, and of national wealth and prosperity.

Inland Trade: Caravans.—The surplus products of agriculture and industry were exported from one district to another in caravans, consisting of bullocks (castrated bulls *Vadhryah*, Rv. viii. 46, 30), pack-horses, camels, dogs, (Rv. viii. 46, 28), asses (Rv. viii. 56, 3) and probably also buffaloes. It may seem strange that the dog was used in Ancient India as a beast of burden; but the reference in the

[1] *Ṛgvedic India*, Chap. xii.

Ṛgveda is clear (*śuneṣitam*, Rv. viii. 46, 28). It should be borne in mind that there was a breed of large and powerful dogs in ancient Sapta-Sindhu, and there was a regular export of them to Persia and Mesopotamia even in later times. Says a writer: "The Babylonians imported Indian dogs. The breed is asserted to be the largest and strongest that exist, and on that account, the best suited for hunting wild lions which they will readily attack. The great fondness felt by the Persians for the pleasure of the chase, by whom it was regarded as a chivalrous exercise, must have increased the value and use of these animals which soon became even an object of luxury."[1] No wonder, therefore, that the ancient Aryans employed these large animals not only to carry their burdens, but also to guard their cattle against the attacks of wild beasts, and their goods against the attacks of robbers during their journey. The ass too was used not only to draw chariots (Rv. i. 34, 9), but also to carry burdens on its back. A Ṛṣi prays for the gift of one hundred asses (Rv. viii. 56, 3). The service of these asses was required not certainly to draw the Ṛṣi's chariots, for he could not have possessed many, but simply to carry his burdens. Some Western scholars are of opinion that the word *Uṣtra* (or camel) probably meant the buffalo. But there is no reason to make this supposition. The *Mahiṣa* (or buffalo) has been distinctly mentioned in Rv. viii. 12, 8 and ix. 33, 1 and other verses. There was a strip of desert-land in the south of ancient Sapta-Sindhu which could only be crossed with the help of camels. It is still one of the beasts of burden in the Punjab and Rajputana, and there is no reason to believe that it did not exist in Vedic times

The caravan, consisting of merchants, their retainers and the above-mentioned beasts of burden, moved on from district to district, selling the commodities they carried, and purchasing such articles as would be wanted elsewhere.

---

[1] *Hist. Hist. of the World*, Vol. I, p. 488.

These merchants were mostly Paṇis, the professional Aryan traders, who were notorious for their greed and sharpness. As cows were sometimes bartered for goods, we may take it for granted that the caravan was gradually augmented by including into it a large herd of cattle.

Contracts for sale.—Contracts seemed to have been made at the time of sale and purchase, and the terms agreed upon could not be violated or altered afterwards. There is a particular reference to this in the Ṛgveda (iv. 24. 9): "A man has realized a small price for an article of great value, and again coming (to the buyer he says) this has not been sold; I require the full price; but he does not recover a small price by a large (equivalent): whether helpless or clever, they adhere to their bargain."[1] The idea is clear. As soon as the bargain is made, there is no going back upon the original terms of the sale. Griffith thus comments: "Both the simple or needy buyer and the shrewd seller make as much as they can out of the bargain."

Images of Gods.—The meaning of the next verse, however, is somewhat curious and obscure: "Who for ten milch-kine purchaseth from me this Indra who is mine? When he hath slain the Vṛtras, let the buyer give him back to me."[2] Wilson translates the verse as follows: "Who buys this, my Indra with ten milch-kine? When he shall have slain (your) foes, then let (the purchaser) give him again to me." Both translations convey nearly the same meaning. Now what is signified by the purchase of Indra for ten milch-kine? Was there any image of Indra that used to be temporarily parted with for a consideration (ten milch-kine in the present instance), and returned after worship? Or, is it merely a metaphorical way of saying that the Ṛṣi, who had obtained the favour of Indra by sacrificing to him, demanded a fee of ten milch-kine for performing a sacrifice to Indra on behalf of any one who sought his favour? It should be borne in

---

[1] Wilson's *Translation of the Ṛgveda.*

[2] Griffith's *Translation of the Ṛgveda.*

mind that the description of the Gods in the Ṛgveda is mainly anthropomorphical, and it is just possible that artists sometimes painted their figures in colours, or carved out their images on stones or wood, or made clay images to represent their various functions. Though Max Müller holds that "the religion of the Veda knows of no idols," *(Chips from a German workshop* i. 38), yet Dr. Ballensen finds in the hymns clear references to images of Gods (*Jour. of the Ger Or. Society* xxii. 587 ff). It is, however, true that image-worship was not in general vogue in Ṛgvedic times. Griffith may, therefore, be right in holding that the verse means "the settlement of the fee to be paid to the priests for obtaining Indra's favours by sacrifice." Wilson gives an English translation of Sāyaṇa's commentary on both the verses, which would bear reproduction here:

"The meaning of this and the following verse (Rv. iv. 24, 9. 10) is thus explained, according to Sāyaṇa, by ancient Ācāryas, skilled in religious doctrine: One (a vendor) who takes a small price for valuable goods, comes aftewards to the buyer, and says, this has not been sold by me, and so saying, he requires the balance of the price, but he, the vendor, does not recover the full price, nor does he get back the article; according to the bargain between them it may not be otherwise; the sale has taken place, and if the bargain has been kept, then it was only to be considered that such is the object of the price, and that is the conclusion; a bargain has been made, and the (stipulated) price given. Therefore, in the first place, an agreement is to be made by me; so reflecting, *Vāmadeva*, having by much praise got Indra into his possessin or subjugation, purposes to make a bargain when about to dispose of him, as in verse 10." But what is meant by "disposing of Indra" is not explained in the above commentary.

From a careful consideration of such evidences as are available, I am disposed to think that there may have existed images of some of the Gods though their worship was not much in vogue, and was sometimes condemned. Maçdonell and Keith observe : " Sale appears to have regularly consisted in barter in the Ṛgveda (iv. 24, 10) : ten cows are regarded as a possible price for an (image of) Indra to be used as a fetish; elsewhere not hundred, nor a thousand, nor a myriad are considered as an adequate price (*śulka*) for the purchase of Indra." (Rv. viii. 1, 5). The translation of the verse last referred to is as follows :

" Wielder of the thunderbolt, I would not sell thee for a large price, not for a thousand, nor for ten thousand, nor oppulent bearer of the thunderbolt, for a hundred, (*i.e.*, for an infinite sum)."

The word used for price is *śulka*. The reference must therefore have been to an image of Indra. In a *mantra* of the Ṛgveda (viii. 100. 3), " Nema Ṛṣi declares that there is no God called Indra. Who hath seen him ? Whom shall we offer our hymns ? " In the next verse, Indra himself says : " Here have I come to thee. Look at me." This may mean that the God bodily appeared before the sage to dispel his doubt about his existence, or simply, his image was shown to him, which was more probable. We come across a word *Mura-devāh* in Ṛgveda (x. 87, 2. 14). Sāyaṇa explains the word as " the destructive herd of Rākṣasas." But it has been translated by Wilson as " those who believe in vain gods." It seems to me that the word " vain " is not the correct rendering of *Mura*, which may mean " senseless " like stocks and stones. The word, therefore, may refer to persons who believed in and worshipped " images " which were lifeless and senseless objects. Of course, such persons have been condemned along with the Rakṣasas, who were supernatural beings, living on raw meat and possessing a power for doing evil. I am, therefore, of opinion that there were images of Gods in Ṛgvedic times, though their worship was condemned by some of the advanced Aryan tribes. The following translation by Wilson of two verses (Rv. viii. 69, 15. 16) probably refers to the mounting of an image of Indra on a golden chariot: "(Indra) like a young boy has mounted his splendid chariot; he makes ready for his father and mother the great deer-like many-functioned cloud. Handsome-jawed (Indra), house-holder, mount thy golden chariot; then let us meet mounted together on that bright, thousand-footed, brilliant, auspiciously moving (car)." The epithets *arvako na kumarakah* (like a small-limbed boy) applied to Indra can only have reference to the small image of the God placed on the car. The word *dampatē* (house-holder), addressed to Indra, probably refers to the house-hold image of the God, worshipped by the Ṛsi, and the reference to his mounting the car with the God lends a strong support to the view that it was only an image of Indra that was placed on the car, intended to be drawn on the occasion of a religious festival. It should be stated here that the verses have been taken from a Vâlakhilya hymn.

High prices.—That the traders in Ancient India sold their commodities for exorhitantly high prices, which made them extremely unpopular, is evident from references in many verses to the practice they followed. One Ṛṣi supplicates Indra as follows: "Gathering up great store of riches, Indra, be thou no trafficker with us, most mighty." (Rv. i. 33, 3). Griffith explains the passage thus: "Do not deal illiberally with us like a petty trader: do not give sparingly, nor demand too much in return."

Trade in the Soma plant.—The Soma plant was brought down from the mountains by savage Aryan nomadic tribes called Śyenas or Garudas, and the Sarpas or Serpents. As the plant was in great demand for the performance of the Soma sacrifice, the shrewd vendors wanted to exact a high price for it. Hence there was a good deal of haggling over its sale. The plant was usually bartered for kine (Rv. viii. 32, 20). In this connection the following observations of Ragozin will be found interesting :—

"The Soma used in India certainly grew on mountains, probably in the Himalayan highlands of Kashmir. It is certain that Aryan tribes dwelt in this land of tall summits and deep valleys in very early times, probably earlier than that when the Ṛg-hymns were ordered and collected, or the already complicated official ritual which they mostly embody was rigidly instituted. From numerous indications scattered through the hymns, it appears probable that this was the earliest seat of the Soma-worship known to the Aryan Hindus, whence it may have spread geographically with the race itself, and that as the plant did not grow in the lower and hotter regions, the aridity of some parts disagreeing with it as much as the steam-laden sultriness of others, they continued to get from the mountains the immense quantities needed for the consumption of the gradually widening and increasing Aryan settlements. A regular trade was carried on with Soma plant, and the traders belonged to the mountain-tribes who were not Aryan,[1] and, therefore, irreverently handled their sacred ware like any other merchandise, bargaining and haggling over it. This is evidently the reason why Soma traders were considered a contemptible class; so much so that, when customs hardened into laws, they were included in the list, comprising criminals of all sorts, breakers of caste and other social laws, followers of low professions, as usurers, actors etc.—of those who are forbidden to pollute sacrifices by their presence They were probably itinerant traders, and the bargain was concluded according to a strictly prescribed ceremonial, the details of which seem singularly absurd and grotesque, until one learns that they had a symbolical meaning. The price (probably for a given quantity, though that is not mentioned) is a cow light-coloured, or, more precisely, reddish-brown, with light-brown eyes, in allusion to the ruddy or 'golden' colour

[1] This can only be true in the sense that though belonging to the same stock, they were not cultured like those who called themselves "Aryans" by way of distinction from the savage nomads.

of the plant—which must not be tied, nor pulled by the ear —*i.e.*, not handled roughly" [1]

Debt and Usury, The Paṇis have been condemned in several verses for their greed, hard-heartedness, irreverence, heterodoxy and niggardliness. They were extremely rich (Rv. iv. 25, 7), but as they never performed the Soma sacrifice, they incurred the displeasure of Indra, and, in fact of all his votaries. These Paṇis or merchants used to lend money to needy people at very high rates of interest. They have been described as "usurers who counted the days for calculating interest" (*bekanātān* [2] *ahardiśah* Rv. viii. 66, 10). As the money-lenders were oppressive, indebtedness was cursed, and prayers were offered to the Gods to make the people free from debt. Macdonell and Keith say: "Ṛṇa, debt, is repeatedly mentioned from the Ṛgveda onwards, having apparently been a normal condition among the Vedic Indians. Reference is often made (Rv. x. 34, 10) to debts contracted at dicing. To pay off a debt was called *ṛṇam saṃ-nī* (Rv. viii. 47, 17). Allusion is made to debt contracted without intention of payment. (Av. vi. 119, 1). The result of non-payment of a debt might be very serious: the dicer might fall into slavery. (Rv. x. 34.) Debtors, like other malefactors, such as thieves, were frequently bound by their creditors to posts (*drupada*, Rv. x. 34, 4), presumably as a means of putting pressure on them or their friends to pay up the debt. The amount of interest payable is impossible to make out. In one passage of the Ṛgveda and Atharva-veda

---

[1] *Vedic India*, pp. 170-171. [2] "The word (Bekanāta) has a foreign appearance, but its provenance can hardly be determined: it might just as well be aboriginal as Babylonian. Hillebrandt thinks, Brünhofer is right in identifying Bekanāta with Bikanir." (Vedic Index, ii. 73) Prof. A. B. Keith is also of the same opinion. Says he: "As little do the Ṛgvedic Indians appear to have been in contact with the Semitic peoples of Babylon. The term Bekanāta which occurs along with Paṇi in one passage has been thought to be a reference to some Babylonian word; though the Indian Bikanir is much more plausible as its origin. "(*Cambridge Hist. of India*, vol. 1, Ch. iv, p. 87).

(Rv. viii. 47, 17=Av. vi. 46, 3) an eighth (*śapha*) and a sixteenth (*kalā*) are mentioned as paid, but it is quite uncertain whether interest or an instalment of the principal is meant. Presumably the interest would be paid in kind. Zimmer thinks that payments of debts were made in the presence of witnesses who could be appealed to in case of dispute. (*Alt. Leben* 181). This conclusion is, however, very uncertain, resting solely on a vague verse in the Atharva-veda." [1] (vi. 32, 3=viii. 8, 21).

Ancestral debts were acknowledged, and had to be repaid by the debtor's descendants. They were both moral and legal obligations. The following prayer, offered to Varuṇa, will bear out our statement : "Discharge, Varuṇa, the debts (contracted) by my progenitors, and those now (contracted) by me ; and may I not, royal Varuṇa, be dependent (on the debts contracted) by another. [The scholiast explains this as follows : May I not obtain enjoyment by the wealth that is acquired by another]. Many are the mornings that have, as it there, not dawned ; make us, Varuṇa, alive in them." (Rv. ii. 28, 9).

"According to Śāyaṇa," says Wilson, "this means that persons, involved in debt are so overcome with anxiety that they are not conscious of the dawn of day ; to them the morning has not dawned ; they are dead to the light of day. The passage is deserving of notice, indicating an advanced as well as a corrupt state of society, the occurrence of debt, and severity of its pressure."

Sea-Trade and the Paṇis.—As there was inland trade, so trade was also carried on with islands and countries across the seas. There are many references in the Ṛgveda to sea-going ships, and to merchants who undertook sea-voyages in quest of wealth. Seekers of wealth sent their ships to the seas (Rv. i. 48, 3). Merchants, eager for gain, put their fleet of merchantmen out to sea in a body (Rv. i. 56, 2). Prayers were

[1] *Vedic Index*, i, pp. 109-110.

offered to the ocean before undertaking sea-voyages (Rv. iv. 55, 6). Ships were hundred-oared (Ṛv. i. 116, 5) and also furnished with "wings," *i.e.*, sails (Rv. x. 143, 5). Most probably these ships were all coast-liners, and seldom ventured out into the vast watery deep, though there is mention of naval expeditions having been undertaken against certain recalcitrant islanders. (Rv. i. 116, 3; read also Sāyaṇa's commentary). There is also mention of islands situated in the midst of the wide ocean (Rv. i. 169, 3; Rv. x. 10, 1). Varuṇa, the Lord of the Ocean, knew the paths of the ships and of the winds (Rv. i. 25, 7). From all these and other references, there can be no doubt that the Ṛgvedic Aryans were well acquainted with the sea, and their merchants made sea-voyages in their ships for the purposes of trade. But what were the seas that were navigated by the Aryan merchants in quest of wealth? I have fully answered this question elsewhere.[1] The Eastern Sea was immediately to the east of the Punjab, covering the whole of the Gangetic trough as far as Assam. The Western Sea covered the present lower valley of the Indus. The Southern Sea covered a portion of present Rajputana, separating the Deccan from Sapta-Sindhu or the Punjab, and the Northern Sea was the Asiatic Mediterranean, north of Bactria. These were the four seas mentioned in the Ṛgveda (ix. 33, 6; x. 47, 3). The Paṇis, or merchants, crossed these seas and traded along the coasts. They bartered their goods for the useful indigenous products of the lands they visited, which were brought to Sapta-Sindhu. Most of the people whom these merchants came across were either savages or half-civilised men, and some of them must have been also cannibals like the present aborigines of the Andaman islands. The idea of *Rākṣasas*, of whom frequent mention is found in the Ṛgveda (vii. 104; x. 87; 182, 3), must have been derived from an observation of their loathsome mode of life and habits. The merchants probably exaggerated their accounts

[1] *Ṛgvedic India*, Chaps. I, II, III.

in the tales they told, and the imaginative mind of the Aryans soon endowed them with three or more heads, (Rv. x. 87, 10), odd and grotesque figures, and also supernatural powers for evil-doing. If *Kikat a* be identified with South Behar, which I doubt, it must have been situated on the southern coast of the Eastern Sea, and the merchants who visited this coast must have brought to Sapta-Sindhu a very poor account of the people found there, who never performed the Soma sacrifice, nor offered the Soma juice, mixed with milk, to Indra. (Rv. iii. 53, 14).[1] There is mention of pearls (kṛśana) in the Ṛgveda (i. 35, 4; 126, 4; x. 68, 1), and if these were not fished up in the local seas, they must have been imported from the Malabar and Coromandal coasts and Ceylon, as pearls are even now found in great abundance in the adjacent seas, as well as the Persian Gulf where pearl-fishing is still carried on on an extensive scale. The merchants must have also imported precious stones, the Indian teak which furnished excellent timber for ship-building, and other valuable and useful commodities from Southern India. Though the Dravidians attained a high degree of civilisation in a later age, I do not think that they were much civilised in Ṛgvedic times. Their frequent contact with the Paṇis must have taught them the rudimentary arts of civilisation, which received a strong impetus, when Aryan settlers from Sapta-Sindhu founded colonies in the various parts of the Deccan. After the drying up of the bed of the Rajputna Sea and the gradual disappearance of the Eastern Sea, the sea-going Paṇis must have left Sapta-Sindhu, and settled on the Coromandal and Malabar coasts, especially as the latter supplied them with abundant materials for ship-building, and played a great part in the uplift of the Dravidians. The Paṇis must have also visited the coasts of the Persian Gulf and Southern Baluchistan, as

---

[1] I have fully discussed the situation of Vedic *Kikata* later on. In my opinion, it was a hilly region in the north of the Punjab, where the Soma plant grew, but where the people never performed the Soma sacrifice. Hillebrandt is also of the same opinion (Vide *Infra*.)

well as the coasts of the Arabian and the Red Seas, accompanied by the civilised Cholas and Pāṇḍyas, the former settling down in Mesopotamia and laying the foundations of the Chaldean or Sumerian civilisation, and the latter in Egypt, along with the Paṇis, who have been described in classical literature as the Punic race. These Paṇis ultimately settled down on the Syrian coast, and were the ancestors of the Phœnicians who were a mixed product of the Paṇis and the Semites. I have elesewhere fully described the gradual expansion of Aryan civilisation in Mesopotamia, Phœnicia and Egypt through the instrumentality of the Paṇis, the ancient Aryan merchants of Sapta-Sindhu, and refer the curious reader to Chapter XI of *Ṛgvedic India.*

Slaves and Dāsas.—The relation of the Aryan merchants with the savage and half-civilised peoples of the countries they visited must have been similar to that of the Spanish, Dutch, Portugese and English merchants during the middle ages with the original inhabitants of the African coasts and the islands of the Atlantic and Pacific Oceans. They bartered their goods, usually trinkets and gaudy things, of which the savages were fond, for the valuable products of their lands, and also kidnapped their men, women and children, whenever any suitable opportunity occurred. There is frequent mention of *slaves* in the Ṛgveda (vii. 86, 7; viii. 56, 3), the kings and nobles possessing hundreds and sometimes giving many of them away to Ṛṣis as valuable presents. These slaves must have been either prisoners of war, or men, women and children kidnapped from foreign countries, as well as the outlying districts of Sapta-Sindhu, and sold by the Paṇis who did not give up their vicious ways even after they had settled down in Phœnicia. For, the Phœnicians were known to the ancients as notorious kidnappers of beautiful women and children from the coasts of Greece and the islands of the Ægean Sea, whom they sold in the markets of Asia Minor, Egypt and Mesopotamia. The mention of "black-skinned slaves" in the Ṛgveda may have reference in some places to these kidnapped slaves from Southern India (Rv. vii. 86. 7; viii. 56, 3). A Ṛṣi prays to Agni for one hundred slaves (*dāsas*, Rv. viii. 56, 3). Another Ṛṣi says that King Trasadasyu, son of Purukutsa, gave him fifty *badhūs*, or young women, who were probably slave-girls. (Rv. viii. 19, 36). The word *Dāsa*, however, does not always mean a 'slave' in the Ṛgveda. It signifies a tribe or people who, though belonging to the Aryan stock, did not subscribe to the orthodox Vedic faith, or perform the Vedic sacrifices. The Yadus and Turbaśas were undoubtedly Aryan tribes who, seceding from the Vedic faith, crossed the ocean and settled on its further shores. But Indra brought them back again safely to Sapta-Sindhu across the waters. (Rv. i. 174, 9; vi. 20, 12; 45, 1), and anointed their chiefs as kings (Rv. iv. 30, 17). They seemed to have been under the special protection of Indra who helped them in their difficulties in various ways (Rv. i. 174, 9; iv. 30, 17; v. 31, 8; viii. 4, 7). But they have been described as *Dāsa* kings (Rv. x. 62, 10), probably because they were looked upon as *Dāsas* (unbelievers) on account of their heterodoxy. All non-sacrificers were called *Dāsas* (Rv. v. 34, 6; x. 86, 19). The verse last referred to distinctly says: "Here I (Indra) come to the sacrifice, looking upon (the worshippers), distinguishing the *Dāsa* and the Ārya; I drink (the Soma) of the (worshipper), who effuses (the Soma) with mature (mind); I look upon the intelligent (sacrificer); Indra is above all (the world)." From this verse it would appear that the Dāsa and the Ārya were so alike in appearance that Indra had to distinguish the one from the other by the mode of his worship only. Vṛtra, as our readers know (*vide* Chap. II) was originally a Brahman and priest of the Gods, and had for his epithet the word *Deva*. But he has been invariably called *Dāsa* in the Ṛgveda, simply because he was an enemy of Indra and acted in opposition to the interests of the settled Aryans. (Rv. vii. 83, 1). There were enemies, both *Aryan* and *Dāsa*, (Rv. x. 38, 3), *i.e.*, sacrificers, as well as non-sacrificers

(Rv. i. 103, 6). There were men, even Ṛṣis like Nema, who did not believe in the existence of Indra, or perform any sacrifice in his honour. (Rv. v. 33, 3; viii. 100, 3). The descendants of the sage Sanaka were opposed to the institution of sacrifice, and hence killed by Indra. (Rv. i. 33, 4). Such men were contemptuously put down as *Dasyus* and *Dāsas*. (Rv. x. 22, 8). Bṛhadratha and Nava-vāstva had probably at first been subscribers to the orthodox Vedic faith, and performed sacrifices, for which they became favourites of Agni (Rv. i. 36, 8). Nava-vāstva appears to have been a son of Kavi Uśanah; but both he and Bṛhadratha were afterwards killed by Indra, probably because of their subsequent heterodoxy, and called *Dāsas* (Rv. x. 49, 6). Macdonell and Keith say that "in many passages the word (*Dāsa*) refers to human foes of the Aryans. The *Dāsas* are described as having forts (*purah* Rv. i. 103, 3; ii. 20, 8; iii. 12, 6; iv. 32, 10), and their clans (*viśah*) are mentioned. (Rv. ii. 11, 4; iv. 28, 4; vi. 25, 2). It is possible that the forts which are called 'autumnal' (*śāradīh*) may be mythical, but it is not essential, for the epithet may allude to their being resorted to in the autumn season." (*Vedic Index*, vol. i, p. 356). It would thus appear that some of the *Dāsas* were as powerful and civilised as the Āryas, their only difference having been cultural and religious. They possessed considerable wealth (Rv. i. 176, 4; iv. 30, 13, viii. 40, 6; x. 69, 5) and could hold their own successfully against the Vedic Aryans, with whom, however, they belonged to the same stock.

As the evolution of the Aryans took place in Sapta-Sindhu, there were many tribes of the stock who could not keep pace with the advanced tribes, called Āryas, and remained in the nomadic and pastoral stages of civilisation. They too were called *Dāsas*, though they could be easily distinguished from their advanced brethren by the colour of their skin, which was dark or brown in consequence of their constant exposure to the sun and the inclemencies of the seasons, inevitable in a nomadic and pastoral state of existence. Hence their colour (*varṇa*) has been referred to in a Ṛgvedic verse (ii. 12, 4) in order to distinguish them from the advanced Āryas or *Ārya varṇa*. (Rv. i. 104, 2; iii. 34, 9). The savage or half-civilised Aryan tribes, known as *Dāsas*, generally lived in secluded inhospitable places, forests and mountains, far removed from the centres of civilisation (Rv. ii. 12, 4. 11; iv. 30, 14; vi. 26, 5). The names of some of the leaders of these *Dāsas* were Samvara, Śuṣṇa, Vetasu, Tugra, Cumuri, Varaśikha (Rv. vi. 26 & 27), Sahavasu (Rv. ii. 13, 8), Arbuda (ii. 14, 4), Varci (Rv. iv. 30, 15), Nava-vastva and Bṛhadratha (Rv. x. 49, 6), all Aryan names philologically. In the battle fought by King Dabhīti with Cumuri, it is said that sixty thousands of the latter's followers were killed by Indra. (Rv. vi. 26, 6). We may conjecture that a large number used also to be taken as prisoners and reduced to slavery. Probably their women also were captured and enslaved. Macdonell and Keith say that "aboriginal women were, no doubt, the usual slaves, for on their husbands being slain in battle, they would naturally have been taken as servants. They would sometimes also become concubines; thus Kavaṣa was taunted with being the son of a female slave (*dāsyāh putrah*) in the Aitareya Brāhmaṇa" (*Vedic Index*, vol. I, p. 357). This conjecture is true; only I would change the word "aboriginal" for "savage Aryan." Ludwig in his Translation of the Ṛgveda (3, 209) considers that in some passages the word *Dāsa* has been applied in the sense of "enemy." (Rv. i. 158, 5; ii. 1, 8; iv. 30, 14. 15 &c.). But Macdonell and Keith say that "it is uncertain." The very names, however, of the Dāsa leaders or chiefs appear to be Aryan, and Ludwig's surmise seems to me to be correct. According to Zimmer [1] and Meyer [2] "*Dāsa* originally meant 'enemy' in general, later developing in Iran into the name of Dahae of the Caspian

[1] *Altindisches Leben* 100 *et seq.*

[2] *Geschichte des Altertums.*

Steppes, and in India into a designation of the aborigines." [1] As the Dahae were closely allied in race and language to the Iranians who formed a branch of the Aryan race, although they may have subsequently mixed with the Mongolians, there can be no doubt that the Dāsas of the Ṛgveda were dissenting Aryan tribes, either civilised or semi-civilised. Many Dāsas were defeated by the Vedic Aryans, and the remnants of the tribes who were dispersed towards the West, must have settled in Iran and the Caspian Steppes in a later age.

"Hillebrandt" [2] say Macdonell and Keith, "argues that as the Dāsas and Paṇis are mentioned together (Rv. v. 34, 6.7), they must be deemed to be closely related tribes, identifying the Paṇis with the Parnians and the Dāsas of the Ṛgveda with the Dahae. This view, of course, necessitates a transfer of the scenes of the Ṛgveda, where Dāsas are prominent, and especially those in which Divodāsa—'the heavenly Dāsa,'—plays an important part, to the far west. Hillebrandt justifies this by regarding the scene of the sixth book of the Ṛgveda as quite different from that of the seventh and the third, in which Sudās, the Bharatas, Vasiṣṭha, and Viśvāmitra appear." [3] The Paṇis have not only been mentioned with the Dāsas, but also with the Dasyus. (Rv. vii. 6, 3). They may have been closely related tribes in the sense that they equally belonged to the Aryan stock, and agreed in differing from the orthodox Vedic faith. But whether the Paṇis could be identified with the Parnians, it is difficult to say. Hillebrandt is probably correct in saying that the scene of the sixth book of the Ṛgveda is different from the seventh and the third, for we find mention of the names of rivers or towns like *Hariyūpīyā* and *Yayyāvatī* which may have been situated towards the west outside the limits of Sapta-Sindhu. It may be surmised that the Aryans

---

[1] *Vedic Index*, i, p. 357.

[2] *Vedische Mythologie*, i, 94.

[3] *Vedic Index*, i, pp. 357-58.

made a war of conquest in that direction, driving before them the Dāsas and the Dasyus.

Dasyus.—The *Dasyus* have also been as frequently mentioned as the *Dāsas* in the Ṛgveda to designate a people hostile to the Vedic Aryans who defeated them with the aid of their Gods. "The great difference between the Dasyus and the Aryans was their religion: the former are styled 'not sacrificing,' 'devoid of rites' 'addicted to strange vows,' 'god-hating' and so forth. As compared with the Dāsa, they are less distinctively a people: no clans *(viśah)* of the Dasyus are mentioned, and while Indra's *Dasyu-hatyā* 'slanghter of the Dasyus' is often spoken of, there is no corresponding use of *dāsa-hatyā*." [1] Futher, "the Dasyu is called *a-karman*, 'riteless" (Rv. x. 22, 8); *a-devayu* 'indifferent to the gods' (Rv. viii. 70, 11); *a-brahman*, 'without devotion' (Rv. iv. 16, 9); *a-yajvan* 'not sacrificing' (Rv. viii. 70, 11); *a-yajyu* (Rv. vii. 6, 3); *a-vrata* 'lawless' (Rv. i. 51, 8; 175, 3; vi. 14, 3; ix. 41, 2); *anya-vrata*, 'following strange ordinances' (Rv. viii. 70, 11)".[2] From a comparison of the *Dāsas* with the *Dasyus*, it seems to me that the former were more civilised than the latter who mostly subsisted on loot and pillage, and stole away the cattle and goods of the settled Aryans, and therefore were more dreaded and hated by them. They were also the remnants of the Aryans, in low stages of development, retaining much of early barbarism in their character. That they belonged to the Aryan stock does not admit of any doubt; for, Indra says in a verse (Rv. x. 49, 3): "*I have deprived the Dasyus of their appellation of Ārya.*" And the Ārya and Dasyn were so alike in appearance that it was difficult for Indra to distinguish the one of from the other (Rv. i. 51, 8). A Ṛṣi says in another verse: "We live in the midst of the Dasyu tribes who do not perform sacrifices, nor believe

---

[1] *Vedic Index*, i, p. 347.

[2] *Ibid* (*Foot-note*).

in anything. They have their own rites, and are not entitled to be called 'men'. O Thou Destroyer of enemies, annihilate them and injure the *Dāsas.*" (Rv. x. 22, 8). They have also been called *a-mānuṣa* in another verse (Rv. viii. 70, 11) *A-mānuṣa* does not mean 'supernatural being,' but 'a being who is so low and bestial as not deserving of the name of *man.*' These Dasyus generally lived on inaccessible mountains or in the deep recesses of forests. Their name was transferred by the Vedic singers to their supernatural foes, Vṛtra and his hosts, who withheld the timely rains and kept the Sun and the Dawn in captivity. But these foes were also designated by the name of *Dāsa.* From the epithet *anāsa*, occurring only once in the Ṛgveda (v. 29, 10), Western scholars have jumped to the conclusion that the Dasyus were "nose-less" or "flat-nosed" like the aboriginal inhabitants of South India. Sayaṇa explains the word as *an-āsa* or mouthless, *i.e.*, devoid of good speech. And this interpretation is supported by the epithet *mṛdhra-vāc* occurring in the same verse, which means "of soft, stammering or unintelligible speech." This epithet is also applied to the Paṇis in Rv. vii. 6, 3; to the Aryan Purus in Rv. vii. 18, 13, and also to hostile persons in Rv. i. 174, 2; v. 32, 8; x. 23, 5. The dialects were different in different localities; and even the same dialect was pronounced differently by the people of the same race living apart from one another. The epithet *anāsa* does not, therefore, imply that the Dasyus belonged to the flat-nosed Dravidian race. The Brāhuis, a solitary Dravidian people living in Baluchistan, must have found their way there in an age later than the Ṛgvedic, when there was free land-communication with South India, or when the Dravidians visited the coasts of Baluchistan and Mesopotamia in their ships for the purposes of trade. In the Aitareya Brāhmaṇa (vii. 18), the word *Dasyu* has been used in the sense of uncivilised peoples. Manu says that many Aryan tribes, in very degraded conditions, were driven out of the Punjab, and lived on the mountains of the Western frontier under the name of *Dasyus*, speaking either the Aryan language, or its corrupted forms which were known as *Mleccha* (Manu Chap. x, 32, 45).[1] It will not do to ignore these interpretations of the word 'Dasyu,' made by very ancient Indian writers. They recognised the Dāsas and the Dasyus as their own kith and kin, with this difference only that they were votaries of another cult, and were placed in a low stage of civilisation and pronounced words incorrectly in a soft, stammering and unintelligible manner which made them incur the odium and ridicule of the cultured and advanced people who called themselves Āryas.

In this connection it would not be inapt and irrelevant to quote the following observations of Mr. P. T. Srinivas Iyengar from his excellent book, *Life in Ancient India in the Age of the Mantras* (pp. 11-12): "A careful examination of the Mantras where the words Ārya, Dāsa and Dasyu occur, indicates that they refer not to race but to cult. These words occur mostly in the *Ṛgveda Saṃhitā*, where 'Ārya' occurs about 33 times in Mantras which contain 1,53,972 words on the whole. This rare occurrence is itself a proof that the tribes that called themselves 'Āryas' were not invading tribes that conquered the country and exterminated the people. For an invading tribe would naturally boast of its achievements constantly. The word 'Dāsa' occurs about 50 times and 'Dasyu' about 70 times. The comparatively more frequent occurrence of these words is due to their use in some of these passages, the first in the sense of 'slave or servant,' and the second of 'robber'; where these words are not used in these meanings, they refer either to demons or to men who were opposed to the Āryas. The word 'Ārya' occurs 22 times in hymns to Indra and 6 times in hymns to Agni; 'Dāsas,' 45 times in hymns to Indra, twice in hymns to Agni; and 'Dasyu' 50 times in hymns to Indra and 9 times

[1] Read also *Ṛgvedic India*, Chap. viii.

in hymns to Agni. The constant association of these words with Indra clearly proves that 'Ārya' meant a worshipper of Indra (and Agni), and 'Dāsa' or 'Dasyu' meant either demons opposed to Indra or the people that worshipped these demons. That the Āryas worshipped Indra and he helped them in their cattle-raids and other quarrels is the constant burden of the Mantras where the word Ārya occurs. The Āryas offered oblations to Indra, through Agni; and next to Indra, Agni was their great helper (Rv. vii. 18, 7; viii. 92, 1. etc.). The Dasyus and Dāsas were those who were opposed to the Indra-Agni cult, and are so explicitly described in those passages where human Dasyus are clearly meant."

Various Aryan tribes in Sapta-Sindhu.—From a careful perusal of the Ṛgvedic hymns it would appear that the people living in ancient Sapta-Sindhu in Ṛgvedic times were divided into many tribes, five of whom developed a homogeneous civilisation, worshipping the same Gods, and performing the same religious rites and ceremonies, though occasionally quarrelling and warring among themselves. The names of these five tribes cannot be distinctly ascertained, but from their joint mention in certain Ṛgvedic verses (i. 108, 8; vii. 18; viii. 10, 5) Zimmer concludes that they must have been the *Anus*, *Druhyus*, *Yadus*, *Turvaśas* and *Purus*.[1] This view has been accepted by Macdonell. In my opinion the above conjecture would be very near the truth, if the *Bharatas* who lived on the banks of the Sarasvatī, Āpayā and Dṛsadvatī and were a powerful and famous tribe in Ṛgvedic times were included in the list, the *Yadus* and *Turvaśas* regarded as one tribe, and the *Purus* and *Tṛtsus* who lived in adjacent districts, and were sometimes allies and acted in concert for putting down the troublesome Dasyus, also counted as one tribe. The Purus lived on the banks of the Upper Indus on the borders of Gandhāra, keeping in check the depredations of the mountainous tribes, the Dasyus. The

[1] *Alt. Laben*, 119-123.

Tṛtsus occupied the country to the east of the Paruṣṇī as Zimmer rightly holds (*Op. cit.*124). The *Bharatas* occupied the country between the Sarasvatī and the Dṛsadvatī, known afterwards as the *Brahmāvarta deśa*, *i.e.*, the country where *Brahman* or the Ṛgvedic hymns were first composed and sacrifices first performed. The *Yadus* and *Turvaśas* and the *Anus* and *Druhyus* also probably lived on the lower valleys of the Sarasvatī, as she then was (Rv. vi. 61, 12). Ludwig identifies the Tṛtsus with the Bharatas. These two tribes may have been amalgamated later on, and the Tṛtsus may have formed the royal house of the Bharatas, as Geldner supposes.[1] But there are evidences in the Ṛgveda of a quarrel having taken place between the two tribes, the Bharatas having formed a confederacy of Ten Kings and advanced against the Tṛtsus, about which we shall write later on. I agree with Zimmer [2] in holding that the Tṛtsus and the Bharatas were two separate tribes who were enemies (Rv. iii. 53, 24). Bloomfield also holds identical views with Zimmer.[3]

In the Ṛgveda we find mention of many other tribes besides those referred to above. The *Krivis* lived on the banks of the Sindhu and the Asiknī.[4] *Pañcāla* is the later name of the Krivis (*Śat. Brā.* xiii. 5, 4, 7). But the Pañcālas were probably a fusion of the Krivis, the Bharatas, the Turbaśas and other tribes in a later age than the Ṛgvedic. The *Kikatas* have been mentioned in the Ṛgveda (iii. 53, 14). It is said that their cows did not yield sufficient milk for mixing with the Soma juice, nor did they offer milk in their vessels to the Gods. Hence they incurred the odium of the Vedic Aryans and were described as *naicaśākha* or 'belonging to a low branch or race.' Their king was Pramagandha. " Hillebrandt[5] thinks that *naicaśākha* refers not to Prama-

1 *Vedische Studien*, 2, 136 *et seq.*

2 *Alt. Leben*, 120.

3 *Jour. of the Amer. Ori. Society*, 16, 41, 42.

4 *Vedic Index*, i, 198.

5 *Ved. Mytho*, 1, 14-16; 2, 241-245.

ganda but to the Soma plant, the plant being called *naicaśākha* 'having shoots turned downwards,' and that the passage refers to a raid against the Kikatas, who were not observers of the milk-cult, or the Soma-cult, with the intention of winning their lands where the Soma grew and where there were cows."[1] Hillebrandt's view seems to me to be correct, and the Ṛgvedic *Kikatas* undoubtedly lived in a mountainous region of Sapta-Sindhu *where the Soma plant grew*. It is not necessary to think with Yāska (Nir. vi. 32) that Kikata was the name of a non-Aryan country. He would have been more near the mark, if he had said that it was a non-Vedic country. Kikata has been in later literature identified with Magadha or South Behar. Very probably the Kikatas of the Ṛgveda subsequently emigrated to South Behar and gave their name to the country of their adoption. I have also elsewhere ventured a guess that even if the Ṛgvedic Kikatas be identified with the people of South Behar, the Aryan merchants, when navigating the Eastern Sea over the Gangetic trough, must have visited the coasts of South Behar and come in contact with these people. But from the context of the Ṛgveda it seems to me that the Kikatas lived in a mountainous region of Sapta-Sindhu in Ṛgvedic times, where the Soma-plant grew.

The *Cedis* were another Aryan tribe who, with their King Kaśu, are mentioned in a Dānastuti of a Ṛgvedic hymn (viii. 5, 37-39), where their generosity is exceedingly praised. It is said that King Kaśu made a gift of one hundred camels and ten thousand cows to the sage Brahmātithi, and employed ten rich nobles in his service. The Ṛṣi says that Kaśu surpassed all other kings in generosity. They probably lived in the south-east corner of Sapta-Sindhu, not far from the desert on one side and the sea on the other, as is indicated by the number of camels given away to the Ṛṣi.

There is no clear mention of the *Matsyas* as a people in the Ṛgveda. Macdonell and Keith say that their name

[1] *Vedic Index*, ii, 38.

appears in one passage of the Ṛgveda (vii. 18, 6) "where they are ranged with the other enemies of Sudās, although it is possible to see merely the sense of 'fish' in that passage."[1]

The *Ajas*, *Yakṣus* and *Śigrus* have been mentioned in the Ṛgveda (vii. 18, 19) as tribes who formed a confederacy under Bheda against Sudas, by whom they were defeated and compelled to pay tribute. Probably, Bheda was one of the Ten Kings who fought against Sudas.

The Vṛcivants were another tribe who were conquered by the Sṛñjaya King, Daivavāta (Rv. vi. 27, 5 *et seq*). The battle took place near *Hariyūpīyā* and *Yayyāvatī*. Probably the Vṛcivants were the ancestors of the Phrygians or Brigges. and lived outside the pale of Sapta-Sindhu proper.

Ludwig in one passage of the Ṛgveda (x. 33, 2) "finds a reference to the defeat of Kuruśravaṇa by the *Parśus*; in another (Rv. vii. 83, 1) he finds a reference to the *Pṛthus* and *Parśus, i.e.*, the Parthians and the Persians. He also sees the Parthians in Pārthava, a name found in one hymn (Rv. vi. 27, 8). The same view is taken by Weber who holds that historical connexions with the Persians are referred to. But Zimmer points out that this conclusion is not justified."[2]

The Viṣāṇins were another Aryan tribe mentioned in the Ṛgveda (vii. 18, 7). In the same verse are also mentioned the *Śivas*, *Alinas*, *Pakthas* and *Bhalānasas*, all of whom are said to have been defeated by Sudās. But Roth thinks that they were his allies. And this conjecture seems to me to be correct. There was the confederacy of Ten Kings against Sudas, and the latter must have formed, for self-defence, an alliance with these Aryan tribes of the North-Western frontier of India, all of whom offered their praise to Indra (Rv. viii. 53, 4). The Śivas were probably identical with the tribe of that name, whom the Greeks found

---

[1] *Vedic Index*, ii, 121.

[2] *Vedic Index*, i, pp. 504-505.

in Alexander's time dwelling between the Indus and the Akesines (Asiknī). "The vil lage of Śiva-pura, mentioned by the scholiast on Pāṇini (iv. 2, 109) as situated in the northern country, may also preserve the name." (*Vedic Index*, ii. 381-382).

The Sṛñjayas were another Aryan tribe who were closely allied with the Tṛtsus. The *Turvaśas* were enemies of both these tribes. Sṛñjaya Daivavāta is celebrated as victorious over the Turvaśas and Vṛcivants.

Other Aryan Tribes: The Phallus-Worshippers.— Besides these tribes, there were others who, though Aryans, were placed in low stages of culture and civilisation, and hence looked upon with anything but favour by the Vedic Aryans. For example, we find the mention of the Śiśnas (Rv. x. 27, 19) or Śiśnadevas (Rv. vii. 21, 5; x. 99, 3) (*i.e.* those whose god was the Śiśna or phallus), who were opposed to Indra-worship and whom Indra defeated. This unmistakably goes to prove that there were tribes living in Sapta-Sindhu in Ṛgvedic times who worshipped the *lingam*, and whom the Vedic Aryans hated for this mode of worship. It is a mistake to suppose that the worship of *lingam* was a monopoly of the Dravidians, and was introduced by them into Northern India, and that a reference to this worship in the Ṛgveda points to the existence of Dravidian tribes in Sapta-Sindhu when the Ṛgvedic hymns were composed. The Phallus-worship was widely prevalent in the ancient world at one time. The Egyptians, Greeks and Romans worshipped Priapus; and the Canaanites and idolatrous Jews worshipped Baal-Peor. These gods represented the Linga-cult. The worship of Bacchus was another form of it. Among the ancient Lydians "Phallic emblems for averting evil were plentiful; even the summit of the tomb of Alyattes is crowned with an enormous one of stone about 9 ft. in diameter."[1] Forlong in his *Rivers of Life* endeavours again and again to

---

[1] *Hist. Hist. of the World*, ii, 434.

show that phallic worship is far more ancient than any other religion known; and he says in one place (vol. ii. p. 38): "The earliest instance I know of phallic worship or reverence, or at all events of phallic drawings, is that mentioned in the *Moniteur* of January, 1865. There it is related that in the province of Venetia, Italy, in a bone cave beneath ten feet of stalagmite, and amidst post-tertiary remains, beside a bone-needle, was found a rude drawing of a phallus, scratched on a plate of an argillaceous compound, surely a primeval idea of the Linga-in-Argha." [1]

Dr. Ginsburgh, in the article "Oath" in Kitto's Cyclopedia, finds reverence for the Phallus, if not worship, in primitive customs as old as the time of Abraham. He says: "Another primitive custom which obtained in the patriarchal age was that the one who took the oath 'put his hand under the thigh' of the adjurer. (Gen. 24, 2; 47, 29). This practice evidently arose from the fact that the genital member, which is meant by the euphemistic expression, 'thigh,' was regarded as the most sacred part of the body, being the symbol of union in the tenderest relation of matrimonial life, and the seat whence all proceeds, and the perpetuity so much coveted by the ancients. (Cf. Gen. 46, 26; Exod. 1, 5, Judges 8, 30). Hence this creative organ became the symbol of the Creator, and the object of worship among all nations of antiquity." [2]

"Originally" says the author of *Phallism* "phallic worship had no other meaning than the allegorical one of that mysterious union between the male and the female, which throughout nature seems to be the sole condition of the continuation of the existence of animated beings. There is no reason whatever for supposing that licentiousness invented the rites incidental to the worship of Pan, Priapus, Bacchus and Venus, whatever may have been made of them

[1] Quoted in *Phallism*, p. 2 London. Privately printed, 1889.

[2] *Op. cit.*, p. 3.

afterwards. 'It is impossible to believe' said Voltaire 'that depravity of manners would ever have led among any people to the establishment of religious ceremonies, though our ideas of propriety may lead us to suppose that ceremonies which appear to us so infamous could only be invented by licentiousness. It is probable that the first thought was to honour the deity in the symbol of life, and that the custom was introduced in times of simplicity," (P. 10).

It would thus appear that the phallic worship was at one time prevalent throughout the ancient world; and it may have prevailed as much among certain Aryan tribes of Sapta-Sindhu, as among the Dravidians, without mutual borrowing. Even in a Ṛgvedic hymn (x.129, 5) occurs the idea of the origin of the Universe from a union of *Svadhā* (Nature) below, and *Prayati* (Power and Will) above, which sowed the seeds from which mighty forces arose. This was the germ of the *Linga-in-Argha* worship which was in later times fully developed. The Vedic Aryans, however, appear to have been opposed to the symbolical worship of this idea, and hated those who worshipped the *Śiśna* or *lingam*. Probably the worship was confined to such tribes as the *Śivas* who lived in the north-west of Sapta-Sindhu, and the name *Śiva* afterwards came to be identified with *lingam* or the god worshipped in that emblem.

The Vṛtras or Serpent-worshippers.—*Vṛtra* has been called *Ahi*, or serpent, in the Ṛgveda. As I have already said, Vṛtra was originally a *Deva* and *Brāhmaṇa* whom Indra killed. Probably he was identified with zigzag lightning which appeared in the form of a hydra-headed serpent. The three heads or mouths of Vṛtra may have probable reference to the forks of lightning, or to the three months of the rainy season. As the flash of lightning is followed by the rumbling of thunder, it was conjectured that Indra hurled the thunder at Vṛtra, as soon as he emerged from his cloud-fort (*pura*), and challenged Indra to a fight. There can be no doubt that before the Indra-cult was firmly established by the agricultural section of the Aryans, Vṛtra was looked upon as a Deva or god by the pastoral and nomadic Aryans who were contemptuously called the Vṛtras by the Vedic Aryans in an advanced state of culture. We frequently come across the word *the Vṛtras* in the plural form in the Ṛgveda. (Rv. vi. 29, 6; 33, 3; vii. 19, 4; 83, 9; ix. 88, 4; x. 83, 7), which either meant 'clouds', or a people who worshipped Vṛtra as a god. The Dasyu chiefs, Cumuri aud Dhuni, have been mentioned along with the Vṛtras, all of whom were killed by Indra. (Rv. vii. 19, 4). The Vṛtras have also been mentioned along with the inimical Dāsas and Āryas (Rv. vi. 33, 3). They have also been called *the Ahis* and mentioned along with the Dasyus. (Rv. ix. 88, 4). From all these references, I am disposed to think that the Vṛtras were a tribe who worshipped the serpent as a God. That they were an Aryan tribe would appear from the fact that Arbuda, a Ṛṣi of the Ṛgveda (x. 94), is called *Kādraveya Sarpa*. He is "mentioned as Grāvastut priest at the snake festival described in the Pañcaviṃśa Brāhmaṇa (xxv. 15). He is obviously the same mythical figure as Arbuda Kādraveya, a seer spoken of in the Aitareya (vi. 1) and Kauṣītakī Brāhmaṇas (xxix. 1) as a maker of mantras." (*Vedic Index* i. 37). That serpent-worship prevailed among a certain Aryan tribe in Sapta-Sindhu in Ṛgvedic times, and a compromise was effected between the Vedic Aryans and this tribe in a later age, is evident from the story told in the Aitareya Brāhmaṇa (vi. 1). The Vṛtras were serpent-worshippers, and, as such, were hated by the worshippers of Indra, particularly when Deva Vṛtra became an enemy of Indra by withholding timely rains for the benefit of his votaries, the settled and agricultural Aryans.

Allied Cults.—It is conjectured by one Vedic scholar[1] that the Śiśna cult and serpent-worship were allied to each

---

[1] Iyengar, *Life in Ancient India in the Age of the Mantras*, p. 129.

other, as they have been referred together in the Ṛgveda: "Thou, heroic Indra, hast caused to flow the abundant waters which had been obstructed by the serpent (Ahi). Through thee, the cows (waters) have rolled on like warriors in chariots. All created things tremble for fear. The terrible (god), skilled in all heroic deeds, has with his weapons mastered these. Indra, exulting, has shattered their cities; armed with the thunderbolt, he has smitten them asunder by his might. Neither demons impel us, Indra, nor, O puissant, of a truth, any evil spirits. The glorious (Indra) defies the hostile beings: let not those Śiśna-devas approach our sacred ceremony. Thou, O Indra, hast surpassed in power, when thou runnest thy course. The worlds have not comprehended within them thy greatness. By thine own might thou hast slain Vṛtra. No enemy hath attained the end of thee in battle. *The earlier gods have yielded to thy divine power;* their powers have yielded to thy divine power; their powers have bowed before thy sovereign might. Indra having conquered dispenses wealth. Let men invoke Indra in the combat." (Rv. vii. 21, 3 7). "This clearly proves" says Mr. Iyengar "that though in many passages Vṛtra and Indra refer to the drought-demon, and the god who with the thunderbolt bursts the clouds, originally they were gods of rival tribes, and the tribes that worshipped Vṛtra, the serpent-god, either also worshipped, or were associated with those that worshipped the Śiśna also." This may be true, but there is no reason to suppose that the serpent-cult or the phallus-worship was "very widespread among the ancient Dravidian-speaking people" only. On the other hand, there are grounds for believing that the cults were Aryan in origin, though the Aryan tribes that worshipped Indra and Fire were at first opposed to them, and waged wars against those who subscribed to these faiths. As I have already said, a sort of compromise seems to have been effected towards the close of Ṛgvedic times between the worshippers of Indra and the serpent-worshippers, when the sage Arbuda, who was a serpent Ṛṣi, presided at a Soma-sacrifice, and composed a hymn in praise of the stones that crushed out the juice from the Soma plant (Rv. x. 94 and Ait. Brā. vi. 1). There was also a lady-Ṛṣi, named Śarpa-Rājñī, who offered a hymn in praise of the God Sūrya or the Sun (Rv. x. 189). Further, there is mention in the Ṛgveda (x. 76) of a Ṛṣi, named *Jaratkarna Sarpa*, *son of Irāvat*, who composed the hymn just referred to in praise of the stones with which the Soma plant was crushed. Our readers will feel no difficulty in identifying him with the Sarpa Ṛṣi Jaratkāru, mentioned in the *Mahābhārata*. The fact that these Ṛṣis, who were serpent worshippers, were also composers of Ṛgvedic hymns points to a compromise effected between them and the worshippers of Indra even in Ṛgvedic times. A similar compromise must also have been effected in still later times when the Vedic Aryans took to Phallus-worship, and identified Skambha with "the golden Phallus standing in the waters" (Av. x. 7) Skambha was the First Principle in creation or "the Secret Prajāpati."

The *Kṛtvans* were another Aryan tribe, who have been mentioned along with the *Ārjīkas* and the five peoples. (Rv. ix. 65, 23). Sāyaṇa says that Kṛtvan was the name of a country.

The Kṛṣṇas.—There seems to have lived in Ṛgvedic times another Aryan tribe, under the leadership of Kṛṣṇa, on the banks of the Aṃśumatī which is identified with the modern Jamunā. Kṛṣṇa was opposed to the Indra-cult, and regarded as an enemy of Indra who waged a protracted war with him. The following verses contain references to Kṛṣṇa: "The fleet Kṛṣṇa lived on the banks of the Aṃśumatī river with ten thousand troops. Indra of his own wisdom became cognizant of this loud-yelling chief. He destroyed the marauding host for the benefit of (Ārya) men. Indra said, 'I have seen the fleet Kṛṣṇa. He is lurking in the hidden region near the Aṃśumatī, *like the sun in a cloud.* O Maruts,

I desire you to engage him in fight and to destroy him.' The fleet Kṛṣṇa then appeared *shining*[1] on the banks of the Aṃśumatī. Indra took Bṛhaspati as his ally and destroyed the fleet and godless army." (Rv. viii. 96, 13-15). It is said that Indra with Ṛjiśvan killed the pregnant wives of Kṛṣṇa. (Rv. i. 101, 1). I do not think that Kṛṣṇa here refers to any person; but the word may mean the 'black cloud,' or Vṛtra; and 'the pregnant wives of Kṛṣṇa' probably means 'the rain-laden clouds.' For it cannot be supposed that Indra was so ungallant himself as to fight with pregnant women and kill them in battle, especially when he expressed the following sentiment elsewhere: "I rob that person of all his wealth and distribute it among my votaries, who incites men to fight with women." (Rv. x. 27, 10). The reference, however, to the killing of fifty thousand Kṛṣṇas in Rv. iv. 16, 13 must have been to men, the followers of the leader and hero of that name.

Vedic and Paurāṇic Kṛṣṇa.—Kṛṣṇa and his army have been described as "fleet" (*caranta*). Hence it is surmised that they were a nomadic pastoral people. It has been mentioned in the Ṛgveda (v. 52, 17) that cattle throve well on the banks of the Yamunā and were famous for their milk. Even in a later age,—the age of the great Epic—we find the same banks teeming with thriving cattle, and the people living a pastoral life. It was on the banks of the Yamunā that the Kṛṣṇa of the Purāṇas was born, who inaugurated a new cult which ran somewhat counter to the teachings of the Vedas (*Bhagavadgīta* ii, 42, 45, 46, 53), and put an end to the worship of Indra (*Bhāgavata Purāṇa* x). Was the Kṛṣṇa of the Purāṇas merely a *replica* of the Kṛṣṇa of the Ṛgveda, who also was an avowed enemy of Indra and lived on the banks of the Yamunā with his wives and followers? Or was the Vedic legend simply engrafted on the life of the

[1] That Kṛṣṇa was not black in colour would appear from his description as *shining* on the banks of the Aṃśumatī.

Paurāṇic Kṛṣṇa who overthrew the Indra-cult, and established a reformed religion? These are questions which it is very difficult to answer. The enmity of Kṛṣṇa of the Ṛgveda with Indra seems to have been based on the fact that the Aryan tribe living on the banks of the Yamunā were a nomadic pastoral people who were not in need of regular rains, as they were not agriculturists, and therefore did not see the necessity of worshipping a new god like Indra. In the Paurāṇic age, the people, living on the banks of the Yamunā, *did* worship Indra and perform sacrifices in his honour for rains, because, though still leading a pastoral life, they had also become agriculturists (*Bhāg. Pur*. x). But the great reformer Kṛṣṇa, probably remembering the old enmity of Indra with the ancient ancestors of his people, and with a view to establish a pure and reformed religion, induced them to give up Indra-worship and depend upon their own *karma* for their welfare (*Bhāg*. x).

The above account constitutes a brief survey of the various Aryan tribes, placed in the different stages of civilisation and culture, that lived in ancient Sapta-Sindhu in Ṛgvedic times. The savage and half savage tribes had their own modes of life, which were condemned by the civilised Aryan tribes in no uncertain terms. As previously referred to, a Ṛṣi thus gave vent to his feelings: "The *Dasyu* practising no religious rites, not knowing us thoroughly, following other observances, obeying no human laws; baffle, destroyer of enemies, the weapon of that slave." (Rv. x. 22, 8. Wilson's translation). Another Ṛṣi sang: "By sacrifices I purify both the sky and the earth. I burn the wide (realms of earth) that are without Indra, and are the haunts of the wicked; wherever the enemies have congregated they have been slain; and utterly destroyed, they sleep in a deep pit." (*Vailasthānam aśeran* Rv. i. 133.1). This was the spirit that animated the advanced Aryan tribes against their less advanced brethern. As already stated, the Five Tribes, though politically independent of one another, developed a homogeneous civilisation, and worshipped the same Gods and performed the same religious sacrifices. I have given a brief account in this Chapter of their village life, trades and occupations, arts and industries, which will go to prove that they were well advanced in civilisation. The other aspects of their domestic, social, communal and political life will be dealt with in the following Chapters.

CHAPTER IV.

FURTHER ACCOUNTS OF THE VEDIC PEOPLE IN ṚGVEDIC TIMES: SOME ASPECTS OF MATERIAL ART AND CULTURE.

Aryans autochthonous to the Punjab.—Our readers have now got an idea of the several tribes of the Aryan stock, that lived in ancient Sapta-Sindhu in Ṛgvedic times. They have also seen that with the exception of the Five Tribes, the others were placed in the different stages of civilisation and culture. Some remained in the pastoral and nomadic stage; others, though settled as agriculturists, did not subscribe to the orthodox Vedic faith; while others again remained in the primitive stage of hunters and robbers. They were the relics and remnants of the gradual process of evolution of the race from the barbarous condition of savages. The existence of all these different stages of evolution of the same race in the Land of the Seven Rivers unmistakably points to the fact that the Aryans were autochthonous, and did not come to ancient Sapta-Sindhu as invaders or aggressors. An invading tribe would be compact and consolidated as one people, with homogeneous civilisation and one common purpose, to enable them to achieve a victory over the indigenous population of the country. In these circumstances there would absolutely be no room for primitive, savage and half-savage tribes of the race. These could not be expected to act in concert with the invaders who had developed a higher type of civilisation, and would make confusion worse confounded by their presence. The existence of these different stages of civilisation of the race in one and the same land can, therefore, be best explained by the supposition that the stock had been autochthonous to the country from time immemorial, that their evolution had been going on from early primitive times, that a group of tribes by a combination of favourable circumstances and environments had developed in long course of time an advanced type of culture, while the other tribes, differently circumstanced and environed, could not keep pace with their advanced brethern, but had lagged far behind in the race, content only to remain in the different stages at which they had arrived. The theory of the Aryan invasion of the Punjab cannot satisfactorily explain the presence in Sapta-Sindhu of the Dāsas, Dasyus, Vṛtras, Śiśnas, Sarpas, Kṛṣṇas, Paṇis, Asuras, Śivas, Viṣāṇins and other tribes more or less advanced,—all belonging to the Aryan stock, and living side by side with the cultured Vedic Aryans. The composition of the Ṛgvedic hymns had taken hundreds, nay thousands of years, as the Ṛgvedic age was divided by the sages themselves into three periods, *viz.*, the Early, the Middle and the Later (Rv. iii. 32, 13; vi. 21, 5), and old songs are referred to as having come down to the Ṛṣis from their primitive ancestors, clothed in the more refined language of the later period (Rv. iii. 39, 2). Such early times are referred to in the hymns as witnessed the discovery and first use of Fire, the birth of Indra, the inauguration of sacrifices, the establishment of marriage laws, and the exchange of a pastoral for a settled agricultural life. With their gradual advancement in culture, some of the old Gods had disappeared or lost their supremacy, and new Gods had taken their place. Indra was admittedly the first and greatest God of Ṛgvedic times; but as he was originally furnished with a stone weapon, and then a bone weapon, his origin must have taken place in Neolithic or later Palæolithic times. All these evidences go to point to the vast antiquity of the Ṛgveda and Ṛgvedic civilisation, and lend a strong colour to the theory that the Aryans were indigenous to the land, and did not come to the Punjab as invaders or immigrants. The presence of the savage and half-savage Aryan tribes in the land during the Ṛgvedic period can only be satisfactorily explained by subscribing to this theory.

An illustration.—The truth of this theory would be best brought home to the mind by an illustration. Let us suppose a large family of savages in the hunting and nomadic stage, living in a country. They would divide themselves into natural groups, and move about the country in search of food and suitable games. Let us further suppose that a branch of the family comes across a patch of forest full of games and affording plenty of food, which the members of the branch would try their best to hold as their own and defend against the intrusion of the other branches. In this forest, some of the hunters would succeed in catching alive a number of young animals, and after taming them, would keep them as live stock for future use in times of necessity. These tamed animals would multiply in course of time and add to the live stock. The owners of this stock would find the rearing up of tamed animals a far more profitable and convenient business than the precarious mode of living by the chase. Their less fortunate brethern would naturally envy their good luck, and try their best to share the stock with them, not certainly with their consent or by mutual agreement, but by raiding or stealing. This would give rise to much heart-burning which would ultimately result in bloody conflicts. The owners of cattle (let us suppose that the live stock mainly consists of cattle) would leave the forest and seek a place of safety, where there are extensive pasture lands and plenty of water for the use of their animals. They would roam about with their cattle from one pasture ground to another, tending them, and guarding them against dangers. In course of time, wild corns would be discovered, which would be found to improve in quality and quantity by cultivation. Accordingly some of the cattle-keepers would take to cultivation and settle down in rude homesteads near their corn-fields. By adopting agriculture as a profession or occupation they would make rapid progress towards civilisation, and ultimately become a civilised people, leaving the other branches of the family far behind in the race and in extremely low stages of culture.

A process of evolution, like the one described above, must have occurred in ancient Sapta-Sindhu among the Aryan tribes before the Ṛgvedic hymns came to be composed. The Five Tribes or branches of the Aryan Family had advanced shoulder to shoulder in the race of life, and attained a comparatively high degree of civilisation, while the other branches of the Family still remained in extremely low stages of culture. Though all belonged to the same stock, they could not but be inimical towards one another, in consequence of their respective mental, moral and communal developments. The Vedic Aryans who were agriculturists and performed sacrifices in honour of their Gods could not tolerate the presence of those who were purely nomadic and pastoral tribes, did not sacrifice to the Gods, and lived by robbery. The latter also lost no opportunity for harassing their advanced brethern; and a constant conflict went on among them, ever since the Five Tribes began to make steady progress in their social and communal life. If we accept this view of Aryan evolution and culture in early Ṛgvedic times, we shall be able to comprehend the truth of the theory that the Aryans were autochthonous to the Punjab. As I have already said, no other theory satisfactorily explains the presence of the savage and half-savage Aryan tribes side by side with the most advanced tribes of the race in the Land of the Seven Rivers.

Result of the struggle with savage Aryan tribes.—It was not with inimical non-Aryan tribes, but with their own kith and kin that the advanced Aryans fought. It was a struggle for their very existence. The savage and half-savage Aryan tribes, who proved themselves to be veritable pests, had to be driven out or got rid of, before the cultured Aryans could think of prospering in life, or making further progress towards civilisation. As I have already pointed out, the struggle had commenced from the very beginning of Aryan civilisation, in fact, from early Neolithic or Later Palæolithic times when Indra was discovered and enthroned as the Supreme God of the agricultural section of the Aryans. It was Indra who carried on the conflict on behalf of his votaries, and succeeded in breaking down their enemies or driving them out of the country. Tribes after tribes of savage Aryan nomads left the country, and passed out into the wider world beyond through the western mountain-passes and Gandhāra, until at the close of Ṛgvedic times a comparatively peaceful atmosphere was established in the country. The whole of the Ṛgvedic period was occupied by this deadly struggle. But it was not barren of results. It is when confronted with enormous difficulties that the human mind becomes most active and determined. Professions and occupations grew up. The successful leaders became Rājas, and Rājanyas; the warriors became Kṣatras or Kṣtriyas; the priests who performed the Soma sacrifices with a view to strengthen Indra in his fight not only with the Dāsas and Dasyus, but also with the Cosmic Forces that tortured the people by withholding timely rains, became a class by themselves, known as Brāhmaṇas, and the generality of the people (*viś*) who preferred peaceful occupations to military life and activities became agriculturists, artisans, and traders. Those of the Dāsas and Dasyus, who had been subdued and had adopted the Vedic faith and civilised life and manners, formed the higher classes of the Śūdras. During this period, arts and industries flourished, healthy social customs were introduced, an elaborate form of worship was established and higher philosophical speculations were indulged in by the sages or Ṛṣis. In a word, the Aryans succeeded in laying the firm foundations of a civilisation which is unique in the world, and has successfully withstood the ravages of time through untold millenniums.

Ṛgvedic civilisation founded in Sapta-Sindhu.—That the Ṛgvedic civilisation was founded, developed and firmly established in the Land of the Seven Rivers does not admit of a doubt. The *mantras* were mostly composed on the banks of the Sarasvatī, the Dṛṣadvatī, the Āpayā, the Sindhu and the other rivers of the Punjab. The frequent mention of these rivers in the *mantras* strongly supports our view. Indra was pre-eminently the God of the Aryans of Sapta-Sindhu. He is said to have been born on a high peak of the Himālaya, where the Soma plant grew. For as soon as he was born, he drank the Soma juice, before even sucking his mother's breasts. (Rv. iii. 48, 2). The Soma plant grew nowhere except on the Mujavat mountain (Rv. x. 34. 1), a peak of the Himālaya, and in the plains of Sapta-Sindhu on the banks of the Sarasvatī and the Sindhu, and on the shores of the Śaryaṇāvat Lake in Kurukṣetra (Rv. ix. 61, 7; 113, 1). The Soma-cult was the peculiar cult of the Aryans of Sapta Sindhu, and subscribed to by only another branch of the Aryans, viz. the Iranians, under the name of *Haoma*, though it was subsequently discarded by them after their migration to Bactria in consequence of a religious schism. This Soma-cult was the oldest (Rv. ix. 42. 4), anterior even to the institution of Sacrifices and the Fire-cult, (Rv. ix. 2, 10), and the Soma was the very essence and spirit of Sacrifice (Rv. ix. 2, 10; 6, 8), the favourite drink of the Gods from ancient times (Rv. ix. 110, 8), the father of Indra (Rv. ix. 96, 5) and the father of all the Gods. (Rv. ix. 88, 10). As there is no trace of the word Soma or the Soma-cult in any of the Aryan languages of Europe, Indra and Soma must have been the sole and exclusive properties of the Aryans of Sapta-Sindhu. As the name of Indra is found in a clay-tablet discovered at Boghaz Keui by Hugh Winckler in 1909, which contains the terms of a treaty made in the Fifteenth Century B. C. by a Mitannian King, it must necessarily have been taken there by a Vedic Aryan tribe from Sapta-Sindhu. The theory of some European scholars that the name of Indra, found in the clay-tablet discovered at Boghaz Keui, must have been left there by a migrating

Aryan tribe who afterwards settled down in Sapta-Sindhu as the Vedic Aryans, is absurd to a degree in the light of the evidences quoted above, and in face of the fact that Indra and Soma were indissolubly connected with each other, and the Soma plant grew nowhere else excepting the Himālaya and the plains of Sapta-Sindhu. It was impossible to think of, or worship Indra without the offer of Soma libations. If Northern Europe, Central Europe or the Arctic region was the original cradle of the Aryan race, and a branch or branches started in their emigration to the South and the East, carrying with them the names of their Gods (including that of Indra) and the modes of their worship, how is it that the names of Indra and Soma are not found in any of the Aryan languages of Europe? How is it again that, while all the other Aryan branches remained in Europe, and found ample room for their growth and expansion, only two branches thought of leaving their cradle, and ventured into the unknown? How is it again that these two branches only made rapid strides towards civilisation and culture, while the other tribes in Europe went on grovelling in darkness and remained in the neolithic stage of culture down to comparatively recent times? Where again is the tradition in the vast Vedic literature, admittedly the oldest of the Aryan race, of this migration from their original cradle in the North? And who were the leaders that safely guided them through vast continents? If they made their appearance in the Punjab as invaders, what were the names of the invading kings, under whom the various Aryan tribes marched in their quest for a suitable home? Would not their names be reverently and gratefully remembered, and handed down from generation to generation by tradition? And how would the presence of the nomadic semi-civilised Aryan tribes in Sapta-Sindhu be explained? These are some of the questions to which no satisfactory answers have been or can be given by Western scholars from their stand-point. And yet they proceed to write elaborate ancient histories of the Aryans of India, and expect their readers to gulp them down as reliable and genuine stuff without any questioning or demur.

Comparison of ancient Aryan culture in India and Europe.—European and American scholars, with only a few exceptions, are extremely loath to take back the date of the composition of the Ṛgvedic hymns beyond 1000 or 1200 B. C., for reasons best known to themselves. What was the state of Ṛgvedic culture and civilisation, as revealed in the hymns? Was it not very high, and, admittedly far higher than the state of culture and civilisation, as found among the various branches of the Aryan people of Europe in the corresponding period? Is it not a fact, as proved by M. Arcelin, that as late as 1150 B. C., stone implements were still exclusively used in Central Gaul, and about 400 B. C. bronze was not yet replaced by iron? Dr. Taylor has thus summarised the state of neolit hic culture among the tribes speaking some forms of the Aryan language in Europe at the beginning of the historic period: "It is believed that the speakers of the primit ive Aryan tongue were nomad herdsmen who had domesticated the dog, who wandered over the plains of Europe in wagons drawn by oxen, who fashioned canoes out of the trunks of trees, but were ignorant of any metal with the possible exception of native copper. In the summer they lived in huts, built of branches of trees, and thatched with reeds; in winter they dwelt in circular pits dug in the earth, and roofed over with poles, covered over with sods of turf or plastered with the dung of cattle. They were clad in skins sewn together with bone needles; they were acquainted with fire, which they kindled by means of fire-sticks or pyrites; and they were able to count up to a hundred. If they practised agriculture which is doubtful, it must have been of a primitive kind; but they probably collected or pounded in stone mortars the seeds of some wild cereals either spelt or barley. The only social institution was marriage; but they were polygamists and practised human sacrifice. Whether they ate the bodies of enemies slain in war is doubtful. There were no enclosures, and property consisted in cattle, and not in land. They believed in a future life; their religion was shamanistic; they had no idols, and probably no gods properly so called; they reverenced in some vague way the powers of nature." [1]

If the Ṛgvedic hymns were composed in Sapta-Sindhu about this period, as alleged by European scholars, what a world of difference is noticed between the two respective cultures. In the Ṛgveda, we find domesticated animals like the horse, cow, goat, sheep, buffalo, ass, camel, dog and the tamed elephant, houses built of stones with a thousand pillars and hundred doors, houses built of wood, houses with mud walls and thatched roofs, iron-forts, the uses of metals like gold, silver, copper, bronze and iron, gold breast-plates, iron breast-plates, and iron mail-coats, gold helmets, weapons like swords and javelins, iron arrow-heads and spears, barricaded enclosures for cattle, chariots drawn by horses, wagons drawn by oxen, foot-soldiers, horsemen or cavalry, camel corps, and possibly also war-elephants, villages governed by leaders (*grāmaṇīs*), towns (*purs*) tenanted by kings and noblemen, ornaments of gold, silver, pearls and precious stones, woolen cloths, cloths woven with golden threads, images of gold, coins in gold and silver, trade by barter, agriculture, and agricultural products, ships and sea-trade, inland trade and caravans, leather and tanning, skins and skin-vessels, money-lending and usury, property in land, stone vessels, and wooden vessels, and cups and dishes made of metal, wooden bedsteads, cushions, blankets, and pillows, a form of popular government, limited monarchy, election of kings by popular suffrage, well-organized social life, laws of inheritance and customary laws, monogamy and polygamy, high morals with occasional lapses, high and dignified position of women, happy domestic life, rights of

[1] Dr. Taylor's *Origin of the Aryans*, pp. 132-133.

women to inherit their husband's properties and to perform religious sacrifices and compose religious hymns equally with men, female liberty, reverance to superiors and respect for women, popular assemblies, clubs for discussion, worship of Gods, elaborate systems of performing sacrifices, a highly developed language and literature, high philosophic speculations on the life here and hereafter, and on the origin of the Gods and of the universe, repentance for evil-doing, and prayers to the Gods for wiping out sins. How could the Aryans of India develop such a high state of culture at the beginning of the historic period, while the Aryan tribes of Europe remained in the barbarous state of half-civilised savages? The treasures of Tutankhamen recently discovered in the royal tomb at Luxor would not reveal such a high degree of culture as we find depicted in the pages of the Ṛgveda Saṃhitā. Either the date of the composition of the Ṛgvedic hymns must be brought down several centuries nearer our present age to allow the immigrant neolithic Aryans sufficient time to develop in Indian soil the neolithic culture brought from Europe, or the theory of the original cradle of the Aryan race in Northern or Central Europe must be given up for good as extremely absurd, incongruous and inconsistent. The real fact of the matter is that the original home of the Aryans was in Sapta-Sindhu, from which Aryan emigration started to Europe in waves after waves from prehistoric and immemorial times, and the advanced Aryan tribes that remained in their original cradle, had developed a culture and civilisation long before any civilisation was born either in Egypt or Mesopotamia. The different distribution of land and water and the existence of a cold climate in Northern India, of which unmistakable evidences are found in the Ṛgveda itself, at once take back the beginnings of Aryan civilisation to the latter part of the Pleistocene, or the Post-Pleistocene period, and we must assign to the composition of the hymns a date which is several millenniums before the Christian Era.

A comparative study necessary.—A comparative study of the neolithic culture of Europe at the dawn of the historic period and of Ṛgvedic culture is necessary in order to be able to fully realise the significance, value and place of the latter in the culture of the world. For Ṛgvedic culture was a veritable world culture, and influenced not only Mesopotamian culture but also the culture of Egypt through the Paṇis and the Dravidians. [1] European culture is immediately indebted to these two cultures for its subsequent growth and development, and is therefore rightly eloquent in its acknowledgment of the debt. But it seems to have lost sight of the original fountain-head, from which all culture proceeded towards the West. The neolithic Aryan savage tribes who migrated to Europe from Sapta-Sindhu got themselves mixed up with Turanian savage tribes, and the indigenous savage populations of Europe, among whom there was also a strong African blend. The amalgamated product was not sufficiently virile and fertile at first to develop an independent civilisation of its own, but took a long time in getting its several elements thoroughly fused into one homogeneous lump and properly fertilized. When that was accomplished, the seeds of material culture, that were brought from Mesopotamia and Egypt and sown into it, vigorously sprouted into plants of luxuriant growth, which have now out-grown and over-shadowed all other culture-plants of the world. No wonder that the European and American savants feel themselves strongly and irresistably attracted to the dead mother-cultures from which their own cultures had drawn their inspiration and sustenance. But the question naturally arises, why have these ancient cultures become dead? Probably because in the first place, they were of exotic growth and not the results of natural independent evolution; and secondly, because the purpose, for which they had come into being, was accomplished. The

[1] *Ṛgvedic India*, Ch. xii & xiii

original Aryan culture has its relics preserved not in underground caves in the midst of deserts and an extremely dry climate, but in the imperishable pages of the Ṛgveda Saṃhitā, which reveal them for all time to come in all their purity, beauty and significance. They belong to a far earlier age than that of Egyptian or Mesopotamian culture, but as they cannot be visualized like the relics gathered from the underground tombs of the ancient Pharaohs, they have less attraction and interest for the ordinary man or woman of the world. None the less, they have an interest, unsurpassed in value, to the patient student of ancient history and culture, and with a view to prove the truth of my assertion, I will now proceed to array and depict such of them as have come to my notice.

Material Art in Ṛgvedic times.—In Ṛgvedic times material art was highly developed, and if the age of the Ṛgvedic hymns be counted by several millenniums before the Christian Era, its development should evoke a feeling of something like awe and wonder in the minds of all persons who bring no bias to bear upon the study of real ancient history. It is my deliberate opinion that Ṛgvedic art was not influenced by any foreign art, for at the time when the hymns were composed, there were no ancient peoples either in Asia or Europe who were as equally advanced as the Vedic Aryans, and could, therefore, furnish models of art for imitation. The Vedic Aryans were autochthones to Sapta-Sindhu which included Gandhāra or modern Kabulisthan on the West, and Bactria on the north. This territory was shut out from the rest of the world by impassable mountains on the west, and lofty mountain ranges and the Asiatic Mediterranean Sea on the north. The south and the east were also hemmed in by seas. Thus isolated and cut off from the outside world, the Aryans were thrown back upon themselves and their own resources, and developed such mental and moral virtues as helped them to inaugurate and develop a civilisation which has no counterpart or parallel in any part of the world and is still unique. I never contend that other peoples, similarly situated and circumstanced, were or would be incapable of developing similar civilisations; but so far, we have not come across the relics of any civilisation, as old as the Aryan, which would bear a favourable comparison with the latter. The Egyptian and the Babylonian civilisations were admittedly very old; but there were traditional accounts, current among the ancient peoples of these countries, of their respective civilisations having been introduced or influenced by foreigners from the East who lived across the ocean. These foreigners undoubtedly belonged to the Punic race, the ancestors of the Phœnicians of history, whom I have identified with the Paṇis of the Ṛgveda. I have elsewhere fully discussed this question, and endeavoured to describe the part they played in the uplift of the Semitic peoples of Western Asia, and the ancient peoples of Egypt (*Rg. Ind.* Ch. xii & xiii); but the civilisations that grew up in those soils were transformed into something new, conformably to the genius of the peoples themselves, though the traces of Aryan influence could be easily discerned and detected in them. As the Paṇis were their teachers, they could only adopt the material culture of the ancient Aryans, and not their moral and spiritual culture, which fact probably accounts for their disappearance after a spasmodic existence of a few millenniums. The spiritual culture of the Aryans still remains to be fully understood and appreciated, for which efforts have begun to be made in Europe and America.

Forts, Palaces and houses.—I will first deal with the material art of the Vedic Aryans. It was perfect so far as it went, supplying all the wants of the people, both cultured and uncultured, and leaving them ample leisure for the pursuit of their avocations or of knowledge in the higher spiritual spheres of life. The rich and the nobles lived in forts made of stones or other hard materials (Rv. iv. 30, 20), and also in beautiful palaces made of wood, which were sometimes burnt down by enemies, or by accident (Rv. vii. 5, 3). The palaces were adorned with pillars which supported the roofs (Rv. iv. 5, 1), and had innumerable doors for light and ventilation (Rv. x. 99, 3). Śamvara had one hundred stone-made forts which were captured by Indra for Dabhīti (Rv iv. 30, 20). Mitra and Varuṇa had a palace with one thousand pillars (*sahasrasthūna*) and filled with vast riches. (Rv. ii. 41, 5; v. 62, 6.) There is also mention of iron forts or cities (Rv. vii. 3, 7; 15, 14; *āyasīvih purvih*). The phrase occurs in the two verses referred to here and also in others addressed to Agni, where prayers are offered to the God for the protection of the people as in a fort or city made of iron. The reference, of course, is to the frequent destruction by fire of houses built of wood, or thatched with inflammable materials. Houses made of stones, or materials hard like iron, were safe in a general conflagration. The *Pur*, of which frequent mention is found in the Ṛgveda (Rv. i. 53, 7; 58, 8; 131, 4; 166, 8; iii. 15, 4; iv. 27, 1; vii. 3, 7; 15, 14 &c.), was ordinarily a fort or stronghold, capable of withstanding a sudden attack or siege, and generally occupied by the King, the members of the Royal Family and the Royal attendants, in which were stored all the valuable things belonging to the Royal household, consisting of hoards of gold, silver, jewels and probably large granaries also. "Such fortifications must have been occasionally of considerable size, as one is called 'broad' (*pṛthvī*) and 'wide' (*urvī*)" *i.e.* it was something like a fortified town capable of accommodating not only the Royal household, but probably the nobles and rich merchants as well. (Rv. i. 189, 2). Such forts were usually made of stone (*aśmamayī*, ii. 30, 20), and thus afforded adequate protection to all the families living within them not only from enemies, robbers or raiders, but also from fire. "Autumnal (*śāradī*) forts are named, apparently as belonging to the Dāsas: this may refer to the forts in that season being occupied against Aryan attacks, or against inundations caused by overflowing rivers." (*Vedic*

Index i. 538). I have proved elsewhere that the autumnal forts which had belonged to Vṛtra and were broken down by Indra referred to the cloudy days of autumn, during which the rains were withheld. (*Ṛg. Ind.* xxiii). Nevertheless, as interpreted by Profs. Macdonell and Keith, there may have existed forts that were occupied by the Dāsa chiefs in autumn, and defended against the attacks of the Vedic Aryans.

Mention is found of *purs* or forts with hundred walls (*śatabhujī*, Rv. i. 166, 8; vii. 15, 14). These walls were certainly not concentric, for in that case a vast space would be enclosed, and the cost of building them would be enormous. What the poets probably mean is that the enclosing wall instead of being a complete circle was a polygon with a hundred sides or arms of equal length, each linked and forming an obtuse angle with the other, where probably stood a bastion for the defence of the wall. I do not find any reason for thinking with Macdonell and Keith that these forts were probably not permanently occupied fortified places "like the fortresses of the madiæval barony," but "probably places of refuge against attack, ramparts of hardened earth with pallisades and a ditch." As the Ṛgvedic times were full of unrest, and wars were constantly going on among all the tribes, Vedic and non-Vedic, forts or fortified towns would be permanently occupied by Kings and Nobles for safety and protection, and defended against attacks and raids. Ramparts of hardened earth with pallisades and a ditch may furnish places of refuge to an army in times of attack, but the Kings and Nobles would naturally prefer to live throughout the year in the fortresses with their families and wealth. The mention of stone-walls and stone-forts undoubtedly points to the fact that they were intended for permanent occupation.

The word *Dehi* occurs in two passages of the Ṛgveda (vi. 47, 2; vii. 6, 5,), meaning "defences thrown up against an enemy, apparently earthworks or dikes." (*Ved. Ind.* i. 379). These defence-works were of a temporary character.

and should be distinguished from *purs*, which were fortresses. Pischel and Geldner[1] think that there may have existed towns with wooden walls and ditches, like the town of Pātaliputra in Chandra Gupta's time, and that fire was used to destroy these walls (Rv. vii. 5, 3). Whether wooden walls existed or not, it is possible that some places were defended by wooden pallisades which used to be set on fire by the enemies. The account of burning out the *Dasyus* or robbers from their hiding place (Rv. vii. 5, 6) probably refers to the burning of the forests, the usual haunts of robbers, in order to compel them to come out to the open where they could be adequately dealt with and punished. That houses were also built of wood does not admit of a doubt. But these were probably thatched with grass, and occupied by families of poor or moderate means. As wooden houses were not safe to live in, having been liable to be destroyed by fire, well-to-do people preferred to have houses built of stones. Vasiṣṭha prayed to Varuṇa that he might not have to live in a mud-house [2] (*mṛṇmayam gṛham*) *i.e.* a house with mud-walls and thatched roof. (Rv. vii. 89, 1). Another Ṛṣi, named Saptagu, prayed to Indra for a big residential house, such as others did not possess. (Rv. x. 47, 8).

The word *gṛha* occurs both in the singular (Rv. iii. 53, 6; iv. 49, 6; viii, 10, 1) and in the plural (Rv. ii. 42, 3; v. 76, 4; x. 18, 12; 85, 26 &c.) in the Ṛgveda and denotes the house of the Vedic Aryan. "*Dama* or *Dam* has also the same sense, while *Pastyā* and *Harmya* denote more especially the house with its surroundings, the family settlement. The house held not only the family, which might be of considerable

---

[1] *Vedische Studien* I. xxii, xxiii.

[2] *Mṛṇmayam gṛham* may also mean an "earthen grave." Burial was a more ancient custom than cremation, and both customs appear to have existed in Ṛgvedic times. But cremation was preferred to burial, as it helped to translate the dead man to heaven directly. (*Vide Infra*) Hence Vasiṣṭha probably prayed to Varuṇa that his dead body might not be consigned to the grave, but that he might be translated to heaven through cremation.

size, but also the cattle (Rv. vii. 56, 6) and the sheep (Rv. x. 106, 5) at night. It was composed of several rooms or isolated huts, as the use of the plural indicates, and it could be securely shut up. (Rv. vii. 85, 6). The door (*dvār, dvāra*) is often referred to, and from it the house is called *Duroṇa*. In every house the fire was kept burning."[1] The entire compound was of course surrounded by a wall or pallisade.

We have seen before that in pastoral times, the cattle and the sheep were kept at night in the *gotra* or *goṣtha*; and only some of the milch-cows were kept in the house. But with the advancement of time, each family probably possessed its own *gotra*, adjacent to the dwelling house, where the cattle and the sheep were kept at night.

We find no information in the Ṛgveda as to how the houses were constructed. But some light on the subject can be thrown from the Atharva-veda. "According to Zimmer, four pillars (*upamit*) were set up on a good site, and against them beams were leant at an angle as props (*pratimit*). The upright pillars were connected by cross beams (*parimit*) resting upon them. The roof was formed of ribs of bamboo cane (*vaṃśa*), a ridge called *viṣūvant* and a net (*akṣu*), which may mean a thatched covering (Av. ix. 3, 8) over the bamboo ribs. The walls were filled up with grass in bundles (*palada*), and the whole structure was held together with ties of various sorts (*nahana, prāṇāha, saṃdaṃśa, pariṣvañjalya*).[2] In connexion with the house, mention is made of four terms which, though primarily sacrificial in meaning, seem to designate parts of the building: Havirdhāna, 'oblation-holder'; Agniśālā, 'fire-place'; Patnīnām Sadana, 'wives' room'; and Sadas, 'sitting room.'"[3] Each house had two wings or sides called *pakṣa*, which probably resembled our *verandāh*. The posts of the Verandāhs were, of

[1] *Vedic Index* i. 229, 230.

[2] Av. ix. 3, 4. 5.

[3] *Vedic Index* i. 230, 231.

course, made of wood, upon which images were carved. Carved images are mentioned in a verse (Rv. iv. 32, 23) which has been translated by Griffith as follows: "Like two slight images of girls, unrobed, upon a new-wrought post, so shine thy bay steeds in their course." Wilson, however, thus translates the verse: "Like two puppets on an arranged, new and slender stage, &c." Whatever may be the correct interpretation, there can be no doubt that images were carved upon wood, and it is quite possible that images of unrobed girls were carved upon the wooden posts that supported the thatch of the Verandah for the purpose of decoration.

From the above account it would appear that a house usually consisted of an outer apartment, called the sitting-room, where the male members of the family assembled, talked or rested; a store-room in which the articles needed at a sacrifice as well as the grains required for daily consumption were stored; an inner apartment, set apart for the exclusive use of the ladies; and a room where the sacred fire was kept burning, called Āṣtrī in the Ṛgveda (x. 165, 3). Besides these rooms there must have been separate bed-rooms for married couples and for grown-up children. The cattle-shed was, of course, situated within the compound of the house, but at a safe distance from the living rooms. Besides these rooms or houses, there was one called *Ā-vasatha*, or dwelling "which appears to be a place for the reception of guests, especially Brāhmaṇas and others on the occasion of feasts and sacrifices." (*Vedic Index* i. 66). The word occurs in the Atharva-veda and the Brahmaṇas. But as the custom of receiving, feeding, and housing guests also prevailed in Ṛgvedic times, we may take it that a separate apartment was reserved for the purpose.

The sage Bharadvāja prays to Indra for the gift of a house which should be *tridhātu* and *trivarūtha*. (Rv. vi.

46, 9). Some say that it seems "as if the houses were constructed of more than one material, *i.e.*, wood, brick and stone." Griffith translates it thus: "O Indra, grant a happy home, triple refuge, triply strong." The meaning is not very clear. Has *tri* or triple been used metaphorically, or literally in the sense that three materials like brick, stone and wood, were used in the construction of the house? The latter sense seems probable. But Sāyaṇa explains *tri-dhātum* by the word *tri-bhūmikam*, i. e. three-storied, or possessing three court-yards or separate apartments. The first that was in the front was probably constructed of stones to make it sufficiently strong against the attacks of enemies or robbers, and the second and third, though constructed of different materials, were equally strong. This may be the probable meaning of the words *tri-dhātu* and *tri-varūtha*. The last word occurs again in Rv. x. 66, 5, where it probably means a house possessing three apartments, one leading to another, so as to afford adequate security to the inmates from outside attacks.

The ladies' apartments in the house were private (*guhā caranti yoṣā*, Rv. i. 167, 3). Of course, their movements were not restrained; but when they did appear before the public, or in the streets, the married ladies decently covered themselves with an outer mantle or shawl (Rv. viii. 17, 7).

The sacred fire was lighted at the time of the performance of nuptials, and it was the duty of the wife to keep it alive till her husband's death. Both the husband and wife daily poured on it libations of *havis*. The question is, if the sons were married during the life-time of their parents, where were their respective nuptial-fires kept? The mistress of the family (*gṛhapatnī*) had her own fire to attend to. Were the nuptial-fires of the sons also kept in the same *Agni-śālā* or Fire-house separately? There is mention in the Ṛgveda of the father giving to his son a strong and comfortable house to live in (Rv. i. 127, 5). Probably, the son's marriage was the occasion when such a house was given him, as it was necessary that the newly married couple should have a separate dwelling to live in. It is most likely that the sacred nuptial fire was brought to this new house or allotted room, where it was tended by the young wife. The verse above quoted would seem to indicate that Fire received oblations simultaneously with the gift of a house to his son by the father. Of course, the son's house used to be built and situated within the same compound, and father and son, and mother and daughter-in-law all lived together and messed jointly.

The fact of the gift of a house to the son at the time of his marriage seems to be further confirmed by the dictum of the sage Viśvāmitra: "The wife is the home." (*jāyedastam*, Rv. iii. 53, 4). As a matter of fact, home and home-life came into being with marriage and the advent of the wife. It should be borne in mind that the newly wedded wife in ancient India was not a mere infant as she is now. She was a young lady, with her own ideas, tastes, and predilections, and she required a separate house not only to live there with her husband, but also to tend the sacred fire, and to store her personal belongings and things, most of which were probably the gifts of her father, mother, brother and relations. Though occupying a separate house, room or rooms, she formed an inseparable member of her husband's family, and had to live with all in friendliness, peace and amity. She had to perform the common household duties, look after her little brothers-in-law and sisters-in-law, care for the comforts of her husband, father-in-law and mother-in-law, superintend the work of the servants, and keep an watchful eye over the feeding and tending of the domestic animals. She was commanded by the officiating priest and the husband at the nuptial altar to perform all these duties cheerfully in her new house, (Rv. x. 85, 43-46), and she set about to discharge them in right earnest.

In this connexion the following observations made by Prof. A. B. Keith in the *Cambridge History of India* (vol. i.

Chap. iv, p. 89) would be found interesting: "The son after marriage must often have lived in the house and under the control of his father, of whom his wife was expected to stand in awe. But, on the other hand, as the father advanced in years, it cannot have been possible for him to maintain a control which he was physically incapable of exercising; and so we find the bride enjoined to be mistress over her step-parents, doubtless in the case when her husband, grown to manhood, had taken over the management of the household from his father's failing hands."

Domestic furniture and utensils.—The furniture and utensils of the house were simple and useful. *Śikyas* or rope-brackets were hung from the roofs for storing such food in vessels as were liable to be attacked and nibbled by rats and mice (Av. ix. 3, 6). *Talpa* was the name for bed or couch (Rv. vii. 55, 8). It was made of wood, and the Taittirīya Brāhmaṇa mentions one made of Udumbara wood. *Proṣtha* was the name for a broad bench over which women lay down to sleep (Rv. vii. 55, 8), and *Vahya* meant "a couch or bed of a comfortable kind used by women." (*Ibid*) (*Vedic Index* ii. 278) The pillow or cushion was called *upa-barhaṇa* (Rv. x. 85, 7). Probably it was stuffed with silk-cotton gathered from the *śamvula* or pods of the Śalmali tree, (Rv. iii. 53, 22), or simply with wool. *Āsandī* was the name for a wooden seat or stool over which a cushion was spread. This word, however, does not occur in the Ṛgveda. There were earthen and metal vessels or jars called *kalaśa* (Rv. i. 117, 12; iii. 32, 15), wooden vessels or troughs called *droṇa* (Rv. vi. 2, 8; 37, 2; 44, 20; ix. 93, 1), skin-vessels for storing water (*bhastrā*, but not occuring in the Ṛgveda) and the Soma juice (Rv. ix. 66, 23), honey (Rv. viii. 5, 19), curd (Rv. iv. 51, 1; v. 83, 7, vi. 48, 18), and wine, called *dṛti* (Rv. i. 91, 10). Women drew water from wells in *kumbhas* which were brought home, probably well poised on their heads (Rv. i. 191. 14). *Kumbhas* were usually made of clay, baked but easily broken (Rv. x. 89, 7), and have been mentioned in several verses. (Rv. i. 116, 7; 117, 6; vii. 33, 13 etc.) The vessels were made of various materials and metals. Silver vessels as well as gourd vessels are mentioned in the Atharva-veda (viii. 10, 23. 29). Gold cups are mentioned in the Ṛgveda. *Ukha* was the name for a cooking pot, usually mentioned in connexion with sacrifice (Rv. i. 162, 13. 15; iii. 53. 22). *Sthālī* was the name for another cooking pot; but the word occurs in the Atharva-veda and the Brāhmaṇas. *Ā-secana* designated a vessel to hold liquids, such as meat-juice (*yūṣan*) (Rv. i. 162, 13). *Dṛṣad* was a flat stone to pound grain upon (Rv. vii, 104, 22; viii. 72, 4), and *Upalā* was the stone-hammer used as pestle. There were also the *Ulūkhala* and *Muṣala* (mortar and pestle) made of wood for husking grain, or pounding the Soma plant. (Rv. i. 28. 6). *Śūrpa* was the name for a wicker-work, flat fan for winnowing grain. The word occurs in the Atharva-veda. (ix. 6, 16; x. 9, 26, &c.). *Udañcana* was the name for a bucket or pail, though the word has been used metaphorically in the Ṛgveda (v. 44, 13). *Titau* was the name for the sieve (Rv. x. 71, 2). used to separate the grain from the straw and refuse. The vessel used for measuring the grain was called *Urdara* (Rv. ii. 14, 11). The word, *Sthivi*, occurring in the Ṛgveda (x. 68, 3), seems to mean a granary for storing grain, from which a desired quantity was extracted when necessary. Macdonell and Keith say that it means a 'bushel' which is a measure of corn. But this meaning is not likely. The valuables were put into boxes (*Kośa* Rv. x. 42, 2). There were also wooden chests, large in size (*Vṛkṣa*) for storing and preserving utensils and sundries. One chest was so large as to accommodate the Ṛṣi, Atri Saptavadhri, who used to be kept confined therein at night by his relatives (Rv. v. 78, 5. 6). The rich possessed a treasure-room paved with rock (*adribudhna ayamnidhi*, Rv. x. 108, 7). The treasure-house was called *Vasāvi* in the Ṛgveda (x. 73, 4). Metal or earthen jars were sometimes filled with gold and silver coins (Rv. iv. 32, 19), and buried underground for security (Rv. i 117, 12).

Besides these, there were wooden spoons, stirring sticks and spits. The *Sruc* was a large wooden sacrificial ladle used for pouring clarified butter on the fire (Rv. i. 84, 18; 110, 6; 144, 1). It was "of the length of an arm, with a bowl of the size of a hand and a beak-like spout." The *Sruva* was "a small ladle used to convey the offering (*ājya*) from the cooking pot (sthālī) to the large ladle (*juhu*). In the Ṛgveda, however, it was clearly used for the Soma libation" (i. 116, 24; 121, 6) *Dravi* was also another name for a ladle (Rv. v. 6, 9; x. 105, 10). *Nīkṣaṇa* was the name for the spit (Rv. i. 162, 13). *Adhi-ṣavaṇa* denoted the pressing board, and one board was placed upon another with the shoots of the Soma plant within for pressing out the juice (Rv. i. 28, 2). *Dhiṣaṇā* denoted a bowl or vat used in preparing the Soma (Rv. i. 96, 1; 102, 1; 109, 3. 4; iii. 49, 1; iv. 34, 1 etc.) These bowls were sometimes decorated with carvings (Av. ix. 49, 9). *Pavitra* was the name for the sieve made of sheep's wool, either woven or plaited, for straining and purifying the Soma juice (Rv. i. 28, 9; iii. 36, 7; viii. 33, 1 &c.). There were undoubtedly spinning wheels or spindles, and also looms in every house, as women wove their own cloths (Rv. i. 92, 3).

Every well-to-do householder had of course a number of servants and slaves. The Gopa or cowherd used to tend the cattle and take them out for grazing. There were servants who ploughed the lands, sowed seeds in them, and reaped the corn when ripe. There were also female servants to assist the women in the performance of their household duties. The women, besides frying grains and cooking foods, churned milk and curds, and made butter out of them (Rv. i. 28, 4). From butter, *ghee* was prepared not only for use as food, but also for pouring as libations into the sacred Fire.

The word *harmya* in the Ṛgveda denotes a house "as a unity including the stabling and so forth (Rv. vii. 56, 16; x. 106, 5), and surrounded by a fence or wall of some sort (Rv. vii. 55, 6). It is several times referred to in the Ṛgveda" (i. 121, 1; 166, 4; ix. 71, 4; 78, 3; x. 43, 3, &c.).

The *śakata* or *śakatī* denoted a cart, (Rv. x. 146, 3) and its creaking sound has been referred to (*Ibid*). Probably the wheels were of a primitive kind, having been made of thick and heavy planks rounded and joined together with a nave-hole in the middle. The *anas* was the name for the cart or the draft-wagon (Rv. iv. 30, 10; x. 85, 10; 86, 18), as opposed to the *ratha* for war or sport with which it is sometimes expressly contrasted (Rv. iii. 33, 9). The wagon is the characteristic vehicle of Uṣas, though she sometimes rides on a chariot. (Rv. ii. 15, 6; iv. 30, 11; viii. 91, 7 &c.). The bridal wagon of Sūryā had a covering (*chadis*) (Rv. x. 85, 10). We may, therefore, take it for granted that the wagon was the usual vehicle for the conveyance of ladies, and each family possessed one or two of such vehicles. The wagon was usually drawn by oxen (*anadvāh*) (Rv. x. 85, 11). The wagon of Uṣas is said to be drawn by ruddy cows or bulls. (Vide *Vedic Index* i. 21, 22).

The horses were stabled probably in a separate shed, near the cow-shed. Horses, cattle, sheep and goats formed the domestic animals of a Vedic householder. The dog also was indispensable and prevented the cattle and sheep from straying, and kept watch of the house at night. It is strange that the cat is not mentioned in the Ṛgveda.

The Presiding Deity of the house.—There are two hymns in the Ṛgveda, addressed to the God *Vastoṣpati* or the deity presiding over the *Vāstu* or house (Rv. vii. 54 & 55). The first hymn runs as follows:

"1. Protector of the dwelling, recognize us; be to us an excellent abode, the non-inflicter of disease. Whatever we ask of thee, be pleased to grant; be the bestower of happiness on our bipeds and quadrupeds.

"2. Protector of the dwelling, be our preserver and the augmenter of our wealth: possessed of cattle and horses, Indra, may we, through thy friendship, be exempt from decay; be favourable to us, like a father to his sons.

"3. Protector of the dwelling, may we be possessed of a comfortable, delightful, oppulent abode, bestowed by thee: protect our wealth, whether in possession or expectation, and do you (Gods) ever cherish us with blessings."

The God Vastoṣpati has been described as the son of Saramā, the divine bitch. This deity performs the same functions as a watch-dog does, and has in fact been identified with it in the following hymn (Rv. vii. 55), which goes to show that the dog was an indispensable animal to the Vedic householder:

"1. Protector of the dwelling, remover of disease, assuming all (kinds of) forms, be to us a friend, the granter of happiness.

"2. White offspring of Saramā, with tawny limbs, although barking thou displayest thy teeth against me, bristling like lancets in thy gums, nevertheless go quietly to sleep.

"3. Offspring of Saramā, returning (to the charge) attack the pilferer or thief. Why dost thou assail the worshippers of Indra? Why dost thou intimidate us? Go quietly to sleep.

"4. Do thou rend the hog: let the hog rend thee. Why dost thou assail the worshippers of Indra? Why dost thou intimidate us? Go quietly to sleep.

"5. Let the mother sleep, let the father sleep, let the dog sleep, let the son-in-law sleep, let all the kindred sleep, let the people (who are stationed) around sleep.

"6. The man who sits, or he who walks, or he who sees us, of these we shut up the eyes, so that they may be as unconscious as the mansion.

"7. We put men to sleep through the irresistible might of the bull with a thousand horns, who rises out of the ocean.

"8. We put to sleep all these women who are lying in the court-yard in litter or the bed, the women who are decorated with holiday perfumes."

Was the above hymn a lullaby-song, sung by a friendly nocturnal visitor who wished perfect rest and quiet sleep to all the members of the household, and freedom from molestation by thieves and pilferers? Or was it an incantation pronounced on the inmates of the house and the watch-dog by thieves so that all might go to sleep leaving them free to pursue their nefarious work? The first interpretation seems more probable, for in verse 3, the son of Saramā (the dog) is asked to return to the charge and *attack the pilferer or thief*, leaving the singer of the hymn quite unmolested and safe, as he is a worshipper of Indra. The composer of the hymn is the great sage Vasiṣṭha himself, who could not certainly be said to entertain a motive for stealing. It seems rather likely that he composed the hymn to ensure quiet sleep and peace to the householders, and went on pronouncing the *mantras*, quite unseen, though occasionally barked and snarled at by the watch-dogs. A conduct like this would be quite consistent with the highly benevolent nature of the renowned Ṛṣi of great spiritual fame.

But the scholiasts give different interpretations of the hymn. According to the *Bṛhad-devatā*, Vasiṣṭha coming by night to the house of Varuṇa intended to sleep there; but the watch-dog barking was about to lay hold of him, when he appeased the animal by this hymn. According to another story, briefly told by Sāyaṇa, and found in the *Nīti-manjarī*, "Vasiṣṭha had passed three days without being able to get any food. On the night of the fourth, he entered the house of Varuṇa to steal something to eat, and had made his way to the larder, the *koṣṭāgāra*, when the dog set upon him, but was put to sleep by these verses, wherefore they are to be recited on similar occasions by thieves and burglars." [1]

This interpretation is highly ingenious. But why should Vasiṣṭha think of stealing food, when he could get it for the mere asking, as he and Varuṇa were great friends, and he

1 Vide *Wilson's Ṛgveda (Eng. Trans.)*

constantly prayed to him for freeing him from sins? And would it not be highly incongruous for the moral and spiritual sage Vasiṣṭha to compose verses that would be used by thieves and burglars as incantations to put the whole household to sleep for the facility of their work? The interpretation put upon the verses does not, therefore, seem to be at all correct. They undoubtedly constitute a lullaby-song, mysteriously uttered to put the whole family to quiet and peaceful sleep and to keep them out of harm. Another suggestion that it was an incantation pronounced by a secret lover upon all the members of the household, including the house-dog, with a view to send them all to sleep so that he might have a free and easy access to his sweet-heart, does not seem probable. There is no mention of this object, nor of the sweet-heart in the hymn, and I take it only to be a simple lullaby-song as explained above. But it must be frankly stated here that verse 6 stands in the way of my explanation being fully accepted. Why should the nocturnal visitor think of shutting up the eyes of the man who sits or walks or sees him, and of making him as unconscious as the mansion? This is a conundrum which is difficult to solve, and must have given rise to various suggestive explanations, none of which, however, seems satisfactory. Does it connote a belief that the power of the incantation would be nullified if the enchanter was seen by any mortal?

CHAPTER V.

FOOD, DRINK, DRESS, SPORTS AND AMUSEMENTS OF THE VEDIC ARYANS.

Food and Drink.—The principal food of the Vedic Aryans consisted of barley-flour and its various preparations, rice and other cereals, fruits, flesh of animals like goats, sheep, cows, oxen, deer, buffaloes and sometimes horses also, honey, clarified butter or *ghee*, curds and other preparations of milk. Their drink consisted of milk, the Soma juice and wines, besides other beverages.

Yava and Dhānya.—*Yava* or barley is frequently mentioned in the Ṛgveda (i. 23, 15; 135, 8; ii. 5, 6; 14, 11; v. 85, 3, &c.) But according to Böhtlingk and Roth's Lexicon, it denoted corn in general. I am, however, not in agreement with this view. *Yava* meant 'barley' and was regularly cultivated by the Vedic Aryans as a principal food grain. (Rv. 1. 23, 15). The verse says that as one who ploughs with steers brings or produces barley, so may Pūṣan bring the six seasons bound closely, through the Soma drops being offered to him. The metaphor does not imply that the corn, known as *yava*, was cultivated in all the six seasons, but it simply means that as surely as ploughing with the help of steers brings forth the crop of barley, so the offering of the Soma juice to the God brings the six seasons regularly and consecutively. That barley throve well when the land was moistened by a shower of rain (probably in winter) has been mentioned in two verses (Rv. ii. 5, 6; v. 85, 3). The other food-grains may have been included under the general appellation of *yava*, the principal food-grain of those times, as the word *dhānya* in a later age implied not only rice or *dhānya*, the principal food grain, but also all other food-grains. But it would be a mistake to suppose that these grains did not exist in Ṛgvedic times and were not cultivated. Even to this day, no worship of the Gods can be performed without *yava*, as it was primarily the grain that was offered to the Gods in early Ṛgvedic times. The same remark holds good with regard to *dhānya* also. This word occurs in Rv. v. 53, 13; vi. 13, 4; and x 94, 13. Another word *dhānā* (always used in the plural) occurs in several verses in the sense of "grains of corn" (Rv. i. 16, 2; iii. 35.3; 52, 5; vi. 29, 4), and in some verses, according to Sāyaṇa, in the sense of "fried barley." But the word *dhānya* cannot but mean the grain of that name, meaning rice. Barley and rice were the two staple crops that were cultivated by the Ṛgvedic Aryans, one in winter or spring, and the other during the rainy season. The word *vrīhi* in the sense of "rice" does not occur in the Ṛgveda; but the word *dhānya* makes up for its absence. It may be that, as the climate of the Punjab was extremely cold in Ṛgvedic times, the cultivation of barley was more successful and yielded bumper crops than that of rice, but it does not follow from this that rice (*dhānya*) was not known nor cultivated by the Ṛgvedic Aryans. Why should the words *yava* and *dhānya* be used to denote grains in general, if there was no distinction between the two? And if there were grains of various kinds, what were their distinctive names? Further, why should not *yava* (barley) and *dhānya* (rice) be included among these grains? The real fact seems to be that as these two kinds of grains formed the staple food-grains, they have been used in the Ṛgveda not only to denote the grains of these names, but also sometimes to include all other grains of minor importance. This, in my opinion, is the most rational view to take of the matter.

Various preparations of food.—As the word *godhūma* or wheat does not occur in the Ṛgveda, we may take it that it was not known in Ṛgvedic times. The principal meals were, therefore, prepared from barley and rice. *Karambha* was a kind of porridge made of fried barley-flour, mixed with curd or ghee. It was offered to Pūṣan, the pastoral God of the Aryans, and may, therefore, be taken as one of their early prepared foods. (Rv. i. 187, 16; iii. 52, 7; vi. 56, 1; 57, 2; viii. 102, 2). *Apūpa* was a kind of cake made of barley or rice, mixed with *ghee* (Rv. iii. 52, 7; x. 45, 9). *Odana* was the name for a mess, usually of grain cooked with milk. (*Kṣīraudana*, Rv. viii. 69, 14; 77, 10). Special varieties are mentioned in the later literature, such as the curd-mess (*dadhy-odana*), the bean-mess (*mudgaudana*), the meat-mess (*māṃsaudana*) &c. *Pakti* was also the name for a kind of cake (Rv. iv. 24, 5; 25, 6. 7; vi. 29, 4). All cooked food was called *pakva* (Rv. vi. 63, 9). *Pacata* also denoted cooked food in the Ṛgveda (i. 61, 7; x. 116, 8).

Milk and its various preparations were also used as food. From the fact that each family possessed a number of cows, and the gift of cows was eagerly sought for by the Ṛṣis, it can be easily surmised that the Vedic Aryans were extremely fond of milk, especially cow's milk It is called *payas* in the Ṛgveda. (i. 164, 28; ii. 14, 10; iv. 3, 9; v. 85, 2; x. 30, 13). Each family must have had an abundant supply of it, as grain cooked with milk (*Kṣīraudana*) formed a favourite dish. *Dadhi* was the name for sour milk and curd (Rv. viii. 2, 9; ix. 87, 1). It was used for mixing with Soma, and *dadhyāśir* (mixed with sour milk or curd) is an epithet of Soma in the Ṛgveda (i. 5, 5; 137, 2; v. 51, 7; viii. 32, 4). It was also mixed with barley-flour for preparing *karambha*. Milk and curd were churned, and *manthā* was the name for a churn (Rv. i. 28, 4). Butter was produced by churning, and *ghṛta* was made from it by melting it on fire. *Ghṛta* is repeatedly mentioned in the Ṛgveda (i 134, 6; ii. 10, 4; iv. 10, 6; 58, 5. 7. 9; v. 12, 1). It was poured on the sacrificial Fire; hence Agni is styled 'butter-faced' (*ghṛta-pratīka* Rv. i. 143, 7; iii. 1, 18), 'butter-backed' (*ghṛta-pṛṣṭha*) (Rv. i. 164, 1; v. 4, 3 &c.) and 'propitiated with butter' (*ghṛta-prasatta*, Rv. v. 15, 1). Whey was called *manthā*, and drunk as a beverage. The word *manthā* in the Ṛgveda (x. 86; 15) also "denotes a drink in which solid ingredients are mixed with a fluid by stirring, usually parched barley-meal (*śaktu*) with milk." (*Ved. Ind.* ii. 131) *Śaktu* in the Ṛgveda (x. 71, 2) probably means groats as opposed to fine meal, according to Macdonell and Keith.

Meat-eating.—Māṃsa or flesh was a regular food of the Vedic Aryans. Considering the fact that they had been a pastoral people before they settled down as agriculturists, and that the climate was extremely cold in Ṛgvedic times, as the year was called *Hima* on account of the predominance of cold-weather conditions throughout the greater part of the year (Rv. i. 64, 10; ii. 1, 11; 32, 2; v. 54, 15; vi. 10, 7; 48, 8.), one need not be surprised that flesh of animals formed a principal item of their food. Goats, sheep, cows and buffaloes were slaughtered for food and at sacrifices, and their flesh offered to the Gods. Agni is called "eater of ox and cow" in the Ṛgveda (viii. 43, 11). The sage Bharadvāja prayed to Indra to grant him and his worshippers food with "go" or the cow as the principal item.[1] (Rv. vi. 39, 1). In the Śatapatha Brāhmaṇa (iii. 4, i. 2), the slaying of a 'great ox' *(mahokṣa)*, or a 'great goat' *(mahāja)* for the entertainment of a distinguished guest has been enjoined. In the *Aitareya Brāhmaṇa* (i.3, 4) there is a passage which distinctly says that when the king or a respected person comes as a guest, one should kill a bull or *Vehat* (i.e. old barren cow) for his entertainment. The great sage Yājñavalkya also expresses a similar view (*Vāj.* i. 109). He was "wont to eat the meat of milch-cows and bullocks (*dehnvanaduha*), if only it was *aṃsala* i.e. 'firm' or 'tender'" (Śat. Brā. iii. 1, 2, 21).[2] Bulls were sacrificed to Indra who was fond of eating their cooked flesh (Rv. x. 27, 2; 86, 13, 14). There was an appointed place for slaughtering bulls and cows (Rv. x. 89, 14). Bulls, cows, and barren cows were slaughtered, and their flesh

---

1 For a different interpretation of this passage see *infra* chap. vi.

2 *Vedic Index* ii. 145

offered as *habya* to Agni (Rv. ii. 27, 5; vi. 16, 47). Buffaloes also were sacrificed to Indra, and their flesh cooked and partaken of by his votaries after having been offered to him. The number of these victims sometimes varied from 100 to 300 (Rv. v. 29, 7. 8; vi. 17, 11). "The ritual of the cremation of the dead required the slaughter of a cow as an essential part, the flesh being used to envelope the dead body." (Rv. x. 16, 7).[1] The horse also was slaughtered at sacrifices, but only occasionally and rarely, the performance of the sacrifice having been very expensive. The flesh was cooked and offered to the Gods, (Rv. i. 162, 3. 10. 11), both roasted (Rv. i. 162, 11) and boiled (Rv. i. 162, 13), and the worshippers and others partook of the meat and juice with great relish. (Rv. i. 162, 12). During the epic period also buffalo-meat was used as food by respectable people and the meat-stalls were crowded with customers.[2] The Mahābhārata refers to an ancient king, named Rantideva, for whose kitchen 2000 cows were daily slaughtered and who acquired great renown by distributing the cooked meat and rice among hungry people.[3] It is said that even down to the time of the Buddha who preached *ahiṃsā* or good will to all living creatures, meat-eating was a prevailing custom, and if some Western scholars are to be credited, the Buddha himself died from a meal of pork, though this view has also been contradicted.[4]

From the above account, it would appear that the Vedic Aryans had no objection to take beef &c. Though the custom of sacrificing cows and bulls continued down to the later Vedic period, even in Ṛgvedic times there seemed to have grown up a revulsion of feeling against the custom. The cow was gradually "acquiring a special sanctity, as is shown by the name *aghnyā* (not to be slain) applied to it in several

---

[1] *Ibid* ii. 147.

[2] *Maaābhārata* (*vanaparva*) ch. 205 Cf. also *Harivamša* (chaps. 146-147).

[3] *Mahābhārata* (*Vana.*) ch. 206 verses 10 and 11.

[4] Fleet, J. R. A. S. (1906) 881-82; Oldenberg. *Buddha* 231, n. 2.

passages." (*Ved. Ind.* ii. 146). The word occurs sixteen times in the Ṛgveda, as opposed to three instances of *aghnya* (masculine). It would thus appear that there was a school of thinkers among the Ṛṣis who set their face against the barbarous custom of killing such useful animals as the cow and the bull. The protest they raised gradually increased in volume till the custom was totally abolished in a later age. The change of climate from cold to hot may also have made the use of beef as food quite unnecessary, and even injurious to health. The flesh of goat and sheep, however, continued to be a principal article of food. Fish does not appear to have been used as food by the Vedic Aryans, though it is mentioned in the Ṛgveda (vii. 18, 6; x. 68, 8), and there is reference to fish being caught in nets (Rv. viii. 67). Probably it was eaten by the lower classes.

The word *śva-ghnin* occurs in the Ṛgveda in the sense of 'hunter' as well as 'gamester' or 'professional gambler,' (i, 92, 10; ii, 12, 4; iv, 20, 3; viii, 45, 38). In a verse (i, 92, 10) it is said that the *śva-ghnī* used to cut down or break the wings of a bird to prevent it from flying away. The term, therefore, included bird-catchers also, who caught birds like partridges, &c., for their flesh to be used as food. Hunters probably killed hares and deer with the object of selling their flesh as food.

Fruits.—Fruits also were eaten, but whether orchards were cultivated is not clear. The forests contained many edible fruits (Rv. x. 146, 5. 6). The translation of the two verses just referred to is as follows: "Araṇyānī (the presiding goddess of the forest) is not (herself) murderous—if no one else assails—but after eating of sweet fruits a man rests there at his pleasure. I laud Araṇyānī, the mother of wild beasts, the unctuous-scented, the fragrant, who yields abundance of food, though she has no hinds to till her" (Muir). In another verse (Rv. iii. 45, 4) "Indra is asked to shower satisfying wealth on his adorers, as a man with a hook shakes down ripe fruits from a tree." (Muir, O. S. T. v. 107). We do not, however, come across the names of any fruits. The berries of the Aśvattha (*ficus religiosa*) are referred to as sweet, and as eaten by birds (Rv. i. 164, 20). Probably the forests were full of wild berries of different species, jujubes, nuts and other kinds of fruits. "Plants (*oṣadhi*, *vīrudh*) are frequently alluded to and are even invoked (Rv. vi. 49, 14; vii. 34, 23; 35, 5; x. 97, 1 ff.), where some of them are spoken of as produced three ages before the gods." (Muir O. S. T. v. 463). They are said to be divine (Rv. x. 97, 4); some of them were flowering and productive and fruit-bearing, but others were not (Rv. x. 97, 5. 15); while some again drove away disease (verse 16), i.e., medicines were prepared from them. There is reference in the Ṛgveda to diggers of lotus-stems (Rv. vi. 61, 2), which probably were also used as food.

From the above account it would appear that the food of the Vedic Aryans was simple, clean, wholesome and substantial. It consisted of barley-flour, rice, milk and its various preparations, flesh of animals, fruits and roots. Honey (*madhu*) was also used with food and drink (Rv. i. 19, 9; 154, 4; ii. 19, 2; 37, 5; iii 8, 1; 39, 6; 43, 3; iv. 38, 10; vii. 24, 2 &c.) in order to sweeten them. From the profusion of sweet-scented flowers in the forests, bee-hives must have been plentiful and the supply of honey abundant. There is mention of *ikṣu* or sugar-cane in the Ṛgveda (ix. 86, 18). Probably it was cultivated, and its juice squeezed out for drink, or made into liquid molasses by heating on fire. Whether sugar was manufactured cannot be ascertained, as the word *śarkarā* does not occur in the Ṛgveda. It is curious that there is no mention of *lavaṇa* (salt) in the Ṛgveda. Macdonell and Keith observe: "This silence (about *lavaṇa*) in the early period is somewhat surprising, if the regions then occupied by the Indians were the Punjab and the Indus valley where salt abounds . . . It is, however, quite concievable that a necessary commodity might happen to be passed over without literary mention in a region where it is very common, but to be referred to in a locality where it is not found, and consequently becomes highly prized." (*Vedic Index* ii. 230). In the *Chāndogya Upaniṣad* it seems to be placed above gold in value (iv. 17, 7), probably because it was not available in the region where the Upaniṣad was composed. From the absence of any mention of salt in the Ṛgveda, some European scholars have come to the conclusion that salt was not used by the ancient Aryans in the preparation of their food. But this, as Macdonell has observed, "is a good illustration of the dangers of *argumentum ex silencio*."[1] The existence of seas near the Punjab, and of the Salt Range in the very heart of the country precludes a supposition like that from being at all probable.

Hymn to Food.—I cannot resist the temptation of quoting here in full the translation of a hymn (Rv. i. 187), addressed to *Pitu* which, in the Ṛgveda "has the general sense of nutriment, whether food or drink."[2]

"1. Now will I glorify Food that upholds great strength, by whose invigorating power Trita rent Vṛtra limb from limb.

2. O pleasant Food, O Food of meath, thee have we chosen for our own; so be our kind protector thou.

3. Come hitherward to us, O Food, auspicious with auspicious help, health-bringing, not unkind, a dear and guileless friend.

4. These juices which, O Food, are thine throughout the regions are diffused. Like winds they have their place in heaven.

5. These gifts of thine, O Food, O Food, most sweet to taste, these savours of thy juices work like creatures that have mighty necks.

6. In thee, O Food, is set the spirit of great Gods. Under thy flag brave deeds were done: he slew the dragon with thy help.

---

[1] Macdonell, *History of Sanskrit Literature* 105 Das, *Ṛgvedic India* 88.

[2] *Vedic Index*. 1. 526,

7. If thou be gone unto the splendour of the clouds, even from thence, O Food of meath, prepared for our enjoyment come.

8. Whatever morsel we consume from waters or from plants of earth, O Soma, wax thou fat thereby.

9. What, Soma, we enjoy from thee in milky food or barley-brew, Vātāpi,[1] grow thou fat thereby.

10. O Vegetable, cake of meal, be wholesome, firm and strengthening: Vātāpi, grow thou fat thereby. O Food, from thee as such have we drawn forth with lauds, like cows, our sacrificial gifts, from thee who banquetest with us." (Griffith).

Drinks: Soma and Surā.—The principal drinks of the Vedic Aryans were Soma and Sura. The Soma plant grew on the mountains, that of the Mujavant being specially renowned (Rv. i. 93, 6; iii. 48, 2; v. 36, 2; 43, 4; 85, 2; ix. 1, 18 &c.). "The plant was prepared for use by being pounded with stones or in a mortar. The former was the normal method of procedure, appearing in the Ṛgveda as the usual one. The stones are called *grāvan* (Rv. i. 83, 6; 135, 7) or *adri* (Rv. i. 130, 2; 135, 5), and were of course held in the hands (Rv. v. 45, 7; ix. 11, 5). ...Sometimes the mortar and pestle were used in place of stones." (*Ved. Ind.* ii. 476). Then the women squeezed the juice out with their fingers (Rv. ix, 67, 8). The juice was afterwards mixed with water, and strained through a sieve made of sheep's wool, which was placed over a *kalaśa*, by stirring it with the fingers. (Rv. ix. 67, 9-12). Thus strained and purified, the juice was mixed with milk or curd and sometimes honey (Rv. ix. 103, 3) and offered to the Gods, and drunk by the worshippers. At first it was the usage to offer the unmixed juice (*śukra, śuci*) to Indra and Vāyu (Rv. i. 137, 1; iii. 32, 2; viii. 2, 9. 10), but this usage was afterwards dropped by the Kaṇvas (Rv.

[1] According to Sāyaṇa, Vātāpi means 'the body.' Griffith thinks, it refers to the fermenting Soma. I accept Sāyaṇa's interpretation.

viii. 2, 5. 9. 10. 28 &c.). It was a favourite drink of the Gods as well as of their votaries. The whole of the Ninth Maṇḍala of the Ṛgveda, and six hymns in other Maṇḍalas are devoted to its praise.

The colour of the juice is described as brown (*babhru*, Rv. ix. 33, 2; 63, 4. 6), tawny, (*hari*, Rv. ix. 3. 9; 7, 6, etc.) or ruddy (*aruṇa*, Rv. ix. 40, 2; 45, 3; *aruṣa*, ix. 61, 21), and its smell fragrant (Rv. ix. 97, 19 107, 2). The juice, as already referred to, was mixed with milk (*gavāśir*), curd or sour milk (*dadhyāśir*) or grain (*yavāśir*).[1] The effect of the drink on the consumers was exhilarating and exciting (Rv. viii. 48). A Ṛṣi exultantly says: "We will drink the Soma, and become immortal; and then we will go to the resplendant heaven, and there be acquainted with the Gods." (Rv. viii. 48, 3). It enabled men to concentrate their mind, made them active, cured their diseases and preserved their characters (Rv. viii. 48, 5). It was also believed to prolong their lives (Rv. viii. 48, 11). But it also had an inebriating effect on the consumers, when probably taken in copious and repeated draughts, ultimately inducing sleep (Rv. ix. 69, 6) and was compared with *mada* or wine (Rv. ix. 68, 3; 69, 3). When singing the praise of Soma, certain Ṛṣis made apparently incoherent prayers for winning beautiful damsels, doubtless the result of an over dose of the drink (Rv. ix. 67, 10. 11. 12). On the eve of a battle, it seems to have been a custom with the warriors to divide the Soma among themselves and drink it, probably for excitement and exhilaration (Rv. ix. 106, 2). Seven women used to squeeze the Soma with their fingers, and sing a song in its praise during the process (Rv. ix. 66, 8).

Surā was the name of an intoxicating spirituous liquor. It has been generally condemned in the Ṛgveda, as, under its influence, men committed sins and crimes (Rv. vii. 86, 6), and became devoid of sense, and drunken (Rv. viii. 2, 12; 21, 14). It has been classed with dicing as an evil (Rv. vii.

---

[1] Hillebrandt *Vedische Mythologie*. i, 219-222.

86, 6). "It was the drink of men in the Sabhā, and gave rise to broils" (*Ved. Ind.* ii. 458). How was it prepared cannot be ascertained. "It may have been a strong spirit prepared from fermented grains and plants, as Eggeling holds or, as Whitney thought, a kind of beer or ale. Geldner renders it 'brandy'." (*Ved. Ind.* ii. 458-59). It was usually kept in skin-vessels, (dṛti, Rv. i. 191, 10). According to the *Taittirīya* Brāhmaṇa, "it was, as opposed to Soma, essentially a drink of ordinary life" (*Ved. Ind.* ii. 458).

Pānta was the name of another drink or beverage in the Ṛgveda (i. 122, 1; 155, 1; vii. 92, 1; x. 88, 1). As it was offered to the Gods, it has been identified by commentators with Soma. But it may have been a drink of a different kind.

Dress.—The skin seems to be the original clothing of the Aryans in primitive times. It was the skin of an animal, a gazelle or goat, that was used as a covering of the human body (Av. v. 21, 7; Śat. Brā. v. 2, 1, 21, 24). The word *ajina* is derived from *aja*, a goat, and the adjective *ajina-vāsin*, 'clothed in skins' denotes the use of skins as clothing (*Śat. Brā.* iii. 9, 1, 12). In the Ṛgveda the Maruts are described as wearing deer-skins (1. 166, 10), and the Munis or ascetics seem to be clad in skins (x 136, 2). The word *mala*, occurring in this verse, has been interpreted in the St. Petersburg Dictionary to mean a 'leathern garment,' being derived from the root *mlā*, to tan. But Ludwig and Zimmer think, it means only a 'soiled garment,' (*Alt. Laben.* 262), which was probably consistent with the character of the hermits.[1] But considering the fact that a very cold climate prevailed in ancient times in the Punjab, we may take it for granted that the soft skins of animals were used as clothing or wraps by the primitive inhabitants. In a *Vālakhilya* hymn, the Ṛṣi Kṛśa praises King Praskaṇva for giving him a hundred white oxen, a hundred bamboos, a hundred dogs, *a hundred dressed hides*, a hundred bunches of *balbaja* grass,

1 *Vedic Index* i, 14, ii, 137.

and four hundred red mares (7, 2-3). The hundred dressed hides must have been meant as materials to make suitable garments from. Even to this day, we find the Tibetans who live on a high and cold plateau use skin-garments for the protection of their bodies. The savages living in hot climate use no clothing, but daub their bodies (like the Andamanese) with mud, or hang bunches of leaves or grass round their waists, like the Juangs of Orissa and the aborigines of Australia. The word *vastra* probably originally meant the skin which protects the *vasā* or fat, and afterwards came to mean a covering or clothing. In the Aitareya Brāhmaṇa (i. 1, 3) we find that a man who had to be initiated in a sacrifice was covered up with a *vastra*, over which the skin of a black buck (*kṛṣṇājina*) was thrown. The author of the *Brāhmaṇa* says that the *vastra* represented the covering of the foetus, and the skin represented the uterus, and the initiate was thus covered up with a view to symbolise his new spiritual birth. This may be true, but the use of the skin-covering may also have reference to the very ancient habit of putting on deer-skins which formed the principal clothing of the people, and the man who was to have been initiated had to put it on in deference to old custom.

We are strengthened in our surmise by the existence of another custom which the initiate had to observe. He had to live in a bamboo hut, specially made for the purpose, and called *prāgvaṃśa*. This undoubtedly points to the time when bamboo huts only were used as abodes by the ancient Aryans. Another curious custom is referred to in the *Śatapatha Brāhmaṇa* (v. 2, 1, 8). The wife of the sacrificer had to wear a garment of *kuśa* grass at the consecration. Of course such dresses were not normally worn, but were relics of a by-gone age when probably grass clothes were used. The conditions that had prevailed in the olden days, when a new custom was first introduced, were carefully remembered, and repeated and reproduced afterwards as far as possible in order to attach sanctity to it. This was probably the reason why a buck-skin had to be thrown over a man as his covering at the time of initiating him in sacrifice. and the wife of the sacrificer had to put on a garment of *kuśa* grass at the sacrifice even in the later ages, when the necessity for their use no longer existed.

During the time of the composition of the Ṛgvedic hymns, the Aryans had greatly advanced in civilisation, and learnt the process of manufacturing cloths from sheep's wool. Their garments mainly consisted of woolen clothes, showing that the climate was still very cold and necessitated the use of warm clothing. *Vāsas* is the most usual word in the Ṛgveda for clothing (i. 34, 1; 115, 4; 162, 16; viii. 3, 24; x. 26, 6 etc.) and the God Pūṣan was called "a weaver of garments" (*Vāso-vāya* x. 26, 6). My surmise is that the process of weaving cloth from sheep's wool was learnt by the Aryans in their pastoral stage, when Pūṣan was their leading God. *Ūrṇā* or wool is very frequently mentioned in the Ṛgveda (iv. 22, 2; v. 52, 9). The Paruṣṇī country and the banks of the Sindhu or the Indus were famous for their wool, (Rv. x. 75, 8), as Gandhara was famous for its sheep, (Rv. i. 126, 7). The Sindhu country was called *Suvāsā* (the producer of beautiful cloths) and *ūrṇāvatī* (the producer of wool). The term for the separate tufts was *parvan* (Rv. iv. 22, 10), or *parus* (Rv. ix. 15, 6), and the epithet 'soft as wool' (*ūrṇā-mradas*) is not rare. (Rv. v. 5, 4; x. 18, 10). The word *ūrṇā* was not restricted to the sense of sheep's wool, but might denote goat's hair also. [1]

"The garments worn were often embroidered, and the Maruts are described as wearing mantles adorned with gold." (Rv. v. 55, 6, *hiranmayān atkān*). [2] Varuṇa also is described as wearing a golden garment. (Rv. i. 25, 13). *Peśas* in the Ṛgveda "denotes an embroidered garment (ii. 3, 6; iv. 36, 7; vii. 34, 11; 42, 1), such as a female dancer would wear.

---

1 *Vedic Index* i. 106.

2 *Ibid*, ii. 291.

(Rv. i. 92, 4. 5). The fondness of the Indians for such raiment is noted by Megasthenes (see *Strabo*, P. 509) and by Arrian (*Indica*, 5, 9.)...So in one passage (Rv. x. 1, 6) a garment (*vastra*) is called *peśana*, with which Roth happily compares the Roman *vestis coloribus intexta*. The making of such garments was a regular occupation of women, as is indicated by the Peśaskarī, the female-embroiderer, figuring in the list of victims at the Puruṣamedha (human sacrifice) in the Yajurveda."[1] The *Taittirīya Brāhmaṇa* interprets the word as 'wife of a maker of gold.' Probably the garments were made of brocades, embroidered with threads of gold by the wife of the goldsmith.

Women were fond of dressing themselves well so as to be attractive to their husbands (Rv. iv. 3, 2; x. 71, 4; 107, 9). The garments were well-made and elegant. (Rv. iii. 39, 2); v. 29, 15.) What were the forms of the male and female costumes, it is very difficult to ascertain. Muir says: "The form of the garments was probably much the same as among the modern Hindus, unless it be that some innovations may have been introduced by the Mahomedans" (O. S. T. v. 462). The Mahomedans may have introduced certain changes in the dress of the civilians; but the Hindus from their conservative instincts must have adhered to the ancient form of their sacrificial garments for the purpose of performing religious ceremonies. We may, therefore, take it that there has been practically no change in the sacrificial garments, excepting perhaps what has been absolutely necessary on account of a change of climate. Macdonell and Keith observe on the point as follows: "The Vedic Indian seems often to have worn three garments—an undergarment (*nivi*), a garment, and an over-garment (*adhivāsa* Rv. i. 140, 9; 162, 16; x. 5, 4) which was probably a mantle, and for which the names *atka* and *drāpi* also seem to be used. This accords with the description of the sacrificial garments given in the Śatapatha

[1] *Vedic Index* ii, 22.

Brāhmaṇa which comprises a *tārpya* perhaps a 'silken undergarment'; secondly, a garment of undyed wool, and then a mantle, while the ends of the turban, after being tied behind the neck, are brought forward and tucked away in front...A similar sort of garments in the case of women appears to be alluded to in the Atharva-veda (viii. 2, 16; xiv. 2, 50) and the Śatapatha Brāhmaṇa (v. 2, 1, 8). There is nothing to show exactly what differences there were between male and female costumes, nor what was exactly the nature of the clothes in either case." [1]

Male and Female costumes.—There were, of course, differences between the two costumes, though they have not been clearly indicated in the Ṛgveda, as there was no necessity for doing so. But they seem to have been suggested in the Śatapatha Brāhmaṇa (i. 2, 4, 13). The female costume consisted of a *nivi* or undergarment, bound in a knot below the navel, over which a garment or cloth was worn in the shape of a skirt or petti-coat, and the whole body was covered by a scarf-mantle or shawl. The male costume consisted of an undergarment, also called *nivi*, which consisted of a piece of cloth wound round the waist, the ends passing between the legs, and tucked up behind, the whole forming something like shorts (*kaupīna*), over which a garment was worn much like a *dhoti* of the present day, and the body was covered by a mantle or scarf. The lower parts of the body immediately below the navel was regarded as unclean (*a-medhya*), and had to be completely covered up from view of the objects of the sacrifice. The wife of the sacrificer, who also took an active part in the sacrifice, wearing as she did a skirt or a cloth arranged like a skirt or petti-coat, could not cover up the "unclean" parts of her body completely from view of the objects of sacrifice lying scattered below on the altar, as her husband did by means of his underclothing; and hence a device was resorted to for yoking her to the sacrifice, as it

[1] *Vedic Index* ii, 292.

were, by means of a triple-plaited rope made of *munja* grass, which was passed round her waist below the navel over her garment, in the shape of a belt (*rāsnā* or *mekhalā*) by the priest known as Agnidhra. The lady thus "yoked" had to sit down near the altar at her appointed place till the termination of the sacrifice, so that the *ājya* or the clarified butter, specially appropriate to the Gods, was visible only to the upper or clean parts of her body. A device like this would not certainly have been necessitated or resorted to, if she had worn breeches or trousers, or worn the *nivi* in the manner of the males. The common female dress, therefore, consisted of a garment worn in the shape of a skirt over the underwear called *nivi*, and a scarf or mantle covering the upper part of the body including the head, and reaching down to the knees or ankles. Whether she wore any head-gear or veil is not very clear. But, considering the severity of the cold climate in ancient Sapta-Sindhu, we may surmise that she wore something like a turban on her head, which was probably of a dainty shape. It is still a custom among the Hindu women of the cis-Sutlej states in the hills to put on dainty turbans on their heads, with no veils over their faces. They look exceedingly pretty in their head-gears, and have very likely preserved the ancient custom. Probably no such turbans were worn at home, as women have been described in the Ṛgveda as appearing with plaits of hairs dangling over their backs (Rv. x. 114, 3). Of course, this does not necessarily imply that they wore no turbans at home. But these were indispensable on ceremonial occasions. Even in Bengal which has discarded head-gears both in the case of males and females, the bridegroom and the bride have to put on special crowns on the occasion of the performance of their nuptials, which is probably a relic of the old custom. The images of the goddesses are still made with special female crowns on their heads, which goes to show that it was a custom among women in ancient India to put on head-dresses.

Ornaments.—Both men and women were fond of wearing ornaments in Ṛgvedic times, though, of course, there were probably some differences in the make of men's and women's ornaments. *Niṣka* is frequently mentioned in the Ṛgveda (ii. 33, 10; viii. 47, 15) as a golden ornament worn on the neck, as is shown by the epithet *niṣka-grīva* (Rv. v. 19, 3). As *niṣkas* were also used as coins, we may guess that they were either of round or square shape and strung together as neck-ornaments. Even to this day, gold coins are strung together and worn on the neck both by men and women in India. *Rukma* was another golden ornament in the shape of a plate or disk worn on the breast (Rv. i. 166, 10; iv. 10, 5; v. 53, 4; viii. 20, 11 &c.), and hung from the neck by a cord which was called *rukma-pāśa* (Śat. Brā. vi. 7, 1, 7, 27; 3. 8, &c.). The epithet *rukma-vakṣas*, 'wearing golden ornaments on the breast,' frequently occurs in the Ṛgveda (ii. 34, 2. 8; v. 55, 1; 57, 5 etc.) The *rukma* appears to have been an ornament for the males, as the Maruts or Wind-gods are described as decorated with it (Rv. v. 54, 11). The women wore golden necklets or neck-chains, or pearl-necklaces, as pearls are mentioned in the Ṛgveda (i. 35, 4; x. 68. 1). The *Sraj* was a garland, ordinarily worn by men, and made either of flowers or golden lace wrought into flowers. (Rv. iv. 38, 6; v. 53, 4; viii. 47, 15). The maker of the *niṣka* and the garland-maker have been mentioned in the same verse as troubled with evil dreams (Rv. viii. 47, 15). They had to execute orders on specified dates and for specified occasions, and as the process of making golden ornaments was necessarily slow and tedious, they were naturally much troubled with anxiety till the orders were duly executed. *Khādi* was either a golden anklet worn both by men and women (Rv. v. 54, 11; 53, 4), or an armlet worn on the arm or wrist like a bangle (Rv. i. 166, 9; vii. 56, 13). It also sometimes signified a ring on the hand (*khādihasta* v. 58, 2). Golden ornaments for the ear (pendants or ear-rings) are also mentioned in the Ṛgveda (viii. 78, 3). They were called *karṇaśobhana*.

Pearls and precious stones are frequently mentioned in the Ṛgveda. Pearls (*kṛśana*) must have been available in large quantities in ancient Sapta-Sindhu, as they are "mentioned as adorning the car of Savitṛ (Rv. i. 35, 4), as well as being used for the adornment of a horse (Rv. x 68, 1). Hence the horse is spoken of as the 'pearled one' (*kṛśanavant* Rv. i. 126, 4)" When pearls were so abundant as to be used for the adornment of a horse, there can be no doubt that they were largely used both by men and women for the adornment of their persons. There is also mention of *maṇis* or jewels (Rv. i. 33, 8), and the followers of Vṛtra are said to have been adorned with jewels. (*Maṇinā śumbhamānāh*) Rv. i. 33, 8). The *maṇi* was also worn round the neck, for in the Ṛgveda (i. 122, 14) occurs the epithet *maṇi-grīva*, 'having a jewel on the neck.' The bridegroom generally adorned his person with golden ornaments, and used scented water or paste as toilette (Rv. v. 60, 4).

Coiffure.—The women dressed their hair in braids (*kaparda*). Sometimes it was woven into four braids which dangled behind on the back. (Rv. x. 114, 3). The word *opaśa* occurs in the Ṛgveda (x. 85, 8; i. 173, 6; viii. 14, 5; ix. 71, 1) and "probably means a 'plait' as used in dressing the hair, especially of women, but apparently in earlier times of men also. The goddess Sinivālī is called Svaupaśā (Rv. i. 173, 6; viii. 14, 5), an epithet of doubtful sense, from which Zimmer[1] conjectures that the wearing of false plaits of hair was not unknown in Vedic times."[2] The conjecture does not seem to be warranted, for the epithet may simply mean that the Goddess wore the plaits in a graceful manner, which highly became her. The epithet *pṛthu-stuka* (Rv. x. 86, 8) meant 'having broad braids,' as the epithet *viṣita-stuka* (Rv. i. 167, 5), applied to Rodasī, meant 'having

[1] *Alt. Leben*, p. 264.

[2] *Ved. Ind.* i. 124-125.

loosened braids.' Geldner[1] thinks that the original meaning of *opaśa* was 'horn.' If this be correct, we may take it that the word implied that the hair after being braided was coiled up in the shape of a horn over the forehead.

Dr. Rajendra Lala Mitra in his *Indo-Aryans* Vol. I gives some drawings from the ancient sculptures of Orissa of the various forms of coiffure in vogue among Indian women more than twelve hundred years ago.[2] Though they were "thought the most attractive and elegant" at the time, some of them appear to us now to be very grotesque and fantastic. As fashion is always changing, though it repeats itself at long intervals, it would be extremely difficult from the meagre description in the Ṛgveda to give an adequate idea of the forms of coiffure fashionable among women in the Vedic age. For example, the word *kurīra* occurs in the wedding hymn of the Ṛgveda (x. 85,8) in connexion with the description of the bride's adornment, and denotes "some sort of female head-ornament." According to Geldner,[3] the word *kurīrin* in the Atharva-veda (v. 31, 2) meant 'a crested animal,' perhaps as Zimmer[4] suggests, the 'peacock.' The word *kurīra*, therefore, probably meant a form of coiffure in which the hair was braided into erect crests. We find drawings in Dr. Mitra's *Indo-Aryans* (Vol. I. pp. 216, 217) of two figures of goddesses, in which the hair appears to have been braided and twisted into rays. In one drawing, "the braids are twisted into six rays, and kept in an erect position by waxing and enclosing sticks or wire within them. A fringe of short hair covers the brow, and on it is placed a triangular tiara with a crest;" in the other, "the rays are greatly multiplied and arranged in a double row, and the tiara is provided with three crests." "In the Yajurveda Samhitā, the goddess Sinīvālī is described by the epithets *Su-kapardā*,

---

1 *Vedische Studien* 1. 131.

2 *Indo-Aryans* Vol. 1. pp. 212-217.

3 *Vedische Studien*, 1. pp. 131, 132.

4 *Alt. Leben*, p. 91.

Su-kurīrā, *Su-opaśā*, as wearing a beautiful head-dress." (*Ved. Ind.* i. 164). Sūryā, who was the daughter of the God Sūrya, had her hair done up into a *kurīra* or crest, and this was probably the fashion of bridal coiffure in Ṛgvedic times. The diadem or tiara that was worn was called *tirīta* (Av. viii. 6, 7).

The men wore their hair long or short according to fashion or pleasure. The Vasiṣṭhas had long hair which was braided and coiled on the right. (*dakṣiṇatas-kaparda*, Rv. vii. 33, 1) The God Rudra (Rv. i. 114, 1. 5) and the God Pūṣan (Rv. vi. 55, 1; ix. 67, 11) are said to have worn their hair in the form of a shell. They have been described as *kapardin*. The same epithet is applied to the Tṛtsus, the tribe to which Vasiṣṭha belonged.[1] (Rv. vii. 83, 8). Men sometimes wore beards or shaved them, as there is mention of razor (Rv. i. 166, 10; viii. 4, 16; x. 28, 9). Indra has been described as wearing beards in the Ṛgveda (Rv. x. 23, 1. 4). *Vaptṛ* in the Ṛgveda denotes a shaver or barber, and there is clear mention of the barber shaving beards in the Ṛgveda (x. 142, 4).

Military accoutrements.—The Gods Maruts have frequently been described as wearing golden helmets (Rv. ii. 34, 3; v. 54, 11; viii. 7, 25). The word for helmet is *śipra* which Sāyaṇa explains by *śirastrāṇa* or helmet. The Ṛbhus are described as wearing iron helmets (*ayah-śipra* Rv. iv. 37, 4). It is therefore evident that warriors used to put on helmets for the protection of their heads. The word *śipra* has also the sense indicating the jaws or the nose. (*Nirukta* vi. 17), and the epithet *su-śipra*, applied to Indra, means, according to Sāyaṇa and Yāska, 'one possessing handsome jaws or nose.' (Rv. i. 9, 3; 29, 2; 81, 4; 101, 10). But Sāyaṇa also interprets the word elsewhere (Rv. iii. 30, 3) as 'having a handsome helmet.' He returns however to the interpretation of 'jaws' in other verses (Rv. iii. 32,

[1] Cf. Muir O. S. T., vol. v, p. 462.

3; 36, 10; viii. 32, 4. 24; 33, 7 etc.) Prof. Aufrecht considers that *śipra* in the dual means 'jaws'; and in certain Ṛgvedic verses (v. 54, 11; viii. 7, 5) the word *siprāh* means 'visors,' the two parts of which are compared to two jaws.[1] In whatever sense the word may have been used, there can be no doubt that even in Ṛgvedic times metal helmets or visors were used by warriors for the protection of their head and face.

There were also breast-plates (*atkāh*) and the Maruts have been described as wearing golden breast-plates (*hiraṇmayān atkān*, Rv. v. 55, 6) which could be donned and doffed at pleasure. Zimmer explains the word elsewhere (Rv. x. 49, 3; 99, 9) as the 'armour of a warrior as a whole.' In other passages it is rendered as garment, because it is said to be 'woven' (*vyuta*, Rv. i. 122, 2) or 'well-fitting' (*surabhi*, Rv. vi. 29, 3; x. 123, 7). Pischel takes the term to mean axe in four places. (Rv. v. 55. 6; vi. 33, 3; x. 49, 3; 99. 9). But the meaning 'breast-plate' seems to be more appropriate. The word *varman* also occurs in the Ṛgveda (i. 31, 15; 140, 10; vi. 75, 1. 8. 18. 19; viii. 47, 8), denoting 'body armour' 'coat of mail' 'corselet.' "It was not a single solid piece of metal, but consisted of many pieces fitted together (*Syūta* Rv. i. 31, 15); it may have been made either of metal plates or, as is more likely, of some stiff material plated with metal".[2] In later literature there is reference to corselets of *Ayas*, *Loha* or *Rajata*.[3]

The warrior had a guard (*hastaghna*) on the left arm to avoid the friction of the bow-string (Rv. vi. 75, 14). Whether the shield was used by the warriors is not clear, though the mention of the word *varūtha* (shield) occurs in the Ṛgveda (vi. 46, 9). There is also no clear record of the employment of greaves or other guards for the legs and feet,

---

1 Muir O. S. T., v. p. 149

2 *Ved. Ind*, i. pp. 60, 61.

3 *Jaiminiva Upaniṣad Brāhmaṇa* iv. 1. 3.

but Grassmann saw greaves in *vatūrinā padā* in Rv. i. 133, 2. It would certainly be strange if there were no greaves or guards for the legs and feet, when the body was protected by armour or coat of mail, the head and face by helmet or visor, and the arm by *hastaghna*. The ordinary warrior was armed with bow and arrows, sword or axe (vāśī, Rv. v. 57, 2) and lance (ṛṣti Rv. v. 57, 2). The arrows were kept in a quiver which was tied on the back across the shoulder. (Rv. vi. 75, 5.) A fuller description of military arms will be given in a subsequent chapter.

Sports: *Hunting.*—Hunting was not merely a pastime, but a necessity among the nomadic Aryans, as it formed, as it were, the main source of their livelihood. I have already said that the wild dog was tamed mainly for the purpose of assisting the primitive Aryans and, for the matter of that, all primitive peoples in the hunt. Flesh of wild animals had originally formed the principal item of food before sheep and cattle were domesticated; and even when domestic animals were available for food, people would resort to hunting not only for the pleasure and excitement which it afforded, but also on economic grounds, as the frequent slaughter of domesticated animals would reduce the live stock before long. Hunting wild beasts became also necessary for the protection of flocks and cattle. "The Ṛgveda is naturally our chief source of information in regard to hunting. The arrow was sometimes employed (Rv. ii. 42, 2), but, as is usual with primitive man, the normal instruments of capture were nets and pitfalls. Birds were regularly caught in nets (paśa,[1] nidha,[2] Jala[3]), the bird-catcher being called *nidhā-pati* 'master of snares' (Rv. ix. 83, 4). The net was fastened on pegs (Av. viii. 8, 5), as is done with modern nets for catching birds. Another name of net

---

[1] Rv. iii. 45, 1; vi. 48, 17. (*Pāśin*, hunter).

[2] Rv. ix. 83, 4; x, 73, 11.

[3] Av. x., 1, 30.

is apparently *mukṣījā*. Pits were used for catching antelopes (*ṛṣya*), and so were called *ṛṣya-da*, 'antelope-catching.' Elephants were captured, as in Greek times, perhaps through the instrumentality of tame females. Apparently the boar was captured in the chase, dogs being used (Rv. x. 86, 4), but the passage from which this view is deduced is of uncertain mythological content. There is also an obscure reference (Rv. x. 51, 6) to the capture of the buffalo (*gaura*), but it is not clear whether the reference is to shooting with an arrow or capturing by means of ropes, perhaps a lasso, or a net. The lion was captured in pitfalls (Rv. x. 28, 10), or was surrounded by the hunters and slain (Rv. v. 15, 3); one very obscure passage refers to the lion being caught by ambuscade, which perhaps merely alludes to the use of the hidden pit (Rv. v. 74, 4)." [1]

Horse-riding and horse-race.—The Vedic Aryans were exceedingly fond of horses, horse-riding and horse-racing. It is surprising to be told by some European scholars, [2] e.g. Prof. Macdonell, that though the horse was employed to draw chariots, it was not used for riding by the Vedic Indians. Macdonell elsewhere says: "No mention is made of riding in battle."[3] Professor Keith also writes in the *Cambridge History of India* (i. 98): "Though horse-riding was probably not unknown for other purposes, no mention is made of this use of the horse in war." Let us examine the truth of these statements. In Rv. i. 162, 7 we come across the following passage:

"Forth, for the regions of the Gods, the *charger with his smooth back is come*; my prayer attends him." (Griffith) Again, "horns made of gold, (*i.e.*, golden manes) hath he: his feet are iron: less fleet than he, though swift as thought, is Indra. The Gods have come that they may taste the oblation

[1] *Vedic Index*, ii. p. 173.

[2] Macdonell *Hist. of Sansk. Lit.*, p. 150.

[3] *Vedic Index* i. p. 42.

of him who *mounted, first of all, the courser.*" (Rv. i. 163, 9).[1] Read again the following translation of two other verses (Rv. v. 61, 2. 3): "Where are your horses, where the reins? How came ye? How had ye the power? Rein was on nose and *seat on back*. The whip is laid upon the flank. *The heroes stretch their thighs apart, like women when the babe is born.*" (Griffith). No better description can be given of riding a horse. There are also many other references to horse-riding in the Ṛgveda. The Aśvins used to come riding on their horses (Rv. viii. 5, 7. 8). Indra has been thus invoked in another verse (Rv. viii. 6, 36): "O Indra, come thou to us from the distant region, riding on thy two handsome horses, and drink this Soma." The translation of another verse (Rv. ii. 27, 22) is as follows: "Adorable Āditya, may I pass (safe) in your car from the illusions which (you desire) for the malignant, the snares which are spread for your foes, (in like manner) as a horseman (passes over a road)." The word used in the verse is *aśvīva, i e.*, 'like a horseman. The Maruts or the Gods of wind rode on fleet horses (Rv. v. 61, 11; 53, 3; 54, 3), as did also Mitra and Varuṇa (Rv. v. 64, 7). Agni also rode on red horses (Rv. ii. 1, 6). Viṣṇu and Indra are said to travel on clouds, as people ride on "trained horses." (Rv. i. 155, 1). There is also mention of a victorious hero returning home on his fleet horse. (Rv. i 158, 3). As regards the employment of horsemen or cavalry in war, there are also further evidences in the Ṛgveda, some of which are quoted below: "Our heroes (leaders), winged with horses, come together." (Rv. vi. 47, 31). The phrase "winged with horses" (*aśvaparṇāh*) evidently means "riding on their fleet horses." These warriors were distinct from those who fought from chariots, for the next passage clearly says: "Let our car-warriors, Indra, be triumphant." (Griffith). There can be no doubt that the poet mentions the two classes of warriors separately. Another verse (Rv. iv. 42, 5) also mentions

---

[1] *Yo arvantam prathamo adhyātiṣthat* (Rv. i. 163, 9).

"heroes with horses": "Heroes with noble horses (*svaśvāh*), fain for battle, selected warriors, call on me in combat. I, Indra Maghavan, excite the conflict; I stir the dust, Lord of surpassing vigour" (Griffith). In another verse (Rv. x. 96, 10) we find Indra riding on his horse, and swiftly proceeding to the battle like the war-horse itself. The Aśvins also ride (Rv. v. 61, 1-3) and are said to have sent fleet horses to the battle-field for Pedu, their protégé (Rv. vii. 71, 5). Riding is also clearly meant in Rv. i. 162, 17, which says: "If one, *when seated*, with excessive urging hath *with his heel* or with his whip distressed thee, all these thy woes, as with the oblations' ladle at sacrifices, with my prayer I banish." (Griffith). There is mention of war-horses in the Ṛgveda (vi. 46, 13. 14; ix. 37, 5: 86, 3; 108, 2; x. 6, 6). In a verse (Rv. vi. 33, 1) a Ṛṣi prays to Indra for the birth of a son who would be mighty, delight-giving, performer of sacrifices, and bestower of gifts, and who riding on a brave steed would successfully encounter the enemies riding on brave steeds in battle.[1] In two other verses chargers are mentioned (Rv. vi. 46, 13. 14): "Indra, in the mighty fray, thou urgest chargers to their speed, on the uneven road and on a toilsome path, like falcons, eager for renown, speeding like rivers rushing down a steep descent, responsive to the urging call, that come like birds attracted to the bait, held in by reins in both the driver's hands." (Griffith). The insertion of the words "in both the driver's hands" is gratuitous. The reins may have been held either by a driver or a rider. In the above verses the riding horses are clearly indicated, because of their furious charge on uneven roads, and down steep descents like rushing streams. Chariots, however strongly made, would be smashed and splintered into bits, if driven on such difficult roads, with such furious speed. *Dadhikras* is the name of the divine

[1] Griffith translates the verse differently thus: "Give us the rapture that is mightiest, Indra, prompt to bestow and swift to aid, O Hero, that wins with brave steeds where brave steeds encounter, and quells the Vṛtras and the foes in battle."

war-horse in the Ṛgveda (Rv. iv. 38, 39, 40 &c.). He represented the war-horses employed both for drawing war-chariots and for riding, and his doings as related in the hymns may be regarded as typical of the feats performed by the war-horses of Ṛgvedic times. "Swift and of varied colour" Dadhikras is compared to "the impetuous hawk." "Swift-rushing, as it were, down a precipice, springing forth like a hero fain for battle, whirling the car and flying like the tempest, he gaineth precious booty in the combats, and moveth, winning spoil, among the cattle .... Loudly the folk cry after him in battles, as it were a thief who steals away a garment; speeding to glory, or a herd of cattle, even as a hungry falcon swooping downward. And, fain to come forth first amid these armies, this way and that with rows of cars he rushes, gay like a bridesman, making him a garland (of the chariots that surround him), tossing the dust, champing the rein that holds him. And that strong Steed, victorious and faithful, obedient with his body in combat, speeding straight on amid the swiftly pressing (hosts), casts over his brows the dust he tosses upward. And at his thunder, like the roar of heaven, those who attack tremble and are affrighted; for when he fights against embattled thousands, dread is he in his striving; none may stay him. The people praise the overpowering swiftness of this fleet Steed who giveth men abundance. Of him they say when drawing back from battle: Dadhikrās hath sped forward with his thousands. Dadhikrās hath overspread the Five-fold People with vigour, as the Sun lightens the waters."[1] (Rv. iv. 38, 2-10). Again, "may he, the true, the fleet, the lover of the course, the bird-like Dadhikrāvan, bring food, strength and light. His pinion, rapid runner, fans him on his way, as of a bird that hastens onward to its aim, and, as it were a falcon's gliding through the air, strikes Dadhikrāvan's side as he speeds on with might. Bound by the neck and by the flanks and by the mouth, the vigorous courser lends new swiftness to his speed. Drawing himself together, as his

[1] Griffith's *Translation of the Ṛgveda*.

strength allows, Dadhikrās springs along the windings of the paths."[1] (Rv. iv. 40, 2-4).

The above spirited verses in praise of Dadhikrās, the typical war-house, indicate the fascination which the horse generally exercised on the imagination of the Ṛgvedic Aryans. Nothing was prized more than swift and spirited horses, and every family possessed a number of them. The horse was indispensable not only for swift locomation, but also for making raids, and attacking an enemy, and protecting the country from tribal invasions. No wonder that the Ṛgvedic Aryans were exceedingly fond of horse-racing and chariot-racing, not only for the sake of the fun and excitement that they afforded, but also for exercising the horses, the riders and chariot-drivers, and keeping them always fit and efficient. Every village must have possessed its own race-course where the horses were regularly exercised, and where races were run on special festive occasions, and prizes given away to the winners. The race-course was called *kāṣṭhā* (Rv. viii. 80, 8), or *āji* (Rv. iv. 24, 8 ; x. 156, 1). and "appears from the Atharva-veda (ii. 14, 6 ; xiii. 2, 4) to have been a quasi-circular one to a mark (*kārṣman*. Rv. ix 36, 1 ; 74, 8) and back again. In the Ṛgveda the course is described as broad (*urvī*) and the distance as measured out (*apāvṛktā aratnayaḥ*, Rv. viii. 80, 8) Prizes (*dhana*) were offered (*dhā*, Rv. i. 81, 3 ; 116, 15 ; vi. 45, 1 ; viii. 80, 8), and eagerly competed for. Other words for victory and the prize are *kāra* (Rv. v. 29, 8 ; ix 14, 1) and *bhara* (Rv. v. 29, 8 ; ix. 16, 5). The person who instituted a race is referred to as *āji-kṛt*, and Indra is called *āji-kṛt*, race-marker (Rv. viii. 53, 6), and *āji-pati*, lord of the race, (Rv. viii. 53, 14). The swift steeds (*vājin*, *atya*), used for the races, were often washed and adorned. (Rv. ii. 34, 3 ; ix. 109, 10 ; x. 68, 11)."[2] They were groomed morning and evening (Rv. vii. 3, 5). The horse has various names in the

---

[1] *Ibid.*

[2] *Vedic Index*, i. p. 54.

Ṛgveda. It was called *atya* (the runner), *arvant* (the swift), *vājin* (the strong), *sapti* (the runner), and *haya* (the speeding). Horses of various colours were known, dun (*harita*, *hari*), ruddy (*aruṇa aruṣa piśanga*, *rohita*), dark-brown (*śyava*), white (*śveta*) etc. Horses were bred and could be obtained in large numbers in Sapta-Sindhu, the regions bordering upon the Sindhu (Rv. x. 75, 8) and the Sarasvatī (Rv. i. 3, 10; ii. 41, 18; vi. 61, 3. 4; vii. 90, 3) having been famous breeding-places of horses. Kings sometimes gave away large numbers of horses to the Ṛṣis. In one *Dānastuti* (Rv. viii. 55, 3), as many as four hundred mares are mentioned as having been presented to the poet. The mares were preferred for drawing chariots, because of their swiftness and sureness (Rv. vii. 69, 1). The chariots of the Maruts were sometimes drawn by mares (Rv. v. 55, 6; 56, 6 etc.). The horses were so much valued that they were on occasions ornamented with pearls and gold (Rv. i. 126, 4; x. 68, 11). Like the horse-race, the Ṛgvedic Aryans were fond of the chariot-race also, for it was "the peaceful preparation for the decisive struggle on the battle-field, for the joyous war in which they delighted, and which plays so large a part in the songs as well as the life of the people." (Kaegi's *The Ṛgveda* p. 19). The hymn, viii. 69, is believed to contain the prayer of a charioteer for victory before the race. (Zimmer, *Alt. Laben* 289 f).

Dicing.—Like horse-racing, the Vedic Aryans were extremely fond of dice-playing. The word *akṣa*, meaning dice, frequently occurs in the Ṛgveda. The dice appear to have been made of Vibhīdaka nuts (Rv. vii. 86, 6; x. 34, 1), and hence were called "brown" (*babhru*), on account of their colour. The dicer is described in the Ṛgveda (x. 34, 12) as "leader of a great horde" (*senanir mahato gaṇasya*) and the number of dice is given as *tri-pañcāśah.* "Ludwig, Weber and Zimmer render it as fifteen, which is grammatically hardly possible. Roth and Grassmann render it as 'consisting of fifty-three.' Lüders takes it as 'consisting of one hundred and fifty,' but he points out that this may be merely a vague expression for a large number."[1]

How the game was played it is very difficult to ascertain from the Ṛgveda. The names of the throws in the later Saṃhitās and Brāhmaṇas are Kṛta Tretā, Dvāpara, Āskanda and Abhibhū.[2] The Śatapatha Brāhmaṇa identifies Kali with Abhibhū (v. 4, 41, 6). "The names of some of these throws go back even to the Ṛgveda and the Atharvaveda. Kali occurs in the latter (vii. 114, 1), and Lüders shows that in a considerable number of passages in the former[3] *Kṛta* means a 'throw' (not 'a stake' or 'what is won,'), and this sense is clearly found in the Atharva-veda (vii. 52). Moreover, that there were more throws (ayāh) than one is proved by a passage in the Ṛgveda (x. 116, 9), when the gods are compared to throws as giving or destroying wealth."[4] In the later Vedic literature we find that a ritual game of dice was played at the Agnyādheya at the Rājasūya ceremonies. "The details are not certain, but it is clear that the game consisted in securing even numbers of dice, usually a number divisible by four, the *kṛta*, the other three throws then being the *Tretā*, when three remained over after division by four; the *Dvāpara*, when two was the remainder; and the *Kali* when one remained. If five were the dividing number, then the throw which shewed no remainder was Kali, the Kṛta was that when four was left, and so on. The dice had no numerals marked on them, the only question being what was the total number of the dice themselves."[5]

Professors Macdonell and Keith say that "there is no reason to doubt that the game as played in the Ṛgveda was based on the same principle, though the details must remain

---

1 *Vedic Index*, i. 2.

2 *Taitt Sam.*, iv. 3, 3, 1. 2.

3 Rv. i 100, 9; 132. 1; v. 60, 1: viii 19, 10; ix. 97, 58; x 42, 9; 43, 5; 102, 2.

4 *Ved. Ind.*, i p. 3.

5 *Ved. Ind.*, i. p. 4.

doubtful. The number of dice used was certainly large (Rv. x. 34, 8), and the reference to throwing fours (Rv. i. 41, 9), and losing by one, points to the use of the Kṛta as the winning throw . . . . No board appears to have been used, but a depression on which the dice were thrown (*adhi-devana, devana iriṇa*) was made in the ground. No dice-box was used, but reference is made to a case for keeping dice in. (*akṣa-vapana*). The throw was called *graha*, or earlier *grābha* (Rv. viii. 81, 1; ix. 106, 3). The stake is called *vij* (Rv. i. 92, 10; ii. 12, 5). Serious losses could be made at dicing; in the Ṛgveda a dicer laments the loss of all his property including his wife. (Rv. x. 34, 2)."[1]

That the game had a fascinating influence upon easy-going and do-nothing young men, and led to great personal and family misery would appear from the gambler's lament in the Ṛgveda (x. 34). The evil habit once contracted was soon developed into a vice which was difficult to eradicate. The loser repeatedly sought out and challenged the winner to play the game again in the desperate hope of a win, and either won or lost the game again (Rv. x. 42, 9; 43, 5). The gambler was chastised by his parents, shunned by his wife, and despised by his friends, and his life became truly miserable and unbearable. Sometimes, when everything was lost, even the wife was staked, and lost; for, other people "paid court" to her. This practice was no doubt a relic of barbarous times, which continued even to a later age, for we find Yudhiṣṭhira in the Mahābhārata staking his wife Draupadī who, when lost in the game, was forcibly brought out from her sanctum by her husbands' brutal cousins, the winners, and subjected to inhuman indignities. In the nomadic and pastoral stages of existence, the cares of life were few; and when there was plenty of food and drink available, the idlers must have invented the game to enable them to while away their time, and to afford them some excitement in their

---

[1] *Ibid.*, i. pp. 4-5.

hum-drum existence. Even to this day, among the nomadic tribes of India, gambling is a besetting vice, which is responsible for thieving, robbery and other crimes. Dicing, as we find in the Ṛgveda, was a relic of far earlier times, and it came to be condemned by thoughtful men in no uncertain terms. It will not be uninteresting to give below a translation of the hymn (Rv. x. 34), which describes the evils of gambling and the woes of the gambler :—

"1. The tumbling air-horn (products) of the great Vibhīdaka tree (*i.e.* the dice) delight me as they continue to roll on the dice-board. The exciting dice seem to me like a draught of the Soma-plant growing on Mount Mujavat. 2. She (the gamester's own wife) never quarrelled with or despised me. She was kind to me, and to my friends. But I, for the sake of the partial dice, have spurned my devoted spouse. 3. My mother-in-law detests me; my wife rejects me. In his need (the gamester) finds no comforter. I cannot discover what is the enjoyment of the gambler any more than I can percieve what is the happiness of a worn-out hack-horse. 4. Others pay court to the wife of the man whose wealth is coveted by the impetuous dice. His father, mother, brothers cry out 'we know nothing of him; take him away bound.' 5. When I resolve not to be tormented by them, because I am abandoned by my friends who withdraw from me,—yet as soon as the brown dice, when they are thrown, make a rattling sound, I hasten to their rendezvous, like a woman to her paramour. 6. The gamester comes to the assembly, glowing in body, and asking himself, 'shall I win?' The dice inflame his desire, by making over his winnings to his opponent. 7. Hooking, piercing, deceitful, vexatious, delighting to torment, the dice dispense transient gifts, and again ruin the winner; they appear to the gambler covered with honey. 8. Their troop of fifty-three disports itself (disposing men's destinies) like the god Savitṛ, whose ordinances never fail. They bow not before the wrath even of the fiercest. The king himself makes obeisance to them. 9. They roll downward; they bound upward. Having no hands, they overcome him who has. These celestial coals, when thrown on the dice-board,[1] scorch the heart, though cold themselves. 10. The destitute wife of the gamester is distressed, and so too is the mother of a son who goes she knows not whither. In debt and seeking after money, the gambler approaches with trepidation the houses of other people at night. 11. It vexes the gamester to see his own wife, and then to observe the wives and happy homes of others. In the morning he yokes the brown horses (the dice); by the time when the fire goes out he has sunk into a degraded wretch. 12. He who is the general of your band, the first king of your troop,—to him I stretch forth (my) ten (fingers) towards the east (in reverence); I do not reject wealth, but I declare that which is right (when I say): 13. Never play with dice, practise husbandry; rejoice in thy property, esteeming it sufficient. 'There, O gamester, are thy cows; (this is) thy wife;' so the adorable Saviṭṛ addresses me. 14. Be friendly, (O dice); be auspicious to us; do not bewitch us powerfully with your enchantment. Let your wrath and hostility abate. Let others be subject to the fetters of the brown ones (the dice)."[2]

We thus find that the allurements of dicing were too great in Ṛgvedic times to be easily resisted. Even Ṛṣis were not impervious to them, for we find a prayer offered to Varuṇa by Vasiṣṭha asking his forgiveness for sins that may have been committed through inadvertence, wine, wrath, dicing or indiscretion. (Rv. vii. 86, 6).

There was probably an appointed place or hall for gambling. The *Sabhā* or public assembly-hall was clearly used for dicing, especially when the assembly was not transacting any public business (Rv. x. 34, 6). In later Vedic literature (*Vaj. Sam.* xxx. 18; *Tait. Bra.* iii. 4, 16, 1) a dicer is called *Sabha-sthāṇu* or 'pillar of the assembly-hall,'

---

[1] Muir is of opinion that the dice were thrown on the dice-board.

[2] Muir's translation (O. S. T. v. 426-427.

doubtless because of his constant presence there. (*Ved. Ind.* ii. 426). There is a verse in the Ṛgveda (i. 124, 7), of doubtful sense, which seems to imply that sometimes widows visited the dicing-hall with a view to gain wealth by gambling. Such conduct on their part was, of course, not approved, as the conduct of a brotherless young woman who sought the company of young men met with public disapproval.

Dancing.—Both men and women danced in Ṛgvedic times, but there is no evidence to show that there was any mixed dancing. There is mention of men dancing with bamboo-sticks held aloft (Rv. i. 10, 1). The dancer was called *nṛta*. Indra danced through excitement at the time of battle (Rv. i. 130, 7). The female dancer was called *nṛtu*. Probably the name was applied to a professional female dancer, who had embroidered garments (*peśamsi*) on at the time of dancing and bared her breasts for attraction (Rv. i. 92, 4). Such shameless dancing cannot be attributed to decent and respectable women who always appeared before the public well-covered. (Rv. viii. 17, 7; 26, 13). In another passage of the Ṛgveda (x. 18. 3), *nṛti* (dancing) is found coupled with *hāsa* (laughter) in the description of the funeral ritual. Professors Macdonell and Keith say: "Though it is clear that a joyful celebration is meant (like the Irish 'wake' or the old fashioned feasting in Scotland after a funeral), it is difficult to be certain that actual dancing is meant." (*Ved. Ind.* i. 457-458). My conjecture on the point is this: After the death of a person, certain rites, like *Śrāddha*, were performed for the spiritual benefit of the departed, and at the end of their performance, dancing and laughter were indulged in for the purpose of chasing away sad and mournful thoughts, and heartening the surviving relatives and restoring them to their normal avocations of life. The verse clearly says: "The offerings that we have made to the Gods to-day have been efficacious. Let us now dance and laugh. We all have attained a long span of life." The performance of the Śraddha of elderly people even to this day is followed by *Saṃkīrtana* (religious music and song) and feasting, undoubtedly a relic of the old custom.

Professor Keith says: "It seems that men also on occasions danced in the open air, as a metaphor alludes to the dust of the dancing feet of men."[1] The metaphor occurs in Rv. x. 72, 6, where the Gods have been described as dancing, which caused clouds of dust to rise. Kaegi[2] says: "Wives and maidens attire themselves in gay robes and set forth to the joyful feast; youths and girls hasten to the meadow when forest and field are clothed in fresh verdure to take part in the dance. Cymbals sound, and seizing each other, lads and damsels whirl about until the ground vibrates, and clouds of dust envelop the gaily moving throng." Men, women and children also loved to swing in swings (Rv. vii. 87, 5; 88, 3), which was a favourite pastime.

Fairs and Merriments.—The word *Samana* frequently occurs in the Ṛgveda. Roth renders it either 'battle' (Rv. vi. 75, 3. 5; ix. 96, 9 etc.), or 'festival' (Rv. ii. 16, 7; vi. 60, 2; vii. 2, 5 etc.). "Pischel thinks that it was a general popular festivity, to which women went to enjoy themselves (Rv. i. 124, 8; iv. 58, 8; vi. 75, 4; vii. 2, 5), poets to win fame (Rv. ii. 16, 7; ix. 97, 47), bowmen to gain prizes at archery (Rv. vi. 75, 3. 5), horses to run races (Rv. ix. 96, 9), and which lasted until morning (Rv. i. 48, 6) or until a conflagration, caused by the fires kept burning all night, scattered the celebrators. (Rv. x. 69, 11; vii. 9, 4). Young women (Av. ii. 36, 1), and elderly women (Rv. vii, 2, 5) sought there to find a husband, and courtezans to make profit of the occasion." (Rv. iv. 58, 8). The extract is made from Macdonell and Keith's *Vedic Index* (ii. 429). Pischel's interpretation of the word (*Vedische Studien* 2, 314) seems to be correct. In some of the Himalayan Cis-Sutlej states, even to this day, are held similar fairs, notably one at Solon and another at Sipi, where women congregate in large numbers and enjoy themselves in various

[1] *Cambridge Hist. of India*, i. 102-103.

[2] *The Ṛgveda*, p. 19. Zimmer, *Alt. Leben* 287 f.

ways. At the Sipi fair, till very recently, women were arrayed in rows, and exposed for sale and knocked down to the highest bidder. The Vedic *Samana* must have degenerated into these modern institutions; for, while at the former, women, both young and elderly, were given an opportunity of selecting their husbands, at the latter they were sold like goods and chattels, and allowed no choice of their own. These fairs having degenerated into veritable slave-marts, the enlightened rulers of the states have rightly put them down with a firm hand.

The Vedic *Samanas* appear to have been popular institutions as they attracted poets, artists, archers and skilful riders of horses, who competed with one another, besides ordinary men and women who had also their own axes to grind. They afforded relaxation, recreation and amusements, and must have been eagerly looked forward to by the ordinary folk, as they gave them an opportunity of meeting one another after long intervals.

Music.—As regards music Prof. Keith says: "Music too had advanced beyond the primitive stage; and already the three types of instrument, percussion, string, and wind, were represented by the drum, used among other purposes, to terrify the foe in battle, the lute, and the flute, the last-named instrument being said to be heard in the abode of Yama, where the holy dead dwell. The hymns themselves prove that singing was highly esteemed."[1] The name of the drum was *dundubhi* (Rv. i. 28, 5; vi. 47, 29. 31), which was used both in war and peace. *Karkari* was the name of a musical instrument (Rv. ii. 43, 3) which was probably something like the lute. The Maruts had *Kṣoṇī* or Vīṇā for their musical instrument. (Rv. ii. 35, 13). It has also been called Vāṇa in another verse, *dhamanto vāṇam*, 'playing upon the lyre.' (Rv. i. 85, 10). Maxmüller, however, has translated it as 'voice,' and remarked: "There is no authority for *vāṇa*

[1] *Cambridge Hist. of India*, i. 103.

meaning either lyre or flute in the Vedas." But this remark seems to be gratuitous. The sounds produced by the Maruts, when blowing, have been compared to the notes produced by playing upon the lyre. The word also means the 'flute,' as a whistling noise is produced when winds blow through the chinks of the doors and the crevices in the walls. Sayaṇa has interpreted the word as a sort of lyre *(īṇā-viśeṣam)*. But probably 'flute' would be the more appropriate meaning. *Veṇu* (flute) may have been a later corruption of *Vāṇa*. The word *Āghāti* occurs in Rv. x. 146, 2, and, according to Professors Macdonell and Keith, means the 'cymbal' used to accompany dancing. Sāyaṇa, however, thinks that it was the name for the Viṇa which emitted different notes when struck at the different *ghātas* or points on the musical scale. That songs were sung does not admit of a doubt. Seven women sang songs in praise of the Soma, when squeezing out the juice from the plant with their fingers. (Rv. ix. 66, 8). The *sāmans* were divine songs sung and set to music. The *gāthās* were songs in verse (Rv. i. 167, 6; viii. 32, 1; 71, 14; 98, 9; ix. 11, 4; 99, 4). The *gāthā-pati* was 'the lord of song' (Rv. i. 43, 4); *gāthā-nī* meant 'leading a song.' (Rv. i. 190, 1; viii. 92, 2); *ṛju-gāthā* meant 'singing correctly.' (Rv. v. 44, 5) and *gāthin* meant the 'singer.' (Rv. i. 7, 1).[1] "The Aitareya Brāhmaṇa (vii. 18) distinguished between Ṛc and Gatha as divine and human respectively. According to the usage of the Brahmaṇas and the liturgical literature, as stated by the St. Petersburg Dictionary, the Gathās are, though religious in content, distinguished from Ṛc, Yajus and Saman as non-Vedic, that is, are not Mantras."[2] The *Dānastutis* were songs sung in praise of kings or nobles who made rich gifts to the poets. They were probably like ballads describing the feats of the heroes.

---

[1] Cf. Hopkin's *Jour of the Amer. Or. So.* 17, 65.

[2] *Vedic Index* i. 224, 225.

It would thus appear that men and women in Ṛgvedic times amused themselves by singing songs, dancing, playing on musical instruments, and attending fairs. The men were fond of horse-racing, hunting and dicing, though the last-named pastime brought endless troubles in its train.

CHAPTER VI.

DOMESTIC AND SOCIAL LIFE, MARRIAGE AND MORALS DURING ṚGVEDIC TIMES.

The domestic life of the Ṛgvedic Aryans has been partially described in some of the preceding chapters. But there were other special aspects of it, which could not be touched upon, and require some elaborate treatment here to enable the reader to obtain an adequate idea of the life as it was actually lived by them.

The wife.—Jāyedastam ("the wife is the home"), exclaimed the great Ṛṣi Viśvamitra in his ecstatic vision of the true source of domestic felicity. (Rv. iii. 53, 4). As it was quite natural to attribute the same source of happiness to the Gods as to men, it was conjectured that Indra had a happy home, presided over by a good, gracious and loving wife, which rang with the dulcet music of her sweet voice and the merry laughter of the children. The poet addresses Indra thus: "Thou hast drunk Soma, Indra, turn thee homeward; thy joy is in thy home, thy gracious consort." (Rv. iii. 53, 6.[1] This graphically describes the domestic felicity that the Ṛgvedic Aryans enjoyed. The wife was not only loving but also obedient, promptly responding to the call of her husband and ministering to his wants. (Rv. i. 122. 2). She dressed herself well and gracefully (Rv. iv. 3, 2; 58, 9), and always put on a smiling countenance (Rv. iv. 58, 8) with a view to please her husband. She carefully prepared and arranged his seat and bed, and looked after his comforts.

---

[1] The verse has been translated by Griffith as above, but it may also be interpreted as follows: "When thou hast drunk the Soma, then, Indra, go home, where lives thy auspicious wife, which rings with the melodious voices (of thy wife and children). *Suraṇam* lit. means "having pleasant sound."

(Rv. iv. 3, 2). She was not only a loving wife, but a loving mother. She was fond of her children whom she loved as a mother only could love them (Rv. vii. 81, 4), and nursed and brought them up with great care. The playful and blooming little darlings (Rv. vii. 56, 16) formed the chief attraction of the home. The little son caught the hem of his father's garments with a view to attract his attention and press his supplication with earnest and lovable words. (Rv. iii. 53, 2). The playful children used to be so much absorbed in their frolics and gambols in the play-ground that they could not feel that they were hungry, and when the mother went to fetch them home for their meals, they would not listen to her call, but push her away by striking her with their little hands. (Rv. x. 94, 14). The mother sometimes found her breasts oozing milk, as the suckling was not at her side; but as soon as it came or was brought to the inner apartments, she cheerfully sat down to give it suck, with caressing words. (Rv. ix. 61, 14). The picture of the mother sitting with her little sons on her lap is indeed very lovely (Rv. vii. 43, 3), as well as that of tumbling urchins advancing towards the father with broken and lisping words pleasant to hear. (Rv. vii. 103, 3). The boys, like the girls, wore golden ear-rings, and bejewelled necklaces. (Rv. i. 122, 14).

The wife has been described in the Ṛgveda as 'the ornament of the home' (Rv. i. 66, 3), which goes to show the great esteem in which she was held. She was an excellent house-wife, rising early with the dawn, and rousing all from sleep, and sending the servants about their respective business. (Rv. i. 124, 4). She at once applied herself to the performance of her household duties, dusting, sweeping, and washing the floors that admitted of washing, and scrubbing and cleansing the cooking pots and utensils. She bathed early, and offered jointly with her husband the morning oblations to the sacred Household Fire, the Lord of the house. Another oblation was offered in the mid-day, and a third in the evening. (Rv. i. 173, 2; iii. 28; v. 43, 15; viii. 1, 29; 13

13). Her first and foremost duty was to keep the sacred Fire burning. As soon as the, cows were milked and the milk brought home in pails, she stirred it over the fire, churned some of it for butter, and proceeded to prepare the meals of the day. The young daughters took charge of the little ones, and duly fed and nursed them. After mid-day meals, she attended to her toilette, dressed herself and the children neatly (Rv. i. 123, 11; 124, 7; iv. 3, 2; 58, 9; x. 110, 5;) with a view to meet her busband, prepared meals for the evening, made beds for the children and put them early to sleep. Often, she had male and female servants under her, whom she employed in their respective duties and treated kindly. (Rv. x. 85, 43). She also looked after the cows and other domestic animals and supervised the work entrusted to their keepers. (Rv. x. 85. 44). Occasionally, accompanied by other women, she rambled about, and climbed the hills to pluck flowers. (Rv. i. 56, 2). She was dutiful to her husband's parents, affectionate to her husband's brothers and sisters (Rv. x. 85, 46), and devotedly attached to her husband (Rv. iv. 58, 8) who was never slow in reciprocating her sentiments. (Rv. i. 73, 3; ii. 16, 8; viii. 2, 19; 35, 5).

"The poetical ideal of the family" say Professors Macdonell and Keith "were decidedly high (Rv. viii. 31, 5-9; x. 34, 11; 85, 18. 19. 41 *et seq.*), and we have no reason to doubt that it was often actually fulfilled. Moreover, the wife on her marriage was at once given an honoured position in the house; she is emphatically mistress in her husband's home, exercising authority over her father-in-law, her husband's brothers, and his unmarried sisters. No doubt the case contemplated is one in which the eldest son of a family has become its head owing to the decrepitude of the parents, his wife then taking the place of the mistress of the joint-family while the brothers and sisters are still unmarried. It is not inconsistent with the great stress elsewhere (Rv. viii. 6, 24) laid on the respect due to a father-in-law, who then is probably regarded as still in possession of his faculties, and controls the house, while his son continues to live with him. The respect would no doubt equally apply if the son had set up a separate family of his own." (*Vedic Index*, i. 484-485).

It was believed that true domestic felicity depended upon the mutual harmony of husband and wife, and their pious performance of the religious duties they owed to the Gods. The following translation of certain Ṛgvedic verses (viii. 31, 5-9) will illustrate our meaning :—

" Gods, may the husband and wife, who with one mind offer libations and purify them, and (propitiate you) with the Soma ever mixed with milk, constantly associated, may they acquire appropriate (sacrificial) viands ; may they be able to offer sacrifice ; may they never be wanting in food (given by the Gods). They retract not (their promises) to the Gods, they withhold not your praise, but offer (abundant) sacrificial food. Blessed with youthful and adolescent offspring, and both having their persons richly ornamented, they pass (happily) their whole life. Offering acceptable sacrifices, obtaining the wealth they solicit, presenting gratifying (oblations to the Gods), for the sake of immortality, enjoying personal union, they (husband and wife) worship the Gods."

The father and son.—The house that did not ring with the merry laughter and joyous shouts of children was not regarded as fit for habitation. Prayers were sent up to the Gods for the birth of children in the house (Rv. vii. 1, 11. 12. 19. 24 ; 4. 10 ; 24, 5 ; viii. 1, 13), and for their long life and prosperity. Sons were coveted not only for the continuity and prolongation of the family line, but also for the spiritual benefit of the dead ancestors who were eager for the oblations offered to them by their lineal descendants (Rv. i. 105, 3). Sometimes, when there was no issue, sons were adopted by a stretch of the legal fiction ; but no real pleasure was felt in these sons, as they were not the flesh and blood of the adoptive parents, and sometimes returned to the original family from which they had come. (Rv. vii. 4, 7. 8). Indeed, it was regarded as a misfortune to have to adopt sons, begot by others. But still the custom existed. The ideal son was he who was a devotee of the Gods and knew how to please them with prayers, who was tall and stout, whose intelligence was keen and deep, who was self-supporting, well versed in the Śāstric lores, brave and spirited, able to defeat his enemies, and pleasant-looking. (Rv. x. 47, 3). The sage Dyumna, son of Atri, prayed for a son who would achieve glory by defeating his enemies in battle (Rv. v. 23, 1. 2). Another sage "prayed for the birth of a son who would be mighty, delight-giving, performer of sacrifices, and bestower of gifts, and who, riding on a brave steed, would successfully encounter his enemies riding on brave steeds in battle" (Rv. vi. 33, 1; *read ante*, Chap. v. p. 224). From the above account it would appear that the sons were trained up not only to be learned, pious and self-supporting, but also to be brave and heroic men who would be able to hold their own against their enemies. With such ideals before them, parents took great care in the upbringing of their sons from their very infancy. The grown-up sons always kept their father's company, sat with him in his room for receiving instructions (Rv. i. 73, 3), and obeyed his orders (Rv. i. 68. 5). Sometimes they were sent to the house of a professional preceptor who imparted to them true knowledge with a view to develop their manhood. (Rv. i. 112. 2). If, unfortunately, any son went astray, the father did not easily give him up for lost, but tried his best by persuasions and admonitions to bring him round. (Rv. ii. 29, 5). In the early times, the father had absolute power over the life and limb of his son, and could inflict on him corporal punishment even to the extent of maiming or blinding him for serious offences. It is related in the Ṛgveda that Vṛṣā-giri blinded his son Ṛjrāśva for destroying one hundred sheep belonging to their co-villagers, though his eye-sight was afterwards restored through the grace of the Aśvins. (Rv. i. 116, 16; 117, 17). It is also related in the *Aitareya Brāhmaṇa* that Ajīgarta driven by extreme poverty, sold his son Śunahśepa to Rohita for being sacrificed to Varuṇa as a vicarious offer (read *ante*,

Ch. ii, p. 106-108), but there is no clear mention of this sacrifice in the Ṛgveda though it is indicated in certain hymns. (Rv. i. 24-30). There can be no doubt, however, that in early Ṛgvedic times the father had absolute power over the life and limb of his son, though it was seldom exercised. He was ordinarily an affectionate father, always anxious for the welfare of his son (Rv. viii. 48, 4), and tried his best to train him up according to the ideal that obtained in those days. He may have been occasionally harsh, nay severe, for the sake of discipline, but he was seldom cruel; and the son, while standing in reverential awe of him, was usually dutiful and devotedly attached to him.

The father was the patriarch of the family, having supreme authority over all. His word was law and had to be implicitly obeyed. Sometimes, when he became too old and unfit for active work, the management of the house-hold naturally passed on to the eldest son who wielded supreme authority, probably under the guidance and advice of his old father, if he still retained his faculties intact. The son's wife then became the *defacto* mistress of the house. In the marriage-hymn of the Ṛgveda, the young wife has been enjoined to exercise authority over her husband's father, mother, sisters and brothers (Rv. x. 85, 46), and the poet must have contemplated a contingency like the above, when she was likely to be called upon to preside over the household. The old parents were treated with due respect and their comforts carefully attended to. (Av. xiv. 2, 16). The daughter-in-law was wealful (*Śambhū*) to her father-in-law, and 'pleasant' (*syonā*) to her mother-in-law.

Exposure of old parents in Ṛgvedic India a myth.—Kaegi in his *Der Ṛgveda* (N. 50) quotes the following remarks of Zimmer to show the treatment accorded by the Germans to the aged, in order to prove the existence of a similar custom among the Ṛgvedic Aryans: "Among the Germans, when the master of the house was over sixty years old, if the signs of the weakness of age were of such a character that he 'no longer had the power to walk or stand, and to ride unassisted and unsupported, with collected mind, free will and good sense', he was obliged to give over his authority to his son, and to perform menial service; the old men might be made by hard sons and cruel grandsons to expiate painfully the love and gentleness they had neglected in their more powerful days; those who had grown useless and burdensome were even either killed outright, or exposed and abandoned to death by starvation. (Grimm *Deutsche Rechtsalt*, p 487 ff.). We have to imagine exactly similar conditions among the Indians, when the texts speak of 'the divided possessions of an old father' and of 'old men exposed.'" (Zimmer, *Alt. Laben*. 326-328).

There is a passage in the Ṛgveda (i. 70, 5) which indicates that the possessions of the old father were divided among his sons in his life-time. Even if we suppose that they were landed property, provisions had to be first made for his and his wife's maintenance. The passages in the later literature (the *Saṃhitās* and *Brāhmaṇas*) however, "all negative the idea that the property of the family was legally family property: it is clear that it was the property of the head of the house, usually the father, and that the other members of the family only had moral claims upon it, which the father could ignore, though he might be coerced by his sons if they were physically stronger...The developed *patria potestas* of the father, which was early very marked, as shown by the legend of Śunahśepa, is inconsistent with the view that the sons were legally owners with their father, unless and until they actually insisted on a division of the property." (*Ved. Ind.* i. 351-352). Even to this day, when landed property is divided among the sons during the father's life-time, a share is reserved for his maintenance, which is equally divided among the surviving sons after his death. Then, again, it should be remembered that even in Ṛgvedic times, sons were coveted, because they would offer oblations to the dead parents and their ancestors. (Rv. i. 105, 3). This was not only a moral but a religious obligation. It cannot, therefore, be at all conceived by any stretch of imagination or comparison with the customs prevailing among the so-called Aryan peoples in other countries that the Ṛgvedic Aryans killed their old and decrepit parents, or exposed and abandoned them to death by starvation. The custom found among the ancient Germans and Romans must have been a relic of the barbarous customs that prevailed among the prehistoric aborigines of Europe, with whom the half-savage Aryan tribes from Sapta-Sindhu had amalgamated. There is no distinct trace of the existence of this barbarous custom in the Ṛgveda, the oldest work extant of the Aryan people.

Hence, there is no reason to believe with Zimmer (*Op. cit.* 327, 328) that the custom of the exposure of the aged prevailed in Ṛgvedic times. He infers its existence "from a passage of the Ṛgveda (viii. 51, 2) and from the mention of the persons exposed (*ud-hitāh*) in the Atharva-veda (xviii, 2, 34). The latter passage may well refer merely to the bodies being exposed after death to the elements (as is done by the Parsis). The former passage merely refers to the individual case of some person who may have been cast out, and proves absolutely nothing as to a habitual or recognised custom, nor can such a custom be inferred from *e g.*, the legend of Cyavana." [1] The Ṛgveda [2] represents Cyavana as an old decrepit man, to whom the Aśvins restored his youth and strength, making him acceptable to his wife, and a husband of maidens.[3] There is nothing to show in the verses that he was abandoned by his sons to die of starvation. It is true that Strabo reports the practice as prevailing in Iran, Bactria and the Massagetae, and that it prevailed among the Norsemen, and conceivably among the early Romans.[4]

---

[1] *Vedic Index*, i. 395.

[2] I 116, 10; 117, 13; 118, 6; v. 74, 5; vii. 68, 6; 71, 5; x 39, 4.

[3] *Ved. Ind.*, i 264.

[4] "Among the Romans there was a period when old men over sixty were thrown down from the bridge into the Tiber." Kaege's. *Der Ṛgveda* Note 50. cf. Grimm, *Deutsche Rechtsalt*, p. 489, 8.

Possibly it formed a stage in the evolution of civilisation in its earliest phase, as there are savages even to this day who kill their old and decrepit parents, because they are looked upon as useless encumbrances. But the Ṛgvedic civilisation had long passed that stage, and was too far advanced to admit of the existence of such inhuman and barbarous practices. Zimmer's conjecture, therefore, may be dismissed as too far-fetched, and unwarranted by fact.

The abandonment of old and helpless parents to their fate by savages was probably a grim necessity in the stage of evolution in which they were placed, when life was nomadic and there were no fixed habitations, and every man, woman and able child had to shift for themselves as best they could, without being burdens on others. "Everyone for himself" could not but be the rule when the excruciating pangs of hunger were felt by all and food was scarce, and the securing of a morsel that would save life necessitated and involved a deadly struggle with equally famishing rivals. Nobody in such a condition would think of, or care for old parents, wife or children, who would be remorselessly abandoned, if unable to carry on the struggle for existence themselves in consequence of old age, infirmity or sickness. Even, if necessary, they would straightway be killed and eaten. This was savage human nature in the early stages of civilisation, to which men and women belonging to far civilised and cultured communities have been sometimes known to revert on occasions of dire and widespread suffering and distress caused by famines. It was to overcome this gruesome and intolerable stage of brutish existence that man struggled, and struggled successfully till he reached the truly human state, and created environments, institutions and opportunities for his development. As I have already pointed out, in Ṛgvedic times the Aryans were well advanced on the high road of culture and civilisation, and had long ago passed the primitive stages of evolution. The abandonment of old and helpless parents, and exposing them to die, unattended and uncared for, could not, therefore, have been a practice among them, consistently with their culture and advancement. If evidence of this inhuman practice be discovered in the Vedic literature, which I extremely doubt, they must be the relics of a stage which they had long out-grown. The brute in man is never killed and reveals itself occasionally even in the most advanced society of the present day, as it may have done in Vedic times. But to infer the existence of a general practice from a solitary instance is not only highly unscientific but extremely absurd.

The exposure of girl-infants also a myth.—There is no passage in the Ṛgveda which can be interpreted to mean that girl-infants were cast away, or exposed to die. "The exposure of girl-infants is asserted by Zimmer (*Alt. Leben* 319, 320) on the strength of a passage in the Kāṭhaka Saṃhitā (xxvii. 9), but it seems clear that the passage has been mis-understood[1] and that it refers merely to laying the child aside, not exposing it, while a boy was lifted up." The traditional rendering of the passage is not that it refers to exposure, but to getting rid of a daughter on her marriage. "It is, however, true that the birth of a girl was not at all popular, not an unnatural sentiment in an early society, and paralleled among other Aryan peoples." (*Ved. Ind.* i. 395).

The daughter.—The daughter was called Duhitṛ, literally 'milker,' because in the early stages of Aryan culture, the principal duty of the grown-up girls was to milk the cows. There is no reason to believe with Professors Macdonell and Keith that "the word appears to be derived from *duh* 'milk' in the sense of one who nourishes a child, rather than as the 'milker' of the primitive family, or the suckling" (*Ved. Ind.* i. 371). The daughter was, in the ancient days, as she is even now, a source of great anxiety to the parents, in as much as she had to be given away in marriage, and her future happiness and welfare entirely depended upon the

---

[1] Böhtlingk, *Zeitschrift der Deutschen Morgenländischen Gesellschaft* 44, 494-495.

character and ability of her husband,—a stranger, who may either turn out to be good or bad—to maintain her properly. As marriage also depended on the choice of the girl, supported by that of the parents, it was often very difficult to select a proper bridegroom for her, who would be worthy of her in every way. Should the girl fail to secure a worthy husband, she had to pass the rest of her life in her father's or brother's house, being entirely dependent on their good will and charity for her maintenance. Sometimes the unmarried daughter was given a share of the paternal property, along with the brothers, for her independent support, (Rv. ii. 17, 7), and this also made her an undesirable member of the family, and she was looked upon with anything but favour by her brothers, or brothers' wives. Moreover, the grown-up unmarried girl, who had lost her parents or had no brother to protect or maintain her, stood the risk of being seduced, or going astray (Rv. iv. 5, 5), which caused not a little anxiety to the parents during their life-time. Hence the advent of a daughter in the family was not an occasion for rejoicing but rather for general gloom and depression. A verse of the Atharva-veda (vi. 11, 3) rightly echoes the general desire for the birth of a son, and not of a daughter: "The birth of a girl, grant it elsewhere; here grant a boy." A boy was preferred to a girl, because he would always remain with his parents, continue the family-line, offer oblations to the manes of ancestors for their spiritual benefit, be a support to his parents in their old age and helplessness, and add lustre and glory to the good name of the family by his noble and brilliant achievements. But these things could not be expected from a girl, for whom a substantial dowry had to be found on the occasion of her marriage, who had to be maintained in case of her husband's poverty or death, and who, in the event of her remaining unmarried, had to be provided for by the apportionment to her of a share of the ancestral property, and always sedulously guarded against going astray. No wonder that the birth of a girl in the family did not cause much rejoicing, and she was put aside, while the boy was lifted up by the parents with expressions of joy and delight.

Training of girls, and Lady-Ṛṣis.—But though she was a source of anxiety to her parents from her very birth, nevertheless she shared the paternal affections equally with her more fortunate brothers. She was fed and nursed by the mother cheerfully, and brought up with her brothers without much distinction. Often she proved herself the very pet of the family, with her sweet temper, merry laughter, and graceful and fascinating manners. The big brothers were fond and proud of her, and the mother was naturally more partial and affectionate to her, because of her prospective separation from her when she would grow sufficiently old to be married, and because she was always sympathetic and helpful to her in her own way. The son, as he grew older, gradually lost close touch with the mother, as he had to remain constantly with the father or with his preceptor, but the girl was always with her, helping her in the performance of her household duties, and sharing her joys and sorrows. A daughter, in these circumstances, could not but be an object of love and attention of her parents, and more especially of the mother. Her education, such as it was in those days, was not neglected, and the cultured classes went so far as to give her a very liberal education equally with the sons, which made her feel and win her rightful place in society. There were lady-Ṛṣis in Ṛgvedic times, who composed verses, performed sacrifices, offered hymns to the Gods, and won honourable places in the galaxy of the noble singers, and occupied glorious niches in the Temple of Fame. Princess Ghoṣā was a celebrated Ṛṣi (Rv. i. 117; x. 39, 40); so were Lopamudrā, (Rv. i. 179); Mamatā (Rv. vi. 10, 2); Apālā (Rv. viii. 91); Sūryā (Rv. x 85); Indrānī (Rv. x. 145) Śacī (Rv. x. 159); Sārparājñī (Rv. x. 189), and Viśvavārā (Rv. v. 28). The last-named lady not only composed verses in praise of Agni or Fire, but even performed the function of a *ṛtvij* or priest at a sacrifice (Rv. v. 28. 1), a privilege which was denied to woman in a later age by a jealous, illiberal and selfish priestcraft. Apālā composed a hymn in honour of Indra (Rv. viii. 91). and offered him Soma herself. Through the grace of Indra she was cured of her skin-disease for which she had been abandoned by her husband. (Rv. viii. 91, 4). Her father's head had become bald, and his corn-fields had lost their productive power. It was through her earnest prayer that Indra was pleased to cure him of his baldness, and produce bumper crops in his fields. (Rv. viii. 91, 5. 6). Women sometimes accompanied their husbands to war, and Viśpalā, the Queen of King Khela, who had lost her leg in a conflict, had it replaced by an iron (*āyasī*) one, through the grace of the Aśvins. (Rv. i. 112, 10; 116, 15; 117, 11; 118, 8; x. 39, 8). Mudgalānī, or Indrasenā, wife of the sage Mudgala, helped her husband in the pursuit of robbers who had stolen their cows, drove the car for her husband when he was put in a tight corner, and taking up her husband's bow and arrows gave them battle, defeated them and recovered the stolen property. (Rv. x. 102). All these instances go to show that women played a very important part in the domestic and social life of the Ṛgvedic Aryans, and they received not only a high intellectual and spiritual, but also a vigorous physical training equally with the men, whom they sometimes surpassed in bravery, intelligence and cleverness. There is a reference in Rv. v. 30, 9 to women-warriors, and it may be surmised that women received some sort of military training, which enabled them to become soldiers. To the eternal credit of Viśvavārā stands the verse in which she offered a prayer to Agni for fixing the nuptial relations on a firm, sound and inviolable basis (Rv. v. 28, 3), which goes to show that noble-minded ladies were anxious to effect social reforms that would purify domestic life, and add to domestic felicity and happiness.

Marriage and status of women.—From the above brief account it would appear that the status of women in Ṛgvedic society was ordinarily high and honourable. Though she was obedient to her husband, and subservient to his will, she was treated by him with proper respect. I have already said that she had the right to perform the sacrifices with her husband. (Rv. i. 28, 3; v. 43. 15; viii. 31, 5-8; x. 40, 101.) The childless widow inherited her husband's property as a matter of right. (Rv. x. 102, 11). The unmarried daughter, who lived all her life in her parents' home with her parents and was called *amājur*, demanded and got a share of the ancestral property for her maintenance. (Rv. ii. 17, 7). But ordinarily she could not claim any share with her brothers. "A son born of the body does not transfer wealth to a sister." (Rv. iii. 31, 2). The former performed excellent sacrifices, while the latter was honoured. But, as in the event of her remaining unmarried, she had to be given a portion of the ancestral property, the brother was naturally anxious to see her married to a worthy young man who would be able to maintain her, and usually gave her suitable dowry and many valuable presents on the occasion of her marriage. (Rv. i. 109, 2). Nevertheless, as the choice of a husband generally rested with the young lady herself, who selected her man from among a number of suitors (Rv. x. 27, 12), and as her marriage was contingent on this selection, it was not unlikely that, failing to make any selection, she remained unmarried. But a spinster was not a desirable member of the family, not only on economic but also on moral grounds, for she stood the risk of going astray. Probably it was from considerations like these that parents and brothers gradually became anxious to see a girl married before she could exercise her own judgment, which probably ultimately led to the custom of infant-marriage. But in Ṛgvedic times no girl was married before she had reached her womanhood. She must be fully developed physically in her father's house (*pitṛ-padam vyaktām*) before her marriage could be thought of. (Rv. x. 85, 21, 22). Sūryā, the daughter of Sūrya, was given away to Soma in marriage, only when she became youthful, and yearned for a husband (*patye śaṃsantīm*, explained by Sāyaṇa as *patim kamaya-mānām paryāptayauvanām iti*, Rv. x. 85, 9). Ghoṣā, the lady-Ṛṣi, married when she nearly passed her youth. From a study of the Vedic marital rituals it appears that the marriage had to be consummated at the earliest on the fourth night after the ceremony, and this would not have been possible if the bride was not a youthful lady. Infant-marriage or rather pre-pubescent marriage was, therefore, uncommon, though probably not entirely unknown in Ṛgvedic times.

In this connection the following remarks of Professors Macdonell and Keith on the subject will be found apposite: "Marriage in the early Vedic texts appears essentially as a union of two persons of full development. This is shown by the numerous references to unmarried girls who grow old in the house of their fathers (*amā-jur* cf. Rv. i. 117, 7; ii. 17, 7; x. 39, 3; 40, 5), and who adorn themselves in desire of marriage, as well as to the paraphernalia of spells and potions used in the Atharva-vedic tradition (Av. iii. 18. = Rv. x. 145) to compel the love of man or woman respectively, while even the Ṛgveda itself (vii. 55, 5. 8) seems to present us with a spell by which a lover seeks to send all the household to sleep when he visits his beloved. [The verses, however, admit of a different interpretation, Read *ante*, Chap. iv, p. 199]. Child-wives first occur regularly in the Sūtra period, though it is still uncertain to what extent the rule of marriage before puberty there obtained. The marriage ritual also quite clearly presumes that the marriage is a real and not a nominal one: an essential feature is the taking of the bride to her husband's house, and the ensuing cohabitation." (Rv. x. 85, 29. 37).[1]

Sometimes a maiden selected a wealthy suitor for her husband, irrespective of his personal attraction, qualifications, or worthiness. Such marriages were condemned. A

---

[1] *Ved. Ind.*, i. 474-475.

respectable girl always selected from among her suitors one whom she really loved, as true love was considered the real basis of conjugal happiness. (Rv. x. 27, 12).

A blind daughter, or a daughter with natural physical defects, could not be easily given away in marriage. But if any one proposed to take her for his wife, no great objection was raised against the proposal. (Rv. x. 23, 11). As has already been pointed out above, the position of the newly wedded wife was one of honour in her husband's home. She was looked upon as the future mistress of the family, and was expected to exercise her benevolent authority over the old parents of her husband and his unmarried brothers and sisters.

It happened sometimes that an unworthy man had to pay a heavy price for his bride (Rv. i. 109, 2), which goes to show that the parents often arranged a match, though they did not perhaps always control the marriage of a son or daughter of mature age. If the parties did not belong to the same *gotra* or were not affiicted with incurable disease, the parents probably never objected to the marriage. There is another verse which also goes to prove that the parents had some control in the selection of a bridegroom for his daughter. If the father had no male issue, he entered into an agreement with his would-be son-in-law that his first male child should be given to him for adoption as his son. (*Putrikā-putra*, Rv. i. 124, 7; iii. 31, 1).

Forms of marriage.—There were several forms of marriage in Ṛgvedic times. One form was usually based on mutual consent, though the final approval of the brother or parents was necessary. The marriage was arranged through an intermediary (Rv. x. 85, 15. 23) "presumably after those concerned had in effect come to an agreement." Another form of marriage was by stealing or capture; but this was not much in vogue, though we come across the story of Vimada who carried off Purumitra's daughter against her father's wish, but very possibly with her own consent.

(Rv. i. 112, 19; 116, 1; 117, 20; x. 39, 7; 65, 12). Then there was a form of marriage called *ārṣa*, when a daughter was married to a Ṛṣi for his vast knowledge and spiritual culture. The story of *Syāvāśva* is an instance in point. And lastly, there was the ordinary form of marriage, which consisted in a daughter being married to a suitable and worthy bridegroom with many valuable presents.

The wedding-ceremony.—The wedding-ceremony, which will be fully described in a subsequent chapter, commenced at the bride's house. (Rv. x. 17, 1). The bridegroom, who dressed himself gorgeously and adorned his person with ornaments, (Rv. x. 78, 7), repaired with his friends and relations to the bride's house, where he met the friends and relations of the bride. "The bridegroom having caused the bride to mount a stone, formally grasped her hand, and led her round the Household Fire (cf. Rv. x 85, 36. 38). This act constituted the marriage, the husband hence being called 'he who takes by the hand' (*hasta-grābha* Rv. x. 18, 8). The festivities being over, the bridegroom took the bride to his house on a car in a marriage procession (Rv. x. 85, 7. 8. 10. 24. 25. 26. 27. 42), all to the accompaniment of suitable stanzas. Then followed co-habitation."[1] The above extract contains too brief an account to give the reader an idea of the elaborate rites performed, and the beautiful *mantras* uttered by the bridegroom and the bride in connection with the ceremony which lasted for several days.

Before the bride mounted the stone, the groom repeated, according to the Gṛhya Sūtras the words: "I am he; thou art she; I the Sāman, thou the Ṛc; I the heaven, thou the earth; here will we unite ourselves and produce offspring." Of course such words addressed to a mere child would be meaningless. They were evidently addressed to one who had attained youth and understood their true import.

---

[1] *Vedic Index*, i. 483-484.

The Ṛgvedic *mantras* clearly describe the *status* of the newly wedded wife, the duties that she was expected to perform in her new sphere and environments, and the necessity of uniting her heart with her husband's for ever. It appears that the bride came to her husband's house to live there permanently, though she was permitted to visit her parents occasionally.

Monogamy and Polygamy.—Monogamy was the rule in ancient Ṛgvedic society, and evidently approved. (Rv. i. 124, 7; iv. 3, 2; x. 71, 1; 104, 3; 105, 8; 186, 7; iv. 3, 2; x. 71, 4 etc.). But a Vedic Indian could have more than one wife (Rv. i. 62, 11; 71, 1; 104, 3; 105, 8; 186, 7; iv. 58, 8; vii. 18, 2; 26, 3; x 43, 1; 101, 11), though it was recognised that a plurality of wives never contributed to domestic happiness, and often made the life of the husband miserable. (Rv. i. 105, 8; x. 33, 2). Polygamy must have been a relic of barbarous times when women were captured, enslaved and married often against their will. Wives were then regarded as chattels, who could be staked at dicing, and over whose life and liberty husbands exercised supreme control. Though polygamy was gradually dying out, the evil custom still persisted in Ṛgvedic times, and the lot of the co-wives was extremely miserable. Each naturally craved the whole-hearted love of her husband, and wished to be his favourite wife; but as this was not possible, the neglected co-wife very often took to the performance of secret rites, and the uttering of incantations with a view to win her husband's love and put down her rival. There are two hymns in the Ṛgveda (x. 145 and 159), said to have been composed by Indrānī and Śacī (both names are identical), which betray the degraded and deplorable state of woman's mind, brought about by the evil custom of polygamy. It appears to have been more confined among kings and nobles (Rv. vii. 18, 7; x. 95, 6) as well as the lower classes than among middle-class men who represented the best culture of the community. If Śacī or Indrānī was the wife of the God Indra, as there is reason to believe from the verses that she was, (Rv. x. 159, 4. 6), it must be admitted that the Gods also indulged in this practice. But it was once remarked by a French cynic that "God created man; but man also created God." The truth of this remark is best illustrated by the fact that the polygamous Aryans in the early stage of their development invested Indra with a plurality of wives. The advanced Ṛṣis, however, credited him with being content with only one loving wife, who was the main source of his domestic felicity. (Rv. iii. 53, 6). There can be no doubt, therefore, that the hymns containing incantations for the suppression of the co-wife, the authorship of which is ascribed to Indrāṇī, must have represented a more primitive stage of society, which partially survived even in Ṛgvedic times.

Polyandry.—As regards polyandry, it must be said that even if the custom had existed in the early stages of culture, there is very little evidence in the Ṛgveda to prove its general existence in Ṛgvedic times. As I have already fully dealt with this subject elsewhere (*ante*, Chap. ii, p. 103-104) I need not repeat my remarks in this place.

Widow re-marriage..—There is no evidence of widow re-marriage in the proper sense of the word, in the Ṛgveda. But a custom seems to have existed, according to which a childless widow could live with her dead husband's brother (devṛ) in order to produce children. (Rv. x. 40, 2). The custom is probably alluded to in a funeral hymn of the Ṛgveda (x. 18, 8), in which the widow is asked to get up from where she lay down beside her dead husband, and return home. The custom of widow-remarriage is also probably alluded to in the Atharva-veda (ix. 5, 27. 28): "When a woman has had one husband before, and gets another, if they present the *aja pañcaudana* offering, they shall not be separated. A second husband dwells in the same world with his re-wedded wife, if he offers the *pañcaudana*" (Muir O. S. T. v. 306). Delbrück thinks that "this very probably refers to a case in which the first husband was still alive, but was impotent or had lost caste (*patita*)." Nevertheless, the later Dharma Sūtras [1] began to recognize ordinary re-marriage in case of the death of the first husband. [2]

Burning of widows.—The burning of a widow on the funeral pyre of her dead husband may have been a custom among the Aryans in the early primitive stages of their civilisation, for we find the custom of killing the widow or widows of a dead man and burying her or them with him, still existing among barbarous tribes. The idea probably was that the dead man must have his wives accompanying him to the next world for providing him with home-comforts. It was from a similar belief that an animal was sacrificed and food-grains offered at the time of the funeral. The custom of burning widows on the funeral pyres of their husbands is clearly referred to in the Atharva-veda (xviii. 3, 1), which contains much ancient history. If the custom existed at the time of the composition of the Atharva-veda, it must have been a revival of the ancient barbarous custom. But during Ṛgvedic times, it seems to have completely disappeared. Pursuant to old custom, however, the widow lay down beside her dead husband on the funeral pyre, but she was asked to get up and go home, as her husband had been dead and it was no use lying by his side. The old custom of burning the widow, however, was subsequently revived and continued down to recent times till it was put down by British legislation.

Exogamy and Endogamy.—"According to Senart, the Aryan people practised in affairs of marriage both a rule of exogamy, and one of endogamy. A man must marry a woman of equal birth, but not one of the same *gens*, according to the Roman law as interpreted by Senart and Kovalevsky,[3]

---

[1] *Vasiṣtha Dharma Sūtra* xvii. 19. 20, 72-74; *Baudhāyana Dharma Sūtra* iv. 1. 16; *Manava Dharma Śāstra*, ix 175

[2] *Vedic Index*, i. 477. For a fuller discussion, read, Chap. xi of this book (*infra*).

[3] *Famille et Propriété Primitives* 19, *et seq*

and an Athenian must marry an Athenian woman, but not of the same *γένος*. In India these rules are reproduced in the form that one must not marry within the *Gotra*, but not without the caste." (*Vedic Index* ii. 268). The remark with regard to India justly applies to the social conditions of post-Ṛgvedic times ; for in Ṛgvedic times, the rules of caste were not fully developed or sufficiently hard and fast. Nobody was certainly not allowed to marry within the same *Gotra*, but love usually transcended the bounds of caste, such as they existed in those days, and there was no bar against inter-marriage, if the match was desirable in every respect. Ṛṣis married kings' daughters, as kings also married the daughters of Brahmans and Ṛṣis. Only the parties should not belong to the same *Gotra*.

Marital relations and Morality.—The wedded couples were expected to be faithful to one another. But the custom of polygamy sometimes brought in its train unchastity on the part of the neglected wife or wives, and we come across many passages in the Ṛgveda, in which the wife has been described to entertain secret lovers. (Rv. i. 34, 3 ; iv. 5, 5 ; ix. 32, 5 ; 38, 4 ; 56, 3 ; 96, 22 ; 101, 12). But "adultery was generally regarded among Aryan peoples as a serious offence against the husband of the woman affected. We accordingly find in the legal literature of India traces of the rule that an adulterer can be slain with impunity, if taken in the act.[1] Weber,[2] however, has adduced some material indicating an indifference to these matters in Vedic times, and Ludwig[3] has adopted the same view. But as Delbrück[4] has clearly shown, the evidence is not convincing ; the cited prescriptions[5] forbidding connexion with another man's wife during a certain rite do not imply that

[1] Leist. *Altarisches Jus Gentium*, 276, *et seq.* 309.

[2] *Indische Studien* 10, 83 *et seq.*

[3] *Op cit.* 5, 573.

[4] *Die indogermanischen Verwandtschaftsnamen* 545 *et seq.*

[5] *Taitt. Sam.*, v. 6, 8, 3 ; *Maitr. Sam.*, iii. 4, 7.

such connexion would otherwise be allowed; the ritual of the Varuṇa-praghāsas,[1] when a wife names her lover or lovers, seems originally to have been a solemn means of banishing the evil brought on a family by a wife's fall; Yājnavalkya's famous saying [2] that no one cares whether a wife is 'unchaste' (*parahpuṃsā*) or not is a mere mistranslation,[3] the expression *parah-puṃsā* really meaning 'removed from the male persons'"[4]

The custom of pubescent marriage that prevailed in Vedic times, and the liberty that women enjoyed, must have been responsible for much laxity of morals among unmarried women, especially those who had no guardians or protectors to prevent them from falling into temptations. After the death of the father, the brother was the natural guardian of an unmarried girl; but, if unfortunately she had no brother, the chances of her being tempted into immoral ways were great. The Ṛgveda refers to this matter (i. 124, 7; iv. 5, 5; viii. 35, 5) as one of frequent occurrence. Clandestine love even among married women was not uncommon (Rv. i. 134, 3; iv. 5, 5; ix. 32, 5; 38, 4; 56, 3; 96, 22; 101, 12, etc.), and the offspring of such unions were often abandoned in secret. (Rv. ii. 29, 1). Pischel and Geldner see many references to *Hetairai* in some passages of the Ṛgveda [5]. Uṣas in one passage (Rv. i. 92, 4) is compared to a *Hetaira* who dances with her breast open in a shameless fashion. Pischel is of opinion that the word *vrā* in some passages of the Ṛgveda refers to women who go to the feast (*samana*, i. 124, 8), or courtezans (*viśyā*, 'of the people' Rv. i 126, 5).[6] It would thus appear that there were dancing women and courtezans in ancient Ṛgvedic society,

---

[1] *Mait. Sam.*, i. 10, 11; *Śata. Brāh.* ii. 5, 2, 20.

[2] *Śat Brah.*, i. 3, 1, 21.

[3] Böhtlingk's Dictionary, S. V.

[4] *Vedic Index*, i. 396-397.

[5] Cf. *Vedische Studien*, i. xxv, 196, 275; 299, 309; 2, 120, 154, 179, etc.

[6] *Ved Ind*, ii. 339-340.

as well as unmarried girls gone astray and married women faithless to their husbands, which probably gave rise to such remarks as "woman's mind is ungovernable" (Rv. viii. 33, 17) "woman's love is always fickle" (Rv. x. 95, 15) and "woman's heart is like that of a hyæna" (*Ibid*). Of course, these remarks were prompted by an observation of the character of the ordinary women of the uncultured classes, most of whom lived a free-and-easy life. But there were also noble types of women among the cultured classes and the decent folk, who were models of feminine virtues, and who were justly honoured and respected by the opposite sex. The above uncomplimentary remarks regarding women had not, therefore, any general applicability. They are, however, significant as revealing a far from ideal state of society in Ṛgvedic times, which stood in urgent need of reforms. These reforms were attempted in a later age, the age of the Sūtras, but the social pendulum was abruptly and violently made to swing to the other extreme with far more disastrous results. Woman's liberty was restricted; she was allowed no choice in the selection of her husband, and she was married at an age when she was incapable of understanding the real significance of marriage and exercising her own judgment and discretion. Womanhood was sacrificed at the altar of supposed social convenience and purity, and out of its ashes arose a race of cribbed, cabined, confined and delicate creatures, too fragile for the propagation of vigorous life, and too ethereal and womanly to be of any earthly use. With her degeneration began the degeneration of the people, which has continued down to the present times with rapid and disastrous acceleration.

CHAPTER VII.

AGRICULTURE AND THE VALUE OF CATTLE IN ṚGVEDIC TIMES.

Indra, the supreme God of the agricultural Vedic Aryans.—The principal occupations of the Ṛgvedic Aryans, as already stated, were agriculture and cattle-keeping. The Pañcajanāh were an eminently agricultural people, as opposed to and distinguished from the other Aryan tribes, some of whom were still in the nomadic and pastoral stage of existence, with low culture, and roamed about the country without any fixed habitations, while others occupied the impregnable forests, from which they occasionally sallied forth with the object of stealing the cattle and agricultural products of the settled and more advanced section of the population. The latter discovered a powerful God to help them in their struggle for existence and self-preservation in the great Indra who was able not only to vanquish their foes, but also to supply them with an abundance of timely rain for carrying on their agricultural operations with success Vṛtra, who had been regarded as a *Deva* and *Brāhmaṇa* in pastoral times when regular rain was not much needed, came to be looked upon by the agricultural section of the people as their mortal enemy, like the savage and half-savage Dāsas and Dasyus who harassed them by stealing their cattle and agricultural products. For it was Vṛtra who withheld the timely rains, brought on distressing droughts that hampered the progress of agricultural work, resulting in a poor produce of food-grains, and shut out, with his black cloud-body, the Dawn and the Sun that marked and indicated the definite times for beginning and performing the sacrifices in honour of the Gods, and especially of Indra, so that he might sufficiently be strengthened in his fight with the deadly demon. Hence Indra, with his terrible thunderbolt, came to be regarded as the only powerful God who was able successfully to cope with the wily stratagems of the dreaded Vṛtra and bring down rain by rending open his cloud-body, and laying him low. Of course, Indra was assisted in his work by some other Gods, notably Viṣṇu, Trita, Parjanya, the Maruts, the Aśvins and Bṛhaspati; but they all required to be strengthened by the libations of Soma throughout the year, which necessitated the holding of an annual session of sacrifice lasting for nine, ten or twelve months until the rains began to fall. And even when the rainy season did appear, a special day-and-night session of a *Sattra* or Soma-sacrifice was held for two or three months to strengthen Indra and his auxiliaries all the better for bringing the fight to a successful and speedy termination. This appears to be the main object of holding the annual and special sessions of sacrifice in Ṛgvedic times and later. We have in a previous chapter referred to a Ṛgvedic verse (v. 45, 11) which says: "I offer to you (Gods) *for the sake of water*, an all-bestowing sacrifice, whereby the Navagvas have completed the ten months' rite."[1]

In another verse, Indra is thus extolled: "Thou art renowned as having slain the Vṛtras. Thou madest flow the floods that were obstructed." (Rv. iv. 42, 7). These floods were rain-waters, obstructed by Vṛtra in his cloud-body, and Indra's renown consisted in having released them successfully for the benefit of his votaries. No wonder, therefore, that Indra appropriated the largest number of hymns of the Ṛgveda, offered to any one single God. He played a two-fold character in Vedic times, first as the leader of the Gods who successfully carried on the cosmic struggle in the sky against Vṛtra for the benefit of the Aryans; and secondly, as the leader and guiding spirit of the human hosts that fought against the Dāsas and the Dasyus on the earth below, who harassed the settled Aryans by stealing their cattle and

---

[1] For an elaborate treatment of the subject, read Das' *Ṛgvedic India*, xii, 475-77, (First Edition).

food-grains. The Vedic Aryans, therefore, felt the necessity for propitiating Indra by singing hymns in his praise, and for strengthening him by the offer of the Soma drink at a sacrifice, to the accompaniment of the recitation of appropriate *mantras* which were supposed to possess the power of vivifying him into activity according to the needs of his worshippers. Of course, Indra would ordinarily perform his functions, even if he were not invoked by songs, or strengthened by the offer of the Soma-drink; but his acts would then be irregular and fitful, and hence unconducive to the requirements of the Aryan people. The latter, therefore, had recourse to *mantras* and the regular performance of sacrifices with a view to *compel* him, as it were, to exercise his functions and regulate his activities in their behalf and for their benefit. The Vedic Aryans realised the value of action on their own part, and did not choose to reman idle; but their action was directed under the divine guidance of Indra and his auxiliaries. If they wanted timely rains for their agricultural work, Indra must be invoked by songs and strengthened by the performance of the Soma-sacrifice; and if they wanted to drive away, kill or defeat the Dāsas and the Dasyus, his aid was similarly invoked so that he might lead their hosts to victory. It was Indra who gave the Aryans new lands for establishing agricultural settlements in, (Rv. iv. 26, 2), distributed the lands conquered from the Dāsas and the Dasyus among his votaries, (Rv. i, 100, 18; ii. 21, 1), poured down timely rains for agricultural work by killing Vṛtra who withheld them, (Rv. iv. 26, 2), and gave them horses, cattle and plenty. (Rv. iv. 28, 5). The Vedic Aryans exerted all their powers for the betterment of their own condition, but they did so under the sure guidance of the divine Indra and the auxiliary Gods, who presided over the different spheres of Earth and Heaven.

Indra-worship simultaneous with the evolution of Aryan agricultural life in the Neolithic Age.—The inauguration of Indra-worship and the Soma-cult appears to be simultaneous with the agricultural stage of Aryan evolution in Sapta-Sindhu. But the Soma-cult had been probably older, as the Soma is called most ancient *(pratnamit)*, and Indra is said to have drunk the Soma-juice as soon as he was born, and before he even sucked his mother's breast. It is remarkable, as we have already said, that Indra's name does not appear among any of the so-called Aryan nations of Europe, which points to his solely Indian origin. No doubt, it appears in the ancient literature of the Iranians, not as *Indra* but as *Āndra*, in the sense of a demon or evil spirit, which marked the difference of religious and material culture of the two branches of the Aryan race, who lived in close proximity of one another. While the Vedic Aryans settled down in Sapta-Sindhu as agriculturists, the majority of the Iranians must have been still in their nomadic stage without feeling any necessity for regular rains. Or, if they knew agriculture, as is evidenced by the existence of such words in the Avesta as *Yao karesh* (Vedic, *Yava-kṛṣi*) and *hahya* (Vedic *Śasya*), it must have been of a primitive kind and confined to the cultivation of one staple crop only, namely *ya a*, which was cultivated in winter and required very little rain for its growth. The cultivation of *dhānya* (paddy or rice), which required copious rain for its growth, was probably unknown to them. Hence Indra, the God of rain and thunder, who came to be lauded to the skies as the supreme God by their neighbours, the Vedic Aryans, was looked upon by them as inimical to their interests and a devil-incarnate. Any way, there can be no doubt that the God Indra was solely the creation of the Vedic Aryans in Sapta-Sindhu, and his discovery was made in early Neolithic times when weapons, fashioned out of rude stones and bones, were freely used by them. (Vide *ante* Chap. ii, pp. 51-56). Indra's thunderbolt, as already stated, had been first made of stone, which was replaced by one made of bone in a later age. The bone-made *vajra* was afterwards replaced by one made of hard metal, bronze or iron. In Ṛgvedic times, the use of iron implements and weapons was common, though the Ṛgveda frequently makes references to ancient times when Indra had been armed first with a stone-made, and afterwards with a bone-made thunderbolt. These ancient times extended back to the early Neolithic Age, when the Vedic Aryans became agriculturists and settled down in rude homesteads near their corn-fields. How long did the Neolithic Age last in Sapta-Sindhu, it is very difficult to ascertain; but there can be no doubt that it lasted for several thousand years, as it did in Europe and other countries. There is reference in the Ṛgveda to ancient hymns, addressed to Indra by the ancestors of the Vedic Aryans, which had come down to their descendants, clothed in new and graceful language. There is further reference to the three ages, during which the Ṛgvedic hymns were composed. Taking all these facts into consideration, one cannot but conclude that Ṛgvedic culture had commenced in Sapta-Sindhu several millenniums before 1200 or 1500 B C, and that the story of Aryan immigration to India from Europe about that period, manufactured by Western scholars, and accepted by their disciples as gospel truth, is a pure myth which has no basis on fact, and upon which no reliable ancient history can be constructed. Most of the Ṛgvedic hymns reveal a comparatively high state of culture, which had no counterpart among the so-called Aryan nations of Europe about 1200 or 1500 B. C. The Neolithic culture of Europe about this period was extremely crude and low, as I have already pointed out elsewhere.[1]

Mode of agriculture in the early Neolithic Age.—The mode of agriculture in Sapta-Sindhu in the early Neolithic Age must have been extremely primitive. The implements of agriculture were made either of stone, bone, or hard wood, tapering to a point, with which the rude cultivator dug the earth, or turned the sod. Captain Cook who visited New Zealand during his First Voyage in the latter part of 1769

---

[1] Vide *ante* Chaps. II & V.

thus describes the mode of tilling the ground adopted by its inhabitants: "A long narrow stake, sharpened to an edge at the bottom, with a piece fixed across a little above it for the purpose of driving it into the ground with the foot, supplies the place both of plough and spade. The soil being light, the work is not very laborious, and with this instrument alone they will turn up ground of six or seven acres in extent."[1] A similar method must have been adopted by the Neolithic Aryans of Sapta-Sindhu for the tillage of their ground which was probably alluvial soil on the banks of the rivers, and therefore could be easily cultivated. The plough must have been a later invention, and used to be drawn either by a pair of horses or oxen. With the invention of the plough, cultivation must have gradually extended from the river-banks to large clearances of the forests, after the Dasyus occupying them had been driven out and the land reclaimed.

The curious reader may ask how a people in the Neolithic stage of civilisation, with no knowledge of the manufacture of iron and the use of iron implements, managed to build houses, construct boats, and manufacture the other necessaries of life. In answer to this query, I will quote again certain passages from Cook's *Voyages of Discovery* to show that human intelligence and ingenuity were quite capable of adjusting themselves to the needs of a people in any stage of civilisation. Writing about the half-savage people of Otaheite, an island in the South Pacific Ocean, Captain Cook's chronicler on board his ship, the *Endeavour*, stated as follows: "The tools which these people make use of for building houses, constructing canoes, hewing stone, and for felling, cleaving, carving, and polishing timber, consist of nothing more than an adze of stone, and a chisel of bone, most commonly that of a man's arm; and for a file, or polisher, they make use of a rasp of coral, and coral sand."[1] These men manufactured cloth from the barks of

[1] Captain Cook's *Voyages of Discovery* (J. M. Dents & Sons, Ltd.), p. 41.

such trees as the mulberry, the bread-fruit tree, and a tree not unlike the wild fig. "The mulberry tree, which the Indians call Aouta, produces the finest cloth, which is seldom worn but by those of the first rank. The next sort, which is worn by the lower class of people, is made of the bread-fruit tree, and the coarsest of the tree resembling the fig tree......The cloth becomes quite white by bleaching, and is dyed of a red, yellow, brown or black colour; the first of which is very beautiful, and equal, if not superior, to any in Europe. Matting of various kinds is another considerable manufacture, in which, in many respects, they excel the Europeans. They make use of the coarser sort to sleep on, and in wet weather they wear the finer. They greatly excel in the basket and wicker-work; both men and women employ themselves at it, and can make it of a variety of patterns." [1]

From the above account it would appear that the Neolithic stage was not incompatible with a comparatively high state of culture, and that the Neolithic Aryans of Sapta-Sindhu, though unacqnainted with the use of iron implements, were yet able to carry on agricultural work and develop the arts of civilised life. But this Neolithic culture of the Aryans had begun long long before the present hymns of the Ṛgveda were composed, and its beginnings were probably simultaneous with the discovery of Indra, the God who killed Vṛtra and brought down timely rains for the benefit of his votaries.

Barley and Paddy, the staple crops.—Barley and paddy (*yava* and *dhānya*)[2] must have been the staple crops of the Vedic Aryans from the very beginning. European

---

[1] *Ibid*, p. 41.

[2] The word *dhānya* occurs in the Ṛgveda (v. 53, 13; vi. 13, 4; x. 94, 13), as well as the word *dhānā*, always in the plural (Rv. i. 16, 2; iii. 35. 3: 52, 5; vi. 29, 4), meaning the grain of that name as well as grains of corn in general. The principal grain (*dhāna* or *dhānya*) was undoubtedly mentioned to include all other grains. (Vide *ante*, Ch. iv)

scholars assert that the two words in the Ṛgveda were the general names for grains of all kinds. This may be true in certain cases; but it does not follow that the Vedic Aryans were not at all acquainted with the particular corns, known as barley (*yava*) and paddy (*dhānya*). On the other hand, there is reason to believe that these were the principal corns that they cultivated and subsisted upon. Barley was, as it still is, a spring-crop, sown in winter, which does not require much rain for its cultivation. A few showers of winter rain are sufficient for it. But the cultivation of paddy (*dhānya*) requires plenty of rain, and begins from the very commencement of the rainy season. It was for the successful cultivation of *dhānya*, one of the staple food-grains of the Aryans, that the regular fall of rain was needed; and it was to ensure this regular fall that Indra, the God of thunder and rain, was invoked, and the sacrifices and various *Sattras*, both annual and periodical, performed. The Himalayan rivers of the Punjab, having their sources in the glaciers, brought down a perennial supply of pure drinking-water to the Aryan inhabitants living on their banks; and those who lived far away from the river-banks had deep wells sunk, from which an abundant supply of drinking water could be drawn. A year-long session of sacrifice was, threfore, not necessary for this purpose; but it was necessary for helping Indra to fight Vṛtra, or the Demon of Drought, and wrest from his cloud-body a sufficient supply of timely rains for the cultivation and growth of one of the staple crops, on which the Vedic Aryans depended for their subsistence; and this staple crop was, and could be none other than paddy or *dhānya*, which grows only during the rains. The ancient Sapta-Sindhu or the Punjab had seas on the South, East and West, and we can suppose that there was no dearth of rains in that country in Ṛgvedic times, as there is at the present day, when the Eastern and Southern seas have receded far away from its boundaries, leaving a vast tract of alluvial country to the east, and an extensive arid desert to the south. The abundance of rains in the Punjab in those days was favourable to the cultivation of paddy in the rainy season, though barley and other winter crops required only moderate rains in the winter. But the rains, as already pointed out, were never regular in coming, and the successful cultivation of paddy, one of the staple crops, depended, as it still does, on the regularity of these rains. Śuṣṇa, another name of Vṛtra, which can be literally translated as the Drought, frequently intervened and withheld the rains, when they were most urgently needed for carrying on agricultural work, and the Vedic Aryans thought it necessary not only to neutralise but also to destroy the evil power of Vṛtra by setting in opposition to it the benevolent power of the great Indra, the wielder of the thunderbolt, who alone was able to vanquish him. Hence arose the necessity for propitiating him by means of *mantras* and the performance of year-long and periodical sacrifices. As paddy is the only principal crop that flourishes in the rainy season, there can be no doubt that it was one of the staple crops of the Ṛgvedic Aryans, and the statement of the Western scholars that *dhānya* did not mean paddy, and that it was not known nor cultivated in Ṛgvedic times, is more fanciful than real.

It may be argued that when there were seas on the three sides of ancient Sapta-Sindhu, there should not have been any serious dearth of rain in that country to necessitate the performance of a year-long sacrifice. But this argument does not hold good in view of the fact that though Bengal and Orissa have the Bay of Bengal and the Indian Ocean in their vicinity, and the annual rain-fall is abundant, there occur frequent distressing droughts, hampering agricultural work and resulting in scarcities and famines, as copious rain-fall depends upon the regular bursting of the *monsoons* (the Vedic *Maruts*). But the monsoons, as a writer says, have the habit of defying all the laws of Nature. If they are irregular and belated, the rain-fall is not useful for the cultivation of paddy. Similar inconveniences were experienced by the

Ṛgvedic Aryans in ancient sea-girt Sapta-Sindhu also; but they proceeded to remedy them and ensure regular rain-fall in their own way, by performing a year-long sacrifice in honour of the great Indra and his auxiliaries, who were supposed to possess the power of overcoming the Drought (Vṛtra or Śuṣṇa) and bringing down timely rains.

The Gods who were auxiliaries to Indra in his great fight with Vṛtra were Viṣṇu, the Sun-god, who heated the sea-water, converted it into vapours and lifted them into the sky above (Rv. viii. 77, 10), the Maruts or Winds (Monsoons), who carried the watery vapours inland from the surrounding seas, *Trita*, the third month of the rainy season when rainfall was incessant, *Parjanya*, the ancient God of rain, and *Bṛhaspati* of "loud speech" (Rv. iv. 50, 5), who helped the worshippers in properly chanting the *mantras* at the sacrifice, held for the propitiation of the Gods. The Sarasvatī, or the country watered by the river of that name, was called *Vṛtraghnī*, the killar of Vṛtra, like Indra (Rv. vi. 61, 3. 7), probably because the early Vedic Aryans lived in that region as agriculturists, when they first noticed and realised the defeat of Vṛtra by Indra. All these Gods, along with Indra, were invoked by *mantras* and strengthened by the offer of the Soma-juice.

Cultivation by irrigation.—Besides the natural supply of water by timely rains, the Vedic Aryans also depended for the cultivation of their lands on artificial irrigation from wells and channels dug for the purpose. There is mention in the Ṛgveda of cultivators who irrigated their lands, and frightened away flocks of birds that picked up the grains sown, by starting up a tremendous din and noise. (Rv. x. 68, 1). The word Kūpa occurs in the Ṛgveda (i. 105, 17), denoting an artificial hollow in the earth, or pit. There is another word, *avata*, which also denotes an artificial well, and frequently occurs in the Ṛgveda. (i. 55, 8; 85, 10. 11; 116, 9. 22; iv. 17, 16; viii. 49, 6; 62, 6; x. 25, 4). Such wells are "described as unfailing (*a-kṣita*) and full of water

(Rv. x. 101, 6). The water was raised by a wheel (*cakra*). of stone to which was fastened a strap (*varatrā*) with a pail (*kośa*) attached to it. When raised, it was poured into buckets (*āhāva*) of wood. Sometimes these wells appear to have been used for irrigation purposes, the water being led off into broad channels, (*sūrmī suṣirā*, Rv. viii. 69, 12.) In some cases they (the wells) must have been deep, as Trita in the myth is said to have fallen into one, from which he could not escape unaided." [1] There is an epithet *khanitrimā* (produced by digging) of *āpaḥ* (waters) in the Ṛgveda (vii. 49, 2), which "clearly refers to artificial water-channels used for irrigation, as practised in the times of the Ṛgveda." [2] So the Vedic Aryans knew the art of irrigating their lands by water, diverted from rivers through artificial channels (or *canals*, as we should now call them), or lifted from wells by means of stone-wheels (*aśma-cakra*)[3], to which buckets were attached (Rv. x. 25, 4). This old device of lifting water from wells is still found in some parts of the Punjab and Rajputana. The mode of irrigation by water, brought through channels or lifted from wells, was probably resorted to in the dry season *i.e.* in winter and spring, when rainfall sometimes was too scarce and scanty for the cultivation of the spring crops, particularly barley which also formed a staple food-grain of the ancient Aryans. There was a brief spell of rains in winter, which furnished an additional reason for holding the year-long session of the *Sattras* with a view to make the winter rain-fall also timely and regular. As the cultivation of paddy required an abundant supply of water, irrigation was probably not resorted to for helping it in times of drought, as extensive areas under cultivation could not be supplied with abundant water by this means. The successful cultivation of paddy solely depended, as it still does, upon copious rain-fall for three months at a stretch, and it was

[1] *Vedic Index*, i. 40, 177; also Macdonell, *Vedic Mythology*, p. 67

[2] *Vedic Index*, i. 214.

[3] Rv. x. 93, 13; 101, 7.

with a view to ensure it regularly that the year-long Sattras were performed. This would furnish the *raison-d'être* of these ancient institutions.

The Vedic method of averting scarcities and famines.— Living by the chase, or hunting wild birds and animals for food, is a precarious mode of livelihood. When games became scarce in a forest, wild men tried to subsist on roots, fruits and edible leaves of trees. But these were not always available in sufficient quantities to appease hunger, or preserve life. The results of such dire distress among savage peoples must have been wholesale deaths by starvation, or what is worse still, cannibalism. The survivors, to avoid repetitions of such distress, must have devised means for catching wild animals alive, and taming them, so that they may be kept as live-stock against days of dire want and distress, which gradually changed their wild nomadic existence as hunters into what is known as pastoral life. This stage was also nomadic, as the pastoral people had constantly to move about with their herds in search of suitable pasturage and places of safety. Pastoral existence was comparatively immune from the frequent visitations of scarcities and famines, but was not altogether free from worries, anxieties, fears and troubles. It was not always easy to protect the herds from the attacks of beasts of prey or from thieves and robbers. Sometimes epidemic diseases, like murrain, broke out among the cattle, thinning their number rapidly and reducing the owners thereof to serious straits verging upon starvation. Gradually, in long course of time, the pastoral people passed on to the agricultural stage which, combined with the pastoral, made existence easier and more comfortable, though it involved more physical and mental exertions and strain, in as much as they had to construct houses, make suitable implements for tilling the land, labour in the fields, mark the seasons suitable for the cultivation of particular crops, devise means for irrigation, make adequate arrangements for feeding and protecting the cattle, and proper provisions against failure of crops through want of timely rains. The agricultural stage not only marked the beginning of the civilised state of mankind, but also formed a fit school for the training of the human mind, and the development of its various latent faculties. It was during this stage of Aryan culture that the communal and tribal laws were by tacit agreement framed and obeyed; right to and private ownership in property self-acquired were respected, and great self-restraint exercised in everything that concerned them and their neighbours. People learnt the value of acting in concert and subordinating their self-interests to the common weal. It seemed as if a new and glorious light had suddenly burst upon their eyes, which helped to awaken them to their environments and made them realize their present condition and ultimate destiny. There was, as it were, a simultaneous rush of physical, mental and spiritual vigour coursing through their entire frames and inner selves, which made them burst out in songs from sheer glee. Manual labour made their physique strong and active, and their mind responsive to every vibration and impulse from outside, which filled it with a healthy inquisitiveness and an eager desire to probe into the various manifestations and mysteries of Nature, and apprehend, as far as possible, their direct relations to the needs and necessities of human life. Speculations were freely indulged in; more new lights received; new paths chalked out, and new Gods discovered; and lastly, a harmony was sought to be established between cause and effect to enable them to interpret the various manifestations of Nature, according to the light vouchsafed to them. Myths rapidly grew up, and clouds and thunders came to be personified into supernatural beings, malevolent and benevolent respectively, so far as they and their interests were concerned. The benevolent powers were picked out and classified into distinct divinities, and the functions of each clearly defined. So were the malevolent powers and their functions discerned, the chief malevolent power being Vṛtra, the withholder of the timely rains which alone could help the life-saving crops to grow and mature. Indra was discovered to be the only God or Asura (Power), who was able to successfully fight with and defeat the malevolent Vṛtra, and his worship was accordingly inaugurated and performed with suitable hymns and sacrifices.

The Vedic Aryans did all that it was possible in human power to do for averting scarcity and famines, and their attendant horrors and sufferings. But they felt their utter helplessness in overcoming their difficulties without divine guide and aid, and the life of the Vedic Aryans during the Ṛgvedic period seemed to be one long series of prayers and sacrifices with the main object of having timely rains for the growth of their staple crops, and for such plenty in food, horses, cattle and gold as constituted their ideal of domestic felicity and comfort, and for the birth of noble sons who would perpetuate the family line and successfully carry on the struggle for existence (Rv. ix. 69, 8). They believed in the *real* existence of Indra and the other Gods whose powers were manifested in Nature in the different hours of the day and night, and they thought it necessary to carefully mark those hours, and duly perform their sacrifices and offer their prayers to the particular God or Gods who indicated their presence by peculiar manifestations of their own. But Indra, being the principal God, pervaded all time and space, and a year-long session of sacrifice was held to propitiate him and harness his divine services in the cause of their general welfare. They believed that Indra, thus propitiated, would help them in having timely rains for the cultivation of their staple crops, and in defeating the Dāsas and Dasyus who harassed them and made their life miserable by their frequent depredations. The Vedic Aryans further believed that it was Indra-worship that made scarcities and famines impossible in the land, and kept the wolf of want from their doors. If they had not believed in the efficacy of his worship, and if their faith had not been strengthened by actual results, through whatever causes, they would never have continued it enthusiastically for thousands of years until the time when Lord Kṛṣṇa was incarnated, who preached his doctrine against Vedic sacrifice and Indra-worship and overthrew Indra from the supreme position which he had hitherto occupied. (Vide *Bhāgavata Purāṇa*, Ch. x). But even Kṛṣṇa could not do away with the ancient custom of Vedic sacrifice and Indra-worship altogether and all at once. It continued spasmodically to exist for hundreds, nay thousands of years, until Lord Buddha succeeded in giving it a temporary check.

It is strange and remarkable that there is no distinct mention of scarcities and famines in the Ṛgveda, which leads one to suppose that they were few and far between in Ṛgvedic times when Indra-worship and the sacrifices, performed in his honour, were greatly in vogue. It is mentioned in the Ṛgveda that Dīrghaśravā, son of Uśij, took to trading for a while for maintaining himself at a time when there was much universal suffering caused by drought until the Aśvins sent down rains. (Rv. i. 112. 11). There is probably another reference in the Ṛgveda to scarcity (Rv. ii. 15, 5), which compelled a large number of helpless people to migrate towards the north and west by crossing the Dhuni or the Paruṣṇī "in quest of wealth." The fact that Indra "stayed the mighty roaring flood from flowing, and carried those who swam not safely over" probably refers to the existence of a long drought which made the rivers low and dry. Beyond these stray references, there is no distinct mention of any widespread scarcity, famine or drought in Ṛgvedic times, which probably were not of frequent occurrence as they are now. Whether this was due to Indra-worship or to favourable meteorological conditions in consequence of the existence of adjacent seas is a matter on which we need not speculate. It will suffice to point out here that the Ṛgvedic Aryans sincerely believed that it was Indra-worship that gave them regular rains in abundance, and made their country immune from the visitations of such dire calamities as famines and droughts.

Methods of agriculture.—Fertile plots of land (*urvarā*) were selected and divided into separate fields (*kṣetra*), which were carefully measured off according to the standard of measurement prevailing in Ṛgvedic times. (Rv. i. 110, 5). Each family possessed a number of fields, which goes to show that there were separate holdings. In the Atharva-veda (viii. 10, 24) Pṛthī Vainya (Pṛthī or Pṛthu, the son of Vena) is credited with the origination of ploughing, *i e.*, he invented the plough, as we know it now, for turning up the soil, preparatory to sowing seeds in. But this does not mean that the art of agriculture was not known to the Vedic Aryans before the time of Pṛthu. If the modern plough, drawn by a pair oxen, was his invention, it must be regarded as a labour-saving improved implement, invented to facilitate agricultural work. The art, however, had existed from Neolithic times, and the mode of tilling the ground had been probably the same as found by Captain James Cook among the rude inhabitants of New Zealand. The Aśvins are said to have taught Manu the art of sowing seeds (Rv. i. 112, 16, Sāyaṇa's commentary), and the Aryan people the art of agriculture by means of the plough (Rv. i. 117, 21). This plough must have been the rude proto-type of the plough which Pṛthu subsequently improved upon. It is significant that in the verse referred to last, it was the Aśvins, and not Indra, who not only taught the Aryans the art of agriculture by ploughing, but also poured down rains for the growth of the crops. Indra's help became necessary when agriculture had far advanced among the Aryans, and copious rains were required for the successful cultivation of such crops as *dhānya* and the different kinds of beans and pulses that flourish only in rain-water. The time, however, was still Neolithic, as Indra was an early Neolithic God. What was the exact form of the Neolithic plough it is very difficult to ascertain; but in Ṛgvedic times it was very much like the modern

Indian plough, drawn by a pair of oxen, and sometimes by a pair of horses. The names of the plough in the Ṛgveda are Sīra (iv. 57, 8; x. 101, 3. 4), and Lāngala (iv. 57, 4). It is described in the Atharva-veda (iii. 17, 3) and some of the Saṃhitās as 'lance-pointed' (*pavīravat* or *pavīravam*), well-tying (*suśimam*) and having a well-smoothed handle (*tsaru*). The ploughshare is called *phāla* (Rv. iv. 57, 8; x. 117, 7), which in Neolithic times must have been made of hard pointed wood. The pole was probably called *īṣā*, like the pole of the chariot, a name which is still used to denote the pole of the plough, to which the yoke or *yuga* (Rv. i. 115, 2; 184, 3; ii. 39, 4; iii. 53, 17 etc.) was fastened and tied with ropes. The animals employed to draw the plough were, as already stated, usually oxen which were yoked and harnessed with traces (*varatrā* Rv. iv. 57, 4), and urged with the goad (*aṣṭrā*, Rv. iv. 57, 4; x 102, 8) by the ploughman. (*kīnāśa* Rv. iv. 57, 8). The furrow was called *sītā* (Rv. iv. 57, 6. 7). In Rgvedic times, the plough was probably a light instrument, drawn only by a pair of oxen; but in later times, it was undoubtedly large and heavy, as we find it mentioned that six (Av. vi. 91, 1) or eight, or twelve (*Tait. Sam.* 1. 8. 7, 1) or even twenty-four (*Kāṭhaka Sam.* xv. 2) oxen were employed to draw it. There is no clear reference in the Ṛgveda to the horse being used to draw the plough, though it was used to draw carts laden with harvested corn. (Rv. x. 101, 7). The horse is eminently fitted to drag the plough over comparatively dry and light soil, but is useless for ploughing lands in knee-deep water and mud, which can only be successfully negotiated by oxen and buffaloes.

Every act of the Vedic Aryans was ceremonial. Before agricultural work was begun, certain verses were uttered to propitiate the Lord of the Field (*Kṣetrapati*) and other deities, supposed to preside over Agriculture, as will appear from the following translation of a hymn (Rv. iv. 57):

" We, through the Master of the Field, even as through a friend obtain what nourisheth our kine and steeds. In such may he be good to us. 2. As the cow yieldeth milk, pour for us freely, Lord of the Field, the wave that beareth sweetness, distilling meath, well-purified like butter, and let the Lord of Holy Law be gracious. 3. Sweet be the plants for us, the heavens, the waters, and full of sweets for us be air's mid-region. May the Field's Lord for us be full of sweetness, and may we follow after him uninjured. 4. Happily work our steers and men, may the plough furrow happily. Happily be the traces bound; happily may he ply the goad. 5. Śuna and Sīra,[1] welcome ye this laud, and with the milk which ye have made in heaven, bedew ye both this earth of ours. 6. Auspicious Sītā,[2] come thou near; we venerate thee that thou mayst bless and prosper us and bring us fruits abundantly. 7. May Indra press the furrow down, may Pūṣan guide its course aright. May she, as rich in milk, be drained for us through each succeeding year. 8. Happily let the shares turn up the ploughland, happily go the ploughers with the oxen. With meath and milk, Parjanya, make us happy. Grant us prosperity, Śuna and Sīra." (Griffith).

Another Ṛgvedic verse (x. 101. 3) about agriculture is as follows:

"Harness the ploughs, fit the yokes; now that the womb is ready, sow the seed therein, and through our praise, may there be abundant food; may (the grain) fall ripe towards the sickle." (Wilson).

This *mantra* was probably uttered at the time of sowing the seed after the ground had been prepared by ploughing and manuring. The priest formally harnessed the ploughs

---

1 "Śuna and Sira: two deities or deified objects who bless or are closely connected with agriculture. According to Yāska, Śuna (the auspicious) is Vāyu, and Sira (plough) is Āditya or the Sun. Professor Roth conjectures that the words mean here ploughshare and plough. Prof. Grassmann translates: 'O Pflug and Lenker' plough and ploughman" Griffith.

2 "Sitā, the Furrow or Humbandru personified, and addressed as a deity" Griffith.

at the time of the ceremony: "The wise (priests) harness the ploughs, they lay the yoke apart, firmly devoted through the desire of happiness" (Rv. x. 101, 4).

Professors Macdonell and Keith say that *śakṛt* in the Ṛgveda (i. 161, 10) denotes dung, and "it is clear that the value of manure was early appreciated." (*Ved. Ind.* ii. 348) Karīṣa in the Śatapatha Brāhmaṇa means "dry cow-dung (ii, i. 1, 7). In the Atharva-veda (iii. 14, 3. 4; xix. 31, 3) we find that the value of the natural manure of animals in the fields was perfectly understood". (*Ved. Ind* i. 139). But in Ṛgvedic times, most of the corn-fields having been alluvial soil, which used to be flooded every year by the spill-waters of the rivers during the rainy season, there was probably not much necessity for manuring them, though lands situated far away from the river-valleys required to be manured. As the number of cattle possessed by the Aryans was large, there was no want of dung for manuring them, and the crops were accordingly rich and abundant. I have already referred to the irrigation of the corn-fields by means of water drawn from wells, or brought through artificial channels, and need not mention it again.

When the corns were ripe, they were cut down with the sickle (*sṛṇī*, Rv. i. 58, 4; x. 101, 3; 106, 6; or *dātra* viii. 78, 10), bound into bundles (*parṣa*, Rv. x. 48, 7) and "beaten out on the floor of the granary (*khala*, Rv. x. 48, 7). The grain was then separated from the straw and refuse either by a sieve (*titau*) or a winnowing fan (Rv. x. 71, 2). The winnower was called Dhānyakṛt (Rv. x. 94, 13) and the grain was measured in a vessel called Urdara (Rv. ii. 14, 11)." [1] The grains were stored in grain-receptacles called *sthivis* (Rv. x. 68, 3). Macdonell and Keith have translated the word as "bushel" (*Ved. Ind.* ii. 487), but its appropriate meaning appears to be a receptacle or store-house for grain, or simply, granary. The passage above

[1] *Vedic Index* i. 182.

referred to clearly says that Bṛhaspati quickly brought out or released the cows from the mountain, just as *yava* is extracted or brought out from a *sthivi*. The surplus grain, or all the thrashed-out grain had to be stored in a place free from dust, worms and mice for future use, from which required quantities were drawn out according to necessity.

Godhūma and Vrīhi not mentioned in the Ṛgveda.—It is remarkable that the word *godhūma* (wheat) is not mentioned in the Ṛgveda. Probably the grain was not known, nor cultivated in Ṛgvedic times, and was not indigenous to the Punjab. It must have been introduced from elsewhere in a later age, for we find it mentioned in the Yajurveda Saṃhitās (*Mait. Sam.* i. 2, 8; *Vāj. Saṃ*. xviii. 12; xix. 22, 89, etc.) and the Brāhmaṇas. (*Śat. Bra.* xii. 7, 1, 2; 2, 9, etc.). In the former, the word is frequently referred to in the plural; but it occurs in the singular in the Śatapatha Brāhmaṇa (v. 2, 1, 6). It is distinguished from 'rice' (*vrīhi*), or 'barley' (*yava*).[1] The absence of any mention of "wheat" (*godhūma*) in the Ṛgveda has an historical significance which seems to have been overlooked by scholars. "The centre of diffusion of wheat," says Mr. H. G. Wells in his *Outline of History* "was somewhere in the eastern Mediterranean region. A wild form is still found in the neighbourhood of Mt. Hermon. When the lake-dwellers sowed their little patches of wheat in Switzerland, they were already following the immemorial practice of mankind. The seed must have been brought age by age from that distant centre of diffusion. In the ancestral lands of the south-east, men had already been sowing wheat perhaps for thousands of years." (pp. 56-57). The reader must here remember that "the lake-dwellings were probably occupied continuously from 5,000 or 4,000 B. C. down almost to historic times" (p. 56). Elsewhere he says. "De Condolle asserts that it is only in the Euphrates-Tigris district that wheat has ever been found growing wild.

[1] *Taittirīya Brāhmaṇa*, i. 3, 7, 2.

It may be that from Mesopotamia as a centre the cultivation of wheat spread over the entire eastern hemisphere. Or, it may be, that wheat grew wild in some regions now submerged. There may have been wild wheat region in what is now the sea-bottom of the Eastern Mediterranean. But cultivation is not civilisation; the growing of wheat had spread from the Atlantic to the Pacific with the distribution of the Neolithic culture by perhaps 10,000 or 9,000 B. C. before the beginnings of civilisation," (pp. 91-92). If there is any truth in the above assertion, then the absence of any mention of wheat in the Ṛgveda must necessarily point to its vast antiquity, and its hymns must, therefore, have been composed in the Punjab several millenniums earlier than 10,000 B. C. If the Indo-Aryans at all emigrated from Europe about 2,000 B. C., as is commonly supposed by modern European savants, is it not extremely strange that they did not bring with them a knowledge of wheat or its cultivation from the very centre through which they had passed, although the Swiss lake-dwellers cultivated it about 5,000 or 4,000 B. C., and had brought a knowledge of it from that centre? The real fact seems to be that the Indo-Aryans never emigrated from Europe to India, as they had been autochthonous to the Punjab, and that the Neolithic Aryan savages who had been compelled to leave their original cradle in the Punjab and emigrated to Western Asia and Europe in the very dawn of the Neolithic age about 20,000 B. C. or even earlier, got themselves acquainted with wild wheat in the regions where it was indigenous and cultivated it in Europe in their crude fashion. As wheat is distinctly mentioned in the Yajurveda Saṃhitās and later Vedic literature, their composition must be put down to a much later period than that of the Ṛgveda, which is quite consistent with the geographical references made in them to the Gangetic provinces to the east of the Punjab, which were of later formation from the bed of the Eastern Sea covering the Gangetic trough in Ṛgvedic times. By the way, it should be recalled that there was an old traditon in ancient Sumeria or Babylonia that the original inhabitants of that country were taught the art of agriculture by a people who had come there in their ships from the east, and I have identified these sea-faring people with the Paṇis of the Ṛgveda and the Dravidians. (vide *Ṛgvedic India*, Ch. xi). As Mr. Wells asserts that the growing of wheat had spread from the Atlantic to the Pacific about 10,000 B. C., the emigration of the Paṇis and the Dravidians to Mesopotamia must have been far earlier than that period; and it is most likely that these Indian merchants brought a knowledge of the cultivation of wheat to India from Mesopotamia about 10,000 B. C. or even later, which undoubtedly corresponded to the Later Ṛgvedic or post-Ṛgvedic age, as the grain has been mentioned in the Yajurveda Saṃhitās and the Brāhmaṇas

As regards *vrīhi*, it may be stated here that it was a species of rice that was sown in spring in moist alluvial beds of rivers or lakes and marshy grounds, and riped before the rains set in. It is known as *Boro-dhān* in Lower Bengal, even to this day, the word *boro* being a corruption of *vrīhi*. *Dhāna* or *dhānya* proper is a crop that is cultivated only during the rainy season and reaped in autumn or winter. There is no mention of *vrīhi* in the Ṛgveda, but, as I have already pointed out, the words *dhāna* and *dhānya* occur several times, meaning rice or paddy, including probably *vrīhi*, and not grains in general. The words *dhānya-bīja* in the Ṛgveda (v. 53, 13) means 'rice or paddy-seed,' and there is no reason why the words should not be understood in that sense. There are several species of rice, of which *vrīhi* is only one, and *āśu* (swift-growing) is another. These rices (especially the latter) are not fit for use in sacrifices; but the white rice that is sown in the rainy season and reaped in autumn (*haimantika*) is the only rice that can be offered in sacrifices, which goes to establish its vast antiquity. Religious rites are always conservative, and no innovations are tolerated in these matters. Hence red or dark rice is carefully eschewed from them, and the only rice that is still used in the performance of *yajñas* is the white rice reaped in autumn or winter, and sown during the rainy season. As I have remarked in this chapter, it was mainly for the cultivation of *dhānya*, and probably *tila* (sesamum) and beans, that timely rains were required, and sacrifices for the propitiation of Indra performed. There would be no need for holding the *Sattras*, if the cultivation of *dhānya* was not necessary. *Vrīhi* seems to have become a general name for rice in a later age. (*Atharva-veda* xi, 4, 13; *Jaim. Brāhm.* i. 43; *Chānd. Upa.* v. 10, 6). And the reason is not far so seek. *Vrīhi*, properly so called, is sown in spring and does not require much rain for its growth. When in a later age the seas disappeared from the vicinity of the Punjab, the rainfall became scanty, and the actual amount of it was not sufficient for the successful cultivation of *dhānya*. The area under its cultivation, therefore, continually diminished, and barley and wheat gradually became the principal crops. But *vrīhi*, or the species of *dhānya* that is sown in spring in marshy grounds, continued to be cultivated and came to be known as rice, and took the place of the Ṛgvedic *dhānya*. Hence in the Atharva-veda, the Brāhmaṇas, and the Upaniṣads, *vrīhi* became the general name for *dhānya*. But as the Ṛgvedic Aryans did not attach much importance to *vrīhi*, because its cultivation was limited only to a very small area and did not yield a bumper crop, there is no mention of it in the Ṛgveda. It should not be inferred from the absence of the name of *vrīhi* in the Ṛgveda that rice was unknown to the Aryans of that age, or that *dhāna* or *dhānya* could mean any other grain than rice. The mistake seems to have arisen from not taking into account the vast geographical and climatic changes that had occurred since Ṛgvedic times before the Atharva-veda and the Brāhmaṇas, etc. were composed. This indirectly proves the vast antiquity of the Ṛgveda. The geographical and climatic changes must have taken thousands of years to have established themselves in their present conditions firmly and permanently. When these became unfavourable to the extensive cultivation of rice or *dhānya*, that of wheat was introduced and substituted for it, as a staple crop.

The value of cattle in Ṛgvedic times.—Cattle was a valuable asset to the Aryans in Ṛgvedic times, and even in the preceding age. The domestication of cattle marked a further step in advance of the hunting stage in which primitive men had been placed. The possession of cattle put them above want and a state of precarious existence. They drank the milk of goats, cows and buffaloes, and their livestock supplied them with meat in times of necessity; for they did not give up all at once the practice of living by the chase. What with the flesh of animals killed in the chase, and what with the meat and milk supplied by their live stock, they managed to eke out a living of tolerable ease and comfort. The possession of cattle, however, gave them an idea of property which they found it extremely necessary to protect. It threw a new burden and responsibility upon them, and restrained their roving spirit and freedom to a certain extent. The cattle had to be regularly taken out for pasturing, and adequately protected from the attacks of wild beasts and robbers. Their advance to the settled agricultural stage further increased the value of cattle. Oxen were indispensable to agricultural work, cow-dung was necessary for manuring the corn-fields, and milk was required not only for daily consumption, but also for offering libations to the sacred Fire twice a day, and for preparing butter and *ghee* from it, to enable them to perform the annual and periodical *Sattras*, so that Indra might supply them with regular rains for the successful cultivation of their crops. Thus cattle formed their most valuable property, and every one earnestly craved to possess a number of them. The larger number of cattle one possessed, the richer one was considered to be. Almost every family possessed a sufficiently large number of cattle; kings owned vast herds of them as personal property, from which they made large gifts to the singers of their praise, and to learned and pious Ṛṣis who performed the sacrifices for them and made them famous in their songs; and thieves and robbers sought opportunities to raid and steal as many of them as possible. The possession of cattle was thus a rage and necessity among the Ṛgvedic Aryans. There are few important hymns in the Ṛgveda in which a prayer has not been offered to the Gods for the gift of cattle. Even the Ṛgvedic Aryans, in their greed for the possession of cattle, sometimes indulged in forays, and prayed Pūṣan to grant them success: "Clear paths that we may win the prize; scatter our enemies afar. Strong God, be all our thoughts fulfilled." (Rv. vi. 53, 4). Again, "Lead on this company of ours, that longs for kine, to win the spoil: thou, Pūṣan, art renowned afar" (Rv. vi. 56, 5).[1]

The value attached to the possession of cattle is accounted for by the reasons mentioned above. But there was another important reason. Cattle constituted the principal wealth, almost the only other wealth of the Ṛgvedic Aryans of the Neolithic Age than their agricultural products. It was not every householder or family that possessed agricultural lands or took to agriculture. These families required the food-grains for their maintenance, and woollen cloths to cover their nakedness and protect them from the rigours of a cold climate that prevailed in ancient times. The kine, therefore, became the media of exchange. The Neolithic Aryans not having been acquainted with metals, there were no coins in current use in the early stages of their civilisation; but as they were eminently a pastoral people, almost every family possessed a sufficient number of cattle, and some of them were exchanged for the necessaries of their life. A cow, therefore, became a unit of exchange, and trade, such as it was in those days, was carried on by barter. The Soma plant was purchased by exchanging kine for a definite quantity of it. Kine were also exchanged for the

---

[1] *Vide ante*, Chap. iii, p. 125.

necessary food-grains and garments. Even wives were sometimes purchased by offering to the parents of the brides a certain number of kine. The value of cattle (*paśu*) was, therefore, very great with the early Ṛgvedic Aryans. Such of the savage or half-savage Aryans as left or were compelled to leave Sapta-Sindhu for Western Asia and Europe also knew the value of cattle as a means of exchange, and we accordingly find the ancient Romans use the word *pecus* or *pecu* (Vedic *paśu*) in the sense of wealth or money. Even when coins were invented as a medium of exchange, they could not do away with the original word for wealth, *viz. pecus* or *pecu*, to mean money; and so *pecunia* came to mean *money* with the Romans and the other races who were indebted to Latin for the growth and development of their languages. We have got the English words *pecuniary*, *impecunious etc.*, all derived from the Latin root *pecus* or *pecu*, originally meaning cattle. The possession of cattle, therefore, denoted wealth as much with the ancient Romans, as with the ancient Ṛgvedic Aryans, and was calculated to keep them above want. A man was considered rich or poor according to the large or small number of cattle that he owned. Gift of cattle to the needy and the spiritually minded Ṛṣis was considered highly meritorious, and the Ṛgvedic princes and kings vied with one another in making very large gifts of cattle to the most deserving. To the gift of cows were afterwards added the gifts of horses, asses, camels, chariots, cloths, gold, silver, and even good habitable houses which could be taken down and carried in parts.[1] Even to this day, the gift of cattle and lands to deserving Brahmans and priests is considered highly meritorious, and the ordinary man, who has neither cows nor lands to give, is enjoined to give their equivalent in money, though very nominal it may be.

---

[1] Rv. i. 126, 1-4; v. 30, 12-15; viii. 1, 32, 33; 3, 21 *et seq.*; 4, 19-21, 5, 37-39; 6, 46-48; 55; 56; vii. 18, 21-24.

The gift of cattle in Ṛgvedic times was prized not only for the milk which the cows supplied, and as a means of bartering, but also for the meat of the oxen, calves and barren cows or cows that miscarried (*vehat*). Beef-eating had been a necessity in pastoral times, but the practice continued, even when it was no longer absolutely necessary, down to later Vedic times until it was altogether abolished on account of the change of climate from cold to hot, and probably also from economical and humane considerations. In Ṛgvedic times oxen and cows used to be sacrificed to the Gods, especially to Indra, in large numbers, and a quantity of their flesh was offered as oblation to Agni, and the remainder partaken of by the votaries in a sumptuous feast. It was also a custom to sacrifice a bull, calf or barren cow in honour of the visit of a distinguished guest. But, although these customs were in vogue, there seem to have gradually grown a strong repugnance and abhorrence against them in the minds of the most thoughtful and considerate, whose privilege it was to lead the van of Aryan progress. The killing of cows came to be condemned even in Ṛgvedic times by some eminent Ṛṣis in no uncertain terms. The cow was pronounced to be *aghnyā* (not to be killed), and the cattle in general as *aghnya* (masculine). The first word occurs sixteen times in the Ṛgveda, as opposed to three instances of *aghnya*.[1] The dictum may not have been accepted or acted upon all at once, but the sentiment was there, which in a later age developed in a general prohibition against cow-slaughter, and resulted in a special sanctity attached to the cow.[1] Griffith's translation of the following hymn (Rv. vi. 28) will be found interesting in this connection :—

"The kine have come and brought good fortune: let them rest in the cow-pen and be happy near us. Here let them stay prolific, many-coloured, and yield through many morns their milk for Indra.

---

[1] *Vide ante*, Chapter v. 204-205.

"Indra aids him who offers sacrifice and gifts: he takes not what is his, and gives him more thereto. Increasing ever more his wealth, he makes the pious dwell within unbroken bounds.

"These (the cows) are ne'er lost,[1] no robber ever injures them: evil-minded foe attempts to harass them. The master of the kine lives many a year with these,—the cows, whereby he pours his gifts and serves the Gods.

"The charger with his dusty brow o'ertakes them not; never to the shambles do they take their way.[2] These cows, the cattle of the pious worshipper, roam over widespread pasture where no danger is.

"To me the cows seem Bhaga, they seem Indra, they seem a portion of the first-poured Soma.[3] These present cows—they, O ye men, are Indra.[4] I long for Indra with my heart and spirit.

"O cows, ye fatten e'en the worn and wasted and make the unlovely beautiful to look on.[5] Prosper my house, ye with auspicious voices. Your power is glorified in our assemblies.[6]

---

[1] "*Na tā naśanti.* Sāyaṇa assigns an imperative meaning to *naśanti* and the other verbs in the indicative mood, which occur in this and the following stanzas: 'Let not the cows be lost: let no thief, etc.'—Wilson." (Foot-note, Griffith's translation.) Sāyaṇa's interpretation seems to be better and more appropriate.

[2] "They are not, or, according to Sāyaṇa, let them not be, carried off in predatory incursions. (Griffith's translation, foot-note).

[3] "The worshipper regards the cows as the deities, Bhaga and Indra, who bring him happiness." (Do. Do.)

[4] *Imā yā Gāvah sa Janāsa Indra.*

[5] This, of course, means that the worn and wasted put on flesh and become vigorous by drinking the milk of the cow.

[6] The evident meaning is that the value and usefulness of the cow are discussed in the *Sabhās* or assemblies. This probably refers to a propaganda against cow-killing.

"Crop goodly pasturage and be prolific; drink pure sweet water at good drinking-places. Never be thief or sinful man your master, and may the dart of Rudra still avoid you."[1]

The last stanza, (which is omitted here), though somewhat obscure in meaning, "appears to refer to the mingling of the milk (the cows) with the juice of the strong Soma (the steer), which, when offered as a libation to Indra, will increase his heroic strength" (Griffith).

The author of the above hymn is the sage Bharadvāja who prayed to Indra elsewhere (Rv. vi. 39, 1) to grant him and his worshippers food with "go" or the cow as the principal item. From the repugnance he felt against cow-killing and his identification of the cow with the Gods Bhaga and Indra, as distinctly expressed in the above hymn (Rv. vi. 28), it seems clear that by the phrase 'food with the cow as the principal item' (*go-agrah*), he meant cow's milk, and all sorts of milk-preparation, *viz. ghee,* butter, curd etc. It was he who probably struck the note against cow-killing for the sake of food, attached a special sanctity to the cow by identifying her with the divinities, Bhaga and Indra. The sentiment was expressed not in a hap-hazard or half-hearted spirit, but with all the earnestness he could command, and it took a firm root in men's mind, and went on growing and flourishing till the custom was altogether abolished in a later age. For, in spite of the growing sentiment of sanctity attached to the cow, the sacrifice of the animal at *yajñas* continued throughout Ṛgvedic times. As is well known, customs, like errors and superstitions, die very hard.

The translation of the following hymn (Rv. x. 169), addressed to the divinity of the cow, will bear reproduction here, and be found interesting, as showing that though the cow was offered as a sacrifice to the Gods, she was looked

---

[1] Cf. Rv. i. 114, 10; "Far be thy dart that killeth men or cattle;" and ii. 33, 14: "May Rudra's missile turn aside and spare us, the great wrath of the Impetuous One avoid us.'

upon with great tenderness verging upon a pathetic attachment :—

"May the refreshing wind blow upon the cows; may they crop the juicy grass; let them drink the nutritious life-sustaining (waters). Rudra, have compassion upon the food which has foot.[1]

"Grant great felicity, Parjanya, to those cows who are of similar forms, of different forms, or of single form, whose names Agni knows through the sacrifice, or those whom the Angirasas created in this world by penance.

"Bring, Indra, to the cow-house (the original word is *goṣṭha* which means 'a standing place for cows' or pasture), the cows who offer their bodies to the Gods, those of whom Soma knows all the properties, those that nourish us with their milk, and those that have calves.

"May Prajāpati, bestowing these (cows) upon me, concurring with the Universal Gods and the Pitṛs, bring the auspicious cattle to our cow-pen. May we be in possession of their progeny." (Wilson).

The above verses clearly indicate the reasons why the cow was valued. She was offered as a sacrifice to the Gods; her milk was necessary for mixing with the Soma juice which was offered to Indra and the other Gods, and it, and its various preparations were used as nutritious food by the Vedic Aryans. Add to this the fact that the cow was a medium of exchange at a time when coins were not in current use, and its dung was used as fertilizing manure and probably also as fuel. All these factors combined to make the cow a most useful and sacred animal. It is noteworthy that one of the verses relates an old fact which probably passed into a myth in the later period of Ṛgvedic times, *viz.*, that it was the Angirasas who created the cow in this world by penance.

---

[1] Wilson says that the phrase means the "cow" and "this seems to favour the notion that cows were sometimes killed for food." But cows also supply milk which is a highly nutritious food.

The Angirasas were a most ancient clan, who first produced Fire, and inaugurated the *yajñas*, and did many other things to advance early Aryan civilisation. Does the reference to their creation of the cow by penance point to the fact that the cow was first domesticated by them and brought to human use? Very probably it does.

There is another Ṛgvedic hymn (x. 19) which also has a touching reference to the cow. The word *go* in this hymn seems to bear a double meaning, for the *Devatā* of some of its verses has been described as either "Waters" or "Cows." Wilson has thus translated the hymn as addressed to Waters:—

"Come back: go not elsewhere: abounding in wealth, sprinkle us; Agni and Soma, you who clothe[1] (your worshippers) again, bestow upon us riches.

"Bring them back again, render them obedient: may Indra restore them; may Agni bring them nigh.

"May they come back to me and be fostered under this (their) protector: do thou, Agni, keep them here; may whatever wealth there is) remain here.

"I invoke the knowledge of the place, of their going, of their coming, of their departure, of their wandering, of their returning: (I invoke) him who is their keeper.

"May the keeper return (with them); he who reaches them when lost; who reaches them when straying; who reaches them when wandering, and returning.

"Indra, come back and bring back (the cattle); give us our cows again, may we rejoice in our cows being alive.

"I nourish you, Gods, who are everywhere present, with curds, with butter, with milk; may all these deities who are entitled to worship reward us with riches.

"Come back (ye cows), bring them back; return (ye cows), bring them back; and (you, cows) coming back,

[1] The meaning is not clear. Punarvasu may be interpreted to mean "you who repeatedly give us wealth."

return; there are four quarters of the earth, bring them back from them."

The main idea of the hymn, as addressed to Waters, seems to be that rains being over, the waters contained in the clouds disappear with them. The clouds are scattered, and go away nobody knows where. Indra who, with the help of Agni, or sacrifice offered to him through Fire, and Soma, *i.e.*, the Soma drink which is offered to him to make him strong and hilarious, brings down the waters or much-needed rains from the clouds, is invoked to bring them back again so that his worshippers may have plenty of corns and wealth. The imagery before the bard's mental eye is that of cows sent out to distant pastures, after they have given plenty of milk, and become dry, when Indra, with Soma and Agni, is invoked to watch their movements, protect them from dangers in their wanderings, and safely bring them back home after they have calved, so that they may give their worshippers an abundant supply of milk again on their return. The metaphor of waters or rains disappearing and coming back again through the help of Indra is actually taken from the most ordinary event of cows, probably dry, being sent out to distant pastures for months under the charge of cowherds. But what an anxiety does the owner feel for their safety, and safe return home after the cows have calved or become "wet?" They may stray, or wander far away and thus be lost. They may break their limbs by falling into pits, be killed by wild animals, or stolen by thieves and robbers. These cows constitute his principal wealth, as they supply him and his family with abundant milk, and many savoury dishes cooked with milk, besides enabling him to prepare the Soma drink which is offered to the Gods as libations to the sacred Fire. Out goes, therefore, his touching prayer to Indra, Soma and Agni, for their safety during their wanderings in unknown places, and safe return home at the end of the period of pasturing in distant regions. The poet has with great skill and dexterity woven this beautiful fabric of his song, which refers to the periodical disappearance and return of the rains, like those of cows sent out to distant pastures.

From the above quotations it would appear that cows were objects of great care with the Vedic Aryans. They were fed on barley and corn (Rv. x. 27, 8), and supplied with pure drinking water drawn from wells and poured into wooden cattle-troughs which were bound with straps for conveniently carrying them from the side of the wells to the cow-pens. The following verses will be found interesting :—

"Set up the cattle-trough; bind the straps to it; let us pour out (the water of the well which is full of water, fit to be poured out, and not easily exhausted.

"I pour out (the water of) the well, whose cattle-troughs are prepared, well fitted with straps, fit to be poured out, full of water, inexhaustible.

"Satisfy the horses, accomplish the good work (of ploughing), equip a car laden with good fortune (meaning probably harvested corn), pour out (the water of) the well, having wooden cattle-troughs, having a stone rim, having a receptable like armour, fit for the drinking of men." (Rv. x. 101, 5-7). (Wilson).

The meaning of the above verses is clear. The well had "a receptacle like armour," *i.e.*, its sides were constructed of stones or some hard materials, so that they might not collapse into the pit. It had a stone rim at the top like a parapet-wall to prevent children and animals from falling into it. The wooden cattle-troughs, provided with straps, were brought to the side of the well, from which pure drinking water, even fit for the use of men, was raised and poured into them. The horses and cattle drank out of these troughs; after which they were yoked to the plough, or to the cart, laden with harvested corn. This probably suggests that horses also were sometimes employed to draw the plough.

The construction of the cow-stall is described in the following verse :—

"Construct the cow-stall, for that is the drinking place of your leaders (the Gods), fabricate armour, manifold and simple; make cities of iron and impregnable, let not the ladle leak, make it strong." (Wilson).

There are so many metaphors and imageries crowded into this one verse that it would appear, at first sight, like the incoherent blurtings of a mad man. The meaning of the verse is this :—

"Construct the cow-stall, for herein will be kept the milch-cows whose milk is poured as libations into the sacred Fire, and mixed up with the Soma juice which is offered to the Gods as drink. The cow-stall is therefore like the drinking-place of the Gods. The walls of the cow-stall should be made as strong as armour for the protection of the animals from the attacks of wild beasts and robbers. But the construction should be quite simple, though extra-strong. It would then be like an iron citadel (or *pur*), quite invincible. As a ladle, with which libations are poured into the Fire as offerings to the Gods, should be strong and by no means leaky, so 'this drinking place of the Gods' should not at all be leaky. In other words, its roof should be made strong and rain-proof." This description of the construction of the cow-stall clearly indicates the great solicitude the Vedic Aryans felt for the safe keeping of their cattle.

I need not further dwell on the great value that the Vedic Aryans attached to their cattle.

CHAPTER VIII.

THE KING AND THE STATE, THE SAGE-PRIESTS, AND WARS AND MODE OF WARFARE.

Evolution of Kingship.—Every tribe, or the people living in one territory with a homogeneous civilisation, had its King, or leader, who maintained peace and order among the population, and protected them from external invasion or agression. Kingship was a natural evolution of leadership of savage, wild people in the hunting and nomadic stages of existence. Man is, by nature, a social animal who is never exclusive and abhors complete isolation from his comrades. Family ties and common interests serve to hold men together in a clan or tribe under the guidance of one of them, who is, by common consent, able to lead them with one united mind for the attainment of one common object. Physical prowess or bravery was an essential qualification of successful leadership in early times, but it was not the only qualification. Palæolithic man was large-brained, as is evidenced by the recent discoveries of human skulls, dug up from caves and burial grounds containing unmistakable evidence of the palæolithic stage of civilisation. The fossilized skulls of Pleistocene man discovered in Australia (Queensland), Sussex (Piltdown), and the Transvaal prove "the existence of large-brained man at a period so remote from our own times as to be measured by hundreds of thousands of years."[1] Writing about the Piltdown man, Dr. Keith says: "If, then, we find a fairly large brain in the Piltdown man, with an arrangement and development of convolutions not very unlike those of modern man, we shall be justified in drawing the conclusion that so far as potential mental ability is concerned, he had reached the modern standard. We must always keep in mind that

[1] *London Times*, January 8, 1921.

accomplishments and inventions which seem so simple to us were new and unsolved problems to the pioneers who worked their way from a simian to a human estate."[1] Regarding the culture of the Piltdown man he observes: "We may rest assured that a brain which was shaped in a mould so similar to our own was one which responded to the outside world as our own does. Piltdown man saw, heard, felt, thought and dreamt much as we still do."[2] It would thus appear that it was not the possession of a mere brute force or extraordinary physical strength and bravery that were sufficient for early man to overcome the difficulties and dangers with which he was beset; he also required a large brain, as large as ours, to *think out* the adequate means for overcoming them with as little loss of energy and life as possible. The "*brainiest*" *man* among the savages, if he happened to possess a strong physique and extraordinary personal valour, was regarded as the fittest man to be their leader, as resourcefulness, coupled with physical bravery, went to make a successful leader. Wild men had sufficient brain to discern and discover these qualities in their leader, and readily gathering round him with loud huzzas, placed themselves under his guidance

---

[1] Keith, *The Antiquity of Man* (1916). In this connection the following observations made by Professor Hermann Klaatsch in his work entitled *The Evolution and Progress of Mankind* (for the first time translated into English in 1923) will be found interesting: "In view of the extraordinary increase in mental power since the dawn of humanity, it will be asked whether we ought to regard primitive man as clever or stupid. The question is justified, but it is wrongly expressed, as the ideas 'stupid' and 'clever' are now so bound up with the impressions of civilised nations, that we cannot apply them to the condition of primitive man. It is much as if a man on the top of a mountain were to try to appreciate the difference in height between the valleys and the foot-hills. Everything seems to him on the same level, whereas there are really considerable differences in altitude. Everything seems very low, because the observer is very high. We cannot possibly put ourselves back on the lower rungs of the ladder up which civilised humanity has climbed. But precisely for that reason we must be on our guard against disdain of our primitive ancestors. Uneducated as they were, they must nevertheless have had the capacity for evolution to which we owe our rise to our present level" Ch. vi, p. 144

[2] *The Antiquity of Man*, p. 429.

and followed him with unswerving obedience. Carlyle, in his picturesque and inimitable style, has thus described the origin of Kingship :

"Neither was that an inconsiderable moment when wild armed men first raised their Strongest aloft on the buckler-throne, and with clanging armour and hearts said solemnly: Be thou our Acknowledged Strongest (well named King, Kön-ning, Can-ning, or man that was able). What a symbol shone now for them, significant with the destinies of the world! A world of true Guidance in return for loving obedience: properly, if he knew it, the prime want of man. A symbol which might be called sacred; for, is there not in reverence for what is better than we, an indestructible sacredness? On which ground, too, it was well said, there lay in the Acknowledged Strongest a divine right; as surely there might be in the Strongest whether Acknowledged or not, considering *who* it was that made him strong."[1]

The following lines from an article I wrote long ago[2] will be found apposite to the subject :—

"In the earliest stages of human civilisation, *personal fitness* alone decided the choice of the people in the selection of a chief; and, as History repeats itself, we find the same principle working in a developed form in modern Republican and Democratical forms of Government. The fundamental principle of Government appears to be an inherent right of the people to govern themselves under the direction and guidance of a leader whom the people choose on account of his personal fitness, and who is invested with certain powers by the people themselves with a view to enable him to carry on the work with which he is entrusted. The rights, privileges and powers of the leader or King are made up of the rights, privileges and powers of the people themselves,—willingly parted with in his favour in return for security and protection of their life, liberty and property."

---

[1] Carlyle, *French Revolution.*

[2] *Modern Review*, Calcutta, Vol. ii, p. 347 (1907).

The Mahābhārata, which is a veritable mine of ancient history, has a passage "which goes to show how the King was created by the ancient Indo-Aryans on the principle of 'Give and Take,' and how the people willingly submitted to be guided by him in return for protecting them and their interests, and maintaining peace and order in the country."[1] The following is a free translation of the passage referred to:—

"In days of yore, when the Earth had no King, the people began to devour one another. At that time, some wise and virtuous men met together and made an agreement among themselves to the effect that they would banish all such men as were harsh-tongued, of angry disposition, adulterous and voluptuous, and addicted to the habit of stealing and misappropriating another's property. Securing the confidence of the people, they lived peacefully for some time; but, in the long run, with a heavy heart, they had to approach Brahmā, the Creator, whom they addressed thus: 'Lord, we are being annihilated for want of a King. Grant us, therefore a King. We all will adore him, and he will protect us in return.' Hearing this prayer of the people, Brahmā asked Manu to take up the duty of protecting them; but Manu declined the honour, saying 'I am always afraid of committing a wrong and sinful act. It is a very difficult task to govern a kingdom, and particularly to keep people on the path of virtue and righteousness.' Then the people addressed themselves to Manu, saying, 'Lord, do not thou be afraid of anything. Sin will never touch thee. We will fill up thy royal treasury by contributing into it heads of cattle, a fiftieth share of gold, and tenth share of grain...... Those, who are capable of bearing arms and riding, will follow thee, as the Gods follow Indra. Thus thou wilt be as powerful as Kuvera himself, and able to protect us with ease. Thou wilt also be entitled to a fourth share of the spiritual benefit which we may be able to acquire under thy

[1] *Ibid*, p. 348.

protection. Protect us therefore, O Lord, like Indra, the chief of the Gods, and sally forth like the blazing sun, to conquer our foes. May their pride be humbled by thee, and may *Dharma* protect us for ever.' The people thus saying, the powerful Manu, who was sprung from a noble race, issued forth from his castle, in a blaze of glory, followed by innumerable armed men, with a view to take up the duty of protecting the people." (*Śānti Parva* ch. 67).

"The above account of willing submission of the people to a King tallies, in substance, with Carlyle's account of wild armed men raising their Strongest aloft on the buckler-throne, and with clanging armour and hearts, saying solemnly, 'Be thou our Acknowledged Strongest.' Both the accounts furnish us with an unmistakable clue to the fundamental principle underlying Government, a deviation and departure from which has, more than anything else, retarded the progress of mankind." [1]

From the above accounts it would appear that leaders or Kings were elected by savage or civilsed communities in ancient times, and the election depended upon their personal qualifications, physical bravery and resourcefulness. These were their *virtues*, literally physical strength and bravery, equivalent to the Sanskrit *vīrya*, and Latin *virtus*, strength. The man who possessed *vīrya* was called *vīra*, or a strong and powerful man. The word *vira* occurs in many Indo-Germanic languages as equivalent to *man*, *i.e.*, man endowed with physical vigour and strength. Dr. P. Giles suggests the adoption of the word *Wiros* for Āryan, "this being the word for 'men' in the great majority of the languages in question." [2] Whether this suggestion is good and wlll be adopted by scholars, it is not for me to say. But it may be stated here that the word *vīra* in Sanskrit does not mean an ordinary man, but a heoric man possessed of superior strength and valour. The leader of the savage Aryan tribes

---

[1] *Modern Review*, ii. 348. (1907).

[2] *The Cambridge History of India*, vol, i. 60.

was probably called *Vīra*, or hero; but, as society gradually advanced in civilisation, he came to be known as *Grāmaṇī*, the leader of a *grāma* or 'body of men.' In the nomadic stage, the *grāma* was moving; but when the people settled down as agriculturists, the *grāma* came to be identified with the territory in which a particular body of men settled down. [1] The leader of the *grāma*, whether moving or settled, was always known as the *Grāmaṇī*. [2] In the early stages, the *Grāmaṇī* was probably elected for his personal qualifications as a leader. But the office seems to have afterwards become hereditary. The *Grāmaṇī* was "the head of the village both for civil purposes and military operations." [3] It was his duty to protect the people, keep them united, maintain peace and order among them, and defend them, with their help, against the attacks of enemies. He had to decide all disputes of a civil nature, put down crimes by punishing the criminals, and make adequate arrangements and organization for the defence of the village, when threatened by invasion. Of course, every able-bodied man in the village thought it his duty to arm himself and follow the leader or *Grāmaṇī*, either on foot or on horseback, according to his social rank, to repel the attack or punish the enemy; and the sinews of war, if the military operations lasted long, were found by the people themselves by individual contributions consistently with one's means and income. And the people probably also contributed a specified portion of their agricultural produce to the Grāmaṇī for the up-keep of his civil and military establishments, such as they were in those days. The Grāmaṇī, of course, had his own lands and cattle for maintaining himself and his family; but his income was supplemented by a portion of the popular contributions also. From the functions he had to

---

[1] Vide *ante*, Chap. ii. p. 111 and iii. p. 124 cf. Rv. i. 44, 10; 141, 1; 149, 4; x. 146, 1, etc.

[2] Rv. x. 62, 11; 107, 5.

[3] *Ved. Ind.*, i. 247.

perform, the office of the Grāmaṇī could not have been hereditary at first. He must have been elected to the office for his personal ability to lead and protect the people. On his death, probably the village-council (*sabhā*) met to elect a fit and competent man to succeed him, and he, who was unanimously considered fit, became the Grāmaṇī. Every village had its own Grāmaṇī, and his authority had been at first quite independent of the others, and there had been probably no co-operation among them, in as much as each village was considered autonomous and independent, and each had its own lands and managed its own affairs as best it could. But sometimes there were quarrels between two villages about their respective boundaries, the possession of any particular piece of land or pasture or cattle, and then a free fight ensued among the inhabitants, resulting in blood-shed and loss of life or limbs. Probably one such quarrel or fight is referred to in a Ṛgvedic verse (vi. 25, 4) which Griffith has translated as follows:

"With strength of limb the hero slays the hero, when bright in arms they range them for the combat, when two opposing hosts contend in battle for seed and offspring, waters, kine or corn-fields."

It was to the interest of the villagers to live in peace with their neighbours; and we can easily imagine that the wisest among them, including the Grāmaṇī, enjoined upon all the duty of exercising self-restraint, and respecting the rights of others as much as they valued and respected theirs, and the necessity of living in peace and amity with the inhabitants of the neighbouring villages. They all spoke the same language, worshipped the same Gods, performed the same religious ceremonies and were placed in the same stage of culture, and regarded, to all intents and purposes, as one people; but their interests, having been different, sometimes jarred against one another, leading to unhappy quarrels, dissensions and bloodshed, which were highly undesirable. A leading and powerful clan of a village may, therefore, have hit upon the happy idea of welding the separate and disjointed villages into one Tribe, under the guidance and control of the clan to whom all quarrels and disputes could be referred for satisfactory solution and decision. Those villages that entered into a mutual compact, recognizing the supremacy of the clan in all matters of internal dispute, ultimately formed into one Tribe, which came to be named after the clan presiding over them. In this way the Five Tribes or Pañcajanāh or Pañcakṛṣṭayah came into existence and were known as the Bharatas, the Anus, the Druhyus etc. after the names of the clans that presided over the village confederacies, or Tribes. The leaders of these clans in the long run became the acknowledged *Rājans* [1] or Kings of the different Tribes named after the clans to which they belonged. The word *Rajān*, by the way, etymologically means 'one who pleases, or secures the contentment of the people by protecting them and their interests, and distributing even-handed justice to all.' (*Rājā prakṛti-rañjanāt*). This was the basic principle underlying the important office he held, and was quite consistent with the fundamental idea of selecting a leader for his physical and mental fitness.

The clan to which the Raja belonged necessarily became the most powerful and prominent, to which the people naturally looked up for help and guidance in times of difficulty, and owed their allegiance. The Gramanis of the several villages that constituted the confederacy under the King were in close touch with the latter, and represented the interests of the villages of which they were the leaders. The village, town or *pur*, in which the King ordinarily resided, became the central seat of Government, and was strongly fortified against attacks. The Gramaṇī of the village or city, where the royal residence was situated, necessarily became more influential than the other Gramaṇīs of the interior

[1] Rv. iii. 43, 5; v. 54, 7, etc.

villages, and was specially honoured by the King, as he formed part of the royal entourage. Professors Macdonell and Keith observe that "the Grāmaṇī's connexion with the royal person seems to point to his having been a nominee of the King rather than a popularly elected officer. But the post may have been sometimes hereditary, and sometimes nominated or elected: there is no decisive evidence available."[1] As I have already pointed out, the post could not but have been elective at first, as only the strongest and most resourceful man was considered fit to be the leader of the people. In later times, when kingly authority was firmly established and centralised, the Grāmaṇī of the capital city may have been nominated by the King, as the latter would naturally prefer to have a man in his entourage and at the head of the capital city, who could be trusted to look to his interests and carry out his behests. It should be remembered that the Grāmaṇī was not only the leader of the people, discharging civil functions, but was also the head of the military contingent of the village, and, as Zimmer[2] says, was often connected with the *Senānī* or leader of the army. Hence it became necessary for the King to nominate a man to this important post, who could be safely trusted by him. The same policy may have been gradually extended to the villages in the interior also; but in Ṛgvedic times it seems that the post of the Grāmaṇī was elective, and his election was probably simply notified to the King for his information and formal approval.

Sage-priests and the part played by them in Tribal evolution.—In the early stages of Aryan culture, every man was his own priest, and performed his daily worship to please the beneficent deities who were supposed to possess the power of granting them plenty, peace, happiness and long life. As the Aryans gradually advanced from the pastoral to the agricultural stage, the problems of existence became

---

1 *Vedic Index*, i. 247.

2 *Altindisches Leben*, 171.

more and more complex, and did not admit of easy solution. The settled agricultural state was certainly far more desirable than a precarious pastoral existence; but domestic ease and comfort entirely depended upon an abundant produce of crops, and this again depended upon an abundant supply of timely rain. Rainfall, however, was not always regular and copious, and the crops were scanty and insufficient in consequence of long droughts, causing great distress among the people. They did not know how to ensure regular and timely rainfall, but there were some wise and thoughtful men among them who seemed to know the mysteries of the Cosmic Powers, and the means of propitiating the benevolent among them by magic utterances (*mantras*) and the performance of mysterious rites, and thus enabling them to overcome the baneful influence of the malevolent powers with a view to bring down timely rains. These men were called *Ṛṣis*, or Seers, whose help was eagerly sought by all classes, especially their leaders, and the rich and powerful. As the rain-maker among certain wild tribes of Africa is the priest and wields great influence among the people, so the Rain-makers in the early stages of Aryan evolution developed into Priests and Ṛṣis, whose help was thought to be indispensably necessary for the production of timely rain, and was sought by the Grāmaṇīs, the Kings, the nobles and the rich. They framed elaborate rules and formulas for the performance of sacrifices with a view to propitiate and strengthen Indra and his auxiliary deities, who alone could defeat the Demon of Drought (Vṛtra) and ensure regular rain-fall. As the leaders and Kings owed their power to the prosperity, happiness and contentment of the people, it was their main interest to requisition the services of the Ṛṣis and Priests in the performance of year-long and periodical sacrifices that had "water" or timely rain-fall for their object. But none but the King and the rich could engage their services, as they and their families had to be supported by rich gifts of cattle, gold, grains and other necessaries of life. Thus the Ṛṣis and Priests became indispensable factors in early Aryan society, and formed a class by themselves wielding great influence over all the leaders of men, Grāmaṇīs and Kings. The Ṛṣis were the Seers who had the mysterious *mantras* revealed to them and had ecstatic visions of the great Cosmic Powers, who regulated and controlled the affairs of the Universe. They had been at first Priests also, performing the sacrifices and chanting the *mantras*. But these offices were afterwards relegated to a special class, who came to be known as Priests or Purohitas, and had different names according to the parts that they had to perform in the sacrifice. The Kings had their own Royal Priests, who in Ṛgvedic times were mostly Ṛṣis, and were held in the highest respect, having precedence even over their Royal masters. The Royal Priest or Ṛṣi wielded great influence over the King and his courtiers and ministers, and his advice was never superseded nor neglected. He possessed the power of propitiating the Gods not only to bring prosperity on the people, but also to secure easy victories to the King over hostile neighbouring States. In Ṛgvedic times we find the renowned Vasiṣṭha and the equally renowned Viśvāmitra as the great Ṛṣis or Priest-leaders of the Tṛtsus and the Bharatas respectively. Every important Tribe had its own Priest-leader. The Kings had implicit faith in them in as much as they possessed, or were supposed to possess the power of bringing down timely rains for the prosperity of the people, and securing glorious victories to them by bringing to their aid the favour of the great Indra. No wonder that they allowed themselves to be guided by their counsels both in peace and war. It was thus that Priesthood, (and in later times Brāhmanism) came to establish its firm influence in Aryan society.

It was the Ṛṣis or Sage-priests, the mighty wise thinkers of old, the "brainiest" among the people, who led the van of progress in the early and subsequent stages of Aryan development. It was they who domesticated the cattle, discovered the use of fire, invented the plough, learnt and taught the art of agriculture, invented and manufactured various implements, made chariots and wagons, discovered the intimate relations of the Cosmic Powers with human welfare, instituted Fire-worship and the various Sacrifices calculated to promote human happiness, evolved the institution of marriage, and established it on a firm and sure basis, discovered the existence of the various beneficent deities and differentiated their individual characteristics, brought them down, as it were, from their distant spheres to exercise their benevolent influence on human affairs, discovered their unity in the One Supreme Deity, permeating the Universe,—the Primordial Source of Creation,—the One and Indivisible, yet manifesting Itself in manifold ways,—and lifted up human hopes and aspirations from the fleeting, evanescent and perishable things of this world to the attainment of calm, serene and everlasting *ānandam* (beatitude), that knows no flow nor ebb and is centred in and co-extensive with Brahman, the Great and Undefinable. It was these great minds that in early Ṛgvedic times fused the disjointed and discordant elements into one homogeneous whole, and united the scattered villages into one confederacy under the supremacy of one vigorous and powerful clan whom they guided by their sage counsels to the attainment of the blessed goal of one united people. It was through their noble and selfless exertions that there came into being in Ṛgvedic times the Five Tribes (*Pañcajanāh* or *Pañcakṛṣtayah*) who possessed a homogeneous civilisation, speaking one language, performing the same sacrifices, and believing in the same Gods, and, though existing as separate Tribes, were looked upon as the different limbs of the great Aryan People that was in the making. The Sage-Masters, realising this ultimate destiny of the Aryans, never missed an opportunity for praying to the great Gods for the well-being of the Five Tribes, [1] upon whom they based their hopes

[1] Rv. x. 60, 4; v. 86, 2; ix 101, 9, etc.

and aspirations for the realisation of their happy and glorious dream, *viz.* the evolution of a noble nation, full of life and vigour, and a civilisation unique in the world. With this object in view they made a persistent attempt to eliminate all discordent elements from the land, and create a peaceful atmosphere, quite conducive to the growth and development of their noble ideals.

To such master-minds as these, Kings and peasants equally bowed their heads in solemn awe and reverence. They had no axes of their own to grind, and were utterly selfless. Unlike the *Patesis* of ancient Chaldea, they had no ambition of being Priest-Kings, exercising supreme political authority and enjoying material pleasure and the best things of this world. They were ascetics, and yet lived as householders with their wives and children on gifts voluntarily made by the King and the Nobles in return for the invaluable services rendered by them. In fact, they lived in perfect detachment from power and pelf, and were worldly, yet not of the world. It is, therefore, sheer blasphemy to say that they flattered and praised the Princes and Nobles, nay the Gods, mainly with an eye to *baksheesh*, as Professor Bloomfield has the temerity irreverently to say.[1] It is an altogether wrong view to take of *Dāna-stutis* or praises for gifts. A man ought not to hoard wealth simply for the sake of personal pleasure and enjoyment, quite unmindful of the wants and sufferings of the poor and the needy, all of whom have a claim on his liberality. (Rv. x. 107). At the present day, the idea may be condemned by some as Socialistic, nay Bolshevistic; but even Socialism and Bolshevism, if not carried to extremes, have their justifications. Liberality has, in all the Scriptures of the world, been enjoined upon as a religious duty; and the Sage-poets of the Ṛgveda have simply dilated upon its virtues. (Rv. x. 117, 5. 6). They hated begging for its own sake, and a Ṛṣi prays to Indra

[1] Bloomfield, *The Religion of the Veda*, Lecture the Second.

that he may never be reduced to such a strait as to be compelled to beg from the rich. (Rv. ii. 28, 11). The praises for liberality had, therefore, the object of stimulating the giver to make a noble and unstinted use of his wealth. (Rv. x. 107, 8-11). Social welfare and advancement depend upon mutual help and obligations. If I do something for you, you must do something for me. It is all a matter of "Give and Take." But the gift should not be always one-sided only, and should be adequately returned. The Sage-poets devoted a major portion of their time to communion with the Gods, and to the performance of sacrifices for the benefit of Princes and peasants alike. They had no time to devote to worldly pursuits, and therefore naturally expected gifts (or *fees*, if you like) from Kings and Nobles, adequate to maintain them and their families according to their rank and station in life. (Rv. x. 107). Work done for niggardly persons is so much time and energy sheerly wasted and lost. One need not, therefore, be surprised if such persons are condemned in the Ṛgveda (Rv. x. 117, 6). It should be borne in mind that it is no crime to earn an honest competency by honest work. The Princes of Ṛgvedic times quite appreciated the invaluable services rendered by the Ṛṣis, and vied with one another to honour them by making rich gifts. The homage paid to them was voluntary and was eminently deserved. The Ṛṣi-priest had the precedence of all in the Royal court, and his consecration preceded even that of the king. This shows the high esteem in which he was generally held.

Election of Kings.—A distinguished Ṛṣi having usually been the moral, spiritual and political guide of the Royal clan that ruled a Tribe, we may take it for granted that no successor to a deceased King was appointed without his knowledge or approval. In fact, we have positive evidence to show that he was the real King-maker. In two hymns of the Atharva-Veda (iv. 22, 3. 5; viii. 7, 6), the Sage-priest (*Purohita*) has been called the King-maker (*Rāja-kṛit*). It was he who suggested the name of a successor to the King probably in consultation with the other members of the Royal clan and court, and his nominee presented himself or was invited for election by the people as their King. In the Ṛgveda, however, we find instances of a son succeeding his father on the throne, [1] which may lend colour to the view that kingship was usually hereditary in Ṛgvedic times. But it was not so always in all the cases. "The monarchy" as Zimmer holds "was elective, though it is not clear whether the selection by the people was between the members of the royal family only, or extended to members of all the noble clans." [2] My humble view is that a Tribe having been named after the ruling clan, the selection was originally confined to its members only, and not extended to members of all the noble clans in the Tribe. As long as a qualified man was available in the Royal clan, there was no need for going outside it for choosing a successor. If the deceased King had a qualified son, the choice naturally fell on him, and he succeeded to the throne, not of course as a matter of right, but by general sufferance. Of course, we may suppose that his father and the Sage-priest took great care in his up-bringing as an ideal future King. A qualified son failing, the selection was made from among the other qualified members of the clan, and then duly announced to the cantons (*viś*). The people or their acknowledged representatives then assembled in the *Sabhā*, or a *Samiti* specially convened for the purpose in the capital city, and there expressed their views or approval. There is a verse in the Ṛgveda (x. 124, 8) which suggests election of a King by the people or subjects themselves. Wilson has translated it thus: "Like subjects choosing a king, they (the waters) smitten with fear, fled from Vṛtra." The sense however is somewhat obscure. The original passage is ***viśo na rājanam vṛṇānā*** which undoubtedly means "like people or subjects

---

[1] *e.g* Vadhryaśva, Divodāsa, Pijavana, Sudās: or Purukutsa, Trasadasyu, Mitrātithi, Kuruśravaṇa, Upamaśravas, etc

[2] *Vedic Index*, ii. 211.

choosing or electing a king." The evident meaning is that as people smitten with fear from the attacks of enemies choose a king to lead and protect them, so the waters fled from Vṛtra (their encompasser) and sought the protection of Varuṇa.[1] There can be no doubt that the Sage-poet had a contigency in his mind when people, without a leader or King, and threatened by enemies, hastened to elect one, capable of protecting them, as their King. There is another hymn (Rv. x. 173) which indicates that the stability of a King on the throne was contingent on the good-will of his subjects. Wilson thus translates the hymn:

"I have consecrated thee, (Rājā); come amongst us, be steady and unvacillating: may all thy subjects desire thee (for their King), may the kingdom never fall from thee.

"Come into this (kingdom), mayest thou never be deposed, unvacillating as a mountain; stand firm here like Indra, establish thy kingdom in this world.

"May Indra, gratified by the perpetual oblation, firmly establish this (prince); may Soma, may Brahmaṇaspati address him (as their votary).

"Firm is the heaven, firm is the earth, firm are these mountains, firm is the entire world, so this King of man be firm.

"May the royal Varuṇa, the divine Bṛhaspati, may Indra and Agni ever give stability to thy kingdom.

"With a constant oblation we handle the constant *Soma*; therefore may Indra render thy subject people payers of (their) taxes."

The above *mantras* were intended to be pronounced by the officiating Priest at the time of the installation of a King. The selection of the King had already been made. The King-elect was present in the assembly (*Samiti*), or at the place

---

[1] The translation given by Dr. B. Shama Sastri in his "Evolution of Indian Polity," (p. 28) is evidently incorrect. It is as follows: 'And they (the Asuras), like people who elect their rulers, have in abhorrence turned away from Vṛtra."

of sacrifice, and his formal election and consecration only remained to be performed. The officiating priest, as the spokesman of the people, invites him to come for formal consecration as their King and expresses a pious hope that he may so act and behave himself as to secure the permanent attachment and good will of his subjects, and that he may occupy the throne firmly and for ever. He winds up his consecrating sermon by further expressing an ardent hope that his subjects may regularly pay their taxes to enable him to carry on the administration of the kingdom and adopt offensive measures against enemies, according to necessity.

The above hymn which was a typical consecration hymn in Ṛgvedic times clearly shows that the King was elected for his personal qualifications only by the people, and depended for the tenure of his office on their good will and contentment. It also shows that the people paid their taxes as long as they were pleased with the administration of their King, and could withhold them, if he proved unjust and tyrannical. The people clearly realised their rights, privileges and duties, and were powerful factors to be reckoned with in the State.

The next hymn (Rv. x. 174) is also significant and would bear quoting here :—

" By the *abhīvarta* oblation, whereby Indra has conquered (everything), do thou, O Brahmaṇspati, bring us to sovereign rule.

" Having overcome our rivals, and those who are our enemies, do thou attack him who assails us, and him who behaves insolently towards us.

" May the divine Savitṛ, may Soma establish thee (*Rājā*) ; may all beings establish thee, so that thou may be supreme.[1]

---

[1] The verbs in this verse have been translated by some in the past-perfect tense ; " The divine Savitṛ and Soma have established thee (*Rājā*), and all beings have established thee, so that thou hast become supreme."

"That oblation whereby Indra became heroic, renowned and eminent, I have offered, O Gods, (to you); may I become freed from rivals. (*a-sapatnah*).

"May I become without a rival, the destroyer of my rivals, obtaining the sovereignty, overcoming (my foes), so that I may reign over these beings and over my people."

The above verses have reference to a sacrifice performed, in which the *abhīvarta* oblation had been offered. The object of this oblation was to make all beings (Gods and men) friendly towards the King. Of the first three verses, the first is addressed by the presiding priest to Brahmaṇaspati, and the second and third to the King, and the last two embody the prayers of the King himself. It appears that though the King was chosen by the people and firmly established on the throne, he was still afraid of the intrigues of his *rivals* (*sapatnah*) and prayed that he might overcome them. There were undoubtedly rival claimants to the throne in the ruling clan, and though one of them was chosen by the people, the disappointed rivals probably intrigued among themselves or with others for his overthrow. The newly elected King had, therefore, a hard and uneasy time of it until he succeeded in either conciliating them or putting them down and removing them out of the way. Sovereign power was clearly insecure in those days.

The Brāhmaṇas contain in them much ancient history and tradition which give us a glimpse of the forms of Government as obtained in early times. We have already seen that the Mahābhārata refers to a time when the people used to govern themselves, and were without a King. In other words, the earliest form of Government was Republican, of course, in its very crude and undeveloped form. This form of Government did not succeed and last long, as the people frequently quarrelled among themselves, which led to bloodshed and mutual annihilation. Then the wisest among them thought and realised that they should all place themselves under one strong ruler or leader who would be able to govern them, maintain internal peace and order, and protect them from outside aggression. And so they chose a King. The *Aitareya Brāhmaṇa* (i. 14), also refers to a similar process of evolution among the Gods: "The Devas said, 'it is on account of our having no King that the Asuras defeat us. Let us elect a King.' All consented. They elected Soma their King. Headed by King Soma, they were victorious in all directions." There is also a significant passage in the *Taittirīya Brāhmaṇa* (i. 5, 9) which is worth reproducing here: "The Devas and Asuras joined in battle. Then Prajāpati concealed his eldest son Indra, lest he might be killed by the mighty Asuras. Prahlāda, the son of Kāyadhu, likewise concealed his son Virocana, lest he might be killed by the Devas. The Devas went to Prajāpati and said: 'there can possibly be no battle for a state having no King' (for its leader). They courted Indra to be their King with sacrifices."[1]

It would thus appear that the election of a King, Chief, or Leader was, and could not but have been the rule in early Aryan communities. Kingship only became hereditary when authority was more centralised in the King, peace reigned in the country for a considerably long time, and people did not much care to know who ruled them so long as they were ruled well. To the extent that the people neglected to exercise their rights and privileges, to that extent monarchy became more powerful, until at last it became hereditary and even absolute.

The original meaning of Rājan: its political significance.—As the Royal clan established its supremacy over all other clans and united all the villages (grāmas) situated within a particular territory into a Tribe, its members were at first known by the name of *Rājan* which originally signified "nobles" and not a "king." (Rv. i. 40, 8; 108, 7: x. 42, 10; 97, 6.) This clan no doubt became powerful as

---

[1] *Vide* Sastri's *Evolution of Indian Polity*, pp. 20-21.

the result of all its members holding together and acting in concert under the direction of one capable leader, and all the members equally shared the glory of federating the villages into one State or Tribe; hence all of them were called *Rājans*. " Zimmer [1] sees traces in one passage of the Ṛgveda (x 97, 6) that in times of peace there was no King in some States, the members of the Royal family holding equal rights. He compares this with the state of affairs in early Germany. But, (observe Professors Macdonell and Keith) the passage merely shows that the nobles could be called *Rājans*, and is not decisive for the sense ascribed to it by Zimmer. Of course this state of affairs is perfectly possible, and is exemplified later in Buddhist times." [2] But the question remains to be answered why *all* of them were designated by the name of *Rājan*, unless it be that all of them held equal rights. My surmise is that so long as the members of the clan were limited in number, it was possible for them to act in concert and equally share the responsibility of the Government, and thus they were called by the common name of *Rājan*. But when in course of time the clan expanded, and the members became too numerous to be able to bear an equal share in the administration of the country, their acknowledged leader was invested with the supreme authority during his life-time, or as long as he was physically and mentally capable of exercising it for the benefit of the people and the State. It was then that the name *Rājan* or *King* came to be specially appropriated by him, and the word *Rājanya* (Rv. x. 90, 12) was applied to designate the other members of the clan, and meant " nobles belonging to the Royal clan." As the office of the King was not hereditary but elective, every capable member stood the chance of being elected King on the demise of the last incumbent. This furnished an incentive to them to keep

---

[1] *Altindisches Leben*, 176, 177.

[2] *Vedic Index*, ii. 217-218.

themselves in a high state of efficiency both in wars and the internal administration of the country, and to act in concert. The Ṛgvedic passage referred to by Zimmer says (according to Wilson's translation) that the *Rājānah* (Princes or Nobles) assembled in battle, or (according to a different translation), in an assembly to discuss public affairs. This would be quite consistent with the theory propounded above.

The elective principle continued uninterruptedly from Vedic times to the Buddhistic Age.—The Atharva-veda though a much later work than the Ṛgveda, contains much ancient history which throws light on many important matters that belonged to a by-gone age. I cannot do better than quote a few passages here to illustrate how a King was elected from the Royal clan, and even invited and brought from a distance by his kinsmen in the event of an eligible member not having been available near at hand :

" To thee hath come the kingship with its spendour on.
Shine as lord, sole ruler of the people.
King! let all regions of the heavens invite thee.
Here let men wait on thee and before thee.

" *The tribesmen shall elect thee for the kingship.*
These five celestial regions shall elect thee.
Rest on the height and top of kingly power; thence
As a mighty man award us treasures.
" Kinsmen inviting thee, shall go to meet thee.
With thee go Agni as an active herald.
Let women and their sons be friendly-minded.
Thou, mighty one, shalt see abundant tribute.

* * * * *

" Speed to us hither from the farthest distance.
Propitious unto thee be Earth and Heaven,
Even so hath Varuṇa this, King, asserted, he who
Himself hath called thee : come thou hither.
" *Pass to the tribes of men, O Indra, Indra.*
Thou with the Varuṇa hast been found accordant.

To his own place this one (Agni) hath called thee
saying,
'Let him adore the gods and *guide the clansmen.*'
"The bounteous paths in sundry forms and places,
All, in accord, have given thee room and comfort.
Let all these in concert call thee hither.
Live thy tenth decade here, a strong kind ruler."[1]

These *mantras* must have been composed by the Sage-priest of the Royal clan which was in need of electing an eligible King from among themselves. As no eligible man was available in the ruling clan, one of their kinsmen, who had probably migrated elsewhere and been living at a distance, was invited by the clan, probably at the suggestion of the Sage-priest himself, to come and occupy the throne, after his due election by the tribesmen or the people. "Kinsmen, inviting thee, shall go to meet thee," and "the Tribesmen shall elect thee for kingship" are highly significant. "Let women and their sons be friendly-minded" is no less significant, in as much as it goes to show that the voices of women also counted, and were an important factor in moulding public opinion. If women did not approve of a particular selection, though they were not invited or allowed to express their own views in the Tribal Assembly, they could yet influence and mould the opinions of their sons who would be summoned to express their views. And this meant a great deal. Hence the Sage-priest prays that "women and their sons" may be "friendly-minded." This shows, beyond the shadow of a doubt, what a living, intelligent and patriotic race were the Vedic Aryans—men, women and their sons—all of whom took a keen and vivid interest in every important matter that related to their tribal welfare.

There is another hymn in the Atharva-veda also referred to by Zimmer and quoted by Dr. Sastri in his *Evolution of*

---

[1] Av., iii. 4, 1. 2. 3 5. 6. 7. The above hymn is quoted by Dr. Shama Sastri in his *Evolution of Indian Polity*, pp. 18, 19, and referred to by Zimmer in his *Altindisches Leben*, 176, 177.

Indian Polity, (p. 19) which goes to show that the King had a share in the village-produce, kine and horses, and was "the sole lord and leader of the people," and that his rivals struggled for precedence. There were undoubtedly several candidates for election as King, and the disappointed candidates gave the elected King a lot of trouble by their secret intrigues against, and sullen indifference to, and non-co-operation with him, and it was necessary for him to overcome them first of all. Below are quoted a few stanzas from the hymn [1]:

"Exalt and strengthen this my prince, O Indra,
Make him sole lord and leader of the people.
Scatter his foes, deliver all his rivals into his hand
In struggles for precedence.
"*Give him a share in village, kine and horses*,
And leave his enemy without a portion.
Let him as King be head and chief of princes,
Give up to him, O Indra, every foeman.

* * * * *

"Supreme art thou, beneath thee are thy rivals,
And all, O King, who were thine adversaries.
Sole lord and leader and allied with Indra, bring,
Conquer thy foeman's goods and treasures.
"Consume, with lion aspect, all their hamlets, with
Tiger aspect drive away thy foemen.
Sole lord and leader and allied with Indra,
Sieze, conquer thine enemies' possessions."

It should be noted here that the above hymn distinctly mentions the name of the tiger, *vyāghra*,[2] which is conspicuous by its absence in the Ṛgveda. I have elsewhere[3] expressed an opinion that the tiger was originally a native of the dense forests of Central and Southern India, which was cut off from the Punjab by the Rajputana Sea and the Gangetic

---

[1] Av., iv. 22.

[2] Vyāghrāpratikeva badhaśva śatrūn (Av., iv. 22, 7).

[3] *Ṛgvedic India*, Ch. v

or Eastern Sea in Ṛgvedic times. It was only when these seas disappeared in a later age, and a land connection was established between Northern and Southern India that it was possible for the tiger to migrate towards the north, and occupy the swampy jungles of Lower Bengal and the *terai* regions of the Himālaya, abounding in games. The mention of the tiger and some eastern provinces of Northern India[1] in the Atharva-veda, therefore, removes the date of its composition by thousands of years from Ṛgvedic times, during which the above-named seas disappeared and the alluvial plains of the Gangetic valley were formed and peopled by Aryan colonists from the Punjab. If the above hymns of the Atharva-veda were composed to meet the requirements of its age, then it must be freely admitted that the custom of the election of Kings by their tribesmen must have continued uninterruptedly for thousands of years from Ṛgvedic times down to the age of the Atharva-veda, though hereditary monarchies also must have been evolved here and there. But in the case of the latter also, the election of a successor indispensably required the popular sanction and approval, of which we find a notable instance in Vālmīki's *Rāmāyaṇa*. When King Daśaratha, the powerful monarch of Kosala, wanted, on account of his extreme old age, to abdicate the throne in favour of his popular eldest son, Rāma, he thought it necessary to summon the Popular Assembly and obtain its sanction to his nomination.[2] It would thus appear that popular opinion could never be flouted either in elective or hereditary monarchies in Ancient India. And *Vox populi* went as strong as ever down to the age of the Buddha, for we find the elective principle still in force among the various Śākya clans. It was only after Alexander's invasion, and the influx of Dravidian adventurers from the south, and of foreign invaders from the north that *Vox populi* became

---

[1] Anga and Magadha.

[2] *Rāmāyaṇa*, ii 2

dumb, or rather was silenced by the loud stentorian voices of the Imperial and Absolute Monarchs. It was driven from all imperial concerns in the capital towns to remote and out-of-the-way villages in the interior, where its feeble tone was heard in the village Panchayets for a long time, even during the period of Mahomedan rule, until it was finally drowned by the victorious and sonorous roll of the British drum, though signs are not wanting of its revival again.

The Royal Court and Retinue.—The Royal Court mainly consisted of those nobles (*Rājans* or *Rājanyas*) belonging to the Royal clan who were the strong supporters of the King: the Royal Priest or Sage (*Purohita*) who guided their counsel; the *Grāmaṇī* of the capital town; the *Sūta* or the Royal charioteer who always accompanied the King in his tours, and drove the car for him in the field of battle; the *Senānī* (lit. leader of an army) who was the General (Rv. vii. 20, 5; ix. 96, 1; x. 84, 2) at the head of the army, responsible for its discipline, and led it to war "when the King became too important to lead every little fray in person;" and others like *Madhyamaśī*, Judge or Arbitrator; *Kṣattṛ*, a distributor of good things (Rv. vi. 13, 2), probably the Royal store-keeper, though Sāyaṇa explains the word occurring in the *Śatapatha Brāhmaṇa* (v. 3, 1, 7) as *antahpurādhyakṣa* or chamberlian; *Saṃgrahitṛ* or Treasurer; *Bhāgadugha*, collector of taxes etc.

The King lived in a big palace, well fortified, and adorned with many doors and pillars, to judge from the description of King Varuṇa's palace in the Ṛgveda. (Rv. ii. 41, 5; vii. 88, 5). He sat on a throne (*Āsandī*) in the Royal court, facing his courtiers on the right and left, all of whom had seats according to their respective ranks. The Purohita who was also the Minister had a seat of honour, probably close to the throne. The King probably personally exercised criminal jurisdiction, as we find references to it in the Sūtras (*Gautama Dharma Sūtra*, xii. 43). "Possibly the jurisdiction would be exercised by a royal officer or even by a delegate, for a

Rājanya is mentioned as an over-seer (*adhyakṣa*) of the punishment of a Śūdra in the *Kāṭhaka Saṃhitā* (xxviii. 4). In civil justice it may be that the King played a much less prominent part, save as a court of final appeal, but evidence is lacking on this head."[1] The Purohita who had his seat close to the throne always advised the King in the discharge of his duties; "he also had the advantage of the Royal ministers and attendants."

Royal pomp and circumstance.—The King attended the court or appeared before the public gorgeously dressed, and bedecked with jewels and gold (Rv. x. 78, 1; cf. Rv. i. 85, 8; viii. 5, 38 etc.). He wore a golden crown on his head which tapered to a point like horn (Rv. v. 59, 3), just like the crowns still worn by Hindu bridegrooms in Bengal on the occasion of the performance of their wedding ceremony. He wore a golden breast-plate (Rv. v. 59, 6 etc.) or mantle and carried the sheathed sword in his hand. In fact, his looks inspired awe in the minds of the spectators. (Rv. i. 85, 8). Sometimes the King mounted the royal elephant with his Minister (Rv. iv. 4, 1) or a royal officer, and went out either a-hunting, or for showing himself to his subjects on any festive occasion. As horses were adorned with pearls and gold, so we can surmise that the royal elephant also was gorgeously bedecked with gold, silver, pearls and jewels, as is still the custom in the Indian Feudatory States. On such occasions, the King was attended by his armed retinue both on foot and on horses and chariots, and the Royal procession must have presented a very picturesque, imposing and impressive appearance. In a word, the pomp and circumstance of Royalty was not lacking in Vedic times.

Bali or Taxes.—The King himself led the army in war and took the field. He fought from his war-chariot, attended on his right by the *Sūta*, or Royal charioteer, upon whose skill in manipulating the chariot in the thick of the battle

[1] *Vedic Index*, ii. 213.

often depended his victory. Body-guards on horses and chariots defended the Royal chariot and the person of the King. "In return for his warlike services the King received the obedience (Rv. i. 67, 1; iv. 50, 8)—sometimes forced (Rv. vii. 6, 5; ix. 7, 5)—of the people, and in particular their contributions for the maintenance of Royalty.[1] The King is regularly regarded as 'devouring the people' (Rv. i. 65, 4; Av. iv. 22, 7; *Ait. Brāh* vii. 29 etc.), but this phrase must not be explained as meaning that he necessarily oppressed them. It obviously had its origin in a custom by which the King and his retinue were fed by the people's contributions, a plan with many parallels. It is also probable that the king could assign the royal right of maintenance to a Kṣatriya, thus developing a Nobility supported by the people."[2] From the existence of the elective system of monarchy in Ṛgvedic times, it cannot be reasonably supposed that the King was oppressive or forced his subjects to contribute more than they could afford to do. But no monarchy or republic can be maintained without the people contributing a definite share of their produce or income to the State coffer; and though such contributions are originally voluntary, they have a tendency of gradually proving irksome to the contributors to the same extent as they forget the fundamental necessity for making them. In Ṛgvedic times when money or gold was scarce, people used to contribute a definite portion of their produce, and a number of cattle and horses to the King. The King, therefore, possessed a huge granary, besides vast herds of cattle and horses, which gradually increased in number as they multiplied. These were probably sufficient to maintain Royalty with dignity in times of peace; but in troublous times when armies had to be moved to the battle-fields, and adequately fed and maintained, the King was in need of special

[1] Cf. Bali-hṛt, 'paying tribute' Rv. vii. 6, 5; x. 173. 6.

[2] *Vedic Index*, ii. 212, 213.

contributions from his subjects, especially the Nobles and the rich among them. If his subjects were unwilling to contribute anything, probably the necessary supplies were "commandeered," as they are done even to this day in most civilised countries. In such cases, the King and his retinue may have been described as "devouring the people." But really the King was not an oppressor. In the *Mahābhārata* we come across a remarkable passage, showing how the King used persuasion instead of force to collect the sinews of war on the occasion of a threatened invasion, which is as follows :—

"The enemy are threatening to invade my territory; and as a public calamity is impending, I ask you to make contributions with a view to enable me to avert it. When the calamity will have been averted, I will return you your money. Should you, however, allow the enemy to come, they will not only rob you of all your wealth, but also carry away your wives and children. In that event, there will be none left to enjoy your property. You are like unto my sons, and I am glad to witness your prosperity. Now that there is an impending calamity, I am asking for your contributions. None ought to prize wealth when danger is threatened." [1]

The King in the above extract wants to open something like the modern State War Loan, repayable to the subscribers by the State afterwards. Whether the King in Ṛgvedic times asked for contributions with a view to repay them after the war was over, cannot be definitely said. Probably the contributions were in the nature of a special War Tax which proved galling to the subjects, and made them describe the King as "devouring the people." Sometimes the unwilling subjects were forced to make their contributions as was done in the case of the subjects of King Nahuṣa, as related in the Ṛgveda (vii. 6, 5). But ordinarily

[1] *Śānti Parva*, Ch. 87.

no force was used except in the case of hostile tribes (Rv. vii. 18, 19), as Zimmer has clearly admitted. [1]

The following extracts from the *Mahābharāta* as regards taxation and the collection of revenue may be applied, *mutatis mutandis*, to describe the attitude of the King towards his people in Ṛgvedic times:

"The King should save his people from the hands of envious and thievish knaves. He ought to fix the rules and rates of taxation, after carefully considering the condition of sale and purchase of goods on the part of the merchants, the margin of their profits, the condition of the roads and ways over which goods are conveyed, and the expenditure which they incur for their maintenance. Taxes should be levied on artisans also with special reference to the nature of their products and the margin of their profits. . . . . . Rules of taxation should be framed in such a way as to enable both the King and the tax-payers to enjoy the fruits of their labour. Actuated by a desire for inordinate gain, the King ought never to allow agriculture, industry and his kingdom to perish. Exorbitant taxation makes the King an object of popular displeasure. How can he, therefore, expect any good? He, who is unpopular with his people, can never gain any object. As a calf, by drinking milk from the udder of a cow, becomes strong and able to carry burdens, but fails to do so, if it does not obtain a sufficient supply of milk, so do the people, by becoming rich in consequence of the levy of moderate taxes by the King, become able to inaugurate many a useful work. But if they are robbed of all their gains by the King, they cannot accomplish any good. So the King should never levy immoderate taxes." [2]

Further, we read in the same epic:

---

[1] *Altindisches Leben*, 166, 167.

[2] *Sānti Parva*, Ch. 87. Quoted in my paper on "Limited Monarchy in Ancient India" in the *Modern Review*, ii. 350-351.

"As the bee collects honey from flowers, without hurting the plant, as men draw out milk from the udder of a cow, without cutting it off, or starving the calf, as a leech insensibly draws blood from the body, as a tigress catches hold of the neck of her cub between her teeth without hurting it, and as a mouse nibbles off flesh from the feet of a sleeping man without being discovered, so should the King imperceptably collect his revenues, without oppressing or annihilating his people." [1]

The Patriarchal system and Kingly form of government. —This attitude of the King towards his subjects which was observed in the Epic Age was the natural development of the patriarchal relations that existed between Royalty and the people in the Vedic Age. A King who owed his position and power to popular suffrage and good will could not afford to be a tyrant.

Professors Macdonell and Keith observe: "The normal, though not universal form of government in early India, was that by Kings, as might be expected in view of the fact that the Aryan Indians were invaders in a hostile territory: a situation which, as in the case of the Aryan invaders of Greece and of the German invaders of England, resulted almost necessarily in strengthening the monarchic element of the constitution. The mere patriarchal organization of society is not sufficient, as Zimmer assumes, to explain the Vedic Kingship."[2] The assumptions made by the learned Professors in this extract are highly gratuitous. In the first place, there is absolutely no evidence in the entire range of the Sanskrit Literature beginning from the Vedas, that the Aryans came to India as invaders or that they had a foreign origin.[3] In the second place, every tribe or body of men,

---

[1] *Śánti Parva*, Ch. 87. Quoted in my paper on "Limited Monarchy in Ancient India" in the *Modern Review*, ii. 350-351.

[2] *Vedic Index*, ii. 210.

[3] Cf. Muir O. S. T., ii. 392.

even if they were not invaders, required a leader or King to protect them from outside aggressions, as men possessing only a primitive culture were not always able to successfully manage their tribal affairs. Thirdly, the system of the election of Kings or tribal chiefs, as prevailed in Ṛgvedic times and the later ages, when there was no question of invasion, unmistakably points to its natural evolution in the land from the pastoral stage of Aryan culture when every pastoral tribe required a Grâmaṇī or leader to guide them from one place to another with their cattle and families. It was only when the several clans settled down as agriculturists in villages that attempts were successfully made to federate them into one Tribe under one leading clan, and the acknowledged leader of that clan was elected as the King. The kingly form of Government was, therefore, the natural outcome, as Zimmer says,[1] of the patriarchal organization of society. The favourite theory of Aryan invasion of the Punjab, to which Western scholars subscribe, need not be brought in to explain the existence of a kingly form of government in Ṛgvedic times.

The Sabhā and Samiti.—A people with democratic instincts like the Vedic Aryans, quite alert to and mindful of their own tribal interests, could not but frequently meet in assemblies to discuss village and public affairs and express their opinions freely on matters that concerned them most intimately. Every important village, therefore, had a permanent institution of its own, which was known by the name of *Sabhā.* (Rv. vi. 28, 6; viii. 4, 9; x. 34. 6). The Sabhā had a house or hall of its own, where the elders and all respectable persons, whether young or old, regularly met not only to talk on important village topics, like cows and probably cultivation, rain or crops, (Rv. vi. 28, 6; viii. 4, 9) but also to while away their idle time in dice-playing, (Rv. x. 34, 6) of which they were exceedingly fond. The Sabhā thus

[1] *Altindisches Leben*, 162.

assumed the character of an assembly as well as a club. We may, therefore, surmise that the ordinary daily sittings of the Sabhā were not formal. It was not incumbent upon every respectable villager to attend the Sabhā. But there were persons who were addicted to dicing, and therefore made it a regular business of theirs to attend it every day and engage in the game,[1] especially when the Assembly was not transacting any public business. Dicing was not a disreputable game in those days, as even Kings indulged in it, and there was even a Royal officer, called *Akṣavāpa*, or Superintendent of dicing, though its evil consequences were too well known to all, and loudly lamented (Rv. x. 34). But it had a fascinating influence on the mind of the weak and the dissolute, who were attracted to the gambling-house (Sabhā), like moths to the blazing fire, and were ruined. The near relations of these men had a horror of the Sabhā, when turned into a gambling-house, and seldom visited it. But it was also a useful institution in other ways. It was a meeting-place for social intercourse (Rv. vi. 28, 6), and also for debates and verbal contests, when young and old, excepting perhaps women,[2] attended its sittings. The exclusion of women from the Sabhā or Assembly was probably due to the fact that besides dicing, wine also was sometimes freely indulged in by the members (Rv. vii. 86, 6; Av. xiv. 1, 35. 36; xv. 9, 1. 2 Cf. Av. vii. 12, 2.) which made them noisy and rowdy. (Rv. viii. 2, 12; 21, 14). Hence an assembly was not regarded as a fit place for women to go to, though there is a passage of doubtful significance in the Ṛgveda (i. 167, 3), which would seem to suggest that women also sometimes attended its sittings on important occasions, when its proceedings were conducted with dignity and decorum. In the period of the Upaniṣads, however, we find women attending assemblies of learned men and taking active parts in the debates.

---

[1] A dicer was called Sabhā-Sthāṇu 'pillar of the Assembly' (*Vaj. Sam.* xxx, 18; *Taitti., Brāh.* iii. 4, 16, 1).

[2] *Maitrāyanī Samhitā*, iv. 7, 4.

"With regard to membership of assemblies" says Dr. Shama Sastri,[1] "there seems to have been no restriction whatever. Whether old or young, educated or uneducated, all seem to have had free admittance into the assembly whenever it was convened. It is also probable that there was no question of quorum, but the presence of every villager was necessary to make the assembly fully authoritative. . . . As the Kṛṣṇa Yajurveda (ii. 2, 2) has prescribed some sacrificial spells for avoiding nervousness in an assembly and for the acquisition of the power of eloquence, it follows that assemblies were convened on a grand scale and that no one was denied the right of expressing his views in the assembly. The priests representing the educated, the nobility representing the agricultural and the trading classes were all present there. As questions of election and banishment of Kings and of restoration of banished Kings were discussed in the assembly, it is doubtful whether Kings attended it or not. If it were a rule that the King should attend it, it would follow that he attended it as its head to preside over its deliberations. But as questions of election and restoration of a King cropped up as subjects of discussion only when there was no King in the Kingdom, some one else, a distinguished priest or a noble, might volunteer himself as its president for the time being; and when the question of the banishment of the tyrannical King was the subject of discussion in the assembly, the tyrant himself might stay away from it in the interests of his own personal safety or dignity. There is, however, no reliable reference found in the Vedas about the King's attendance in the assembly as its president The Ṛgvedic references to the presence of a Rājā in the midest of an assembly (ix. 92, 6; x. 97, 6) can be taken to mean either as the presence of a noble in the midst of an assembly, or as the presence of the King in festal assemblies or congregations, or battles, as interpreted by

---

[1] *The Evolution of Indian Polity.* Sec. iv, pp. 77-78.

Sāyaṇa (Rv. ix. 92, 6). On no account can the two passages be taken to mean that the King attended the assembly as its president."

The *Sabhā* was essentially an assembly of the people, but probably not of all the people, irrespective of class or culture, as guessed by Dr. Sastri, but only of the respectable and cultured section of it, the accredited leaders, though every one could be present there as visitor or spectator. "According to Ludwig, [1] the Sabhā was an assembly not of all the people, but of the Brahmins and Maghavans ('rich patrons.') This view can be supported by the expressions *Sabheya* 'worthy of the assembly' applied to a Brahmin," [2] *rayih sabhāvān*, 'wealth fitting for the assembly, [3] and so on." [4] A Ṛgvedic verse (viii. 4, 9) clearly says: "He who is thy friend, Indra, is verily possessed of horses, of cars, of cattle, and is of goodly form: he is ever supplied with food-comprising riches, and delighting all, he enters the assembly (*sabhā*)." The phrase *rayih sabhāvān* (Rv. iv. 2, 5) is also highly significant. Those who were fit to attend an assembly and took part in its deliberations were called *sabheyas*, and the birth of a *sabheya son* was earnestly desired by fathers (Rv. i. 91, 20; vii. 5, 18). The Sanskrit word *sabhya*, now in use to mean 'a member of an assembly' or as an epithet to mean 'cultured,' must have been derived from the Vedic word *sabheya* 'worthy of the assembly.' Hence I am disposed to think with Ludwig that the *sabhā* was originally an assembly of the rich, respectable and cultured men of a village or town, whose opinion had some value and weight. Of course, when the assembly had no important business to transact, its hall was

---

[1] Translation of the Ṛgveda, 3, 253-256. He quotes for his view Rv. viii. 4, 9; x. 71, 10. Cf. also Rv. vii. 1, 4.

[2] Rv. ii. 24, 13. cf. i. 91. 20.

[3] Rv. iv. 2, 5.

[4] *Vedic Index*, ii 426, 427

used as a club for "social intercourse and general conversation," as well as for playing the game of dice. Sometimes, a sacrifice also was held in the hall and libations were offered to the sacred Fire which was accordingly called *sabhya.* (Av. viii. 10, 5; x. 55, 6). It was probably on occasions like this that the King also was invited to and attended the assembly.

The word *Samiti,* like *Sabhā,* occurs several times in the Ṛgveda (i. 95, 8; ix. 92, 6; x. 97, 6; 166, 4; 191, 3). Hillebrandt holds that the Sabhā and the Samiti were indistinguishable and meant the one and the same thing. [1] But Ludwig [2] thinks that the Samiti was the popular assembly which could be attended by all, irrespective of class, rank and wealth.—primarily the *viśah* (the people),—not excepting of course the Maghavans and Brahmins, if they also desired to attend it. The etymological meaning of the word supports this view. *Sam-iti* literally means a meeting which is attended by all persons. When both the words are used in the Vedas, there must have been some difference in their meanings. The King also attended the Samiti (Rv. ix. 92, 6) as well as the Nobles. (Rv. x. 97, 6, *rājānah samitavira*). Zimmer thinks that it was at the *Samiti* that the King was elected. A Ṛgvedic verse (x. 173, 1) clearly says: "May *all the people* wish thee for their King." [3] If this view be correct (and I am disposed to think that it is), then it must follow that the *Samitis* were held on special and important occasions in the capital towns, and attended by all the people or their representatives, living in the town as well as the interior villages. The Sabhās were local and permanent institutions, but the *Samitis* were held on extraordinary occasions when all the people (*viśah*) were invited to assemble and come to a unanimous decision on an important

---

[1] *Vedische Mythologie,* 2, 123-125.

[2] Translation of the Ṛgveda, 3, 253 *et seq.*

[3] *Viśastvā sarvā vāñchantu,* (Rv. x 173, 1)

matter. They were like the Congresses and Conferences of our present time.

Frays and wars.—It seems that every young man and able-bodied person in Ṛgvedic times would bear arms and fight. Even women sometimes emulated their brothers and husbands in these matters and fought against their enemies when necessary, and also accompanied their husbands to the field of battle. The names of Mudgalānī, and Viśpalā will naturally occur to the reader's mind in this connection. (Rv. x. 102, 2, 11; i. 116, 15). Mudgalānī actually drove her husband's car in pursuit of some robbers, and defeated them with the help of his bow and arrows. Viśpalā, the wife of King Khela, who had accompanied her husband to the field of battle and lost her leg in fighting, had it replaced by one of iron through the grace of the Aśvins. Sarasvatī, the Goddess of Speech, (or the River, or Agni of that name) has been described in the Ṛgveda as Vṛtraghnī or the killer of Vṛtra, (Rv. vi. 61, 3. 4) and took part with Indra in his fight against that demon. In a hymn of the Ṛgveda (x. 125), popularly known as the Devī-Sūkta, Vāc, the Goddess representing the Primordial Force of the Universe, says that she stretches Rudra's bow and fights for the good of mankind. (Rv. x. 125, 6). These descriptions of fighting Goddesses must have been inspired by actual facts—the examples of fighting women in Ṛgvedic times. There must have been a stage in the evolution of Aryan civilisation when it was necessary for every man and woman to defend themselves and their property from attacks and aggressions; but in course of time, the fighting came to be relegated to the sterner sex only for obvious reasons, as women were not always free and physically fit and able to engage in or carry on the fight for a long time. In the pastoral and early agricultural stages, there were frequent frays and fights over the possession of land, cattle and even women and children between clans and clans, and tribes and tribes

(Rv. vi. 25, 4), resulting in bloodshed, broken heads and much heart-burning. Sometimes there were raids made by a hostile tribe or robbers, who suddenly swooped down upon the unwary inhabitants, and carried off their cattle, goods and even women. A free fight ensued between the villagers and the raiders who were hotly pursued until they were punished, or given up as too strong for the pursuers. The existence of a state of society like this made life and property highly insecure, and necessitated every youth and able-bodied man to be a good fighter, brave and dashing, and well armed to be able to meet a sudden emergency. Parents, as well as Ṛṣis prayed for the birth of brave sons who would be "very powerful, the slayers of the Dasyus and the destroyers of cities" (Rv. x. 47, 4). One Ṛṣi thus prays to Indra: "When wilt thou gather men with men, O Indra, heroes with heroes, and prevail in combat? Thou shalt win triple kine in frays for cattle, so, Indra, give thou us celestial glory." (Rv. vi. 35, 2). Thus a militant and warlike spirit prevailed among all classes from Ṛṣis down to the commonest people, all of whom trained themselves and their sons in the art of fighting. As already stated, the great Ṛṣi, Mudgala, and his wife pursued the robbers who had stolen their cattle, and after defeating them in a fray, succeeded in recovering their kine (Rv. x. 102). We shall not, therefore, be wrong in inferring that every village had some kind of organization for training men in the use of arms, the art of riding, physical culture, skilful driving of chariots, and the rudimentary arts of warfare. Horse-racing and chariot-racing were indulged in probably not so much for amusement, as for the necessity of developing and promoting a skill in horse-riding and chariot-driving. We may surmise that the Grāmaṇī, who was both the civil and military leader of the village, took a lead in the matter, and organized his village contingent, not only for the defence of the village, but also for taking an active part in any war that the King might wage against a powerful enemy.

Offensive weapons.—The primitive weapons of men were at first those furnished by Nature's own armoury, viz. teeth, nails and fists. These were gradually replaced by clubs, stones, flint-flakes, bones and horns of animals. Slings were afterwards invented to throw stones at and disable an adversary from a long distance. The bow and arrow were subsequent inventions, and were found to be more effective than slings. At first the arrows were horn-tipped, or, simply, pointed hard wood, tipped with poison, as horns were not plentiful. The poison had a deadly effect as soon as mixed with the blood of the person hit. Mr. Henry Stanley, the great African explorer, has given instances in his work *Through Darkest Africa* of the quick and deadly effect of even bruises and scratches made by poison-tipped arrows, discharged by the cannibals and the pigmies of the Congo Forest. When metals came to be known and manufactured, the arrow-heads were made either of copper, bronze or iron. Swords, spears, daggers, lances and axes also were made of metal and used as weapons of offence. In the Ṛgveda we find mention of weapons made of wood, stones, bones, horns and metals, showing the different stages through which Ṛgvedic culture had passed. Indra's *vajra* had been first made of stone and then of bone before it was made of metal. [For *stone* read: Rv. ii. 14, 6; vii. 104, 5; for *bone*, Rv. i. 84, 13; for *iron*, Rv. i. 52, 8; 80, 12; viii. 85, 3; x. 48, 3; 96, 3, etc.] The *vajra* was adamantine, undecaying, fiery, scorching, and never-failing. Unlike the stone weapons hurled by the Aryan fighter against his enemy, it was "undecaying," because it always came back to Indra's hand and could be used again and again. It was, therefore, the greatest, the deadliest, the dreadest and the most effective weapon that the Aryans could imagine. As fighters, possessed of limited human powers, they could only use the sling to throw stones, or the bow to discharge arrows against their adversaries. They also used the club or bamboo stick to batter an enemy with. But this could only be used in a hand-to-hand fight. (*Muṣṭihatyā* Rv. i. 8, 2). They also made use of *astras* (weapons like swords, spears etc.) in such fightings to conquer their "embattled foes." (Rv. i. 8, 4). The cavalry did terrible execution among the enemy's infantry in all such cases. The word *arvatā* in the above verse literally means "with a horse" and is explained by Śāyaṇa to mean "fighting on horse-back." Griffith, however, remarks that "horses seem to have been used in war as drawers of chariots only, and *arvatā* here stands for *rathena*, with a car or chariot." But this interpretation is wrong in the face of the many evidences cited elsewhere about horse-riding and horsemen fighting in battles. I am deliberately of opinion that cavalry formed an important unit of the army in Ṛgvedic times.

The principal weapon of the Ṛgvedic warrior was his bow (*dhanus*, Rv. viii. 72, 4; 77, 11; ix. 99, 1; x. 18, 9, etc.), and arrow (*iṣu* Rv. ii. 24, 8; viii. 7, 4). "The last act of the funeral rite included the removal of the bow from the right hand of the dead man." (Rv. x. 18, 9). This goes to show that the bow and arrow were the constant companions of a man in Ṛgvedic times, who probably never went out to any long distance without them and never laid them aside until his death. Considering the insecure condition of the time, it was probably necessary for a man always to go out armed. The *dhanus*, which was also called *dhanvan*. (Rv. ii. 24, 8; 33, 10; vi. 59, 7; viii. 20, 2, etc.), "was composed of a stout staff bent into carved shape (*vakra*), and of a bow string (*jyá*) made of a strip of cow-hide (Rv. vi. 75, 11) which joined the ends. The tips of the bow, when the string was fastened, were called *ārtni*. Relaxed when not in actual use, the bow was specially strung up when needed for shooting."[1] The arrow which was called *iṣu*, *bāna* (Rv. vi. 75, 17) *śaru* (Rv. i. 100, 18; ii. 12, 10; iv, 3, 7 etc.) *śarya* or *śaryá* (Rv. i. 119, 10; 148, 4; x. 178, 3)

---

[1] *Vedic Index*, i. 388, 389.

usually consisted of three parts, viz., the shaft (*śalya*) which was made of a reed, still known as *śara*, the head of which was either of horn (Rv. vi. 75. 11), or of metal, —copper, bronze or iron, (*ayo-mukham*), and the feather-socket (*parṇa-dhi*) to which feathers were stuck up or fastened to make it fly swiftly through the air. (Rv. vi. 46, 11). It was shot from the ear (Rv. vi. 75, 2) and "so is described in the Ṛgveda as 'having the ear for its place of birth' (*karṇa-yoni*, Rv. ii. 24, 8). The arrow was about five spans or three feet long." [1]

The quiver or arrow-holder was called *iṣudhi* (Rv. i. 33 3; vi. 75. 5) which was carried by every bowman slung on his back (Rv. vi. 75, 5). It was probably also called *niṣaṅga* (Rv. iii. 30, 15; v. 57, 2; x. 103, 3), as the word *niṣaṅginah* in the sense of 'having quivers' occurs in Rv. v. 57, 2. The word, *niṣaṅga*, had probably also the sense of "sheath of a sword." The archer used a leathern hand-guard, called *hastaghna* (Rv. vi. 75. 14) on his left hand for its protection from the impact of the bow-string. The points or tips of the arrow-heads were sometimes poisoned (*digdhā*, Av. iv. 6, 7; v. 18, 8; cf. Rv. vi. 75, 15) like those of the pigmies of the Congo Forest, showing that the practice was a relic of ancient barbarous times.

Āyudha was a general name for weapons, but as the bow and arrow were the principal weapons of the Vedic fighter, the word was used in the Ṛgveda to designate them only. (i. 39, 2; 61, 13; ii. 30, 9; vi. 75, etc). Every warrior was armed with the bow and arrow, besides possessing other weapons. The arrow was discharged from a distance, and the other weapons like the sword, the battle-axe, lance and spear were used in hand-to-hand fighting. The club alsc was probably used in such fighting; but it was a most primitive weapon, and gradually gave place to swords, lances, etc.

---

[1] *Ibid*, i. 81, 82.

The word *pavīra,* according to the Nirukta, denotes a 'lance' (xii. 30). But it has evidently the meaning of 'sword' in the Ṛgveda (x. 60, 3). The verse, referred to here, has been thus translated by Wilson: "Who, whether armed or unarmed with a sword (*pavīravān*), overcomes adversaries in fight, as (a lion destroys) buffaloes." The word *pavi* in the Ṛgveda (i. 34, 2; 88, 2, etc.) means a metal tire with sharp edge. But it also occasionally means a weapon (Rv. v. 52, 9; vi. 8, 5; x. 180, 2) like a share for breaking down rocks (Rv. v. 52, 9), or javelin to be hurled against an enemy, (Rv. x. 180, 2). The *pavīra* was something like a sword which was also known by the name of *asi* (Rv. i. 162, 20; x. 79, 6; 86, 18, etc.). Though it denoted the sacrificial knife, yet it was also used in war (Av. xi. 9. 1). The word *kārpāṇa,* meaning a sword, occurs in Rv. x. 22, 10, with which Indra is said to have fought the Vṛtras. There can be no doubt that a weapon like the modern sword was used in fighting. The word *kārpāṇa* is the same as the modern *kṛpāṇa* (sword).

The *cakra* or discus was another weapon used in war, and hurled against an adversary with sure effect. (Rv. viii. 96, 9). It was one of the weapons of Indra, and of the Gods in later Paurāṇic lore. The discus was sharp-edged, and rapidly turned on the point of the digit finger of the right hand, before being hurled against an enemy. The use of this weapon required great practice and skill, and it at once cut down that limb against which it was aimed. It is said that Kṛṣṇa cut down Śiśupāla's head with the help of his *cakra* or discus.

The lance was called *sṛka* in the Ṛgveda (i. 32, 12; x. 180, 2). Probably this word has been corrupted in Bengali into *sarki.* The word *srakti* has been used in the sense of a spear in the Ṛgveda (vii. 18. 17). *Ṛṣti* also denotes a weapon, held in the hands of the Maruts (Rv. i. 37, 1; 64, 4, 8; v. 52, 6; viii. 20, 11), and Zimmer thinks that it denotes a spear. (*Alt. Leben*, 301). *Śakti* was another name of the spear in the Ṛgveda (Rv. vi. 75, 9). But it was like a long *ankuśa* (or elephant-goad). (Rv. x. 134, 6). The *ārā* was Pūṣan's characteristic weapon, being a goad with a pointed metallic end. (Rv. vi. 53, 1). As Pūṣan was essentially a pastoral God, we may take it that this sort of weapon was used to pierce an enemy with by the pastoral Aryans.

The word *vāśī* in the Ṛgveda is probably used in the sense of a hachet (viii. 29, 3), as it is held by the God Tvaṣṭṛ, the divine carpenter. It is also used in the sense of the carpenter's knife in the Atharva-veda (x. 6. 3). The word is still used by carpenters in Bengal to denote their hatchet. It is described in the Ṛgveda as a weapon of the Maruts, (i. 37, 2; 88, 3; v. 53, 4), which, therefore, might have been used by the Ṛgvedic Aryans as a weapon of war also. The *paraśu* was used to cut down wood (Rv. i. 127, 3; vii. 104, 21; x. 28, 8) and was like an axe and sometimes used in battles. There is another word *parśu* which originally meant a rib-bone. Sāyaṇa says it denotes "the rib-bone of a horse, the edge of which is as sharp as a sword, and fit for cutting." Probably it afterwards denoted an iron sickle made after the rib of a horse and was used in war as a weapon, as there is mention of warriors, armed with large and heavy sickles, *pṛthu-parśu*, proceeding to battle (Rv. vii. 83, 1). Another name of the axe in the Ṛgveda is *svadhiti*, used for dissecting the sacrificial horse (i. 162, 9. 18, 20), and also for cutting wood. (ii. 39, 9; iii. 2, 10; v. 7, 8, etc.). But it was also a weapon of war, as Indra with its help is said to bring forth excellent water. (Rv. x. 92, 15). The word in this verse probably means the thunderbolt; but it also may mean the axe, with which Indra was probably supposed to cut the clouds open. It has been described as the best of all weapons. (Rv. ix. 96, 6).

Pāśa was another weapon used in war; but it was not metallic. It was made of rope and was like a noose which the horsemen probably used for capturing the combatants of the enemy by flinging it over their necks from a distance.

(Rv. ix. 83. 4). It must have been a very primitive weapon, as the Gods like Varuṇa, Soma etc. were armed with it. There is reference in the Ṛgveda (x. 4. 6) to daring robbers seizing travellers in the forests with cords which may mean 'nooses.'

The noble warriors put on coats of mail called *drāpis*. (Rv. i. 25, 13; 116, 10; iv. 53, 2; ix. 86, 14; 100,9). The word *kavaca* is used in the Atharva-veda in the sense of a corselet or breast-plate (Av. xi. 10, 22), and was probably the same as the *drāpi* of the Ṛgveda. The word *varman* also occurs in the Ṛgveda in the sense of 'body-armour' 'coat of mail' or 'corselet.' (Rv. i. 31, 15; 140, 10; vi. 75, 1. 8. 18. 19; viii. 47, 8; x. 107, 7, etc). Though the rich and noble warriors clad themseves in *drāpis* or *varmans* to protect their bodies, and put on the *śiprā* (helmet) to cover and protect their heads in war, (Rv. i. 101, 10; iv. 37, 7; ii. 2, 3; 34, 3; x. 96, 4, etc.), the ordinary soldiers had probably no such protections. They fought with their bows and arrows from a distance, and when they came to close quarters, they probably fought with their swords and axes, after slinging their bows on their backs. They had no occasion to carry the *varūtha* (shield) with them, as it was likely to prove a heavy encumbrance to them, and hamper their free and easy movements. The shield, therefore, was not in much use in Ṛgvedic warfare, though it was probably known, as the word *tri-varūtha* (three-shielded or thrice strong) occurs in a verse (vi. 46, 9). The name of the shield in later literature is *carman*, as it was made of strong hide like that of the rhinoceros, and the frequent joint use of the words *asi-carma* (sword and shield) goes to show that it was used by the swordsman only in self-defence.

The horseman had only the sword and the lance or spear as his principal weapons, as it was not easy for him to manipulate the bow and arrow from horseback, though they also may have been used. The warriors who fought from their chariots invariably fought with their bows and arrows. They kept also swords, lances or spears in their chariots for use in sudden and unexpected emergencies. But the bow and arrow were considered the most important, formidable and effective weapon by the Vedic Aryans. A Ṛgvedic verse (vi. 75, 2) runs as follows: "May we conquer the cattle (of the enemies) with the bow: with the bow may we be victorious in battle: may we overcome our fierce exulting (enemies) with the bow: may the bow disappoint the hope of the foe: may we subdue with the bow all (hostile) countries." I cannot do better than subjoin here Wilson's translation of the other verses of Sūkta 75 of the Sixth Mandala of the Ṛgveda which will give the reader an idea of the weapons and mode of Ṛgvedic warfare:

"When the mailed warrior advances in the front of battles, his form is like that of a cloud.[1] With thy body unwounded, do thou (evidently addressed to the leader or King) conquer; may the strength of the armour defend thee. 2. (Here follows the translation of the verse regarding the importance and effectiveness of the bow as quoted above) 3. The bow-string, drawn tight upon the bow, and making way in battle, repeatedly approaches the ear (of the warrior), as if embracing its friend (the arrow), and proposing to say something agreeable, as a woman whispers (to her husband). 4. May the two extremities of the bow, acting consentaneously, like a wife sympathising (with her husband), uphold (the warrior), as a mother nurses her child upon her lap; and may they, moving concurrently, and harassing the foe, scatter his enemies. 5. The quiver, the parent of many, of whom many are the sons, clangs as it enters into the battle: slung at the back (of the warrior), prolific (of its shafts), it overcomes all shouting hosts. 6. The skilful charioteer, standing in the car, drives his horses before him whithersoever he will: praise the efficacy of the reins, for the reins from the back (of the car compel the studs) to follow the intention (of the driver). 7. The horses raising the dust with

[1] As the mail-coat was made of iron, it was natural for the poet to compare the warrior to a cloud.

their hoofs, rushing on with the chariots, utter loud neighings, retreating not (from the charge), but trampling with their fore-feet upon the enemies, they destroy them. 8. The spoil borne off in his car, in which his weapons and armour are deposited, is the appropriate oblation of the warrior; therefore let us, exulting, daily do honour to the joy-bestowing car. 9. The guards [1] (of the chariot), revelling in savoury (spoil), distributors of food, protectors in calamity, are armed with spears (*śaktivantah*), resolute, beautifully arranged, strong in arrows, invincible, of heroic valour, robust, and conquerors of numerous hosts. 10. May the Brahmans, the progenitors, presenters of the *Soma*, the observers of truth, protect us: may the faultless heaven and earth be propitious to us: may Pūṣan preserve us from misfortune, let no calumniator prevail over us. 11. The arrow puts on a (feathery) wing: the (horn of the) deer is its point: it is bound with the sinews of the cow: it alights where directed: whenever men assemble or disperse, there may the shafts fall for an advantage. 12. Straight-flying (arrow), defend us: may our bodies be stone: may Soma speak to us encouragement: may Aditi grant to us success. 13. Whip, with which the skilful (charioteers) lash their thighs and scourge their flanks, urge the horses in battles. 14. The ward of the fore-arm protecting it from the abrasion of the bow-string, surrounds the arm like a snake with its convolutions [2]. May the brave man, experienced in the arts of war, defend a combatant on every side. 15. This praise (be offered) to the large celestial arrow, the growth of Parjanya, [3] whose point is anointed with venom, whose blade is iron. 16. Arrow,

---

[1] "*Pitarah* is the only substantive in the text which both scholiasts render *pālayitārah*, guards, defenders, a body of spearmen, *śaktivantah* apparently, attendants on the war chariot of the chief" Wilson's *Ṛgveda Samhita*, Footnote.

[2] "Mahidhara suggests another interpretation and explains *hastaghna*, a shield, as well as the guard of the fore arm" Wilson. But in the above verse "hand-guard" is more appropriate.

[3] "The stem of the arrow, formed of the *śara* reed or grass, growing in the Rainy Season." Wilson's *Ṛgveda* (foot-note).

whetted by charms, fly when discharged: go: light amongst the adversaries: spare not one of the enemy. 17. Where arrows alight like shaven-headed boys: may Brahmaṇspati, may Aditi, grant us happiness; grant us happiness every day. 18. I cover thy vital parts with armour; may the royal Soma invest thee with ambrosia: may Varuṇa amplify thy ample felicity: may Gods rejoice (at beholding thee) triumphant. 19. Whoever, whether an unfriendly relative or a stranger, desires to kill us, may all the gods destroy him: prayer is my best armour." (Rv. vi. 75).

The above hymn discloses the following facts:—

(1) the warrior chief was mailed or had iron armour on his body: (2) the bow was considered the most effective weapon; (3) the bow-string was drawn up to the ear before the arrow was shot; (4) the hosts indulged in shouting probably to defy the enemy and muster courage; (5) the quiver, full of arrows, was slung at the back of the warrior; (6) the latter had an arm-guard to protect his arm; (7) the charioteer skilfully drove the chariot to all places of vantage; (8) the chariot was defended by guards who were skilfully arranged, and armed with spears and bows as their weapons. The carrying of spears by the guards probably points to their having been horsemen who followed the chariot in its rapid movements on the battle-field. The bowmen were probably foot-soldiers who also ran with the car and kept up a "running fight" with the enemies by discharging their arrows on the assailants of the King. (9) The arrows were all feathered, and were either horn-tipped or iron-bladed, and were besmeared with deadly poison; (10) the efficacy of *mantras* on arrows was believed in; (11) "the brave men" or heroes, who occupied the position of captains, led and defended the combatants on every side.

The composition of the Army and mode of warefare.— The army appears to have been composed of Infantry, Cavalry, Charioteers, and also probably of an Elephant corps and a Camel corps; but about these last two, there are no reliable proofs. The Infantry was called *Patti*, for the word is mentioned in the Atharva-veda (vii. 62, 1) "to designate the foot-soldier in war as opposed to the *Rathin* 'charioteer,' the latter defeating the former." [1] In early Ṛgvedic times, there was probably no regular army maintained by the King or the State. The King must have some armed retinue in his employ for the protection of his castle, person and property; but in times of war, the people (*viśah* or *vaiśyas*) volunteered to enlist themselves as soldiers—foot-soldiers, horsemen and charioteers—not always from a sense of duty or spirit of patriotism, but probably also from a love of adventure for its own sake, and for the loot and plunder that war-like expeditions generally opened out bright prospects of. Of course, these warriors equipped themselves with their own weapons, horses and chariots, and each band was under the command of its own selected leader or captain; but all the captains of the different bands were under the direction of the General (*Senānī*) or the King who, on all important occasions, himself took the command. Besides these volunteers, there were, of course, the village contingents, all of whom assembled in the capital town under the lead of the Grāmaṇīs. [2] These village contingents also provided

---

[1] *Vedic Index* i. 489

[2] "In war, the Vaiśyas (the people in general) must have formed the bulk of the force under the Kṣatriya leaders...The aim of the Vaiśya's ambition was, according to the Taittirīya Saṁhitā, (ii. 5 4, 4) to become the *Grāmaṇī*, or village headman a post probably conferred by the King on wealthy Vaiśyas, of whom no doubt there were many. It is impossible to say if in Vedic times a Vaiśya could attain to nobility or become a Brahman." (*Vedic Index* ii. 334). As there were no castes, properly so called, in the Vedic times and the people were called by the general name of Viśah, there is no reason to suppose why those who afterwards became Brahmans and Kṣatriyas had not sprung from them. As regards the Grāmaṇī, he had been a natural leader of the people at first, and afterwards came to be appointed by the King, having been selected from among the leading men, the Vaiśyas. The Grāmaṇī in the later times was invariably a Vaiśya. It is strange and remarkable that the leaders of the Gandhavaniks, the Vaiśyas of Bengal, are still called Grāmaṇīs, a title which they appear to have inherited from Vedic times.

themselves with and brought their own arms, horses and chariots. But when engaged in active service, the army had to be fed and supplied with regular daily rations which, we can suppose, were supplied by the State, or collected from the voluntary contributions of the people themselves. It is also possible that supplies were often "commandeered" from the inhabitants of the villages through which the royal army marched, which must have given rise to the description of the King as the "devourer of the people" (Rv. i. 65, 4; Av. iv. 22, 7). Of course, there were also raids and forays for the supply of provisions when soldiers in active service were in need of them.

Beside the Infantry, there was also the Cavalry, about whose absence in the Army of the Vedic Aryans, Western scholars are almost unanimous. But I have fully discussed the question in another Chapter (vide *ante* Chapter v. pp. 222-227), and have proved beyond doubt that horsemen formed an important unit of the Army in the Vedic Age, and took part in active fighting. Their charge was most dreadful, as they swept down like a hurricane, broke through the line of the enemy, and scattered and sent them flying in all directions like chaff before the wind. The following translation of two Ṛgvedic verses (vi. 46, 13. 14) gives a graphic description of a cavalry charge: "Indra, in the mighty fray, thou urgest chargers (*arvataḥ*) to their speed, *on the uneven road and on a toilsome path*, like falcons, eager for renown, *speeding like rivers rushing down a steep descent*, responsive to the urging call, that come like birds attracted to the bait, held in by reins in both the hands (of the riders)." This could not have been the description of a charge, made by war-chariots "on the uneven road and on a toilsome path," "speeding like rivers, rushing down a steep descent." Chariots, however strongly built, would be smashed and splintered into bits, when furiously driven on such difficult roads.

The war-chariots were mainly occupied by warriors belonging to the noble clans and could only be successfully manœuvred on dry and hard plains and battle-fields. They were generally made of hard wood like *śiśu* and *khadira* and covered up with cow-hides (Rv. vi. 47, 26. 27) for additional protection. From the large use of war-chariots in the Vedic Age and later in battle-fields, we can safely surmise that military expeditions and wars were generally undertaken in the dry seasons,—winter, spring or summer—as wet grounds, sloppy roads and flooded fields would be quite unsuitable for chariots or horses.[1] The number of chariots, however, was limited in comparison with the number of horsemen or foot-soldiers upon whom generally fell the brunt of the battle. Verily, the battles were soldiers' battles, in those days.

We have seen that elephants were tamed and ridden in Ṛgvedic times. Whether they were used in battles, as in subsequent times down to the time of the invasion of India by Alexander the Great, and even later, is not quite clear from a perusal of the Ṛgveda. That these animals were kept by the King and the Nobles for riding and show in the processions (Rv. iv. 4. 1) does not admit of a doubt. But their general use as a corps in Vedic times is not evident. There are two verses in the Ṛgveda which describe elephants as "fighting"; but they do not go to prove that they were used in wars. Describing the Aśvins, one verse says: "You are like two mad elephants bending their fore-quarters and smiting the foe." (Rv. x. 106, 6). Another verse says: "He who wishes thy enmity fights as the elephant in the mountain." (Rv. viii. 45, 5). There is however, one other verse which suggests that elephants were probably employed in wars. The translation of the verse in question (Rv. x. 44, 9), made by Wilson, is as follows:—"I bear this thy well-made goad (*ankuśa*) (excited) by which, *Maghavat*, thou urgest on the slayers of powerful foes. (*i.e.* elephants,

1 "The Taittirīya Brāhmaṇa (i. 8, 4. 1) contains the statement that the Kuru-Pañcāla Kings, who, like the Brahmins of those tribes, stand as representatives of the good form, used to make their raids *in the dewy season*," (*Ved. Ind.* ii, 211, 222), *i.e.*, in *Hemanta* or the beginning of winter.

Airāvat, etc.)." Wilson says in the foot-note that the word *śapharujah*, occurring in the verse, really means 'striking with the hoof.' *i.e.* trampling under foot. From this we can suppose that elephants also were sometimes used in wars to assail the enemies and trample under their feet such as came in their way.

Camels were used in Vedic times as beasts of burden (Rv. viii. 46, 28), and were probably employed in war-time to carry the supplies and stores to the battle-fields. But there is a significant passage in the Ṛgveda which lends colour to the view that there were also Camel corps, and warriors rode on camels to pursue and chase away the enemy. The passage is as follows: "Thee then, O Pūṣan, like a swift one on his way, I urge with lauds that thou mayst make the foe-men flee, *drive, camel-like, our foes a-far.*[1] (Rv. i. 138, 2). The cavalry was, indeed, quite able to pursue an enemy; but in desert tracts, the camels were more useful for this purpose, and probably there were Camel corps in Ṛgvedic times for special employment in wars in the desert country. Chariots and horses would be worse than useless on sandy plains.

Besides these units of the army, there were, of course the drummers, the flag-bearers, the camp-followers, and the men of the Supply and Transport Department. There were frequent raids and frays, for which we may rest assured, the army was not mobilized; but when a war took place between two States, it had to be completely mobilized. The drum was called *dundubhi*, which is an onomato-poetic word, so called on account of the sound it emitted when struck. It is frequently mentioned in the Ṛgveda (i. 28, 5; vi 47, 29. 31), and was probably accompanied by a sort of fife. *Karkari* (Rv. v. 43, 3) was probably the name of a wind instrument of music which emitted a shrill, sharp and loud sound like that of a clarion. Professors Macdonell and Keith think

---

[1] Griffith's *Translation of the Ṛgveda.*

that it was probably the name of a lute. But it was more like a flute or a clarion than stringed instrument. The sound of *karkari* has been compared with that of a francoline partridge or the neighing of a horse. (Rv. vi. 43). However this may be, there can be no doubt that there was some sort of war-music in Ṛgvedic times, and the *dundubhi* or the drum was the principal instrument. The following verses praise the *dundubhi* :—" Send forth thy voice aloud through earth and heaven, and let the world in all its breadth regard thee: O Drum, accordant with the Gods and Indra, drive thou afar, yea, very far our foemen. Thunder out strength and fill us full of vigour: yea, thunder forth and drive away all dangers. Drive hence, O War-drum, drive away misfortune. Thou art the fist of Indra: show thy firmness. Drive hither those, and these again bring hither:[1] the War-drum speaks aloud as battle's signal. Our heroes, winged with horses, come together. Let our car-warriors, Indra, be triumphant." (Rv. vi. 47, 29-31). From these verses it appears that the loud, deep, and sonorous sound of the *dundubhi* spread to a long distance and heartened the combatants. It was also used as a battle's signal, calling upon all fighters to assemble. The horsemen assembled with their horses and the charioteers with their chariots.

The war-flag (*dhvaja* Rv. vii. 85, 2; x. 103, 11) used to be unfurled, and carried aloft on a pole before a marching army, and held high when the actual battle began and continued. As long as it was held high and visible to all the combatants, no defeat was indicated. The lowering of the flag or its capture probably indicated defeat or surrender. A verse (Rv. vii. 83, 2) says: "Where men assemble with uplifted banners, in whatever conflict, there is something unfavourable; where living beings, looking to heaven, are in fear, there, Indra and Varuṇa, speak to us encouragement."

---

[1] "Drive to us the cows of the enemy and send our own cows home in safety. *Gaḥ*, cows, is understood with *amuh*, those, and *imah*, these" (Griffith). The above translation of the verses is made by Griffith.

(Wilson). The meaning is probably this: Where both the contending armies meet with banners uplifted, there is a firm determination on the part of each army to fight to the bitter end; and it is then that the combatants, anxious for the safety of their life and limb, look up in fear to heaven for their protection by the Gods. The translation of the next three verses is as follows: "The ends of the earth are beheld laid waste; the clamour has ascended, Indra and Varuṇa, to heaven; the adversaries of my people approach me: having heard my invocation, come for my defence. Indra and Varuṇa, you protected Sudās, overwhelming the yet unassailed Bheda with your fatal weapons: hear the prayers of these Tṛtsus in time of battle, so that my ministration may have borne them fruit. Indra and Varuṇa, the murderous (weapons) of my enemy distress me; foes amongst the malignant (assail me); you two are sovereigns over both (celestial and terrestrial) wealth; protect us therefore on the day of battle." (Rv. vii. 83, 3-5). It was customary on the eve of a battle to offer prayers to Indra, Varuṇa and the other Gods for protection and victory (Rv. v. 35, 6-7; vii. 27, 1), and the Royal priest who accompanied the army to the battle-field performed the Soma-sacrifice and offered libations of the drink to Indra. All the combatants were given a share of it, not only to invigorate them like Indra, but also to excite them to fight, as the drink had an exhilarating effect on the consumers. (Rv. vi 47, 6; ix. 106, 2). The combatants danced in their wild excitement, keeping time with the loud and sonorous sound of the war-drums, before the actual engagement took place, as there is clear mention, in the Ṛgveda, of Indra dancing in the battle-field (i. 130, 7), and of men dancing with bamboo-sticks held aloft. (i. 10, 1). The bamboo-stick must have played an important part in Ṛgvedic India, as it does even now in Modern India, as an effective weapon of offence. Those combatants, who could not procure any arms, probably used their bamboo-sticks with terrible effect in hand-to-hand fighting. These men danced their weird

44

war-dance not only to excite and encourage themselves and their comrades to fight bravely, but probably also to terrify the enemy with loud yells. The army was led by the *Senānī*, or the leader of the host, very probably on horseback, so as to make himself visible to all. A verse says: "The leader of the host, a hero, advances in front of the chariots intent on seizing cattle (of the enemy); his army exults." (Rv. x. 96, 1). The victorious hero's horse galloped in all directions (Rv. ix. 100, 4), urged by the rider who probably thought it necessary to encourage the fighters by his personal presence. Another verse gives a vivid picture of the battle-field at the time of action: "The drum utters its sound; the leathern guard twangs, the tawny bow-string leaps to and fro: let the hymn be raised to Indra" (Rv. viii. 69, 9).

I cannot resist the temptation of giving here the translation of a war-hymn (Rv. x. 103), which will give the reader an idea of how the Gods were invoked on the eve of a battle, and how the soldiers were encouraged to imitate the war-like Gods and hurl themselves upon their enemy with a firm determination to win victory:

"1. The fleet-going Indra, like a formidable bull sharpening (his horns), the slayer of foes, the exciter of men, loud-shouting, ever-vigilant, the chief of heroes, overthrew at once a hundred hosts. 2. With Indra, the loud-shouting, the vigilant, the victorious, the war-like, the unconquerable, the daring, the hurler of arrows, the showerer, (as your ally), conquer, ye warriors, ye leaders, that (hostile host) and overcome it. 3. Indra, with the arrow-bearing (Maruts), armed with swords, the subduer, the warrior, who encounters a multitude (of foes), who conquers those who encounter him, the drinker of the *Soma*, the strong-armed, having a powerful bow, who shoots with well-aimed arrows, (conquer with help).[1] 4. Come with thy chariot, Bṛhaspati, who art the

[1] So Sāyaṇa supplies the ellipeses; Mahīdhara supplies "may he protect us."

slayer of Rakṣasas, discomfiting thy enemies, crushing (hostile) hosts and demolishing (them), victorious in battles, be the defender of our chariots. 5. Known by his strength, mighty, heroic, over-powering, vigorous, enduring, fierce, attended by heroes, attended by mighty men, the offspring of strength, the possessor of water, do thou, Indra, ascend thy triumphant chariot. 6. Imitate in heroism, ye kindred warriors, follow, friends, in prowess this Indra, who is the breaker of mountains, the acquirer of water, armed with the thunderbolt, conquering the swift (foe), destroying (the enemy) by his might. 7. May Indra, bursting open the clouds with force, pitiless, heroic, with hundredfold anger, invincible, the overthrower of armies, irresistible, protect our armies in battles. 8. May Indra be the leader of these (hosts), may Bṛhaspati, Dakṣiṇā, Yajña, and Soma go before, let the Maruts march in the van of the destroying and victorious armies of the Gods. 9. (May) the mighty forces of the showerer Indra, of the royal Varuṇa, of the Ādityas and Maruts (be ours). The shouts of the magnanimous and victorious deities, the subverters of worlds, have arisen. 10. Excite, Maghavan, my weapons, (excite) the spirit of my heroes: slayer of Vṛtra, let the speed of the horses be accelerated, let the noises of the chariots be increased. 11. When the banners are intermingled, may Indra be our (defender), may those arrows which are ours be victorious, may our warriors be triumphant; God, protect us in battles. 12. Bewildering the mind of our foes, Apvā, seize their limbs and depart, proceed against them, burn in their hearts with sorrow, let our enemies be covered with thick darkness. 13. Advance, warriors, and conquer; may Indra grant you happiness, may our arms be strong, so that you may be invincible."

These are really stirring words to excite even the most craven spirits. What with these, and what with the bright vision of the war-like Gods ready to aid them with their powerful divine help in the coming conflict, what with the stirring example of the victorious feats of the Gods themselves, and what with the exhilarating influence of the Soma drink, redoubled by the exciting war-music, the warriors for the time being lost all thoughts of fears or of themselves, and plunged headlong into the fight.

War-tactics.—Sometimes when it became necessary to surprise an enemy, the soldiers advanced by bending their bodies low or by crawling on the ground, so as not to be visible to or discovered by them. (Rv. ix. 64, 29). A tactic like this was only possible on uneven and undulating grounds. But when an army met an army, the battle was usually fought on an even plain or field. When after a decisive victory the enemy were put to flight, they were hotly pursued by the victors, horsemen pursuing horsemen, chariots pursuing chariots, and foot-soldiers pursuing foot-soldiers. Many were killed, and many taken as captives. The victors pursued them even into their own territory, and if the villages remained undefended, freely indulged in loot and pillage. Herds of cattle and horses were captured and driven to the camp of the victors, and gold and everything found valuable were plundered. (Rv. i. 63, 6). We can surmise that young women, boys and girls also were taken as captives, and enslaved. There is frequent mention of slaves in the Ṛgveda (vii. 86, 7; viii. 56, 3). The King and nobles possessed very large numbers of slaves, some of whom were sometimes given away to deserving Ṛṣis A sage prays to Agni for the gift of one hundred slaves. (Rv. viii. 56, 3). Trasadasyu, son of Purukutsa, once presented fifty slave-girls (*badhūs*) to another sage. (Rv. viii. 19, 16). These slaves must originally have been prisoners of war. Slaves were in great requisition in ancient Sapta-Sindhu for performing the household duties of the rich and nobles, and carrying on their agricultural work. The booty of war was probably shared by the King with his nobles, the leaders and the privates. It was when glorious victories were achieved, and there was plenty of booty to give. that Kings amply rewarded the priests and bards by cracked and seething, so he pours out foam."[1] (Rv. iii. 53, 17-22). On the meaning of the last verse, Professor Wilson remarks: "The construction is elliptical: the ellipsis is supplied by the scholiast: as the tree is cut down by the axe so may the enemy be cut down: as one cuts off without difficulty the flower of the Śimbala, so may he be destroyed· as the caldron when struck, and thence leaking, scatters foam or breath from its mouth, so may that hater, struck by the power of my prayer, vomit foam from his mouth." Griffith says that "the phrases are probably, as Ludwig explains, merely proverbial expressions for threat, full of sound and fury, followed by insignificant results." The last verse of the above hymn (Rv. iii. 53, 24) has been thus paraphrased by Prof. Wilson, following Sāyaṇa: "These sons of Bharata, Indra, understand severance (from the Vasiṣṭhas), not association (with them); they urge their steeds (against them), as against a constant foe; they bear a stout bow (for their destruction) in battle." This shows the deep hatred that the Viśvāmitras bore against the Vasiṣṭhas which resulted in the formation of a confederacy of Ten Kings against Sudās, of which Viśvāmitra became the guiding and moving spirit. But this was not the only cause of the war; there were other causes at work, of which Viśvāmitra took advantage with a view to gain his main object, *viz.*, the crushing of Vasiṣṭha, and the overthrow of the King whom he served.

Other causes.—The extensive conquests of Sudās, his uniform good luck and success, and his suzerainty over the subject States had excited the jealousy of his rivals, and created a deep discontent in the minds of those whom he had subdued. They all had been eager to accomplish his complete overthrow; but there was none to take the initiative in the matter and concert adequate measures. At this psychological moment, Viśvāmitra, who had left Sudās's court in high dudgeon, egged them on to avenge themselves upon Sudās by forming a strong confederacy,

[1] Griffith's Translation of the Ṛgveda.

and advancing against his kingdom with their united forces. His suggestions were eagerly accepted and acted upon. A confederacy of Ten Kings was immediately formed, and adequate preparations made for advance. As Viśvāmitra had been till recently the principal Purohita and trusted adviser of Sudās, the guidance of the confederacy naturally devolved upon him. It is very difficult to ascertain the names of the Ten kings who formed the confederacy, but there is evidence of the following tribes having joined it, *viz.*, the Anus, the Druhyus, the Bharatas, the Yadus, the Turvaśas, the Purus, the Śimyus, the Ajas, the Śigrus and the Yakṣus. (Rv. vii. 18.) Bheda, the Chief of a tribe on the Yamunā, also took a leading part in the war. The Ajas, the Śigrus and the Yakṣus were probably non-sacrificing Aryan tribes living in the north of Sapta-Sindhu.

The news of the formation of a strong confederacy against Sudās did not take a long time to reach him. He found almost all the principal Aryan tribes, including the Purus, arrayed against him, and considered the situation very grave and serious for him. He thought that the strong alliance must be met by a similarly strong counter-alliance; otherwise the result was surely to be disastrous. Almost all the important tribes living on the east, west and south of his kingdom and three tribes living on the north had joined the confederacy. He, therefore, naturally approached some northern Aryan tribes (all of whom did not probably subscribe to the Vedic faith) for help, and formed an alliance with the Parśus and the Pṛthus (Rv. vii. 83, 1) and the Alinas, the Pakthas, the Bhalānas, the Śivas, and the Viṣāṇins who, according to Zimmer, lived to the north-east of modern Kafiristan. Ludwig is of opinion that the Pṛthus and the Parśus can be identified respectively with the Parthians and the Persians of later times; but on this point there is a difference of opinion. [1] As regards the Alinas, the Bhalānas,

[1] Zimmer, *Altindisches Leben*, 134 *et seq.*, 434, 435.

The main cause of the war.—It appears that the great Ṛṣi Viśvāmitra had been for sometime the *Purohita* (principal priest) of Sudās, King of the Tṛtsus. He had received many gifts from Sudās, for which he was praised. He had performed sacrifices for him, which won him the favour of Indra. (Rv. iii. 53, 9). "Come forward, Kuśikas," says Viśvāmitra, addressing himself to his sons, "and be attentive; let loose Sudās's horse to win him riches; east, west and north, let the King slay his foemen, then at earth's choicest place perform his worship." (Rv. iii. 53, 11). The verse clearly indicates that Sudās was about to embark on an extensive conquest of the territories lying in the east, west and north of Sapta-Sindhu. The southern direction has not been mentioned, because immediately to the south of Sapta-Sindhu lay the dreary and uninhabited desert and the sea. Divodāsa had already brought under his subjection many territories, and Sudās was only treading in his footsteps with the object of bringing the whole of Sapta-Sindhu under one rule, and of establishing one mighty Aryan empire. Probably this was also the ambition of Viśvāmitra, as the division of the country into a number of small independent States really retarded the progress and advancement of the people as a whole. Sudās must have been eminently successful in his conquests, and Viśvāmitra's dream was about to be realised. But he had a very powerful rival in Sudās's court in the person of Vasiṣṭha, with whom he had a difference. What was the nature of the difference, it is very difficult to ascertain from the Ṛgveda, and various scholars have variously speculated on the subject. "It seems that the Vasiṣṭhas were pioneers in adopting the rule that Purohitas should act as Brahman priests[1] at the sacrifice: the Śatapatha Brāhmaṇa (xii. 6, 1, 41) states that the Vasiṣṭhas were once the only priests to act as Brahmans, but that later any priest could

[1] Vasiṣṭha was Brahman at the sacrifice of Śunahśepa, *Ait-Brāh*, vii. 16; *Śāṅkhāyana Śrauta Sūtra*, xv. 21, 4.

serve as such."[1] Vasiṣṭha, having been a Tṛtsu (Rv. vii. 83, 8), afterwards became the principal priest of the Royal family, and acted as Brahman priest, a right which was probably denied to Viśvāmitra, and this led to a dispute which ended in Viśvāmitra's leaving Sudās's court with all the Kuśikas, and going over to the Bharatas to which clan he originally belonged. This incident was probably developed in the Epics and the Purāṇas as a quarrel over the fact that though Viśvāmitra was a *Ṛṣi* and *Rājarṣi*, he was not acknowledged as a *Brāhmaṇa* by Vasiṣṭha. However this may have been, it is an undoubted fact in Ṛgvedic history that though Viśvāmitra had at first been the Purohita of the Tṛtsus, he was ousted from the position by Vasiṣṭha, or the Vasiṣṭhas, and, in his rage, left Sudās's court, and joined the court of the Bharatas who were probably Sudās's enemies. When about to depart from the sacrificial hall of Sudās, he thus invoked good luck for the several parts of the chariot or wain on which he was going to travel :—

" Strong be the pair of oxen, firm the axles, let not the pole slip, nor the yoke be broken. May Indra keep the yoke-pins from decaying : attend us, thou whose fellies are uninjured. O Indra, give our bodies strength, strength to the bulls who draw the wains, strength to our seed and progeny that they may live, for thou art he who giveth strength. Enclose thee in the heart of *Khayer* (*Khadira*) timber : in the car wrought of Śinśapā put firmness. Show thyself strong, O Axle, fixed and strengthened, throw us not from the car whereon we travel. Let not this sovran of the wood leave us forlorn or injure us. Safe may we be until we reach our homes and rest us and unyoke. With various aids, do come to us, Indra ; with best aid speed us, Maghavan, thou Hero. Let him who hateth us fall headlong downward ; him whom we hate let vital breath abandon. He heats his very axe, and then cuts a mere Semul blossom off. O Indra, like a caldron

[1] *Vedic Index*, ii. 276.

made to penetrate into the country. Indra is credited, in one instance, with having destroyed ninety or ninety-nine forts of the enemy, and demolished seven fortified cities in another, and also with having performed other heroic deeds. A Ṛgvedic verse (i. 53, 9) mentions the fact of an attack having been made on King Suśravā by Twenty Kings who had united their forces numbering 60,099 strong with a view to defeat the powerful Prince; but they themselves were defeated by Suśravā in the long run, through the active and merciful help of Indra. (Rv. i. 53, 10). The great commentator, Sāyaṇa, does not give any account of Suśravā, or of the war that the Twenty Kings waged against him. Probably, Suśravā had belonged to an earlier period of the Ṛgvedic Age, and already become a mythical hero (like Rāma or Yudhiṣṭhira at the present day), when the above verses were composed. Hence no detailed account of this terrible war is available beyond the fact that Twenty Kings had united their forces to defeat him but were unsuccessful.

The War of Ten Kings with Sudās.—But the war of Ten Kings with Sudās has been mentioned in the Ṛgveda with some details, as it was undoubtedly a comparatively recent occurrence and remembered by many, even in the later period of Ṛgvedic times. The details, however, are scattered in fragments in several hymns and verses. We shall endeavour to knit them together into a succinct narrative in this Chapter.

But before we do so, it will be necessary to give here a brief account of some of the principal Aryan tribes of that time. The Tṛtsus were one of the Five Tribes mentioned in the Ṛgveda. They appear to have lived on the banks of the Paruṣṇī, the modern Rāvi. The Bharatas lived on the banks of the Sarasvatī, the Dṛsadvatī, and the Āpayā in their upper courses, and the Yadus and the Turbaśas lived probably lower down near the mouth of the Sarasvatī, close to the sea-shore. It has been related of them that they had once crossed the sea (probably the

Rajputana Sea, as it then was), and lived on its further shores, very likely in modern Gujrat, and their Kings remained unanointed, whereupon Indra crossed the sea and brought them back again to the shores of Sapta-Sindhu (Rv. i. 54, 6; iv. 30, 19; vi. 20, 12), and rescued them from barbarism, into which they had probably been relapsing, cut off as they had been from their own kith and kin. They resettled on the bank of the Sarasvatī in its lower course, where they performed many sacrifices. But, as they had been at first heterodox in faith, they have been described in a Ṛgvedic verse (x. 62. 10) as belonging to the *Dāsa* tribe, for any one who did not subscribe to the Ṛgvedic faith was put down as a *Dāsa*. The Anus and the Druhyus probably lived in the tract of country between the Sarasvatī and the Śatadru. The Purus lived on both the banks of the upper Indus on the borders of Gandhāra, and kept in check the depredations of the troublesome Dasyus, or mountainous Aryan tribes, in which work they were occasionally assisted by their neighbours, the Tṛtsus. (Rv. i. 63. 7). The Purus also appear to have been settled on the bank of the Sarasvatī (Rv. vii. 96, 2). Whether this place had been the original settlement of the tribe, from which they afterwards migrated to the banks of the Sindhu, cannot be definitely said. Probably this tribe lived in both the regions. King Purukutsa was the son of Durgaha, and appears to have been made a prisoner of war, and to have died in captivity. (Rv. iv. 42, 8). His queen, after the performance of a sacrifice according to the direction of seven Ṛṣis who had probably taken charge of the kingdom during the interregnum, was blest with a son whose name was Trasadasyu (the Frightener of the Dasyus), and who subdued all the wild Aryan tribes and became their leader. (Rv. iv. 42, 8; viii. 19, 37). Trasadasyu was thus the posthumous son of Purukutsa, and in his days became so famous by his wars and victories that he looked upon himself, and was also looked upon by the people, as equal to Indra in prowess and glory. In fact, he was regarded as *Ardhadeva* or half-God. (Rv. iv. 42, 8). He was believed to be invincible in war, and under special divine protection. (Rv. iv. 42, 6). The Purus appear to have been afterwards allied with the Kurus by marriage, and King Kuruśravaṇa was called *Trāsadasyava, i.e.*, a descendant of Trasadasyu (Rv. x. 33, 4). The latter's father, Purukutsa, who had at first been an ally of King Sudās, was afterwards prevailed upon to join the confederacy of Ten Kings against him, and in the war that followed was probably taken prisoner and died in captivity.

Of the several Aryan tribes living in Sapta-Sindhu at this time, the Purus, the Tṛtsus and the Bharatas appear to have greatly distinguished themselves. The most famous Kings of the Tṛtsus were Divodāsa and his grandson, Sudās, son of Pijavana, and hence nicknamed *Paijavana.* It is surmised by some Western scholars[1] that the Tṛtsus and the Bharatas were one people, *i.e.*, belonged to one clan or tribe, in support of which they quote certain verses (Rv. vi. 16, 4. 5. 19). But Bharata, mentioned in the fourth verse, had no connection with Divodāsa, mentioned in the fifth and nineteenth verses. King Bharata worshipped Agni (Fire) on the bank of the Sarasvatī; hence, one name of Agni is Bhāratī, a name which was, in a later age, transferred to the Goddess Sarasvatī, presiding over *Vāc* or Speech. Similarly, another name or epithet of Agni, as worshipped by Divodāsa, was *Daivadāsa* (Rv. viii. 103, 2). In Rv. vi. 16, the Ṛṣi Bharadvāja has simply referred to the fact that King Bharata and King Divodāsa both became famous in Ṛgvedic times by having been "energetic supporters of the Fire ritual." The Tṛtsus and the Bharatas should not, therefore, be regarded as one tribe. They might have originally belonged to one clan, called the *Tṛtsus*, but in Ṛgvedic times the two branches appear to have been distinct, and there is evidence of the existence of tribal feuds, which led Viśvāmitra to make a united and determined effort by the formation of a strong

[1] Macdonell and Keith, *Vedic Index*, i. 363.

coalition of Ten Kings, for curbing the growing and aggressive power of the Tṛtsu King, Sudās, grandson of Divodāsa.

The great Divodāsa had been a warlike prince who had been engaged in a series of wars with the Yadus and the Turvaśas (Rv. ix. 61, 2), whom he ultimately subdued; also with Śamvara, the great Asura chief, whose ninety-nine forts he demolished with the help of Indra (Rv. i. 130, 7; vi. 26, 5); and with the Paṇis, the Pārāvatas, and the Bṛsayas who were nearly exterminated. (Rv. vi. 61, 1, *et seq*). Hillebrandt has inferred that the last three tribes belonged to Arachosia, and the Sarasvatī river mentioned in the hymn was the *Haraquaiti*, flowing through that region. But the inference is wrong, as the battle really took place on the banks of the Sarasvatī flowing through the Punjab. The Paṇis, as I have elsewhere said,[1] lived on the high banks of the Gangā, probably on the coast of the Eastern Sea, covering the Gangetic trough, and the Pārāvatas lived on the banks of the Yamunā, as mentioned in the Pañcaviṃśa Brāhmaṇa. (ix. 4, 11).[2] It is, therefore, certain that the battle with the Paṇis and the Pārāvatas took place on the banks of the Sarasvatī in the Punjab and not in Arachosia, and that Divodāsa led his victorious army towards the east, as far as the coast of the Eastern Sea. But Divodāsa, who had for his allies Āyu and Kutsa, King of the Purus (Rv. ii. 14, 7), once suffered a reverse in a battle with Tūrvayāna, to whom they had to submit. (Rv. i. 53, 10). With this one exception, he was all along helped in his war-like expeditions by the mighty Indra. Tūrvayāna appears to have been the King of the Pakthas (Rv. x. 61, 1, *et seq*). Divodāsa also became renowned for his hospitality and liberality which earned for him the title of *Atithigva*, or 'Entertainer of guests.' Sudās, his grandson (some say, son), shared the glory and fame of his illustrious ancestor, as a liberal and powerful prince.

---

[1] *Ṛgvedic India*, Chaps. vi & vii.

[2] Vedic Index, i. 519.

in his territory by the confederacy of Ten Kings, the latter cut the embankment of the river Adinā with a view to flood his territory, but the waters could not be diverted through the breach, and flowed in its channel as usual, to the great chagrin and disappointment of the invaders. (Rv. vii. 18, 8. 9). This miracle was attributed to the power and mercy of the great Indra. It would thus appear that the Vedic Aryans were acquainted with many of the modes of modern warfare. Of course, they were not so improved and elaborate as they are now. But still they were the best and most effective, consistently with their knowledge, culture and the resources available in their time. In the next Chapter I will give an account of the great war that the Ten Kings waged against Sudās, the King of the Tṛtsus. The account has been given in fragments only in the Ṛgveda, which I will attempt to knit together as far as possible into a succinct narrative.

CHAPTER IX.

WARRING ARYAN TRIBES AND THE WAR OF TEN KINGS WITH SUDĀS, KING OF THE TṚTSUS

Frequent wars and raids among Aryan Tribes.—The ancient Aryans having been divided into numerous tribes (of whom five only had developed a homogeneous civilisation and were known as Pañcajanāḥ), there were frequent quarrels and raids among themselves. Sometimes these quarrels were the results of personal or tribal jealousies; or, sometimes a powerful King of one tribe cherished the ambition of extending his dominion over the neighbouring States by waging a war of conquest, when the latter formed themselves into a confederacy to check his ambition and victorious progress. Thus, what with the murderous depredations of the Dasyus, *i.e.*, the savage Aryan tribes living by robbery, and what with the frequent raids and wars made by the neighouring civilised Aryan States, the lot of the people was far from happy and peaceful. They always lived in a state of military preparedness, and were ready, at a moment's notice, to take the field and fight their enemies. There are many hymns and verses in the Ṛgveda, which relate to fightings, wars or conquests, and there was no Ṛgvedic Ṛṣi of importance, who did not compose prayers for the defeat or destruction of enemies. Indra was the principal God, to whom was attributed the credit of achieving victories in almost all wars. It was he who broke down the forts of the enemies, conquered their territories, brought them under subjection, or destroyed them, root and branch. The whole country seemed to have been dotted with forts and strongholds, and each State had a string of forts on its borders. It was the main object of an invading army to demolish these forts first of all, before any attempt was giving them cattle, horses, gold, jewels, precious cloths, slaves, chariots, asses, camels and even dogs. Sometimes the presents were carried by long strings of pack-animals, including the large species of dogs that used in ancient times to carry burdens on their backs.

The carnage in the battle-fields was sometimes awful. In one battle Indra is said to have slaughtered fifty-thousand black foes. (Rv. iv. 16, 13). He is also credited with destroying the ninety-nine cities of Śamvara (Rv. i. 54, 6). He is further said to have killed hundreds, nay thousands of warriors who fought under an Asura chief, named Varci, whose power was thus completely broken. (Rv. vii. 99, 5). The dead bodies were probably collected and thrown into pits (*vailasthānam*, Rv. i. 133, 1), dug up in the battle-fields. The verse just referred to says: "The foes have fallen where they had collected, and lie in the pit of death, pierced and mangled." Another verse says: "Do thou, Maghavan, beat off the aggressive host's strength; cast them within the narrow pit, the deep and narrow pit." (Rv. i. 133, 3). [1] Wilson translates the first verse of Rv. i. 133 thus: "By sacrifices I purify both the sky and the earth. I burn the wide realms (of earth) that are without Indra, and are the haunts of the wicked. Wherever the enemies have congregated, they have been slain; and utterly destroyed, they sleep in a deep pit." The scholiast considers the word *vailasthānam* in the first and the third verses as equivalent to *Śmaśāna* or 'burning ground,' probably on the supposition that burial was not an ancient custom of the Aryans. But in battle-fields, it was not possible to burn

---

[1] Griffith says that "the hymn is a prayer for the destruction of witches, goblins and evil spirits of various sorts." The witches might have possessed bodies; but goblins and evil spirits had no physical bodies which could be "pierced and mangled and cast into the pit of death." The *amitrāh* or foes were men, and their dead bodies were thrown into pits. If this was the custom of disposing of dead bodies in the battle-fields in ancient times probably their remains may yet be discovered at places by deep excavations.

down all the dead bodies. They were simply cast into deep pits and buried. Sometime in war-time, cities or fortresses were besieged, and all supplies cut off. (Rv. i. 53, 8). Those fortresses that were constructed of wood were sought to be destroyed by fire. In a Ṛgvedic verse (vii. 5, 3) " Vaiśvānara or Fire has been described to have pierced the citadel of the enemy, when the black people came out pell-mell, through consternation and distress, leaving their dinner unfinished ;" and in verse 6 of the same hymn " Agni is said to have driven out the Dasyus from their hiding places by burning and blazing fiercely." The black people referred to in this verse " were undoubtedly the sun-burnt Aryan Dasyus who lived in the deep recesses of the forests for self-protection, but who were afterwards expelled in consequence of the forests being set on fire." [1] Fire, then, was frequently used to destroy fortified cities, when besieged, and forests which were the haunts of the marauding robbers in Ṛgvedic times. Even in the Epic Age, we find in the Mahābhārata the description of a terrible conflagration, started by Arjuna and Kṛṣṇa, for the destruction of the great forest of Khāndava with all its wild and savage denizens. In the Rāmāyaṇa also there is description of the fine city of Lankā having been destroyed by fire by the besiegers.

There was another way of harassing the enemy in Ṛgvedic times. There were many populous cities and villages on the fertile banks of the rivers of the Punjab. When an enemy's hosts invaded these territories, they sometimes attempted to discomfit and defeat the inhabitants very easily by cutting the embankments or artificial dykes, constructed for the protection of the low-lying villages, and thus flooding them. There is mention in the Ṛgveda of one such attempt having been unsuccessfully made by an invading army. When the great King Sudās was attacked

---

[1] Das' *Ṛgvedic India*, Chap. vii.

the Pakthas, etc., Roth thinks that they were Sudās's allies in the great war, [1] and Zimmer at first agreed with this view, [2] though he subsequently changed his opinion. They might have been the enemies of the Tṛtsus at first, as Divodāsa's fight with Tūrvayāṇa, King of the Pakthas, goes to show. (Rv. i. 53, 10). But Sudās, in view of the impending danger to his kingdom, must have formed a new alliance with them, and assigned to some of them the task of keeping the advance of the Purus from the north-west in check by invading his territory. It is perfectly reasonable to surmise that in the predicament in which Sudās was placed, he did not think it either prudent or safe to rely on his unaided arms alone, but that he was obliged to seek the help of other powerful tribes in this unequal contest. Sudās was the special protégé of Indra, and as the tribes, the Alinas, Pakthas, etc., mentioned in Rv. vii. 18, 7, "glorified that Indra who recovered the cattle of the Ārya from the plunderers, who slew the enemies in battle," the inference would be natural that they were Sudās's allies. However this may be, there can be no doubt or question that the Tṛtsu King, guided by the sage counsel of Vasiṣṭha, made adequate preparations to meet the united army of the confederacy, and arrayed his forces on the northern bank of the Paruṣṇī.

The advance of the Confederates' hosts.—The confederates' hosts advanced, under the guidance of Viśvāmitra, from the east, and had to cross the Śatadru and Vipāś in their upper courses, before they could reach the southern bank of the Paruṣṇī. But these two rivers were found to be in high flood, and it was difficult for the united army to cross them without the help of boats. As the expedition was undoubtedly undertaken in the dry season (probably in autumn), when the waters of the rivers were naturally at a low level, the leaders of the confederacy had

[1] *Zur Litteratur und Geschichte des Weda*, 95.
[2] *Altindisches Leben*, 126.

probably hoped, nay expected, to ford them easily without the help of boats, and so no provisions had been made for ferrying the army, horses, chariots, cars and bullocks across the streams. The flood in the two rivers was probably due to sudden heavy rain-fall on the mountains at their sources, and was in the nature of a freshet which temporarily obstructed the advance of the united army. At this juncture Viśvāmitra offered a prayer to the two rivers, beseeching them to bend low so as to give the army an easy ford :—

"Hear then, sisters, what the poet says: I come to you from far with loaded wagons. Now bend ye low, give me an easy ford: let not your waves touch my axle-tree, O Rivers." (Rv. iii. 33, 9).

The Rivers listened to Viśvāmitra's supplication, saying :

"We will heed thy word, O Ṛṣi, that comest to us from far with loaded wagons; I bend low before thee as a willing slave, as to her lord submits the bride." (Rv. iii. 33, 10).

The Bharatas, "filled with the ardour of battle" and intent upon winning cattle (Rv. iii. 33, 11), crossed the rivers as soon as the flood subsided, and reached the country between the Vipāś and the Paruṣṇī. Encamping themselves on the southern bank of the latter, they had recourse, first of all, to a stratagem. There had been an embankment or dyke along the northern bank of the Paruṣṇī (probably also called the *Adīnā* at this place) to protect the fertile low-lying lands and the villages and towns of the Tṛtsus, nestled among them,* and the leaders of the invading army formed the plan of creating a breach in the embankment by cutting it open, higher up the river, so as to divert its waters through it, flooding the entire low-lying plains of the Tṛtsus, and thus secure an easy victory by embarrassing them. Had the season been rainy and the river in high flood, their stratagem would have been highly successful. But the season having been dry, and the water-level low, in spite of the recent flood that caused the Śatadru and the Vipāś to swell and obstruct the progress of the Bharatas, the current could not be diverted through the breach, but flowed on in its natural channel. The fact has been referred to in two Ṛgvedic verses by the Tṛtsu bard, Vasiṣṭha, and the failure of the stratagem attributed to the mercy of the great Indra :

"The evil-disposed and stupid (enemies of Sudās), crossing the humble, Paruṣṇī river, have broken down its banks ; but he (Sudās) by his greatness pervades the earth, and Kavi, the son of Cayamāna, like a fallen victim, sleeps (in death).

"The waters flowed their regular course to the Paruṣṇī, nor (wandered) beyond it ; the quick courser (of the King) came to the accessible places, and Indra made the idly-talking enemies, with their numerous progeny, subject among men (to Sudās)." (Rv. vii, 18, 8. 9).[1]

From the above verses it would appear that Kavi, a leader of the confederacy, undertook, or was deputed to effect a breach in the embankments ; but Sudās was too alert and vigilant for him, and quickly appearing on horseback with his brave contingents to oppose him, engaged him in battle in which he was killed. Thus the plan of the enemies to flood the Tṛtsu country was frustrated, and the situation saved.

The Battle and Sudās's glorious Victory.—Sudās probably did not think it prudent to cross the Paruṣṇī with his entire army, and give battle to his enemies encamped on the southern bank. This step would have been highly unwise, and probably fatal, as he was threatened on the north and west by the Purus, under Purukutsa, and in fact, was surrounded on every side by his enemies. With the assistance of his allies, he had, therefore, to keep the advance of the powerful Purus in check. The river Paruṣṇī that ran between his encamped army and the main army of the

---

[1] Wilson's Translation of the Ṛgveda.

confederacy, encamped on the other bank, afforded him some sure protection. But the situation had been getting serious, critical, nay intolerable, and something had to be immediately done to save it, and decide the issue in his favour. He, therefore, had recourse to a stratagem, boldly concieved and carried out. He detached a portion of his valiant army, crossed the river higher up with it, probably under cover of darkness (Rv. vii. 33, 3), and suddenly appearing at the rear of the enemy's camp, surrounded it, and surprised them, dealing a fierce and determined attack. The army of the confederacy had not expected an attack like this, and were not prepared to meet it. Panic at once seized the ranks, and a general confusion ensued in the camp. The leaders were at their wit's end, and found it impossible to rally the panic-stricken soldiers in battle-array and hurl back the terrible onslaught of the attackers. As the camp had been surrounded, there was no way for escape in any direction, excepting the river, and a general stampede ensued in that direction. Men fled precipitately for their lives, hotly pursued by the attackers, who did terrible execution among them, killing their General Bheda.[1] Numbers hurled themselves into the Paruṣṇī and were either drowned or carried away by the rapid currents. Those who safely reached the northern bank were at the mercy of Sudās's army encamped thereon, and were either killed or captured. Śruta, Kavaṣa, Vṛddha, and Druhyu, some of the valiant leaders of the confederacy, "were drowned in the waters." (Rv. vii. 18, 12). Twenty-one leaders were slain, "as a well-looking priest lops the sacred grass in the chamber of sacrifice." (Rv. vii. 18, 11), and thus was the annihilation of the vast army of the confederacy completed. "The warriors of the Anus and Druhyus intending (to carry off the) cattle, (hostile) to the pious (Sudās), perished to the number of sixty-six thousand six hundred and sixty: such are the glorious acts of Indra." (Rv. vii.

---

[1] Rv. vii. 33, 3. Elsewhere it is said that Bheda was killed afterwards. (Rv. vii. 18, 18-19).

18, 14). The carnage in the field of battle must, therefore, have been terrible. "The hostile Tṛtsus (meaning the *Bharatas*), ignorantly contending with Indra, fled routed, as rapidly as rivers on a downward course, and being discomfited, abandoned all their possessions to Sudās.[1] Indra has scattered over the earth the hostile rival of the hero (Sudās), ...and baffled the wrath of the wrathful enemy, and the (foe) advancing on the way (against Sudās) has taken the path of flight." (Rv. vii. 18, 15. 16).

Indeed, the victory achieved by Sudās over the confederacy of the Ten kings was highly brilliant and glorious, for all the odds had been against him. Though allied with some of the tribes of the north-west, who were probably employed to keep the advance of Purukutsa in check, he fought against the allied hosts almost single-handed, and, by stratagem, completly routed them, killing almost all their leaders. People were unwilling to believe that such a victory could be achieved by a mere man, or a human hero. He must have been actively assisted by Indra and the Gods; otherwise this miracle would not have happened. And there were ample grounds for this popular belief. When Sudās, after crossing the river with his select contingents, surrounded the enemy's camp from behind, foul weather suddenly appeared with high winds, which undoubtedly made confusion worse confounded, creating great disorder among the enemy's ranks. This fact is undoubtedly indicated in the following two verses:

"They who ride on parti-coloured cattle (the Maruts), despatched by Pṛśnī, and recalling the engagement made by them with their friend (Indra), came like cattle from the pasturage, when left without a herdsman: the exulting *Niyut*

---

[1] The verse may also be translated thus: "The Trtsus, allied with Indra, rushed forth like waters rapidly flowing in their downward course. The ignorant enemy, having been routed, abandoned all their possessions to Sudās." This quite tallies with the context. Wilson's translation as quoted above does not seem to have been correctly made.

steeds brought them quickly (against the foe). The hero, Indra, created the Maruts (for the assistance of the Rajā), who, ambitious of fame, slew one-and-twenty men on the two banks (of the Paruṣṇī), as a well-looking priest lops the sacred grass in the chamber of sacrifice." (Rv. vii. 18, 10. 11).

This divine help has been freely acknowledged by the Vedic bard, Vasiṣṭha, in several verses of which the following one is remarkable :

" Indra has effected a valuable (donation) by a pauper : he has slain an old lion by a goat : he has cut the angles of the sacrificial post with a needle : he has given all the spoils (of the enemy) to Sudās." (Rv. vii. 18, 17).

Though the battle was won, and the allied army completely routed, nay annihilated, Sudās did not immediately lie on his oars, but followed up his victory by an invasion of the territories of his enemies, and " quickly demolished their strongholds and their seven cities." (Rv. vii. 18, 13). The territory of the Anus was annexed (Rv. vii. 18, 13) ; the Turvaśas, the Druhyus and the Bharatas were humbled ; "the subjugation of the turbulent Bheda, who holds men praising that (Indra) as guilty of wickedness " was effected, and " the dwellers on the Yamunā and the Tṛtsus glorified Indra when he killed Bheda in battle" (Rv. vii. 18, 18. 19). As regards the Ajas, the Śighrus and the Yakṣus, they too were subjugated and they " offered to him (Indra) as a sacrifice the heads of the horses (killed in combat)." (Rv. vii. 18, 19). According to the scholiast, this last passage means that " they presented the best horses taken."

The booty which Sudās collected in the course of his victorious march was immense, and freely distributed among the sages and his friends. Vasiṣṭha thus praises Sudās for the valuable gifts made to him :

" Praising the liberality of Sudās, the grandson of Devavat, the son of Pijavana, the donor of two hundred cows, and of two chariots with two wives, I, worthy (of the gifts), circumambulate thee, Agni, like the ministrant priest in the chamber (of sacrifice).

"Four horses having golden trappings, going steadily on a difficult road, celebrated on the earth, the excellent and acceptable gifts (made) to me by Sudās, the son of Pijavana, bear me as a son (to obtain) food and progeny.

"The seven worlds praise (Sudās) as if he were Indra: him whose fame (spreads) through the spacious heaven and earth: who, munificent, has distributed (wealth) on every eminent person, and (for whom) the flowing (rivers) have destroyed Yudhāmadhi in war."[1] (Rv. vii. 18, 22-24).

Verily, Sudās was one of the most famous Kings in Ṛg-vedic history. As a result of his wars, all the important Aryan tribes of Sapta-Sindhu were brought under one rule, if only for a time, and the Tṛtsus and the Bharatas probably amalgamated as one people. The discomfiture of Viśvāmitra was complete, and the Vasiṣṭhas rose in popular esteem and deservedly became famous for their piety and high spiritual powers.

---

1 Wilson's Translation of the Ṛgveda.

CHAPTER X.

MANNERS, CUSTOMS, RITES AND BELIEFS: FAMILY-LIFE; WEDDING RITES; CHILD-LIFE; HOSPITALITY AND LIBERALITY; STUDENT-LIFE AND LEARNING; ORIGIN OF THE IDEA OF RELIGION; THE REGION OF YAMA OR HEAVEN; NIRṚITI OR HELL; BURIAL-RITES; DEMONS AND GOBLINS; CREMATION-RITES; TRANSMIGRATION KARMA AND REBIRTH.

Some of the manners and customs of the Aryan people have been described in the previous chapters, and I propose to deal with others in this.

Family-life.—The type of family-life, as I have already said, was patriarchal. The father was the head of the family as long as he lived, or was physically able to discharge his duties. When he became too old or decrepit, his place was taken by the eldest son (Rv. i. 70, 5), who not only maintained his old parents in comfort with due regard to their helpless condition (Rv. vii. 18, 23), but also took proper care of all the members of the family and the dependents. He gave away his unmarried sisters in marriage, bestowing upon them suitable dowries, and maintained and took proper care of them as long as they remained unmarried. A fatherless and brotherless spinster was considered unlucky and pitied, as she was in danger of being seduced and going astray. (Rv. i. 124. 7; iv. 5, 5). Hence a daughter who failed to secure a husband and remained unmarried was entitled to and given a portion of the ancestral property for her maintenance, which she shared equally with her brothers. This enabled her to live an honourable and independent life in the event of her father's or brother's death, and keep her above want. The absence of any provision for her maintenance compelled her, when helpless, to seek employment elsewhere, probably among environments which made her fall into temptations. A young helpless girl was (as she still is) the object of sinful attention of undesirable characters who missed no opportunity for seducing and ruining her, and was thus reduced to becoming a prostitute. (Rv. i. 124, 7; iv. 5, 5). The putting away of illegitimate children is referred to in the Ṛgveda (Rv. ii. 29, 1), and according to Professors Macdonell and Keith, "expressions like *Kumārī-putra* 'son of a maiden' (*Vāj. Sam.* xxx. 6; *Tait. Brāh.* iii. 4, 2, 1) and the 'son of an unmarried girl' (*agrū*) spoken of in the Ṛgveda (Rv. iv. 19, 9; 30, 16. 19; ii. 13, 12), point in the same direction." [1]

For these reasons, the birth of a girl in a family was never popular. As previously stated, there is a prayer in the Atharva-veda which asks for the birth of sons and not of daughters. (Av. viii. 6, 25). The Aitareya Brāhmaṇa (vii. 31, 1) also says that "daughters are the cause of misery." Though sons were desired, yet daughters, when born, were not neglected. They were brought up along with the sons, and were the objects of parental affections, though undoubtedly they caused greater anxiety to the parents for the reasons stated above than the sons. Zimmer [2] has inferred from a passage in the *Kāthaka Saṃhitā* (xxvii. 9) that girl infants were exposed to die, but, as pointed out by Böhtlingk, the passage has been misunderstood, as "it refers merely to laying the child aside, not exposing it, while a boy was lifted up," and "the traditional rendering of the passage is not that it refers to exposure, but to getting rid of a daughter on marriage." [3]

It sometimes happened that brothers quarrelled among themselves even in the life-time of their parents, and in an event like this, the family property was partitioned among them by the father, of course, after reserving a share for

---

[1] *Vedic Index*, i. 395-396.

[2] *Alt. Leben*, 319, 320; Kaegi *Der Ṛgveda* n. 49; Schrader *Prehistoric Antiquities*, 389, 390, &c.

[3] *Vedic Index*, i. 305; also foot-note 34.

himself and his wife for maintenance during their life-time. (Rv. iii. 45, 4). As soon as a son was married, he and his wife were given a separate house or room to live in, though they all messed jointly.

Wedding rites.—In the Tenth Maṇḍala of the Ṛgveda there is a hymn (*Sūkta* 85) which describes the marriage of Sūryā, the daughter of Sūrya (or the Sun), with Soma, (the Moon), [1] and contains *mantras* that were applied to wedding rites. The *mantras*, however, have not been given in the Ṛgveda in their succinct order, consistently with their application to the different parts of the ceremony which extended over four days at least. We find, however, the details in the *Gṛhya Sūtras* which, we can safely surmise, have recorded them in the order in which they were actually observed during the ceremony since Ṛgvedic times. It should be remembered in this connection that the conservative instincts of an old nation like the Aryans never suffered a departure from old ritual forms and traditional practice, although they had no significance in a later age when customs had materially changed. For example, the same ancient *mantras* that were applicable to post-pubescent marriages of youthful damsels in Vedic times are still uttered at the time of the weddings of girls who are mere infants and given away in marriage before they even reach their

[1] What is the meaning of the marriage of the daughter of the Sun with the Moon? Does Sūryā represent the light of the Sun, and were the Vedic Aryans aware that the Moon was lighted by the borrowed rays of this luminary? And has this fact been poetically described as the marriage of Suryā with the Moon? I have no doubt that the Ṛṣis of the Ṛgveda were acquainted with the above scientific fact. There is a verse in the Ṛgveda (i. 84. 15) which strongly corroborates this view. Its meaning is as follows: "The (solar rays) found on this occasion the light of Tvaṣṭṛ, verily concealed in the mansion of the moving Moon." Griffith explains *Tvaṣṭṛ's Bull* as "an obscure expression for the Sun," and says "the purport of the verse may be that when, after the rains, the bright moonlight night came, men recognized the fact that the light was borrowed from the Sun." Hence this fact must have been poetically described as the marriage of the Sun's daughter with the Moon.

teens, thus reducing them to mere mockery. We shall not, therefore, be wrong, if we infer that the details of the wedding rites as found in the *Gṛhya Sūtras* were substantially the same as practised in Ṛgvedic times. In fact, most of the *mantras* in the Sūtras have been taken from the Ṛgveda itself without any modification or change.

The preliminary part of the marriage, of course, consisted in the selection of the bride and bridegroom. In Ṛgvedic times a girl was never married before puberty, and was allowed liberty to make a choice of her husband from among the youthful suitors of those families that were not *sa-gotra*, or otherwise barred from a matrimonial alliance with her family. Of course, the selection was mutual either from love or other considerations. But we may take it for granted that love formed the chief and dominant factor in the matter of selection. The bridegroom's friends then approached the bride's father, to whom the formal proposal was made, as was done in the case of Sūryā by the Aśvins on behalf of Soma. (Rv. x. 85, 9. 15. 23). If the bride's father approved of her selection of her future husband, the preliminaries were settled and an auspicious day fixed for the performance of the ceremony.

Sometimes when the bridegroom proved to be an unsuitable match either on account of his physical deformity, age, mental or moral disqualification, poverty or other causes, the bride's father demanded from him a heavy fee as the price of the bride. (Rv. i. 109, 2). Sometimes again a bride chose for her husband a wealthy man (but otherwise disqualified probably on account of disparity of age) for the sake of his wealth only, and not for love. But all such matches were condemned. (Rv. x. 27, 12). On the other hand, the father of a bride who was naturally deformed or blind had also to give a handsome dowry to the bridegroom for taking the hand of his daughter in marriage. The usual mode of selection however was based on mutual attraction and love within certain restrictions, for which ample opportunities were afforded to the young people on the occasions of public sacrifices, as in the case Śyāvāśva, or in *Samanas* (public fairs) which were visited by them in large numbers. Sometimes a willing bride was forcibly carried away from the protection of an unwilling father or guardian by the bridegroom and his people, which often resulted in a free fight between the two parties (Rv. i. 116, 1), but such occurrences were rare.

As the selection depended upon mutual attraction and love, there was probably no room in ancient times for making matches on "the actual calculation and determination of the Kūtas,"[1] which require an expert knowledge of Astrology. Though Astronomy and Astrology existed in some forms in Vedic times, that part of the latter science which dealt with the *Kūtas* was probably not much developed, or if developed, not much consulted for the purpose of selecting a bride or bridegroom, for the selection was made by the young people themselves. It was only when post-pubescent marriage came into disuse through various causes that the actual calculation and determination of the Kūtas, which were twelve in number,[2] became absolutely necessary with a view to making suitable matches, and securing the happiness and welfare of the young couples. And this custom has since then been in vogue.

Now to return to the wedding rites in Vedic times, when youthful maidens were married to young men. An auspicious day having been fixed for the performance of the wedding, the bridegroom, well-dressed, well-scented, and well-adorned with gold ornaments and jewels (Rv. v. 60, 4), proceeded in a car, with his friends and relations, in a procession to the bride's house. The guests, of course, were received with due *éclat*, and honoured with a sumptuous feast. Then the wedding rites began at the auspicious hour.

---

1 R. Raghunath Rao's, *Aryan Marriage*, p. 172

2 *Aryan Marriage*, p. 72 ff.

It should be borne in mind here that the *Gṛhya Sūtras* have enjoined marriage on *Snātakas*, *i.e.*, those young bachelors who have finished their education, and are about to enter on their duties as householders. "One of the duties of the householder, in the old days absolutely essential, is the daily performance of the Agnihotra,[1] which requires the constant companionship of the wife. It is, therefore, prescribed that the Fire before which the wedding is concluded should be carried immediately to the husband's home and maintained there constantly by the couple."[2] The young bride, therefore, was old enough to be able to suffer the pangs of separation from her parents and relatives, and live with her husband constantly in her new home, tending the sacred Fire with him. She was also sufficiently advanced in intelligence to be able to understand the meaning of the *mantras* uttered by her husband and the presiding priest on the occasion of the performance of her wedding rites.

The wedding rites began by the bridegroom uttering his *saṃkalpa* which, "as a psychological act, is the determination to direct and control one's energies in such ways as will secure the attainment of the object in view."[3] The *saṃkalpa* was as follows: "This woman will I now marry to acquire the wealth of *Dharma* and *Prajā*." The meaning is clear. The object of the bridegroom in marrying the maiden was to acquire spiritual powers, to advance in spirituality with her, and to beget children for continuing the family line.

At the first meeting of the bride in her house, the bridegroom had to observe her limb by limb and pronounce the following *mantras*: "Look upon me, (thy husband) with no angry eye; be not hostile to (me) thy lord; be tender to animals, be amiable, be very glorious (or beautiful in thy person); be the mother of males; be devoted to the Gods; be

---

1 *Āśvalāyana* (i. 9. 1-2); *Āpastamba* (ii. 5, 14-15).

2 V. S. Srinivasa Sastri's *Marriage After Puberty*, p. 5.

3 *The Aryan Marriage*, p. 20.

the bestower of happiness; be the bringer of prosperity to our bipeds and quadrupeds." (Rv. x. 85, 44).[1]

Before giving her away, the father solemnly extracted the following promise from the bridegroom: "In the attainment of *Dharma*, *Artha* and *Kāma*, she is not to be transgressed."[2] The bridegroom promptly responded: "Transgress her I will not." (*nāticarāmi*). The bride's father repeated the same admonition for the second and the third time, and the bridegroom made the same response as above stated. Then the girl was given away by the father to the bridegroom with many suitable presents cows, clothes, ornaments, beds, bedsteads, &c., (Rv. x. 39, 14; 85, 13. 20. 31. 38).

On this solemn occasion of the gift, the eyes of the bride's parents and relations were naturally filled with tears at the thought of parting with her for ever, when the bridegroom uttered the following *mantra*: "Why weep they when they ought rather to rejoice? Let them think of the attachment that will subsist between us through long years to come. They have brought about this marriage so that it may end in our embrace."[3]

Next was placed on the girl's head a ring of *darbha*, and on it rested the hole of a yoke, into which a gold coin was thrown. The yoke was probably the emblem of subjection of the wife to her husband, and the gold coin with the water poured on it was the emblem of prosperous and peaceful life. As the yoke was held over the bride's head, and the gold coin and water poured into the hole, the bridegroom uttered the following *mantra*: "May this gold prove a blessing to thee. May the yoke prove a blessing to thee. May the hole of the yoke prove a blessing to thee. May this

---

1 This *mantra* was also probably uttered at the conclusion of the ceremony, when the bridegroom really acquired the status of husband.

2 *Dharmārtha-kāmeṣu nāticaritavyā.* (*The Aryan Marriage*, pp. 23-24).

3 *Marriage After Puberty*, p. 5. For the *mantra* read Appendix I, p. 9.

purificatory water prove a blessing to thee. Do thou unite thy body with mine (at the coming intercourse.)"[1]

Next followed the *kankana-bandhana* ceremony which was of great importance, as from this time forth until the *samāveśana* (sexual union) was performed, the bride and the bridegroom could suffer no pollution, as they had the *kankana* or *rakṣā*.[2] In the course of the ceremony, some *mantras* were uttered, one of which was as follows: "Go thou to my house; be thou there its mistress; control thou the beings that are in it, issuing orders for the sacrificial rites." Later on the bridegroom said: " First, *Soma* had thee for his bride; the *Gandharva* obtained thee next; *Agni* was thy third husband; thy fourth (husband) is I, born of man. *Soma* gave thee to the *Gandharva*; the *Gandharva* gave thee to *Agni*, and *Agni* has given thee to me, for wealth and sons." (Rv. x. 85, 40. 41). Sāyaṇa explains the verses thus: "While yet the desire for sexual intercourse has not arisen, Soma enjoys a girl; when it has just begun, the Gandharva takes her, and at marriage transfers her to Agni, from whom man obtains her (possessing capacity) for producing wealth and sons." The Smṛtis are more explicit; for Atri says: "Women are first enjoyed by the Gods, Soma, Viśvāvasu, and Agni; only then do men enjoy them. But the women are not tainted thereby. When hair has appeared (on the pubes), Soma enjoys a maiden; the Gandharva enjoys her when the breasts are developed, and Agni when she has had the menstrual discharge."[3] These different stages of a woman's physical and mental development are further explained thus: "Soma is Śasyādhipati, the Lord of the Vegetable world; and presides also over the mind...The physical growth of the girl, including that of the hair, was under the care of Soma. The mind of the girl was also developed under his guidance...The Gandharva is the master

---

[1] *Op. cit.*, p. 5.

[2] *Aryan Marriage*, pp. 24-25.

[3] *Marriage After Puberty*, pp. 5 and 6.

of graces. It is his function to make the woman's body beautiful, and to add richness of tone Under his care the pelvis develop, the breasts become round and attractive, the eyes begin to speak the language of love, and the whole body acquires a rich hue. His work is advanced, and he hands her on to Agni. Who is Agni? He is the Lord of Fire, the Lord of the *Agni-tattva.* Nature is radiant with colour and joy in spring and summer; animals breed in spring... Agni is the Fructifier. It is he who brings about the menstrual flow, and women then can bear children. Agni then gives her to man, her fourth Pati or Lord."[1] This seems to be the correct explanation of the Ṛgvedic verses referred to above. It would thus appear that girls were married in Vedic times when they became youthful women, able to discharge their duties as wives, and capable of bearing children.

After the above *mantras* were uttered, came the ceremony of *Panigrahaṇam*, or taking the bride's hand. The bridegroom took the bride's hand in his own, and walked with her seven steps uttering certain *mantras*, one of which is as follows: "I take thy hand for good fortune that thou mayest attain old age with me, thy husband. The all-knowing Gods, Bhaga, Aryaman, Savitṛ have given thee to me, that I may be the master of a household." (Rv. x. 85, 36). After this communication he led her round the Fire and chanted more *mantras* till the *Saptapadī* ceremony was gone through. After the seventh step, the husband (for the bridegroom was now the husband of the bride) thus addressed his wife: "Now we have taken the seven steps together, be thou my companion. Let us be companions. Let me have thy companionship. May I never part from thee, nor thou from me. Let us be united; let us always take counsel together with glad hearts and mutual love. May we grow in strength and prosperity together. Now are we one in mind, deeds and

[1] *The Aryan Marriage*, pp. 26-27.

desires. Thou art *Ric*, I am *Sāman*; I am the sky, thou art the earth; I am the semen, thou art its bearer; I am the mind, thou art the tongue. Follow me faithfully, that we may have wealth and children together. Come, thou of sweet speech."[1] This *Saptapadī* was the most important part of the ceremony, as it established "an indissoluble link between the husband and the wife."[2]

After this, the *Lāja Homa* (or oblations to the sacred Fire with *lāja* or fried paddy) was performed. One of the *mantras* uttered by the priest is as follows: "I set thee free from the noose of Varuṇa, wherewith the adorable Savitṛ had bound thee; in the place of sacrifice, in the world of good deeds I unite thee, unharmed, with thy husband." (Rv. x. 85, 24). The presiding priest uttered also these *mantras*: "May Pūṣan lead thee hence, taking thee by thy hand; may the Aśvins convey thee away in their car; go to the dwelling (of thy husband), as thou art the mistress of the house; thou, submissive (to thy husband), givest orders to his household. In this (thy husband's family) may affection increase with offspring; be watchful over the domestic Fire in this house; unite thy person with this thy husband; and both growing old together govern your household...Let not the robbers who approach the husband and wife reach them; may they by easy roads pass the difficulty; may enemies keep aloof. Fortunate is this bride, approach, behold her; having given her your congratulations, depart to your several homes" (Rv. x. 85, 24. 26. 27. 32. 33).

The garment in which the bride was married had to be given up to the priest: "This garment is inflaming; it is

---

[1] *Marriage After Puberty*, p. 7.

[2] *The Aryan Marriange*, p. 30. Some say that after the *Saptapadi* ceremony, the bride had to mount a stone which was emblematic of her remaining fixed and immovable in her husband's family like the stone, and look at the Dhruva star (the fixed Polar star) pronouncing the following *mantra* "*Om dhruvamasi dhruvādham patikule bhuāsam*," *i.e.*, O Polar star, thou art fixed; may I also remain fixed in my husband's family.

pungent; it is like stale Soma; it is like poison; it is not fit for use. The Brahman, who knows Sūrya, verily desires the bridal garment." (Rv. x. 85, 34). It consisted of three parts, the *āśasana* (border-cloth), the *viśasana* (head-cloth) and the *adhivikartana* (divided bodice), of which the Brahman relieved her (Rv. x. 85, 35). Sāyaṇa explains *āśasana* as *tūṣādhāna*, the receptacle of the fringe, which was of different colour. *Viśasana* is that which is to be placed on the head, that which is to be placed at the end of the fringe or border. *Adhivikartanam* is the garment which they cut into three pieces." If Sāyaṇa's explanation be correct, we here get an idea of the bridal dress. There was a skirt to which a border of different colour was attached. Probably the border, which was of embroidered work, was detatchable. Then there was a veil that covered the head of the bride, and there was a garment cut into three pieces which served the purpose of a bodice or jacket.

The first day's ceremony having been over, the married couple started for their home in a car; and as the wife mounted it, she was told by the husband: "Thou shalt be my mistress henceforth and bear me ten sons. Be mistress of thy father-in-law and mother-in-law. Be mistress of these and of the other daughters-in-law of the house, of the children, property and all." [1]

On reaching home, the couple resumed the ceremonies before the sacred Fire which had been duly brought from the bride's house, and performed the *Pradhāna Homa.* He poured libations on the Fire with appropriate *mantras*: (1) "This to Soma (who has nourished my wife so well). (2) This to the Gandharva (who has adorned my wife so well). (3) This to Agni (who has given me this *yuvatī* or youthful maiden). (4) This *kanyā*, O Sūrya, has passed from her father's family to her husband's. Her maidenhood she has resigned. Do thou be propitious. I set thee free from

[1] *Marriage After Puberty*, pp. 7 & 8 cf. Rv. x. 85, 46.

thence, (*i.e.*, from thy father's family), not from hence, (*i.e.*, my family). I place thee here firmly bound: grant, Indra, Showerer, that this (damsel) may have excellent children and be very fortunate.[1] (6) O Indra, Showerer, make this bride the mother of sons, pleasing to me (her husband); give her ten sons; make her husband the eleventh (member).[2] (7) May Agni, foremost of the Gods, come. May he free and save her offspring from the cords of death. When Agni makes her know no sorrow for loss of progeny, may Varuṇa acquiesce. Be ye, Agni and Varuṇa, propitious. (8) May the *Gārhapatya Agni* protect her, grant her progeny, long life, make her a mother on whose lap children nestle and play; awake her only to feel the joy of owning sons. Be thou propitious. (9) In thy house, O bride, be there no cries of sorrow at night. Be the criers other than thee and thine. Be there no dishevelled hair and beating of breast for thee. Shine, O bride, in thy husband's house with thy husband alive and with sane-minded children surrounding thee. To all this, O Surya, the Guardian of brides, do thou look. (10) May Dyaus nourish thy loins *(pṛṣtha)*, Vāyu thy thighs, the Aśvins thy breasts. May Sūrya protect thy child at the breast. May Bṛhaspati keep thee ever-clothed. May the Viśvedevāh be Guardian-angels at thy back. (11) Barrenness, infant-deaths, sins, causes of sins, these all, O bride, do I now throw unto thy enemies like unto the garland of flowers faded through use, which is thrown to the tree-tops by thee. May Sūrya, the Guardian of brides, help in this."[3]

The bridegroom had to perform another Homa at the time of first entering into or occupying with the bride the quarters or house set apart for them. This Homa was called the *Gṛha-praveśa Homa.* Some of the *mantras* are as follow:

"(1) May my dearest wife, that has come into our house with all the cows and horses given her by her father, live

---

[1] Rv. x. 85, 25.

[2] Rv. x. 85, 45.

[3] *The Aryan Marriage*, pp. 30-35.

long with her long-lived lord. May she attain heaven by her progeny. May she bring forth many a child. With her wealth ever-increasing, may she, O Agni, tend the Holy Fire for a hundred winters." (2) "May this Agni of my *Upāsana*, who has his shining house, who unceasingly increases my strength, who guards my home, give unto us, husband and wife, wealth, strength and progeny, as he did to the Devas." (3) "O Prajāpati, make thou our progeny happy. O Indra, O Agni, grant us the happiness of never witnessing the death of our children, during the life-time of us two, husband and wife." (4) "O bride, thee Bṛhaspati hath given unto me. Protected by me, do thou ever have me in thy mind. Do thou unite with me, and begetting sons, live thou long." (5) "May love grow in this house with progeny. Be thou ever ready here for the discharge of thy duties as *Gṛhiṇī*. Unite thy body with mine thy lord's. Grow thou old here, and teach sacrificial law to thy sons and grandsons with a gladdened heart."[1]

The marriage-rites did not end with the bringing of the wife to her husband's home, and the performance of the above-named Homas. There was still another ordeal which the couple had to pass through, and which shows how they had to exercise self-restraint—the very basis of matrimonial happiness—for a few days, and in some cases, even for a year. The ordinary rule, however, was the observance of *three nights' brahmacarya, i.e.*, abstinence, or, as the author of *The Aryan Marriage* prefers to call it, continence.

The original *Saṃkalpa* (or determination) of the marriage was not the attainment of intellectual or spiritual love, with no thought of the body, but the attainment of domestic felicity by the possession of a youthful loving wife who would be the husband's help-mate and soul-mate in the discharge of his duties as a householder and in the performance of his daily worship of the sacred House-hold Fire, and who would

[1] *Op cit.*, pp 39-42.

be the mother of healthy, virtuous and noble sons for continuing the family-line. With this object in view the husband chose his wife and brought her home after going through certain wedding rites. As both the husband and wife were youthful, and attracted to each other by love, it is quite natural to suppose that they would be very eager to come into physical contact with one another, and wish the rites to be soon over. But no, they had yet to learn and realise that true love was not passionate, or passion-born, but was based on perfect self-restraint. They had to lead a life of continence for a period, the minimum being three days, and the maximum one year. The longer the period of continence, the better was the chance of obtaining a superior type of son, a Ṛṣikalpa, a Ṛsi or even a Deva.[1] This *brahmacarya* had to be observed under really trying circumstance. The pair were not allowed to take any food with salt, and for three nights at least had to sleep together on the floor, abstaining from intercourse and observing *brahmacarya.*[2] They had to wear ornaments for obvious reason, and lie on the same bed with *Viśvāvasu Gandharva* occupying the middle position, which consisted of "a rod of the *Udumbara* tree, coated with sandal paste, and covered with cloth." This rod was supposed to be inhabited by Viśvāvasu Gandharva, and was the witness of the pair's *brahmacarya*. On the fourth night after the performance of the *Pakva Homa* (if the night was auspicious), the pair retired to a gaily decorated room, and a *mantra* of great significance was then recited: "Rise, O Viśvāvasu, from this our bed, rise, we pray. Seek thou a girl that is tender in years, and that needs thy assistance. Leave thou this bride, my wife, unto me, and let her unite herself to me. O Gandharva, this bride, now united to me, her husband, prostrates to thee, and begs this favour of thee. Depart and find thou an immature girl that still dwells in

---

[1] *Baudhāyana*, i. 7. 11.

[2] *Śankhāyana*, i. 7. 5; *Āśvalāyana*, i. 8, 10-11; *Jaimini* 20, 6; *Gobhila* ii. 3. 15. &c.

her father's house. Such a one is verily thy portion, nay thy brith-right."[1] Besides this verse the Ṛgveda has another which has thus been translated by Wilson: "Rise up from hence, Viśvāvasu; we worship thee with reverence, seek another maiden, with large hips; leave the bride (to me) her husband" (Rv. x. 85, 22). After this, both the husband and wife performed the *Śeṣa Homa*, preparatory to *Samāveśana* or sexual union. *Ahutis* or oblations were devoutly offered to Agni, Vāyu, Āditya, Prajāpati, Prasavādi Devatās, Madhvādi Devatās, Cittādi Devatās, Bhuh, Bhubah, and Svah. This Homa was "intended to put the parties in the proper frame of mind for the sexual act. The two parties must be steady in their minds, and their powers must be at the highest point. There must be no lascivious thoughts, and the idea of animal gratification must be thrown entirely into the back-ground. Both must consciously and deliberately *will* with all their might that the progeny shall be spiritual."[2]

As generally there should be no sexual intercourse unless the wife desired it, she was made to utter the following *mantra* first:

"Know I what thou hast in thy mind; lovingly do I view thee as one knowing my mind, thee that hast had thy birth in *tapas* and that art enriched in *tapas*. Here in my house, do thou enrich me with progeny and wealth, being born in thy son, that hast a desire for sons." Responded the bridegroom thus: "Know I what thou hast in thy mind; lovingly do I view thee as one seeking impregnation in thy body during the Ṛtu period (period of menstruation), thee

---

1 *The Aryan Marriage*, p. 45. Cf. Rv. x. 85, 21. Sāyana has explained *vyaktām* in the verse as *stanodgamādirāhityenāproudhām*, but *vyaktām* (fully outlined or expressed) really conveys the idea of physical development and not the absence of it, as maiden "with broad hips" in the next verse clearly implies. It is Viśvāvasu who takes charge of the girl when she is physically developed, and only hands her over to Agni when she menstruates. After this event the girl is handed over to her husband for producing progeny.

2 *The Aryan Marriage*, p. 46.

that hast had me in thy mind. A youthful woman, (*yuvatī*) thou art...and be thou born in thy son, desirous as thou art of a son." (Rv. x. 183, 2). Then the following prayers were offered by the husband: "May the Viśvedevāh unite our hearts; May the Udaka Devatās, Vāyu and Dhātṛ unite our hearts: May Sarasvatī vouchsafe to us appropriate speech." (Rv. x. 85, 47). "O Prajapati, enter thou my body. O Tvaṣṭṛ, Fashioner of Forms, enter thou my body with Viṣṇu and other Devas. O Indra, come thou with thy friends, the Viśvedevāh, and enter thou our bodies with them to grant us our wish. Parents of a numerous progeny are we to be." "May Prajāpati grant us progeny till we grow old. May Sūrya make us each love the other. O bride, live thou long in the house of thy husband; and enjoy thou the companionship of thy husband ever more. May we be happy in the wealth of our bipeds and quadrupeds." (Rv. x. 85, 43). [1]

The wedding rites ended with the performance of the *Śeṣa Homa* and the consummation of the marriage on the fourth night. I will not deal with further details, as they may appear too indecent for modern taste, but will ask the reader to satisfy his curiosity by reading the two excellent books on Aryan marriage from which I have made so many quotations, for which I beg to apologise to the authors. These wedding rites are still observed by the higher castes of the Hindus, but with what a mockery! The bride now is a mere infant, and does not understand the meaning or significance of the various *mantras* uttered, or the various rites performed at the time of her marriage, minus of course the *Śeṣa Homa*, which is now deferred till she attains her puberty when the *Garbhādhāna* ceremony is gone through. As no account of Vedic culture would be complete without a description of the ideal of marriage as it was conceived by the ancient Vedic Aryans, and of the details of the rites that

[1] *The Aryan Marriage*, pp. 48-49.

were (and are still) gone through, I have taken some pains to give it here as briefly as possible, even at the risk of incurring the odium and displeasure of my fastidious readers.

Marriage is one of the most solemn rites that man has to go through in his life. On it depend his personal happiness, domestic felicity, birth of noble progeny who will continue the family-line after him, his moral and spiritual culture, and the full development of his true manhood. The preparations for entering into married life, and acquiring ability to perform the sacred and onerous duties inseparable from it, as enjoined by the Vedic Scriptures on every young man who wishes to be an ideal householder, were such as were calculated to subordinate the lower self to the higher, and develop those moral and spiritual traits in his character that enabled him to ascend higher and higher in the ladder of progress till he reached the final goal of life,—the highest, the blest, and the most beautiful,—which is the full realisation of the unity of the Ego or individual self with the One Universal Self, called Brahman. With this one supreme end of life in view, the ancient Ṛṣis of the sacred Land of the Seven Rivers, the real *Seers* that ever graced the world, prescribed rules and regulations for every important affair of our life, so as to guide humanity to the attainment and realisation of the *summum bonum* of human existence. The ideal is indeed extremely difficult to reach and realise, and, to our eternal shame be it admitted, there have been many lapses in the past, as there have been lapses in the present; but still the ideal is there—*Brahmacarya* or self-restraint from beginning to end—which is worth holding up before Humanity for all time to come. It will not do to take a superficial view of a rite or custom, and scoff at it as immoral, indecent or obscene; for there is really nothing immoral, indecent or obscene in an act that is primarily responsible for and the sole cause of our creation and being, and of the creation and continuity of animal life. Marriage is the most solemn affair in a man's or woman's life, upon which depend his or her worldly, moral and spiritual welfare, and final emancipation from the bonds that tie him or her down to the earth. It is certainly not a thing to be donned or doffed at one's pleasure. It is an eternal bond that binds two souls together for ever, and each suffers for the other's lapses or derelictions. It is not a contract with the Hindus, but a sacrament, and there is no breaking away or parting from the union.

Child-life.—There is very little mention in the Ṛgveda of child-life, or of the various rites and ceremonies that were performed from the conception of the child in the mother's womb, through the different stages of development of the foetus, till its birth, and from its birth till it grew up sufficiently old to be able to take care of itself. But there is elaborate description of all the rites performed for the well-being and long life and health of the child in the various Smṛtis, which contain records of old customs obtaining from the very dawn of Aryan civilisation.

There was a popular belief in Ṛgvedic times that there were evil spirits, goblins, Rākṣasas, &c., that were always on the look-out for an opportunity to destroy the foetus in the mother's womb and bring about abortion or mis-carriage, thereby causing the death of both mother and child. Against the attacks of these evil spirits, unseen and malignant, and for the adequate protection of the foetus, certain *mantras* or incantations were uttered, some of which are to be found in the Ṛgveda itself. The Atharva-veda, which is a veritable repository of popular beliefs and ceremonies, contains many such incantations. The following is a translation of some of the *mantras* taken from the Ṛgveda (x. 162) :

"1. May Agni, the destroyer of the Rākṣasas, consenting to our prayer, drive hence (the evil spirit) who (in the form of sickness) assails thine embryo, who, as the disease *durnāman*, [1] assails thy womb. 2. May Agni, concurring in

---

[1] Nirukta, vi. 12. Yāska gives the meanings of the Lexicons to *durnāman*, *viz.*, a worm, disease, hæmorrhoids.

our prayer, destroy the cannibal who, as sickness, assails thine embryo, who, as the disease *durnāman*, assails thy womb. 3. May we exterminate from hence the evil spirit, who destroys the impregnating energy, the germ as it settles, the moving embryo, who seeks to destroy (the babe) when born. 4. May we exterminate from hence (the evil spirit) who, separates thy thighs, who lies between husband and wife, who, entering thy womb, devours (the seed)......6. May we exterminate from hence (the evil spirit) who, having beguiled thee by sleep or darkness, approaches thee, and seeks to destroy thy offspring."[1]

The belief in the evil spirits, always bent upon destroying the embryo, or the life of the child when born, still continues among the Hindus of all classes, either ignorant or enlightened, especially among their women-folk who scrupulously follow old customs and rites, and resort to many strange and uncanny devices to ward off their malignant influence over the foetus, and the child when born. It would be a very interesting and curious literature, if these rites and customs were studied and faithfully recorded, as they would go to show that the present descendants of the ancient Aryans have very little changed their faith in this respect since pre-Ṛgvedic times, millenniums ago. However this may be, there were and still are so many rites and ceremonies in connection with child-life, as would fill quite a volume, if elaborately recorded. Some of the principal rites relate to the principal events of the life of a child, *viz.*, (1) when it is first brought out from the lying-in room on the fifth, eighth or ninth day to see the light of the sun, and is exposed to the sun's rays; (2) when on the twenty-first or the thirtieth day, it leaves the lying-in room and is carried to the house or the living rooms; (3) when on the third month, it has to be given a name; (4) when on the sixth or seventh month it has to taste its first rice, and cuts its teeth; (5) when in the

---

[1] Wilson's *Translation of the Ṛgveda.*

fifth year, the tonsure or the first shaving of the head (Rv. vi. 75, 17) as well as the perforation or piercing of the ears take place; (6) when in that year or afterwards, it is first taught the alphabets; (7) when in the eighth year or afterwards, the boy becomes a *Dvija*, *i.e.*, puts on the sacred thread, becomes a *Brahmacārin* and is taken to the house of the Guru or spiritual preceptor for the study of the Vedas, and so on. In ancient times, the boy soon after his *upanayanam* left his father's home and resided in the house of his preceptor for at least twelve years as a *Brahmacārin*, abstaining from fish, flesh or the luxuries of life, and subsisting on food begged from house-holders, which he shared with his preceptor. It was a hard and rough life that he had to lead, often subjecting himself to privations, so as to effectually restrain, if not to kill the promptings of the flesh common among youths, and steady his mind for the acquirement of spiritual knowledge. This was the period of probation of the future citizen and householder, and we know of no better school than this for the purpose. It is a pity that the Ṛgveda does not contain any elaborate account of child-life or of the life led by the youths; but the *Smṛitis* do, and as they contain accounts of *old customs remembered*, they must have truly represented what had actually existed in very ancient times. Still in the Ṛgveda, we find pictures of young pupils standing reverently round their preceptor for receiving their lessons or instructions (Rv. i. 112, 2), and pronouncing words in the manner in which the preceptor pronounced them. (Rv. vii. 103, 5). Indra says in another verse (Rv. i. 170, 1). that what is carefully studied (*adhītam*) to-day is forgotten to-morrow. This may mean that what is learnt *by rote* is soon forgotten, or it may imply that the meaning of a *mantra*, recorded in a book, which is explained by the preceptor today, is forgotten tomorrow. The question is whether the art of writing and books existed in Ṛgvedic times. I have discussed this question elsewhere, and have come to the conclusion that the Ṛgvedic Aryans were most likely acquainted with the art of writing, and probably there were books or *granthas* in which the *mantras* were recorded.[1] The statement in a Ṛgvedic verse (x. 71, 4) that there are men who hear and *see* speech without understanding its meaning unmistakably points to the existence of books and the art of writing. However this may be, there can be no question that young men passed their youthful days in the house of their preceptor, receiving instructions from him as to the true import of the *mantras*, the significance of sacrifices, and the duties of a householder, &c. The instruction was practical, and when their education was finished, they returned home, with the permission of their *Guru*, to enter upon the second stage of their life by taking a suitable wife and performing the duties of a householder.

Hospitality and Liberality.—The Vedic Aryans were a hospitable people, and hospitality was looked upon as a religious duty. The guest was served and adored as men served and adored Agni, and even as they served and groomed their fleet horses morning and evening. (Rv. vii. 3, 5). The niggardly misers were doomed to destruction (Rv. ix. 63, 5). The translation of the following hymn (Rv. x. 117) regarding the virtues of hospitality will be found interesting: "1. The Gods have not assigned hunger as (the cause of) death,[2] for death approaches the man who has eaten; the riches of one who gives do not diminish; he who gives not finds no consoler. 2. He who, possessed of food, hardens his heart against the feeble man craving nourishment, against the sufferer coming to him (for help), and pursues (his own enjoyment even) before him, that man finds no consoler. 3. He is liberal who gives to the suppliant desiring food, wandering about distressed; to him there is an ample (recompense), and he contracts friendship with his adversaries. 4. He is not a friend, who gives not food to a friend, to an associate, to a

[1] *Journal of the Department of Letters*, vol. x, (Calcutta University).

[2] This probably proves that famines and deaths from starvation were rare in Ṛgvedic times.

companion; let him turn away from him, that is not a (fitting) dwelling; let him seek another more liberal lord. 5. Let the very rich man satisfy his suitor, let him look forward to a more protracted route (according to the scholiast, the road of virtue), for riches revolve from one man to another, as the wheels of a chariot turn round.[1] 6. The inhospitable man acquires food in vain. I speak the truth, it verily is his death. He cherishes not Ārya man nor a friend; he who eats alone is nothing but a sinner. 7. The ploughshare furrowing (the field) provides food for the ploughman; a man travelling along a road acquires (wealth for his master) by his movements; a Brahman expounding (the Veda) is better than one not expounding it; (so) let the man who gives become a kinsman to the man who gives not, (literally, 'the loving kinsman will prevail over him who loves not.') 8. He who has but one foot takes a longer time on a journey than he who has two; he who has two feet comes after him who has three; he who has four feet comes up overtaking the two-footed (and three-footed), beholding their traces as he passes by[2]. 9. Two hands are alike but they do not perform the same work; two cows calving at the same time do not yield the same milk; two twins have not the same strength: two persons of the same family do not display equal liberality."[3]

The above hymn is ascribed to Bhikṣu, said to be the son of Angiras. As the great sage, Angiras, is said to have instituted the Fire Sacrifice (Rv. i. 45, 3; 71, 2-3; 83, 4), he must have belonged to the First or Early Age of Ṛgvedic civilisation. In fact, he was looked upon as a semi-mythical being in the Later Age of the Ṛgvedic period. The custom of hospitality of the Aryans must, therefore, have existed

[1] Probably the meaning is "let him look further along the path of life, and he will see riches deserting the rich and going to others. Fortune is fickle"

[2] "The term 'foot' here is explained by the Scholiast as being metaphorical for portion or wealth. The man who has four times the riches of another should be four times as liberal." Wilson.

[3] Wilson's *Translation of the Ṛgveda.*

from the very beginnings of Aryan civilisation, and is still in vogue among their descendants, thousands of years after. The great King Divodāsa acquired the title of *Atithigva* (or Hospitable to guests) on account of his remarkable hospitality. (Rv. i. 51, 6; 112, 14; iv. 26, 3; vi. 47, 22). As meat was a principal item of food in ancient pastoral times and even later, it was usually the practice to kill an animal, a cow or a goat, for the entertainment of the guest or guests, especially when they happened to be distinguished persons.[1] A Ṛṣi prays to the Gods to remove, among other things, "illiberality." (Rv. x. 63, 12). Some of the kings, mentioned in the Ṛgveda, were exceedingly liberal to the Ṛṣis who performed sacrifices for them, giving, on particular occasions, large amounts of gold coins, hundreds of cows, horses, camels, dogs, asses, ornaments, valuable cloths, chariots, houses to live in, and even male and female slaves for their service. (Rv. i. 126, 1-4; v. 30, 12-15; vii. 18, 21-24; viii. 1, 32-33; 3, 21 *et seq.*; 4, 19-21; 5, 37-39; 6, 46-48; 55; 56, &c.). The *Bhojas* or givers of enjoyment have thus been praised in the Ṛgveda (x. 107, 8-11):

"The givers of enjoyment do not die, they do not go to destruction, they suffer no injury; the givers of enjoyment suffer no pain. Dakṣiṇā[2] gives them all this world and the entire heaven.

---

[1] Cf. *Ait. Brah.* (i. 3. 4); *Yājnavalkya* (i 109); *Mahābhāratam* (*Vana.* Ch. 206, verses 10, 11) in which Rantideva is described to have killed 2,000 kine daily for his kitchen and distributed food mixed with meat to hungry people; also *Uttara-Rāma-Caritam* of Bhavabhūti.

[2] *Dakṣiṇā* is the fee paid to priests at a sacrifice. "A cow—a prolific (*dakṣiṇā*) one—was the usual fee on such an occasion" (*Vedic Index*, i. 336) Murray in his English Dictionary also traces the meaning of the English word "fee" as "cow," "money" "payment for service." Kātyāyana in his *Śrauta Sūtra* (xv. 2. 13) and Lātyāyana (Śrauta Sūtra, viii. 1, 2) also say that when nothing is specified, a cow is the *dakṣiṇā*. It should also be remembered that the food cooked on *dakṣiṇāgni* (the fire to the south of the altar) was partaken of by the priests, and this may have been the original form of *dakṣiṇā*. The cow may have been substituted for it later on.

"The givers of enjoyment first won the cow, the source (of food); the givers of enjoyment have won a bride who was beautifully attired; the givers of enjoyment have won deep potations of wine; the givers of enjoyment have conquered those who, without being challenged, advance to meet them.

"For the giver of enjoyment they deck out a fleet horse; to the giver of enjoyment is presented a maiden beautifully adorned; to the giver of enjoyment belongs this dwelling, adorned like a lake full of lotus flowers, delightful as a dwelling of the gods.

"Horses capable of bearing heavy burdens bear the giver of enjoyment; a well-constructed chariot rolls along (for the giver) of the *dakṣiṇā*; O Gods, protect the giver of enjoyment in combats; may the giver of enjoyment be the victor over his foes in battles."

In the face of such praises, one would wonder if the ancient Aryans did not cultivate the spirit of hospitality and liberality. The Paṇis were condemned for their illiberality and selfishness. (Rv. vi. 61, 1) and for their greed and usury (Rv. viii. 77, 10), though Bṛbu, a Paṇi chief, was praised for his generosity and gifts to Ṛṣis. (Rv. vi. 45, 33).

Student-Life and Learning.—I will attempt again to give here a further fuller account of student-life and learning as depicted in the Ṛgveda. That there was some sort of institution in Ṛgvedic times for instructing the youths appears from stray references in the Scripture. For example, we come across the following verse (Rv. i. 112, 2) which Wilson has translated as follows: "Earnest and exclusive adorers stand, Aśvins, round your car, (to benefit) by your bounty; as (disciples listen) to the words (of a teacher) for instruction." Whether the art of writing and books existed in those days is still a matter of controversy: and even if we admit that they existed, the instruction imparted by the teacher to his pupils was chiefly verbal, as it was religious in character and appertained to ***mantras*** which had to be correctly pronounced and recited in order to make them efficacious in the performance of rites and ceremonies. Referring to the croakings of frogs on the advent of the rains, a curious verse (Rv. vii. 103, 5) says how one frog imitates the croaking of another "as a learner (imitates) his teacher." Another verse (Rv. vii. 87, 4) says: "The cow (speech) has thrice seven appellations: the wise and intelligent Varuṇa, giving instruction (*śikṣan*) to me, his worthy disciple, has declared the mysteries of the place (of Brahma)."

From the above references it would appear that there were in Ṛgvedic times private educational institutions, conducted by renowned teachers and sages, which were attended by young men, eager to master the sacred lore, who probably lived in the houses of the teachers themselves for a sufficiently long period to enable them to be proficient in learning. Some sort of discipline must also have been enforced on the pupils who had to observe the rules of *brahmacarya*, abstaining from luxury and voluptuous thoughts and actions. The word *Brahmacārin* occurs in the Ṛgveda (x. 109, 5), probably in the technical sense of a religious student. Professors Macdonell and Keith observe that "the practice of studentship doubtless developed, and was more strictly regulated by custom as time went on, but it is regularly assumed and discussed in the later Vedic literature, being obviously a necessary part of Vedic society." [1]

"The Atharva-veda has in honour of the Brahmacārin a hymn (xi. 5) which already gives all the characteristic features of religious studentship. The youth is initiated (*upa-nī*) by the teacher into a new life; he wears an antelope skin, and lets his hair grow long; he collects fuel, and begs, learns and practises penance. All these characteristics appear in the later literature. The student lives in the house of his teacher (*acārya-kula-vāsin*; *ante-vāsin*); he begs, looks

[1] *Vedic Index*, ii. 75.

after the sacrificial fires, and tends the house. His term of studentship might be long extended: it was normally fixed at twelve years, but much longer periods, such as thirty-two years, are mentioned. The age at which studentship began varied...One of the duties of the Brahmacārin was chastity."[1]

Though the practice of *brahmacarya* may not have existed in its developed form in Ṛgvedic times, we may safely surmise that all the elements that go to make up the life of a religious student were there. It was undoubtedly from this class of students that the various priests, Brahmans, Adhvaryus, Udgātṛs, &c., were recruited. The Brahmans were "observant of their vows, practising penance throughout the year." (Rv. vii. 103, 1). Unless they practised *brahmacarya* in their student-life in the house of their preceptors, it would be quite impossible for them to observe vows and practise penance throughout the year, when performing the duties of Brahmans. As girls were never married until they developed into youthful maidens, we may take it for granted that no young man, at any rate, of the higher classes, ever thought of marriage, until he reached youthful maturity, and returned from the abode of his preceptor after a long residence there, well practised in *brahmacarya* and declared fit to enter upon the stage of householder, and to take a wife with whom he had to perform his daily religious duties and worship.

The disciplinary education of girls also does not appear to have been neglected. Some of them appear to have received as sound a religious instruction as young Brahmacārins, for we find the names of Lady-Ṛṣis like Ghoṣā (a princess), Apālā, Lopamudrā, and Visvavārā, the last performing a sacrifice, offering oblations to Agni, and performing the duties of Hotṛ. The story of Śyāvāśva must be in the recollectiun of our readers, to whom King Rathaviti and his Queen refused to give their daughter in marriage until he could be declared a Ṛṣi by the Gods.[2] The physical

[1] *Op. cit.*, ii, 75-76.

[2] Vide *ante*, Chap. iii, pp. 134-135

and military training of young men were also not neglected, as they were taught to ride horses and wield arms. The art of elocution was also taught to young men, so that they might successfully take part in the debates held in *Sabhās* and *Samitis*.

A mere ability to get by heart and pronounce correctly the ***mantras*** learnt from the preceptor, without apprehending their true sense and meaning, was not considered the high standard of learning and wisdom. The following verses (Rv. x. 71, 2-9), as translated by Wilson, will be found interesting :

"When the wise create Speech through wisdom, winnowing (it) as (men winnow) barley with a sieve, then friends know friendship : good fortune is placed upon their word.

"(The wise) reached the path of Speech by sacrifice, they found it centred in the Ṛṣis ; having acquired it, they dispersed it in many places ; the seven noisy (birds) meet together.[1]

"One (man) indeed *seeing* Speech has not seen her ; another (man) hearing her has not heard her ; but to another she delivers her person as a loving wife well-attired presents herself to her husband.[2]

"They call one man firmly established in the friendship (of Speech), they do not exclude him from (the society of) the powerful (in knowledge) ; another wanders with an illusion that is barren, bearing Speech that is without fruits, without flowers.

---

[1] "The seven metres, *Gāyatrī*, &c., are here referred to. The previous words refer to the diffusion of learning ; those who have studied the Veda have afterwards taught it to others." Wilson.

[2] Seeing Speech evidently connotes the idea of ***written Speech*** (or verses), proving the existence of the art of writing in Ṛgvedic times, at any rate, in the later period. Read my article on the "Art of Writing in Ancient India" published in the *Journal of the Department of Letters*, Vol. x, (Calcutta University, 1923).

"He who has abandoned the friend who knows the duty of friend,[1] in his Speech there is not a particle (of sense); what he hears he hears amiss; for he knows not the path of righteousness.

"Friends ('persons having equal knowledge' *Sāyaṇa)* possessing eyes, possessing ears, were (yet) unequal in mental comprehension; some seemed like pools reaching to the mouth, others reaching to the loins, others like pools in which one can bathe.

"Although *Brāhmans* (the original word is *Brāhmaṇāh)* who are friends concur in the mental apprehensions which are conceived by the heart (of the wise), yet in this (assembly) they abandon one man (to ignorance of the sciences) that are to be known, others again who are reckoned as ***Brāhmans*** (the original word is *Brāhmaṇāh)* wander (at will in the meanings of the Veda).

"Those who do not walk (with the Brahmans) in this lower world, nor (with the Gods) in the upper world,—they are neither Brahmans nor offerers of libations; they, devoid of wisdom, attaining Speech, having sin-producing (Speech), becoming ploughmen, pursue agriculture"

Wilson makes the following observations on the hymn from which the above verses have been quoted: "The knowledge of Brahma is identical with the study of the Veda, so that the subject of the hymn is the eulogy of the understanding of the Veda as essential to divine knowledge. This mystification and panegyric of the Veda by the Veda itself clearly belongs to a period more recent than that of the earlier Maṇdalas of the Ṛgveda." Wilson's observations appear to be just. We find in the above verses that a true comprehension of the meaning of the Vedic verses was essential to the qualifications of a Brāhmaṇa, and not a mere

---

[1] *Sacividam* is explained by Sāyaṇa as "the teacher who is the friend of the Veda because he shows his gratitude to the Veda by preventing the destruction of tradition."

ability to recite them without understanding their significance. A class of wise and learned Vedic teachers arose, who were the custodians of the real import of the sacred verses, and it was necessary to approach them and associate with them with the devout earnestness of a pupil in order to be able to grasp it. The study of such philosophical subjects as were concerned with the solution of the mystery of human life, here and hereafter, and its intimate relation with the Gods and Pitṛs (ancestors) was also considered essential and encouraged. We find some hymns in the Ṛgveda which have dealt with cosmological and philosophical questions, and a proper comprehension of these was deemed necessary as an indispensable equipment of a true Brāhmaṇa.

A perusal of the translation of the above verses would further convince the reader of the fact that the language in which the *mantras* were composed was not the ordinary spoken dialect of the people in Ṛgvedic times, for it could not be understood by them either by seeing written speech or hearing it from the mouths of the learned. In fact, the speech was archaic in character and was found "centred in the Ṛṣis" who alone could compose the *mantras* in the seven recognised metres and explain them. Those who were eager to acquire wisdom approached the Ṛṣis who taught them the significance of the *mantras* and initiated them into the mysteries of true knowledge and wisdom. The language of the *mantras* was therefore sacred, old and mystic, and not intelligible to ordinary people.

Origin of the Idea of Religion.—Death is looked upon by almost all men of all countries with the greatest amount of fear and dismay, as it cruelly removes them from their dearest and nearest, from their valued possessions and familiar environments, and from this bright and sun-lit earth to some unknown region, where they have to make their dismal journey alone and unattended, without any loving sympathy to stand them in good stead in their sorrows and tribulations. It is this fear of death which is surely to come sooner or later to every living person, either savage or civilised, rich or poor, wise or ignorant, old or young, that set men a-thinking and a-speculating from the earliest dawn of the history of human civilisation about the nature of the next world to which the dead depart, and the condition in which they exist. A belief in the continuance of individual life, even after death, seems to be ingrained in the human mind, and the idea of final extinction, like the flame of a lamp blown out, is repugnant to it. The appearance of dead persons to their near relations in dreams went a great way in confirming this belief which naturally conjured up the existence of an invisible world—the world of spirits or the dead. This belief and the belief in the existence of some superior Power or Spirit who controls our life and death, and is the bestower of our happiness or misery, were the root-causes of the birth and growth of Religion. With these fundamental beliefs for its basis, men have built up their ideas of Religion, which vary differently according to the different stages of their mental development, and invented customs, rites or ceremonies which, in their opinion, are best calculated to conduce to their happiness and well-being, not only in their present life, but in the life after death. It is not my purpose here to discuss or explain the various forms of Religion that prevail in different human communities; but I will confine myself solely to an exposition of some beliefs, customs and rites of the ancient Indo-Aryans which give us glimpses of their ideas of Religion and of Life after death.

Yama and Yamī.—Yama in the Ṛgveda appears to be the deity who presides over the invisible world of the dead—"the abode where the Fathers and Yama dwell" which is "situated in the midst of the sky (Rv x. 15, 14), in the highest heaven (Rv. x. 14, 8), in the third heaven, the inmost recess of the sky, where is *eternal light*"[1] (Rv. ix. 113, 7-9). He

[1] Macdonell's *Vedic Mythology* 77.

is described as a King (Rv. ix. 113, 8), but he lives with another King, Varuṇa, the Moral Governor of the Universe, both of whom the dead man sees on reaching heaven. (Rv. x. 14, 7). His father is Vivasvat and his mother Saraṇyu (Rv. x. 14, 5). Elsewhere he is described as the son of Gandharva and the water-nymph, *Apyā Yoṣā*, and as having a twin sister, named Yamī (Rv. x. 10). Yama chose death and abandoned his body (Rv. x. 13, 4), and "passed to the other world, finding out the path for many, to where the ancient fathers passed away"[1] (Rv. x. 14, 1-2). He is also called 'lord of settlers' (Viśpati) and 'our father' (Rv. x. 135, 1).

According to the Atharva-veda (xviii. 3, 13) he was the first of mortals to have died. The Vedic conception of Yama, therefore, is far from terrible. He was lord of death, and King of the dead, no doubt. But he had been himself a mortal, and having abandoned his body, found out the path for many. The world of the dead, though unknown, has, therefore, no horror for those who have not as yet passed on to it. The ancient fathers live there, as well as the ancestors of the dead person, all enjoying happiness, according to their pious and benevolent acts on earth.

But who are Vivasvat and Saraṇyu, and Gandharva and Apyā Yoṣā? Though there is no single hymn in the Ṛgveda, addressed to Vivasvat, his name occurs in it thirty times, and he is described as the father not only of Yama, but also of the Aśvins (Rv. x. 17, 2), and in post-Vedic literature as well as in the Ṛgveda (Vālakhilya iv. 1) itself, as the father of Manu. In the Yajurveda (*Vāj. Sam.* viii. 5) and the Brāhmaṇas, he is called *Āditya*, and in the post-Vedic literature, identified with the Sun. Gandharva in the Ṛgveda is brought into a relation with the Sun (x. 123, 6; 177, 2; i. 163, 2). He and Vivasvat therefore are identical; so are Saraṇyu and Apyā Yoṣā (water-nymph) identified with Uṣas. Yama and Yamī were the twin brother and sister born of these parents, and

---

[1] *Op. cit*, 77.

probably represented light and darkness respectively. The dialogue in Rv. x. 10 between Yama and Yamī discloses an eager desire on the part of the latter to come into incestuous connection with the former, but Yama sternly sets his face against her unholy and sinful proposal, and rebukes her roundly for it. The union was therefore never effected; but both brother and sister lived in the highest heaven in the world of the dead *(Vāj. Sam.* xii, 13). As darkness follows light, with the object of coming into contact with it, but never succeeds in doing so, so was Yamī baffled in her desire. As both Yama and Yamī lived in the highest heaven, the world of the dead was both bright and dark, the pious and virtuous at once proceeding to the bright region to revel with Yama, Varuṇa and the ancient Fathers, and the sinful proceeding to the dark region probably presided over by Yamī of sinful mind, in order to purge their sins, and suffer punishment for their misdeeds in life. Probably Yamī is identical with Nirṛti who is the personification of Sin (Rv. i. 24, 9; 38, 6; vii. 104, 9; x. 18, 10 and much dreaded by all right-minded men, as the evil deity is represented to preside over the dark abyss into which all sinful persons are cast after death to suffer punishment. But this dark region has not been the subject of any direct description in the Ṛgveda, though it is hinted at here and there. The Ṛṣis have only depicted the bright region of Yama in glowing and vivid colours, as will appear from a description of it in the Ṛgveda.

The Region of Yama or Heaven.—The following Ṛgvedic verses (ix. 113, 7-10), describe Heaven or the region where Yama presides :—

"Where light is perpetual, in the world in which the Sun is placed, in that immortal imperishable world place me, Pavamāna; flow, Indu, for Indra.

"Where Vivasvat's son is King, where the inner chamber of the Sun (is), where these great waters (are), there make me immortal; flow, Indu, for Indra.

"Where wishes and desires (are), [1] where the region of the Sun (is), where food and delight (are) found, there make me immortal; flow Indu, for Indra.

"Where there are happiness, pleasures, joy and enjoyment, where the wishes of the wisher are obtained, there make me immortal; flow, Indu, for Indra." [2]

It has been stated above that the Pitṛs or ancient Fathers dwell with Yama in his happy abode (Rv. x. 15, 14). This abode being situated in the region of the Sun (Rv. ix. 113, 9), "the Fathers are united with or guard the Sun (Rv. x. 107, 2; 154, 5), or are connected with the rays of the Sun (Rv. i. 109, 7), and Suns shine for them in heaven (Rv. i. 125, 6). They are connected with the step of Viṣṇu (Rv. x. 15, 3), and pious men are said to rejoice in the dear abode, the highest step of Viṣṇu" (Rv. i. 154, 5).[3]

There is a tree in Heaven beside which Yama drinks the Soma juice with the Gods (Rv. x. 135, 1). "Heaven is regarded as the reward of those who practise rigorous penance *(tapas)*, of heroes who risk their lives in battle (Rv. x. 154, 2-5), but, above all, of those who bestow liberal sacrificial gifts. (Rv. x. 154, 3; i. 125, 5; x. 107, 2)...In heaven the deceased enter upon a delectable life (Rv. x. 14, 8; 15, 14, etc.), in which all desires are fulfilled, and which is passed among the Gods (Rv. x. 14, 14), particularly in the presence of the two Kings, Yama and Varuṇa (Rv. x. 14, 7). There they unswervingly overcome old age (Rv. x. 27, 11). Uniting with a glorious body they are dear and welcome to the Gods. (Rv. x. 14, 8; 16, 5; 56, 1). There they see father, mother, and sons. (Av. vi. 120, 3; x 14. 8; 16, 5; 56, 1). The life is free from imperfections and bodily frailties (Rv. x. 14, 8). Sickness is left behind and limbs are not lame

1 According to Sāyaṇa, "where the desired gods and the inevitably solicited Indra, etc., exist."

2 Wilson's "Translation of the Ṛgveda." *Indu* here stands for the drops of the Soma.

3 Macdonell's *Vedic Mythology*, 73.

or crooked (Av. iii. 28, 5)...In the heaven of the Blest, the Ṛgveda further says, the sound of the flute and of songs is heard (Rv. x. 135, 7); Soma, *ghee* and honey flow for them (Rv. x. 154, 1)...It is the world of the righteous (Rv. x. 16, 4), where righteous and godly men, familiar with rites (*ṛta*), dwell in peace. There they are united with what they have sacrificed and given (*iṣṭapūrta*), especially reaping the reward of their pious gifts to priests." (Rv. x. 154, 1). [1] No account of Heaven or Yama's region would be complete without mentioning his messengers as related in the Ṛgveda. "A bird either the owl (*ulūka*) or the pigeon (*kapota*) is said to be the messenger (Rv. x. 165, 4; 123, 6) of Yama, apparently identified with Death. [2] The messenger of Yama and of Death would therefore appear to be the same. (Av. viii. 8, 11). Yama's regular messengers, however, of whom a fuller account is given (Rv. x. 14, 10-12) are two dogs. They are four-eyed, broad-nosed, brindled (*śabala*), brown (*udumbala*), sons of Saramā (*sārameya*). They are guardians that guard the path (Rv. x. 14, 11), or sit on the path. (Av. xviii. 2, 11). The dead man is exhorted to hasten straight past these two dogs and to join the fathers who rejoice with Yama (Rv. x. 14, 10); and Yama is besought to deliver him to them and to grant him welfare and freedom from disease. Delighting in lives (*asutṛp*), they watch men and wander about among the peoples as Yama's messengers. They are entreated to grant continued enjoyment of the light of the Sun. Their functions, therefore, seem to consist in tracking out among men those who are to die, and in keeping guard on the path over those who enter the realm of Yama...There does not seem to be sufficient evidence for supposing that the two dogs of Yama were regarded as keeping out the souls of the

---

[1] *Op. cit.* 74. Macdonell observes: "To the celestial life of the Blest in the Saṃhitās and Brāhmaṇas corresponds in the Upaniṣad the lower and transient bliss of the heaven of the Gods which is followed by rebirth, only those who know the truth attaining to immortality and the changeless joy of unending peace by absorption into the world soul." *Op. cit.*

[2] Yama is identified with Death (*Mṛtyu*) Rv. i. 165. 4.

wicked, though it is quite possible that they were so regarded." [1] The belief that Yama was identified with Death, and that he had foot-fetter (*padbīśa*), like Varuṇa's bond (Rv. x. 97, 16), and also these dread messengers, made him, to a certain extent, an object of fear in the Ṛgveda.

Nirṛti or Hell.—There is no definite mention of Hell (*Naraka*) in the Ṛgveda. But, as Macdonell observes, "if in the opinion of the composers of the Ṛgveda the virtuous received their reward in the future life, it is natural that they should have believed at least in some kind of abode, if not in future punishment, for the wicked, as in the case of the Avesta. As far as the Atharva-veda and the Katha Upaniṣad are concerned, the belief in hell is beyond doubt. The Atharva-veda (ii. 14, 3; v. 19, 3) speaks of the house below, the abode of female goblins and sorceresses, called ***naraka loka***, in contrast with ***svarga loka***, the heavenly world, the realm of Yama (xii. 4, 36)...It is in the Atharva-veda several times described as 'lowest darkness' (viii. 2, 24) as well as 'black darkness' (v. 30, 11) and 'blind darkness' (xviii, 3, 3). The torments of hell are also once described in the Atharva-veda (v. 19), and with greater detail in the Śatapatha Brāhmaṇa (11. 6, 1); for it is not till the period of the Brāhmaṇas that the notion of future punishment appears plainly developed. The same Brāhmaṇa further states that every one is born again after death, and is weighed in a balance, receiving reward or punishment according as his works are good or bad (11, 2, 7, 33). This idea is also Iranian." (*Ved. Myth.* 75). The Aryans of the Ṛgvedic period probably loved to contemplate on everything that was *bright*: bright day, bright sky, bright sun, bright stars, bright phenomena of Nature, bright Gods, bright fire, and bright heaven where the virtuous go after death to revel with Yama and the Pitṛs, and which is filled with "eternal light," joy and bliss. Like children, they

[1] *Op. cit.*, 77.

abhorred and dreaded darkness, and everything connected with it,—Vṛtra in the shape of darkness or black clouds, black Dāsas, black Asuras, black daws, black owls that flew in the darkness of night, wolves and thieves that prowled about at night, *râkṣasas*, *piśācas* and goblins that loved darkness and became powerful at night, and black night itself with all its unseen horrors and dangers. As worshippers and lovers of Light, they avoided as much as possible the mention of Darkness, Hell or its dark denizens. This, however, does not prove that they had no idea of darkness or hell or of the dark fate that awaited evil-doers. They knew the dreaded character of Nirṛti, the personification of Sin, which, according to Max Muller, "was conceived, it would seem, as going away from the path of right, the German Vergehen. Nirṛti was personified as a power of evil or destruction" (*Ṛgveda* vol. i). According to Sayaṇa, Nirṛti is the deity of Sin (*Pāpa-devatā*). One prayer in the Ṛgveda (i. 24, 9) says: "Keep afar from us Nirṛti, with unfriendly looks; and liberate us from whatever sin we may have committed." Another prayer says: "Let not the most powerful and indestructible Nirṛti destroy us: let her perish, with our (evil) desires." (Rv. i. 38, 6). Vasiṣṭha curses his calumniator as follows: "May *Soma* give to the serpent, or toss upon the lap of Nirṛti, those who with designing (accusations) persecute me, a speaker of sincerity, and those who by spiteful (calumnies) vilify all that is good in me. May he be deprived of bodily (existence) and of posterity; may he be cast down *below* all the three worlds..." (Rv. vii. 104, 9. 11). Another verse refers to "bottomless darkness:" "Indra and Soma, chastise the malignant (evil-doers), having plunged them in surrounding and inextricable (lit. bottomless) darkness, so that not one of them may again issue from it; so may your wrathful might be triumphant over them." (Rv. vii. 104, 3). Again, "may the cruel female fiend who, throwing off the concealment of her person, wanders about at night like an owl, fall headlong down into the unbounded cavern (endless abyss)." (Rv. vii. 104, 17). There is yet another verse which goes to show how the "deep abyss" or hell was produced: "Like women who have no brethern, going (about from their own to their paramour's house), women adverse to their lords, going astray, so the wicked, false (in thought), false (in speech), they give birth to this deep abyss of hell)." (Rv. iv. 5, 5). No further quotations are necessary to prove that the Ṛgvedic Aryans had clear ideas of hell, though they did not think it fit to give a detailed description of the tortures and torments to which the sinful were subjected there. As I have already pointed out, Nirṛti was probably the same as Yamī of sinful desire, representing darkness or hell, as Yama represented righteousness (*ṛta*) *i.e.* light or heaven. The couple Yama and Yamī, as twin brother and sister, therefore represented Heaven and Hell respectively, and were juxtaposed like Day and Night.

Cremation and Burial.—Fire was regarded by the ancient Aryans as the messenger of the Gods on earth, and carrier of the oblations that were offered to them through him. (Rv. i. 60 1; x. 12; 2 etc.) The material things that constituted *habya* could not be bodily and directly conveyed to the Gods in heaven; hence the services of a heavenly messenger and carrier like Agni were requisitioned. This analogy was also extended to human corpses, as well as to the carcasses of the animals that were sacrificed to the Gods. After a man died, it was thought necessary to send his body to heaven, and this could only be done by consigning it to Fire. After the body was consumed by Fire and reduced to ashes, the dead man could assume a new body in the world of Yama and join the Pitṛs and his ancestors. This seems to be the fundamental idea of cremation, It would be a mistake to suppose that cremation was adopted by the ancient Aryans on sanitary or other grounds. The idea was essentially and originally religious. Before Fire was discovered or brought to human use, corpses used to be cast away as a rule, or buried under ground, or exposed to be devoured by carnivorous birds and beasts. The custom of burial must, therefore, have preceded the custom of cremation; and the latter probably came into vogue after the cult of Fire-worship had been fully established. One branch, however, of the ancient Aryans. *viz.*, the ancestors of the Iranians, retained the old custom of exposing the corpse to be devoured by birds, even after they had become staunch Fire-worshippers, for they believed Fire to be too sacred to be polluted by such an unclean thing as a corpse. But the Vedic Aryans did not agree with them in this view, and, anxious as they were to see their beloved dead go to heaven and join his ancestors, they consistently thought it right to consign his dead body to Fire in order to transfer it to heaven in a subtler and more resplendant form befitting his new environments. The old custom of burial, however, still continued to exist to some extent, though the trend of public opinion seemed to be strongly in favour of cremation. Hence, in early Ṛgvedic times, both customs existed side by side, as would appear from a careful study of the *mantras* relating to funeral rites.

Burial-rites.—The following Ṛgvedic *mantras* (x. 18. 10-13), as translated by Wilson, indicate the existence of the custom of burial in Ṛgvedic times. Addressing the dead body carried to and lying in the burial ground, the priest says:—

"Go to this thy Mother-Earth, the wide-spread, delightful Earth; this virgin (Earth is) as soft as wool, to the liberal (worshipper); may she protect thee from the proximity of Nirṛti.[1]

"Earth, rise above him;[2] oppress him not; be attentive to him (and) comfortable;[3] cover him up, Earth, as a mother covers her child with the skirt of her garment.

---

[1] The meaning probably is: "you performed many sacrifices and worshipped the Gods, paying liberal fees to the priests. Hence, may Earth protect thee from the proximity of Nirṛti."

[2] *i.e*, so as to give him breathing room; whilst this verse is being recited, dust is to be scattered over the grave; see Āśvalāyana-Gṛhya-Sūtra iv. 5.

[3] *Sūpavañcanā*=deceiving well. Sāyaṇa says: "Treat him kindly for the sake of the sacrifice; " fondle him, lull him to rest The alternative explanation *Supratiṣṭhā bhava* seems te mean "be a good resting place.'

"May the earth heaped over him lie light: may thousands of particles (of dust) envelope him; may these mansions distil *ghee* for him; may they every day be an asylum to him in this world.

"I heap up the earth around thee, placing (upon thee) this clod of earth; may I not be injured: may the Pitṛs sustain this thy monument: (*sthūṇā*): may Yama make thee a dwelling here."

Sāyaṇa says that the above *mantras* were uttered at the time when, after the collection of the bones or ashes of the dead man, they were put into an urn, and buried in a grave; and in this opinion he is supported by the Āśvalāyana Gṛhya Sūtra (iv. 5). This may have been a later custom for aught we know, and may be regarded as a relic of the ancient custom of burial which was being replaced by the custom of cremation, and also as a compromise between the two customs. It will be seen later on that at the time of cremation, *mantras* were uttered with the object of sending the dead man to heaven, the dominion of Yama, situated in the highest heaven. If he had already been cremated and gone to heaven, why, very soon afterwards at the time of burying his ashes and bones, should he be asked again to "go to this thy Mother-Earth, the wide-spread delightful Earth?" Would not such a procedure be inconsistent and contradictory? The perusal of the original *mantras* thus leaves no doubt in the mind that they were in ancient times uttered at the time of burial: otherwise, they would be quite meaningless. If it be at all possible for the dead corpse to suffer any pain, it must have suffered extreme agony at the time of its cremation, and the burnt bones or ashes would suffer no further pain or agony at the time of their burial in a grave, enclosed in an urn provided with a lid, over which earth was heaped up. But the *mantras* become quite sensible when they are applied to the burial of a corpse. The dead body was still there, as would appear from a perusal of verse 9 in which the mourners have been described as taking away the bow from the dead man's hand, and it was quite natural for them not to have been able as yet to dissociate themselves from their feeling and belief that the dead man, who had been quite alive a few hours ago, could not feel any pain so soon afterwards. It was, therefore, not unnatural for them, while performing their last melancholy duty towards him, to entertain tender feelings for him, and address him as follows: "Go to this thy Mother-Earth, the widespread delightful Earth: this virgin Earth is as soft as wool." The Earth also is besought "to oppress him not" and "to be attentive to him and comfortable" and "to cover him up as a mother covers her child with the skirt of her garment." Then, again, it is prayed that the earth heaped over him may lie light. It is probable that after burial a monument or *tumulus* (sthūṇā) was raised over the grave, and the Pitṛs were besought "to sustain it." and Yama "to make thee a dwelling here." The last verse (*mantra* 14) of the above hymn is very curious. Wilson has translated it as follows. "At the decline of the day they have placed me (in the grave) like the feathers of an arrow; I have restrained my declining voice as (they check) a horse with a bridle." What is the real significance of this verse? Śayaṇa gives a different interpretation of it and the *Bṛhaddevata* still another, which do not seem to be quite relevant to the context. According to the *bṛhaddevatā*, the meaning of verse 14 is as follows: "Like a feather of an arrow, they (the Fathers, as in the previous verse) have placed me in the days which come towards or approach, (*i.e.* in future days); I have caught the words that comes towards, (*i.e.* the future word), even like a horse with a rein."[1] According to this interpretation, these are the words of the Ṛṣi of the hymn, named Saṅkusuka, which, however, are vague in meaning. What is meant by "I have caught the word that comes towards, *i.e.*, the future word," and what

[1] Pandit Bidhusekhar Sāstri's translation, quoted by Dr. S. K. Chatterjee in the *Modern Review*, March 1925.

is its relevancy to the context? In some editions of the Ṛgveda, the following commentary of Sāyana on this verse occurs, though Wilson remarks as follows: "No comment on this." Sāyaṇa says that this is a prayer addressed to Prajāpati by the Ṛṣi Sankusuka, and means: "O Prajāpati, the Gods have placed me in this adorable day (which by *upalakṣaṇā* means *samvatsara*, or the whole year) firmly in the world, as feathers are tied firmly at the base of the shaft of an arrow. So, condescend to accept my words of adoration (prayer) as a horse is caught or held by its reins." Sāyaṇa's comment appears to be more sensible than that of the *Bṛhaddevatā*.

Wilson translates *pratīcīne ahani* as 'at the decline of day,' (when the sun declines down the *western* horizon), and *pratīcīm vācam jagrava* as "I have restrained my declining voice." The soliloqy has been ascribed to the dead man interred in the grave, and I have accepted this interpretation. Even if this be not the correct meaning, there can be no question about the existence of the custom of burial in Ṛgvedic times, as is evident from a perusal of the other verses. According to Wilson's interpretation, the buried man seems to say to himself after hearing all the prayers and wishes of the mourners: "You have placed me in the grave at the decline of day, when darkness is approaching: or in a grave where day has declined, *i.e.* which is dark. And you have placed me in a slanting (*i e.* not fully stretched) posture, as feathers are tied slantingly to an arrow, and this posture is far from comfortable to me. But what do complaints now avail? My voice is dumb."

Whether this interpretation be correct or not, there can be no doubt that the foregoing *mantras* refer to the burial of a dead person, and not merely of his ashes or bones after cremation. In fact, the dead body has been distinctly referred to in the hymn, and not his ashes and bones. It is noteworthy that the dead man is not asked to go to Yama's world in the highest heaven where Yama, Varuṇa and the Pitṛs dwell in great happiness and enjoyment of bliss, nor to join his ancestors in that blessed region, but he is simply asked to go to Mother-Earth, "the wide spread and delightful Earth," and to live in the mansion created for him, which, it is hoped, would prove to be "an asylum to him in this world." The Pitṛs are simply requested "to sustain this thy monument" (*sthūṇā*), and Yama is besought "to make thee a dwelling here." There is no question here of the dead man enjoying any bliss for his good actions or suffering any pangs or punishment for his misdeeds. He is merely asked to rest there in peace probably till the end of Time, though from the supposed soliloquy of the dead man, an eternal peaceful sleep in a dark mansion was considered to be a far from ideal existence even for the dead, and rather impossible, because, forsooth, he stood badly in need of the help of the Pitṛs, and the protection of Yama from disturbance. The idea savours of the spirit that actuated the ancient Egyptians in a later age to make mummies of dead bodies, and preserve them in underground caves or vaults, with all their belongings that they made use of during their life-time. A peaceful eternal sleep in the bosom of Mother-Earth, free from the sorrows and tribulations, and the cares and anxieties of life, was this the ideal of existence for the dead in ancient times?

This ideal, if it existed, was no doubt a good one, so far as it went, but somewhat crude and primitive The soul or spirit of the dead man was believed to survive, but in a perfectly dorment and quiescent state. Did it ever become self-conscious, and realise whom did it belong to, and what it did during the life-time of its possessor? And did it feel misery and happiness, when recalling the performance of misdeeds and virtuous actions respectively in its late existence? These are questions which have not been anticipated, nor answered in the above-quoted burial-verses. Perfect peace and rest is only possible for the pure and virtuous and those who are not troubled by any desires and their non-fulfilment; but the spirit of the wicked could not but be restless, chafing at its limitations, dashing about in fruitless rage, and seeking every opportunity for giving a free vent to its evil propensities. It was believed that wicked men, after death, became ghosts, goblins and frightful demons called *rākṣasas*, etc., of which we find frequent mention in the Ṛgveda and the later Saṃhitās, and against whose malignant influence protection was sought by means of prayers, charms and incantations.

Demons and Goblins, etc.—These earth-bound or terrestrial demons and goblins are called in the Ṛgveda by the general name of *rākṣasas*. They have "the form of dogs, vultures, owls and other birds (Rv. vii. 104, 20-22). Becoming birds, they fly about at night (*Ibid*, verse 18). Assuming the form of a brother, husband, or lover, they approach women and desire to destroy their offspring (Rv. x. 162, 5). They also lie in wait for women in the shape of a dog or an ape (Av. iv. 37, 11). Thus they are dangerous during pregnancy and child-birth (Av. viii. 6)......They have mostly human form, their head, eyes, heart, and other parts being mentioned; but they have frequently some kind of monstrous deformity, being three-headed, two-mouthed, bear-necked, four-eyed, five-footed, fingerless, with feet turned backwards, or with horns on their hands." (Av. viii. 6).[1] They have been described in the Ṛgveda also as three-headed, and three-footed (Rv. x. 87, 10), as eating raw-meat, (*Ibid*. 7. 19), hindering the performance of sacrifices (*Ib*. 8), exciting men and women to vilely abuse one another (*Ib*. 13), and as eating human flesh, and the flesh of animals, and drinking the milk of cows by stealth (*Ib*. 16). They are also known by the name of *Yātudhāna*. (Rv. vii. 104, 15. 16) *Amāda* and *Kravyād*, *i.e.*, eaters of raw-meat. "In order to satisfy their greed for flesh and blood, the *Rākṣasas* attack men,

[1] *Vedic Mythology*, 70.

usually by entering them. Agni is besought not to let the Rakṣas enter into his worshippers. (Rv. viii. 49, 20)......Agni, being the dispeller of darkness as well as the officiator at the sacrifice, is naturally the God who is oftenest opposed to them, and who is frequently invoked to burn, ward off or destroy them. (Rv. x. 87, 3-6). In this capacity he (as well as some other deities) receives the epithet of *rakṣohan* 'Rakṣas-slayer'...These evil spirits injure not only spontaneously but also at the instigation of men. Thus the Ṛgveda speaks of the yoker of Rakṣas, *rakṣoyuj* (vi. 62, 9), and refers to the Rakṣas and Yātus of sorcerers (vii. 104, 23; viii. 60, 20)." [1]

There was another class of evil spirits, named *Piśācas*. The name occurs only once in the Ṛgveda (i. 133, 5) as *Piśācī*. According to the *Taittirīya Saṃhitā* (2, 4, 1, 1.), there are three hostile groups of evil spirits, *viz.* Asuras, Rākṣasas, and Piśācas who are opposed to the three classes of Gods, men and Pitṛs respectively. The Piśācas, therefore, are connected with the dead. They are described in the Atharva-veda as *Kravyād*, eaters of raw flesh or corpses (v. 29, 9). Besides these, there were a lesser group of demons called *Arātis*, according to Hillebrandt, and "a group of injurious demons, the *Druhs*, both male and female," mentioned in the Ṛgveda, about twelve times. "They are Indo-Iranian, their name occurring in the Avesta as *Druj*."[2]

These evil spirits are, as a whole, unconnected with the phenomena or forces of Nature, seeming partly at least to be derived from the spirits of dead enemies.[3] "Less personal than the demons mentioned above, and probably due to a more advanced order of thought, are the hostile powers which are concieved as a kind of impalpable substance of disease, childlessness, guilt, and so forth, which, flying about in the

---

1 *Op. cit.*

2 *Op. cit*

3 *Op. cit.* cf. Oldenberg, *Die Religion des Veda* (62-2.

air, produce infection, and to deflect which to enemies is one of the chief tasks of sorcery."[1] There is a verse addressed to Apvā in the Ṛgveda (x. 103, 12), which Wilson has translated as follows: "Bewildering the mind of our foes, Apvā, seize their limbs and depart, proceed against them, burn in their hearts with sorrow, let our enemies be covered with thick darkness."[2]

These evil spirits having been believed to have mostly originated from the wicked souls of dead persons buried in the earth, did the ancient Aryans think of restricting their number in the terrestrial region by widely introducing the custom of cremation, and conveying the dead to the dominions of Yama or Nirṛti, there to enjoy or suffer the fruits of their individual actions in life? Cremation is even now regarded by their descendants as absolutely necessary for the welfare of the souls of the dead, excepting those of infants who are sinless and pure, and of holy mendicants or *Sādhus* who are supposed to have overcome their desires and evil propensities during their life-time, and are therefore accorded a burial as perfectly harmless. But in the case of ordinary men and householders, want of cremation is looked upon with horror, as retarding the progress of their souls in the other world (*sadgati*). The cremation ceremony is also called *Aurdvadehik kriyā*, or the ceremony that releases the soul from the body *for its upward journey to heaven*. Unless this ceremony is performed, the departed soul is believed to linger among its late environments, and hover about without consolation, and in great distress as a *preta*. I will now give a brief description of the funeral rites as were performed at the time of cremation in Ṛgvedic times.

Cremation-rites.—It appears that the body of a dead person was carried by his relations and friends to the

---

[1] *Op cit.*

[2] Apvā, according to Sāyaṇa, is a goddess; according to Roth, it is a disease; and according to Mahidhara, it means "sickness or fear."

cremation ground, followed by his widow and her female relations having their husbands alive. The dead body was washed, clothed, and laid on the funeral pyre preparatory to being cremated. According to the Atharva-veda (xviii. 4, 31) the dead man was provided with ornaments and clothing for use in the next life. Even to this day, it is the custom to wrap the dead body in a new cloth, and put some gold into its mouth. Then the widow stretched herself beside the corpse, as either betokening a desire to be burnt along with her lord, without whom, she naturally thought in the highest paroxysm of her grief, it would be impossible for her to live, or as representing the relic of an ancient barbarous custom, (still existing among certain barbarous tribes), which caused the wife or wives of the departed also to be immolated with the dead husband to enable them to bear him company in the next world.[1] After this the priest or the person officiating at the funeral rites uttered the following *mantras* :

"Depart, Mṛtyu, by a different path ; by that which is thine own, and distinct from the path of the Gods : I speak to thee who hast eyes, who hast ears : do no harm to our offspring, nor to our male progeny.

"If, avoiding the path of death, you go (on the path of the Gods), assuming a longer and better life, (my friends), then may you, (O sacrificers), diligent in sacrifice,

---

[1] "The belief in some sort of survival after death seems to have arisen in very early pre-historic times. The placing of the dead bodies in a sleeping position or in the embryonic position, and the depositing in many instances of objects of food point to the notion that the dead would awaken to enjoy some kind of continued existence, or would in some way be born again. The idea of survival or rebirth or new birth is therefore very much more ancient than we used to imagine. Another idea that proves to be of great antiquity is that for the re-awakening, dead persons require not only a supply of food, but also the companionship of wives and attendants. In other words, what is known as Sati-burial has a long history."

Prof. M. A. Canney in his *Stephanos Nirmalendu Ghosh Lecture* delivered at the Calcutta University, January 1925. (Published in the *Calcutta Review*, July 1925.)

enriched with progeny and affluence, be cleansed and pure.[1]

"May those who are living remain separate from the dead: may our invocation of the gods to-day be successful: let us go forward (or with our faces to the east) to dancing and laughter, assuming a longer and better life.[2]

"I erect this circle (of stones) for the protection of the living, that none other of them may approach this limit: may they live a hundred years, occupied by many holy works, and keep death hidden by this mound.

"As days pass along in succession; as seasons are duly followed by seasons; as the successor does not abandon his predecessor, (*i.e.*, as a son does not leave his father by dying first), so, *Dhātṛ*, support the lives of these (my kinsmen).

"(Ye kinsmen of the dead man), choosing old age, attain length of life, striving one after the other, how many soever you may be: may *Tvaṣṭṛ*, the creator of the good races of men, being at one (with you), grant you, (busy) at this (sacrifice), a long life.

"Let these women who are not widows, who have good husbands, enter (anointed) with unguent and butter. Let women without tears, without sorrow and decorated with jewels, first proceed to the house.[3]

"Rise, woman, (and go) to the world of living beings: [Sāyaṇa: 'go to the home of the living, *i.e.*, thy sons,

---

[1] "*Śuddhah*, according to the comment, means pure from the decay caused by the sins accumulated in a former life; *pūtah* pure from that caused by the sins of the present life." Wilson The occasion was seized and thought fit for a brief sermon, enjoining on the necessity for holy living and holy doing.

[2] The evident meaning is "Let us not be overwhelmed with unavailing grief, but let us go on performing our worldly duties cheerfully, which will ensure us a better and longer life."

[3] The women were first asked to leave the cremation or burial ground and go home Their presence during the ghastly ceremony to be presently performed was dispensed with, to spare their womanly feelings. So was the widow asked to leave the dead body and go home.

grand sons, etc.']: come, this man near whom thou sleepest is lifeless; thou hast enjoyed this state of being the wife of thy husband, the suitor who took thee by the hand.

"Taking his bow from the hand of the dead man, for the sake of our vigour, energy and strength, (I say) thou art there; may we (who are) here, blessed with male offspring, overcome all the enemies who assail us." (Rv. x. 18, 1-9).

After these verses follow the burial verses which have already been quoted. As the custom of burial preceded that of cremation, the burial verses must be very old. They were also uttered at the time of cremation, and probably utilised afterwards for the collection of the bones or ashes and burying them under ground in an urn, with a monument raised over it. With regard to the taking of the bow from the hand of the dead person, it is surmised that he must have been a *Kṣatriya*. But as the caste-system was not fully developed in olden times when every adult male was a warrior, the surmise does not appear to be correct.

After the married women and the widow had left the place, the following verses were addressed to the dead man at the time of cremation:

"Depart, depart, by the former paths by which our forefathers have departed; there shalt thou behold the two monarchs, Yama and the divine Varuṇa, rejoicing in the *Svadhā*.

"Be united with the Pitṛs, with Yama; and with the fulfilment of thy wishes in the highest heaven, discarding iniquity, return to thine abode, and unite thyself to a luminous body." (Rv. x. 14, 7, 8). The "abode" mentioned in the last verse probably refers to the abode of Yama where he is asked to unite himself to a luminous body. But the verse also admits of a different interpretation which is as follows: "After enjoying bliss in the highest heaven with Yama and the Pitṛs, and having all your desires fulfilled there, come back again to this thy terrestrial abode (*puna rastamehi*), discarding iniquity and being united to a luminous body; in other words, incarnate yourself again as a pure and virtuous man. The verb *ehi* means 'come' as opposed to *yāhi* 'go,' and may have reference to his coming back to earth, after being reborn in a pure and luminous body. Max Müller has translated the verse in his "Essay on the Funeral Rites of Brahmans" (*Jour. of the Ger. Or. Society* for 1855 p. xiv) as follows: "Leave evil there, then return home, and take a form" etc. But Muir says: "This rendering appears to make the departed return to this world to resume his body, though in a glorious state, which does not seem to bring out a good sense." (O. S. T. v. p. 293-94). I fail to see why it does not. It is quite natural for the bereaved to desire that the departed would return home to them in a luminous and glorious body, after purging all his evils and sins in the region of Yama and enjoying heavenly pleasures there for a time. It should be borne in mind that the ancient Aryans were fond and desirous of living on earth for a hundred years or even a longer period, which was a pleasant place to live in, and where they could look upon the Sun. Compare Rv. x. 57. 4: "May thy spirit (Subandhu) come back again to perform pious acts; to exercise strength, to live; and long to see the Sun."

After addressing the above two verses (x. 14, 7-8) to the departed, the evil spirits were scared away from the cremation-ground by the following *mantra*:

"Depart from hence, begone, go far off, (evil spirits); the Pitṛs have assigned this place to him (the departed), Yama has given him a place of cremation, consecrated by days, streams and nights." (Rv. x. 14, 9). The use of the word "streams" probably means that the cremation-grounds were usually situated on the banks of flowing rivers. After this the dead man was thus addressed again:

"Pass by a secure path beyond the two spotted four-eyed dogs, the progeny of Saramā, and join the wise Pitṛs who rejoice joyfully with Yama.

"Entrust him, O King, to thy two dogs, which are thy protectors, Yama, the four-eyed guardians of the road,—(him who is) renowned by men, and grant him prosperity and health.

"The messengers of Yama, broad-nosed, and of exceeding strength, and satiating themselves with the life (of mortals), hunt mankind; may they allow us this day a prosperous existence here, that we may look upon the Sun." (Rv. x. 14, 10-12).

The last sentence of the last verse has been otherwise explained as follows: "May they now restore to us that fair life to look upon the Sun," (till speaking of the departed worshipper.)

Very probably a brief sacrifice was performed on the cremation-ground, in honour of Yama and the Pitṛs with the utterance of some *mantras*. (Rv. x. 14, 1-6, and 13-16).

It would appear that the dead body used to be wrapped up in the hide of a cow recently slain, and covered with its fat and marrow, before it was consigned to the fire, the underlying idea being that by this device, the body would not be directly attacked by the fire, but would be sufficiently heated to quicken it into life, and send it to heaven, though, as a matter of course, it was thoroughly consumed and reduced to ashes by the blazing fire. Of course, it can be safely presumed that this was done only in the case of rich persons who had performed sacrifices during their life-time, and it could not have been the practice followed in the cremation of ordinary mortals, on account of the prohibitive expense involved in the killing of a cow or bull. When cow-killing came to be forbidden in a later age, the practice probably assumed the harmless form of *Vṛṣotsarga* at the time of performing the *Śrāddha* ceremony of a distinguished man, which consists in dedicating a bull and releasing it to roam and graze freely about. These dedicated bulls are known as Brahmani bulls. When the funeral pyre was quite a-blaze, the following *mantras* were addressed to Agni:

"Agni, consume him not entirely; afflict him not; scatter not (here and there) his skin, nor his body;[1] when, *Jātavedas*, thou hast rendered him mature, then send him to the Pitṛs.

"When thou hast rendered him mature, then give him up, *Jātavedas*, to the Pitṛs; when he proceeds to that world of spirits (or, according to Sāyaṇa, when he obtains the quickening of life, wrought by Agni), then he becomes subject to the will of the Gods.

"Let the eye repair to the Sun; the breath to the wind, go thou to the heaven or *to the earth*, according to thy merit; or go to the waters if it suits thee (to be) there, or abide with thy members in the plants.[2]

"The unborn portion; burn (lit. heat or warm) that, Agni, with thy heat; let thy flame, thy splendour, consume (lit. heat) it; with those glorious members which thou hast given him, Jātavedas, bear him to the world (of the virtuous).[3]

"Dismiss again to the Pitṛs, Agni, him who, offered on thee, comes with the *svadhās*: putting on (celestial) life, let the remains (of bodily life) depart: let him, Jātavedas, be associated with a body.

"Should the black crow, the ant, the snake, the wild beast, harm (a limb) of thee, may Agni, the all-devourer, and the Soma that has pervaded the Brāhmaṇas, make it whole.

---

[1] Wilson says: "There may be here an allusion to the spiritual, or (in the language of the later psychology) subtile body, *sūkṣma śarira*; the scholiast only says 'do not reduce him to ashes.'"

[2] "The scholiast no doubt understands here the doctrine of transmigration" Wilson.

[3] *Ajo bhāga* has been translated by some European scholars as "the goat is thy portion," the idea being that a goat was sacrificed and offered to Agni. Macdonell says: "Agni is besought to preserve the corpse intact and to burn the goat (*aja*) which is his portion. A goat is also immolated with the sacrificial horse to go before, as the first portion for Pūṣan, and announce the offering to the Gods ere it reaches the highest abode." (Rv. i. 162, 2. 4; 163, 12. 13). But Sāyaṇa explains *Aja* as the *antarapuruṣa*, which has no body, no organs of sense, *i.e*, the unborn soul which cannot be *burnt* by Agni, as Wilson has wrongly translated. The word is *tapasva* which means 'heat it' or 'quicken it by heat.' 'Burn or consume' cannot be applied to it.

"Enclose the mail of Agni with the (hide of the) cow; cover it with the fat and marrow: then will not (Agni), bold, exulting in his fierce heat, proud, embrace thee round-about to consume thee (to ashes)." (Rv. x. 16, 1-7).

After the corpse was consumed, the fire was thus dismissed:

"I send the flesh-devouring Agni to a distance; let him bearing away sin repair to (the realm of) King Yama; but let this other Jātavedas who is known (by all) convey the oblation to the Gods.[1]

"The flesh-devouring deity Agni, who has entered your dwelling, I turn him out, for the worship of the Pitṛs, upon beholding this other (Agni) Jātavedas; let him celebrate the sacrifice (to the *Pitṛs*) in the most excellent assembly." (Rv. x. 16, 9. 10).

Lastly, the funeral fire was extinguished by pouring water on it, when the following two *mantras* were uttered:

"Cool again, Agni, the spot which thou hast burned, there let the water-lily grow, and the ripe *Dūrvā* with its many stalks.

"(Oh Earth), cool and filled with cool (herbs), gladsome and filled with gladsome (trees), be thronged with female frogs and give joy to this Agni" (Rv. x. 16, 13. 14).

From the above description it appears that bodies were cremated on low hollow grounds where water would collect in the rainy season and water-lilies grow, and in other seasons, the Dūrvā grass would spread with its green stalks.

From all the funeral verses quoted above, we can safely deduce the following inferences: (1) that the custom of burial was older than the custom of cremation and continued to exist for sometime after the latter had been introduced;

[1] The "flesh-eating" or funeral Fire was quite distinct from the Fire that used to be lighted for the worship of the Gods. The former was evidently looked upon with disfavour.

(2) that a sort of compromise was afterwards effected between the two customs by collecting the bones and ashes of the dead person from the cremation-ground, and then ceremoniously burying them in a grave in a closed urn, and a monument or *tumulus* was raised over it; (3) that the feasibility of translating the dead person from this earth to heaven or the region of Yama and the Pitṛs was suggested by the offering of oblations, intended for the Gods and Pitṛs, on the sacrificial Fire which was supposed to carry them directly to the deities and ancient Fathers respectively; (4) that the conception of Yama was not that of a terrible God in Ṛgvedic times; (5) that his region was bright, resplendant and full of bliss, and those who departed there assumed luminous bodies and lived in great happiness; (6) that Yamī, (twin sister of Yama), having been depicted as entertaining sinful desires, represented darkness, as Yama represented light, because he was just, righteous and virtuous; (7) that as Yama and Yamī lived in the highest region of the sky, it must have been divided into two portions, one bright and the other dark, the latter probably presided over by *Yamī* or *Nirṛti*, as the former was presided by Yama and Varuṇa; (8) that though there is no direct reference to Hell in the Ṛgveda, a dark region like that of Yamī was conceived as a place of torment, and this was probably the origin of the idea of Hell, which was fully developed in the later Vedic literature; (9) that the idea of enjoying in heaven the fruits of one's virtuous conduct during one's life-time on earth is prominent in the Ṛgveda; (10) that the wicked persons after death became evil spirits who suffered torments in various ways; (11) that the custom of burning widows on the funeral pyres of their husbands did not exist in Ṛgvedic times, though it may have existed in earlier barbarous ages, as is indicated by the custom of the widow lying prostrate beside her dead husband, till she was raised by the hand by a near relation, and asked to go home to live with her children and grand-children; (12) that the dead body, before being consigned to the funeral pyre, was

wrapped up in a cowhide, and covered with fat and marrow (probably of a slain cow) to prevent Agni from consuming it quickly and scattering its skin and bones, as it was deemed necessary to send the whole body to heaven through the help of fire; (probably it may also have been a device to keep the ghastly scene of the burning corpse out of view of those who attended the funeral); (13) that the corpse was supposed to possess an unborn portion, probably the soul, which was not liable to be consumed by fire, but which required to be heated and quickened into life to enable it to proceed to heaven, though, according to the Atharva-veda (ix. 5, 1), before it could complete its course from earth to the third heaven, it had to traverse a vast gulf of darkness; (Muir. O. S. T. v. 303); (14) that there were two four-eyed dogs of Yama in heaven to keep watch at the gate, and to track new victims of Death on earth, showing that the wild dog had been domesticated and employed to keep watch and help in the chase, before the conception of Yama's region with dogs as his gate-keepers was formed; and lastly, (15) that the theory of transmigration and of re-birth or re-incarnation, as subsequently developed in the later Vedic litarature and the Purāṇas, was adumbrated in the Ṛgveda, about which I will now write.

Transmigration, Karma and Rebirth or Incarnation.— It is generally assumed that there are no ideas of transmigration, *karma* and rebirth in the Ṛgveda. But such an assumption is belied by the existence of many suggestions and even positive proofs on the points in the sacred Scripture. For example, the idea of death and rebirth of an individual in the next world, and even in this, is common, and was probably derived from the sight of the daily phenomenon of the Sun, the bright luminary of the sky, being born in the morning, growing powerful and resplendent in the noon, losing power in the afternoon, and gradually decaying till he drops down dead in the darkness of the night, only to be re-born with a fresh lease of life the very next morning. The birth, waxing, waning and death of the Moon, and his re-birth also gave the Vedic bards an idea of birth, death and re-incarnation of the human soul. Rv. x. 85, 18 says; "These two (the Sun and Moon) wandering in thought one after the other, youthful, sportive, approach the sacrifice; one (of them) looks over all worlds, the other regulating the seasons *is born repeatedly*." The next verse also is significant: "New every day (the Moon, some commentators say, the Sun) is born; the manifester of days, he goes in front of the dawns; he destributes their portion to the Gods as he goes; the Moon protracts a long existence." (Wilson). The following two verses from the Ṛgveda (x. 72, 8. 9) will more clearly explain our meaning: "8. Of the eight sons of Aditi who were born from her body, she approached the Gods with seven, and cast out *Mārtāṇḍa* (the eighth). 9. With seven sons Aditi approached the former generation (of Gods): she again produced Mārtāṇḍa for birth as well as for death." The last verse does not appear to have been correctly translated by Dr. Muir from whose work (O. S. T. vol. v, p. 49) the above translation is taken. *Pūrvam yugam* in the verse, does not mean "the former generation of Gods," but simply "in former age or times." The last sentence, when correctly translated, would read as follows: "And (she) produced Mārtāṇḍa for repeated birth and death" (*prajāyai mṛtyave tvat punaḥ mārtāṇḍam ābharat*). Verse 8 clearly says that eight sons were born from Aditi's body, of whom seven were taken to the Gods and became Devas or *Devāḥ Ādityāḥ*; but she cast out the eighth child, Martaṇḍa, because he could not become immortal or be free from death like the other seven, and was subject to birth and death, and that and that again, *i.e.*, repeated birth and death. And this is the characteristic of the Sun (Martaṇḍa) which the ancient Ṛṣis observed, because he is born every morning and dies, or almost becomes dead, in the evening, and is re-born the very next morning. So the idea of death and re-birth was not foreign to the old bards, and was naturally extended to men who were also mortals, and died to be born again. The same idea is probably expressed in Rv. i. 164, 31: "I have beheld the unwearied protector of the Universe, the Sun, *travelling upwards and downwards by various paths*; invested with aggregative and diffusive radiance, he revolves in the midst of the regions." (Wilson). The idea is probably clearer in Rv. i. 164, 32: "He (man), whilst yet enveloped in his mother's womb, is subject to many births, and has entered upon evil" (Wilson). The soul was regarded as immortal, and the body or bodies in which it was enveloped as mortal or perishable. There is a significant verse (Rv. i. 164, 38) which shows that the Vedic Aryans clearly conceived that the immortal soul, in conjunction with the mortal body, went to the higher or lower spheres: "The immortal, cognate with the mortal, affected by (desire of) enjoyment, goes to the lower or the upper sphere: but (men beholding them) associated, going everywhere (in this world together), going everywhere (in other worlds together), have comprehended the one, but have not comprehended the other." In other words, they have not distinguished between the body and the soul. According to the Scholiast, they have not made any distinction between the three kinds of bodies with which the soul is invested, the gross body, the subtile body, and the union of the two. (Wilson's *Ṛgveda*, foot-note). What is important for us to note in this verse is the assertion that the soul in conjunction with the body, and affected by desire (the germ of *karma*), goes up to heaven, and comes down to the earth below, again and again.

That a dead person assumed a new resplendent body in the region of Yama in order to live and revel with him and the blessed fathers has already been referred to. (Rv. x. 14, 8). I have also pointed out that the last sentence of the verse just quoted admits of an interpretation which suggests re-incarnation or rebirth on the earth below, after a sufficiently long residence in Yama's region. (Vide *ante* pp. 415-416). Verse 12 also would seem to suggest a similar idea when the two sons of Saramā are prayed "to restore to us that fair life (of the dead) to look upon the Sun", *i.e.*, to enable it to re-incarnate on earth in a new-body. If the soul of the departed person could create a new body for itself in heaven consistently with its meritorious actions, it was natural to believe that it could also create a new body for itself on the earth below at the end of the period of its enjoyment of heavenly bliss according to its capacity. This idea seems to have been fully developed in the later Brāhmaṇa period and that of the Upaniṣads. "To the celestial life of the Blest in the Saṃhitās and Brāhmaṇas corresponds in the Upaniṣads the lower and transient bliss of the heaven of the Gods which is followed by re-birth, only those who know the truth attaining to immortality and the changeless joy of unending peace by absorption into the world-soul......One who reads the Veda in a particular way is said to be freed from dying again and to attain identity of nature (*sātmatā*) with Brahma (*Sat. Brāh.* 10, 5, 6, 9). As a reward for knowing a certain mystery a man is born again, in this world. (*Op. cit.* 1, 5, 3, 14). Thus we have in the *Śatapatha Brāhmaṇa* the beginnings of the doctrine of retribution and transmigration. [Our readers, however, will find that the germs of the doctrine are traceable in the Ṛgveda itself]. That doctrine (as well as the doctrine of hell) is not only to be found in the earliest Sūtras,[1] but appears fully developed in the later Brāhmaṇa period, that is to say, in the oldest Upaniṣads, the Chāndogya, the Bṛhadāraṇyaka, and especially the Kaṭha Upaniṣad. In the last named Upaniṣad, the story is related of Naciketas, who pays a visit to the realm of Death and is told by the latter, that those who have not sufficient merit for heaven and immortality, fall again and again into the power of death and enter upon the cycle of existence (*saṃsāra*), being born again and again with a body or as a stationary object. He who controls himself reaches Viṣṇu's highest place."[2]

---

1 Hopkins, *Religions of India*, 204.

2 Macdonell, *Vedic Mythology*, 74.

The following verse of the Ṛgveda gives us conceptions which contain the germs of the theories of metempsychosis, re-birth, and *Karma* :

"Let the eye (of the dead man) repair to the sun ; the breath to the wind : go thou to the heaven, or *to the earth according to thy merit*, or go to the waters if it suits thee (to be) there, or abide with thy members in the plants." (Rv. x. 16, 3).

In this verse we find that not only do the dismembered subtle parts of the dead man go to different regions, but he with his whole body either goes to heaven or to earth or to the waters according to his merit (*dharmaṇā*), or according to what will conduce to his welfare (*apovā gaccha yadi tatra te hitam*), or he abides in the plants. The dead man goes to heaven to enjoy bliss for his meritorious acts, or he returns to the earth as a mortal reborn ; or he goes to the waters as an acquatic animal, or becomes a plant, if that suits him. Do not these conceptions give us clear ideas of the doctrines of transmigration, *Karma*, and rebirth ?

Subandhu was a Ṛṣi who, according to Sāyaṇa, was put to death by certain *Māgāvins* by the performance of magical rites. His three surviving brothers who were also Ṛṣis composed hymns to resusciatate him into life and thus invoked his spirit :

"May (thy) spirit (Subandhu) come back again to perform pious acts ; to exercise strength ; to live ; and long to see the Sun.

"May our progenitors, may the host of the Gods, restore (thy) spirit : may we obtain (for thee) the aggregate of the functions of life." (Rv. x. 57, 4. 5).

As Subandhu did not die a natural death, but was believed to have been suddenly killed by magic, his brothers thought that his spirit could be called back to the dead body by *mantras*, and composed four hymns containing many pathetic and touching prayers for restoring him to life. His spirit or soul was sought to be called back from heaven, the region of Yama, from the earth, from the four regions of space, from the watery ocean, from the advancing rays of light, from the plants, from the Sun and the Dawn, from the great mountains, and from the remotest regions whither it may have gone or wandered away from the body. The invocation is concluded by the following verse: "Although thy spirit have gone far away to what has been, or to what is to be, we bring back that (spirit) of thine to dwell here, to live (long)." (Rv. x. 58, 12).

The following prayers also are significant: "Asunīti,[1] give us back the (departed) spirit: extend our life that we may live (long): establish us that we may (long) behold the Sun: do thou cherish the body with the *ghi* (that we have offered).

"May earth restore the (departed) soul to us: may the divine heaven, may the firmament (restore it): may *Soma* restore the body to us: may Pūṣan restore to us speech, which is prosperity." (Rv. x. 59, 5. 7).

It appears from the perusal of the next hymn that Agni restored Subandhu to life; for Agni says: "I bring the spirit of Subandhu from Yama, son of Vivasvat, for life, not for death, but for security." (Rv. x. 60, 10).

There is a verse addressed by Ṛṣi Bṛhaduktha to his deceased son Vājin (Rv. x. 56, 1), and its "purport is to enjoin the reunion of the vital with the external elements, vital warmth with fire, vital breath with air, the soul animating the body with that animatig the Sun. Sāyaṇa cites a passage of Śruti (Rv. i. 115, 1) declaring the Sun to be the soul of the animate und inanimate world; and another declaring the Sun to be the supreme birth-place of the Gods. His explanation 'on the entrance of the body' into the Sun, may imply the Vedanta notion of

[1] A goddess: literally "conductress of breath or souls;" *i.e.*, who prolongs life.

bodily existence after death by means of the Sūkṣmaśarīra (the subtile body)." (Wilson). The translation of the verse is as follows:

"This (light) is one (portion) of thee, and this other is one (portion); with thy third light enter into (outer radiance); on the entrance of the body into (the Sun), the supreme birth-place of the Gods, become lovely and beloved."

The third verse refers to the reward that is brought by good acts, and to heaven that is attained in consequence of them. "Thou art, Vājin, strong through food; thou art well-beloved: urged thereto, follow (the object of thy) praise; urged thereto, proceed to heaven: urged thereto, pursue the duties that are the most important and sure of reward: urged thereto, follow the Gods: urged thereto, follow (the light), descending (from heaven)."

As regards suffering in hell for evil-doing, I have already discussed the matter when writing about Nirṛti (see *ante*, p. 402). As the performance of sacrifices and pious acts had for its reward a happy existence in bright heaven, so evil-doing led the doer to suffering in dark hell, "the bottomless pit." (vii. 104, 17). It has been distinctly stated in the Ṛgveda (iv. 5, 5) that unmarried brotherless girls who go astray, married women who become unchaste and are inimical to their husbands, all wicked and sinful men, and all men who are false in thought and false in speech, "give birth to this deep abyss of hell" (*idam padam ajantā gabhīram*). In other words, but for sinful acts, evil doing, evil thinking, and false speech there would be no hell. But as these are rampant in the world, hell is as real for the sinful and wicked as heaven for the pious and pure. "Nothing, however, is said as to the eternity of reward or punishments," according to Macdonell. (*V. M.*, 169).

The following passages will show how the performance of sacrifice led the sacrificers to heaven, and non-performance of it led men to the lower regions:

"They go separately (to the world of the Gods); first those, who offer oblations to the Gods, have attained reputation difficult to surpass: those, who have not been able to ascend the ship of sacrifice, have gone down (in the world), wretches (plunged) in debt.

"Thus may those others, the ignorant, go downwards, where restive horses are yoked; otherwise (is it with those) who before (death) are near unto liberality, among whom precious gifts (to the Gods) are numerous." (Rv. x. 44, 6-7).

There is also a prayer for the protection "of the luminous paths (of the Gods), constructed by sacred acts." (Rv. x. 53, 6).

I need not multiply further evidences to prove that the ideas of transmigration, re-birth and *Karma* were well adumbrated in the Ṛgveda. The sacred Scripture was regarded even in those days as authoritative, and as a repository of all true knowledge, and any deviation from it was regarded in later times as sacrilege, and an innovation that could have no religious or spiritual sanction, and was therefore not worth listening to. The Brâhmaṇas and the Upaniṣads would possess no Scriptural value, if they dealt with doctrines which had not been adumbrated or sanctioned in the Ṛgveda.

CHAPTER XI.

A FURTHER ACCOUNT OF SOME MANNERS, CUSTOMS AND BELIEFS OF THE ṚGVEDIC ARYANS.

The status of widows.—I have already said that a widow, if she had no son, could succeed to her husband's property, as a matter of right. There is no reference to the remarriage of widows in the Ṛgveda; but she could live with her husband's brother for begetting a son, if she chose. (Rv. x. 40, 2). There is, however, no reference in the Ṛgveda to this union being performed with any particular rites. The son, born of such union, was of course regarded as the legitimate son of the dead husband.

The Manu-Saṃhitā says that the laws of marriage have no reference to the remarriage of widows and that King Vena in ancient times caused widows to be forcibly remarried, a procedure which was strongly resented by the twice-born castes. (Manu. ix. 65, 66). He, however, makes an exception in the case of a girl whose fiancé dies soon after she has been betrothed or engaged, (*vagdattā*), and lays down the rule, that in such an event the younger brother (*devara*) of the dead fiancé can take her for his wife, after going through the proper wedding rites. Manu enjoins on every father not to give away his daughter in marriage to any body else, after she has been once given away by the performance of marriage rites to another, as no gift of the same thing can be made twice over. (ix. 69, 71).

From a careful study of the Ṛgveda, it appears to me that the custom of widow-remarriage, in the true sense of the word, did not exist in Ṛgvedic times, but the widow could live with her husband's younger brother to beget a son for her husband, if she chose. It was not the custom for the widow to live with any other man for the purpose than her husband's younger brother who was called *devṛ* or *devara*. The usual word in the Ṛgveda is *devṛ* (x. 40, 2; 85, 44. 46), but in later Sanskrit literature, it is *de-vara*. The word *vara* in the Ṛgveda frequently occurs in the sense of a 'wooer' (Rv. i. 83, 2; v. 60, 4; ix. 101, 14; x. 85, 8. 9) or 'the prospective husband.' Does the word *de-vara* denote the sense of second (*dvi*) *vara* or wooer or husband? It is a question for philologists to solve. Anyhow, it is still the custom with a Hindu bridegroom (*vara*) in Bengal to go to wed a girl, accompanied by his younger brother who, of course, remains still unmarried, and is called *nit-vara* (probably a corruption of the word *nitya-vara*) and in some places *mit-vara* which may be a corruption of the word *mitra-vara* *i.e.* the bridegroom's "best man." Among certain lower classes of Hindus in Orissa, the father is unwilling to give his daughter in marriage to a bridegroom who has got no younger brothers, apprehending perpetual widowhood for her in the event of her husband's death. But if she has a *devara*, she can easily live with him as his wife, when her husband dies. Some low-class Hindus of the United Provinces and Bihar also allow the widow to live with her husband's brother as his wife. Probably these customs are the survivals of the ancient Ṛgvedic custom of the widow living with her husband's brother for begetting a son.

Though the custom of widow-remarriage may not have existed in Ṛgvedic times, there is a reference to it in the Atharva-veda (ix. 5, 27. 28): "When a woman has had one husband before and gets another, if they present the *pancaudana* offering, they shall not be separated (after death). A second husband dwells in the same world with his re-wedded wife, if he offers the *aja pancaudana*" (Muir O. S. T. V. 306).

King Vena, referred to by Manu as having forced all widows to marry, is mentioned in the Ṛgveda (x. 93, 14), though he is described there as a generous patron, and not as a social iconoclast. The name of Pṛthī also is mentioned in the Ṛgveda (i. 112, 15), with his epithet *Vainya* (Rv. viii. 9, 10), or descendant of Vena Pṛthī or Pṛthu is "the name of a semi-mythical personage who is mentioned in the Ṛgveda and later as a Ṛṣi, and more especially as the inventor of agriculture, and the lord of both worlds, of men and animals. He bears in several passages the epithet Vainya, 'descendant of Vena,' and must be regarded as a culture-hero rather than as a real man. According to other accounts, he was the first of consecrated Kings."[1] If Vena was the ancestor of Pṛthu, he must have belonged to the very earliest time, when, it is possible, widows took, or were encouraged to take husbands in remarriage. But in later Ṛgvedic times, the custom did not exist, except in a very modified form as mentioned above. In later times, however, the custom appears to have been revived, as can be gathered from the Atharva-veda. But later on, it was not at all encouraged, as we learn from Manu. Parāśara, however, still later on, sanctioned the custom in a modified form. It would thus appear that widow-remarriage never came into vogue as a national custom among the higher classes of the Aryans, though it was and is still tolerated among the lower classes. We can surmise the reasons why the custom did not come into vogue in Ṛgvedic times. Girls were usually married when they became youthful; hence very probably the number of girl-widows was extremely small. Those who became widows, if youthful, could live with their husband's younger brothers for producing progeny. As the custom was sanctioned, no scandal was attached to it, and hence there was no need for re-marrying widows. As widows inherited their husband's properties, a remarriage or union within the same family was probably also regarded as prudent from a worldly point of view. The widow also was

---

[1] *Vedic Index* ii. 16.

probably unwilling to sever herself from her old associations and environments, and pass on to a family where she would be like a stranger and not quite at home. Hence the custom of the young widow allying herself with the younger brother of her husband for the sake of progeny answered all the purposes for which re-marriage was necessary. As regards widows possessing sons and daughters, they had no hankering after remarriage, and passed their time in bringing them up and settling them in life. These were probably some of the reasons why the re-marriage of widows did not come into vogue in Ṛgvedic times.

But the marriage of infant-girls came into vogue from the end of the Sūtra period. There is a discussion in some Sūtras [vide *Gobhila-Gṛhya Sūtra* (3, 4, 6): *nagnikā tu śreṣṭhā*] as to the proper marriageable age of girls, and Gobhila is of opinion that infant-girls only should be married. Gobhila's son also justifies his father's preference for a *nagnikā*. Gautama in his Dharma Sūtras is also of the same opinion. It is curious that Gobhila, Gautama and Uśaṣti in the Chāndogya-Upaniṣad all belong to the Sama-veda school of teachers. All the Smṛtis from Manu downwards enjoin the necessity of marrying girls before puberty. Parāśara who is regarded as an authority for the Kali Yuga also supports the marriage of infant-girls. As the marrige of infant-girls gradually came into vogue, the number of girl-widows also increased, and instances of such widows going astray must have been common, which probably roused Parāśara to lay down a rule that such girl-widows should be re-married, especially when the custom of producing progeny by childless widows with the help of their *devaras* had fallen into disuse. In the circumstances of Aryan society in the days of Parāśara, he was undoubtedly justified in enjoining re-marriage of girl-widows, though conservative leaders did not in their blindness to the social evils brought on by enforced widowhood accept the wholesome safe-guard prescribed by him. Modern tendency is to enhance the marriageable age of girls, but it should be sufficiently enhanced to an age when girls can think for themselves and are able to bear children soon after marriage. If widow-remarriage be looked upon with disfavour by the leaders of the present-day Hindu society, it is very likely that young women also will share the feelings of their elders, when they are widowed after they have become mothers, and are burdened with the care of bringing up their children. Such young widows will not ordinarily think of re-marriage, nor will be preferred by suitors on account of their encumbrances. They will reconcile themselves to their lot and will generally be unwilling to change their old associations and environments, or to leave their darling children in the care of others for doubtful happiness in the company of strangers. But in the case of childless young widows, the rule of Parāśara should be followed, if such widows are willing to remarry. A married life is far more respectable, moral and socially wholesome than a life of sin, intrigue, incest and immorality, which not only sends the soul to eternal perdition but eats into the very vitality of domestic and social purity. A social canker can never make a nation healthy, growing and vigorous.

Liberty of women.—Though women enjoyed greater freedom in Ṛgvedic times than they do now, there seems to have been a wholesome restraint upon their movements. The apartments in which they ordinarily lived were secluded, ensuring privacy, and when they went out on an errand, or or some friendly call, they did so probably covered with a cloak (viii. 87, 7; 26, 13), and accompanied by chaperons or escorts. They sometimes attended *Sabhās*, probably in company with their husbands or other elderly relations, and also took part in sacrifices with their husbands. Frequently they climbed hills with other women to pluck flowers, and occasionally went to *Samanas* or fairs for fun. It was, however, regarded as scandalous for a woman to pass the night in a stranger's or another man's house (Rv. i. 123, 8), and adultery was regarded as "a serious offence against the husband of the woman affected." An adulterer could be slain with impunity if taken in the act, and traces of this rule can be found in the later legal literature of the land. (*Vedic Index* ii. 396). Love was as much jealous in ancient days as it is in modern times, and suspicion of the fidelity of the wife often led to family dissension and unhappiness, and sometimes to separation also, until the innocence of the wife was proved, when a reconciliation was effected through the medium of mutual friends (Rv. x. 68, 2). There is a curious and somewhat unintelligible hymn in the Ṛgveda (x. 109) which refers to the sin of Bṛhaspati, which resulted in his wife, Juhu, losing the affections of her husband who deserted her. Bṛhaspati led the life of a *Brahmacārin*, and his sin having been expiated, his wife was restored to him by the Gods and the seven Ṛṣis who spoke about her purity. This legend gives us a hint as to how reconciliation between separated husbands and wives used to be effected.

Criminal offences and punishments.—Thieves and robbers were common in Ṛgvedic times. A thief was called a *Taskara* or *Stena*, who generally took advantage of the darkness of night to commit his crime, unseen. (Rv. i. 191, 5). He also stole cattle (Rv. vi. 28, 3) and burgled into houses, though he was not always successful in his operations on account of the presence of watch-dogs. (Rv. vii. 53, 3). There were also highwaymen who haunted the woods and robbed unfortunate travellers who happened to go through them, by tying them with ropes. (Rv. x 4, 6). There was another class of thieves, called *Tāyus*, who though not as daring as *Taskaras*, yet stole cows, under cover of darkness in night, and also clothes. (Rv. iv. 38, 5). They were not professional thieves, but appear to have been driven to the crime through indebtedness (Rv vi. 12, 5). When robbers attacked in a body and drove away cattle, they were pursued by the villagers, and a free fight took place between the parties. The punishment of thieves, when caught, "appears primarily to have been left to the action of the robbed. The practice of binding them in stocks seems clearly referred to." (cf. Rv. i. 24, 13. 15; vii. 86, 5).[1] When hauled up before the King, they probably sometimes had their backs scorched (Rv. v. 79, 9), with a view to mark them as thieves. It also appears that they were sometimes thrown or rolled down from a high precipice according to the gravity of their offence, which either killed them outright or crippled them for life. (Rv. i. 129, 6). But capital punishment was usually carried out by decapitation. Prof. Macdonell and Keith are of opinion that in later times and probably earlier also as in other countries, a more severe penalty for theft could be exacted, and death inflicted by the King. (*Gautama-Dharma Sūtra* xii. 43-45; *Āpast. Dharma Sūtra*, i. 9, 25, 4. 5). The stolen property was returned to the person robbed, if it could be recovered. In later times, the King had to compensate for the loss, if the property could not be recovered. (*Agni Purāṇa* ch. ccxxiii), which was a fine conception of the duties and obligations of the King as the protector of the people.

In the primitive state of Aryan society, punishment for a crime ordinarily rested with the person or persons injured, who took revenge for the injury done as best they could. If a man was killed by another, the relations of the murdered man pursued the murderer who, if caught, was killed outright by way of revenge. We may suppose that sometimes the relations of the murderer mustered strong to protect him, and a free fight ensued between the two parties resulting probably in further bloodshed and loss of life. Sometimes a compromise was effected between the parties, by the murderer and his friends paying to the relations of the murdered man heavy compensation in the shape of a certain number of cows and bulls, probably on the intervention of the King. This was known as *Vaira*[2] and *Vaira-deya*[3]

---

[1] *Vedic Index*, i. 304.

[2] *Pañca. Brah.* xvi. 1, 12; *Tait. Sam.* i. 5, 2, 1; *Kāthaka Sam.* ix. 2.

[3] Rv. v. 61, 8, on the exact sense of which, cf. Max Müller S. B. E. 32, 361.

which "seem to have in the later Saṃhitās and the Brāhmaṇas the definite and technical sense of 'wergeld,' the money to be paid for killing a man as compensation to his relatives. This view is borne out by the Sūtras of Āpastamba and Baudhāyana. Both prescribe the scale of 1000 cows for a Kṣatriya, 100 for a Vaiśya, 10 for a Sūdra, and a bull over and above in each case." Of course, the crime for slaying a Brāhmaṇa was considered too heinous for a wergeld. (*Āpast.* i. 9, 24, 7 *et seq. Baudhā*, i. 10, 18, 18). "The Ṛgveda (ii. 32, 4) preserves the important notice that a man's wergeld was a hundred (cows), for it contains the epithet *śata-dāya*, 'one whose wergeld is a hundred.'"[1] This goes to show that the criminal authority of the King was very weak in those days. The acceptance of compensation for manslaughter also points to the fact that the sphere of private revenge was being gradually diminished by public opinion and the royal authority.[2]

The father, having complete power over the life and limbs of his son, could part with the latter's life or liberty for an adequate compensation, as in the case of *Śunahśepa*, or punish him by mutilating a limb, as in the case of Ṛjrāśva who was blinded by his father for slaying one hundred rams for a she-wolf. (Rv. i. 116, 17; 117, 16. 17). There was no law nor authority to restrain him from doing these cruel acts. There is a curious verse (Rv. v. 34, 4) which says that even the offer of an oblation made to Indra by a patricide, matricide or fratricide is acceptable to the God, who condones the most sinful acts. This goes to show that there was no machinery of the law which could bring the perpetrator of such heinous crimes to justice. He was suffered to live, probably because there was none to take revenge upon him for these misdeeds, and it was not the business of the State or the King to punish him for offences which in modern times

---

[1] *Vedic Index*, ii. 331.

[2] *Op. cit.*, ii. 332.

would justly be looked upon as offences against the State. Very likely, the King did not move in these matters on his own initiative, unless he was specially approached by some one for justice. Professors Macdonell ane Keith observe: " The crimes recognized in Vedic literature vary greatly in importance, while there is no distinction adopted in principle between real crimes and what now are regarded as fanciful bodily defects, or infringements of merely conventional practices. The crimes enumerated include the slaying of an embryo (*bhruṇa*), the slaying of a man (*vīra*), and the slaying of a Brahmin, a much more serious crime. Treachery is mentioned in the *Pañcaviṃśa Brāhmaṇa* as being punishable by death, as it was punished later. But there is no trace of an organized criminal justice vested either in the King or in the people...In the Sūtras, on the other hand, the King's peace is recognized as infringed by crimes, a penalty being paid to him, or, according to the Brahminical text-books, to the Brahmins. It may therefore reasonably be conjectured that the royal power of jurisdiction steadily increased; the references in the Śatapatha Brāhmaṇa to the King as wielding punishment (*daṇḍa*) confirm this suposition. Whether, as the analogy of other systems suggests, the King was assisted in the judicial duties, as he undoubtedly was later, by assessors, presumably of the Brahmin caste, cannot be made out clearly."[1]

Civil Law.—Civil disputes were probably decided in early times by private arbitration and later on by the King as the Chief Civil Judge, in conjunction with the elders of the tribe. The idea of private arbitration is conveyed by the word *madhyamā-śī*, 'lying in the midst,' which occurs in the Ṛgveda (x. 97, 12).[2] In the later Vedic literature we come across the words *praśnin*, *abhi-praśnin* and *praśnavivāka*,[3] which were probably equivalent to the plaintiff, the defendant,

[1] *Vedic Index*, i. 391-392.

[2] *Vedic Index*, i. 394.

[3] *Vaj. Sam.*, xxx. 10; *Tait Brah.*, iii. 4, 6, 1.

and the arbitrator or judge. Disputes regarding land, inheritance, transfer of chattels, sale or barter, debt, and other questions of a civil nature were decided by the judge or arbitrator on the basis of evidence and according to custom. In the absence of direct evidence, ordeals were sometimes resorted to for the decision of a case, but ordeals were seldom employed for deciding a civil dispute, though we come across one instance in which the dispute between Vatsa and his rival as to the true Brahmanical descent of the former was settled by his walking unharmed through the flame of a fire. (*Pānc. Brāh.* xiv. 6, 6).[1] In criminal cases, however, the procedure was frequently adopted. In the Chāndogya Upaniṣad (vi. 16) the ordeal of the red-hot axe is mentioned as applied in an accusation of theft.[2] Branding a thief with red-hot iron as punishment has already been referred to. For non-payment of a debt, a debtor could be enslaved (Rv. x. 34), and even bound by the creditor to a post, presumably as a means to put pressure on him or his friends to pay up the debt. (Rv. x. 34, 4). Indebtedness was dreaded as a great evil by the Ṛgvedic Aryans, and frequent prayers were offered to the gods to keep them free from debts.

Magical Rites and Incantations.—There seems to have been a general belief in the efficacy of magical rites and incantations among the Ṛgvedic Aryans. Diseases were sought to be warded off or cured and impending misfortunes averted by means of incantations. The malignant influences of *rakṣas*, goblins and evil spirits (Rv. x. 85) and even the bites of poisonous snakes and insects (Rv. i. 191) were also sought to be neutralized by this means There are certain hymns in the Ṛgveda on these subjects, a translation of some of which is given below :

"1. I banish disease (phthisis) from thine eyes, from thy nose, from thy ears, from thy chin, from thy head, from thy brain, thy tongue. 2. I banish disease from thy neck,

[1] *Vedic Index*, i. 394.

[2] *Op. cit.*, i. 392.

from thy sinews, from thy bones, from thy joints, from thy upper arms, from thy soulders, and from thy forearms. 3. I banish disease from thy entrails, from thy anus, from thine abdomen and from thy heart, from thy kidneys, from thy liver, from thy (other) viscera. 4. I banish disease from thy thighs, from thy knees, from thy heels, from thy toes, from thy loins, from thy buttocks, from thy private parts. 5. I banish disease from thy urethra, from thy bladder, from thy hair, from thy nails, from thy whole person. 6. I banish disease from each limb, from each hair, from each joint where it is generated, from thy whole person." (Rv. x. 163).

Not only were incantations pronounced but rites also were performed to eradicate the disease, as are still done by orthodox Hindus, according to Tāntric directions. We, therefore, find germs of Tāntric worship in the Ṛgveda, and it is a mistake to suppose that the Tantras were of comparatively modern development. Read the following translation of Rv. x. 161 :

" 1. By means of the oblation I set thee free to live safe from undeveloped consumption and from royal consumption; and if the seizer have already seized him, then do you, Indra and Agni, set him free. 2. If he be of wasted life, or already dead, or be come to the verge of death, I bring him back from the lap of Nirṛti; I have made him strong enough to live for a hundred years. 3. *I have rescued him with an oblation* having a thousand eyes, conferring a hundred years, giving life for a century, so that Indra may conduct him beyond all harm for a hundred years. 4. Regaining thy strength, live for a hundred autumns, a hundred winters, a hundred springs; may Indra, Agni, Savitṛ, and Bṛhaspati, (propitiated) *by this century-yielding oblation*, give this man back (to us) for a hundred years. 5. I have rescued thee, I have found thee; come back again, thou who art young again: sound in body, I have obtained for thee all thy sense, thy whole life."[1]

[1] Wilson's translation.

Similarly, *mantras* were uttered for the averting of abortion (Rv. x. 162), for the dissipation of bad dreams (Rv. x. 164), for the destruction of a rival (Rv. x. 166), for winning the love of the husband (x. 159), and for the averting of Misfortune (or Alakṣmī. Rv. x. 155). The translation of a few verses from the last-named hymn is given below :

"1. Miserable, ill-favoured, deformed, ever-railing (goddess), go to thy mountain ; with these exploits of Śirimbiṭha (the name of a Ṛṣi), we scare thee away. 2. May she be scared away from this (world), scared away from the next (world), the destructress of all embryos ; sharp-horned Bṛhaspati, approach, driving away distress. 3. The wood which floats by the sea-shore far off, remote from man, seize that, (O goddess), hard to destroy, and therewith go to a distant shore.[1] 4. Utterers of discordant sounds, when swiftly moving you departed, all the enemies of Indra were slain, disappearing like bubbles," &c.

There seems to have been a great prejudice against owls and their screechings, which were considered inauspicious as bringing evil on the cattle and inmates of the house, and *mantras* were uttered to counteract their evil influence. (Rv. x. 165). The bird was regarded as a messenger of the God of Death. The same prejudice still obtains against the black owl, though the white barn-owl is looked upon as a messenger of Lakṣmī or Good Fortune.

There are a hymn in the Ṛgveda (i. 191) which deals with antidotes against poison, and certain *mantras*, the recitation of which was calculated to destroy the effects of poison in the body, injected by the bite of serpents and the sting of scorpions or other venomous insects. The antidote consisted in some drugs which were supposed to possess

[1] The sea was known to the Ṛgvedic Aryans and it was probably a custom to go to the sea-shore and there size a floating log or drift-wood on which Alakṣmī was deported to a foreign land. Sāyaṇa expands the wood to "the wooden body of the deity called *Puruṣottama* (Viṣṇu)." But this explanation does not seem to be probable.

properties not only to neutralise the effects of poison but also to kill the venomous creatures. The *mantras* are as follow: "Those (who move with their) shoulders, those (who move with their) bodies, those who sting with sharp fangs, those who are virulently venomous; what do you here, ye unseen, depart together far from us.

"The all-seeing Sun rises in the east, the destroyer of the unseen, driving away all the unseen (venomous creatures) and all evil spirits.

"The Sun has risen on high, destroying all the many (poisons); Āditya, the all-seeing, the destroyer of the unseen, (rises) for (the good of) living beings.

"I deposit the poison in the solar orb, like a leather bottle in the house of a vender of spirits: verily, that adorable (Sun) never dies; nor (through his favour), shall we die (of the venom); for, though afar off, yet drawn by his coursers, he will overtake (the poison): the science of antidotes (*Madhulā*, as synonymous with *Madhu-vidyā*) converted thee, (Poison), to ambrosia.

"I recite the names of ninety and nine (rivers), the destroyers of poison; although afar off, (the Sun), drawn by his coursers, will overtake the poison: the science of antidotes has converted thee (Poison) to ambrosia.

"May the thrice-seven pea-hens, the seven-sister rivers, carry off, (O Body), thy poison, as maidens, with pitchers, carry away water.

"May the insignificant mongoose (carry off) thy venom (poison): if not, I will crush the vile (creature) with a stone: so may the poison depart (from my body), and go to distant regions." (Rv. i. 191. 7-10, 13-15).

It should be noted here that the Ṛgvedic Aryans observed the proverbial enmity between pea-cocks and snakes, and mongooses and snakes, and therefore their names were invoked in the above incantations.

When a man became seriously ill, certain rites were performed for his cure, and the following *mantras* were recited:

"1. O Gods, raise again the man, O Gods, who has sunk; O Gods, give life again to the man, O Gods, who has committed sin. 2. Those two winds blow to the region which are far beyond the ocean; may the one bring you vigour, may the other blow away all evil. 3. Breathe, wind, medicinal balm; blow away, wind, all evil; for thou art the universal medicine, thou movest as the messenger of the Gods. 4. The wind speaks: I have come to thee with pleasures and protections; I have brought thee fortunate vigour, I drive away thy disease. 5. May the Gods give (us) protection in this world, may the company of the Maruts protect us, may all beings grant protection so that this (person) may be free from sin. 6. Waters verily are medicinal; waters are the dissipators of disease; waters are the medicine for everything; may they act as medicine to thee. 7. The tongue (being cleansed) by the ten-branched hands (of Prajāpati) is the forerunner of speech; with those (hands) the removers of disease, we touch thee." (Rv. x. 137).

It will be seen from a perusal of the above verses that air and water were sought to be purified by *mantras* so as to make them conducive to the health and speedy recovery of the diseased person and passes were made with the fingers of the two hands over his body, so as to drive away the disease. The waters, when impregnated with *mantras*, were considered as possessing powers to purify a man, and were sprinkled over his head. The following verses on the efficacy of waters will be found interesting:

"1. Since, Waters, you are the sources of happiness, grant to us to enjoy abundance, and great and delightful perception. 2. Give us to partake in this world of your most auspicious juice, like affectionate mothers. 3. Let us quickly have recourse to you, for that your (faculty) of removing (sin), by which you gladden us: waters, bestow on us progeny. 4. May the divine waters be propitious to our worship, (may they be good) for our drinking: may they flow round us, and be our health and safety. 5. Waters, sovereigns of precious (treasures), grantors of habitations to man, I solicit of ye medicine (for mine infirmities). 6. Soma has declared to me: all medicaments, as well as Agni, the benefactor of the Universe, are in the waters. 7. Waters, bring to perfection all disease-dispelling medicaments for the good of my body, that I may long behold the sun. 8. Waters, take away whatever sin has been (found) in me, whether I have (knowingly) done wrong, or have pronounced imprecations (against holy men), or have spoken untruth. 9. I have this day entered into the waters: we have mingled with their essence. Agni, abiding in the waters, approach, and fill me (thus bathed) with vigour." (Rv. x. 9). (*Wilson*).

Medicine and Surgery.—It appears from a perusal of the above hymns that dirtressing and serious diseases were regarded as the result of sins, and it was deemed necessary to remove the effect of sins by the performance of specific rites and the recitation of *mantras*. But the use of medicines also was not discarded. It appears that there were professional medical men who had a special knowledge of medicinal herbs, from which they prepared different nostrums for different diseases, with beneficial results, and their services were in great requisition.

Rudra, in the Ṛgveda, is a fierce deity (ii. 33, 9. 11) and destructive like a terrible beast (ii. 33. 11). He is the ruddy (aruṣa) boar of heaven (i. 114, 5). He is a bull (ii. 33, 7. 8). He is exalted (vii. 10, 4), strong (i. 43, 1), strongest of the strong (ii. 33, 3), unassailable (vii. 46, 1), unsurpassed in might (ii. 33, 10), rapid and swift. He is young (ii. 33, 1; v. 60, 5), and un-aging (vi. 49, 10). He is called *asura* (v. 42, 11), or the great *asura* of heaven (ii. 1, 6). He is self-glorious (i. 129, 3), rules heroes (i. 114, 1. 2) and is a lord (*īśāna*) of this vast world (ii. 33, 9), and father of the world. (vi. 49, 10). He makes the streams flow over the earth and, roaring, moistens everything (x. 92, 5). He is intelligent (i. 43, 1), wise (i. 114, 4) and beneficent (ii 33, 7). He is several times called bountiful, *mīḍhva* (i. 114, 3), is easily invoked (ii. 33, 6) and auspicious, *Śiva* (x. 92, 9). But malevolence is also frequently attributed to him in the Ṛgveda. He is implored not to slay or injure in his anger his worshippers, their parents children, men, cattle or horses (i 114, 7, 8), but to spare horses (ii. 33, 1), to avert his great malevolence and his bolt from his worshippers, and to prostrate others with them (ii. 33, 11, 14). He is besought to avert his bolt when he is incensed, and not to injure his adorers, their children and their cows (vi. 28, 7; 46, 2-4), and to keep from them his cow-slaying, man-slaying missile (ii. 33, 1). In the Atharva-veda, he is even said to assail with fever, cough and poison. In the Ṛgveda, he is described as possessing firm limbs (ii. 33 11), beautiful lips (ii. 33, 5), a fat belly, a dazzling appearanec (i. 114, 5), brown colour (ii. 33, 5), wearing braided hair, shining like the brilliant Sun, like gold (i. 43, 5), and holding the thunderbolt in his arm. His lightning shaft discharged from the sky traverses the earth (vii. 46, 3). He is said to be armed with a bow and arrows (ii. 33, 10, 11, &c.), which are strong and swift. The Maruts are described as his sons (i. 114, 6, 9; ii. 33, 1), who are called Rudras or Rudriyas. In a passage of the Ṛgveda (ii. 1, 6), Rudra is one of the several deities identified with Agni. Though thus described as a dreaded and maleficent deity, yet he has a beneficent side. For, he is besought not only to preserve from calamity (v. 51, 13), but to bestow blessings (i. 114, 1, 2; ii. 33, 6) and produce welfare for man and beast. (i. 43, 6). *His healing powers are mentioned with especial frequency.* He grants remedies (ii. 33, 12), he commands every remedy (v. 42, 11) and has a thousand remedies (vii. 46, 3). He carries in his hand choice remedies (i. 114 5), and his hand is restorative and healing (ii. 33, 7).

He raises up heroes by his remedies, for *he is the greatest physician of physicians* (ii. 33, 4), and by his auspicious remedies his worshipper hopes to live a hundred winters (ii. 33, 2). He is besought to remove sickness from his worshippers' offspring (vii. 46, 2), and to be favourable to man and beast, that all in the village may be well-fed and free from disease. (i. 114. 1).[1]

Rudra has been variously identified by scholars with Agni, the Storm-God, Storm and Agni, chief of the souls of the dead, and even with a God of mountain and forest. But from the above brief descriptions of Rudra, it appears to me that he has been conceived as the Solar God, presiding over the hottest months of the year, when the rays of the Sun are fierce, and burn like fire, when men and animals suffer from the effects of abnormal heat, and become sick, when at the end of the sultriest day, clouds gather on the horizon, and thunder-storms break out, uprooting trees, blowing down houses, killing men and animals by lightning, and presenting a general appearance of devastation. This was the maleficent side of the God Rudra. His beneficent side consisted in clearing up the atmosphere, blowing away the germs of diseases, cooling down the temperature by showers of rain, improving public health and causing medicinal herbs and grass and corn to grow. These two different aspects of the God alternately made him the most dreaded, as well as the most beneficent. He was Rudra (the Fierce) as well as Śiva (the beneficent). It is remarkable that the hottest months of the year are even to this day appropriated to the special worship of Śiva or Rudra. As many epidemic diseases break out during these months, and the out-break stops only as soon as the atmosphere is cleared by thunder-storms and rains, Rudra who is the father of the Maruts (Storms) and wields the thunderbolt, is rightly regarded as "the greatest physician of physicians," and the owner

---

[1] *Vide* Macdonel's *Vedic Mythology* 28.

of remedies and medicinal plants which grow up as soon as the parched up earth is saturated with moisture. It would thus appear that medicines (*bheṣaja*), or medicinal herbs were used in Ṛgvedic times for the treatment of diseases, and Rudra was looked upon as the *Deva who presided over the Science of Medicine*.

There is a verse in the Ṛgveda, which, when translated, would read as follows: "We different men have all our various imaginations and designs. The carpenter seeks something that is broken, *the doctor a patient*, the priest some one who will offer libations." (Rv. ix. 112, 1). This goes to show that there were men who were physicians by profession, and treated patients for a fee, and were anxious to have a large number of patients. A Ṛṣi declares. "I will give to thee, Oh physician, a horse, a cow, a garment—yea, even myself." (Rv. x. 97, 4). The verse shows the nature of fees that a good physician received from his patients. There is a whole hymn (Rv. x. 97) devoted to the praise of medicinal plants or herbs from which the following extracts are made:

"1. I think of the hundred and seven applications of the brown-tinted plants, which are ancient, being generated for the Gods before the three ages. 2. Mothers (of mankind), a hundred are your applications, a thousandfold is your growth; do you who fulfil a hundred functions make this my (people) free from disease. 3. Rejoice, plants, bearing abundant flowers and fruits, triumphing together (over disease) like victorious horses, sprouting forth, bearing (men safe) beyond (disease). 4. 'Plants!' thus I hail you, the divine mothers (of mankind). I will give to thee, Oh physician, a horse, a cow, a garment—yea, even myself. 5. Your abode is in the Aśvattḥa, your dwelling is established in the Palāśa, you are assuredly the distributors of cattle, in as much as you bestow them on the physician. 6. Where, plants, you are congregated like princes (assembled) in battle, there the sage is designated a physician, the destroyer of evil spirits, the extirpator of disease. 7 The *Aśvavatī*, the *Somavatī*, the *Urjayantī*, the *Udojasa*—all these plants I praise for the purpose of overcoming this disease.[1] 8. The virtues of the plants which are desirous of bestowing wealth issue from them, man, (towards) thy body like cattle from the pen. 9. Verily *Iṣkṛti* is your mother, therefore are you also *Niṣkṛtis*; you are flying streams; if (a man) is ill, you cure him. 10. The universal all-pervading plants assail (diseases) as a thief (attacks) a cow-shed, they drive out whatever infirmity of body there may be. 11 As soon as I take these plants in my hand, making (the sick man) strong, the soul of the malady perishes before (their application) as (life is driven away from the presence) of the seizer of life. 12. From him, Oh plants, in whom you creep from limb to limb, from joint to joint, you drive away disease like a mighty (prince) stationed in the midst of his host. 13. Fly forth, sickness, with the jay, with the blue jay, with the velocity of the wind; perish along with the iguana. 14. Let each of you, plants, go to the other, approach the one (to the vicinity) of the other; thus being all mutually joined together, attend to this my speech. 15. Whether bearing fruit or barren, whether flowering or flowerless, may they, the progeny of Bṛhaspati, liberate us from sin. 16. May they liberate me from the sin produced by curse, from the sin caused by Varuṇa, from the fetters of Yama, from all guilts caused by the Gods. 17. The plants, falling from heaven, said, 'The man, whom living we pervade, will not perish.' 18 The plants which have the *Soma* for their King, and are numerous and all seeing, of them thou (O *Soma*-plant) art the best; be very bountiful to the affectionate heart. 19. Plants, which have the *Soma* for your King, who are scattered over the earth, the offspring of Bṛhaspati, give vigour to this

[1] "These, says Sāyaṇa, are the four principal plants. Mahīdhara explains them as 'the giver of horses (or of wealth), the yielder of Soma, the giver of strength (or life), the restorer of vigour. The last two might be termed 'tonic' and 'stimulant.'" Wilson.

(infirm body). 20. Let not the digger hurt you, nor (the sick person) for whom I dig you up; may all my bipeds and quadrupeds be free from disease. 21. Both the plants that hear this (prayer), and those which are removed far off, all coming together, give vigour to this (infirm body). 22. All the plants, together with the Soma their King, declare, 'We save him, O King, to whom the *Brāhmaṇa* administers us.' 23. Thou (Soma) art the best of the plants, to thee (all) trees are prostrate; may he be prostrate to us, who attacks us." (Wilson).

The Ṛṣi of this hymn is Bhiṣaj (the physician), the son of Atharvan. It would appear from a perusal of the verses that the Ṛgvedic Aryans were fully acquainted with the virtues and uses of various medicinal plants in the cure of diseases. Their applications were a hundred and their juices were either extracted or decoctions made from them. Mixed together, they were given to the patients as medicine. The science of Hindu Medicine was founded in early Ṛgvedic times; but it is a matter for wonder that the medicinal virtues of plants could be discovered and utilized in the treatments of diseases at such an early period of history, when there were no science-laboratories, and the facilities for scientific experimenting were so few and far between.

That the ancient Aryans had a fair knowledge of Anatomy would appear from the fact that the victims of sacrifices had to be cut up and dissected by the sacrificing priests themselves, and the different parts of the carcass offered as oblations to Agni. When human sacrifices were in vogue, the body of the human victim also had to be cut up and dissected, and the different parts offered as oblations to Agni. This gave them an idea, nay a knowledge, of the different internal organs and the arrangement of the bones of the body, Whether this knowledge was sufficient for developing a skill in Surgery is more than we caṇ say; but we find references made in the Ṛgveda to the amputation of legs, and their substitution by iron legs. This wonderful feat together with other wonderful performances have been attributed to the twin divinities, the Aśvins, who played the parts of divine physicians and worked wonders. The blind was made to see, the lame to walk, and the old and decrepit was restored to youth. The following references give an account of their wonderful healing powers: The sage Cyavana, grown old and deserted, they released from his decrepit body; they prolonged his life, restored him to youth, rendered him desirable to his wife and made him the husband of maidens (Rv. i. 116. 10). Ṛjrāśva had been blinded by his father for killing one hundred and one sheep and giving them to a she-wolf to devour. The Aśvins restored his eye-sight (Rv. i. 116, 16), and cured Parāvṛj of blindness and lameness (Rv. i. 112, 8). When Viśpalā's leg had been cut off in battle like the wing of a bird, the Aśvins gave her an iron one instead. (Rv. i. 112, 10; 116, 15). They cured Ghoṣā of an incurable skin-disease, and gave her a husband when she was growing old in her father's house.[1] Though these wonderful cures are attributed to the divine physicians, the Aśvins, we can safely surmise that there were real *human* physicians in Ṛgvedic times who possessed remarkable healing powers, and such surgical skill as enabled them to perform an amputation of a leg and replace it by an iron one. It was customary with the ancient Aryans to attribute their own feats to the Gods, and thus Rudra and the Aśvins came to be regarded as the divine physicians with whose help the ancient Aryans developed the Sciences of Medicine and Surgery.

---

[1] *Vedic Mythology*, 21 : Muir's O. S. T., p. 243 ff.

CHAPTER XII.

THE VEDAS AND VEDIC GODS, PHILOSOPHICAL SPECULATIONS REGARDING THE ORIGIN OF THE UNIVERSE AND REALISATION OF THE UNITY OF THE GODHEAD.

The Vedas.—The word *Veda* literally means "Knowledge," and in the sense in which it is appllied to the sacred Scriptures of the ancient Aryans, it means "Sacred Knowledge." The Vedas comprise not only the three principal Scriptures *viz.*, the Ṛgveda, the Yajurveda and the Sāmaveda, but also the fourth Veda, known as the Atharva-veda, and the Brāhmaṇas of each Veda, the Āraṇyakas, the Upaniṣads, and the Sūtras which are known as the Śrauta Sūtras, the Dharma-Sūtras, and the Gṛhya Sūtras, as well as the six Vedāngas, known as *Śikṣā*, *Kalpa*, *Vyākaraṇa*, *Jyotiṣ*, *Chandas* and *Nirukta*. The Vedic literature, properly so called, therefore covers an extensive period, beginning from the earliest Scripture which is admittedly the Ṛgveda down to the time of the Vedāngas. This period may be computed at some 15,000 to 20,000 years, during which Vedic culture was gradually evolved and developed. The present Saṃhitās of the Four Vedas are said to have been given distinctive shapes by the great sage Kṛṣṇa Dvaipāyana, well-known as Veda-vyāsa, who, with the help of his disciples, sorted and classified the *mantras*, according to their nature, purport and applicability about 5,000 years ago, though the *mantras* known as Ṛc, Sāma and Yajur had existed from time immemorial, and were chanted at or applied to the performace of particular sacrifices from memory by their custodians, generation after generation. Though the Ṛk-*mantras* are admittedly the oldest, there appear to have existed still older *mantras*, known as *Nivits* and *Nigadas*, traces of which are still to be found in the Ṛgveda and in some of the Brāhmaṇas.[1] The language of the

[1] Vide *ante*, Chap. i, p. 40, *et seq.*

Vedic literature however reveals unmistakable proofs of different and distinct stages of evolution and development, though the changes were necessarily extremely slow on accouut of the reluctance of religious teachers to introduce them, as the language had a peculiar sanctity attached to it by hoary tradition. In fact, the sacred *mantras* were believed by the ancient Aryans, and are still believed by their descendants, to have been revealed by the Creator himself, and are not attributed to any human agency or authorship. The ancient sages, or Ṛṣis, who were so spiritually advanced as to have been in direct communion with the Universal Soul, or Brahman, are said to have simply discovered the *mantras*, (or rather they were revealed to them) in the diction and metre in which they are still found, and any attempt to change a syllable or interpose a word was and is still regarded as a sin and sacrilege, especially as a procedure like this was believed to mar the power and reduce the efficacy of the *mantras*. Hence the unchangeability of Vedic language in the *mantras*, though an undoubted change is noticeable in the later Vedic literature, from the Atharva-veda and the Brāhmaṇas downwards.[1]

Apauruṣeya.—It is generally believed that the Vedas, as simple revelations from the Supreme Being, are *apauruṣeya*, *i.e.*, are not ascribable to the authorship of any human sage, or sages and hence infallible. The *mantras*, it is said, embody eternal truths and verities, and were *seen*, *i.e.*, vividly realised by the Ṛṣis or Seers who were in touch with the Supreme Being, and clothed in inspired language which was not the language of their own coining or making, but which naturally gushed forth, as it were, from their inmost souls. Though each hymn has its own Ṛṣi, the latter is not regarded as its author, but as *seer* of the *mantras* comprised in the hymn. Different schools of thought in a later age discussed this subject threadbare from different standpoints, and came to

[1] *Ante*, Chap. i, p 40.

the conclusion that on the whole the Vedas should be regarded as *apauruṣeya* and infallible, though, of course, there were some dissenters from this view, whose number however was extremely small.

Truth is always Truth, and hence eternal, emanating as it does from the Fountain-head of all Truths, which is God or Brahman. As the Vedic Ṛṣis were highly spiritual men and in close touch with this Fountain-head of all Truths, the moral and spiritual Truths that they realised and that were revealed through them, must have been pure, unsullied and eternal also. In this sense, the Vedas may be called eternal and *apauruṣeya*; but the language in which these truths were embodied, though inspired, was nevertheless the language of the Ṛṣis, which was coloured by their own thoughts, imaginations and modes of expression. Hence in many *mantras* we find a distinct individualistic touch which makes them *pauruṣeya* to a large extent. There is reference to individual wants, cravings and aspirations, praises for liberal gifts, curses upon enemies and evil-doers, exultation for victories, and repentence for sins, and to ancient and contemporary history, and even to the croakings of frogs on the advent of the rains, most of which came within the range of the sage-bard's individual knowledge or experiences, and had nothing eternal or *apauruṣeya* about them, requiring the aid of divine inspiration But the discovery of the Devas or Gods, the description of their powers and various functions, and their intimate relations to human affairs, the realisation of their underlying unity in one Godhead, the utility of sacrifices made to the Gods and the efficacy of prayers, the unravelling of the mysteries of life and death and of the origin of the Universe, the discovery and realisation of *Ṛta* or the Moral Order of the Universe—these and similar other things must be attributed to divine inspiration and put down as *apauruṣeya*. The Vedas, therefore, may be described as both *pauruṣeya* and *apauruṣeya*, fallible as well as infallible,—partly fallible, in so far as they are the result of defective human thoughts and reasoning, and partly infallible in so far as they relate to permanent and eternal truths which know no change, and are unaffected either by time or circumstance. It is the treatment of these eternal truths, moral as well as spiritual, in a remote age when the human race was in its infancy, that adds to the value of the *mantras*, and their historical significance.

The Devaṣ.—The distinguishing trait of the budding Aryan mind was its inherent love of Light and of everything that was conducive to human happiness and welfare. Like children, they hankered after light, and turned away from darkness. The blue and bright expanse of heaven, *(Dyāvā)*, the broad sun-lit earth with its green meadows, luxurious vegetation, and flowing rivers, (*Pṛthivī*), the bright and glorious Sun, (*Sūrya*), the beautiful Dawn, preceding sun-rise, (*Uṣas*), the glimmering light on the eastern horizon, struggling with darkness for expression before the appearance of the Dawn, (the *Aśvins*), the bright star-bespangled sky at night, (*Varuṇa*), the bright fire dispelling darkness, (*Agni*), the zigzag lightning in the sky, the glorious Moon adorning the heaven at night, the vast and glittering expanse of waters in the ocean (*Varuṇa*), the life-giving waters that flow in the rivers, the cooling rains from heaven that make the grass and corn grow and vegetation thrive, (*Āp*), the breezes that mitigate the effect of sultry heat *(Vāyu)*, the storms that rush through heaven presaging the advent of rains, (*Maruts*), the deafening and dreaded thunder as it rolls and rends open the clouds and brings down rain (*Indra's Vajra*), the invigorating draught of the Soma-juice (*Soma*), the rivers that bring down pure drinking-water from the mountains (*Nadyah*),—all these natural phenomena and objects made deep impressions on the susceptible minds of the ancient Aryans, who believed them to be suffused with life and intelligence, and endowed with a power for doing good, if approached in a spirit of adoration and humility. Their mind became highly imaginative, and connecting causes with effects, wove up myths round the different natural phenomena and objects that strongly impressed them. Each natural phenomenon having been believed to be presided over by an indwelling spirit, called *Deva* or *Devatā* (from the root *div*, to shine), the latter was sought to be propitiated by appropriate songs or praises, which were afterwards accompanied by sacrifices in order to move the Devatā into benevolent activity on behalf of the worshippers. The appearance of a *Devatā* in physical Nature synchronised with the time of his special worship, and the worshippers kept themselves ready with oblations and songs to be promptly offered to the deity on his appearance. The first deity to appear at the fag-end of night was the twin Gods, the *Aśvins*, (regarded as one *Devatā*), when light was struggling with darkness for expression in the distant horizon, and oblations with appropriate *mantras* were offered to them. These Gods were justly regarded as the divine physicians who cured blindness, generally associated with darkness, lameness, associated with physical inactivity at night, decrepit old age, associated with the torpor of death-like sleep, and diseases of various sorts that became less painful as night wore into dawn. They were also regarded as the principal helpers of Indra in his fight with the demon of darkness (Vṛtra) who was supposed to have imprisoned in his dark bosom the bright and beautiful Dawn and the glorious and resplendent Sun that resuscitated men into life and activity and provided them with joy and happiness. The *Aśvins* came riding on fleet coursers, and soon vanished, followed by the first faint flushes of the Dawn who changed her dark complexion into bright, (Rv. i. 123, 9) and soon became *Vyuṣṭhā* (full-blown) or refulgent, like a beautiful heavenly maiden in the glory of her eternal youth. She roused all living creatures from sleep, as if resuscitating them from death into life, scattering joy and happiness everywhere, and presaging the advent of the glorious orb of the day, who followed her as a lover follows his beloved, or as a son follows his mother. The appearance of the Dawn on the horizon was the signal for the performance of sacrifices for her propitiation, and the offering of appropriate oblations and songs. The hymns addressed to the Dawn in the Ṛgveda are the most beautiful from a poetical point of view, which can favourably compare with such hymns in any literature of the world, in their refreshing grandeur and simplicity. The Dawn soon disappeared, followed by the Sun, not all at once, but in three different stages of his rising, first as *Udeṣyat*, or giving promises of his appearance, next as *Udyat*, *i.e.*, about to appear or rise, and lastly as *Udita i.e.* risen. All these different stages were signalised by appropriate songs and the offering of suitable oblations. The Sun dwelt in the highest heaven, and lighted up not only that region with his bright and glorious rays, but also the middle-region or *antarikṣa*, and the lower region or the Earth. He had seven rays, and seven horses to draw his chariot which had seven wheels or only one wheel. (Rv. i. 164, 2. 3). He had three principal aspects during the three principal divisions of the day, one in the morning as Creator, when Nature appeared as *recreated* after her extinction or apparent annihilation in the darkness of the night, one in the mid-day as Protector by causing plants and corns to grow and sucking up watery vapours from the ocean, (Rv. vii. 36, 1), and storing them for precipitation as rain, and another soon after mid-day till evening when he assumed a fiery appearance like that of Rudra till he annihilated himself and all creation with him in the darkness of the night. It was necessary to resuscitate him into life, and rescue him from the clutches of darkness, and the task was assigned to *Indra* who, with the help of the other Gods, engaged himself in a fight with the demon of darkness (*Vṛtra*). This demon assumed many forms, one of which was clouds, in which he not only imprisoned the Sun and the Dawn for three or four months during the rainy season, but maliciously withheld the timely rains also, that were needed for the cultivation of crops. The task of releasing the Sun, the Dawn, and the waters also fell on Indra who waged a long and terrible fight with the demon for months together till he became victorious. It was felt necessary to strengthen Indra and the Gods, who were his allies in his fight with Vṛtra, by the performance of appropriate sacrifices and the offering of the invigorating drink of the Soma-juice with appropriate *mantras*. Indra thus came to be regarded as the Supreme God, and as the creator of the Sun and the Dawn and the bright heaven, and releaser of the "waters of life." He was all-powerful, all-pervading, the wielder of the dreaded thunderbolt, and the leader of all the Gods. He was so bright and refulgent in his glory that a thousand Suns could not rival him, and he came to be identified with the Sun in heaven, the Lightning in *antarikṣa*, and Fire on earth, which were regarded as his three bodies. (Rv. i. 103, 1). But he was in fact greater than all of them. There was only one rival of him, *viz.*, *Varuṇa* who was identified with the bright blue sky with his eye as the Sun in the day-time, and a thousand glittering eyes in the shape of stars at night, and with the aerial ocean above and the terrestrial ocean below, and described as the upholder of heaven, the creator of the Sun and the Dawn, the guider of the ships on the ocean, the observer of men's actions, the punisher of evil-doers, and the upholder of *Ṛta* or the Moral Order of the Universe. He was undoubtedly more ancient than Indra, representing an earlier stage of the evolution of Aryan culture, and came to be associated with Indra when the latter was discovered. Indra ultimately ousted Varuṇa from his supremacy, and himself became the Supreme Deity.[1] *Mitra* was the early name of the Sun-God, and his name is found coupled with that of Varuṇa. Savitṛ was also another name of the Sun-God (Rv. iv. 14, 2; vii. 63, i. 2. 4; x. 158, 1-4), but he appeared to have illuminated the upper regions of heaven at night, when

[1] Vide *ante* Chap. ii, pp. 84-85.

the terrestrial Sun had set. (Rv. ii. 38, 3. 4; i. 35, 2). He sent all creatures to sleep and also roused them in the morning. (Rv. iv. 53, 3, 6; vii. 45, 1). Sāyaṇa is of opinion (*vide* his comments on Rv. v. 81, 4) that before his rising, the Sun was called Savitṛ, but from his rising to setting, Sūrya. Professor Macdonell says that "Savitṛ was originally an epithet of Indian origin applied to the Sun as the great stimulator of life and motion in the world, representing the most important movement which dominates all others in the Universe, but that as differentiated from Sūrya, he is a more abstract deity. He is in the eyes of the Vedic poets the divine power of the Sun personified, while Sūrya is the more concrete deity, in the conception of whom the outward form of the Sun-body is never absent owing to the identity of his name with that of the orb." (Cf. i. 35, 9; 124, 1).[1] *Aditi* was probably the name of the Primordial Force of Nature, who was the mother of the Gods, and especially of the eight Ādityas *viz.*, Varuṇa Mitra, Bhaga, Dakṣa, &c., all of whom, excepting the eighth, were divine. The eighth Āditya was Mārtāṇḍa, or the terrestrial Sun, who was cast out by Aditi for repeated births and deaths, as he was born every morning and died in the evening, only to be reborn on the next day. (Rv. x. 72, 9). The seven Ādityas were the seven divine Suns who lighted up the seven different regions of heaven (Rv. ix. 114, 3). *Fire* or *Agni* was another deity who has been more frequently praised in the Ṛgveda than any other deity, excepting Indra. Fire on the earth below, Lightning in *antarikṣa*, and the Sun in heaven were all one and the same substance (Rv. i. 103, 1), giving glimpses and idea of the splendour of *Brahman*, the Supreme God, from whom they borrowed or derived their lights. Fire was the deity, through whom *Brahman* and all the Gods could be worshipped in every household everyday, and oblations offered to the Gods, because Fire consumed them and carried their essence

[1] Macdonell's *Vedic Mythology*, 15

to the Gods for whom they were meant. Every householder kept up the sacred Fire burning in his home and daily oblations were offered to him twice or thrice by the husband and wife until their death. On the occasion of the performance of any special sacrifice, Fire was ceremoniously lighted up and libations of *havis* and the Soma-juice, as well as oblations were offered to him with appropriate *mantras* for the propitiation of some particular God or Gods. He was regarded as the Purohita or priest of the sacrifice. *Pūṣan* was another deity representing the beneficent power of the Sun, manifested chiefly as a pastoral deity. Like Rudra, he had braided hair (Rv. vi. 55, 2) and a beard (Rv. x. 26, 7). He carried an awl (Rv. vi. 53, 5. 6. 8) or a goad (Rv. vi. 53, 9; 58, 2) and his car was drawn by goats instead of horses (Rv. i. 38, 4; vi. 53, 3. 4). He moved onward beholding the Universe (Rv. ii. 40, 5) and made his abode in heaven (Rv. ii. 40, 4). He was the lord of the road (Rv. vi. 53, 1) and removed dangers, wolves and way-layers from the paths. (Rv. i. 42, 1-3). He conducted the dead on the far path to the Fathers, showing them the way. (Rv. x. 17, 3-5). He was prayed to disperse foes and make the paths lead to booty (Rv. vi. 53, 4), to remove foes, to make the paths good and to lead to good pasture. (Rv. i. 42, 7. 8). He was also called Paśupā or protector of cattle (Rv. vi. 58, 2). Hence it is rightly surmised that Pūṣan was the name of the Sun when the Aryans were a pastoral people, moving from place to place with their cattle in search of pasture. (*vide* Macdonell's *Vedic Mythology*). Viṣṇu, who occupied a supreme position in the later Vedic literature, held a subordinate position in the pantheon of the Gods in the Ṛgveda. He took three steps, one on earth, one in mid-heaven, and the third in the highest heaven which was invisible to men, but visible to the Gods, like an eye fixed in heaven (Rv. i. 22, 20). It was his dear abode, where pious men rejoiced and where there was a well of honey. (Rv. i. 154, 5) and where the Gods rejoiced (Rv. viii 29, 7). According to Yāska's predecessor, Aurṇavābha

(Nir. 12, 19), the three steps meant the rising, culminating and setting of the Sun. There is an alternative view, prevailing throughout the younger Vedas, the Brāhmaṇas as well as post-Vedic literature, and supported by Yāska's predecessor Śākapūṇi and endorsed by some European scholars, which "interprets the three steps as the course of the solar deity through the three divisions of the Universe" *(Ved. Myth.* 17). Though Viṣṇu is not clearly connected with any natural phenomenon, "he was originally conceived as the Sun, not in his general character, but as the personified, swiftly moving luminary which with vast strides traverses the whole Universe." (*Ved. Myth.* § 17). Viṣṇu was allied with Indra in the latter's fight with Vṛtra (Rv. vi. 69; vii. 99, 5. 6; i. 155, 2). Indra about to slay Vṛtra says "Friend, Viṣṇu, stride out vastly" (Rv. iv. 18, 11), and in company with him, slew Vṛtra (Rv. vi. 20, 2). The *Maruts* or the winds were also the Gods who helped Indra in killing Vṛtra, and bringing down rains from the clouds. There is a host of other Gods mentioned in the Ṛgveda which either represented natural phenomena or abstract ideas of them. Their characterstics and powers have been fully dealt with by Professor Macdonell in his excellent work *Vedic Mythology*, to which I would refer the reader for further information.

Classification and number of the Devas.—The *Devas* or Gods have been divided into three distinct classes, and their number put down as thirty-three in the Ṛgveda (i. 139, 11). The verse referred to says: "Gods who are eleven in heaven; who are eleven on earth; and who are eleven dwelling with glory in mid-air, may ye be pleased with this our sacrifice." These thirty-three Gods have also been mentioned elsewhere (Rv. i. 34, 11; iii. 6, 9). Following the triple classification, "Yāska (Nir. 7, 5) divides the different deities or forms of the same deity enumerated in the fifth chapter of the Naighantuka, into the three orders of *pṛthivīsthāna*, terrestrial, (Nir. 7, 14-9, 43), *antarīkṣasthāna*, *madhyamasthana*, aerial or intermediate (10, 1-11. 50), and *dyusthāna*, celestial.

(12, 1-46). He further remarks that in the opinion of his predecessors who expounded the Veda (*nairuktāḥ*), there are only three deities, Agni on earth, Vāyu or Indra in air, Sūrya in heaven. (This view may be based on such passages as Rv. x. 158, 1: 'May Sūrya protect us from heaven, Vāta from air, Agni from the earthly regions'). Each of these, he continues, has various appellations according to differences of function, just as the same person may act in the capacity of *hotṛ*, *adhvaryu*, *brahman*, *udgātṛ*. Yāska himself does not admit that all the various Gods are only forms or manifestations of the three representative deities, though he allows that those forming each of the three orders are allied in sphere and functions."[1] According to the *Śatapatha Brāhmaṇa*, the thirty three Gods were 8 Vasus, 11 Rudras, 12 Ādityas, Dyus, and Pṛthivī (7, 5, 7, 2). The *Aitareya Brāhmaṇa* substitutes *Prajāpati* and *Vaṣatkāra* only for Dyus and Pṛthivī (1, 2, 4). The Gods have, according to their attributes, also been divided into four *castes* like men in some of the Brāhmaṇas and Saṃhitas. Agni and Bṛhaspati are regarded as Brāhmaṇas (*Tait. Brah.* 3, 5, 3; *Tait. Sam.* 2, 2, 9, 1); Indra, Varuṇa and Soma etc. as Kṣatriyas; the Vasus, Rudras, Ādityas, the Viśvedevāḥ and the Maruts as Vaiśyas; and Pūṣan as Sūdra. (*Śat. Brāh.* 14, 4, 2, 23-25). Though the number of the Gods was originally 33, divided into three main groups, their aggregate "could not always have been regarded as exhaustive, for in a few passages[2] other Gods are mentioned along with the 33. In one verse (Rv. iii. 9, 9.=Rv. x. 52, 6) the number of the Gods is by way of a freak stated to be 3339."[3] We do not think that this number was stated by way of a freak. The number gradually increased as new Gods were discovered and added to the pantheon, until at the present day it is three hundred and thirty millions or infinite. From One, the Deity became three

[1] Macdonell's *Vedic Mythology*, 10.

[2] Rv. i. 34, 11; 45 2; viii. 35, 3; 39, 9.

[3] Macdonell's *Vedic Mythology* 10.

(Rv. i. 164, 46), and from three it became thirty-three, and from thirty-three it became 3,339, and now it has become infinite in number. The conception was something like that of "polytheistic Monotheism," or the conception of the One God in infinite manifestations, or even Pantheism regarding the Deity as representing not only all the Gods but Nature as well.[1] This One God was called *Prajāpati* who was not only above all Gods, but embraced all things. (Rv. x. 121, 8-10).

Anthropomorphic accounts of the Gods and their images. —Though the Devas were regarded as so many manifestations of the One God, each manifestation was differentiated from the others by certain characteristics and attributes inherent and peculiar to it, which went to make up its individuality and physical appearance. The function of each Deva also was different from that of the others; hence the *mantras* that were uttered for his propitiation formed a separate group and were quite appropriate to his nature and character. For example, Indra had a beautiful nose (*su-nāsika*) and his jaws or lips were symmetrical (*su-śipra*). He had tawny beards (Rv. ii. 11, 1; x. 23, 1. 4), and tawny hair (Rv. x. 96, 5, 8), and wore a golden helmet on his head (Rv. viii. 92, 4). He had a capacious belly as he could consume vast quantities of the Soma drink (Rv. ii. 16, 2), when he was compared to a lake. (Rv. iii. 36, 8). He was armed usually with the dreaded thunderbolt which had been first made of stone, then of bone, and lastly was made of gold and iron, showing the different stages of culture through which the ancient Aryans had passed. He had a pair of bay horses on which he rode, as befitting a warrior and leader of hosts, or which drew his car which was golden (Rv. vi. 29, 2). But he always fought from his car and the epithet, *ratheṣṭhā* (car-fighter), is exclusively appropriated to him. He had long arms, which were far-extended and great (Rv. vi. 19, 3; viii. 32, 10; 70, 1), as

[1] *Ibid.*

well as strong and well-shaped. Besides weilding the thunder-bolt, he also used the bow and arrows in war (Rv. viii. 45, 4; 66, 6. 11; x. 103, 2. 3) and sometimes carried the *aṁkuśa* (hook) as a weapon. (Rv. x 44, 9). His whole appearance is tawny (Rv. x. 96), though he is occasionally described as golden (Rv. i. 7, 2; viii. 55, 1). Indra had a wife named Śacī or Indrāṇī (Rv. i. 82, 5. 6; iii. 53, 4. 6; x. 86, 9. 10), and he enjoyed great domestic felicity. (Rv. iii. 53, 4. 6).

The above brief description of Indra's appearance is sufficiently anthropomorphic, and it was not unnatural that images were made of him, worshipped, and sometimes sold for an adequate value. As I have already pointed out elsewhere, (*vide* Chap. iii, pp. 143-145), the worship of the images of Gods was not unknown in Ṛgvedic times. "Did the Vedic Indians make images of their Gods?" asks Dr. Muir.[1] Professor Müller (*Chips from a German Workshop* i. 38) answers the question in the negative. "The religion of the Veda" he says, "knows of no idols. The worship of idols in India is a secondary formation, a later degradation of the more primitive worship of ideal Gods." On the other hand, Dr. Bollensen finds in the hymns clear references to images of the Gods. (*Journal of the German Oriental Society*, xxii. 587ff). He writes: "From the common appellation of the Gods as *divonaras* 'men of the sky' or simple *naras* (*Luras*?) 'men,' and from the epithet *nṛpeśas* 'having the form of men'[2] (Rv. iii. 4, 5), we may conclude that the Indians did not merely in imagination assign human forms to their Gods, but also represented them in a sensible manner. Thus in Rv. ii. 33, 9, a painted image of Rudra is described: *sṭhirebhir angaih pururūpah ugrah babhrus śukrabhih pipiśe hiraṇyaih.* 'With strong limbs, many-formed, awful, brown, he is painted with shining golden colours.' Rv. i. 25, 13 (where it is said of Varuṇa, that wearing a golden

---

[1] O. S. T. v. 453.

[2] Cf Sāyaṇa's Commentary on Rv. iii. 4, 5.

coat of mail, he veils himself in his radiance; spies sit round him'), appears also to refer to a sensible representation.... Still clearer appears the reference to representations in the form of an image in Rv. v. 52, 15, *nū manvānah eṣām devān aścha* (the editions of prof. Müller and Aufrecht both read *achhā*). 'I now pray to the Gods of these (Maruts).' Here it seems that the Maruts are distinguished from their Gods *i.e.* from their images.'......' Besides the common expression *vapus, tanu, rūpa* ('body' and 'form'), there is in the oldest language one which properly denotes an image of the Gods *viz. Śandṛś.* Much more is added in support of the same view." Personally I have no doubt that the anthropomorphical description of the Gods in the Ṛgveda was not merely imaginary, but also suggested their sensible representations.

The description of Rudra also is anthropomorphical. Professor Macdonell thus describes his physical features: "He has a hand (Rv. ii. 33, 7), arms (Rv. ii. 33, 3) and firm limbs (Rv. ii. 33, 11). He has beautiful lips (Rv. ii. 33, 5), and (like Pūṣan) wears braided hair. (Rv. i. 114, 1. 5). His colour is brown (*babhru*, Rv. ii. 33, 5) and he is multiform (Rv. ii. 33, 9). He shines like the brilliant Sun, like gold. (Rv. i. 43, 5). He is arrayed with golden ornaments (Rv. ii. 33, 9) and wears a glorious multiform necklace." (*niska*, Rv. ii. 33, 10) (*Vedic Mytho.* § 28). Besides these physical features, he is also described as "soft-bellied" (Rv. ii. 33, 5) "wielder of the thunderbolt" (Rv. ii. 33, 3) armed with a bow and arrows (Rv. ii. 33, 10) and a javelin (*heti*, Rv. ii. 33, 14), destroyer of sins (Rv. ii. 33, 2. 3), owner of medicinal plants, and the chief physician amongst physicians, (Rv. ii. 33, 4), white-complexioned (Rv. ii. 33, 8), father of the Maruts (Rv. ii. 33, 1), and omniscient and divine. (Rv. ii. 33, 15). His epithet *Tryambaka* occurs in the Ṛgveda (vii. 59, 12), though only once. The Vājasaneyī Samhitā clothes him in a skin (3, 61) and makes him a dweller on the mountains. (16, 2-4).

I have elsewhere described Rudra as the prototype of the later Vedic and Paurāṇic Śiva. (*Vide* Chap. xi, *ante*). It is, therefore, a mistake to suppose that Śiva was not a Vedic but a non-Aryan God. The Ṛgvedic description of Rudra exactly tallies with the Paurāṇic description of Śiva, and, as it is anthropomorphic, undoubtedly suggests points for making his image.

The anthropomorphic description of Pūṣan and Varuṇa have been briefly referred to above. But "the anthropomorphism of Varuṇa's personality is more fully developed on the moral than on the physical side. The descriptions of his person and his equipments are scanty, more stress being laid on his activity. He has a face, an eye, arms, hands and feet. He moves his arms, walks, drives, sits, eats and drinks. The poet regards the face (*anīkam*) of Varuṇa as that of Agni (Rv. vii. 88, 2). The eye of Mitra and Varuṇa is the Sun (Rv. i 115, 1; vi. 51, 1; vii. 61, 1). The fact that this is always mentioned in the first verse of a hymn suggests that it is one of the first ideas that occur when Mitra and Varuṇa are thought of. The eye with which Varuṇa is said in a hymn to Sūrya (Rv. i. 50, 6) to observe mankind, is undoubtedly the Sun...Varuṇa wears a golden mantle (*drāpi*) and puts on a shining robe...In the *Śatapatha Brāhmaṇa* (13, 3, 6, 5) Varuṇa is represented as a fair, bald, yellow-eyed old man...Mitra and Varuṇa's abode is golden and situated in heaven, (Rv. v, 67, 2; i. 136, 2) and Varuṇa sits in his mansion (*pastyāsu*) looking on all deeds. (Rv. i. 25, 10. 11). His and Mitra's seat (*sadas*) is great, very lofty, firm with a thousand columns (Rv. v. 68, 5; ii. 41, 5), and their house has a thousand doors (Rv. vii. 88, 5). The all-seeing Sun, rising from his abode, goes to the dwellings of Mitra and Varuṇa to report the deeds of men (Rv. vii. 60, 1. 3) and enters their dear dwelling (Rv. i. 152, 4). It is in the highest heaven that the Fathers behold Varuṇa (Rv. x. 14, 8)...In marked contrast with Indra, Varuṇa has no myths related of him, while much is said about him (and Mitra) as upholder of the physical and moral order. Varuṇa is a great lord of the laws of Nature. He established heaven and earth and dwells in all the worlds (Rv viii. 42, 1. The three heavens and the three earths are deposited within him (Rv. vii 87, 5. He and Mitra rule over the whole world, (Rv. v. 63, 7), or encompass the two worlds (Rv. vii. 61, 4)...They are lords of order (*ṛta*) and light, who by means of order are the upholders of order. (Rv. i. 23, 5)...As a moral Governor, Varuṇa stands far above any other deity. His wrath is roused by sin; the infringement of his ordinances, which he severely punishes (Rv. vii. 86, 3. 4). The fetters (*pāśah*) with which he binds sinners are often mentioned. (Rv. i. 24 15; vi 74, 4; x. 85, 24)."[1] Varuṇa was undoubtedly the encompassing sky, with his eye as the Sun. He was afterwards identified with the aerial ocean above and the terrestrial ocean below.[2]

The description of Uṣas, the Goddess of Dawn, is also anthropomorphic, consistently with her natural appearance in the sky. "Uṣas" says Professor Macdonell "is the most graceful creation of Vedic poetry and there is no more charming figure in the descriptive religious lyrics of any other literature...Arraying herself in gay attire, like a dancer, she displays her bosom (Rv. i. 92, 4. cf. vi. 64, 2) Like a maiden decked by her mother she shows her form (Rv. i. 123, 11). Clothed in light, the maiden appears in the east, and unveils her charms. (Rv. i. 124, 3.4). Effulgent in peerless beauty, she withholds her light from neither small nor great (*ib.* 6). Rising resplendent as from a bath, showing her charms, she comes with light, driving away the darkness (Rv. v. 80, 5 6). She is young, being born again and again, though ancient; shining with an uniform hue, she wastes away the life of mortals (Rv. i. 92, 10). As she has shone in former days, so she shines now, and will shine in future, never aging,

[1] Macdonell's *Vedic Mythology*, 12.

[2] *Vide* Chap. ii, pp. 81-82 (*ante*).

immortal." (Rv. i. 113, 13.15). She has been alternately described as the mother of Sūrya, having generated Sūrya, Sacrifice and Agni (Rv. vii. 78, 3), because she precedes the Sun, and also as the wife of Sūrya, because the latter follows her as a young man a maiden. (Rv. i. 115, 2; vii. 75, 5; iv. 5, 13). I have elsewhere pointed out that she was the prototype of the Paurāṇic Umā or Durgā.[1]

It is further useless to multiply instances of the anthropomorphical descriptions of the Vedic gods. Though images may not have been made of all of them, their conception in the Ṛgveda was sufficiently anthropomorphical to warrant a supposition that their worshippers had mental visions of them as glorified or divine human beings, possessing supernatural powers. Each manifestation of Nature, therefore, had a presiding deity of its own, distinct from every other manifestation and its presiding deity, and possessing supernatural powers commensurate with its peculiar functions and character. The natural object or phenomenon, through which the deity manifested itself, was however quite distinct from the deity, as the body is distinct from the soul.

The visible bodies and invisible spirits of the Gods.— The sage poets of the Ṛgveda clearly conceived the presiding deities as distinct from the visible material objects through which they manifested themselves.[2] The visible resplendent Sun was the external body of the real divine Sun who was subtle and invisible. The Sun has been described as "the soul (*ātmā*) of all that moves and stands." (Rv. i. 115, 1: *Sūrya ātmā jagatastaṭhuṣaśca)* In Rv. x. 85. 16, we come across the following sentiment: "Sūryā, the *Brāhmans* know thy two chariot-wheels in their season; the single wheel that is concealed the sages know it also." (Wilson). Now Sūryā was the daughter of Sūrya, the Sun, and probably

[1] *Ṛgvedic India*, chaps. xiii, xxii and xxiv.

[2] I am much indebted to Professor Kokileśwar Sāstri's excellent article in Bengali on *Advaitavāda*, published in the *Journal of the Department of Letters*, vol. viii. (Calcutta University) for some of the materials of this section.

stands for the dazzling light of the Sun. Of her two chariot-wheels, one was visible, and the other invisible which sages only could conceive in their mind. Another verse is as follows: "When, Gods, you filled the worlds (with your radiance) as clouds (fill the earth with rain), then you brought forth the Sun *hidden in the ocean.*" This refers probably to the manifestation of the Sun at the time of creation from his subtile and unmanifested state which was invisible. Again "Ignorant, I inquire of the sages who know (the truth); not as one knowing (do I enquire), for the sake of (gaining) knowledge: what is that One alone, who has upheld these six spheres in the form of the unborn" Rv. i. 164, 6). Wilson comments on this verse as follows: "The *One* may be, according to the Scholiast, the orb of the ungenerated Sun, on which the six seasons depend; or the *Satyaloka,* whence there is no return, and which may be considered as the stay of the other six worlds or regions; or agreeably to the Vedanta views, 'the One' is the sole form of the unborn Creator, which is the same with the Universe." There is another significant verse (Rv. i. 50, 10) which describes the light of the Sun as *ut*, i e., the material light which is visible on earth, and *uttara*, i.e., the light that is diffused in the higher regions of the sky, and visible to the Gods, and *uttama*, i.e., the most excellent which is the light of Brahman or the Primordial cause of the Universe. Wilson again comments on this verse as follows: "Here, again, we may have an allusion to a spiritual Sun." This verse has been quoted in the *Chāndogya Upaniṣad* also where it has been remarked that the real Sun never rises nor sets.

Agni or Fire also has two sources of production, one in the lowest region (*avare*), and another in the highest (*parame*). The translation of Rv. ii. 9, 3 is as follows: "We adore thee, Agni, in thy loftiest birth (place), and with hymns in thine inferior station: I worship that seat whence thou hast issued: the priests have offered thee, when kindled, oblations." Wilson comments on the above as follows:

"Agni is worshipped in heaven as the Sun; in the firmament as Lightning, and as the sacrificial Fire kindled on the altar." The explanation is plausible; but the verse may also mean that the material Fire on earth below is the manifestation of the divine Fire in the highest heaven. Rg. x. 45, 2 says: "We recognize thy threefold station, Agni, and thy three (forms): we recognize the many stations occupied by thee; we know what thy supreme secret appellation (is): we know the source, whence thou hast proceeded." In Rv. x. 16, 9 a distinction has been made between the funeral Fire that consumed the dead body and the invisible essence of Fire that carried oblation to the Gods and is all-knowing.

The *Soma* too was both material and spiritual. The juice of the material Soma plant was drunk, but the immaterial or spiritual Soma could never be drunk by any body. "He who has drunk thinks that the herb which men crush is the *Soma*; (but) that which the Brāhmans know to be *Soma*, of that no one partakes ..Concealed by means of coverings, protected by the *Bārhats*,[1] O Soma, thou abidest listening to the grinding-stones. No terrestrial being partakes of thee." (Rv. x. 85, 3-4). Again the divine spirit of the Soma is referred to in the following verses: "Like a horse urged on to battle, do thou (Soma), who art all-knowing, rush from heaven to the receptacle whose mother is the cloud." (Rv. ix. 86, 3) "All-seeing (Soma), the mighty rays of thee, who art the lord, encompass all the sphere; pervading (all things) thou flowest, *Soma*, through thy functions; thou rulest lord of the whole world" (Rv. ix. 86, 5). "Thundering like the summit of the sky (the *Soma*) roars, by whose support both heaven and earth (are upheld); the Soma flows acquiring Indra's friendship; purified, he alights upon the pitchers. The light of the sacrifice, he distils sweet (juice) delightful (to the Gods), the parent of the Gods, the generator (of all), possessed of ample wealth; he supports the hidden wealth of heaven and earth, the most exhilarating, the exciting (*Soma*),

---

[1] The Bārhats are the guardians of *Soma*, *Svāna*, *Bhrāja*, *Ānghārya*, etc.

the nourisher of (Indra), the juice." (Rv. ix. 86, 9. 10) "Wearing a coat of mail (i.e., clothed in light) reaching to heaven, the adorable Soma, who fills the firmament (with rain), placed in the waters, generating heaven, passes with the water, (and) worships its ancient parent (Indra)." (Rv. ix. 86, 14). "All these are the offspring of thy celestial effluence ; thou art the ruler of the whole world ; so, purified (Soma), this universe is in subjection to thee ; thou, *Indu*, art the foremost, the supporter of the house. Thou, O Sage, art the ocean, thou art omniscient ; these five regions (rest) on thy support ; thou sustainest both heaven and earth ; the Sun, O Pavamāna, (nourishes) thy luminaries." (Rv. ix. 86, 28. 29). "O Soma, Pavamāna, thine are the thrice eleven universal Gods abiding in the secret heaven." (Rv. ix. 92, 4). From these references to *Soma*, it would be abundantly clear that Soma was something infinitely higher than the mere plant that grew on the mountains from which juices were extracted for drink and exhilaration.

Similarly Indra also had two forms, one visible in the Sun, the sky, and thunderstorms, and another subtle, invisible and mysterious. "That mighty mysterious form, desired of many, wherewith thou (Indra) hast engendered the past, and (engenderest) the future, the ancient manifested light, the beloved of Indra, into which the five (orders of beings) delighted enter." (Rv. x. 55, 2). This was his secret and invisible form or place of abiding which only the wise could obtain glimpses of or know : "I have looked down upon the secret and fearful place of his abiding ; I have repaired, desiring him, (to the place of) the self-sustainer ; I have inquired (of him) from others : they, the leaders (of rites), the searchers after wisdom, have said to me, let us have recourse to Indra." (Rv. v. 30, 2,.

Like Indra, Viṣṇu also had a visible and invisible form He took three steps, of which the first two were visible, and the third which was in the highest heaven was invisible to mortals but always visible to the Gods. (Rv. i. 22, 20). This was his dear abode, where pious men rejoiced, and where there was a well of honey. (Rv. i. 154, 5).

Vāta or Vāyu had also a physical form which manifested itself in wind. "(I proclaim) the greatness of the impetuous Vāyu; his voice spreads thundering around; he moves along sweeping the sky, tinting purple (the quarters of the horizon), he advances, raising the dust of the earth." (Rv. x. 168, 1). The sage-poet, unable to trace his origin, at first asks in perplexity "Where has he been generated? Whence was he manifested?" but answers as follows: "The soul of the Gods, the germ of the world, this divinity moves according to his pleasure: his voices are heard, his form is not (seen); let us worship that Vāta with oblations." (Rv. x. 168, 3. 4). Vāta, in another hymn, (Rv. x. 186), has been described as possessing healing balm, and able to bring happiness and prolong human life. He had the treasure of immortality in his house. (*tē gṛhē amṛtasya nidhirhitaḥ*).

The *Maruts* were the strong winds or storms that brought down rain. They rose from the ocean and shed rain. (Rv. i. 39, 9). Their appearance was bright like the Sun or the blazing Fire. (Rv. vi. 66, 2; vii. 59, 11). The Maruts were decorated with garlands and other ornaments. (Rv. v. 53 4). They had spears on their shoulders, anklets on their feet, golden ornaments on their breasts, fiery lightnings in hands, and golden helmets on their heads. (Rv. v. 54, 11). These were their physical features and appearance; but their spiritual nature is referred to in a verse in which they are said to have saved men from sin. (Rv. i. 166, 8).

The physical appearance of the sky or the vast and limitless void over our head was known by the name of *Dauḥ* or *Dyāvā* But this physical sky was the manifestation of an unseen or invisible sky, known as *Parama Vyoma*. It was in this *Parama Vyoma* that Indra upheld Dyāva and Pṛthivī, (Rv. i. 62, 7) and it was in this region that Agni was first produced and became revealed to *Mātariśvan*, (Rv. i.

143, 2) who brought him (Agni) down to earth and gave him to the Bhṛgus. (Rv. i. 60, 1). By the way, Mātariśvan is the name of Agni in three passages of the Ṛgveda, (i. 96, 4; iii. 5, 9; 26, 2). But he has also been distinguished from Agni and named separately, as in the verse: "One Being the wise call variously; they speak of Agni, Yama, Mātariśvan." (Rv. i. 164, 46). Yāska has identified him with Vāyu, and Sāyaṇa has explained the word etymologically as *Mātari antarikṣe śvasiti prāṇiti vartate iti yāvat*; *i.e.*, one who breathes in the sky; in other words, air or atmosphere. And this view is supported by the verses in which Agni is said to have revealed himself to Mātariśvan who brought him down to earth for the use of man. (Rv. i. 60, 1; 93, 6; 128, 2; 141, 3; iii. 2, 13; 9, 5; vi. 8, 4; x. 46, 9). It has been further said that Mātariśvan produced by friction the hidden Agni. (Rv. i. 141, 3; 71, 4: 148, 1). In one verse (Rv. iii. 29, 11), Agni is said to have become the swift flight of wind. In another verse (Rv. x. 109, 1), Mātariśvan is spoken of as boundless and wandering *(salila)*. From all these references, my opinion is that Mātariśvan was really air or wind, though he is occasionally identified with Agni, because Agni cannot be produced and cannot burn without the help of wind or air. But Mātariśvan was not the material wind or *vāta*, but the very essence of it, produced by the vibration of *Mahākāśa* or ether in the *Parama Vyoma*; and it was by the vibration or friction of Mātariśvan that Agni was produced.

It would thus appear that there are usually two aspects of the Gods in the Ṛgveda, one physical or material, and the other subtile and spiritual, which have earned for them the epithet of *Dvijanmā* or twice-born. (Rv. vi. 50, 2). It is therefore a mistake to suppose that the Ṛgvedic bards were mere worshippers of crude physical nature in all its different aspects. They really looked upon them as the different manifestations under different names of the one, all-pervading and underlying Spirit that was intelligent, active and highly beneficent, and revealed Itself outwardly as the Sun, the

Sky, the Pṛthivī, the Maruts, Agni, Indra, Varuṇa, Uṣas and so forth. This point will be futher elaborated later on.

Unity in diversity; "*Polytheistic Monotheism.*"—This invisible world of the Soul constitutes the one underlying principle of all physical existence, life and manifestations, and the Ṛgvedic bards had a clear conception of it. I have already said that the Sun has been described in the Ṛgveda, (i. 115, 1) as the *ātmā jagataḥ* or the "Soul of the world" or "the Soul of all that moves or is immoveable" (*ātmā jagatastaṣthuṣaśca*) and identified with the Gods Indra, Mitra, Varuṇa and Agni, as will appear from the translation of the following verse, (Rv. i 164, 46) : "They call him (the Sun) Indra, Mitra, Varuṇa, Agni, and he is the heavenly nobly-winged Garutman. To what is One, sages give many a title : they call it Agni, Yama, Mātariśvan." (Griffith). Garutman is, of course, the celestial bird, the Sun. Griffith thus comments on this verse : "All these names, says the poet, are names of one and the same Divine Being, the One Supreme Spirit under various manifestations." Elsewhere the Sun has been described as *Ekaiva vā mahān ātmā devatā Sūryaḥ i.e*, the Divine Sun is the One great Spirit. As the Sun is *Agni*, so the latter also is *Sarvā devatāḥ, i.e.*, Agni is all the divinities. "Agni when born is Varuṇa, when kindled is Mitra." (Rv. v. 3, 1). Again, "Agni is one, though kindled in various ways : one is the Sun, pre-eminent over all ; one Dawn illumines this all ; *one is that which hath become this all*" (*ekam vai idam vi babhūva sarvam*). (R. viii. 58, 2). It will thus appear that there was in the mind of the Ṛgvedic bards a clear conception of unity in the midst of diversity. The burden of the song in Rv. iii. 55 is *mahaddevānām asuratvamekam, i.e.*, "great and incomparable is the divine nature of the Gods," (Muir), or as Wilson has translated the passage "Great and unequalled is the might of the Gods." I would prefer to translate the passage thus : "Great and *one* is the might of the Gods," in other words, the great might of the Gods proceeds from One Source. And this idea has been elaborated in what is popularly known as the ***Devī Sūktam***, (Rv. x. 125), of which the Deity is ***Paramātmā*** or the Universal Soul, and the Ṛṣi is ***Vāc***, personified Speech or the Word that proclaimed or manifested the Supreme Being, and was inseparable from Him, representing His might or function. This is how *Vāc*, or the Primordial Force of Brahman, proclaims herself:

"1. I proceed with the Rudras, with the Vasus, with the Ādityas, and with the Viśvadevas; I support both Mitra and Varuṇa, Agni and Indra, and the two Aśvins. 2. I support the foe-destroying Soma, Tvaṣṭṛ, Pūṣan and Bhaga; I bestow wealth upon the institutor of the rite offering the oblation, deserving of protection, pouring forth the libation. 3. I am the Sovereign Queen, the collectress of treasures, cognizant (of the Supreme Being), the chief of objects of worship; as such the Gods have put me in many places, abiding in manifold conditions, entering into numerous (forms). 4. He who eats food (eats) through me; he who sees, who breathes, who hears what is spoken, does so through me; those who are ignorant of me perish; hear thou who hast hearing, I tell thee that which is deserving of belief. 5. I verily of myself declare this which is approved of by both Gods and men; whomsoever I will, I render formidable, I make him a Brahman, (according to Sāyaṇa, Brahmā, the Creator), a Ṛṣi, or a sage. 6. I bend the bow of Rudra, to slay the destructive enemy of the Brahmans (chanters of hymns at a sacrifice). I wage war with (hostile) men, I pervade heaven and earth. 7. I bring forth the paternal (heaven) upon the brow of this (Supreme Being),[1] my birth place is in the midst of the waters;[2] from thence I spread through all beings, and touch this heaven with my body. 8.

---

[1] This passage has been orherwise translated thus: "I bring forth the paternal (heaven), (which is) the brow of this world."

[2] ***Apswantah samudre***: In the midst of the waters of the ocean. These waters must have been in their subtile form in the ***kāraṇa-samudra***, or causal ocean at the beginning of creation.

I breathe forth like the wind, giving form to all created worlds; beyond the heaven, beyond this earth (am I), so vast am I in greatness."[1]

This Goddess, *Vāc*, represented the Active Principle, or the Creative Force of the Supreme Being, and was the origin of the later Vedic Umā, or the Paurāṇic Durgā, the Primordial Śakti (Ādyā Śakti), from whom everything proceeds and who pervades everything and is conterminous with the Supreme Being Himself who is without beginning or end, and vaster than the Universe. This Primordial Force manifests itself in various forms as Indra, Agni, Varuṇa, the Aśvins, the Maruts, Mitra, Bhaga, Pūṣan, Tvaṣṭṛ, Rudra, Sūrya, etc., and gives forms to all created worlds. Nothing exists or can exist without its help or support. These manifestations, though diverse in character, are really one in essence. All objects, material and immaterial, owe their origin to it. The Ṛgvedic bards realised the presence of this Universal Soul not only in the Gods, but in men, animals, trees, mountains, and all natural phenomena. Professor Macdonell says that "by the end of the Ṛgvedic period a kind of polytheistic monotheism had been arrived at. We find there even the incipient pantheistic conception of a deity representing not only all the Gods but Nature as well. For the Goddess Aditi is identified not only with all the Gods, but with men; all that has been and shall be born, air, and heaven (Rv. i. 89, 10); and Prajāpati is not only the One God above all Gods, but embraces all things (Rv. x. 121, 8.10). This pantheistic view becomes fully developed in the Atharva-veda (x. 7, 14.25), and is explicitly accepted in the later Vedic literature."[2]

Prajāpati.—Prajāpati is called Hiraṇyagarbha in the Ṛgveda. The latter term means "the Golden Embryo, or He who had the golden germ, *i.e.*, He who was in the golden mundane egg as an embryo, Brahmā, the Creator." (Wilson).

---

[1] Wilson's translation.

[2] *Vedic Mythology*, § 10.

The following hymn (Rv. x. 121) is addressed to Prajāpati (Hiraṇyagarbha) :—

"1. In the beginning there arose the Golden Child. He was the one born lord of all that is. He established the earth and this sky :—Who is the God to whom we shall offer our sacrifice ?[1]

"2. He who gives breath, (*i.e.*, life). He who gives strength ; whose command all the Gods revere ; whose shadow is immortality, whose shadow is death :—Who is the God, &c.

"3. He who through his greatness is the one King of the breathing and awakening world ; He who governs man and beast :—Who is the God, etc.

"4. He whose greatness the Himavat, the Samudra, the Rasā proclaim ; He whose these regions are, as it were, his two arms :—Who is the God, etc.

"5. He through whom the sky is bright and the earth firm ; He through whom the heaven was established,—nay the highest heaven ; He who measured out the aerial space :—Who is the God, etc.

"6. He to whom the two battle-hosts, sustained by his support, look up trembling in spirit, there where the risen Sun shines :—Who, etc.

"7. When the mighty waters pervaded the universe, holding the germ and begetting fire, thence He arose, who is the sole life of Gods ; Who is the God, etc.

"8. He who by his might looked even over the waters which gave strength and lit the sacrifice ;—He who alone is God above all the Gods :—Who is the God, etc.

"9. May He not harm us, the Creator of this earth ; who, ruling by fixed ordinances, created the heaven ; who also created the bright and mighty waters :—Who is the God to whom we shall offer our sacrifice ?

---

[1] The last sentence has been otherwise translated by Wilson, following the commentators : "Let us offer worship with an oblation to the divine Ka" (or Prajāpati).

"10. No other than thou, Prajapati, hast given existence to all these beings; may that object of our desires for which we sacrifice to thee be ours, may we be the possessor of riches."

The Puruṣa-Sūkta.—Prajāpati, then, is the Creator, (Paurāṇic Brahmā) of the Universe, and of all animate and inanimate things that exist. He is thus regarded as the mighty Generative or Male Principle, the *Puruṣa*, or the Giant Being who is identified with the entire Universe, and even greater than it, who divided himself, or was divided by the Gods into all the component parts that constitute the Universe—the Sun, the Moon, the Earth, man, animals, plants, and even the four natural classes into which mankind is divided. The Puruṣa "is the victim whom the Gods offer up and the dissection of whose body—which is simply *the material to work with*, the whole of pre-existing Matter, with its latent possibilities for generating life—produces the various parts of the Universe with their denizens, of course with special reference to our habitable earth, as far as known to the Āryas of India."[1] The hymn in which the sacrifice of the Puruṣa has been related is called the *Puruṣa-Sūkta* (Rv. x. 90) and thus reads in translation:

1. "Puruṣa of the thousand heads, the thousand eyes, the thousand feet, covered the earth in all directions and extended ten finger-breadths beyond. 2. Puruṣa is this whole universe, whatever has been, and whatever shall be and a possessor of the immortality which groweth great by food (offered in sacrifice?) 3. So great is Puruṣa, yea, greater still. One quarter of him is all that hath been made, three quarters of him are the immortals in heaven. 4. With three feet Puruṣa mounted up, with one foot he remained here, then he spread out on all sides and became that which eateth and that which eateth not. 5. From him the Virāj

[1] Ragozin's *Vedic India*, p. 420.

was born, and from the Virāj again Puruṣa.[1] As soon as he was born, he reached out beyond the earth at both ends. 6. When the Gods prepared the sacrifice with the Puruṣa as the offering, the spring was the sacrificial butter, the summer was the fuel, the autumn was the (accompanying) oblation. 7. On the sacrificial grass they anointed the victim, that Puruṣa who was born in the beginning; him the Gods sacrificed, whose favour is to be sought, and the Ṛṣis. 8. When the sacrifice was completed, they collected the fat dripping from it; it formed the creatures of air, and the animals that live in forests, and those that live in villages (wild and domestic). 9. From this sacrifice when completed were born the Ṛg-hymns and the Sāma-hymns, and the incantations (probably the future Atharvan); and the Yajus were born from it. 10. From it were born the horses and all the cattle that have two rows of teeth, the kine were born from it; from it the goats and sheep were born. 11. When they divided Puruṣa, into how many parts did they cut him up? What was his mouth? What were his arms? What were his thighs and feet called? 12. The Brāhmaṇa was his mouth; the Rajanya was made from his arms; the Vaiśya—he was his thighs; the Sūdra sprang from his feet. 13. The Moon was born from his mind; the Sun from his eye; Indra and Agni from his mouth; from his breath the wind was born. 14. From his navel came the air; from his head sprang the sky; from his feet the earth, from his ear the regions; thus they formed, the worlds. 15. When the Gods bound Puruṣa as victim, preparing the sacrifice, seven enclosing bars of wood were placed for him, thrice seven layers of fuel were piled for him. 16. So the Gods through sacrifice earned a right to sacrifice; *these were the first*

[1] "The *Viraj* is a ponderous and solemn sacred metre, said to consist of forty syllables. That metre is born of sacrifice, and sacrifice of metre is a familiar mystical conception. This is the explanation given by the Śatapatha Brāhmaṇa; it commends itself by its simplicity and its conformity to Vedic modes of thought and speech." Ragozin's *Vedic India*, p. 420 (Foot-note).

ordinances. Those mighty ones attained to the highest heaven, where the ancient Gods abide, whose favour is to be sought."

The conception of the Puruṣa or the Giant Divine Being, who is conterminous with and even greater than the Universe, from whose body the whole creation including the Devas sprang, is essentially pantheistic, and was probably an old conception like that of Prajāpati, Viśvakarmā and Paramātmā. But the idea of His sacrifice by the Gods and Ṛṣis must have been of later origin, when human sacrifice was probably in vogue, and the four castes were fully developed. The idea, however, is somewhat self-contradictory in so far as the Gods and Ṛṣis who are said to have been created by him, took part in His sacrifice, although they were produced from one or another of his severed limbs. The real idea was probably this: The Primordial Being or Brahman is Infinite and Limitless from His very nature. But as soon as He thought of Creation and revealed Himself in Creation, He conditioned His Infinitude and Limitlessness to a certain extent, which was undoubtedly *the greatest act of sacrifice* that man could think of. Without this great Sacrifice on the part of Brahman, there would have been no creation — no earth, no sky, no Sun or Moon, no Gods, no Ṛṣis, no men, no castes, no animals—birds or beasts—no Ṛks, Sāmans or Yajus—and the One only would have remained absorbed in Himself for ever in the midst of primitive darkness, and limitless vastness. The Creation, therefore, was the result of Brahman's Supreme Sacrifice, and this became the model of all sacrificial institutions invented by men for their own benefit, and the benefit of the Universe. The Vedic bard has described this great Sacrifice in language and sentiments which were necessarily somewhat crude and imperfect. Nevertheless, the Sūkta is the great Pantheistic hymn in which the Universe, in its entirety and parts, has been identified with Brahman, the Supreme Being.

Viśvakarman, the Creator.—This Puruṣa, or the Supreme Divine Being, was also named Viśvakarman or the

Creator. The idea of creation connotes four things, *viz.*, (1) the Creator; (2) the object created; (3) the material from which the object is created; and (4) the place where the creation takes place. The Vedic bard looked upon the Creator as the greatest Artisan or Architect, and he was naturally puzzled to think about the material or materials employed by the Creator in creating the Universe, and the place where such creation took place. He was also unable to comprehend or describe the Great Artisan or Architect Himself. The translation of the following verses (Rv. x. 81) will speak for itself:—

2. "What was the station? What was the material? How was it done? so that the beholder of all, Viśvakarman, (was) generating and disclosed heaven by his might[1] 3. Having eyes everywhere, and having a face everywhere, having arms everywhere, and having feet everywhere, he traverses (heaven) with his arms, (earth) with his swift-moving (feet), and exists a God without companion, generating heaven and earth. 4. Which was the forest, which the tree, from which they, (*i.e.*, the makers of the world directed by Parameśvara) fabricated heaven and earth? Inquire, Sages, in your minds what (place) he was stationed in when holding the worlds." (Rv. x. 81). Again we read, (Rv. x. 82). "2. Viśvakarman, of comprehensive mind and manifold greatness, is all-pervading, the Creator, the arranger and the supreme supervisor; him in whom the desires of their (senses) are satisfied with food, they call (him) supreme beyond the Seven Ṛṣis. 3. He who is our preserver, our parent, the creator (of all), who knows our abodes (and knows) all beings, who

---

[1] "In the first verse it is said that after *pralaya*. the Creator made all things anew. It is now asked—where was the scene of action, what were the materials and how was the work performed? In this world, says the commentator, a potter must have his shop, his clay, his wheel: so what site, matter, and implements had Īśvara? Sāyana intimates that the questions imply a negative answer, and says they mean that nothing of the kind was necessary." (Wilson).

is the name-giver of the Gods—he is one; other beings come to him to inquire, (*i.e.*, to ask who is the Supreme Lord?) 4. Those ancient Ṛṣis who adorned (with light) these things in the animate and inanimate world, offer to him wealth (of sacrifice) as praisers with abundant (laudation). 5. What was that embryo which was beyond the heaven, beyond this earth, beyond the Gods, beyond the *Asuras*, which the waters first retained, in which all the Gods contemplated each other? 6. The waters verily first retained the embryo in which all the Gods were aggregated, single deposited on the navel of the unborn (Creator), in which all beings abode. 7. You know not him who has generated these (beings), (his life) is another, different from yours;[1] wrapped in fog, and foolish speech, (do they) wander (who are) gluttonous and engaged in devotion."[2] (Wilson).

From the above verses, the following facts are deduced: (1) that creation has no beginning nor end, in the same way as the Creator has no beginning nor end; (2) that the Universe merges in temporary apparent extinction at the time of *Pralaya*, but it really merges in the Creator in whom it remains in a dormant or quiscent state; (3) that at the time of a new creation, the Gods and the divine Ṛṣis come first into existence, who help the Creator in creating animate beings and inanimate things; (4) that the creation evolves out of the Creator Himself; (5) that the Creator, though all conscious, has not the same *individual* consciousness as sensient beings, who are conditioned and limited by their own *individual* consciousness only; and (7) that the Creator

[1] Sāyaṇa comments on this verse as follows: "The assertion that we know *Viśvakarman* in the same way as men say 'I am *Devadatta* I am *Yajnadatta*' is false; for the essence (*tattva*) of *Viśvakarman Parameśvara* is not endowed with conscious individual existence, but he is a different entity from you who are sensient beings, who have individual consciousness and so forth."

[2] Mahidhara explains this verse as follows: "You who are engaged in the enjoyments of this world or the next, being subject to false knowledge or ignorance, have no knowledge of Truth." Sāyaṇa also has a similar explanation.

cannot be apprehended by those who are engaged in the enjoyments of this world, or of the next, as such enjoyments do not conduce to that self-concentration which is the key to real divine knowledge, and only serve to keep the mind wandering away from God and this perception of the Truth.

Vedic Cosmogony.—And this naturally leads us to Vedic Cosmogony, as conceived by the Ṛṣis. There is a remarkable hymn in the Ṛgveda (x. 129) of which the deity is the *Paramātman* (the Universal Soul) and the Ṛṣi is Prajāpati Himself, and which reads as follows in translation:

"1. Nor Aught nor Naught existed then; not the aerial space, nor heaven's bright woof above. What covered all? Where rested all? Was it water, the profound abyss? 2. Death was not then, nor immortality; there was no difference of day and night.[1] That One breathed breathless in Itself, *i.e.*, existed, but without exerting or manifesting Itself; and there was nothing other than It. 3. In the beginning there was darkness in darkness enfolded, all was undistinguishable water.[2] That One, which lay in the empty space, wrapped in nothingness, was developed by the power of heat (tapasas).[3] 4. Desire first arose in It,[4] that was the

---

[1] "That is, time was not yet, because time is known only by the alternation of day and night. Therefore in Genesis I., the first work of creation is to 'divide the light from the darkness.'" Ragozin's *Vedic India*, P 427.

[2] "Compare all this to Genesis I., 2: "And darkness was on the face of the deep, and the spirit of God was moving (or brooding) on the face of waters." Ragozin's *V. I.*

[3] Wilson translated *tapasas* as "through the power of austerity," and says the word "is said to mean not penance, but the contemplation of the things which were to be created."

[4] "Desire (to manifest itself) is the first stirring of sentient will, which must itself precede action. The word is *Kāma.* It became (from obvious association) the word for "love" and the name of the Love God. The Greek language and mythology present an exactly parallel case: Eros, the name of the Love-God, originally means 'desire.' And by the light of this marvellous effort of Vedic thought, the [illegible] features [illegible] in Hesiod's Theogony acquire [illegible] new [illegible] race of Immortals [illegible] Night, whom the briny deep bore. Foremost [illegible] and next broad-bosomed Earth (*pṛthivī*)...and Eros, most beautiful of Immortals..' This Eros is the Cosmogonic Kāma (Desire) of our hymn, the prompter of the act of creation" Ragozin's *V. I.* P 247-428 (Foot-note).

primal germ of mind, which poets, searching with their intellects, discovered in their hearts to be the bond between Being and Not-Being. 5. The ray of light which stretched across these worlds, did it come from below or from above? Then seeds were sown and mighty forces arose, Nature beneath, and Power and Will above. 6. Who indeed knows? Who proclaimed it here—whence, whence this creation was produced? The Gods were later than its production—who then knows whence it sprang? 7. He from whom this creation sprang, whether He made it or not, the All-Seer in the highest heaven, He knows it, or He does not."[1] (Max Muller).

The Vedic thinkers conceived primeval Chaos, unquickened as yet by the first fiat of Creative Will, yet brooded over by the Divine presence, which their great poetic gift enabled them to clothe in such words as, to use Max Müller's enthusiastic expression, "language blushes at, but her blush is a blush of triumph." "One of the great beauties of this matchless piece" says Ragozin "is that while reaching the uttermost bounds of philosophical abstraction, it is never obscure unless to the absolutely uninitiated."

As already stated, the Vedic bards conceived creation as the result of *desire (kāma)* in the mind of the Brahman. Before creation, chaotic matter was in a quiscent state, resting in the bosom of the Great One, without any signs of life or activity. As soon as desire for creation arose in the Divine Mind, there was a simultaneous stir, movement and activity in the entire chaotic mass, the result of vibration proceeding from His desire. Rays of light were stretched

---

[1] The last sentence can be explained thus: If the Creator knew that He had made the creation, He would be conditioned by His knowledge or individualistic consciousness Creation like the Creator, has neither beginning nor end. But the creation of a thing implies its beginning, though the Universe really has no beginning. Therefore to say that the Universe was created by Brahman would be to limit and condition creation and Brahman Himself. Hence the poet says: "He knows it, or He does not."

out across, below and above. "This, according to Sayaṇa, refers to the suddenness of creation, which was developed in the twinkling of an eye, like the flash of the Sun's ray. It was so quick, he continues, that it was doubtful whether the things in the central space (understood by the word 'across') were created first, or those above, or those below; in other words, creation took place simultaneously in all the three portions of the Universe. Sāyaṇa tries to reconcile this with the received notion of creation in a series (*viz.* that from *ātmā* came the *ākāśa*, and from the *ākāśa* the wind, from the wind fire, etc.), by saying that this was the order in which things were created, but the development of the world was like a flash of lightning, so that the series could not be distinguished." [1]

In the above hymn, it has been said: "Then seeds were sown and mighty forces arose. Nature (*Svadhā*) beneath, and Power and Will (*Prayati*) above." This probably implies that the Brahman divided Himself into two halves, one half was His Will and Power (*Puruṣa*), and the other half Nature (*or Prakṛti*) in whom seeds were sown for the evolution of creation. This *Svadhā* or Nature was probably the same as Aditi, the mother of the Gods. "Aditi, who was thy daughter, Dakṣa, was born; after her the Gods were born adorable, freed from the bonds of death. When, Gods, you abode in this pool [2] well arranged, then a pungent dust went forth from you as if you were dancing. When, Gods, you filled the worlds (with your radiance) as clouds (fill the earth with rain), then you brought forth the Sun hidden in the ocean." (Rv. x. 72, 5-2). These verses indicate the creation of the Gods as the result of vibration proceeding from the Creator. The Gods looked as if they were dancing and thereby raising, as it were, clouds of dust.

---

[1] Wilson's *Translation of the Ṛgveda*, foot-note.

[2] *i.e.*, when the world was yet subtile water as it was before creation, and the Gods were properly speaking uncreated.

Everything was in rapid motion and whirling at the beginning of creation, and the Sun was afterwards revealed as the result of this vibration.

This vibration is the same as the Primordial Force, of which all the Devas were the component parts. Indra, Agni, Soma, Rudra, the Maruts, the Sun, the Dawn and the Aśvins, etc., were constantly vibrating and in motion. But this vibration was not the result of blind and unintelligent Force. "From kindled heat (*tapasaḥ*) were born Right and Law (*Satya* and *Ṛta*, the Cosmic Order), and Night, then the watery flood. And from the watery flood the coursing year was born, disposing day and night, the ruler of all that close the eyes. And in their order the Creator formed the Sun and the Moon, and heaven and earth, the regions of the air and light" (Rv. x. 190).

So it was this Cosmic Order (Ṛta) that had been first born before creation took place according to this Order. From Ṛta were born Soma (Rv. ix. 108. 8), Dyāvā-Pṛthivī (Rv. x. 65, 8) the Maruts (Rv. iii. 54, 13; vii. 66, 13), Agni (Rv. iv. 5, 9), Bṛhaspati (Rv. ii. 23, 3), Sūrya (Rv. v. 62, 12), Uṣas (Rv. vii. 74, 1), Mitra and Varuṇa (Rv. i. 2, 8; vii. 61, 2; v. 64, 1) and the Viśvedevāḥ. This Ṛta or the Cosmic Order, proceeding from the Brahman, still rules and upholds the Universe regulating the course of the Sun, Moon, Dawn, the Winds, Year, Days and Nights, Seasons and Stars, and the birth, growth and decay of Vegetable and Animal life.

We have endeavoured to give in this Chapter a brief account of the ideas that the ancient Vedic bards entertained regarding the Universal Soul (*Paramātman* or *Brahman*), and the creation of the worlds and of Gods, men, animals and vegetation. The ideas, of course, were slowly and gradually evolved until at the end of the Ṛgvedic period the Vedic cosmogony was fully adumbrated, and unity in the midst of diversity realised.

CHAPTER XIII.

YAJÑA OR VEDIC SACRIFICE.

No account of Ṛgvedic culture would be complete without a brief reference to Yajña or Sacrifice that played such a large and important part in the life of the Vedic Aryans. They were an eminently sacrifice-loving people, performing sacrifices daily, fortnightly, monthly, seasonally, annually, and on all important occasions and at the happenings of all the principal events of life *viz.*, birth, teething, tonsure, marriage, conception, initiation, illness, death and so forth. In a word, it may be said that the life of the Vedic Aryans was made up of a series of sacrifices, which it was incumbent upon them to perform.

The meaning and origin of Yajña.—Yajña means sacrifice,—sacrifice of something that one considers to be useful or valuable in favour of an invisible Being or Spirit who is supposed to be fond of it, and capable of awarding a desired boon to the performer. The early conception of this Being or Spirit seems to have been awful. Grant Allen, in his *Evolution of the Idea of God*, traces the conception of this awful Being to the worship of the Old Man of a savage tribe, who had been its powerful leader and also its terror in his life-time, and who was thought capable, even after his death, of exercising his influence, either for good or for evil. His memory was, therefore, cherished with mixed feelings of awe and reverence, and his spirit sought to be propitiated by the offer and sacrifice of such things as he was fond of. Sir E. B. Tyler, in his *Primitive Culture*, "gave his attention mainly to the disposition of primitive man to ascribe a soul to every object, animate and inanimate."[1] The world,

[1] H. G. Wells' *Outline of History* i. 77 (George Newnes, Ld.)

according to this conception, was full of spirits, mostly malevolent, who delighted in being satiated with the blood of their human and animal victims. Hence, when any epidemic broke out among men and animals, causing sudden deaths, or a devastating famine occurred, it was ascribed to the malevolent influence of a particular blood-thirsty Evil Spirit or Spirits, who required to be propitiated by the offer of blood. Hence a fowl, a pig, or even a human being was sacrificed for his or their propitiation. This was the germ of *Yajña* or Sacrifice.

Writing on this subject, Mr. H. G. Wells says: "(Neolithic) men were becoming aware that personally they needed protection and direction, cleansing from impurity, power beyond their own strength. Confusedly in response to that demand, bold men, wise men, shrewd and cunning men were arising to become magicians, priests, chiefs and kings. They are not to be thought of as cheats or usurpers of power, nor the rest of mankind as the dupes. All men are mixed in their motives ; a hundred things move men to seek ascendancy over other men, but not all such motives are base or bad. The magicians usually believed more or less in their own magic, the priests in their ceremonies, the chiefs in their right."[1] Further on he says that the mind of these Neolithic men became "full of the fear of some ancient Old Man who had developed into a tribal God, and also obsessed by ideas of sacrificial propitiation and magic murder. No doubt, the rein-deer hunter was a ruthless hunter and a combative and passionate creature, but he killed for reasons we can still understand. Neolithic man, under the sway of talk and a confused thought-process, killed on theory ; he killed for monstrous and now incredible ideas; he killed those he loved through fear and under direction. These Neolithic men not only made human sacrifices at seed-time ; there is every reason to suppose they sacrificed wives and slaves at the

---

[1] *Op. cit.*, p. 77.

burial of their chieftains; they killed men, women, and children whenever they were under adversity and thought the Gods were a-thirst. They practised infanticide. All these things passed on into the Bronze Age."[1]

Evolution of Yajña.—The above description probably gives a correct sketch of the development of the idea of sacrifice among savage men, and for the matter of that, among savage Aryans. But at the dawn of the Neolithic Age, we find the Aryan mind concieving the existence of benevolent Spirits or Gods, as arrayed against the influence of malevolent Spirits or Demons. The Gods or *Devas* were bright, powerful, benevolent and beneficent, while the Demons or Rakṣasas were dark and malevolent, always seeking opportunities for committing mischiefs, and constantly striving for supremacy over the *Devas*. There was a constant struggle going on between these two sets of powers, and the Āryans thought it right and obligatory to strengthen the Gods in their struggle with the malevolent Powers by the offer of prayers and such drinks and victuals as they found capable of strengthening them in their own life. Hence arose the necessity of Sacrifice. But this Sacrifice also carried with it the echoes of the beliefs and barbarities of a by-gone age, which they had outlived, in as much as we find occasionally even in Ṛgvedic times stray references to human sacrifice, in addition to the sacrifice of animals and the offer of oblations or *puroḍāśas* (cakes), and the libations of *havya* (*ghṛta*) or milk and the Soma-drink.

The discovery and use of *Agni* (Fire) greatly impressed the imaginative mind of the Neolithic Aryans, as Agni was not only bright and gloom-dispelling like the Sun, Dawn, Stars, and Lightning, but it could also be very easily produced, whenever required for domestic or ritual purposes, by a very simple process, *viz.*, the attrition of two dry sticks or the striking of two flints. Moreover, it was found instantly to consume everything consigned to it. On account of its

[1] *Op. cit.*, p. 78.

brightness and heat, it was identified with the Sun in the sky and Lightning in the clouds, and came to be looked upon as a deity on earth, who could be easily approached and worshipped, and through whom the oblations and libations, offered to the other distant Gods, could be easily and quickly conveyed to them. Hence, *Agni* came to be established as a Household Deity or *Gṛhapati*, the Lord of the house. He was also regarded as the Divine Priest of the Sacrifice *(yajñasya purohitaḥ)*, and an intermediary between Gods and men. Every Vedic house-holder was a sacrificer, and sacrificed to the Gods through Agni. It was highly necessary for, and obligatory on him to be a staunch Fire-worshipper, and keep the sacred Fire burning and alive in his house by throwing into it *samits*, or pieces of sacrificial wood, and pouring upon it libations of *havis* (*ghee*) and milk, and oblations thrice, or at least twice daily, along with his wife. For, the light of Agni dispelled gloom, the abode of Evil Spirits or Demons, *(Asuras* and *Rākṣasas)*, which earned for the deity the title of *Rakṣohan* or Killer of Demons. The man who ceremoniously kindled the sacred Fire, and kept it burning all his life was called *Āhitāgni*. He could also worship the other Gods through this Agni, according to prescribed formulas, with the help of priests who were experts in the art of performing the different parts of the various sacrifices (*yajñas* that had different objects in view. Elaborate formulas were drawn up in a later age for the performance of these *yajñas*, which are found so correctly embodied in the *Yajur-veda*, and explained in the *Brāhmaṇas* and *Sūtras* viz. the *Gṛhya Sūtras* and the *Śrauta Sūtras* that even at this distance of time the Vedic *yajñas* can be performed as faithfully as they were done thousands of years ago. The *Gṛhya Sūtras* contain rules for the performance of all sacrifices in connection with the important events and incidents of our home-life, viz., birth, marriage, initiation (*upanayanam*), conception, death etc., as well as of our civic and social life, *e.g.*, the dedication of newly-dug tanks and wells and of fruit-bearing and shady trees for the benefit of the public. The *Śrauta Sūtras* deal with elaborate formulas in connection with the performance of such sacrifices as *Agni-hotra*, *Iṣṭi-yāga*, *Paśu-yāga*, *Agni-ṣtoma*, *Aśva-medha*, *Rāja-sūya*, etc.

The Āhitāgni.—It was incumbent on every Vedic householder to be an *Āhitāgni*, or one who ceremoniously consecrated Fire for daily worship in his house along with his wife, and jointly worshipped that deity daily till death. In his boyhood, he had to live in his preceptor's house for the study of the Vedas, and the ceremony performed at the time of his first going there was known as *Upanayanam*. Here he had to pass through a course of rigorous training and discipline under the direction of his preceptor, and the period of this training and discipline was known as *Brahmacarya*. During his stay with his preceptor, he had to throw a piece of *samit* or dry sacrificial wood into his tutor's House-hold Fire every evening, probably with a view to be well practised in Fire-worship when the time should come for him to have his own Fire at home. On his *Samāvartanam* or return home from his preceptor's house, he had to kindle the sacred Fire, before which he had to perform the *Lāja-homa* at the time of his marriage. This Fire was called *Gṛhya*, *Āvasathya* or *Smārta Agni*.

Agnyādhāna.—After his marriage, he had to kindle and worship daily what was known as *Śrauta Agni*, which married men alone were privileged to do. The ceremony performed in connection with the first kindling of this sacred Fire is known as *Agnyādhāna* or *Agnyādheya*. For this purpose a new house, called *Agni-śālā*, is built, in which a four-sided altar or *Vedī* is raised. The northern and southern sides of the altar are long and concave in form, so that the size of the altar is like that of the trunk of a woman, with a narrow waist, and the upper and lower parts symmetrically bulging out at both ends. On the west of this altar is marked the place for the *Gārhapatya Agni* or House-hold Fire in the shape of a circle, three square feet in area; on the east is the place for the *Āhavanīya Agni*, marked in the shape of a square, and on the south is the place for the *Dakṣināgni*, marked in the shape of a semi-circle, but both of equal area with the circle on the west.[1] The first-named Fire is the representative of the house-holder, the second that of the Gods, to which all oblations meant for them are offered, and the third, i.e., the *Dakṣiṇāgni*, that of the Pitṛs, to which offerings intended for the Pitṛs are made. The house-holder (*yajamāna*) performs on the previous day a purificatory rite, and towards evening enters into the *Agni-śala* with his wife, where they both pass the night. The *Adhvaryu* brings Fire and puts it in the Gārhapatya circle where the Yajamāna keeps it burning the whole night by throwing into it pieces of *samit*. Two pieces of fire-sticks are also brought there, and kept ready for use early in the next morning. As soon as the day dawns, a horse is brought, and the Adhvaryu comes and extinguishes the Fire. He then proceeds to produce Fire by the attrition of the two fire-sticks (*araṇis*), the Yajamāna holding the lower *araṇi*, and his wife first, and then the Adhvaryu afterwards producing Fire with the help of the other *araṇi* by rotating it in a groove in the lower. The Fire, thus produced, is caught in pieces of dry cow-dung, placed in an earthen pan, which the Yajamāna kindles by blowing air from his mouth.

The priests whose services are requisitioned at this *Yajña* are (1) the *Hotṛ* or *Hotā* whose duty it is to invoke the Gods by the recitation of Ṛgvedic *mantras*, and who is well versed in the Ṛgveda; (2) the *Adhvaryu* whose duty it is to pour libations etc. (*āhuti*) upon the Fire, and prepare the necessary *havyas* for the sacrifice, to the accompaniment of Yajur-vedic *mantras*, and who is an expert in the Yajur-veda; (3) the *Udgātṛ* who is well practised in singing Sāma-mantras, and thoroughly versed in the Sāma-veda; and lastly, (4) the Brahman or Brahmā, the chief *Ṛtvik*, who presides at the

[1] According to some, the place for the *Gārhapatya Agni* should be square and that for the *Āhavaniya Agni* circular in shape.

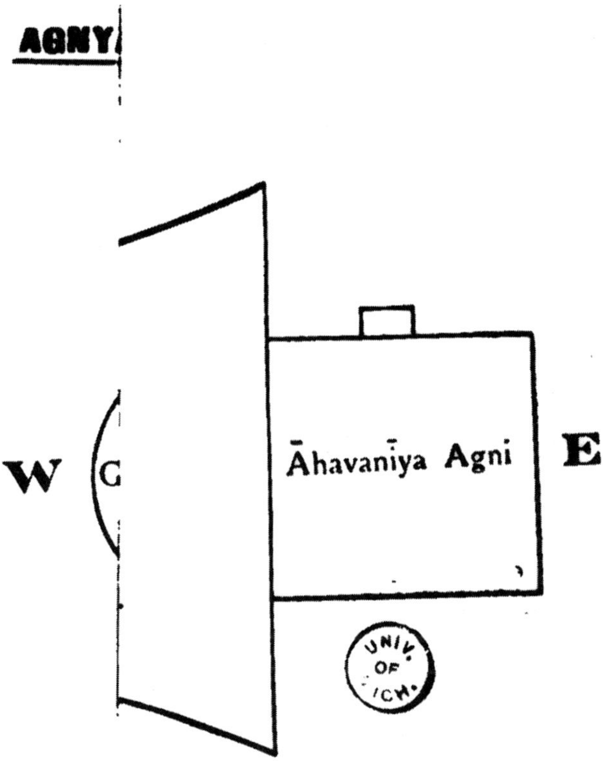
AGNY
W
C
Āhavanīya Agni
E

ceremony, and superintends the work of the above-named three *Ṛtviks*, being well versed in the three Vedas.

After the Fire is kindled by the Yajamāna, the Adhvaryu throws some sacrificial wood into it and deposits it in the Gārhapatya enclosure, to the accompaniment of some Sāma-songs, sung by the Brahmā. After that, the Adhvaryu takes a portion of the Gārhapatya Fire, and, preceded by the horse, and followed by the Yajamāna, proceeds to the place of the Āhavanīya, all the while the Brahmā singing Sāma-songs. The horse is then made to face westward, and to put one of its fore feet into the Āhavanīya enclosure when the Adhvaryu touches its fore-foot with the Fire, and puts it in the enclosure, all the while the Brahmā singing Sāma-songs. Next, the Adhvaryu goes back to the Gārhapatya Agni, and bringing a portion of it, puts it in the semi-circular enclosure for the Dakṣiṇāgni. This done, the Brahmā sings three Sāma-songs, and the whole party walks round the altar thrice, with their right arms towards the Vedī (*pradakṣiṇam*), after which the horse is set free.

Next follows *Pūrṇāhuti Homa*. For this purpose, some *ghṛta* is heated on the Gārhapatya Fire, and the Adhvaryu, sitting near the Āhavanīya Fire, takes some *ghee* with a wooden ladle or spoon known as *juhū*, and pours it upon the Fire to the accompaniment of Yajur-mantras, all the while the Yajamāna touching him. This is what is called *Pūrṇāhuti*, and with it the rite of *Agnyādhāna* ends. The Yajamāna has to observe the rules of abstinence for some days after this, and to keep the Gārhapatya Agni constantly burning, though the other two Fires are allowed to go out, to be rekindled only from the Gārhapatya on particular occasions. From this time onward, the householder is known by the name of *Āhitāgni*, and privileged to perform all Śrauta ceremonies, and the worship of the Devas and Pitṛs. [1]

[1] This account of *Agnyādhāna* has been condensed with slight alterations from Pandit Ramendra Sundar Trivedi's excellent work *Yajña-kathā* written in Bengali.

The horse in the above ceremony is the emblem of the Sun. It is brought into the *Agni-sālā* before sun-rise, and taken from the west side of the altar to the east, and made to face westward with a fore-foot placed in the Āhavanīya enclosure, all of which is emblematic of sun-rise. The fact that the Adhvaryu puts a portion of the Gārhapatya Agni into the Āhavanīya enclosure after touching its foot with the Fire goes to show that Fire on earth is regarded as identical with the Sun in heaven, and the Sun being identical with Indra and Viṣṇu, two of the supreme Gods of the Aryans, the Fire put and kindled in the Āhavanīya enclosure is fit for worshipping these deities, as well as the other Gods, and all libations and oblations offered to this Fire are conveyed directly to the Gods themselves. Fire-worship is a very ancient cult with the Aryans, having been inaugurated in Neolithic times, but the taming of the horse must have been earlier still, as it performs a very important part in the ceremony of *Agnyādhāna*. Fire-worship also prevailed among the Iranians, and the ancient Greeks and Romans, which goes to show that the two last-named branches of the Aryans must have left their original cradle in Sapta-Sindhu for Europe in Neolithic times after the cult of Fire-worship had been introduced in the mother-land.

Agnihotra.—After the performance of the ceremony of *Agnyādhāna*, which marks his initiation into the Fire-cult, it is incumbent on the initiated house-holder, called *Āhitagni*, and his wife to perform twice daily the *Yāga* known as *Agnihotra*. From the Gārhapatya Agni which is kept constantly burning, a portion of the Fire is taken by them to the Āhavanīya and Dakṣiṇāgni enclosures respectively, and kindled morning and evening, upon which libations are poured. The morning libation to the Āhavanīya Agni is offered to Sūrya (the Sun) with the recitation of the following *mantra*: *Bhūrbhuvah svah Om Sūrya-jyotih jyotih Sūrya Svāhā*; and the evening libation is offered to Agni with the recitation of the following *mantra*: *Bhūrbhuvah svah*

Om Agnir-jyotih jyotiragni Svāha. The libation consists of pure milk of a cow, specially reserved for the purpose. The milk is held in an earthen vessel and heated on the Gārhapatya Fire. Two wooden ladles, one small, called *sruva*, and another large, called *Agnihotrahavanī*, are brought. The milk is taken from the vessel with the help of the small ladle, and poured into the large one four or five times, and then the contents of the large ladle or spoon are poured upon the Āhavanīya Fire, after feeding it with a *samit*, in two instalments. The first instalment is accompanied by the recitation of one of the two mantras quoted above, addressed to Sūrya or Agni, as the case may be, and the second instalment is accompanied by no recitation of any *mantra*, as the offering is made to Prajāpati who is simply to be contemplated in the mind. But the whole of the contents of the large ladle should never be poured upon the Fire, and a little remnant left, which is to be drunk by the house-holder.

After offering libations to the Āhavanīya Fire, the house-holder sits before the Gārhapatya Agni and pours the first libation upon it with the help of the small ladle only in the name of *Agni Gṛhapati* (Lord of the House), and the second in the name of Prajāpati. Then sitting before Dakṣināgni, he pours upon it the first libation in the name of *Agni Annapati* (Lord of Food), and the second in the name of Prajāpati. At the end of the evening ceremony, after drinking the remnant of *havis*, and throwing three pieces of *samit* into each of the three Fires, the house-holder pays his homage to Agni, and goes out of the *Agni-śala*.

The performance of Agnihotra being obligatory on every house-holder, it must be daily attended to by him, and in the event of his unavoidable absence or illness, by his representative, either a son, grand-son, or daughter's son. According to some, even after the death of his wife, the ceremony should be continued by him till his own death, though, according to others, he may delegate his authority to any of his lineal representatives to perform it. For, its performance implies the repayment of the debts we owe to the Ṛṣis, the Gods and the Pitṛs. The ceremony itself is very simple, as our readers have seen, involving no cost or trouble, and can be performed by all, rich and poor alike. All that is necessary is a little pure milk, and a few pieces of dry wood. Even if milk be not available, a little curd, or a few grains of rice can be offered to the Fire. When nothing is available, one can offer one's *śraddhā* (adoration) to Agni with the words: *Aham śraddhām juhomi*, *i.e.*, "I offer thee my *śraddhā* or adoration." *Śraddhā-Homa* has been extolled in the Scriptures.

Iṣṭi Yāga.—The house-holder, initiated as *Āhitāgni*, has to perform many other Śrauta Yāgas, one of which is named *Iṣṭi-Yāga*, which must be performed every fortnight *i.e.*, on the full moon and new moon days. The former is called *Pūrṇamāsa Yāga*, and the latter *Darśa Yāga*. The rites performed for each are similar. The first offering, or *āhuti*, is intended for Agni, and it is called *puroḍāśa*, which is a cake made from barley or rice meal. The Ṛtvik, known as Adhvaryu, takes a few handfuls or ladlefuls of rice or barley, and puts them into a mortar (*udukhala*). After separating the chaff from the grain by husking them with the help of a pestle (*musala*), he winnows them with a wicker-fan and collects the whole grains only, leaving aside the chaff and broken grain-particles. Then the grains are grounded and powdered on a flat stone-slab (*dṛṣad*) with the help of a round stone hammer (*upalā*), and the meal is made into a thick paste, from which cakes are prepared by baking them on fire in small earthen dishes or pans called *kapālas*, which are usually square in shape, but some of which are rounded off by rubbing on stone into semi-circular shapes. For the first offering of *puroḍaśa* to Agni, seven semi-circular pans are arranged on the altar round a square one, all in touch with one another, and eight cakes are put into them. This is known as the *Aṣṭa-kapāla-puroḍāśa*. For the second offering which is intended for Agni and Soma, eleven such pans are arranged as stated above, and eleven cakes are put into them; but these cakes must be prepared by baking them on the Gārhapatya Agni in the *kapālas* themselves. Then the cakes are steeped in *ghee*, and the pans properly arranged on the altar strewn with *Kuśa* grass. All these things are done by the Adhvaryu himself, to the accompaniment of particular Yajur-mantras. The offering of these eleven cakes is called *Ekādaśa-kapāla-puroḍāśa.*

The services of four Ṛtviks are required for the performance of the Iṣti-Yāga. The first is the Adhvarju who builds, as it were, the body of the *Adhvara* or *Yajña* with the help of Yajur-mantras; the second is the Hotṛ who calls or invokes the Gods with the help of Ṛgvedic *mantras*, the third is the Brahman who superintends the work of the first two, and the fourth is called *Agnīt*, an assistant to the Brahman. The services of the Udgātṛ are not required, as it is not necessary to sing Sāma-songs during the performance of the ceremony.

The following articles are required for the Iṣti-Yāga; (1) Some pieces of sacrificial wood, or *Samit*, three of which are necessary for encompassing the Āhavanīya Agni, and are named *paridhi*; (2) a few bundles of *Darva* or *Kuśa* grass which is strewn over the altar for depositing the sacrificial articles upon, only one bundle remaining whole, named *prastara*, over which the ladle named *juhū* is kept; (3) *ājya* or *ghee*, purified for sacrifice, the earthen pot in which it is kept being called *ājya-sthālī*; (4) four wooden ladles, the first of which is called *dhruvā*, because it remains fixed or immovable on the altar, the second is called *sruva*, small in size, which is used for taking *ājya* from the *dhruvā*, the third is called *juhū* into which *ājya* taken from the *dhruvā* is poured, and the fourth is called *upabhṛt*, smaller in size than the *juhū*, and held by the Adhvaryu in the left hand under it to prevent any *ājya* from falling on the ground; (5) *agnihotra-havanī*, the large ladle mentioned in the description of

Agnihotra, which is used in the Iṣṭi-Yāga for the purpose of bringing *yava* or rice; (6) mortar and pestle for husking grain; (7) *Sūrpa* or a wicker-fan for winnowing chaff from the grains; (8 *dṛṣad-upalā* or the flat stone slab and stone hammer for pounding the grains; (9) *Śamyā*, a piece of wood which is put under the stone-slab to make it a little sloping; (10) a piece of black buck-skin which is spread below the mortar and the stone-slab and (11) a wooden sword called *sphya*. All these sacrificial articles are carefully arranged by the Adhvaryu over the altar, strewn with *Kuśa* grass.

On the previous day, the Yajamāna invites Agni for performing the ceremony by throwing into each of the three Fires a piece of *samit*. In the afternoon after shaving, he takes his bath and some light food, and then standing before the sacred Fire takes a vow never to speak an untruth, and similar vows. He sleeps in the Agni-Śālā with his wife.

On the morning of the day on which the Iṣṭi-Yāga is to be performed, the first thing the Yajamāna does is formally to appoint the Brahman to perform the sacrifice. The latter takes his seat on the south of the Āhavanīya Agni, the Yajamāna sitting on his left and his wife sitting on the south of Gārhapatya Agni. On the north of the altar, the Hotṛ and the Agnīt take their seats. The Adhvaryu also has his seat assigned there, but he cannot sit down, as he has constantly to move about, doing this and that work in connection with the sacrifice When the Brahmā takes his seat, some water is procured with the face towards the east, which is kept in a pot beside the Āhavanīya Agni on the east. This water or *ap* is called *praṇītā* which is supposed to act as *vajra* towards the Rākṣasas and Asuras

We will now suppose that the Adhvaryu has, in the meantime, got every thing ready for the sacrifice, prepared the *puroḍāśas*, arranged them in *kapālas* over the altar, and kindled the Āhavanīya Agni, to the accompaniment of

Samidhenī Ṛg-mantras, recited by the Hotṛ. The ceremony now begins with the performance of some minor yāgas. First is the *Prayāja yāga*. The Adhvaryu offers five *ahutis* of *ghṛta* to the following five Devatās: *Samit*, *Tanūnapāt* or *Narāśamsa*, *Idāḥ*, *Varhiḥ* and *Svāhākāra*. Next, one *ahuti* of *ghṛta* is offered to Agni, and another to Agni and Soma, after which commences the principal *yāga*. The first set of *purodāśas* is offered to Agni, and the second set to Agni and Soma. Between the offerings of these two sets of *purodāśas*, *ahutis* of *ghṛta* are offered to Agni and Soma respectively with *mantras* muttered in a low voice. Hence this *yāga* is called *Upāmśu yāga*. Then comes the *Sviṣṭakṛt yāga*, in which portions of the *purodāśas* broken and deducted at the time of offering them are offered to *Sviṣṭakṛt* or *Rudra*. The Sviṣṭakṛt is followed by the *Anuyāja* in which *āhutis* of *ghṛta* are offered to the Gods *Vṛhiḥ*, *Narāśamsa* and *Agni*.

The rites are performed in the following manner: The Adhvaryu usually stands near his seat to the north of the altar. Whenever any *yāga* has to be performed, he comes to the south of the altar with the *juhū* in his right hand, and the *upabhṛt* in his left, held below the *juhū*, and directs the Agnīt to request the Gods to hear. The Agnīt then stands up with the wooden sword, named *sphya* and thus replies: "Well, the Gods are ready to hear." Then the Adhvaryu directs the Hotṛ to invoke the Gods, which he does by reciting two *mantras*, the first of which is a Ṛg-mantra, called *anuvākyā*, and the other either a Ṛg- or Yajur-mantra, called *Yājyā*, because it is really the *mantra* of the *Yāga*. For instance, if Agni is to be worshipped, the Hotṛ, before reciting the *mantra*, says: "We worship Agni." This part of the recitation is called *Āgū*. Then muttering the *Yājyā*, he says: "Let Agni eat and convey the offering to the Gods." (*Agne vīhi vauṣat)*. This is called *Vaṣatkāra*. Simultaneously the Adhvaryu throws into the Fire either the *ājya* or the *purodāśa*, *i.e.*, whatever may be the offering. Then the Yajamāna utters the renunciation *mantra (tyāga-mantram)* saying: "This is given to Agni and is not mine," whereupon the Adhvaryu returns to his seat. This rule is followed in the case of performing every Yāga.

At the time of offering an *āhuti*, it is the practice to keep a little remnant of it. When *puroḍāśas* are offered, remnants are kept which are shared by the four Ṛtviks, special portions being allotted to each. Two pieces of these remnants are reserved for the Brahmā and the Yajamāna who partake of them at the end of the sacrifice.

The whole bundle of *Kuśa* grass on the altar, which is named *prastara*, represents the body of the Yajamāna. After the performance of Anuyāja, the *prastara* is thrown into the Āhavanīya Agni, and when it is burnt to ashes, the Yajamāna is supposed to go to heaven, and there mix with the Gods. When the bundle is burning, the Hotṛ, with the permission of the Adhvaryu, recites some *mantras* which are called *Sūktavāk*, and when it is burnt to ashes, pronounces benedictions which are called *Śamyu-vāk*. The three *samits* called *paridhi*, that encompassed the Āhavanīya Agni, represents the body of the *Deva-Hotṛ* or Agni. These are cast into the Fire, and the Deva-Hotṛ leaves the place of sacrifice. Then the Adhvaryu performs a Homa with *ājya* in the name of the Viśvadevāḥ, which is known as the *Samsrava Homa*. This brings the ceremony, so far as the Yajamāna is concerned, to a close.

So far, all the Yāgas have been performed on the Āhavanīya Agni. Now comes the turn of the Gārhapatya Agni, near which the Yajamāna's wife has been sitting. With the exception of the Brahmā, all the three Ṛtviks offer *āhutis* of *ājya* to this Agni in the names of Soma, Tvaṣṭṛ, the Deva-Patnīs (the wives of the Gods) and Agni Gṛhapati. It is quite in the fitness of things that the mistress of the house should be mindful of the wives of the Gods and Agni Gṛhapati, the Lord of the house, as well as of Tvaṣṭṛ who creates and fills the house with children, and of Soma who imparts comely appearance to the new-born babies. The remnant of *havis* offered to them is partaken of by her. Then benedictions are pronounced, and the *Samsrava Homa* is performed. This *Yāga* is called *Patnī Samyāja*.

The Adhvaryu now comes before the Dakṣiṇāgni, and there performs an Ājya-Homa. The remnant of the paste, from which *puroḍāśas* were made, is now offered to Agni in the name of the Viśva-devāh. All the Devas who were invoked by the Hotṛ not having left the place as yet, the Adhvaryu pours a little *ājya* on the Āhavanīya Agni, which is a signal for their departure. This ceremony is called the *Samiṣta Homa*. The *kuśa* grass, strewn over the Vedī, is now collected and thrown into the Fire, the water in the pot scattered over the altar, and the chaff and broken grain-particles thrown away for the Rākṣasas who claim them as their own.

The Yajamāna, it will be recollected, has been supposed to have attained Deva-hood after the sacrifice. He is now eager to attain the state of Viṣṇu, and, therefore, like Viṣṇu, takes three steps towards the east as far as the Āhavanīya Agni. Then looking towards the east which is the region of the Gods, he says: "I have merged myself in *jyotih* (light)." After that, he offers the following prayer to Gṛhapati Agni: "Make me the ideal lord of the house; and let my son spread (perform) this heroic *karma* after me." Then going before the Āhavanīya Agni, he relinquishes the *vrata* adopted by him the previous day and coming out of the Agni-śālā, partakes, with the Brahmā, of the remnants of *puroḍāśa* reserved for them. Thus is ended the Iṣti-Yāga.

It is now necessary to give *dakṣiṇā* or fee to the Ṛtviks. At first, it was not expensive, for with the commencement of the Yāga, rice sufficient for the four Ṛtviks was put into a vessel which was placed over the Dakṣiṇāgni which kept it boiling. When rice was cooked, it was placed before them who partook of it at the close of the ceremony. This constituted their *dakṣiṇā*, so called because the food was cooked over the Dakṣiṇāgni. As society advanced and ideas became complex, the rice cooked over the Dakṣiṇāgni was discarded, and a milch-cow was substituted for it, which afterwards gave place to its money-equivalent in gold and silver (*kāñcana-mūlyam*).[1]

Paśu-Yāga.—It will not be possible for me to give full details, in a small chapter like this, of all the important Śrauta-Yāgas that the Vedic Aryans used to perform. The description of the Paśu-Yāga, the Soma-Yāga, the Puruṣa-Yajña,, and the other Yajñas would fill quite a volume, and the details would be tiresome and bewildering to the ordinary reader to a degree. It will suffice to mention here in connexion with the Paśu-Yāga that, in addition to the altar used for the performance of the Iṣti-Yāga, another new altar had to be made to the east of the Āhavanīya Agni, which was known as the *Pāśuka Vedī*, over which again a small altar had to be raised, with earth dug out from the ground on the north of it. Farther away to the east of the Pāsuka Vedī, a *Yūpa* or sacrificial post had to be driven into the ground, to which the animal to be sacrificed was tied. Fire taken from the Āhavanīya Agni was then placed in the centre (*nāvi*) of the raised small altar; but fresh fire had also to be produced by the attrition of *araṇis*, and mixed with it, when the whole was converted into Āhavanīya, and the old Āhavanīya then took the place of the Gārhapatya. A larger number of Ṛtviks and their assistants were employed for the performance of this Yāga, and a larger number of Gods invoked. The man who sacrificed the animal was called *Śamitā*. The animal, however, was not killed with any sacrificial knife, but strangled to death. Then the fat near the navel of the animal (*vapā*) was extracted by the Adhvaryu and offered to Fire with many formalities and *mantras*.

---

[1] I am indebted for the above details to Pandit R. S. Trivedi's *Yajña-Kathā* Read also Hillebrandt's *Ritual-literatur* and Keith's account of Yajñas as performed according to the formulas of the *Black Yajurveda*.

Animal sacrifice was prevalent among the Vedic Aryans in ancient times, and cows, oxen, rams, goats, buffaloes and horses etc. were sacrificed to the Gods. This custom must have been a relic of pastoral times, when meat was the principal item of food of the Aryans, and it was quite natural for them to offer to the Gods the same kind of food as they themselves found to be useful and nourishing. Sometimes at big sacrifices performed by Kings and Nobles, as many as three hundred buffaloes and one hundred bulls used to be slaughtered, and their meat partaken of by the votaries. Horses were seldom sacrificed, and the cost of performing a Horse-sacrifice (*Aśvamedha Yajña*) was so prohibitive that none but Kings could perform it. But the sacrifice of bulls and cows etc. continued and was common, though, with the introduction of agriculture, it came gradually to be disfavoured on account of the great usefulness of the animals. The milch-cow especially was excluded from the list of victims, and earned the name of *Aghnyā*, *i.e.*, unfit for sacrifice, even in Ṛgvedic times. In course of time there grew up a strong revulsion of feeling against the slaughter of animals in general, and we find the author of the *Śatapatha Brāhmaṇa* indulging in the theory that after the Devas had performed the great sacrifice of the Puruṣa, the Giant Man, or the Creator, from whose divided limbs arose the different parts of creation (*ante* Ch xii. p. 477), the essence of Yajña departed from Him, and entered into the horse. After the sacrifice of the horse, it entered into the cow, and from the cow it went into the sheep, and rom the sheep it went into the goat, and from the goat it went into the earth, where it found a lodgment or resting place in *Yava* and *Vrīhi*, *i.e.*, barley and rice. The offer of cakes (*puroḍāśas*,), made from barley or rice, is as efficacious as the sacrifice of animals, to which cakes are compared. This theory, or account of the subsequent development of sacrifice, is very interesting, as showing the different stages through which it had passed in ancient times. The Puruṣa probably represented man and human sacrifice must have been in vogue in early times, as it is still in vogue among savages who partake of the flesh of the victims in order to imbibe their strength and spirit. Then followed the sacrifice of animals, *viz*, the horse, cow, sheep, and goat in succession, until, out of a strong revulsion of feeling against animal sacrifice, grew the desire of sacrificing grains only, or cakes prepared from them.[1] It is a mistake to suppose that with the preaching of the doctrine of *Ahimsā* by Lord Buddha, sacrifice of animals fell into disuse. The sentiment against animal sacrifice had already existed and developed, and the Buddha only gave expression to that sentiment by preaching universal love and kindness to all created beings, which, however, was carried to an absurd excess by his followers, as well as by the votaries of the Jain religion. Fruits, flowers, rice and sweets are the offerings, usually now made to the deities in all temples, either Hindu, Jain or Buddhist. The sacred Fire has probably been substituted by a lighted lamp, fed with *ghee* or oil, which is kept burning during Puja or worship.

But to return to our account of Vedic sacrifice. The initiator of the sacrifice as well as those engaged in performing it partake of the remnants of the *puroḍaśas* or *ājya* and

---

[1] As already stated, in Vedic times the animal was not sacrificed with a knife, but it was bound to a post (*Yūpa*) and strangled to death. The Yajamāna and the Ṛtviks had to turn their faces away from the place of slaughter, as the sight was extremely revolting. *Mantras* were uttered before the act of sacrifice which go to show that the performers of the animal sacrifice knew it to be a cruel act but tried to reconcile their conscience with such words addressed to the slaughterer as follow: "Kill the animal, kill it, kill it; it is no sin, no sin, no sin. The merits of this sacrifice will come to us, and its demerits, if any, will go elsewhere." Similar sentiments are expressed even to this day at the time of sacrificing an animal: "*Paśus* have been created for sacrifice; hence for sacrifice they are to be killed; and their killing at a sacrifice brings no sin to the worshipper; as this killing is no killing at all, but it helps the animal to go to heaven." Killing by strangulation was resorted to in ancient times, probably because there was no sharp metallic knives in the Neolithic age. With the manufacture of steel knives, sacrifice was made by decapitating the victim, as it is done even to this day.

milk, offered to the Gods, in order to be able to imbibe their spirit, and be at one with them. This would remind one of the Christian Eucharist sacrifice, at which bread and wine are offered, which are supposed to be converted into the flesh and blood of Christ for the time being, and partaken of by the votaries in order to be at one with their Saviour.[1] It will be interesting to refer to a similar sentiment that prevailed among the votaries of Mithra (*Mitra*) in Persia and the Roman Empire in Europe in the early part of the Christian Era.[2] "They placed before the mystic a loaf and a cup full of water over which the priest pronounced the sacred formulas. This oblation of bread and water, with which they mingled wine, is compared by the Christian apologist with the Christian Communion."[3] Of course, this custom was strongly condemned by the early Christian Fathers as emanating from the Devil himself. One of them wrote as follows: "The wicked devils have imitated the Christian institution in the mysteries of Mithras, commanding the same thing to be done. For bread and a cup of water are placed with certain incantations in the mystic rites of one who is being initiated." There was of course, no imitation, as Mithraism was older than Christianity. The rite was only a relic of ancient custom, once prevalent among mankind, and particularly among the Aryans.

Puruṣa-medha or Human Sacrifice.—There is no direct reference to human sacrifice in the Ṛgveda, though the custom may have been hinted at in some hymns (Rv. i, 24-30), and may have existed in pre-Ṛgvedic times. It seems however to have been condemned by the Ṛgvedic Aryans who

[1] Christ said that he was "the bread of life," and further declared: "He that eateth my flesh and drinketh my blood, dwelleth in me and I in him." The Vedic sacrificer also declared at the end of his sacrifice: "I have merged myself in Light, and am at one with Viṣṇu." After that, he partook of the remnant of *puroḍāśa* or cake.

[2] Read *ante* Chap. ii, p. 94.

[3] Prof. Groten's *Christian Eucharist* quoted in Pandit Trivedi's "Yajña-katha."

did not also burn widows on the funeral pyres of their husbands. Though public opinion was strong against it, the custom may have persisted in secret, and there seems to have been a recrudescence of it in later time. For we find the rite of human sacrifice mentioned in the *Vājsaneyī Samhitā* of the White Yajur-veda. "The passage in it bearing on the subject is supposed to describe the different kinds of human victims, appropriate for particular Gods and Goddesses. The section, in which it occurs, opens with three verses which, the commentator says, were intended to serve as *mantras* for offerings of human victims. Then follows a series of one hundred and seventy-nine names of Gods in the dative case, each followed by the name of one or more persons in the objective case; thus 'to Brahma a Brāhmaṇa, to Kṣatra a Kṣatriya,' etc. The copula is nowhere given, and it is quite optional with the reader to supply whatever verb he chooses. The whole of these names occurs also in the *Taittirīya Brāhmaṇa* of the Black Yajurveda, with only a few slight variations, and in some cases having the verb *ā-labhate* after them. This verb is formed of the root *labh*, to kill, with the prefix *ā*, and commentators have generally accepted the term to mean 'slaughter,' though in some cases it means 'consecration after slaughter.'" [1].

It is true that there is a passage in the *Śatapatha Brāhmaṇa* of the White Yajurveda, in which the human victims at a *Puruṣa-medha* are "recommended to be let off after certain *mantras* had been repeated over them" (a process which may have been adopted later on, when a a strong feeling against human sacrifice grew up); but this does not conclusively prove that the custom had not existed before. The *Aśvamedha* or Horse-sacrifice required the immolation of a human being,[2] which probably accounts for its abolition in the *Kali-yuga*.

---

[1] Dr. R. L. Mitra's *Indo-Aryans* ii, 80.

[2] The *Taittiriya Brāhmaṇa* says: "He (the initiator of the Horse-sacrifice) immolates a man; (the form of) a man is (like that of) Virāt, the type of the animated creation. By the immolation of the man is Virāt immolated."

"The *Puruṣa-medha* was celebrated for the attainment of supremacy over all created beings. Its performance was limited to Brahmans and Kṣatriyas. It could be commenced only on the tenth day of the waxing moon in the month of Chaitra, and altogether it required forty days for its performance, though only five out of the forty days were specially called the days of the Puruṣa-medha, whence it got its name of *Pañcāha*. Eleven sacrificial posts were required for it, and to each of them was tied an animal fit for Agni or Soma, (a barren cow), the human victims being placed between the posts."[1]

The *Śatapatha Brāhmaṇa* says: "Now, if a Brāhmaṇa performs the ceremony, he should give (all his property) to the most learned. The Brāhmaṇa includes every thing; the knower of every thing is included in every thing; the *Puruṣa-medha* includes every thing, (and it is) for the attainment and subjugation of every thing." He is then enjoined to retire to a forest, and separate himself from mankind. If he likes to live in a village, he should produce fire by the rubbing of two sticks, return home and continue to perform the rites he was used to, not speaking with anybody, excepting the learned and those dear to him.

Though the rite was condemned, discontinued, and only occasionally resorted to on such occasions as the performance of the *Aśva-medha*, it seemed to have established a firm hold on the mind of the superstitious, and during the Paurāṇic age, was again practised under the name of *Nara-bali* to please the Goddess Chandikā. *The Kālikā Purāṇa* clearly enjoins on the necessity of performing human sacrifice with a view to please the deity, and gives very gruesome and horrifying details as to how the victim should be selected, brought, consecrated and sacrificed to the Goddess by decapitation. Though sacrifice of a human being is now regarded as deliberate murder, and the culprit

[1] Dr. R. L. Mitra's *Indo-Aryans* ii, 79.

is tried and punished for culpable homicide, amounting to murder, fanatics are not wanting, who feel no compunctions for sacrificing even their own sons and daughters before the Goddess to secure an object dear to their heart, and we occasionally read reports in the newspapers about the commission of this most revolting and diabolical crime, which goes to show that human nature, in spite of its veneer of culture, sometimes harks back to the barbarous custom of brute-like savages.

The Aśvamedha and the Soma-Yāga.—The performance of the Aśvamedha was only occasionally resorted to by Kings in order to celebrate a victory or establish their suzerainty, and continued down to the early Christian Era, the last Hindu King, said to have performed it, having been the great Samudra Gupta of the Gupta Dynasty. The later ancient Law-givers have prohibited it, along with some other ancient customs, for the Kali-Yuga. Another most important Śrauta-Yajña in Vedic times was the *Soma-yāga*, which has been described in the Ṛgveda as *pratnamit*, (ix. 42,4) or the most ancient, and as anterior to all sacrifices (*Yajñasya pūrvyah*, ix. 2,10). The performance of this Yāga was most complicated, requiring quite a troop of priests bearing various names, each of whom had to be given a number of cows, besides gold and silver, which made it a most expensive affair. A very large space was required for its performance, and as such space was not ordinarily available in the house, an open space outside the village was selected for the purpose. The rite sometime lasted for only one day, when it was called *Aikāhika*, sometimes for twelve days, when it was called *Ahīna*, and sometimes for more than twelve days, for a whole year, or even more—when it was called *Sattra*. The rite, known as *Agniṣṭoma* had to be performed in one day, though the completion of its preliminaries took full four days.

The Soma Sacrifice had for its offering the juice of the plant, known as Soma, ceremoniously prepared, and mixed with milk, or curd, and honey, though, in connection with its performance, animals also had to be sacrificed. The Soma plant has not been correctly identified with any plant to-day and those who still perform the sacrifice use substitutes for it. Another branch of the Aryans, the Pārsis, also performed the Soma-sacrifice in ancient times, and perform it even to this day, under the name of *Haoma*, with substituted plants, as the real plant is not available. Even in the time of Zoroaster, the real Soma plant was not easily available, and the *Haoma* ceremony had to be performed with the juice of the leaves of the pomegranate tree. In Ṛgvedic times, however, the plant was available in large quantities, which grew not only on the Himalayan peak, known as Mujavat (identified by some with the modern *Kailāsa*, situated near Lake Mansorovar in Tibet), but also in the plains of ancient Sapta-Sindhu, especially on the banks of the Sarasvatī, the Indus, the Ārjīkyā and the Śaryaṇāvat Lake in Kurukṣetra. (Rv. ix. 65, 22-23). The plant that grew on Mount Mujavat, however, was regarded as the best, which earned for it the general title of *Maujavata*, and was greatly valued and demanded by the performers of this sacrifice. The plant died down to its roots in winter and summer, and flourished again in rain-water during the rainy season. It was probably a phosphorescent plant, emitting a bright light at night (Rv. ix. 85, 12; 86, 14), with reddish-brown leaves, which justified its comparison with *Suparṇa* (the Eagle with golden wings) and with *Gandharva* or the Sun. (Rv. ix. 85, 11). Its resplendent appearance at night, and its waning and waxing during the year probably suggested its comparison with the moon which wanes and waxes, and becomes bright at night. As the Moon was supposed to contain the ambrosia (*amrita*) for the Gods, which made them immortal, so the juice of the Soma plant also had an exhilarating effect on its consumers. Hence in course of time, the Soma probably came to be identified with the Moon. However this may have been, there were traders in Vedic times who made it a regular business of theirs to import the plant from the mountain, and exchange it for cows. Probably in consequence of the change of the climate of Sapta-Sindhu from cold to hot, the plant subsequently became extinct in the plains of the Punjab, though it may still be obtainable in the lofty heights of the Himālaya, if a diligent search for it were made. The Soma-juice, producing as it did a cheering effect on the consumers, which raised their drooping spirits, and enabled them to fix their minds on high spiritual matters and realise vividly the presence of the Gods, was eagerly drunk by the performers of the sacrifice, and even by soldiers just on the eve of a battle. (Rv. ix. 166, 2) It has been described as the most favourite drink of the Gods and specially of Indra who was always eager to have an offer of the juice, and was said sometimes to drink it in such enormous quantities as to justify his comparison to a "lake." The main object of the Soma sacrifice was to strengthen Indra in his fight with Vṛtra, and bring down timely rains from the reluctant clouds for helping agricultural work. The sacrifice was sometimes continued for nine months, ten months or even twelve months to ensure timely rain-fall. The priests who were originally engaged in the sacrifice for *nine* months were called the *Navagvas*, and those who performed it for *ten* months were called the *Daśagvas*; but afterwards the practice was for all—either the Navagvas or the Daśagvas,—to perform the sacrifice for ten months only until the rains began to fall. There was, however, a school of thinkers who held that the sacrifice should be performed for full twelve months, instead of ten, as Indra required to be particularly strengthened when he was in the thick of the fight with Vṛtra, the Demon of Drought.[1]

The Soma has been described in the Vedic Scriptures as the "King," because the deity presiding over it really helped Indra to overcome Vṛtra, and grant plenty and happiness to

---

[1] *Ṛgvedic India.* Chs. xxi and xxii.

the people. He was not only the King of the people but also of the Gods, as he led the latter to victory over the Asuras. Hence every Vedic Aryan worshipped the Soma and was fond of drinking the Soma-juice not only for securing good fortune, but also for obtaining immortality. In a later age when the plant became scarce, the drink came to be restricted to the Brahmans only, the Kṣatriyas drinking the juice of the leaves of the *Ficus Indicus*, or the Fig-tree, and the Vaiśyas drinking curd as substitutes of the Soma-juice with equal religious efficacy. Those of my readers who desire to know fully the details of the Soma-sacrifice and of other sacrifices are advised to read the *Aitareya Brāhmaṇa* the *Śatapatha Brāhmaṇa*, the *Āśvalāyana Śrauta Sūtra* and the *Kātyāyana Śrauta Sūtra*. Mr. Trivedi's *Yajña-Kathā* also gives a pretty good idea of what the Soma-sacrifice and other Vedic sacrifices were like.

Some causes of the decline of Indo-Aryan Culture.— The extreme love of artificial ritualism that the later Vedic Aryans developed caused them to direct their attention mainly to the forms of things rather than to their spirit, and seemed to smother their natural cravings for higher spiritual knowledge. This also helped to make Brahmanism or Priestcraft strong, powerful and gradually autocratic. Hence towards the end of the Vedic period, there grew up a reaction in the minds of the thoughtful against meaningless ritualistic performance of the various Vedic sacrifices, and attaching an undue importance to them. Higher speculations about the human soul, (*Jivātmā*), and the Universal Soul (*Paramātmā or Para-Brahman*), and their intimate relation to each other, were indulged in, and beatific visions obtained in the domains of higher spiritual culture, which were embodied in simple and rapturous language in the pages of the *Upaniṣads*. Lord Kṛṣṇa raised, later on, a strong protest against the performance of sacrifices for merely gaining worldly fortune and advantages, to the impoverishment of the soul, and directed his votaries to realise God in their own souls, by purifying their mind and controlling all selfish desires and other disturbing elements and influences by the practice of *Yoga* and the cultivation of the habit of looking on all things as emanating from, and permeated by God. He, however, appreciated the real significance and value of *Karma* and Sacrifice, as it was through these means that the *Para-Brahman* was said to have created this Universe. Lastly, came Lord Buddha who openly revolted against Brahmanism and its galling domination, and preached the noble doctrines of equality, fraternity, and good will and love towards all created life, and declared that salvation or *Nirvāṇa*, which meant freedom from the endless cycles of birth and death and human miseries, could only be attained by rigid self-control, and holy doing and holy thinking. When, again, the beauty of the pure tenets of Buddhism was lost sight of by age-long accretions of doctrinarianism and meaningless formalities growing upon them, and the hankering after a pure spiritual life was starved, there was another re-action in the mind of its votaries, which was taken advantage of by orthodox Brahmanism to resuscitate the old Vedic religion, not certainly in its ancient form, but in a form acceptable to the people, which was a compromise between the Vedic religion and Buddhism. Hence the inauguration of the Paurāṇic religion, and of the Tāntric mode of worship was the result. Buddhism thus gradually lost its hold on the mind of the people and was ultimately banished from India. But the Paurāṇic religion too having failed fully to satisfy the spiritual hankerings and the social needs of the people on account of its highly exclusive character and rigid narrowness, liberal reformers in the persons of the great Śankara, Śrī Caitanya, Rāmānuja, Vallabhācārya, etc., rose at different periods of history either to preach the religion of the Upaniṣads (*Vedantism*), or to proclaim social equality and the doctrine of pure love (*bhakti*) to God, which could be cultivated by all men irrespective of caste or creed, not with the help of any complicated religious rites and formalities, but by leading pure and austere lives, practising good will and love towards all creatures, and earnestly and constantly taking the name of the Lord, without any thought of the self, or the good things of this world. The result was the gradual growth of that spirit of *Vairāgya*, or indifference to all mundane affairs, which probably carried in it the fatal germs that have gradually weakened and emasculated the national life of the Hindus, and brought about their present helplessness and degradation. A revival of Hindu national life probably lies in the direction of the *full realisation of God as the Creator of this wonderful Universe with its immutable laws* (*Ṛta*), which certainly is not a mere delusion or *māyā*, but is a real and necessary factor in the growth of our life and well-being; and while people should make full use of all their faculties and opportunities to improve their surroundings and add to human happiness and culture by constant devotion to action, divested of all selfish desires, they should not be wedded to worldliness to such an extent as to forget that they are of God and godly, and that God alone is the be-all and end-all of human existence. The early Ṛgvedic Aryans succeeded in developing a wonderful culture in the remote past, not by looking upon the world as *māyā*, or life as "an empty dream," but by vividly realising their existence and trying to make life happy and comfortable as much as possible in this world. They constantly prayed to the Gods that they might live and look upon the Sun for a hundred years, and enjoy all the good things of the world. They domesticated cattle, developed the art of agriculture, invented and manufactured all necessary implements, created industries, carried on inland and foreign trades, fought their enemies, and laid down their lives in the defence of their hearths and homes. While they did all these things, they were not unmindful of their spiritual needs and culture, and developed a unique religious system which was calculated to satisfy the hankerings of the soul. Action was wedded to Contemplation, and their material and spiritual cultures harmoniously advanced side by side. They believed that they could create their own destiny by means of *karma*, and hence took to it in right earnest. On the other hand, Buddhism, Vaiṣṇavism, and the Vedantic doctrine of *māyā* created a tendency in the mind of the people to look upon this life as a bundle of miseries, and the world as a place of suffering; and to be able to effect a permanent escape from them anyhow became the principal goal of their existence and activities. Hence they ceased to take any interest in the things of this world, and swayed by maudlin sentiments, became pessimists and slaves of a powerful and designing priestcraft. Their emasculation having been completed, their subjection to foreign domination followed as a matter of course. None could domineer over them, if they had not weakened themselves, and none could enslave them if they had not enslaved themselves beforehand. The robust optimism of the Ṛgvedic Aryans, and their refreshing joy of life are sadly wanting in the present race of their descendants, which have to be sedulously cultivated in order to be able to hold up their heads before the modern progressing races of the world. The good points of the other subsequent Hindu cultures also should form a precious heritage to enrich their spiritual life in the present age and the ages to come. A happy blending and assimilation of these two important factors in their life would once more bring their ancient culture to the fore-front of the world in no distant time.

CHAPTER XIV.

ṚGVEDIC POETRY.

Poetical faculty is a rare and divine gift. It has been said that poets are born, and the saying is true in so far as the poetical faculty is a natural gift and cannot be cultivated. The art of poetry, though born with the faculty, can however be cultivated, and improved by cultivation. The faculty is the soul, and the art the form in which the faculty works and displays itself. Both the faculty and the art are indispensable to the production of true poetry. The poet is endowed with fine sensibility, and a mass of delicate nerves that respond to the subtlest vibrations in Nature and produce in the mind noble imageries and impressions which are not perceived by the less gifted. Hence the true poet possesses the faculty of an inner sight, *a second sight*, if we may so describe it, that sees beauties and wonders where others do not even suspect their existence, and unravels the meaning of what appears to be mysterious to ordinary mortals. The poet has therefore his fits of raptures and ecstasies which raise his mind and soul to lofty and sublime heights, from which he sees things in their true light and perspectives. He describes his impressions and experiences in language which is sometimes clear and rapturous, but which often becomes mystic and unintelligible on account of its very imperfections and inability to convey the subtle and delicate sentiments as vividly as they are perceived. Every true poet is a *seer* and the Vedic poets were all *seers* or Ṛṣis who saw and realised high moral and spiritual truths, and gave expression to them in appropriate rhythmical language called verses or *mantras*. These Ṛṣis were probably the oldest poets that the world has ever produced, and flourished in an age so remote from our own that it can be measured by more than ten thousands of years.

They were a specially gifted class,—these Ṛṣis—who loved to spend their time in self-culture, self-concentration and contemplation of the sublimest things in Nature. The first appearance of the bright Dawn in the eastern sky at the end of Night was hailed with rapturous strains like the following (Rv. i. 113) :

"This light has come, of all the lights the fairest,
The brilliant brightness has been born, far-shining.
Urged onward for God Savitṛ's uprising,
Night now has yielded up her place to Morning.

"The sisters'[1] pathway is the same, unending;
Taught by the Gods, alternately they tread it.
Fair-shaped, of different forms and yet one-minded,
Night and Morning clash not, nor do they linger.

"Bright leader of glad sounds, she shines effulgent ;
Widely she has unclosed for us her portals.
Arousing all the world, she shows us riches ;
Dawn has awakened every living creature.

"There Heaven's Daughter has appeared before us,
The maiden flushing in her brilliant garments.
Thou Sovran lady of all earthly treasure,
Auspicious Dawn, flush here today upon us.

"In the sky's framework she has shone with splendour,
The Goddess has cast off the robe of darkness.
Wakening up the world with ruddy horses,
Upon her well-yoked chariot Dawn is coming.

"Bringing upon it many bounteous blessings,
Brightly shining she spreads her brilliant lustre.
Last of the countless mornings that have gone by,
First of bright morns to come has Dawn arisen.

---

[1] Night and Dawn.

"Arise! the breaṭh, the life, again has reached us;
Darkness has gone away and light is coming.
She leaves a pathway for the Sun to travel;
We have arrived where men prolong existence."

The above is a free and concise translation of the beautiful original verses, made by Professor Macdonell, but it scarcely approaches the grace and rhythm of the originals. Dr. Muir has a metrical sketch of Uṣas, as represented in the various hymns, addressed to her, in which "there is little of which the germ will not be found in the originals." I cannot resist the temptation of quoting the sketch in extenso here, as it will give the reader a true insight into the thoughts and sentiments of the Vedic bards:

"Hail, Uṣas, Daughter of the Sky,
Who, borne upon thy shining car,
By ruddy steeds from realms afar,
And ever lightening, drawest nigh:

"Thou sweetly smilest, Goddess fair,
Disclosing all thy youthful grace,
Thy bosom bright, thy radiant face,
And lustre of thy golden hair:—

("So shines a fond and winning bride,
Who robes her form in brilliant guise.
And to her lord's admiring eyes,
Displays her charms with conscious pride.

"Or virgin by her mother decked,
Who, glorying in her beauty, shows
In every glance, her power she knows
All eyes to fix, all hearts subject:—

"Or actress, who by skill in song
And dance, and graceful gestures light,
And many-coloured vestures bright,
Enchants the eager, gazing throng:—

"Or maid who, wont her limbs to lave
In some cool stream among the woods,
Where never vulgar eye intrudes,
Emerges fairer from the wave) :—

"But closely by the amorous Sun
Pursued and vanquished in the race,
Thou soon art locked in his embrace,
And with him blendest into one.

"Fair Uṣas, though through years untold
Thou hast lived on, yet thou art born
Anew on each succeeding morn,
And so thou art both young and old.

"As in thy fated ceaseless course
Thou risest on us day by day,
Thou wearest all our lives away
With silent, ever-wasting force.

"Their rounds our generations run
The old depart, and in their place
Springs ever up a younger race.
Whilst thou, immortal, looked on.

"All those who watched for thee of old
Are gone, and now 'tis we who gaze
On thy approach ; in future days
Shall other men thy beams behold.

"But 'tis not thoughts so grave and sad
Alone that thou dost with thee bring,
A shadow o'er our hearts to fling ;—
Thy beams returning make us glad.

"Thy sister, sad and sombre Night,
With stars that in the blue expanse
Like sleepless eyes mysterious glance,
At thy approach is quenched in light ;—

"And earthly forms, till now concealed
Behind her veil of dusky hue,
Once more come sharply to view
By thy illuming glow revealed.

"Thou art the life of all that lives,
The breath of all that breathes; the sight
Of thee makes every countenance bright,
New strength to every spirit gives.

"When thou dost pierce the murky gloom,
Birds flutter forth from every brake,
All sleepers as from death awake,
And men their myriad tasks resume.

"Some prosperous wake in listless mood,
And others every nerve to strain
The goal of power or wealth to gain,
Or what they deem the highest good.

"But some to holier thoughts aspire,
In hymns the race celestial praise,
And light, on human hearths to blaze,
The heaven-born Sacrificial Fire.

"And not alone do bard and priest
Awake;—the Gods thy power do confess
By starting into consciousness
When thy first rays suffuse the east;

"And hasting downward from the sky,
They visit men devout and good,
Consume their consecrated food,
And all their longings satisfy.

"Bright Goddess, let thy genial rays
To us bring stores of envied wealth
In kine and steeds and sons, with health
And joy of heart and length of days." [1]

---

[1] Muir's O. S. T., vol. V, 196-198.

The following is a metrical translation of the verses of a hymn (Rv. i. 50), addressed to the Sun :—

" By lustrous heralds led on high
The omniscient Sun ascends the sky,
His glory drawing every eye,
All-seeing Sun, the stars so bright
Which gleamed throughout the sombre night,
Now scared like thieves, slink fast away,
Quenched by the splendour of thy ray.
Thy beams to men thy presence show :
Like blazing fires they seem to glow.
Conspicuous, rapid, source of light,
Thou makest all the welkin bright.
In sight of Gods and mortal eyes,
In sight of heaven thou scal'st the skies.
Bright God, thou scann'st with searching ken
The doings all of busy men.
Thou stridest o'er the sky ; thy rays
Create, and measure out our days ;
Thine eye all living things surveys.
Seven lucid mares thy chariot bear,
Self-yoked, athwart the fields of air,
Bright Śurya, God with flaming hair.
That glow above the darkness we
Beholding upward soar to thee,
For there among the Gods thy light
Supreme is seen, divinely bright." [1]

Savitṛ has sometimes been identified with the setting Sun in the Ṛgveda (Rv. ii. 38), as will appear from the following translation of some verses :—

" Borne by swift coursers, he will now unyoke them,
The speeding chariot he has stayed from going,
He checks the speed of them that glide like serpents :
Night has come on by Savitṛ's commandment.

[1] *Ibid.* pp. 160-161.

The weaver rolls her outstretched web together,
The skilled lay down their work in midst of toiling,
The birds all seek their nest, their shed the cattle ;
Each to his lodging Savitṛ disperses." [1]

The following is a translation of the celebrated *Sāvitṛī or Gāyatrī* mantra (Rv. iii. 62, 10) which is repeated even to this day by every orthodox Brahmin :—

" We contemplate that excellent
Glory of Savitṛ, the God,
That he may stimulate our thoughts."

The following stanzas are from a hymn addressed to Night (Rv. x. 127) :—

" Night coming on, the Goddess shines
In many places with her eyes :
All-glorious she has decked herself.

" Immortal Goddess, far and wide
She fills the valleys and the heights :
Darkness with light she overcomes.

" And now the Goddess coming on
Has driven away her sister Dawn :
Far off the darkness hastes away.

" Thus, Goddess, come to us to-day,
At whose approach we seek our homes,
As birds upon the tree their nests.

" The villagers have gone to rest,
Beasts, too, with feet and birds with wing :
The hungry hawk himself is still.

" Ward off the she-wolf and the wolf,
Ward off the robber, Goddess Night :
And take us safe across the gloom."

---

[1] Macdonell's *Hist. of Sansk. Lit.*, p 79.

The following is a translation of a hymn addressed to Araṇyānī or the genius of the Forest (Rv. x. 146). The first stanza has been translated by Dr. Muir, and the last four by Professor Macdonell who observes that the wierd sights and sounds of the gloaming are therein described "with a fine perception of nature." I have myself attempted a translation of the second stanza :—

"Thou seemest, Goddess, here to stray
Forlorn among these trackless woods,
These dark and dreary solitudes.
Why dost thou not inquire the way
That leads to cheerful human haunts ?
Is there nought here thy courage daunts ?

"A lowing sound like bull's is heard,
And this is answered by a screech,
The two combined make music wierd,
As if the lyre is played to preach
The praise of Forest-Goddess wild.

"Sounds as of grazing cows are heard,
A dwelling-house appears to loom,
And Araṇyānī, Forest-nymph,
Creaks like a cart at even-tide.

"Here some one calls his cow to him,
Another there is felling wood ;
Who tarries in the forest-glade
Thinks to himself 'I heard a cry.'

"Never does Araṇyānī hurt
Unless one goes too near to her :
When she has eaten of sweet fruit
At her own will she goes to rest.

'Sweet-scented, redolent of balm,
Replete with food, yet tilling not,
Mother of beasts, the Forest-nymph,
Her I have magnified with praise."

Parjanya was the god of rain, and his activity is described in very vivid strains (Rv. v. 83) :—

" The trees he strikes to earth and smites the demon crew,
The whole world fears the wielder of the mighty bolt.
The guiltless man himself flees from the potent God,
What time Parjanya thundering smites the miscreant.

" Like a car-driver urging on his steeds with whips,
He causes to bound forth the messengers of rain.
From far away the lion's roar reverberates,
What time Parjanya fills the atmosphere with rain.

" Forth blow the winds, to earth the lightning flashes fall,
Up shoot the herbs, the realm of light with moisture streams,
Nourishment in abundance springs for all the world,
What time Parjanya quickeneth the earth with seed.

Thunder and roar : the vital germ deposit :
With water-bearing chariot fly around us :
Thy water-skin unloosed to earth draw downward,
With moisture make the heights and hollows equal." [1]

The following is a free translation made by Dr. Muir of the hymn addressed to Frogs (Rv. vii. 103) :

" As Brahmans, who a vow fulfil,
The frogs had now a year been still.
Like dried and shrivelled skins they lay,
Faint, parched with heat for many a day,
Expecting, long in vain, the showers
Withheld by Air's malignant powers.
But autumn [2] comes ; Parjanya rains
In copious streams, and floods the plains.
Clouds veil the sun, the air is cool,
The ponds, long empty, now are full.
There float the frogs, their bodies soak ;
Afar is heard their merry croak.

---

[1] Macdonell's *Hist. of Sansk.* Lit., P. 92.

[2] *Prâvrit* in the verse does not mean Autumn, but the Rainy Season.

Well drenched, they jump aloft in glee,
And join in noisy colloquy.
They leap upon each other's backs,
And each to t'other cries co-ax.
As teachers first call out a word,
Then boys repeat what they have heard,
Just so the frogs croak once more
What other frogs had croacked before.
Sounds diverse issue from their throats,
Some low like cows, some bleat like goats,
Though one in name, of various sheen,—
For one is brown, another green.
As Brahmans at a Soma-rite
Around the bowl in talk unite,
This day the frogs their pond surround,
And make the air with noise resound.
The priests who sweated o'er a pot
Soon quit the fire they find too hot,
The frogs so long oppressed by heat,
Emerge in haste from their retreat.
From rules divine they never swerve,
But all the seasons' laws observe.
When autumn comes, their sufferings cease,
From scorching heat they find release.
The frogs that bleat, and those that low,
Brown, green, on men all wealth bestow.
The kine that on our pastures graze,
We owe to them, with length of days."

The above quotations will suffice to give our readers an adequate idea of how closely did the Ṛgvedic bards observe Nature, and how faithfully and felicitously did they describe her striking features. With regard to the hymn on Frogs, it may be remarked by critics that it is too commonplace a theme to write verses upon. But an element of wonder is observable in the mind of the bard that the frogs should remain in hiding and silence for a large part of the year, and only come out and revel in noisy croakings on the advent of the rains, which fact makes him conclude that,

From rules divine they never swerve,
But all the seasons' laws observe.

This is the precious moral that he draws from their habits, and wishes to impress upon the mind of those who disregard *Ṛta* or the immutable law and order of the Universe that upholds everything. When even such insignificant creatures as frogs obey this "divine rule," how much more should it be obeyed by men! Like a true poet, he is willing and ready to take a lesson even "from the meanest thing that moves" and profit by it. As the frogs are the heralds of the rainy season which makes the corn grow, and provides abundant grazing to the kine, they are rightly praised as the bestowers of wealth and kine. The poet who is evidently a priest, engaged in sacrifice, and is a Guru or teacher of the young, compares the frogs with the lads when learning their lessons from the teacher, and with those Brahmans who observe a religious vow of silence for a long period. Though the comparisons may be regarded as grotesque, yet they have the effect of raising the subject of the poem to a high standard of excellence—an art which only great poets are endowed with.

I will now attempt to give an idea of Ṛgvedic poetry that deals with complex subjects, or subjects that are not apparent to our physical senses but can only be grasped by our intellectual, moral and spiritual faculties.

Varuṇa is generally identified with the nightly sky or the terrestrial ocean below; but he is greater than either. He is the supreme lord of the Universe, producing and upholding everything, and governing the world according to Ṛta, or the immutable laws framed by him.

" Lo, reared of old by hands divine,
High towers in heaven a palace fair;
Its roof a thousand columns bear;
A thousand portals round it shine.

"Within, enthroned in godlike state,
Sits Varuṇa in golden sheen;
To work his will, with reverent mien,
His angel hosts around him wait.

"When I behold this vision bright,
I deemed the God was clad in flame,
Such radiance from his presence came,
And overpowered my aching sight.

"Each morn, when Uṣas starts from sleep,
He mounts his car, which gleams with gold;
All worlds before him lie unrolled,
As o'er the sky his coursers sweep.

"He, righteous lord, the sceptre wields,
Supreme, of universal sway,
His law both men and Gods obey;
To his decree the haughtiest yields.

"He spread the earth and watery waste;
He reared the sky; he bade the Sun
His shining circuit daily run:
In him the worlds are all embraced.

"By his decree the radiant Moon
Moves through the nightly sky serene,
And planets sparkle round their queen;[1]
But whither have they fled at noon?

"The rivers flow at his behest,
And yet—admire his wondrous skill—
The ocean-bed they cannot fill,
Although their currents never rest.

---

[1] "In Indian Mythology the Moon is a God, not a Goddess; but I have in this line adhered to customary English phraseology." Muir.

"The path of ships across the sea,
The soaring eagle's flight, he knows,[1]
The course of every wind that blows,
And all that was or is to be.

"Descending, ceaseless, from the skies,
His angels glide this world around;
As far as earth's remotest bounds,
All-scanning, range their thousand eyes.

"This mighty lord who rules on high,
Though closely veiled from mortal gaze,
All men's most secret acts surveys;
He, ever far, is ever nigh.

"Two think they are not over-heard
Who sit and plot, as if alone;
Their fancied secrets all are known,
Unseen, the God is there, a third.

"Whoe'er should think his way to wing,
And lurk, unknown, beyond the sky,
Yet could not there elude the eye
And grasp of Varuṇa, the King.

"For all within the vast expanse
Of air that heaven and earth divides,
Whate'er above the heaven abides,
Lies open to his piercing glance.

"The ceaseless winkings all he sees,
And counts, of every mortal's eyes;
In vain to wink a creature tries
Unless the God the power decrees.

---

[1] Compare Proverbs xxx. 18: 'There be three things which are too wonderful for me; yea four, which I know not; 19. The way of an eagle in air; the way of a serpent upon a rock; the way of a ship in the midst of the sea; and the way of a man with a maid.'" Muir.

" To thoughtful men who truth discern,
And deeply things divine explore,
The God reveals his hidden lore ;
But fools his secrets may not learn.

" He marks the good and ill within
The hearts of men—the false and true
Discerns with never-erring view :
He hates deciet, chastises sin.

" His viewless bonds, than cords and gyves
More hard to burst, the wicked bind ;
In vain, within their folds confined,
To cast them off the sinner strives

" And yet the God will not refuse
His grace to one who inly moans,
When fetter-bound, his errors owns,
And for forgiveness meekly sues.

" But where is, Lord, thy friendship now ?
Thine ancient kindness, O, restore ;
May we, so dear to thee of yore,
No longer dread thy frowning brow.

" Thine ire we did not madly brave,
Nor break thy laws in wanton mood ;
We fell, by wrath, dice, wine subdued :
Forgive us, gracious Lord, and save

" Absolve us from the guilt, we pray,
Of all the sins our fathers wrought,[1]
And sins which we commit by thought [2]
And speech, and act, from day to day.

From dire disease preserve us free,
Nor doom us to the house of clay,
Before our shrivelling frames decay :
A good old age yet let us see.

---

[1] See Exodus xx. 5, Deuteronomy v. 9, and Ezakiel xviii. 1, ff.

[2] Rv. x. 37, 12.

In vain shall hostile shafts assail
The man thy shielding arm defends ;
Secure, no wrong he apprehends,
Safe, as if cased in iron mail.

" As mother birds their pinions spread
To guard from harm their cowering brood,
Do thou, O Lord, most great and good,
Preserve from all the ills we dread." [1]

We make no apology to our readers for quoting in full this excellent metrical sketch made by Dr. Muir, as it will enable them to obtain a clear idea of Varuṇa as conceived by the ancient Ṛṣis—Varuṇa, the Supreme God who was the Creator of Heaven and Earth, and the Sun, Moon and Stars, and the Moral Governor of the Universe who ruled everything according to the immutable laws framed by him. He was all-seeing and all-knowing and he punished every wrong-doing, and impure and unholy thought, and there was no escape for anybody, excepting those who became penitent and implored his forgiveness. This conception of Varuṇa was that of a God who was both dreaded and loved—dreaded for his inexorable decrees, and loved for his mercy and forgiveness, whenever he was approached in a truly penitent spirit ; and this conception was more ancient than that of Indra, and also more popular, as Varuṇa never made any distinction between class and class, and was kind to all men, if only they were good and righteous. There were no dogmatism in his cult, as in that of Indra-worship, and no narrowness and bigotry. Hence Varuṇa was universally worshipped by the Aryans, and his worship spread over Western Asia and even Greece, having been promulgated by the Paṇis, the ancient Aryan merchants, and ancestors of the Phoenicians of history, who remained his staunch votaries to the end, and never acknowledged the supremacy

[1] Muir's *Original Sanskrit Texts* v. 76a-76d.

of Indra for which they suffered great persecutions at the hands of the orthodox Vedic Aryans. The Iranians also were his staunch followers, and their Supreme God, Ahura Mazda, is said to be none other than Varuṇa himself, the great Asura of the Ṛgveda. Be that as it may, there can be no question teat Varuṇa's ancient conception was grand, which closely approaches the modern conception of God who is the upholder of the moral order of the Universe and punishes those who transgress it, but who at the same time is gracious and merciful to those who repent for their sins and implore his forgiveness. The following stanzas from a hymn (Rv. vii. 89) addressed to him will be found interesting :—

" May I not yet, King Varuṇa,
Go down into the house of clay,
Have mercy, spare me, mighty Lord.

" Thirst has come on thy worshipper
Though standing in the water's midst ;
Have mercy, spare me, mighty Lord.

" O Varuṇa, whatever the offence may be
That we as men commit against the heavenly folk,
When through our want of thought we violate thy laws,
Chastise us not, O God, for that iniquity."

The worship of Indra was first introduced by the Vedic Aryans when their angle of vision had changed owing to a change of culture in consequence of their having settled down as agriculturists, and when they wanted the help of a powerful God who could supply them with abundant rains regularly. It was then that Vṛtra came to be looked upon as a powerful malevolent deity whom it was necessary to kill in order to release the needful rains that he withheld in his cloud-body. Indra thus became the wielder of the thunderbolt with which he carried on the struggle with Vṛtra, and laid him low. The following metrical sketch made by Dr. Muir describes how Indra, attended by the Maruts, set out to encounter Vṛtra —

"Amid the plaudits, long and loud,
Which burst from all the heavenly crowd,
Charmed by the sweet and magic sound
Of hymns pronounced by bards renowned,
Viewed by admiring troops of friends,
The valiant God his car ascends.
Swept by his fervid bounding steeds,
Athwart the sky the hero speeds.
The Marut-hosts his escort form,
Impetuous spirits of the storm.
On flashing lightning-cars they ride,
And gleam in warlike pomp and pride :
Each head a golden helmet crests,
And glittering mail adorns their breasts ;
Spears on their shoulders rest, their hands
Bear arrows, bows and lightning brands.
Bright tinkling anklets deck their feet,
And thought than they is not more fleet ;
Like lions' roar their voice of doom ;
With iron force their teeth consume.
The hills, the earth itself, they shake,
All creatures at their coming quake ;
Their headlong fury none can stay,
All obstacles are swept away.
The forest's leafy monarchs tall
Before their onset crashing fall,
As when in fierce destructive mood
Wild elephants invade a wood."

Then began a terrible conflict with Vṛtra, at the end of which

"Pierced, cloven, crushed, with horrid yell,
The dying demon headlong fell
Down from his cloud-built tower.

Now bound by Śuṣṇa's spell no more,
The clouds discharge their liquid store ;
And, long by torrid sun-heams baked,
The plains by copious showers are slaked ;
The rivers swell, and sea-ward sweep
Their turbid torrents broad and deep.
The peasant views, with deep delight
And thankful heart, the auspicious sight.
His leafless fields, so sere and sad,
Will soon with waving crops be clad,
And mother Earth, now brown and bare,
A robe of brilliant green will wear.
And now the clouds disperse, the blue
Of heaven once more comes forth to view.
The Sun shines out, all Nature smiles,
Redeemed from Vṛtra's power and wiles ;
The Gods with gratulations meet,
And loud acclaim, the victor great ;
While Indra's mortal votaries sing
The praises of their friend and King "

The Vedic poets thus proclaim Indra's greatness :

" A hundred earths if such there be,
A hundred skies fall short of thee,
A thousand Suns would not outshine
The effulgence of thy light divine.
The worlds which mortals boundless deem,
To thee but as a handful seem.
Thou, Indra, art without a peer
On earth, or yonder heavenly sphere."

The following is a brief description of Indra's relations to his worshippers :

" Thou, Indra, art a friend, a brother,
A kinsman dear, a father, mother.
Though thou hast troops of friends, yet we
Can boast no other friend but thee.

With this our hymn thy skirt we grasp,
As boys their father's garments clasp.

* * * *

With faith we claim thine aid divine,
For thou art ours, and we are thine."

The Soma, the favourite drink of Indra, and for the matter of that of the Vedic Aryans, has thus been praised:

"This Soma is a God; he cures
The sharpest ills that man endures.
He heals the sick, the sad he cheers,
He nerves the weak, dispels their fears;
The faint with martial ardour fires,
With lofty thoughts the bard inspires,
The soul from earth to heaven he lifts;
So great and wondrous are his gifts.
Men feel the God within their veins,
And cry in loud exulting strains:

"We 've quaffed the Soma bright,
And are immortal grown;
We 've entered into light,
And all the Gods have known.
What mortal now can harm,
Or foeman vex us more?
Through thee beyond alarm,
Immortal God, we soar."[1]

The following lines are nearly literal translation of Rv. x. 119 and show the hilarious effect produced on Indra by the Soma-drink:—

"Yes, yes I will be generous now,
And grant the bard a horse and cow.
I 've quaffed the Soma-draught.
These draughts impel me with the force
Of blasts that sweep in furious course.

[1] The last ten lines are a literal translation of Rv. viii. 48, 3.

I 've quaffed the Soma-draught.
They drive me like a car that speeds
When whirled along by flying steeds.
These hymns approach me fondly now,
As hastes to calf the mother-cow.
I turn them over as I muse,
As carpenter the log he hews.
The tribes of men, the nations all
I count as something very small.
Both worlds, how vast soe'er they be,
Don't equal even the half of me.
The heaven in greatness I surpass,
And this broad earth, though vast her mass,
Come, let me as a play-thing seize,
And toss her wheresoe'er I please.
Come, let me smite with vigorous blow,
And send her flying to and fro.
My half is in the heavenly sphere,
I 've drawn the other half down here.
How great my glory and my power!
Aloft into the skies I tower.
I 'm ready now to mount in air,
Oblations to the gods to bear:
I 've quaffed the Soma-draught."[1]

Agni or Fire is the God to whom 200 hymns have been addressed in the Ṛgveda, the largest number being 250, all addressed to Indra. The following extracts from a metrical sketch made by Dr. Muir will give the reader an idea of how this God was looked upon and worshipped by his votaries:

" Great Agni, though thine essence be but one,
Thy forms are three; as fire thou blazest here,
As lightning flashest in the atmosphere,
In heaven thou flamest as the golden Sun.

[1] Dr. Muir's Translation. *O. S. T. V.*

"It was in heaven thou hadst thy primal birth,
By art of sages skilled in sacred lore
Thou wast drawn down to human hearths of yore,
And thou abid'st a denizen of earth.

"Sprung from the mystic pair,[1] by priestly hands
In wedlock joined, forth flashes Agni bright;
But—O ye Heavens and Earth, I tell you right,
The unnatural child devours the parent brands.

* * * *

And yet this orphaned God himself survives:
Although his hapless mother soon expires,
And cannot nurse the babe, as babe requires—
Great Agni wondrous infant, grows and thrives.

* * * *

"In every home thou art a welcome guest;
The household's tutelary lord; a son,
A father, mother, brother, all in one;
A friend by whom thy faithful friends are blest.

"A swift-winged messenger, thou callest down
From heaven, to crowd our hearths, the race divine,
To taste our food, our hymns to hear, benign,
And all our fondest aspirations crown.

"Thou, Agni, art our priest, divinely wise,
In holy science versed; thy skill detects
The faults that mar our rites, mistakes corrects,
And all our acts completes, and sanctifies.

"Thou art the cord that stretches to the skies,
The bridge that spans the chasm, profound and vast,
Dividing Earth from Heaven, o'er which at last
The Good shall safely pass to Paradise.

* * * *

---

[1] The two pieces of fuel by the attrition of which fire is produced, which are represented as husband and wife.

" Preserve us, lord, thy faithful servants save
From all the ills by which our bliss is marred ;
Tower like an iron wall our homes to guard,
And all the boons bestow our hearts can crave.

" And when away our brief existence wanes
When we at length our earthly homes must quit,
And our freed souls to worlds unknown shall flit,
Do thou deal gently with our cold remains.

" And then thy gracious form assuming, guide
Our unborn part across the dark abyss,
Aloft to realms serene of light and bliss,
Where righteous men among the Gods abide."

And this naturally leads us to the conceptions that the Vedic bards formed of Yama, the God of Death, and of our future life. The following metrical sketch made by Dr. Muir will undoubtedly be found interesting :

" To great king Yama homage pay,
Who was the first of men that died,
That crossed the mighty gulf, and spied
For mortals out the heavenward way.

" No power can ever close the road
Which he to us laid open then,
By which in long procession men
Ascend to his sublime abode.

" By it our fathers all have passed ;
And that same path we too shall trace,
And every new succeeding race
Of mortal men, while time shall last.

" The God assembles round his throne
A growing throng the good and wise—
All those whom, scanned with searching eyes,
He recognizes as his own."

The following stanzas give the purport of the *mantras* addressed to the dead at funeral ceremonials :

" Departed mortal, speed from earth
By those old ways thy sires have trod,
Ascend, behold the expectant God
Who calls thee to a higher birth.

" First must each several element
That joined to form thy living frame
Flit to the region whence it came,
And with its parent source be blent.

" Thine eye shall seek the solar orb,
Thy life-breath to the wind shall fly,
Thy part ethereal to the sky ;
Thine earthy part shall earth absorb.

" Thine unborn part shall Agni bright
With his benignest rays illume,
And guide it through the trackless gloom
To yonder sphere of life and light.

" On his resplendent pinions rise,
Or soar upon a car aloft,
By Wind-gods fanned with breezes soft,
Until thou enterest Paradise.

" And calmly pass without alarm,
The four-eyed hounds that guard the road
Which leads to Yama's bright abode ;
Their master's friends they dare not harm.

" All imperfections leave behind
Assume thine ancient frame once more,
Each limb, and sense, thou hadst before,
From every earthly taint refined.

" And now with heavenly glory bright,
With life intenser, nobler, blest,
With large capacity to taste,
A fuller measure of delight.

" Thou there once more each well-known face
Shalt see of those thou lovedst here
Thy parents, wife, and children dear,
With rapture shalt thou soon embrace.

" The Fathers, too, shalt thou behold,
The heroes who in battle died,
The Saints and Sages glorified,
The pious bounteous kings of old.

" The Gods whom here in humble wise
Thou worshippedst with doubt and awe,
Shall there the impervious veil withdraw
Which hid their glory from thine eyes.

" The good which thou on earth has wrought,
Each sacrifice, each pious deed,
Shall there receive its ample meed
No worthy act shall be forgot.

" In those fair realms of cloudless day ;
Where Yama every joy supplies,
And every longing satisfies,
Thy bliss shall never know decay."

The difference between Ṛgvedic and secular poetry is this : while the latter revels in pure and simple imagination and is mostly without any real substance, the former is real and earnest, and based on the cardinal principles of a living faith. To a Vedic worshipper the Gods are as real as his human friends and neighbours, and the future existence of the soul after death as real as his own existence on this earth. And this adds to the supreme value of Vedic poetry.

I have already given elsewhere literal prose translations of the cosmognic hymns of the Ṛgveda ; but I cannot resist the temptation of subjoining below a few metrical translations made by Professor Macdonell. Three of the seven stanzas of Rv. x. 81 are as follow :

" What was the place on which he gained a footing ?
Where found he anything, or how, to hold by,

What time, the earth creating, Viśvakarman,
All-seeing, with his might disclosed the heavens?

" Who has his eyes and mouth in every quarter,
Whose arms and feet are turned in all directions,
The one God, when the earth and heaven creating,
With his two arms and wings together wields them.

" What was the wood, and what the tree, pray tell us,
From which they fashioned forth the earth and heaven,
Ye sages, in your mind, pray make inquiry,
Whereon he stood, when he the worlds supported?

The answers to some of these queries have been summed up in a verse of Rv. x. 72 :

" Even as a smith, the Lord of Prayer,
Together forged this universe :
In earliest ages of the Gods,
From what was not arose what is."

The following is a translation of the celebrated Song of Creation :

" No-being then existed not, nor being;
There was no air, nor heaven which is beyond it;
What motion was there? Where? By whom directed?
Was water there, and fathomless abysses?

" Death then existed not, nor life immortal;
Of neither night nor day was any semblance.
The One breathed calm and windless by self-impulse;
There was not any other thing beyond It.

" Darkness at first was covered up by darkness;
This universe was indistinct and fluid.
The empty space that by the void was hidden,
That One was by the force of heat engendered.

" Desire then at the first arose within It;
Desire, which was the earliest seed of spirit.
The bond of being in non-being sages
Discovered searching in their hearts with wisdom.

"Who knows It truly? Who can here declare It?
Whence was It born? Whence issued this creation?
And did the Gods appear with its production?
But then who knows from whence it has arisen?

"This world-creation, whence it has arisen,
Or whether it has been produced, or has not,
He who surveys it in the highest heaven,
He only knows, or e'en He does not know it."

This song of Creation is probably the grandest of all similar songs to be found in any literature of the world and it reaches a height of imagination and speculation unsurpassed by any similar song. The last line "He only knows, or e'en He does not know it" seems to have been misunderstood by some critics. If Brahman is all-knowing, they argue, how is it that even He does not know how and whence did this creation proceed? It undoubtedly proceeded from Brahman, as indicated in the previous verses; but Brahman Himself is limitless, transcending all time, space and thoughts. To say, therefore, that He knows Himself fully is to condition His limitlessness. The Vedic bard, realising this, suddenly exclaims "Or even He does not know it." This really enhances the sublimity of the poem, and does not lessen its grandeur in any way.

I will not stop here to give specimens of incantations and other poems on mundane subjects, some of which are to be found in the Ṛgveda. From the translation of the hymns and verses quoted above, it will be clear to our readers that Ṛgvedic poetry is not as primitive as it is sometimes supposed to be, but it reveals a very high order of human culture at an extremely remote period of the world's history, when humanity in general was in its early infancy, and light was struggling with darkness for mastery and expression. No wonder that people believed that the *mantras* of the Ṛgveda were divine revelations, and could not be ascribed to human agency.

CHAPTER XV.

CONCLUDING REMARKS.

I have endeavoured in this small volume to give my readers an idea of Ṛgvedic culture and of its vast antiquity. They have no doubt found that this culture was of a high order, exceedingly remarkable, considering the age in which it was developed, when the world was "wrapped up in its winter sleep," and the few who had been awake moved in the gloaming more like distorted shadows of humanity than human beings themselves. It is simply wonderful to contemplate that at such an early dawn of the history of mankind, the Aryans, of all peoples in the world, should have been chosen to lead the van of human civilisation, and develop a culture which still furnishes models for imitation to not a few of the so-called civilised races of mankind. And yet this culture, though very old, was not the oldest, for its beginnings must be taken back several thousands of years earlier than the Ṛgvedic period. I will not repeat here the arguments that I have elsewhere advanced to prove that Ṛgvedic Culture had made its beginnings more than 25,000 years ago, and passed through all the different stages of evolution before it reached the form in which we find it in the Ṛgveda. I have no doubt that scholars will gradually realise that his culture is the oldest of all living or dead cultures of the world, and that it influenced nearly every great culture that history or tradition knows of.

I cannot do better than conclude this work by quoting the following observations of Professor Max Muller :—

"There is perhaps too litttle of kings and battles in the Veda, and scarcely anything of the chronological frame-work of history. But poets surely are better than kings, hymns and prayers are more worth listening to than the agonies of butchered armies, and guesses at truth more valuable than unmeaning titles of Egyptian or Babylonian despots."[1]

And again :—

"The real history of man is the history of religion: the wonderful ways by which the different families of the human race advanced towards a truer knowledge and a deeper love of God. This is the foundation that underlies all profane history: it is the light, the soul, and life of history, and without it, all history would indeed be profane."[2]

Considered from this point of view, the history of Ṛgvedic Culture has a value of its own, which cannot be sufficiently appraised.

---

[1] *Chips from a German Workshop*, vol. i, p. 5 (1868).

[2] *Ibid*, p 21.

BIBLIOGRAPHY.

CHAPTER I.

The *Ṛgveda Samhitā*; Das' *Ṛgvedic India*. Wallace's *Geographical Distribution of Animals with a study of the relations of living and extinct Faunas as elucidating the past changes of the Earth's Surface*, vol. I, (1870); H. F. Blanford "*On the Age and Correlations of the Plant-bearing Series of India, and the former existence of an Indo-Oceanic Continent*" in the *Quarterly Journal of the Geological Society*, vol. xxxi (1875); *Encyclopaedia Britannica*, xii (9th Edn.); Wadia's *Geology of India* (1919); *Memoirs of the Geological Survey of India*, xlv, part I. H. G. Wells' *Outline of History*; Keith's *Antiquity of Man*; Tilak's *Arctic Home in the Vedas*; *Modern Review* (Calcutta), vol. xxx, Nos. 1 and 2; Macdonell's *History of Sanskrit Literature*; Prof. Winternitz's Readership Lecture delivered at the Calcutta University and published in the *Calcutta Review*, Nov. 1923. *Journal of the Department of Letters*, vol. viii. (Calcutta University); "*The Hindu Nakṣatras*" in the *Journal of the Department of Science*, vol. vi (Calcutta University); Tilak's *Orion*; The *Aitareya Brāhmana*: Introduction by Dr. Martin Haug, vol. I, (1863)

CHAPTER II.

The *Ṛgveda Samhitā*: Das' *Ṛgvedic India*; E. O. Jame's. *Introduction to Anthroplogy* (1919); Henry Drummond's *Ascent of Man*; Muir's *Original Sanskrit Texts*, vol. v; Griffith's *Translation of the Ṛgveda*; M. N. Dutt's *Translation of the Ṛgveda*; Bloomfield's *Religion of the Vedas*; *The Scientific American* (1922); Captain Cook's *Voyages of Discovery*; Dr. Haug's *Introduction to the Aitareya Brāhmaṇa*; *the Aitareya Brāhmaṇa*; Dr. Muir's references to the doctrines of *Anaxagoras* and

Euripedes, to the *Theogony of Hesiod* and to the *Fragments of Æschylus* in O. S. T., vol. V; the *Atharva-veda*; the *Taittirīya Samhitā*; the *Śatapatha Brāhmaṇa*; Weber's *Indische Studien*, vol. iii: Max Muller's *Chips from a German Workshop*; Prof. Macdonell's *Brahmanism and Buddhism*; published in the *Hindustan Review*, vol. xlvii (1923); *Historians' History of the World*, vol. i; Lord Avebury's *Prehistoric Times*; Westermarck's *History of Human Marriage*; Howard's *History of Matrimonial Institutions*; *The Mahābhāratam*; Shama Śhastri's *Evolution of Indian Polity*; Macdonell's *Vedic Mythology*, The *Rāmāyanam*; Macdonell & Keith's *Vedic Index*; The *Chāndogya Upaniṣad*; The *Vājsaneyī Samhitā*; Zimmer's *Altindisches Leben*; H. G Wells' *Outline of History*;

CHAPTER III.

Macdonell and Keith's *Vedic Index*, vols. i & ii; Maine's *Ancient Law*; The *Taittirīya Samhitā*; the *Taittirīya Brāhmaṇa*; The *Ṛgveda Samhitā*; Griffith's Translation of Do.; Macdonell's *History of Sanskrit Literature*; the *Aitareya Brāhmaṇa*; the *Bhāgavata Purāṇam*; Muir's *O. S. T*, (vol. v), the *Atharva-veda*; the *Śatapatha Brāhmaṇa*; the *Gopatha Brāhmaṇa*; Das' *Ṛgvedic India*; *Hist. Hist. of the World* vols. I & II; Wilson's *Translation of the Ṛgveda*; Ragozin's *Vedic India*; *Cambridge History of India*, vol. I; Zimmer's *Altindisches Leben*; Meyer's *Geschichte des Altertums*; Hillebrandt's *Vedische Mythologie*; P. T, Srinivas Iyengar's *Life in Ancient India in the Age of the Mantras*; Geldner's *Vedische Studien*; Macdonell's *Vedic Mythology*; *Journal of the American Oriental Society* 16; *Phallism* (London, 1889); *Kitto's Cyclopedia*; Forlong's *Rivers of Life*; the *Moniteur* (Jan. 1865) the *Bhagavatgītā*.

CHAPTER IV.

The *Ṛgveda Samhitā*; the *Zend-Avesta*; Dr. Taylor's *Origin of the Aryans*; Das' *Ṛgvedic India*; Macdonell &

Keith's *Vedic Index*, vols. I & II; Geldner's *Vedische Studien* I; The *Atharva-veda*; Griffith's *Translation of the Ṛgveda*; Wilson's *Do.*; the *Bṛhad-devatā*; Sāyaṇa's *Commentary on the Ṛgveda*; the *Nīti Manjarī*; *Cambridge History of India*, vol. I.

CHAPTER V.

The *Ṛgveda Samhitā*; Macdonell and Keith's *Vedic Index*, Vols. I & II; the *Mahābhāratam*; *Journal of the Royal Asiatic Society* (1906); Oldenburg's *Buddha*; *Harivamśam*; Macdonell's *History of Sanskrit Literature*; Das' *Ṛgvedic India*; Griffith's *Translation of the Ṛgveda*; Śāyaṇa's *Commentary on the Ṛgveda*; Hillebrandt's *Vedische Mythologie* I; Zimmer's *Altendisches Leben*; the *Śatapatha Brāhmaṇa*; the *Aitareya Brāhmaṇa*; the *Taittirīya Brāhmaṇa*; Geldner's *Vedische Studien* I; Mitra's *Indo-Aryans*; vol. I, Muir's *O. S. T.*, vol. V; the *Atharva-veda*; the *Taittirīya Samhitā*; *Cambridge History of India*; vol. I; *Journal of the Amer. Or So.* 17.

CHAPTER VI.

The *Ṛgveda Samhitā*; the *Aitareya Brāhmaṇa*; the *Atharva-veda Samhitā*; Kaegi's *Der Ṛgveda*; Zimmer's *Alt. Leben*; Grimm's *Deutsche Rechtsalt*; Macdonell and Keith's *Vedic Index*, vols. I & II; *Vasiṣtha Dharma Sūtra*; *Baudhāyana Dharma Sūtra*; *Mānava Dharma Sūtra*; Senart's *Famille et Propriete Primitives*; Weber's *Indische Studien*; the *Taitt. Samhitā*; the *Maitr. Samhitā*; the *Śatapatha Brāhmaṇa*; Böhtlirgk's Dictionary; Geldner's *Vedische Studien*.

CHAPTER VII.

The *Ṛgveda Samhitā*; Das' *Ṛgvedic India*; Captain Cook's *Voyage of Discovery*; Macdonell and Keith's *Vedic Index*, vols. I & II; Macdonell's *Vedic Mythology*; the *Bhāgabat Purāṇa*; the *Taitt. Samhitā*; the *Kāthaka Samhitā*; Griffith's *Translation of the Ṛgveda*; Wilson's *Do.*; the *Taitt. Brāhmaṇa*; the *Vāj. Samhitā*; the *Śat. Brāhmaṇa*;

the *Mait. Samhitā ;* H. G. Wells' *Outline of History ;* the *Atharva-veda Samhitā* ; the *Jaim. Brahmaṇa ;* the *Chānd. Upaniṣad.*

CHAPTER VIII.

The *Ṛgveda Samhitā* ; the London *Times* Jan. 8, 1921 ; Keith's *Antiquity of Man ;* Hermann Klaatsch's *Evolution and Progress of Mankind ;* Carlyle's *French Revolution ;* the *Modern Review* (Calcutta), vol. II ; the *Mahābhāratam ; Cambridge History of India ;* Macdonell and Keith's *Vedic Index*, vols. I & II ; Zimmer's *Alt. Leben ;* Bloomfield's *Religion of the Veda ;* Shāma Shāstri's *Evolution of Indian Polity ;* the *Aitareya Brāhmaṇa ;* the *Taitt. Brāhmaṇa ;* the *Atharva-veda Samhitā ;* Das' *Ṛgvedic India ;* the *Rāmāyaṇam ; Gautama Dharma Sūtra ;* the *Kāthaka Samhitā ;* the *Śatapatha Brāhmaṇa* ; Muir's *O. S. T.*, vol. II ; the *Mait. Samhitā* ; Ludwig's *Translation of the Ṛgveda* ; Hillebrandt's *Vedische Mythologie* ; Henry Stanley's *Through Darkest Africa* ; Wilson's *Translation of the Ṛgveda* ; Griffith's *Do.* ; Sāyaṇa's and Mahīdhara's Commentaries on the Ṛgveda.

CHAPTER IX.

The *Ṛgveda Samhitā ;* Macdonell and Keith's *Vedic Index*, vols. I & II ; Hillebrandt's *Vedic Mythologie* ; the *Pancavimśa Brāhmaṇa ;* Zimmer's *Altindisches Leben* ; Roth's *Zur Litteratur und Geschichte des Weda ;* Wilson's *Translations of the Ṛgveda* : Griffith's *Do.*

CHAPTER X.

The *Ṛgveda Samhitā* ; Macdonell and Keith's *Vedic Index*, vols. I & II ; Zimmer's *Alt. Leben* ; Kaegi's *Der Ṛgveda* ; Schrader's *Prehistoric Antiquities* ; the *Kāthaka Samhitā* ; the *Vāj. Samhitā* ; the *Taitt. Brāhmaṇa* ; Raghunath Rao's *Aryan Marriage* ; Srinivasa Sastri's *Marriage after Puberty* ; *Āśvalāyana Gṛhya Sūtras* ; *Āpastamba Gṛhya Sūtras* ; *Buadhāyana* ; *Śānkhāvana* ; *Jaimini* ; *Gobhila* ;

Yāska's *Nirukta*; Wilson's *Translation of the Ṛgveda*; *Ait. Brāhmaṇa*; *Yājnavalkya*; the *Mahābhāratam*; *Kātyāyana Śrauta Sūtra*; Macdonell's *Vedic Mythology*; the *Atharvaveda Samhitā*; the *Taitt. Samhitā*; Oldenberg's *Die Religion des Veda*; *Journal of the German Oriental Society for 1888*; Muir's *O. S. T.*, vol. V; Hopkin's *Religions of India*. Prof. M. A. Canney's *Stephanos Nirmalendu Ghosh Lecture* (1925) published in the *Calcutta Review* (July 1925).

CHAPTER XI.

The *Ṛgveda Samhitā*; the *Manu Samhitā*; the *Atharvaveda Samhitā*; Macdonell and Keith's *Vedic Index*, vols. I & II; *Gobhila Gṛhya Sūtras*; *Chānd. Upaniṣad*; *Gautama Dharma Sūtra*; *Āpastamba Dharma Sūtra*; *Agni Purāṇam*; *Pancavimśa Brāhmaṇa*; *Taittirīya Samhitā*; *Kāthaka Samhitā*; *Vāj. Samhitā*; *Taitt. Brāhmaṇa*; Wilson's *Translation of the Ṛgveda*; Macdonell's *Vedic Mythology*.

CHAPTER XII.

The *Ṛgveda Samhitā*; Wilson's *Translation of the Ṛgveda*; Sāyaṇa's *Commentary on the Ṛgveda*; Macdonell's *Vedic Mythology*; the *Śatapatha Brāhmaṇa*; the *Aitareya Brāhmaṇa*; the *Taitt. Brāhmaṇa*; the *Taitt. Samhitā*; Muir's *O. S. T.*, vol. V; *Journal of the German Oriental Society* XXII; Max Muller's *Chips from a German Workshop*, vol. I; Das' *Ṛgvedic India*, Chaps. XIII, XXII, and XXIV; *Journal of the Department of Letters*, vol. VIII (Calcutta University); Ragozin's *Vedic India*.

CHAPTERS XIII, XIV & XV.

Ṛgveda Samhitā; Macdonell's *History of Sanskrit Literature*; Muir's *Original Sanskrit Texts*, vol. V; the *Old Testament*; *Chips from a German Workshop* vol. I. R. S. Trivedi's *Yajnā-kathā*; Grant Allen's *Evolution of the Idea of God*; E. B. Tyler's *Primitive Culture*.

Index.

A

Abhibhū 228
Abhi-praśnin 437
Abhi-varta 310, 311
Abraham 165
Adhi-devana 229
Adhi-ṣavaṇa 195
Adhi-vāsa 213
Adhi-vikartana 378
Adhvara 495
Adhvaryu 490, 492, 494, 495, 496, 497, 499, 500
Aditi 57, 85, 338, 339, 422, 457, 474, 483, her eight sons 57
Adīnā 351, 362
Adultery, regarded as a serious offence, 257, 433; punishment of adulterer ... 434
Agastya 4
Aghā 38
Aghnya 205, 286
Aghnyā ... 204, 286, 501
Agni 67, compared to a horse 69, produced by Atharvan and kindled by Dadhyanc 74; identified with lightning and the sun 74, son of stone 74, *dvimātrika* 75, produced by the friction of two sticks 75, water, the source of Agni 76, as a God 91, 92, 108, 160, 186, 290, 309, 375, 379, 380, 411 417-19, 457 467, 468, 471, how produced 487, how Agni came to be established as a household deity 483
Agni *Annapati* 493
Agni Āhavanīya ... 490-93, 495, 496, 498, 500
Agni *Gṛhapati* 493
Agni *Vaiśvānara* ... 29
Agni Āvasathya ... 489
Agnihotra ... 373, 489, 492, 493
Agnihotra-havanī... ...393, 495
Agni Śālā 180, 191, 485, 490, 492, 493, 496
Agni-stoma 489, 506
Agni-tatva ... 376
Agnidhra 215
Agnīt ... 495, 496, 497
Agnyādhāna ... 489, 491, 492
Agnyādheya 228, 489
Agriculture in the Neolithic age, its mode 265; marks the beginning of civilised life 272; Vedic methods of agriculture 275
Agrū 369
Ahi, as Vṛtra 65, 166, in the plural 167
Ahi-hantā 61
Ahimsā 204, 502
Ahīna 506
Ahura-Mazda 89, 528
Aikāhika 506
Airāvat 343
Aitareya Brāhmaṇa, 41, 78, 106, 107, 122, 211, 235, 241, 312, 509
Aja-Panchaudana ... 255
Ajas 163, 360, 361
Ajigarta ... 107, 108, 241
Ajihanta 61
Ajina 210
Ajina-vāsin 210
Akesines (Asiknī) ... 164
Akṣa 227
Akṣa-vapana 229
Akṣa-vāpa 325
Akṣu 189
Alakṣmī 440
Alexander, the Great 164, 317, 342
Alinas ... 163, 360, 361
Allen, Grant 485
Allyattes 164
Amājur 250, 251
Amśa 56
Amkuśa ... 335, 342, 462
Amshasponds 89, 90
Amśumatī 169
Anas 196
Anadvan 196
Anatomy 448
Anāsa 32, 158
Anāyudhah 32
Andamanese 211
Andrews R. C. 177
Anga 28
Angiras 136, in the plural 74, originators of Fire-worship 74, 289; created the cow 290, 389

PAGE.
Anglo-Saxon 43
Animal Sacrifice 109
Anjanā 103, 104
Antarikṣa 66
Antahpurādhykṣa ... 318
Antevāsin 392
Anthropomorphic accounts of Gods ... 461 *et seq*
Anus ... 46, 112, 160, 161, 301, 354, 360, 364, 466
Anuvākyā 497
Anuyāja 497
Ap. 453
Apālā ... 248, 249, 393
Aphrodite 79
Apūpa 203
Apvā 347
Apauruṣeya 451, 452
Apyā Yoṣā 398
Arachosia 356
Araṇi ... 75, 490, 500
Araṇyānī, ...205, 520
Arātis 44
Arbuda ... 155, 167 169
Arcanānā 134
Arcelin, M. 180
Ardha-deva 354
Aristotle 98
Arjuna 350
Arjunī 38
Army, how composed in Vedic times ... 339 *et seq*
Arrian 213
Arrows, horn-tipped ... 331
Artha 374
Arvant 227
Aryaman ... 56, 84 376
Aryan clans 47, savage Aryan tribes 47, their dispersion 48; Aryans 14, 16, 17, 19, 20, 21, 22, their cradle in Sapta-Sindhu 179, eastward advance of Aryans from the Punjab 29; Neolithic Aryans 30, Aryans autochthonous to Sapta-Sindhu 48, 173, 176 Aryan immigration to India from Europe, a myth 264, Aryan culture in ancient India and Europe compared ... 180 *et seq*
Aryo-Mongolian 18, 32
Aśma 55, 114
Aśma-cakra ... 127, 270
Aśva 55
Aśva-medha, ... 489, 501, 504, 506
Aśva-parśu 52
Aśvattha ... 206, 446
Aśvavāti 449

PAGE.
Aśvins 53, compared to horse 69; 94, 108, 136, 223, 224, 241, 244, 261, 274, 275, 329, 377, 379, 453, 459; as divine physicians ... 449
Aṣṭa-kapāla-puroḍāśa ... 494
Asanga 136
Asi 333
Asiatic Mediterranean Sea ...5, 6, 32, 67, 150
Asi-carman, ... 336
Asiknī 161
Assyria 25, 140
Astrā (goad) 276
Astras 332
Asuniti 426
Asuras ... 47, 89, 94
Asura-Maghavan 89
Asura Mahān 89
Atharvan ... 54, 73, 74, 448
Atharva-veda 25, 28, 30, 71, 244, 247, 255, 278, 307, 314, 317, 402, 444; spells in—28, the age of the— ... 30
Atithigva ... 356, 390
Atka ... 212, 213, 220
Atri 67, 91, 94, 132, 134, 241, 375
Attys 94
Atya ... 226, 227
Aurdhva-dehika-kriyā ... 412
Aurnavābha 458
Auśija 136
Avata (well) 269, mode of raising water from well ... 270
Averting scarcities, Vedic method of— 271
Avesta 36, 402
Avratah 32
Ayah śipra 219
Ayas 220
Ayodhyā 29
Ācārya 144
Ācārya-kula-vāsin ... 392
Ādityas, six in number 57, eight 57, 124 twelve 460; also 80, 89, 90, 382, 398, 441, 457, 473
Ādyā Śakti 474
Āghāti 235
Āgū 497
Āhāva (bucket) 270
Āhitāgni ... 488, 489 491, 494
Āhuti ... 490, 494
Āji 226
Āji-kṛt 226
Āji-pati 226
Ājya ... 95, 215, 495
Ājya-Homa 499
Ājya-sthālī 495
Ākāśa 483
Āmāda 410

PAGE.

Āndra 66, 263
Āñjaneya 103
Āpastamba 435
Āpayā ... 161; 178, 353
Āpta 61
Āptya Tṛta 58, earlier than Indra 60
Āraṇyakas ... 24, 25, 28
Ārā (goad) 335
Ārjikas 169
Ārjikīyā 507
Ārtni 332
Ārṣa-marriage 253
Āruṇi 29
Ārya ... 153, 154, 159, 160, 167, 361, 389
Ārya-varṇa 155
Āśu (dhānya) 281
Āśvalāyana Gṛhya Sūtra ... 406
Āstrī 109
Āsandi ... 193, 318
Āsecana 194
Āskanda 228
Āyu 356
Āyudha (bow and arrow) .. 333
Āvasatha 190

B

Baal 94
Baal-Peor 164
Babylonia ... 25, 140, 141
Babylonians .. 95, 142
Babylonian civilisation ... 185
Bacchus 164
Bactria ... 5, 48, 116
Bagaios 93
Baksheesh 306
Balbuja (grass) 210
Balder 95
Balders-baal 95
Balder's Fire 95
Baleshaugen 95
Balestranden 95
Balhika 28
Bali (Taxes) 319
Baltic 95
Barhats 408
Barley, a staple grain ... 266
Baudhāyana ... 52, 436
Bāṇa (arrow) 332
Begging condemned 306, 307
Bekanāta 148
Bel 95
Belcher, Edward 75
Belt, Great and Little ... 95
Belteberga 95
Benfy 95
Bhaga 56, 91, 93, 287, 376, 472

PAGE.

Bhakti 513
Bhalānasas ... 163, 360
Bhara 226
Bharadvāja 132, 190, 203, 288, 355
Bharatas 45, 105, 156, 160, 161, 301, 304, 353, 355, 358, 359, 360, 362, 364, 366
Bhastrā 72, 193
Bhāgadugha 318
Bhāgavata Purāṇa ... 132
Bhāratī 355
Bhāvya 136
Bheda 163, 345, 360, 366
Bheṣaja 446
Bhikṣu 380
Bhiṣaj ... 127, 448
Bhṛgu 136
Bhṛgus introduced Fire-worship 74, as carpenters 130, as chariot-makers ... 139
Bhojas 390
Bhruṇa 437
Bhuh 382
Bhuvah 382
Bibhindu 140
Black Yajurveda 504
Bloomfield, Prof. 16, 91, 103, 161, 306
Boghaz Keui ... 115, 178
Bogu 93
Bollensen, Dr. 462
Bolshevism 306
Borodhāna 281
Bṛbu ... 139, 391
Bṛhadāraṇyaka Upaniṣad ... 424
Bṛhaddevatā 198, 407, 408
Bṛhadratha ... 154, 155
Bṛhadukta 426
Bṛhaspati 37, 60, 170, 261, 269, 279, 309, 346, 357, 379, 380, 434, 439, 440, 447, 484
Bṛsayas 356
Brahman, in the sense of the Supreme Deity, 384, 395, 424, 478, 482, 484, 504, in the sense of the officiating priest 128, 129, 131, 490, 491, 495, 496, 498, as Creator 294, 474
Brahmacarya 380, 381, 384, 387, 392, 393, 489
Brahmacārin 387, 392, 393, 434
Brahmaṇaspati 57, 93, 309, 310, 311, 338
Brahmātithi 162
Brahmāvarta 161
Brāhmaṇas, 24, 25, 28, 41, 42, 52
Brāhmaṇas the first twice-born caste, 128, 131, 132, 177, 358, 395, 396, 418, 477, 504, 505
Brāhmaṇi bull 417
Brāhuis 158

PAGE.

Bridal dress 378
Bronze Age 487
Buddha 44, 274, 317, 502 510
Buffaloes slaughtered and their meat eaten 204
Bugash 93
Buhler, Dr. 62, 94
Burial preceded cremation ... 405
Burial rites ... 405, 408
Burning of widows ... 256

C

Caitanya ... 510
Cakra ... 270, 334
Camel-corps ... 340, 343
Canning (man that was able) .. 296
Caravans ... 141, 142
Carlyle ... 296, 298
Carmamna 127
Carman 336
Caste system ... 45, 46, 129
Cattle, value of— .. 283 *et seq.*
Cows media of exchange, 284, cattle as wealth, 109, cows identified with Bhaga, Soma and Indra, 287 construction of sheds for cattle 293, cows slaughtered and their meat eaten 203
Cavalry 339
Cayamana 363
Cedis 46, 102
Celts 77
Celtic 22
Chádis 196
Chaldea 17, 306
Chaldeans 95 152
Chambal 3
Chandiká 505
Chandra Gupta 183
Chaos (primeval) ... 482
Chandogya Upanisad 424, 432, 438, 467
Charioteers ... 339, 341
Chariot-race ... 226 227
Chellean period 8, 49
Child-life ... 385 *et seq.*
Child-wives occur in the Sûtra period 251
Cholas 22
Christ 503
Christian Eucharist; communion 503
Chàttadi devatas ... 384
Civilisation, Stone and Bone age of Aryan— ... 55
Civil Law 437
Cloth, made of skin and wool... 72
Coiffure 217

PAGE.

Coins 140
Composition of the army 339 *et seq.*
Congo Forest ... 331, 333
Constantine 94
Contract of sale 143
Cook, Captain ... 75 76 264
Cosmic order 484
Costumes, male and female ... 213, 214, 215, 216
Creation, song of— ... 537
Cremation, idea of— ... 404
Cremation rites, 412—421, its want looked upon with horror 412
Crete 31
Criminal offences ... 434
Cro-Magnon race ... 10, 11
Cro-Magnards ... 10, 17, 18
Cumuri ... 155, 167
Cyavana ... 244, 449
Cyclopes 78

D

Dabhiti 155, 186
Dadhi 202
Dadhici, sage 52, 53, 54, 55, 70, 114 his renunciation 53, with a horse-head 53, identified with the horse ... 54, 55
Dadhikras 54, 55, 224, 225, 226
Dadhikrávan 225
Dadhyanc 52, 114, kindled fire 74
Dadhyaśir 202
Dadhyodana 202
Dahae identified with the Dasas 155, 156
Dakṣa 56, 483
Daitya 103
Daivadása ... 355, 356, 357, 361
Daivaváta 163, 164
Dakṣiṇá 129 347 390, 391, 499
Dakṣiṇágni ... 129, 490, 491, 492, 493, 499, 500
Dam 18
Dampati 146
Dancing ... 232, 233
Daṇḍa 437
Danaides 79
Darbha ... 134, 135, 374, 495
Darwin 98
Darśa-yága 494
Daśagvas 508
Daśaratha 317
Dasyus 19, 47, 84 86 92 93, 133, 156, 157, 158, 159, 160, 174, 177 188, 260, 261, 262, 273 350, 325 described as riteless and not sacrificing 157, 7 : deprived of their name as Ârya 157, compared with Vṛtra 158, 167

PAGE.

Daughter, etymological meaning of 246, allowed choice of husband 247; unmarried daughter given a share of paternal property 247, 250; stood the chance of going astray 247: birth of daughter looked upon with disfavour 247: but became a pet of the family 248; her education not neglected ... 248
Daughter-in-law, position of ... 242
Dauh 470
Dáma 188
Dána-stuti ... 227, 235, 306
Dása 9, 47, 84, 86, 92, 93, 128, 133, 152, 50, 260, 261, 262, 273, 354; does not mean a 'slave,' but a 'tribe' 153, 154, 155, 156; also an 'enemy' 155 and civilised or uncivilised Aryan tribe, dissenting from Vedic faith 156; in the plural 174, 177
Dātra 278
Debt 148, ancestral debt repayable 149, debtor how punished 438
De Condeile 279
Dehi 187
Delbruck ... 255, 257
Demeter 79
Demons 410
Devas 77, 453; their classification and number 459; the number of deities three 460; thirty-three Devas 460; caste of the Devas 460; their number mentioned as 3339 (ibid); their visible bodies and invisible spirits 466; their anthropomorphic description 461. The word *Deva* as an epithet of Vṛtra 64, 65, 114: *Devah Ādityah* 57, 422; *Deva Hotṛ* 498; *Deva Patnis* 498; Devas and Asuras identical ... 58
Devara 429, 430
Devatá 454
Devayāni 136
Devāpi 130
Devavat 366
Devi-Sūktam ... 329, 473
Devṛ 430
Dhanus (bow) 332
Dhanvan (bow) 332
Dhāna 281
Dhānā ... 126, 201

PAGE.

Dhānya 126, 200, 263, a staple grain 266; 275. ... 281
Dhānya-bija 281
Dhānya kṛt 278
Dharma ... 373, 374
Dharma-Sūtras 256
Dhāstra 132
Dhātṛ 383, 414
Dhiṣanā 195
Dhruvā 495
Dhuni 167, 274
Dhvaja 344
Dicing ... 228, *et seq.*
Dirghaśrava (son of Uiśj) ... 274
Disposal of dead bodies ...404, 405
Diti 103
Divodāsa 156, 355, 356, 357, 361
Divonaras 462
Dog, taming of the—70; earlier than the conception of Yama 71; as a beast of burden 141; killing lions 142; four-eyed dogs guarding Yama's region 410, and messengers of Yama ... 417
Domestic life 96
Drāpi... ... 213, 336, 464
Draupadī 105, 229
Dravi 195
Dravidians 22, 141, 151, 158, 164, 166, 183
Dress ... ... 210 *et seq.*
Droṇa 193
Dṛṣad... ... ...194, 494
Dṛṣadvatī ... 160, 161, 178, 353
Dṛti 72, 193
Druhs... 411
Druhyus ... 46, 112, 160, 161, 301, 354, 360, 364, 368
Druj 411
Drummond, Henry ... 50, 51
Druṇa 126
Drupada 148
Duhitṛ 123
Dundubhi ... 128, 234, 343, 344
Durgā ... 466, 474
Durgaha 354
Durnaman ... 385, 386
Duroṇa 189
Dūrvā 419
Düsseldorf 8
Dvāra 189
Dvāpara 228
Dvija 387
Dvita 58
Dyāvá ... 56, 57, 67, 77, 453, 470
Dyāvā-Pṛthivi ... 77, 79, 81, 484
Dyaus ... 77, 79, 379

PAGE.

Dyaus-Pitar 77
Dyus ... 56, 57, 67, 77

E

Early Aryan Gods ... 77
Earth and Sky looked upon as Mother and Father ... 77
Eastern Sea ... 2, 6, 16, 150
Education of girls... ... 393
Educational institutions ... 392
Eggeling 210
Egypt 23, 25
Egyptian civilisation 182, 183
Ekata ... ... 5[illegible]
Ekādaśa-kapāla-purodāśa ... 495
Election of kings ... 307 *et seq*
Elephant corps ... 339, 342
Endogamy 257
Eoanthropus 8
Eoliths 7
Eolithic ... ... 32, 4[illegible]
Esquimaux 75
Euphrates-Tigris 27
Euripedes 78
European Mediterranean Sea .. 5, 6
Evans, Sir Arthur ... 31
Evil Spirits, three classes of ... 411
Exogamy ... 102, 256, 257
Exposure of old parents a myth 242, 243
—of girl-infants also a myth ... 246

F

Fairs 233
Fairguni ... 61, 62, 93
Family life described, 237, 238, 239 368, 369, 370
Father and Son 240, 241, Father patriarch of the family 242
Fiorgyn ... 61, 62, 93
Five Tribes ... 32, 46, 111, 112 171, 173, 176, 305
Fire, origin of 73; evidence of its existence in early Pleistocene 73, the youngest of Gods 73, first produced by Atharvan 73; worshipped by Bhṛgu and Manu 74; identified with the sun and lightning 74. son of stone 74 produced by the friction of two dry sticks by the Aryans 75; also by the Tasmanians ... 75
First Glacial Age ... 7
——-Ice Age 7
——-Interglacial period ... 7

PAGE.

First True men 9, 18
Fish 205
Foetus, incantation for protecting the ... 385, 386
Food, hymn to 207, 208; food of Ṛgvedic Aryans 200 *et seq*
Forlung 164
Four Seas 2
Fourth Glacial Age ... 8, 17
Fourth Ice Age 5
Fruits 205

G

Gambler's lament ... 230
Gandhāra ... 5, 17, 18, 19, 48, 116, 135, 160, 177, 184, 212, 354
Gandharva ... 375, 381, 398
Gaṅgā 26, 356
Gāna 26
Garbhādhāna 383
Garden of Eden 117
Gārgya, ... 132
Gārhapatya Agni ... 379, 489, 491, 492, 493, 495, 496, 498
Garudas 103
Garutman 472
Gāthā 235
Gāthā pati 235
Gāthā-nī 235
Gāthin 235
Gaul 5, 6
Gaura 222
Gautama 432
Gautama-Dharma-Sūtra ... 318
Gāyatri 519
Geldner 38, 161, 188, 210, 218
Gens ... 120, 256
Germans, treatment of old parents by ancient 242, 243
Germanic nations ... 20, 22
Ghee 126
Ghoṣā 136, 248, 250, 393, 449
Ghṛta 202
Giles P. 298
Ginsburgh, Dr. 165
Glacial Age, first, 7, fourth ... 17
Goat the first animal tamed ... 69
Gobhila 432
Gobhila Gṛhya Sûtra ... 433
Gobi desert 117
Goblins 410
Godhūma, 210; not mentioned in the Ṛgveda 27[illegible]; its historical significance 279, 280
Gomati (the Gomal river) ... 135
Gopā ... 122, 125
Goṣṭha 110, 114, 119, 121, 122, 123, 189

PAGE.

Goṣṭhī ... 109, 110, 119, 120, 121
Goṣṭhī-patī 119
Gotama Ráhūgaṇa ... 29
Gotra in the sense of cloud) 58; (in the sense of cow-shed) 109, 110, 114, 122, 123, 124, 89; in the sense of clan) 102, 100, 110, 111, 119, 120, 121, 257 ...
Gotra-pati ... 110, 124
Gṛbha 229
Graha (throw of dice) ... 229
Grāma 44, 111, 119, 121, 124, 209; (self contained) .. 126
Grāmaṇī ... 44, 111, 121, 124, 133, 181, 299, 300, 301, 302, 303, 304, 318, 324, 330, 340
Granthas 388
Grassmann ... 221, 227
Grávan 208
Grávastut 167
Greece 24
Gṛha ... 121, 189
Gṛha-praveśa-homa ... 370
Gṛha-pati 121 485,—Agni ... 489
Gṛha-patnī ... 121, 128, 489
Grihiṇī 380
Gṛhya-Agni 489
Gṛhya Sūtras ... 253, 370, 371, 373, 483
Griffith 74, 359
Grimaldi cave 10
——— man 17
——— race ... 10 11, 18
Grimm 243
Gṛtsamada 132
Gupta Dynasty 506
Guru 388

H

Hahya 263
Haimantika 281
Haoma 178, 507
Haraquaiti 356
Haris' candra, story of ... 107
Hariyūpiya 156, 163
Harmya 188, 195
Hastaghna ... 72, 220, 221, 333
Hastagrábha 253
Haug, Martin 40
Havirdhána 489
Havis 128, 191, 458 488
Havya ... 204, 404, 487, 490
Hàya 227
Head-gear (female) ... 215
Heaven described... 400, 401
Heidelberg 7, 8
Heidelbergensis, Homo ... 7, 8

PAGE.

Helius 94
Hell or Nirṛti 402, how produced 404, 427
Hephaistos Indian ... 43
Here 79
Hermon Mt. 279
Hesiod 78 79
Hetairai 258
Heti 463
High prices 146
Hillebrandt 65; his theory of Vṛtra ... 55, 156, 356
Hima (in the sense of 'year')... 2, 203
Himavat 475
Hiraṇyagarbha 474
Home, origin of 96; home described 237, 238
Homo Heidelbergensis ... 7, 8;
——— Neanderthalensis 8, 10, 17,
———Sapiens 9; ———Primigenius 49
Horse, tamed before the discovery of Indra 68; highly prized by Aryans 69; horse-bone, used as weapan 53; 54; horse-riding and horse-race 222 *et seq* 226, 227; horse, slaughtered in sacrifice, and its meat eaten .. 204, 506,
Horus 94
Hospitality ... 388 *et seq.*
Hota 490
Hotṛ ... 134, 490, 493, 496, 497, 498
Howard 98
Human Sacrifice, seldom resorted to by Ṛgvedic Aryans 106; but practised in lates times ... 503, 504, 505,

I

Iberians 18, 32
Ice-Age, First 7, Fourth ... 5
Idáh 457
Idols 144
Ignus 92
Ikṣu 206
Ilá 132
Illegitimate children put away, 258, 369
Images of Gods ... 143, 144 145
Image-worship ... 144 462
Indo-Aryans ... 20, 23, 25, 39
Indo European 36
Indo-Iránian 36
Indra 37, 38, 84, 85, 87, 92, 108 109, 112, 114, 115, 223, 224, 289, 290, 291, 309, 312, 314,

PAGE.

315, 344, 345, 346, 347, 399, 400, 529 *et seq*; Indra with stone and bone weapons 31; his first conception 52; his origin from the horse 55; his birth-story 56, 178: drinks soma-juice as soon as born 57, 178; his principal feat 57; incurs odium for killing Vṛtra 57; deprived of the Soma-juice 57; forcibly partakes of the Soma-juice 57; Indra and Vṛtra myth unravelled 58: Indra's discovery 58; a God of the agricultural Aryans 63; releases the captive waters and the Sun and the Dawn 63; gives fertile lands to the Aryans 63; kills the Dásas and Dasyas 63; distinguished from Parjanya and Trita 63; supersedes them 63, 93; his supreme position established 63; looked upon as the devil-incarnate by the Parsees 64, 66; his existence doubted by the Paṇis 88, and by certain Ṛṣis 89; his name coupled with that of Pūṣan 125; Indra-Varuṇa 84; Indra Maghavan 85; purchase of Indra 143; Indra's image probably carried in car 146; his name occurring in a clay-tablet found at Boghaz Keui 178; his happy home 237; the supreme God of the agricultural Aryans 260 *et seq*; his two-fold functions 261; his worship simultaneous with the evolution of agriculture in the Neolithic age 262, 263; Indra, the sole creation of the Vedic Aryans 263; his discovery made in the Punjab in Neolithic times 263; his existence fully believed in and realised 273; Indra destroys 99 forts and 7 cities 353; had two forms, one visible and another invisible 469; his physical description 461; origin of the Indra cult 56

Indrāṇī ... 248, 254, 462

PAGE.

Indu ... 399, 400, 469

Incantation for suppression of co-wife 255

Infant-marriage, how it developed in later times 250; not known and existing in Ṛgvedic times ... 250, 432

Infantry 339

Interglacial period, first ... 7

Inter-marriage ... 133, 136 137

Iran 15, 19

Iranian 14, 39, 91, 93, 115, 492, 523

Irāvát 169

Irrigation, cultivation by ... 269

Iśāna 27, 444

Iṣā 276

Iṣkrti 447

Iṣṭa-pūrta 401

Iṣṭiyāga ... 489, 494-500

Iṣu 332

Iṣudhi 333

Iyengar P. T. S. ... 159

J

Jabālā 103, 104

Jábála 103, 104

Jain religion 502

Jāla 221

James E. O. ... 49, 72, 73, 75, 98

Jana 111, 114, 120

Janapada 111

Janitrī 77

Japa formula 41

Japan 22

Jaratkāra 103

Jaratkārṇa Sarpa ... 169

Jaratkāru 103, 169

Jātavedas 418, 419

Java 7

Jāyedastam (wife is the home) 97

Jīvātmā 509

Juangs 22, 211

Juhū ... 195, 434, 491, 495, 497

Jupiter 37, 78

Jyā 332

K

Kadraveya 103

Kadraveya Sarpa 167

Kadru 103, 104

Kaegi 227, 233, 242

Kāfiristhān 360

Kakṣivanta 136

Kailāsa 507

Kalaśa ... 127, 193, 208

Kalā 149

Kali 228

	PAGE.
Kalivuga ...	432, 504, 506
Kālikā Purāṇa ...	... 505
Kamadyu ...	... 136
Kāma ...	374, 481, 482
Kanvas ...	... 208
Kankana ...	... 375
Kankana-bandhana	... 375
Kanyā ...	... 378
Kaparda ...	... 217
Kapardin ...	... 219
Kapāla ...	494, 495, 496
Kapota ...	... 401
Karambha ...	... 201
Kāra ...	... 226
Karīṣa ...	... 278
Karkari ...	...234, 343
Karma ...	171, 421, 423, 425
...	428, 510, 512
Karmāra ...	126, 130
Karṇa-sobhana ...	... 216
Kārpāṇa ...	... 334
Kārṣman ...	... 226
Karuma ...	... 130
Kaśu	... 162
Kāshmir ...	... 5, 116
Kāṣṭhā ...	... 226
Katha Upaniṣad ...	402, 424
Kāthaka Saṃhitā	246, 319
Kātyāyana Śrauta Sūtra	... 509
Kauṣitakī Brāhmaṇa	...132, 167
Kavaca ...	... 335
Kavaṣa ...	132, 155, 364
Kavi	132, 363
Kāyadhu ...	... 312
Keith ...	8, 116, 192, 294 295
Ketkar V. B. ...	... 37
Khadira ...	...342, 358
Khala ...	... 278
Khanitrimā Āpah	... 270
Khaver ...	... 358
Khādi ...	... 216
Khādi-hasta ...	... 216
Khāndava ...	... 350
Khela (King) ...	...249, 329
Kikata 151, 161, not identified with Magadha but situated in Sapta-Sindhu ...	162
Kināśa (ploughman) ...	276
King, election of 307 *et seq*, described as 'devourer of the people' ...	... 320
King-maker ...	... 307
Kingship, evolution of	294 *et-seq*
Kitchen-midden ...	... 22
Klaatsch, Herman	... 295
Konow, Sten ...	20, 21, 22, 24
Kośa ...	194, (pail) 270
Kosala ...	... 29
Kossaeans ...	... 93, 94
Kostāgāra ...	... 198
Kovalevsky ...	... 256
Kravyād ...	...410, 411
Krivi ...	... 72, 161
Kronos ...	... 78
Kṛpāṇa ...	... 334
Kṛśa	... 210
Kṛṣṇas (a tribe) ...	...169, 174
Kṛṣṇa 169, 170; a cloud 170; (Vedic and Purnánic)	...170, 171
Kṛṣṇa (Lord) overthrew Indra-worship	274, 334, 350, 409
Kṛśana (pearl) ...	151, 217
Kṛta	...228, 229
Kṛtvans ...	... 169
Kṣatra ...	128, 177, 318, 504
Kṣatriya ...	68, 132, 133, 177,
...	320, 415, 504, 509
Kṣetra ...	...121, 275
Kṣetrasya pati ...	... 121
Kṣetrapati ...	... 276
Kṣiraudana ...	... 202
Kṣoṇī ...	... 234
Kula	110, 119, 121
Kula-pá ...	...119, 121
Kumārī-putra ...	... 369
Kumbha ...	127, 193
Kūpa 269, mode of raising water from ...	... 270
Kurīra ...	... 218
Kurīrin ...	... 218
Kurus ...	26, 105, 355
Kurukṣetra ...	53, 114, 178, 507
Kuru-Pañcālas ...	... 29
Kuruśravaṇa ...	163, 355
Kuśa	52, 211, 495, 496
Kuśikas ...	357, 358
Kūtas	... 372
Kutsa (Ṛṣi) ...	... 41, 356

L

	PAGE.
Lady Ṛṣis 104, Ghoṣā, Lopamudrā Mamatā, Apālā, Sūryā, Indrāṇī Śacī, Sārpa Rājñī, Viśvavārā ...	248
Lāja ...	... 377
Lāja-homa ...	377, 489
Lakṣmī ...	... 440
Land of the Seven Rivers	... 15
Lāngala (plough)	... 276
Lankā ...	... 350
Lavaṇa (Salt) ...	... 206
Liberality ...	388 *et seq*
Linga-in-Argha ...	165, 166
Lingam ...	... 164
Lion-hunting ...	... 222
Lithuanian ...	36, 61, 93
Loha ...	... 220

PAGE.

Lopa-mudrā ... 104, 248, 393
Love-story, Vedic 134, 135
Lüders 227
Ludwig .. 155, 161, 163, 210, 227, 257, 327, 359
Luxor 182
Lydians 94, 182

M

Mada 209
Madhu 206
Madhulā 441
Madhu-vidyā 53, 441
Madhvādi devatās ... 382
Madhya-deśa 29
Madhya-māśi 318, 437
Magadha 28
Māgávins 425
Maghá 38
Maghavan ... 85, 224, 327, 328, 343, 347
Magical rites 438, incantations 439—443
Máhabhárata ... 99, 229, 297, 311, 322, 350
Mahádeva 27
Mahája 203
Mahákáśa 471
Mahá-kula 110
Mahenjo Daro 137
Mahiṣa 142
Mahokṣa 208
Maine, Sir H. S. 120
Mala 210
Mamatá 248
Mámsa 203
Mámsaudana 202
Maná ... 140, 141
Maṇi 217
Maṇi-griva 217
Mansarobar, Lake ... 507
Manthá (churn) 202, (whey) ... 202
Mantras ... 24, 40, 43, 113, 129, 131 etc
Manu 41, 158, 398, 429, 431; kindled fire 74, learns the art of sowing seeds from the Aśvins 275, takes up kingship ... 297, 298
Manu-Sanhitá 429
Marital relations ... 257, 259
Marriage 96, 251, 252—by contract 101—of Heaven and Earth 78, forms of— 252, 253
Mártāṇḍa 422
Maruts ... 60, 67, 68, 93, 104, 135, 210, 212, 219 223, 227, 201, 268, 269, 365, 366, 442, 453, 463, 484, 529; sons of Rudra ... 444 etc

PAGE.

Marutvatīya Nivid ... 41
Mása 126
Massagetae 244
Mátara 77
Mátariśvan ... 470, 471
Máthava Videgha 29
Matsyas 162
Maujavata 507
Máyá ... 511, 512
Max Müller Prof.... 91, 416, 539
Medeus 94
Medicine 443
Megasthenes 213
Mekhalá 215
Mentone 10
Mesopotamia ... 13, 14, 17, 142, 152, 280
Mesopotamian civilisation ... 184
Metempsychosis 424
Mexico 25
Milanippe 78
Miocene ... 1, 33, 34, 35
Mitannian 115
Mithilā 29
Mithra ... 89, 90, 94, 503
Mithraism in Roman Empire 94
Mitra ... 56, 67, 80, 81, 82, 84; 89, 90, 91, 94, 125, 186, 223, 456, 464
Mitra-Varuṇa 114
Mitra, Dr. R. L. ... 218, 504, 505
Mit-vara 430
Mlā 210
Mleccha 159
Monarchy elective ... 308
Mongolia 6
Mongolian ... 11, 18, 32, 49, 68
Mongoloid type 32
Monogamy ... 98, 99, 254
Monotheism, polytheistic ... 461
Monsoons ... 268, 269
Moon-worshipper ... 86
Morality ... 257, 258, 259
Montelier 31
Mousterian ... 9, 72, 73
Mṛdhra-vác, epithet applied to Dasyus, Paṇis and Purus... 158
Mṛga (constellation) ... 37, 38
Mṛtyu 413
Mudga 126
Mudgala ... 130, 249, 330
Mudgalāni (Indrasenā) 249, 329
Mudgaudana 202
Muir Dr. ... 53, 138, 213, 515
Mujavat 28, 116, 178, 208, 230, 507
Mukhopādhyāya, D. M. ... 37
Mukṣija 222
Mundavers 22
Munja (grass) 215
Mura-devah 145

	Page.
Murderer, punishment of ...	435
Musala ...	194, 494
Music ...	234, 235
Musti-hatya	332

N

Nāciketas	424
Nagnikā	432
Nahana	189
Nahuṣa	321
Naicaśākha	161
Naraka	402
Naras	462
Narāśamsa	497
Nāsatyas	114
Navagvas ...	60. 261, 508
Navavástva ...	154, 155
Neandeathal 5, 8, 9;—Race 8,10—men	12
Neanderthaler Age ...	5
Neanderthalers ...	5, 6, 8, 18
Neanderthalensis, Homo	8, 10, 17
Negroid 10, 17;—Race ...	13
Nema (Ṛṣi) ...	89, 145, 154
Neolithic 4, 48;—men 11, 12, 13, 19, 5';—Age 12—Age in Crete 31—Aryans 18, 19, 31, 32, 113; culture of Neolithic Aryans 67—Age in India 264; culture in—265	
Nidhā	221
Nidhāpati	221
Nigadas ...	40, 42, 440
Nikṣaṇa	195
Nilsson	95
Nippur	95
Nirṛti or Hell ...	402-405, 412, 439
Nirukta ...	219, 334
Nirvāṇa	5.0
Niṣādas	45
Niṣangā	333
Niṣka	127, 140, 141, 216, 463
Niṣka-grīva ...	140, 216
Niṣkṛtis	447
Níti-manjarí	198
Nitvara	430
Nivi	213, 214
Nivids 40, 42, 43, more ancient than Ṛgvedic hymns 41, Marutvatíya Nivids 41; 450.	
Nṛta	232
Nṛtu	232
Nṛti	232
Nripeśas	462

O

Oceanos	78
Odana	202
Offensive weapons	330 *et seq.*
Ogni	92
Old Man, tribal ...	485, 496
Oldenberg	86
Opaṣa ...	...217, 218
Ordeals	438
Original Cradle of humanity .	116
Orion (constellation) ...	37
Ornaments ...	217, 218
Oṣadhi	206
Osborn H. F.	117
Otaheite	265
Ouranos ...	79, 90, 91
Ouranus	89, 95
Owls, regarded as inauspicions	440

P

Pacata	202
Faijavana	355
Pakṣa	189
Pakthas ...	163. 856, 360, 361
Pakva	202
Pakva-Homa	381
Palada	189
Palāśa	446
Palæolithic men, Later 10, 12 32, 294 ——Age 5,——stage 12——Aryans	32
Pan	165
Pañca- carsaṇyah ...	45
Pañca-janāh	32, 45, 46, 67, 111, 301, 305, 352
Pañca-kṛṣṭayah	32, 45, 46, 67, 68, 111, 301, 305
Pañca-kṣitayah ...	... 45. 111
Pañcāha	505
Pañcālas ...	27, 29, 161
Pañcudana ...	255, 430
Pañcauimśa Brāhmaṇa	167, 437
Pañcāyat	318
Pāndavas	105
Pándyas ...	22, 152
Paṇis 88, 139, 140; sceptical of Indra's existence 88, 94; as traders 139; as ship-builders 139; called ' Bekanātas' 148; 149, 151, 156, 174, 183, 185, 281, 356, 391	
Pāni-grahaṇam	375
Pāṇini	1, 33, 36, 43, 44 etc.
Pānta...	210
Pāpa-devatā	403
Parama-Brahman ..	509, 510
Paramātmā	473, 476, 481, 484, 509
Parama Vyoma ...	470, 471
Paraśu (axe)	335
Psrāśara ...	431, 432, 433
Parāvṛj	449
Pārāvatas	356
Paridhi ...	495, 499

PAGE.

Parimit 189
Parisvañjalya 189
Parjanya 83, 91, 92, 93, 261; earlier than Indra 60, 61; originally meant 'rain-cloud 61; as God of thunder and rain 61, 62, 79; superseded by Indra 61; distinct from Indra 61, 67, 92; 269, 277, 289, 338, 521
Parṇa-dhi (feather-socket) ... 333
Parnians 156
Parṣu 279
Parsis 66
Parśu (rib-bone of a horse) 52; (sickle) 335
Parsus (a tribe) ... 163, 360
Pārthava 163
Parthians ... 163, 360
Partition of family-property in father's life-time ... 369
Parus 212
Paruṣṇī (Rāvi) 161, 212, 353, 361, 362
Parvan 212
Pastya 188
Paśu 285
Paśu-yāga ... 489, 500, 501
Pāśa ... 221, 335, 465
Pāśuka-Vedī 500
Pātali-putra 188
Patanjali ... 1, 33, 35, 36
Patesis 306
Pathaspati 124
Patnī-samyāja 409
Patnīnām-sadanam ... 189
Patria potestas ... 106, 108, 243
Patriarchal System 96, 242, 329
Pauruṣeya 451
Pavamāna ... 399, 469
Pavi 324
Pavíra (lance or sword) ... 334
Pavitra 195
Payas 202
Pecu 285
Pecus 285
Pedu 224
Perkunas ... 61, 62, 92, 93
Persia .. 12, 13, 14
Persians 25, 360. Old Persian (language) ... 33, 35, 36
Peru 25
Peśas 212
Peśaskārí 213
Peśamsi 232
Peśana 213
Petrie, Flinders ... 24, 25, 36
Phala 276
Phalguni 38
Phallus 165

PAGE.

Phallus-worship 164
Pharaoh 184
Phœnicians ... 88, 91, 95, 152, 185
Phrygian ... 93, 94, 163
Physicians, professional ... 446
Pijavana ... 355, 367
Piltdown ... 8, 294, 295
Pirrauru 102
Piśācas ... 403, 411
Piśāci 411
Pischel 38, 188, 220, 233, 258
Pithecanthropus erectus ... 7
Pitara 77
Pitṛs ... 289, 396, 400, 402, 404, 409, 415—18, 420, 490
Pitu 207
Plants, medicinal... ... 446
Pleistocene man 294
Pleistocene Sea ... 3, 35, 182
Pliocene ... 1, 7, 8, 34, 35
Polygamy ... 98, 99 254
Polyandry 98, 99, 103, 104, 254
Polynesian 13
Polytheistic monotheism 461, 472
Post-glacial 32
Post-pleistocene ... 3, 34, 182
Post-pubescent marriage ... 371
Pṛśni 365
Pṛthi 431
Pṛthi Vainya 275
Prithiví ... 56, 67, 79, 453
Pṛthu (King) invented the plough ... 275, 431
Pṛthus (tribe) ... 163, 360
Pṛthu-parśvavah 52, 335
Pṛthu-stuka 217
Pradakṣiṇam 491
Pradhāna Homa 378
Prahlāda 312
Prajá 373
Prajāpati ...41, 68, 108, 289, 312, 380, 382, 383, 460, 474, 475, 476, 481, 493
Prakṛti 97, 483
Pralaya 479, 480
Pramaganda 161
Praṇītā 496
Prāgvamśa 211
Prāṇāha 189
Prasavādi-devatas ... 382
Praskaṇva 210
Praśna-vivāka 437
Praśnin 437
Prastara 495, 498
Prātardoha 122
Pratimit 189
Pravargya Vidyā ... 53
Prayati 166, 483

PAGE.

Prayāja Yāga 497
Preta 412
Priapus 164, 165
Priest-kings 306
Promiscuous intercourse 97, 98; condemned by the Aryans 99
Property belonged to the father and not to the family ... 243
Prostha 193
Puliyers 22
Punic race 152, 185
Pur 45 122, 181, 186 187, 188
Purāṇas ... 44 132, 358
Pūrṇāhuti Homa ... 491
Pūrṇamāsa yāga 494
Purohita 304, 307
Puroḍāsas ... 487, 494, 496 497, ... 499, 501, 502
Purus 46, 132, 158 160, 354, 355, 356, 361, 365
Purukutsa ... 348, 354, 355, ... 363, 365
Purumintha 135
Purumitra 136, 252
Pururavā 101
Puruṣa .. 97. 476 *et seq.* 483, ... 501
Puruṣa-medha ... 213, 503—505
Puruṣa-sūkta ... 476
Puruṣa-yajna 500
Pūṣan 124 125, 126, 128, 200, 202, 212, 219, 277 284, 335, 338, 377, 426, 458 464, 473; joint worship of Pūṣan and Indra 126
Puṣkarāruṇi 132
Puṣkariṇi 123
Pyrenees 5

Q

Quaternary ... 1, 33, 34, 35

R

Ṛbhus 94, 138
Ṛc 235, 253, 377
Ṛgveda ... 1, 15, 16, 19, 26, 27; Three Ages in the— ...16, 40, 46, 113, 174
Ṛgvedic culture 15, 18; beginning of—16, 19, Ṛgvedic Aryans, 16, 19; difference of worship in the Ṛgveda and Yajurveda 27; Ṛgvedic civilisation founded in Sapta Sindhu 178 Ṛgvedic poetry ... 513 *et seq.*

PAGE.

Ṛjiśvan 170
Ṛjrāśva 241, 449
Ṛṇa 148
Ṛṇam smni 148
Ṛṣis, 40, 41, 43, 129, 130, 132, 133, 135, 136, 303, 304, 513, 514
Ṛṣti (spear) 334
Ṛṣya 222
Ṛṣyada 222
Ṛta ... 81, 452, 456, 484, 523
Ṛtvij 248, 490, 491, 494
Ragozin, Z. A. ... 146 482
Rāhūgaṇa, Gotama ... 29
Raids 329, 330
Rajata... 220
Rājan ... 112, 301, 312, 313, 138 (Rājā) ... 177, 301, 309
Rāja-kṛt 307
Rājanya 128, 130, 132, 177, 313, 318, 319, 477
Rājarṣi 358
Rajputana sea 354
Rājaśūya ... 228, 489
Rakṣas 438
Rakṣohan 411, 488
Raksoyuj 411
Rākṣasas, 32, 145, 385, 410, 411; their forms and habits 410
Rāma ... 105, 317, 353
Rāmānuja 510
Rāmāyaṇa 317, 350
Rantideva 204
Rasā 475
Rāsnā 215
Ratha 196
Rathaviti ... 134, 135, 393
Rathesthā 461
Rathin 340
Rathyā 122
Rayi 141
Rebirth ... 421, 422, 423
Reindeer men 11, 12
Re-incarnation ... 421, 422
Religion, origin of the idea of 396, 397
Rheia 78
Rodasi 104, 217
Rohita, story of 107, 241
Rome... 24
Romans 22, treatment of old parents by— 244
Roth 89 233, 361
Royal court and retinue ... 318
Royal pomp 319
Rudra, 27, 219, 288, 289 329, 443, 463, 473; identified with Agni, 444, 445, as the greatest physician 445; as a

PAGE.

solar God 445; his maleficent side 445; his beneficent side 445; presiding over the science of Medicine 446; (in the plural) 444; 473; Eleven—— ... 460
Rudriyas 444
Rukma 216
Rukma-pásá 216
Rukma-vakṣa 216

S

Sabhá 210, 231, 308, 324, 325, 327, 394; exclusion of women from Sabhás 325; distinction between Sabhá and Samiti 328, 433
Sabhá-sthánu 231, 325
Sabhya 327, 328
Sabheya 327
Śacī ... 248, 254, 462
Sacrifice, human 27; —to the Manes 27,—universal ... 27
Sadas 189
Sadgati 412
Sadánírá 29
Sage-poets 305
Sage priests ... 302 *et seq* 315;
Sa-gotra 124
Sahavasu 155
Śakatí 196
Śáka-puni 459
Śakṛt (dung) 278
Śakti (spear) 334
Saktu 203
Śakuni 105
Śákya 317
Śálá 123
Śalya (shaft) 333
Samanas 233, 234, 250, 372, 433
Sáman ... 26, 235, 253, 377
Samávartanam 489
Samaveśana 375, 382
Samrát 80, 84
Sámaveda 25, 26; difference between Sáma-veda and Ṛgveda 26
Samdamśa 189
Samgava ... 122, 123
Samgrahitṛ 318
Samiṣta Homa ... 499
Samit 488, 489, 490, 495, 497, 498
Śamitá 500
Samiti ... 30, 309, 328, 394
Sámidhení 497
Samkalpa 373, 380
Samkīrtana 232
Samsrava Homa ... 498, 499
Samudra Gupta 506

PAGE.

Samvara ... 155, 186, 349, 356
Śamvala 193
Śamyá 496
Śamyu-vák 498
Sanaka 154
Sandṛś 463
Śankara 510
Sankasuka 407, 408
Sanskrit 43, 44
Śapha 149
Sapta-Sindhavah ... 1, 14, 15, 19, 29
Sapta-Sindhu ... 30, 33, 47 48, 55, 63, 67, 89, 91, 114, 115, 117, 141, 142, 149, 150, 151, 173, 184, 227, 507, 508
Saptagu 188
Sapti 227
Sapta-padí 376, 377
Saramá 88, 197, 198, 416, two sons of— 423
Saranyu 398
Sarasvatí, ... 2, 3, 60, 160, 161, 178, 227, called Vṛtraghní 269, 329, 353, 356, 383, 507
Śarkarí 206
Sarpas (a tribe) 102, 174
Sárpa-rájní 169, 248
Śaru (arrow) 332
Śarya (arrow) 332
Śárya (arrow) 332
Śaryanavat Lake (in Kuru-ksetra) 53, 55, 114, 178, 507
Śaśíyaśi 134, 135
Śastras 41
Śaśvatī 136
Śasyádhipati 375
Śata-dáya 436
Śatadru 361, 354
Śatam 68
Śatapatha Bráhmaṇa 87, 211, 214, 278, 318, 402, 424, 437, 460, 464, 501, 504, 505, 509
Sattras 112 129, 261, 267, 270 annual and periodical 60, their utilitarian origin 60, performed to propitiate Indra 62, year-long session of— ... 267, 282, 283, 506
Satya 484
Satya loka 467
Savitṛ ... 38, 108, 230, 231, 376, 439, 456, 457, 514, 518, 519
Śávitri 519
Sáyam-doha 122
Sáyaṇa ... 38, 46, 52 83, 94, 134, 136, 139, 145, 191, 198, 201, 219 235, 407, 408
Scania 95

PAGE.

Scandinavia 95
Scarcity, averting of 271; few and far between in Ṛgvedic times 274
Second Interglacial period ... 7
Secret Prajápati ... 169
Semites 17
Semetic people 13
Semul 358
Senání ... 302, 318, 340, 345
Senart 256
Séṣa-homa .. 382, 383
Seven Ṛṣis 479
Shámá Shástrī ... 103, 326
Śigrus ... 163, 360, 366
Śikya 193
Sinbala 359
Simsapá 358
Simyus 360
Sindhu ... 137, 141, 161, 178, 327, (Country) 136
Siniváli ... 217, 218
Sipī Fair 234
Sipra ... 219, 220
Śiprá (helmet) 336
Sirá (plough) ... 276, 277
Sirimbitha 440
Siśna 166
Śiśnas (a tribe) ... 164, 174
Śiśna-cult 167
Śiśna-devas ... 164, 167
Śiśu 342
Śiśupala 334
Sitā (wife of Rama) 105; (furrow) ... 276, 277
Śiva (sun of the night) 87; (God) 444, 445
Śivas (a tribe) 163, 166, 174, 360
Sivapura 164
Skambha 169
Skin-cloths and utensils 71, 210, 221
Slavs 77
Slavonic 22
Smārta-Agni 489
Simaśāna 349
Smṛtis ... 385, 387
Snake-worship 27
Snataka 373
Socialism 306
Socrates 78
Sol 94
Soma 54, 85, 147, 208,—cult earlier than Indra-cult 57, 263; came to be detested by Parsis 61; afterwards shared by the Vedic Aryans and the Iranians 178; the oldest 178; the plant grew on the Mujavat and the banks of the Sindhu, Sarasvati and Saryaṇāvat lake 178, 179; Soma the father of Indra 178; its juice the favourite drink of the Gods 178; the word not occurring in any Aryan language of Europe 178
Soma-juice partaken of by soldiers on the eve of battle 345; preparation of the Soma juice 208, 209; its effect on consumers 209; the word occurring in pages 287, 289, 290, 309, 312, 336, 346, 370, 371, 375, 377, 401, 403, 418, 426, 443, 447, 448, 453, 468, 469, 473, 494 498; identified with the Moon 507; as king 508, 509; Soma-traders 147
Soma sacrifice 25, 26; its inauguration 60; its object 507, 508 *etc.* also 500, 506
Soma-book 25
Somavatī 447
Sone (river) 3
Songs and singing ... 235
Sons, desired 240, 241, 243;—adopted 240; ideal—241, 307, 330 training of sons 241; father's authority over sons 108, 241; sons not legal owners of property with the father ... 243
Speech 394 *et seq.*; *seeing* speech connotes the existence of the art of writing .. 394
Spencer 98
Sphya ... 496, 497
Sports ... 221, 222 *et seq.*
Sṛka (lance) 334
Sṛni (sickle) ... 278
Sṛnjaya ... 163, 164
Śraddhā 417, 494; Śraddhā homa 494
Śrāddha 232
Sraj 211
Śrauta-Agni 489
Śrauta-Sûtras ... 488, 489
Śrauta-Yāga ... 494, 531
Srakti (spear) 334
Sruc 195
Śruta 364
Sruva ... 195, 495
Stanley, Henry 331
Starcke 98
Stena 434
State War Loan 321

	Page.
Sthālī	194
Sthibi ...	126, 194, 278, 279
Sthūnā	406
Stone Age	4
Strabo	244
Student-life ...	391 *et seq.*
Subman	7
Subandhu ...	416, 425, 426
Subrahmanya	41
Sudās	130 163, 177, 345, 351, 352, 353, 355, 356, 357, 358, 359, 360, 361, 362, 363, 364, 365, 366, 367
Śūdra	68, 128, 133, 319, 477
Suhasta	136
Su-kapardā	218
Su-kurīrā	219
Sukráchárya	136
Sūkṣmaśarīra	427
Sūktam	42
Sūktavāc	498
Śulka	145
Sumeria	281
Sumerians ...	17, 137, 152
Sun, identified with Indra, Mitra, Varuṇa, Agni, Yama Māturiśvan his three aspects, 472 ...	455
Sun-worshippers	86
Śuna	227
Śunahśepa, story of	106, 07, 241, 243, 436
Sundhyu	136
Su-opaśa	219
Śūrpa ...	194, 496
Surā ...	208, 209
Surgery ...	443, 444, 448
Sūrya ...	91, 94, 124, 378, 379, 383, 453, 466, 484, 518
Sūryā, marriage of	370, 371; 38 196, 219, 248, 250
Sûryash	94
Susa	31
Su-śipra	219
Suṣṇa ...	155, 268, 269, 530
Suśravā	353
Sūta ...	318, 319
Sūtras ...	24, 25, 28, 42, 52
Suvāsā (epithet of the Sindhu country)	212
Svah	382
Svadhā ...	166, 483
Svadhiti (axe)	335
Svaghnin	205
Svahākāra	497
Svanaya Bhavya	136
Svarāt	84
Svargaloka	402
Svarbhānu	94
Svasara	123

	Page.
Svayamvara	136
Śvetaketu	100
Śviṣṭakṛt	497
Śviṣṭakṛt Yāga	497
Śyavāśva	134, 135, 253, 372, 393

T

Taittirīya Brāhmaṇa ...	37, 72, 122, 212, 312, 504
Taittirīya Samhitá	52, 68, 72, 80, 411
Takṣa	126
Talpa	193
Tantra	126
Tanūnapāt	497
Tapas	382
Taranta	134
Tárpya	214
Taskara	434
Tasmanians	75
Taxes 319; how levied	322, 323
Taylor Dr.	180
Tāyus	434
Ten Kings 130, 161, 163; confederacy of ...	351, 359, 360
Ten periods of Vedic culture	25
Teutons	73
Thieves, punishment of	434 435
Third Interglacial period ...	8
Thraetaona	61
Three ages of the Ṛgveda ...	16, 21
Tibetan plateau	5
Tila	282
Tilak B G.	37, 38
Tirita	207
Tishtrya	67
Tiṣya (star)	37
Titau (seeve) ...	194, 278
Totem ...	102, 103, 110
Tṛtsus ...	46, 112, 130, 160 161, 164, 219, 345, 353-358, 361, 362, 364, 366, 384
Trade, inland 141; in Soma plant 146, 147; Sea-trade	149, 150,
Traitana ...	58, 61, 63
Transmigration	421
Trasadasyu ...	348, 354
Trāsadasyava	355
Treachery, punishable by death	437
Tretá	228
Tridhátu ...	190, 191
Trinil	7
Trita 58 63, 107, 261, 269, 270; Aptya—58; earlier than Indra	60, 61
Tritas	61
Triton	61
Trivarūtha ...	90, 191

PAGE

True man 6, 18; First true man 9, 18
Tryamvaka 463
Tsaru (handle of the plough) ... 276
Turanians 48, 68
Turkestan 5
Turvaśas ... 46, 128, 153, 160, 161, 164, 353, 356, 360, 366
Tūrvayāna ... 356, 361
Tūṣādhāna 378
Tutankhamen 182
Tvaṣṭṛ ... 53, 85, 126, 130, 139, 335, 383, 414, 473, 498
Twenty Kings, war of ... 353
Tyler E. B. 485

U

Udaka-Devatas 383
Udañcana 194
Uddālaka 100
Udeṣyat 455
Udgātṛ 26, 490
Udita 455
Udojasa 447
Udukhala 494
Udumavara 381
Udyat 455
Ukhā ... 127, 194
Ulūkhala 194
Umā ... 466, 474
Upabarhaṇa 193
Upabhṛt ... 495, 497
Upalā ... 194, 494
Upamit 189
Upanayanam ... 387, 488, 489
Upaniṣads ... 24, 25, 28
Upāṁśu Yāga 497
Uranos 91
Urdara ... 194, 278
Urjayanti 447
Urṇā 212
Urṇāvati 212
Urvarā ... 137, 275
Urvaśī 101
Uṣas 101, 108, 130, 196, 298, 308, 453, 465, 484, 515; as mother of Sūrya 466; as his wife 466
Uśaṣti 432
Uśij ... 136, 274
Uṣṭra 142
Usury 148

V

Vāc ... 43, 132, 329, 355, 473, 474
Vadhri 141
Vahya 193

PAGE

Vailasthānam 349
Vainateya 103
Vainya ... 275, 431
Vaira 435
Vaira-deya 435
Vairāgya 511
Vaiśvānara 89, 350
Vaiśya ... 68, 133, 340, 477, 509
Vājasaneyī Samhitā ... 27, 463, 504
Vājin ... 226, 426, 427
Vajra ... 31, 51, 54, 114, 331; originally stone-made 51, 55 and then bone-made 51; Indra's—52, 54; as golden 53; as *dyasa* (iron) 55; as *Caturaśri* Śatāśari, Śataparvan, Sahasra-bhṛṣṭi ... 53, 55
Vajrin (Indra) 60
Vala ... 67, 91, 94, 95
Valka 72
Valkala 72
Vālakhilya ... 510, 398
Vālmīki 105
Vallavācārya 510
Vāmadeva ... 132, 144
Vapā 500
Vaptā 127
Vaptṛ 219
Vara 430
Varaśikha 155
Varatrā ... 270, 296
Varci 155
Varcivants ... 163, 167
Varma 90, 91
Varenya 90
Varhī 497
Varman ... 220, 336
Varuṇa 42, 56, 67, 76, 80, 82, 84; his powers and functions 81; moral governor of the universe 81; lord of the seas 8.; supreme lord of the universe 81; his powers usurped by Indra 84, 85; son of Aditi 84; causes of the decline of his powers 86; identified with the moon 86; 88-91; 107, 108 125, 149, 150, 186 188, 198, 199, 212, 223, 231, 241, 309, 3 4, 336, 344, 345, 377; worshipped by the Paṇis as Supreme God 88; identified with Ahura Mazda 89; as Āditya 89; 309, 398-409, 415, 453, 456, 462, 464, 513 *et seq.* ... ...
Varuṇa-praghāsas ... 258

PAGE.

Varütha ... 220, 336
Vaṣatkára ... 460, 497
Vasá 211
Vasávi 194
Vasiṣtha 81, 84 130, 132, 156, 188 108, 169; (in the plural) 219; 231, 304, 357, 358, 359, 366, 367, 403
Vasus, eight ... 460, 473
Váṇa ... 234, 235
Vása 212
Vása-váya 212
Váśi (hatchet) 235
Vástoshpati ... 196, 197
Vástu 196
Váta 470
Vátápi 208
Vatsa 238
Váya 126
Váyu 208, 309, 382, 383 453, 470
Vedangas 450
Vedas 24, 450
Vedī ... 489, 491
Vedic culture, ten periods of ... 25
Vedic cosmogony .. 481-434
Vedic Sacrifice ... 485 *et seq*
Vehat ... 203, 286
Vena ... 429, 430
Veṇu 235
Venus 165
Vereṫraghna 67
Vergehen 403
Verual Equinox 37
Vetasu 155
Vibhíndaka 227
Vidadaśva 135
Videha 29
Videgha 29
Vij 229
Vimada ... 135, 252
Vimána 126
Vīṇá ... 234, 235
Viṇatá ... 103, 104
Vindhya Hills 4
Vipás ... 361, 362, 363
Vīra 298, 299, 437
Viráj 477
Virocana 312
Virtus 298
Vīrya 298
Viś 128
Viśah ... 111, 119, 328, 340
Viṣanins ... 163, 174, 360
Viśasana 378
Viṣita-stuka 217
Viṣṇu 60, 87, 93, 223, 261, 269, 383, 400, 424. 458, 459, 492, 499; had two forms, one visible and another invisible 469

PAGE.

Viśpalá ... 249, 329, 449
Viśpati ... 112, 398
Viṣumant 189
Viśvadevah 108, 379, 383, 473, 484
Viśvakarmá ... 478, 479
Viśva-rūpa ... 57, 58, 61
Viśva-vārá ... 248, 249, 393
Viśvámitra 16, 97, 130, 132, 156, 192, 237, 304, 355, 357, 358, 359, 361, 362, 367
Viśvávasu 375, 381;—Gandharva 381
Viśyá 258
Vivasvat ... 398, 399
Voltaire 166
Vox populi 317
Vṛcaya 137
Vṛddha 364
Vṛṣā-giri 241
Vṛṣā-kapi ... 37, 38, 92, 93, 113
Vṛṣotsarga 417
Vṛtra 51, 53, 54, 63, 66, 83 86, 87, 114, 153, 207; killed 99 times 52; demon of drought 57; a Brāhmaṇa 57; son of Tvaṣṭṛ 57; Vṛtra and Indra myth unravelled 58; as priest of the Devas and Asuras 58; his three mouths 58; assumes malevolent form 59; captures the Sun, Dawn and Waters 59; war with Indra 60; as Deva 64, 65; as God of pastoral Aryans 64, 167; black-skinned 65; Hillabrandt's theory of Vṛtra 65; vanquished by Tishtrya 67; becomes a malevolent power 87, 260; as Deva and Brāhmaṇa 260, 403; (in the plural) 166, 167, 171, 261; 508; Vṛtra's many forms 455, 456.
Vṛtraghnī ... 269, 329
Vrā 258
Vrāja ... 119, 120, 121
Vrājapati 119
Vrīhi 201; not mentioned in the Ṛgveda 279, 281, 282; 501
Vyāghra 316
Vyūṣṭhā 454

W

Wadia 3, 35
War of Ten Kings with Sudas. 353 *et seq*.

PAGE.

War-tactics ... 348, 349, 350 351
War-tax 321
Waters, hymn to remove diseases ... 290, 291, 442
Weapons, offensive 331 *et seq*.
Weber 227, 257
Wedding ceremony ... 253
Wedding rites ... 370 *et seq*
Well, construction of ... 292
Wells H. G. ... 4, 5, 8, 9, 11,, 12, 17, 19, 30. 31, 35, 279
Wergeld 436
Westergaard 90
Westermarcke 98
Wheat, not mentioned in the Ṛgveda 279 ; its historical significance 279, 280.
White Yajurveda ... 504
Whitney 210
Widow (childless) inherited husband's property, 250; remarriage of widows 254; burning of widows 256; their status 429.
Widow-remarriage 254, 429, 430, 431, 432
Wife, description of 237, 239, her authority 242
Wilson Prof. 359
Winckler, Hugh .. 115, 178
Winternitz M. ... 1, 33, 34, 35 39, 42, 43, 44
Wiros 298
Woman, not cause of human downfall 97 ; regarded as chattel 105; uncomplimentary remarks about women 106; status of women 449; 250; women fought in battles 329; liberty of women 433.
Woman-warrior ... 249
Writing, art of ... 387, 388

Y

Yadus ... 46, 112, 128, 153, 160, 161, 353 356, 360, 397, 398, 400
Yajamāna 490, 491, 496, 497, 498
Yajña 282, 288, 289-347, 485 *et seq*; its meaning 486; its evolution 487; passes from animals to grains 501, 502.

PAGE.

Yajna-Kathā 509
Yajur-veda 25, 26, 27; its age 30; 41 42, 218, 488; White Yajurveda 504; Black Yajurveda 326;
Yajus 41, 235
Yakṣus ... 163, 360, 366
Yama 70, 100, 234, 408; his pair of four-eyed dogs 70, 401; his conception later than the taming of dogs 70; myth of Yama and Yamī 100; Yama's conception not fearful 398; Yama's region described 399; his messengers 401; Yama identified with Death 401, 402, 404; 412, 415, 416, 418, 420, 426, 471, 534.
Yamī 100, 101, 397, 398, 420; represents darkness, as Yama light 399; identical with Nirṛti (Hell) 399, 404.
Yamunā 26, 169, 170, 356, 366
Yaokaresh 263
Yava 126, 200 *et seq*; 251, 267 279, 497, 501.
Yayāti 136
Yayyāvati ... 156, 163
Yājñavalkya ... 203, 258
Yājyās 42, 497
Yāska . 162, 219, 459
Yātus 411
Yātudhāna 410
Yima 90
Yoga 509
Yojana 37, 129
Yoni-kūta 103
Yudhiṣthira ... 105, 229, 359, 367
Yuga (yoke) 276
Yūpa ... 106, 500, 502
Yuvati 378

Z

Zend-avesta ... 61, 89 90
Zeus 79
Zimmer 149, 161, 163, 189, 210, 217, 218, 227, 242-244, 246, 302, 303, 313-315, 322, 334, 360
Zoroaster 507
Zoroastrianism 94

ERRATA.

PAGE.	LINE.	FOR.	READ.
53	18	byegone	bygone
77	28	coferred	conferred
101	19	ths	this
103	31	Jabāla	Jabāla
139	32	othodox	orthodox
144	30	possessin	possession
145	12	oppulent	opulent
181	23	woolen	woollen
183	28	irresistably	irresistibly
226	30	race-marker	race-maker
361	9	his	their
497	16	Vrhiḥ	Varhiḥ
528	6	teat	that

BY THE SAME AUTHOR

ṚGVEDIC INDIA

Demy 8vo., p. 616, Rs. 10-8.

(An outline of the Early History of India as depicted in the Ṛgveda, examined in the light of the results of modern Geological, Archæological and Ethnological investigations, and drawn from a comparative study of the civilisations of the Deccan, ancient Airyana, Babylonia, Assyria, Phoenicia, Asia Minor and Pre-historic Europe).

Prof. A. V. William Jackson of Columbia University.—" There is much in the volume to engage special study by one interested in the early history of India and of Iran."

Prof. V. Giuffrida-Ruggeri of Naples University.—I beg you to accept my compliments for this original and daring work."

Prof. G. Sergi of Rome University.—" I have read your book with great pleasure, and many things I have learned because of the great richness of facts and doctrine about the social conditions of the Aryan peoples of India at the time of the Ṛgveda."

Dr. James Lindsay in the J. R. A. S. for Oct. 1921.—" This is an interesting work by one who is well versed in Vedic lore ....The work in whole affords ample proof of the author's learning and industry as a Ṛgveda scholar."

The Time's Literary suppplement (May 12, 1921).—" In his striking Birdwood Memorial Lecture last month Sir Edward Grigg said that in all form of research the patience and peculiar subtlety of the Indian intellect promise great results. These qualities are well displayed by the Lecturer in Ancient Indian History and Culture to the Calcutta University in this further volume.

The Madras Mail (5th August 1921).—" He has written a substantial tome of 600 pages, which is a solid contribution to the literature bearing on this branch of research.......No review of Mr. Das's book can conclude without an acknowledgment of the learning, the powers of original thinking, and the acute critical skill that he has displayed in writing a work of such vast importance to scholars and students interested in antiquarion historical research."

The New India (*12th March 1921*).—" The book bears evidence of wide research and a judicious use of the resultant materials."

The Bombay Chronicle (*8th May 1921*).—" If Mr. Tilak's work constituted a landmark in the history of Indian scholarship, a like compliment may be paid to the author of " Ṛgvedic India " : and if future volumes will be as replate with information, as the one under review, their value to the student of the early history of the Aryans will be unsur. passed."

The Vedic Magazine (*April 1921*).—" Every lover of India who reads this scholarly work will find his pride in her past stimulated and his faith in her future rejuvenated and revitalised."

The Man of December 1921.—" We must recognize that Das has done a good service to British Anthropology."

Only a few copies of the First Edition are left. *Second Edition in the Press.*

Book your order early with

R. CAMBRAY & Co.,

BOOKSELLERS & PUBLISHERS,

15, College Square, Calcutta.

BENGALI WORKS BY THE SAME AUTHOR.

		Price. Rs.	A.
1.	SĪTĀ (Third Edition, illustrated) A study of Sītā's life and character after Vālmīki ...	1	4
2.	PALĀŚBAN (Third Edition) A domestic novel of great purity and beauty.	1	8
3.	KUMĀRI (with author's portrait) A beautiful Social Romance.	2	0
4.	ARAṆYA-VĀSA (Romantic life in the wilds of Chotanagpur)	1	4
5.	DURGĀ-RĀṆĪ (A Social Romance) ...	0	12
6.	PRABHĀ-VATĪ (A Drama based on classical sources).	1	0
7.	GĀTHĀ (A volume of beautiful poems) ...	0	12
8.	THE VAIŚYA CASTE (in English) ...	1	4

[*To be had of all principal booksellers in Calcutta*].